HISTORIC HOUSES
Castles & Gardens

IN GREAT BRITAIN AND IRELAND

Editor: Deborah Valentine

Published by:
Reed Information Services
Windsor Court, East Grinstead House, East Grinstead,
West Sussex RH19 1XA
Telephone: (01342) 335794 Fax: (01342) 335720
Telex: 95127 INSFER G

REED
INFORMATION
SERVICES

Registered in England Number 181427
Registered Office: Church Street, Dunstable, Bedfordshire LU5 4HB

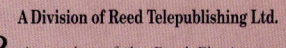

A Division of Reed Telepublishing Ltd.

A member of the Reed Elsevier group

Blenheim Palace

Home of the 11th Duke of Marlborough,
birthplace of Sir Winston Churchill

Open daily 1030am-5.30pm (last admission 4.45pm) mid March to 31st October 1995

A visit to Blenheim is a wonderful way to spend a day. An inclusive ticket covers the Palace tour, Park, Gardens, Herb Garden, Butterfly House, Motor Launch, Train, Adventure Play Area and Nature Trail. Optional are The Marlborough Maze and Rowing Boat Hire on Queen Pool. Car parking is free for Palace visitors and there are excellent Shops, a licensed Restaurant and two Cafeterias. Events for 1995 include the annual Grand Charity Cricket Match, in aid of the Oxfordshire Association of Young People, between a Celebrity XI and an Oxford University XI on 28th May and The Blenheim International Horse Trials which take place on 14th, 15th, 16th and 17th September. Further details from The Administrator's Office (Dep HHCG), Blenheim Palace, Woodstock, Oxon OX20 1PX. Telephone: 01993 811091.

The right to close the Palace or Park without notice is reserved.

This view of Blenheim's north front is taken from the new Blenheim Palace Guide Book, published by Jarrold.

INTRODUCTION

This richly illustrated full colour guide to Historic Houses Castles and Gardens has been published annually for some 40 years and contains information on over 1300 beautiful properties and gardens open to the general public.

Many of the properties listed are privately owned or in the care of the National Trust, English Heritage, National Trust for Scotland, Scottish Border Heritage, CADW - Welsh Historic Monuments and Irish Heritage.

New features include a 16 page map section, colour tinted by county for easier recognition, with the position of properties or gardens marked with a recognised symbol. The map gives general locations only and some properties now include a location map at the bottom of their entry. A colour tint has also been added for those properties offering accommodation or conference facilities.

1995 is a year for celebration. The National Trust is 100 years old and the article on page v outlines this achievement. An achievement which is marked by no less than four Sandford Awards. Although a grand national total of thirteen awards is announced this year for excellence in Heritage Education, Martyn Dyer's article on page xxvii is dedicated to the National Trust winners. Also celebrating this year is the British Tourist Authority's year-long Festival of Arts and Culture, bringing alive our country's wonderful culture in over 500 exhibitions and special events being displayed around the country. This is explained in our article on page xi.

It is not often that a 'brand new' castle bursts upon the scene. Alton Castle perched on a rocky precipice high over the River Churnet in Staffordshire, is one such. Stephen Weeks talks about this romantic castle for visitors on page xv.

To see our heritage in the most grand of houses is one thing but to 'Listen to our Heritage' is quite another. Our article by Natalie Cox of Soundalive brings properties to life on page xxi.

Haddon Hall in Derbyshire was the winner of the Historic Houses Association/Christie's Garden of the Year Award and is featured on our title page. More information about Haddon Hall can be found on page 33.

All admission charges quoted are subject to change without notice. All dates are inclusive i.e. May to September. Opening times and dates apply to 1995 only.

CONTENTS

Cover picture: Speke Hall, Merseyside by courtesy of the National Trust	*Title Page picture:* Haddon Hall, Derbyshire Winner Christie's/HHA Garden of the Year Award presented in 1994

1895-1995
The restoration period

The splendour of the British landscape is celebrated the world over. Our country homes and historic places attract admirers in their millions each year.

It's hard to imagine otherwise.

Yet, in 1895, our national assets - unique and irreplaceable - were under threat. And were it not for the labours of three visionary Victorians, the Britain we know and love might be a very different place indeed.

Powis Castle.

Together they founded the National Trust to preserve places of historic interest and natural beauty for ever, for everyone.

One hundred years later, as Britain's leading conservation charity, we care for some 400 historic properties and gardens, 547 miles of breathtaking coastline and over half a million acres of magnificent countryside.

National treasures painstakingly restored, lovingly maintained, and preserved, for generations more to enjoy.

For a free Centenary Map Guide and information on any National Trust properties, events or for membership details telephone:

0181-464 1111.

Alternatively write to:

The National Trust, Centenary Information Office, P.O. Box 39, Bromley, Kent BR1 1NH.

Elisabeth Vigee Lebrun, self-portrait 1791.

THE NATIONAL TRUST CENTENARY

A NATIONAL CELEBRATION

The National Trust's Centenary year, 1995, is for us all to celebrate. The statistics speak volumes. The Trust owns over 200 stately homes; 162 gardens; 25 wind & water mills; 51 abbeys, priories, churches & chapels; 39 inns & public houses; not to mention, all the thatched cottages & barns, castles & keeps, Roman baths & villas, clock towers & gazebos. The National Trust protects almost 550 miles of coastline and 590,000 acres of open countryside in England, Wales & Northern Ireland, along with all or part of 60 villages & hamlets, as well as whole islands, lighthouses, moats & mazes. Trust property - from Orford Ness on the Suffolk Coast to Crom on Lough Erne - includes 99 National Nature Reserves & 466 Sites of Special Scientific Interest, home to all 14 native species of bat, 71 species of rare birds & 52 species of butterflies. The land encompasses limestone pavements & salt marshes, 4,000 acres of freshwater lakes & ponds, and over 63,000 acres of woodland.

The hills above Watersmeet, Myrtleberry Cleave

Our Heritage

The Trust protects the property in its care for the benefit of the nation, and "inalienably", which means that the looking after is now and forever. Annual income stands at £140 million, but need for expenditure far outstrips this. The worth of the Trust's holdings is, literally, invaluable. Three quarters of all properties owned by the Trust are inadequately endowed, which is to say, there is not enough money in the property's coffers to fund repairs and upkeep. The need for support from members, visitors, donors and volunteers is ever growing.

Every aspect of the Trust's work is expected to maintain the high standards set by its visionary founders, a remarkable Victorian trio: Miss Octavia Hill, social reformer; Sir Robert Hunter, solicitor and campaigner for commons and forests; Canon Hardwicke Rawnsley, a vicar who founded the Lake District Defence Society. These three joined forces, and on 12th January 1895 the National Trust was registered with the Board of Trade. The Duke of Westminster proved prophetic when he said, "mark my words, Miss Hill, this is going to be a very big "thing".

The Trust buys its First Property

Beginnings were modest. The Trust's first acquisition in February 1895 was Dinas Oleu - 4.5 acres of steep and rocky fell overlooking Barmouth in North Wales, given by Mrs Fanny Talbot, a friend of Ruskin. Alfriston Clergy House, four miles from the English Channel in East Sussex, was the first building purchased by the Trust - a 14th century half-timbered and thatched dwelling costing £10 in 1896. This set a trend: the Trust cares as much for vernacular and domestic architecture as for the stately and grand.

14th century thatched and half-timbered house beside the village green, Alfriston Clergy House

Beatrix Potter, best known as an author and artist, was otherwise known in the Lake District she loved as Mrs William Heelis. During her lifetime, she gave generously to the National Trust and, on her death in 1943, left the Trust 14 farms and 4,000 acres to its care. Today, visitors can enjoy bed and breakfast at one of the Trust's tenanted farms in Coniston, Yew Tree Farm, once owned by Beatrix Potter; visit the Beatrix Potter Lake District show and exhibition at Packhorse Court, Keswick; study her children's book illustrations at the Beatrix Potter Gallery in Hawkshead and at her modest 17th century house, Hill Top near Ambleside (where she based many of her stories), and walk the fells she donated, among the Herdwick sheep which won her prizes.

Two decades after the National Trust Act of 1907 - when the Trust gained its powers of inalienability - two more Acts of 1937 and 1939 allowed owners to donate property and possessions in lieu of taxes. Under this arrangement, the Country House Scheme, the Trust acquired Wightwick Manor, built from 1887 with William Morris and pre-Raphaelite influences. Next came Blicking Hall, near Norwich, a 17th century house with its entire estate.

Chinese bridge in the China garden at Biddulph Grange

Lizard Lighthouse seen from along the coast

After wartime's 'Dig for Victory', came hard post-war years, continuing the threat to gardens. In 1948, the Trust and the Royal Horticultural Society launched the National Gardens Scheme to acquire and maintain this precious and living heritage.

Gardens in the Trust attract over 8 million visitors every year, and are kept in trim by teams of hard working and dedicated gardeners, some trained through the Trust's own Careership Scheme. Students may learn how to maintain exotic Eastern gardens, complete with pagodas and ornamental bridges, as at Biddulph Grange Garden in Staffordshire, or to tend camellias and conifers at Bodnant in North Wales, or even the delicate skills of topiary needed at Hidcote Manor in Gloucestershire.

Enterprise Neptune, launched in 1965 to save unspoilt coastlines, celebrates its 30th birthday in 1995, having raised an impressive £18 million and protected one in six of every mile of coastline around England, Wales & Northern Ireland.

With so much to care for, the Trust's responsibilities grow and grow. Natural disasters, such as the great storms of 1987 and 1990 do not help and neither do the man-made. In 1989, an accidental fire caused by workmen, gutted Uppark, a 17th century mansion on the West Sussex/Hampshire border. On 1st June 1995, this property will re-open after a £20 million restoration programme (funded from insurance cover) for which the National Trust has employed teams of craftsmen and rediscovered long forgotten, traditional skills.

At Ightham Mote in Kent, leadwork and lime mortars are being applied as they might have been when the Great Hall was new in the 14th century. In 1995 the painted ceiling of the 16th century Tudor chapel will be restored, and visitors can continue to see conservation in action and study the phases of work in a fascinating exhibition. By contrast, in London, visitors to Hackney have viewed the revitalising of Tudor Sutton House, while in Richmond, 17th century Ham House has re-opened with its Stuart splendour intact, but protected by 1990s technology for security and environmental monitoring.

In 1994 the Trust won two Europa Nostra Awards; one for Speke Hall in Merseyside, where the timber-framed house and its grounds have been restored; the other for footpath restoration in the Peak District, where erosion from constant wear and tear had taken its toll.

Restoration and Unusual Properties

At Dolaucothi Gold Mines in Dyfed, it is now possible to study ancient and modern mine workings, complete with authentic miners' helmets and lamps. Not far away at Dinefwr, the Victorian-Gothic mansion is undergoing repair. An exhibition of work in progress is open, as is the ancient deer park with its White Park cattle.

Carpet of Azaleas and Rhododendrons at Bodnant Garden, Gwynedd

(Ian Shaw/National Trust Picture Library)

The Trust's policy in recent years has been to slow down the rate of acquisition in order to consolidate existing resources. That said, new and unusual properties include Patterson's Spade Mill in Northern Ireland and Finch Foundry in Devon, the last working water powered edge tool works in the country. Porthdinllaen on the Llyn Peninsula in North Wales joined the portfolio last year with a full complement of six houses, an inn, lifeboat station, cliffs, moorings and beach.

In the Cotswolds, Chastleton a 17th century manor house, acquired for the National Trust in 1991 by the National Heritage Memorial Fund, is under restora-

(Andreas Von/National Trust Picture Library)

The interior of the Lucy travelling coach in the coach house. Charlecote Park, Warwickshire

tion with plans to open to the public in 1996-7. In Sussex, Nymans, the home of the late Countess of Rosse, is receiving equal attention. There are plans to open her 20th century house, which looks more like a Medieval manor, but in the meantime visitors can enjoy the newly designed, marquee-style restaurant and shop. In Hampstead in London, the home of architect Erno Goldfinger, which he built for himself and his wife in 1937, will open to the public in 1996 as the Trust's first Modern Movement house.

Activities for all Ages

Throughout the 16 regions of the National Trust, there are activities for all ages and tastes. Theatre in

Education by the Young National Trust Theatre, enjoyed by 7,000 school children every year, part of an extensive and developing education programme aimed at students of all ages. Fetes, fairs and concerts on summer days and nights. Walks with wardens, tours with gardeners and the ever popular `Putting to Bed' days when visitors can watch the painstaking preparations for closing up a house over the winter months.

After all the walking along miles of coastline, tramping across fells and dales, as well as exploring the ins and outs of country houses and their estates,

Trelissick garden, Trelissick, Cornwall

there is the unmissable attraction of the Trust's 130 restaurants and tearooms serving traditional home-made food. For those who need to work off the excesses of too many cream teas, volunteers can always join the Trust's Acorn Camps and Working Holidays. To get away from it all, there are over 200 National Trust holiday cottages, some of them part of National Trust estates: from Cotehele on the Tamar River to Castle Ward on Strangford Lough; from the Laura Ashley decorated Mote Cottage at Ightham Mote to former gardeners' homes at Trelissick Garden in Cornwall. There is even the National Trust Travel Collection launched in 1994 with Page and Moy, where supporters can enjoy tours of historic Britain as well as venturing further afield to Barbados, Italy and the Confederate States.

The restaurants, cottages and holidays are all part of the Trust's enterprise activities, as are the 208 shops, 170 at historic houses and gardens, and 38 in the high

street which sell an extensive range of exclusive merchandise inspired by the treasures in the Trust's care. All profits from these activities directly benefit the Trust's charitable work.

The Trust does not only protect the past, but also looks forward to treasures of the future. The Foundation for Art was established in 1986 to commission and acquire contemporary art; under its patronage artists document and respond to the Trust's properties, at times selling their work to raise funds for the Foundation.

It is not possible to mention the full range of the Trust's work and the opportunities it offers to its members and visitors ; there is so much going on, so much careful repair and conservation, so much enthusiastic and committed provision of access and enjoyment. So much variety. The National Trust is Britain's largest conservation charity and a world leader in the field of caring for all that is precious in the natural and built environment, for the last century and for the years to come.

Detail of cottage garden from the Holnicote Estate, Somerset

Visit the best!

Arundel Castle

Family home of the Dukes of Norfolk
For details see West Sussex Section

THE FESTIVAL OF STATELY STARS

by the British Tourist Authority

The year-long Festival of Arts and Culture aims to present - to overseas visitors, as well as to the British themselves - the rich diversity of our heritage and contemporary arts, which make the country such a wonderful cultural centre. It covers the performing arts, and the incredible calendar of arts festivals; museums and galleries (they are putting on over 500 exhibitions and special events); crafts and customs; religious heritage; literature (Swansea hosts the UK Year of Literature and Writing); and the cinema - Cinema 100 begins towards the end of the year, commemorating the first century of British moving pictures.

The World of Beatrix Potter   Bowness-on-Windermere, Cumbria

A great many historic houses and gardens will be playing a prominent role in this year's Festival of Arts and Culture, the biggest nation-wide celebration of its kind ever staged in Britain. They are themselves works of art, and an integral part of the country's cultural and social history, and they will be the setting for a variety of performances this summer. In addition, of course, 1995 is the centenary year of the National Trust, which is holding a bewildering array of events - from classical and jazz concerts and plays, to lectures, Fetes Champetres and children's days - to mark 100 years of conserving buildings and gardens, landscapes and coastline.

Anniversaries

The centenaries of the National Trust and the cinema are just two of a number of contrasting anniversaries which fall in 1995, and thus enrich the Festival programme. Others include 100 years of Westminster Cathedral and Belfast's Grand Opera House; the bicentenaries of the poet John Keats' birth, and the death of the innovative potter Josiah

Wedgwood; and the tercentenary of one of England's finest composers, Henry Purcell. It is also, of course, 50 years since World War 11 ended in Europe; while north of the border, events commemorating the 250th anniversary of the Jacobite Rebellion led by Bonnie Prince Charlie include a major exhibition at Glasgow's Art Gallery and Museum (June 3 - August 27). Aberdeen celebrates the quincentenary of its university with a series of exhibitions. Going back even further, Durham's theme is "1,000 years of arts, culture and architecture": two years ago, the city celebrated the 900th anniversary of its beautiful cathedral - now it is the millenium of the founding of its diocese.

Some of the Festival events being staged in historic houses and gardens are given in this guide, but throughout 1995 - when you travel to any part of England, Scotland, Wales or Northern Ireland - be sure to call at local tourist information centres for details of all kinds of Festival events in that area. All activities and events are to be enjoyed in this very special year.

Sculpture, Chichester Cathedral, Chichester Festivities

National Trust

The National Trust spent a long time working out its party plans, and they have surely come up with something for almost everyone. There will be Fetes Champetres at West Wycombe Park (July 7-9), Claremont Landscape Garden (July 12-15), Stourhead (July 19-22) and Mottisfont Abbey Gardens (September 8-9); Son et Lumiere at Polesden Lacey (June 16-18) and Lyveden New Bield (September 9); several open-air opera and theatre productions; and music, music, music - whether you prefer 100 years of jazz and dance (Dyrham Park, June 30-July 1), Gilbert and Sullivan (Tattershall Castle, July 15), a centenary concert with fireworks by the Bournemouth Sinfonietta (Kingston Lacy, July 14), a folk festival at Felbrigg Hall (May 28), or the Enterprise Neptune 30th anniversary jazz concert at Plas Newydd on Anglesey (August 26).

Fireworks. Open air concert Leeds Castle, Kent

The Trust's programme also has a series of lectures at the Purcell Room and other London venues from February to December: speakers include Viscount Norwich, Sir Nicholas Goodison, David Bellamy ("The Natural History of the National Trust") and the Duchess of Devonshire ("Behind the scenes at a country house"). A centenary exhibition will be on view at the National Gallery from November 22 to March 10, 1996; and another opens this March at the Royal Cornwall Museum, Truro. During their centenary year, the National Trust will also be unveiling the completion of its largest-ever conservation project, when Uppark in West Sussex reopens to the public. This 17th century house suffered near-terminal damage in a terrible fire in 1989, but the Trust was determined it would not perish.

Wedgwood, Keats and Purcell

The bicentenary of Wedgwood's death will be marked with a big exhibition, "Josiah Wedgwood - The Man and His Mark" at the City Museum & Art Gallery, Stoke-on-Trent (June-September); the Victoria & Albert Museum has another exhibition opening in June; and the bicentenary will also be commemorated at the Lady Lever Art Gallery, Merseyside. There will be Keats exhibitions at Dove Cottage and the Wordsworth Museum, Cumbria (July-September), and the Guildhall Gallery, Winchester (June-July); while Purcell's music will be much in evidence at concerts, including those of the long-established Stately Homes Music Festival (May-September), which is working with the Purcell Tercentenary Trust to present recitals and chamber music at various country houses. There will also be a Purcell Festival in All Saints' Church, Tudeley, Kent (November 17-25).

Festival Events at Historic Houses, Castles & Gardens

In the same county, Leeds Castle again has an impressive programme of musical and other events; while Canterbury Cathedral will, for the very first

Royal Opera House. Elite Syncopations

time, be the setting for a Shakespeare play ("Romeo and Juliet", August 7-20). the comparably youthful Westminster Cathedral's centenary celebrations, from February to October, include an exhibition of items from the Vatican, an international festival of flowers with music (May 17-20), and concerts by resident and visiting choirs and BBC orchestras.

A stately home with its own 1995 anniversary is Wilton House near Salisbury, which is celebrating its

Barbara Hepworth Sculpture Garden. St.Ives, Cornwall

450-year-old Tudor origins (according to legend, Shakespeare once acted there, in "As You Like It"). Further west, a house of much later vintage opens to the public for the first time at Easter: High Cross at Dartington Hall near Totnes, dates from the 1930's and its interest is not limited to architecture. It contains Leonard and Dorothy Elmhirst's outstanding 20th century collection, including paintings by Ben Nicholson and David Jones; pottery by Bernard Leach and Hamada; fine books and some interesting letters. The house and collections will be open most of the year.

Literary Heritage

Our literature will also have a central place in the Festival of Arts and Culture, with Swansea the host for the UK Year of Literature and Writing - the fifth of the Arts Council's "Arts 2000" series. The main emphasis is on the spoken and written word, from ancient Welsh tales to the poetry of Dylan Thomas and the thrillers of Dick Francis, but there will also be events featuring music, dance and sculpture. Swansea's Maritime & Industrial Museum has exhibitions on "The Art of the Book" (February-March) and "The Printed Word (April-September). The West Country, long the home of writers and the setting of their works, has also adopted the literary heritage as its Festival theme. Dorset County Museum, Dorchester, which already has a reconstruction of Hardy's study, is opening a new literary gallery; Devizes Museum is highlighting Wiltshire writers; and Porlock Museum celebrates "Local Authors, Past and Present".

A new permanent exhibition opens in April at the Shakespeare Centre, Stratford-upon-Avon; while throughout the year "Emigrants", a large-scale exhibition on two centuries of emigration to North America, is on display at the Ulster American Folk Park, Omagh.

Add to all that the wealth of arts festivals taking place all over the country, and one gets the feeling that 1995 is going to be a very good year.

England's Fairytale Castle

Alton Castle

See entry under Staffordshire. Open all year round from May 1st 1995.

A ROMANTIC CASTLE - A FAIRYTALE FOR VISITORS

by Stephen Weeks

Alton Castle - the East Elevation

A Castle Awakes from its Centuries Old Slumber

The chance of recreating a major historic English castle occurs rarely. Many castles in England had fallen into ruin even before the Civil War in the 17th century; others met their end during the war. Those few that survived went on to be embellished or restored as seats of the nobility - Arundel, Alnwick, Raby, Warwick... Alton Castle, in Staffordshire, once the seat of the great Talbot family, Earls of Shrewsbury, literally fell asleep as in the fairytale of *Sleeping Beauty*. In the 1840's it was nearly awoken by the great Victorian architect Augustus Welby Pugin, but it wouldn't be until this year that it finally emerged from its centuries old slumber.

And when a building has been forgotten about, so is its history. When the current Alton Castle Project began in early 1993, a researcher began the daunting task of uncovering over eight hundred years of history... and there's still more to find, for before the Castle's present huge rock-cut moat and curtain wall were built by Bertram de Verdun, a Norman knight, around 1175, there was a Saxon stronghold on the site, whose last heiress with the romantic name of Rohesia, married this first of the de Verduns. Sir Bertram rode off on a crusade with Richard the Lionheart, never to return. He was buried at Acre, having died in battle at Jaffa in the Holy Land in 1191. And so the Castle descended - often through the female line (as heirs were liable to get themselves killed in battle) until it reached - by marriage in 1408 - the mighty English warrior Sir John Talbot, who became the first Earl of Shrewsbury. By this time the Castle had endured at least one siege and many an intrigue - for Alton is extremely lucky in having a chronicler who wrote of the day to day affairs of the

xv

place and its owners. Actually, the chronicler was a monk in the nearby Abbey of Croxden that Sir Bertram had also founded. Apart from such dramatic events as a bell falling and cracking, life in themonastery was pretty serene, and therefore the monastic diary is full of the more interesting events of the Castle! The Croxden Abbey Chronicle will be a major source of vivid detail for interpreting the Castle's early history for visitors, a researcher's dream!

A Smouldering Ruin

With the coming of the Talbots, the Castle's history then went hand in hand with the great events of the day: the Castle's illustrious owners were at battles from Agincourt to Bosworth, had connections with the great from Joan of Arc to Mary Queen of Scots, and - of course - supported King Charles in the Civil War: which caused Cromwell's men to bombard it, and leave it a smouldering ruin in the 1640s. This glorious period of chivalry, however, is that which inspired the romantic vision of medieval history and soaring castles that is the stuff of every child's dream. In 1844, the 16th Earl of Shrewbury, aided and abetted by Pugin - who had given London the romantic medieval inspired interiors of the rebuilt Houses of Parliament - decided to recreate that dream of lost romance at Alton.

Ruins of the 12th century castle with Pugin's building behind

Some years before, the 15th Earl had taken a fancy to the old rabbit warren on the abandoned Castle's estate, rebuilding an agent's house first as Alton Lodge. A few gothic bits later and it became Alton Abbey. Many battlements later and it became Alton Towers - and, with its magnificent gardens, the prin-cipal seat of the Premier Earls of England. His heir, John, the 16th Earl, was similarly smitten with the building bug, and having built a new Catholic church, school and monastery by the Castle site, decided to rebuild the Castle itself in a fantastic goth-ic style inspired by the surviving medieval castles in France and on the Rhine. In 1844 work started, with Pugin working directly off the foundations of the ruined medieval fortress. It is not known who was going to live there - the Earl himself, for weekends? his widow? or his heir, Bertram? But it didn't matter. The 16th Earl was, he thought, fabulously wealthy. But by the 1850's the Irish famines would dry up the rent stream from the vast holdings there gained in the 15th century, and in 1852 both the 16th Earl and Pugin his architect died. The dream Castle was still not quite a reality, with one tower unfinished and the interior still to fit out.

Castle 'For Sale'

Nervous executors hastily completed the building with simple materials and let it to the convent next door. In 1924 the ailing Shrewsbury Estate sold up. Alton Towers went, as did the Castle and thousands of acres. In 1989, the Catholic school that had lodged itself in the Castle closed, and the Castle's future became uncertain. It was put up for sale, only the second time since its first recorded appearance in the Domesday book nine hundred years before. The success of Alton Towers as a garden and `theme park' nearby made a future as a guest house or themed attraction seem possible - but the closeness of such a powerful visitor base also made it possible to mount a project that would complete Pugin's vision, and furnish it to show the Earls of Shrewbury's illustrious history as it might have been lived-in.

The Alton Towers' sale catalogues list the armour, tapestries, pictures, artefacts that were disposed of. Sadly, the Shrewsburys were still selling in the 1960s, when the last of the family portraits went. Our valiant researcher has traced many of these now - some in attics, others on the walls where they left (as valueless) in a former house family now an institu-tion, others in salerooms. Some will return to Alton; others will be expertly copied by a team of Indian master painters who have studied early paint tech-niques using their own hand-ground pigments.

It is the revival of the people who lived in the Castle which will make the place complete. A recreation

Alton's magnificent Vaulted ceilings

cannot simply stop at plaster ceilings or oak panelling: those you can find in town halls! But again, a Castle shouldn't just be a line-up of dowdy portraits of the 12th Earl or 1st Duke or last Countess, and it is in the presentation of the Castle medieval inhabitants that the real thrill of the Castle will lie for the visitor.

Dungeons, Battlements and High Turrets

Any visit to a castle should include entering through a strong gatehouse, climbing to high turrets and battlements, descending to deep dungeons. A castle should have winding stone stairs, lofty halls, and cellars cut into the bedrock. Alton has all these experiences! I had no hesitation in suggesting that all visitors should have the option of climbing to the battlements, and from there seeing the beautiful River Churnet winding through the countryside directly below the 200 foot precipice on which the Castle is built. And I also have had no hesitation in ensuring that a smouldering or blazing (*that* depending on season) log fire is always alight in the great hall hearth. But of those warriors that made the Castle, there are no portraits. Portraits only began as

likenesses in the 16th century in Britain, so the task has been to find images from a wide variety of sources. Theobald de Verdun in the 13th century left his seal showing him riding his great battle horse on a document sent by the barons to the Pope. John Talbot gave a wedding gift to Margaret of Anjou, bride of King Henry VI, that consisted of a volume of romances, illustrated with scenes that included the King giving Talbot his sword and thus creating him Earl. That one scene alone has become the basis for one of the castle's most stunning interiors.

The chapel that Pugin built in the castle was opened out into the hall for the use of the school as one large space. Whilst the Castle does have a smaller chapel now, the hall-as-chapel was an imbalance. The new emphasis on heraldry and chivalry provided the key to changing the chapel into a recreation of King Henry VI's Throne Room, using the illumination from The Shrewsbury Book for an exact reference for the throne with its elaborate embroidery, the dais and even the design of the wall hangings around the room.

The recreation of John Talbot's sword was an even greater challenge. The leading expert on medieval swords was called in, and gradually enough information was pulled together to ensure the result - forged

Just one of Alton's lofty turrets

Stained-glass window in Alton's Chapel

by an armourer in Essex - is absolutely accurate. Even the inscription on the sword has been discovered and is reproduced. As for Bertram de Verdun, as I write this, investigations are taking place in Acre and Jaffa for anything that might be recovered from Richard 1st's crusader army. Something is bound to turn up! History, as seen - and touched - through items of the period can be vivid and exciting. At Penhow Castle, in Wales, where I live, I have recovered meat bones from dishes eaten in the reign of Richard 111 - and they are very popular with adults and children alike, who can touch those very bones from five hundred years before.

They may be meat bones yet to the found at Alton. Certainly there is a filled-in ravine in front of the drawbridge and gatehouse that has yet to be explored. It is hoped that later in 1995 excavations of the moat and ravine will begin, and visitors will be able to watch the process.

Pugin and the Middle Ages

The other story that must be told at Alton is, of course, that of the genius of the new building's architect, Pugin. Last year's exhibition of his work at the V & A Museum in London rose the general level of awareness of his work. Alton Castle was his great

unfinished masterpiece. Fortunately, he left many designs for wallpaper, furniture, carpets, fabrics, tiles, joinery - and it has been relatively simple to copy or adapt these for Alton. Pugin made true medieval Gothic the style that rules the second half of the 19th century, and he opened people's eyes then (as now) to the colourful world of the middle ages. Such colour work requires elaborate stencil painting and Roderick Gradidge, an architect with specialist knowledge of Victorian interiors, has advised on the overall look of the interior. Generations of use as a school had left the Castle with lino floors, emulsioned corridors and rows of washbasins. A Pugin interior, even in a clifftop castle, is a warm, glowing thing. A team of stencil painters has recreated the feel that the great architect would have wished for this special castle, although no actual designs or plans exist from this time.

But local architect David Slade had the job of making the Castle function for the exacting requirements of an historic house opening for the first time in 1995. To begin with the carriage drives laid by Pugin were never used by the school. The romantic Riverside Drive, that turns sharply and becomes The Ascent - climbing by rocky outcrops and eventually (after a mile!) providing the visitor or guest with his or her first tantalising glimpse of the Castle... this drive had to be dug out from nearly two feet of leaves and debris. It also had to be made to conform to the requirements of the modern motor car. Then there was the problem of catering.

Fairytale Castle for all to Enjoy

The Castle itself has few large rooms, and those that it has are in full use telling their historic story, but

One of the Chapel's sculptures

Alton Castle - as seen from the Castle's park

any historic attraction today is under increasing pressure to service all kinds of catering needs - a far cry from the days, not so long ago, when homemade teas in thick china cups were served by the local WI in the old kitchens. Fortunately, near to the Castle, was an old school hall, and this has been converted into The Moot Hall - a recreation of the hall that once stood in the outer ward of the Castle, now part of Alton village, and which was demolished in 1845. By using a relatively modern building, and disguising it with a brilliant gothic design by Roderick Gradidge, an efficient catering establishment is being created. Following a `Candlelit Tour' of the Castle (which run all through the year, including the Christmas season), the Moot Hall will serve a popular "Wars of the Roses Feast" - a carefully researched medieval supper and entertainment, themed on the exploits of the Talbots throughout that turbulent period of the 15th century. An important aspect of introducing anything for sale at an historic house is seeing that all `products' are not only of good value, but fit into the general ambience of a house, rather than - in the case of catering - a restaurant or hotel. The limited number of guest suites in the Castle, as another example, will have no reference to being in what is, effectively, a guest house: they will be furnished as country house bedrooms - and dinner will be served to all house guests at a set time from one menu at one long table. Fortunately, guests who are staying in the Castle will be able to eat in the Castle itself - with the food being hauled up in a lift designed by Pugin from a kitchen in the rock-cut basement below! Work on the guest accommodation was second priority to the public rooms, and is proceeding this summer. And now the Act of Parliament has been passed that allows marriages to be solemnised in castles, then the highly decorated chapel will have a new role. There can be nothing more romantic than castles in any event, and Alton - under the imaginative hand of the visionary architect Pugin - was conceived to be the epitome of romance, a true fairytale castle. **Now the dream is underpinned with sand, cement and solid marketing!**

Editor's Notes

Stephen Weeks is a film-maker, writer and conservationist. In 1973- at age 25, and after directing his third feature film - he bought partly ruined Penhow Castle in Wales as his home and which he has made the subject of a successful repair and presentation programme. This began his work in pioneering audio-tours, and in setting up Monumental Trust to revive other buildings in need.

RAINBOW FAIR *presents*

LISTEN TO YOUR HERITAGE

By Natalie Cox

For some time now there has been great debate and great interest in interpretation within leisure management and National Institutions, museums and the like. Interpretation is the buzz word of the nineties and it has many connotations. To a large degree the audio and audio visual guides and information sectors have taken second place to the more avant garde display, set work and printed material now available. This has largely been due to the technology of the replication equipment lagging behind.

A Museum and Heritage attraction - talking signpost

It is also that the visitor has been used to seeing, reading and touching exhibits rather than experiencing a total generic atmosphere together with documentary, anecdotal and descriptive audio information. The ability for the user to interact and to choose their pathway to revisit an object or scene has hitherto been unavailable in the marketplace. The wonderful Walkman cassette systems, which in themselves provide useful information and experiences, can only assist the visitor on a chronological walk. The advent of transmission and infra-red systems improved the lot of the audio tour industry, but still presented enormous headaches in installation and operation, particularly in the Heritage industry.

For the last two and a half years a British company has been working to overcome this problem by developing an interactive random access machine which takes the effort out of audio tours and gives control to the visitor. The company also specialises in Sets-Designs-Animations-Talking Images-Projections-SFX-Audio and Audio Visual. The Company was originally set up in 1989 in Teddington, Middlesex by Malcolm Dexter-Tissington. Malcolm is not your usual managing director of a museum and leisure-based company, he has been described as Lateral Inventor in the Sinclair mould; music performance and production, children's books, and technology products have all played their part in shaping his career.

Malcolm was educated in Surrey. Excelling in sport, music, and technology, he represented his area in several activities. He began his career in Australia as a professional footballer; injury forced a premature end to this, and a spell as coach of a second division side followed before he joined the Sports and Fashion conglomerate, Speedo.

The marketing and promotional skills necessary to fulfill his position presented Malcolm with countless opportunities to shine in the Australasian market. His successes included the now legendary "Paris Album Collection" which eventually went worldwide with the "super pop group" **Supertramp**.

Malcolm's work in the arts and heritage industry really began from a chance meeting in 1973, when he was spotted by the eminent Australian conductor David Cubbin. Drawing on his musical talents, (he first sang as a chorister in Sir Malcolm Sargent's festive presentation at the opening of the Fairfield Halls in Croydon, then was a member of the rock group "Angels") Malcolm performed solo roles in Opera and Oratorio throughout Australia.

Because classical music requires such intensive training and education Malcolm needed to go back into education to further supplement his musical skills. This meant from very early in the morning on assignments, off to rehearsals at 10am, back to swotting 12-2pm and off to opera rehearsals in the

The Petersen Car Museum

afternoon back to university in the evenings for over fours years to gain his tertiary qualifications. He wasn't to know at the time, but part of the studies and associated activities meant learning and being involved with concert management and promotion, theatre production, design, sound recording, and special effects.

By 1981 Malcolm's singing career had taken in some 20 countries and over 50 roles totalling more than 700 performances. He was fortunate to be awarded the 1981 Queen Elizabeth II Silver Jubilee Scholarship to study in Juilliard Center, New York, and at the Cantica Studio in Kent, two of the world most prestigious music foundations. The Hoffmans Music Masters award followed shortly after when Malcolm returned to base in England.

Most classically trained performers experience the wonderfully termed period of "resting" (to the uninitiated - out of work), and during the early period of 1984 Malcolm helped out a national charity by promoting a series of Gala concerts. The sponsor of these concerts was so pleased with the result of these performances that Malcolm was invited to spearhead their 1985 musical activities which culminated in directing and producing the National UK tour of "Requiem" by Andrew Lloyd Webber.

This led to Malcolm joining the leisure production company, Living Images, a specialist design and build production company which designed, created and produced Heritage, Museum and Leisure based displays and components.

As part of their technical services and production team he was responsible for some thirty projects from military museums (Royal Air Force), Cartoon Grottos (Shoe People) to the design of visitor attrac-

tions - Checkpoint Cheltenham - other projects included the conception and the production of the world's first projected waterfall with pool and cameo for the natural history documentary for the Museum of the North in Llanberis, North Wales.

Malcolm's talents in specialist audio production enabled the company to capture a specific generic section within its product market and he produced custom audio, audio-visual presentations for its unique displays. Examples of this can be seen at the Royal Green Jackets tableaux of the Waterloo scene where a combination of interactive CD and lighting is used on the one hand and an interactive "1815" rifle range using lasters and I/R on the other.

Not being content with being a workaholic, Malcolm during what appears to be his "sleep" time has written two series of books for children; the first 26 books are to be released in 1995 along with a cartoon series for television, and the second series called Nicholas and his Magic Hat, is currently being completed. Malcolm has also written over 20 songs, plays and musicals; his production company Attwood/Plenty Publications also publishes classical works of young Australian composers.

The Interpreter™ in use

A dugout scene at the Royal Irish Regimental Museum in Ballymena

When Malcolm started his own design and build company in 1989 he had already built up an impressive client list, to which he was able to add significantly, incorporating new clients such as various Ministry of Defence departments, the First Leisure Corporation, Ulster Museum, Oriel ynys mon and many other Museum and Heritage attractions. New and innovative products have been introduced to the market by Malcolm such as the **Talking Signpost, Talking Envelope** and the **Communicator**, the first in a line of solid state audio tour guide systems.

The **Interpreter**™ is the latest and the most successful of Malcolm's innovations. It is a solid state, state-of-the-art audio tour guide system. It has no moving parts and consequently requires minimal maintenance. It is an ideal companion for visits to museums and galleries, historic houses and castles - in fact anywhere a tour guide is needed. It can be used outside too, for town tours, gardens, parks, zoos, woodland trails and nature reserves.

The system came into operation in April 1994 and was first seen at the D-Day Museum in Portsmouth. It has subsequently been used in the Queens Gallery at Buckingham Palace, St. George's Hall, Liverpool and The Miniatures Museum in Los Angeles. During 1995 the Palace of Versailles and Muse Orsay in Paris open, along with the Petersen Car Museum in California. The Bird House at Harewood House is amongst the many UK attractions scheduled to open at the begining of the tourist season. Additional contracts are being negotiated in Australia, Japan, Spain, Eire and Germany. Contrafts are currently under negotiation with Gracelands in Memphis and the Heritage-President Jackson's home in Nashfield.

The D-Day anniversary activities in June of this year provided a rigorous testing ground for the *Interpreter*™. The brief was to produce a tough system that would kept to keep the staffing costs down, but provide maximum variety and random selection of the tour in five translations.

The unique Overlord Embroidery, the largest of its kind in the world, runs the full circumference of the room. In a separated area in the centre of the room an audio visual presentation is given every fifteen to twenty minutes.

This presented difficulties in providing the method of tour to be used. Many visitors wanted to break from their appreciation to take in the Audio Visual display, then return to any one of the 34 panels of the Embroidery. This meant that the sound systems had to cope with a wide range of technical facilities.

The MkV *Interpreter* ™ with a total running time of 60 minutes and the facility to carry up to 999 different messages, provided a solution to this problem. Without a cassette to rewind or fast foward to the appropriate place, visitors simply used the numeric keyboard, tapping in the number of the panel of their choice to call up the information on that section of the Tapestry. Added to this feature, the high quality soundtrack brings voices, music and sound effects together in any number of languages, providing the

Reminiscing in the War Room

visitor with the information they require in an interesting, atmospheric format.

The versatility of *Interpreter*™ system, and its several formats available, mean that longer running times of up to six hours are possible.

The distribution of *Interpreter* ™ is so simple that virtually no staff training is needed and this overcame the need for high staffing of the D-Day Museum. It takes only one member of staff to distribute the handset from the mother station which charges them every night. A unique driving logic drains the batteries and recharges each handset, thereby eliminating time dating. Using the *Interpreter* ™ at D-Day is made easier for the staff by having the facility of a full 10 hour battery use per day, which enabled 250 machines to service 16,000 visitors with a choice of five tours in the peak period after the D-Day Anniversary.

Another feature is that if the visitor requires another tour or language, all they have to do is simply insert the handset into a pod and in a few seconds the new, relevant commentary or tour is loaded. The Museum hope to add new commentaries and languages by using satellite stations.

In keeping with Malcolm's 25 years involvement with the Heritage, Museum and Tourist Industry, 1995 will see the first of four new products: the *Interpreter*™ MkVII a Fixed River Transit System installed in France. This will be closely followed by two new products for the Heritage Industry - all conceived, designed and produced by Malcolm, whose team produces all their products in the UK - no mean achievement given the stiff competition in technological products from the Far East markets. Preliminary research and development has also commenced on a Vision Wand System.

One thing is for sure - sleeping in Teddington will not be a problem for Malcolm and his team.

For more information contact the Soundalive Group on 0181-977 8222.

THE GARDENS AT
HATFIELD HOUSE Hertfordshire

"There are nearly 14 acres of formal and informal gardens dating back to the late 15th century. From 1609 to 1611 John Tradescant the Elder laid out and planted the gardens for Robert Cecil, the builder of the House. Today the gardens, much embellished in the last years, contain many of the same plants growing in knot gardens typical of the period, arranged in the court of the 15th century Palace where Queen Elizabeth I spent much of her childhood. There are herb and sweet gardens, a parterre of herbaceous plants and roses, fountains, statuary and a foot maze or labyrinth, the whole enclosed in ancient rose-brick walls, topiaried yews, holly and pleached limes.

A wilderness garden, planted with forest and ornamental trees, blossoms in the spring with crabs, cherries, magnolias and rhododendrons underplanted with many flowers and bulbs, the whole providing colour and interest (for there are many rare and unusual plants) for all seasons."
"Photographs by Mick Hales, Garry Rogers and Jeremy Whitaker."

"I feel at home here as I gaze down and respond to the feeling of total delight which it gives me . . . "   Sir Roy Strong

"Hatfield's gardens are the most completely beautiful and fit for their purpose of any great house in England." "Tradescant" of the RHS Journal.

FOR DETAILS SEE HERTFORDSHIRE SECTION

HERITAGE EDUCATION TRUST

CENTENARY YEAR WINNERS

The National Trust's commitment to education has been dramatically signalled by the announcement of the 1994 winners of Sandford Awards, sponsored by Reed Information Services and administered by the Heritage Education Trust. Of a grand national total of thirteen awards, four have gone to National Trust properties: Dunham Massey and Moseley Old Hall in England, Chirk Castle in Wales, and Castle Ward in Northern Ireland. And for good measure to complete the geographical spread a Sandford Award will also be presented to Culzean Castle & Country Park owned by the parallel but quite separate National Trust for Scotland. Dunham Massey Hall & Park will host the National Presentation Ceremony of the Heritage Education Trust in March, 1995, the centenary year of the National Trust.

Dunham Massey

Opportunities for all at Dunham Massey

Costumed senior servants provide tutelage in Victorian cooking, laundering, praying and eating inside while rangers explain park management outside: this is all part of a comprehensive and active education programme which uses both the Hall and its surrounding environment. Pauline Mills is the Education Co-ordinator responsible and her plans for development of the existing programme envisage a 'learning from portraits' element. In addition Dunham Massey also offers a complete day modified for adults based on the children's Living History Experience package as part of teachers' In-service training (INSET).

Local schools are fortunate indeed to have such an amenity on-hand where pleasure, understanding and knowledge are available in equal and generous proportions. The Sandford Award judge records that

parties of pupils make use of the singular educational opportunities at Dunham Massey from most surrounding Local Education Authorities. Salford and Stockport come in for especial praise for forging excellent working relationships with the property through teachers and advisers. Dunham Massey is also in partnership with Grand Metropolitan Estates which contributes to education through sponsorship. The opportunities for Heritage Education in Cheshire are now immense and Dunham Massey brings to five the total number of Sandford Award holders in the County: there is now really no reason why any Cheshire school child should be deprived of the unique learning opportunities offered through the existence of education resources and facilities of quality in historic buildings.

Chirk Castle Every Child's Dream

Dungeons where prisoners hung in chains, arrow slit windows, murder holes, drum towers, armour—these are just some of the authentic aspects of history which at Chirk comprise what the Sandford Award judge described as every child's dream of a border castle.

This dream becomes a reality in the hands of the skilled helpers and volunteers who now implement the education programme masterminded by Jill Burton, the National Trust Education Officer who is also responsible for the education programme at Erddig, Sandford Award 1991. What is so striking at Chirk Castle is the versatility of the education programme. In setting it up the local history adviser and a development group comprising both primary and secondary teachers was established. A programme was devised focussing on the National Curriculum as it then was: money was spent and materials produced. Then the government changed the history curriculum. Inevitably some of the material will go to waste. But schools can and do use their discretionary time to take a broader view of Heritage Education, for the authorities at Chirk are only too willing to adapt to any reasonable request to fit in with the needs of individual schools which can be accommodated by the Castle's background. The range of options on offer is really impressive and includes houses and households, castles, war and society, Tudors and Stuarts, Britain 1500-1960 and local history. Another very interesting trend is a steady increase in the number of foreign pupils thought to be the result of an English language tour operator in Chester. In response the ever adaptable Jill Burton and her team are setting up programmes in German, French and Dutch, with Italian to follow. Their initiatives could do much to offset the sometimes none too laudable reputations of some foreign language schools on the south coast.

Long-term Education Commitment

It is a crucial part of the Sandford Award scheme to encourage long-term commitment to education at historic properties throughout the UK and to set, maintain and improve standards. A Sandford Award is not seen as a one-off prize but as a marker of serious commitment to the community at large in one of the most important ways possible, namely through education. Sandford Award holders must after five years apply for review if they wish to remain listed.

Children at Croxteth taking part in the 'Spring Awake' theme week run by the education team

Llancaiach Fawr Manor

Sandford Award judges will then be looking for evidence not only of the maintenance of standards but also of improvement and development of the educational services and facilities which originally earned recognition. Again the National Trust has scored in 1994. Of the four Awards to be made at the 1995 National Presentation Ceremony to National Trust properties, two will be to properties which already hold Awards from earlier years: both Moseley Old Hall and Castle Ward will be adding a third Award to their collection.

The First National Presentation Ceremony of the Heritage Education Trust

Moseley Old Hall near Wolverhampton received its first Sandford Award in 1983 when it was also the venue for the first National Presentation Ceremony organised by the Heritage Education Trust which had been set up in 1982 to take over the administration of the Sandford Award from the Council for Environmental Education. Lord Montagu, himself on the eve of taking up his position as first Chairman of English Heritage, was Guest of Honour to present the Awards. On that occasion there were just two other Sandford Award winners: Hopetoun House in Scotland and Bickleigh Castle in Devon. Each has received subsequent Awards and both are still listed by the Heritage Education Trust for the excellence of their education services.

Since its own first Award in 1983 Moseley Old Hall has demonstrably developed its education by appointing a part-time education assistant, enlarging the range of its activities for children and initiating training for new guides and helpers as well as up-dating teachers' packs. Moseley Old Hall has one

Castle Ward

enviable claim to fame: Charles II really did sleep there, spending two days at the Hall following his flight after the Battle of Worcester in 1651. It would have been all too easy for the education programme to rest on this laurel. It does not do so and presents instead an impressive range of activities illustrative of a wide span of seventeeth century life and work including the plague and domestic duties in Stuart times.

Co-operative Education Themes in Northern Ireland

Castle Ward in Co.Down, Northern Ireland is the only Sandford Award holder in the Province. Its link with Heritage Education is a strong one and of long-standing: it won its first Sandford Award in 1980, two years before the Heritage Education Trust was set up and while the Award scheme was guided by the informal 'Sandford Group' and administered by the Council for Environmental Education. It was off the mark at once following the setting up of the Quinquennial Review procedure by the Heritage Education Trust in 1986 and won its second full Sandford Award in 1987. Its third Award in 1994 seals its commitment to education.

Developments at Castle Ward are founded on co-operation. Together National Trust staff and colleagues in the South Eastern Education and Library Board—the education authority for the area—have worked to develop and sustain a very valuable service for schools. This idea of co-operation extends into the work done with children of which a particular feature is bringing together Roman Catholic and Protestant children under a cross-community scheme. This in turn provides

opportunities for developing education for mutual understanding and cultural heritage, both of which are statutory curricular themes within the Northern Ireland curriculum. And now British Telecom has stepped in with new sponsorship arrangements with the Department of Education for Northern Ireland which will underwrite development work for the next three years.

A National Education Resource

The work of the National Trust in setting up educational amenities in so many of the properties in its care is inspirational. It is a relatively new but most important development and it is not alone in responding to the challenge of the Sandford Award . Private owners, charitable trusts, small limited companies, industrial giants, local authorities, deans and chapters, museum and gallery authorities all feature in the full list of Sandford Award holders. Together this comparatively small band makes a huge contribution to national education.

Culzean Castle

If you would like to support the work of the Heritage Education Trust and be kept informed of developments you may register on the mailing list by sending a cheque for £6.50p payable to the Heritage Education Trust to Martyn Dyer, Chief Executive, Heritage Education Trust, the University College of Ripon & York St. John, College Road, Ripon HG4 2QX. Telephone (01969) 650 294. Those on the mailing list receive NIMROD, the periodical of the Heritage Education Trust, newsletters and the chance to apply for an invitation to the annual National Presentation Ceremony.

Sandford Award Holders
1994

The following properties received Sandford Awards in the years in brackets after their names in recognition of the excellence of their educational services and facilities and their outstanding contribution to Heritage Education. Two or more dates indicate that the property has been reviewed and received further recognition under the system of quinquennial review introduced by the Heritage Education Trust in 1986. Any property which wishes to retain its listing must apply for review of its educational services and facilities five years after the date of its last award.

Sandford Award holders may now apply jointly with a school for the Reed Award for children with special educational needs. Under this award the Heritage Education Trust will also be able to make financial grants to selected Reed Award winners deemed by the Directors of the Trust to be of exceptional merit. The annual closing date for both awards is 31st January.

ASTON HALL, *Birmingham* (**1993**)

*AVONCROFT MUSEUM OF BUILDINGS, *Bromsgrove, Worcestershire* (**1988**) (**1993**)

*BASS MUSEUM VISITIOR CENTRE AND SHIRE HORSE STABLES, *Burton upon Trent, Staffordshire* (**1990**)

BEAULIEU ABBEY, *Nr. Lyndhurst, Hampshire* (**1978**) (**1986**) (**1991**)

BEWDLEY MUSEUM, *Worcestershire* (**1992**)

BICKLEIGH CASTLE, *Nr. Tiverton, Devon* (**1983**) (**1988**)

BLAKESLEY HALL MUSEUM, *Birmingham* (**1993**)

BLENHEIM PALACE, *Woodstock, Oxfordshire* (**1982**) (**1987**) (**1992**)

BOUGHTON HOUSE, *Kettering, Northamptonshire* (**1988**) (**1993**)

BOWHILL HOUSE & COUNTRY PARK, *Bowhill, Nr. Selkirk, Borders, Scotland* (**1993**)

BRONTË PARSONAGE MUSEUM, *Haworth, Nr. Keighley, West Yorkshire* (**1993**)

BUCKFAST ABBEY, *Buckfastleigh, Devon* (**1985**) (**1990**)

CANTERBURY CATHEDRAL, *Canterbury, Kent* (**1988**) (**1993**)

*CASTLE MUSEUM, *York, North Yorkshire* (**1987**) (**1993**)

CASTLE WARD, *County Down, Northern Ireland* (**1980**) (**1987**) (**1994**)

CATHEDRAL & ABBEY CHURCH OF ST. ALBAN, *St. Albans, Hertfordshire* (**1986**) (**1991**)

*THE CECIL HIGGINS ART GALLERY AND MUSEUM & *THE BEDFORD MUSEUM, *Bedford, Bedfordshire* (**1989**) (**1993**)

CHILTERN OPEN AIR MUSEUM, *Chalfont St. Giles, Buckinghamshire* (**1994**)

CHIRK CASTLE, *Chirk, Clwyd , Wales* (**1994**)

CLIVE HOUSE MUSEUM, *Shrewsbury, Shropshire* (**1992**)

COLDHARBOUR MILL, *Working Wool Museum, Cullompton, Devon* (**1989**) (**1994**)

COMBE SYDENHAM, *Nr. Taunton, Somerset* (**1984**) (**1989**) (**1994**)

CRATHES CASTLE AND GARDENS, *Kincardineshire, Scotland* (**1992**)

CROXTETH HALL AND COUNTRY PARK, *Liverpool, Merseyside* (**1980**) (**1989**) (**1994**)

CULZEAN CASTLE AND COUNTRY PARK, *Ayrshire, Scotland* (**1984**) (**1989**) (**1994**)

*DOVE COTTAGE AND THE WORDSWORTH MUSEUM, *Grasmere, Cumbria* (**1990**)

DRUMLANRIG CASTLE AND COUNTRY PARK, *Dumfriesshire, Scotland* (**1989**)

DULWICH PICTURE GALLERY, *London* (**1990**)

DUNHAM MASSEY, *Altrincham, Cheshire* (**1994**)

ERDDIG HALL, *Nr. Wrexham, Clywd, Wales* (**1991**)

GAINSBOROUGH OLD HALL, *Gainsborough, Lincolnshire* (**1988**) (**1993**)

GEORGIAN HOUSE, *Edinburgh, Lothian, Scotland* (**1978**)

GODOLPHIN , *Helston, Cornwall* (**1993**)

HAREWOOD HOUSE, *Leeds,West Yorkshire* (**1979**) (**1989**) (**1994**)

SIR HAROLD HILLIER GARDENS AND ARBORETUM, *Ampfield, Nr. Romsey, Hampshire* (**1993**)

HELMSHORE TEXTILE MUSEUM, *Lancashire* (**1990**)

HOLDENBY HOUSE, *Northampton, Northamptonshire* (**1985**) (**1991**)

HOPETOUN HOUSE, *South Queensferry, Lothian, Scotland* (**1983**) (**1991**)

KINGSTON LACY HOUSE, *Wimborne, Dorset* (**1990**)

LAUNDRY COTTAGE, *Normanby Hall Country Park, South Humberside* (**1994**)

LICHFIELD CATHEDRAL AND VISITORS' STUDY CENTRE, *Lichfield, Staffordshire* (**1991**)

LLANCAIACH FAWR MANOR, *Nelson, Mid Glamorgan* (**1994**)

*MACCLESFIELD MUSEUMS, *Macclesfield, Cheshire* (**1988**) (**1993**)

MOSELEY OLD HALL, *Wolverhampton, West Midlands* (**1983**) (**1989**) (**1994**)

NATIONAL WATERWAYS MUSEUM, *Gloucester, Gloucestershire* (**1991**)

NORTON PRIORY, *Cheshire* (**1992**)

*OAKWELL HALL COUNTRY PARK, *Birstall, West Yorkshire* (**1988**) (**1993**)

PENHOW CASTLE, *Nr. Newport, Gwent, Wales* (**1980**) (**1986**) (**1993**)

*THE PRIEST'S HOUSE MUSEUM, *Wimborne Minster, Dorset* (**1993**)

*QUARRY BANK MILL, *Styal, Cheshire* (**1987**) (**1992**)

ROCKINGHAM CASTLE, *Nr. Corby, Northamptonshire* (**1980**) (**1987**) (**1992**)

ROMAN BATHS MUSEUM, *Bath, Avon* (**1994**)

ROWLEY'S HOUSE MUSEUM, *Shrewsbury, Shropshire* (**1993**)

RYEDALE FOLK MUSEUM, *Hutton le Hole, North Yorkshire* (**1993**)

THE SHUGBOROUGH ESTATE, *Stafford, Staffordshire* (**1987**) (**1992**)

TATTON PARK, *Knutsford, Cheshire* (**1979**) (**1986**) (**1991**)

*TOWER OF LONDON, *Tower Bridge, London* (**1978**) (**1986**) (**1991**)

*WIGAN PIER,*Wigan, Lancashire* (**1987**) (**1992**)

WIGHTWICK MANOR, *Wolverhampton, West Midlands* (**1986**) (**1991**)

*WILBERFORCE HOUSE AND GEORGIAN HOUSES, *Hull, Humberside* (**1990**)

WIMPOLE HALL, *Nr. Cambridge, Cambridgeshire* (**1988**) (**1993**)

1994 Results
Full Sandford Awards

CHILTERN OPEN AIR MUSEUM
CHIRK CASTLE
DUNHAM MASSEY

LAUNDRY COTTAGE
LLANCAIACH FAWR MANOR
ROMAN BATHS MUSEUM

Quinquennial Review
1994
Full Sandford Awards

At Quinquennial review Full Awards are made where the educational services and facilities are deemed to have been developed or improved since the date of the previous Award. The classification 'listing retained' indicates that the educational services and facilities are deemed to have retained their original level of excellence.

CASTLE WARD
COLDHARBOUR MILL
CROXTETH HALL AND COUNTRY PARK
MOSELEY OLD HALL

CULZEAN CASTLE AND COUNTRY PARK
COMBE SYDENHAM
HAREWOOD HOUSE

Quinquennial Review
1994
Listing Retained

DRUMLANRIG

BICKLEIGH CASTLE

Croxteth Hall from the air. In 1994 the Hall and Country Park won their third Sandford award for excellence in Heritage education.

The Sandford Awards and the Reed Awards are both administered by the Heritage Education Trust and sponsored by Reed Information Services.

Application forms and full details of the two Awards and details of the work of the **Heritage Education Trust** from: **Martyn Dyer, Heritage Education Trust, the University College of Ripon & York St. John, College Road, Ripon HG4 2QX telephone 01969 650 294.**

For details of museums shown above listed with a star, please refer to **Museums & Galleries in Great Britain and Ireland, 1995 edition.**

Palace of Holyroodhouse
Edinburgh

The ridge, known as the Royal Mile, that slopes downwards from Edinburgh Castle, comes to a majestic conclusion at Holyroodhouse where Palace and Abbey stand against the spectacular backdrop of Salisbury Crags.

See Lothian Section for further details.

Historic Houses Castles and Gardens
in Great Britain and Ireland

 The National Trust Denotes properties in the care of the National Trust

ENGLISH HERITAGE
 Denotes properties in the care of English Heritage

 Denotes properties in the care of the National Trust for Scotland

 Denotes property owned and administered by a member of the Historic Houses Association

Denotes property in the care of CADW - Welsh Historic Monuments

Denotes property under the auspices of Irish Heritage

 Denotes guided tours of the building

 Denotes the major part of the property is suitable for wheelchairs

 Denotes educational services recognised by the Heritage Education Trust

 Denotes that all property is a recipient of the Sandford Award

 Denotes property is open all year

AVON

BARSTAPLE HOUSE (TRINITY ALMSHOUSES)
(Bristol Municipal Charities)
Bristol   map **14** U17
Telephone: (0117) 9265777 (Warden)

ENGLISH HERITAGE

Victorian almshouse with garden courtyard.

Location: Old Market Street, Bristol; ½ m from City centre on A420.
Station(s): Bristol Temple Meads (¾ m).
Open: GARDEN & EXTERIOR OF BUILDINGS ONLY, now extensively renovated. All the year week-days 10-4.
Admission: Free.
The Almshouse is occupied mainly by elderly residents & their rights for privacy should be respected.

BECKFORD'S TOWER
(The Beckford Tower Trust)
Bath   BA1 9BH   map **14** U18
Telephone: (01225) 338727

Built 1827 by William Beckford of Fonthill. A small museum (first floor) illustrating Beckford's life; fine views from Belvedere (156 easy steps).

Location: 2 m from Bath Spa Station via Lansdown Road.
Station(s): Bath Spa (2 m).
Open: Apr-end Oct Sat Sun & Bank Hol Mon 2-5. Parties other days by arrangement.
Admission: Adults £1.50 children/OAPs 75p.

Humphrey Repton (1752-1815)
Artist and garden designer

His work can be seen at the following properties included in Historic Houses Castles and Gardens:-

Corsham Court
Uppark
Sezincote

CLAVERTON MANOR
(The American Museum in Britain)
nr Bath   map **14** U18
Telephone: (01225) 460503

A Greek Revival House high above the valley of the River Avon. Completely furnished rooms showing American decorative arts from the late 17th to the mid 19th centuries. Galleries of special exhibits. Paintings, furniture, glass, silver, textiles, miniature rooms and Folk Art. Dallas Pratt Collection of Historical Maps, Special Exhibitions, American gardens.

Location: 2½ m from Bath Station via Bathwick Hill; 3¼ m SE of Bath via Warminster Road (A36) & Claverton village. Bus 18 (to University) from bus station - alight The Avenue, 10 mins walk to Museum.
Station(s): Bath Spa (2½ m).
Open: End Mar-beginning Nov every day (except Mons) 2-5 Gardens open throughout the season 1-6 (except Mon).
Admission: House and Grounds £5 children £2.50 and OAPs £4.50 (1994 prices) Grounds and Galleries only £2 children £1. Adult and Educational parties by previous arrangement with the Secretary.
Refreshments: Teas with American cookies. Light lunches at weekends.

CLEVEDON COURT 🌿 The National Trust

Tickenham Road, Clevedon   BS21 6QU   map 14 U18
Telephone: (01275) 872257

A 14th century manor house incorporating a 12th century tower and a 13th century hall with terraced 18th century garden; rare shrubs and plants. The home of the Elton family. Important collections of Nailsea glass and Eltonware.

Location: 1½ m E of Clevedon on the Bristol Road B3130.
Station(s): Yatton (3 m).
Open: 2 Apr-28 Sept Wed Thurs & Sun also Bank Hol Mons 2.30-5.30 (last adm 5).
Admission: £3.40 (children under 17 must be accompanied by an adult).
Refreshments: Tea-room in Great Hall open 2.30-5 (not NT).
No dogs. Unsuitable for wheelchairs. Coaches by appointment. Guided evening tours by prior arrangement.

DYRHAM PARK 🌿 The National Trust

nr Bristol and Bath   SN14 8ER   map 14 U18   &
Telephone: (0117) 9372501

Late 17th century house set in an ancient deer park. The Blathwayt furniture and Dutch paintings in a fine series of panelled rooms.

Location: 12 m E of Bristol approach from Bath/Stroud Road (A46), 2 m S of Tormarton interchange with M4, 8 m N of Bath.
Station(s): Bath Spa 8 m.
Open: Park Daily 12-5.30 (or dusk if earlier) last adm 5. *Closed* Christmas Day. House & Garden 1 Apr-29 Oct Daily (except Thurs & Fri) 12-5.30. Last admission 5 or dusk if earlier.
Admission: House Gardens & Park £4.80 Children £2.40 *Parties must book.* Park only £1.60 Children 80p.
Refreshments: Lunches and teas in new licensed stable restaurant.
Dog walking area provided but no dogs in deer park. Wheelchairs provided. Braille guide. Children's guide. Activity trail guide. National Trust shop.

ENGLISHCOMBE TITHE BARN

(Dr Jennie Walker)
Englishcombe   BA2 9DU   map 14 U18   &
Telephone: (01225) 425073
Fax: (01225) 425073

Early 14th century cruck framed tithe barn. Recently restored mediaeval graffiti.

Location: Adjacent to Englishcombe Village church 1 m S.W. of Bath.
Open: Suns and bank hols from Good Fri to Aug bank hol 2-6pm.
Admission: Adult £2.50 child £1.50 (accompanied by an adult) disabled free.
Events/Exhibitions: Telephone for confirmation.
Car parking facilities.

HORTON COURT 🌿 The National Trust

Horton   BS17 6QR   map 14 U18   &

A Cotswold manor house restored and altered in the 19th century. 12th century hall and late Perpendicular ambulatory in garden only shown.

Location: 3 m NE of Chipping Sodbury, 3/4m N of Horton, 1 m W of Bath/Stroud Road (A46).
Station(s): Yate 5 m.
Open: HALL & AMBULATORY ONLY 1 Apr-28 Oct Wed & Sat 2-6 (or sunset if earlier).
Other times by written appointment with the tenant.
Admission: £1.50 Children 80p. *No reduction for parties.*
No dogs. Unsuitable for coaches. Wheelchairs - ambulatory only. No WCs.

NUMBER ONE, ROYAL CRESCENT

(Bath Preservation Trust)
Bath   map 14 U18
Telephone: (01225) 428126

Number 1 was the first house to be built in the Royal Crescent, John Wood the Younger's fine example of Palladian architecture. The crescent was begun in 1767 and completed by 1774. The house was given to the Bath Preservation Trust in 1968 and both the exterior and interior have been accurately restored. Visitors can see a grand town house of the late 18th century with authentic furniture, paintings and carpets. On the ground floor are the Study and Dining Room and on the first floor a Lady's Bedroom and Drawing Room. A series of maps of Bath are on the second floor landing. In the basement is a Kitchen and a Museum Shop.

Location: Bath, upper town close to Assembly rooms.
Open: Mar 1-Oct 29 Tues-Sun 10.30-5 Oct 31-Dec 10 Tues-Sun 10.30-4 last adm half an hour before closing. Private tours out of hours with refreshments if required by arrangement with Administrator.
Admission: Adults £3.50 children/students/OAPs/adult groups £2.50 school groups £2 family ticket £8.
Museum. Shop.

SHERBORNE GARDEN (PEAR TREE HOUSE)

(Mr & Mrs John Southwell)
Litton   BA3 4PP   map 14 U18
Telephone: (01761) 241220

3½ acres landscaped into several gardens of distinctive character. Cottage garden, rock garden, large ponds with moisture gardens, pinetum, mixed wood. Collections of acers, birches, species roses, clematis. Special collection of hollies (over 180 varieties). Picnic area.

Location: Litton, 8 m North of Wells on B3114 off A39.
Open: Suns & Mons June through September. Also for National Garden Scheme April 2 May 7 June 4 Oct 1 11-6. Other times by appointment.
Admission: £1.50 Chd free. Parties by arrangement. Free car parking.
Refreshments: Home-made teas on National Gardens Scheme days (except in Apr and May) and for parties; at other times tea/coffee available.
Suitable for the disabled. Dogs on leads.

Sir John Van Brugh (1664-1726)

Architect. His work can be seen at the following properties included in historic Houses Castles and Gardens:-

Blenheim Palace
Castle Howard
Claremont
Grimsthorpe Castle
Seaton Delaval Hall

BEDFORDSHIRE

CHICKSANDS PRIORY

(Ministry of Defence Property Administered by RAF Commander)
Shefford   map **5** S22   △
Telephone: (01234) 824195

Chicksands Priory was founded by Payne De Beauchamp and his wife Countess Rohese for Nuns and Canons of the English Order of Gilbertines c 1150. Dissolved and surrendered 1538, it was sold by Henry VIII for £810 11s 8d to the Snowe family 1540. Acquired by the Osborne family in 1576, it so remained their family home until sold to The Crown, 1936. 13th and 15th century monastic remains survive with architectural work by Isaac Ware (1740) and James Wyatt (1813). Stained glass, Chinese wallpaper, Coade statuary have been uncovered since the Anglo-American Group of Friends opened the building to the public, 1975. The 18th century Venetian Prayer Book purchased by Sir Danvers Osborn, 3rd Baronet, is shown in the refurbished Private Chapel. Ghosts of former inhabitants are said to haunt the building; a plaque boasts of a walled up Nun within the cloisters and remains of monastic residents are buried in the still landscaped gardens. Game larder, Orangery and grapevines are on show exclusive of guided tour of the interior, which takes approximately 45 minutes. Past visitors to Chicksands include St Thomas Becket, King James I, HRH Princess Alice, Duchess of Gloucester, the Duke of Bedford, Terence, Cardinal Cooke. Following intensive external restoration by the Ministry of Defence, The Friends are decorating and restoring the interior.

Location: In RAF Chicksands 1¼ miles from Shefford. Entrances on A507 Shefford to Ampthill Road and on A600 Shefford to Bedford Road.

Open: 1st & 3rd Suns of Month Apr-Sept 2-5 last tour 4.30. Guided tours only.

Admission: No adm charge - donations for interior decoration requested, suggested donation £1 per adult. Parties by appointment only.
Refreshments: Light refreshments at Priory. Nearest hotels at Biggleswade, Bedford & Hitchin, all being 7 miles from Chicksands.
Car parking. Unsuitable for wheelchairs. *Friends of Priory licensed to open Priory to public and redecorate interior.*

CECIL HIGGINS ART GALLERY & MUSEUM

(Gallery jointly owned and administered by Bedford Borough Council and the Trustees of the Cecil Higgins Art Gallery)
Castle Close, Bedford   MK40 3NY   map **5** S22   ♿ Ⓢ
Telephone: (01234) 211222
Fax: (01234) 221606

Re-created Victorian Mansion, originally the home of the Higgins family, wealthy Bedford brewers. Rooms displayed to create a 'lived-in' atmosphere, including many items from the Handley-Read Collection, and a bedroom with furniture designed by William Burges (1827-1881). Adjoining Gallery with changing displays of watercolours, prints and drawings from own outstanding collections, and permanent displays of English and Continental ceramics and glass. Situated in pleasant gardens leading down to the river embankment.

Location: Centre of Bedford, just off The Embankment.
Station(s): Bedford Midland (1 m). Bus Station: (½ m).Trains from London (St.Pancras), and King's Cross Thameslink - fast trains 36 mins. United Counties X4 Bedford/Milton Keynes - Buckingham - Bicester - Oxford; X3 Northampton - Bedford - Cambridge; Coach link from London Marylebone Station.
Open: Tues-Sat 11-5 Sun 2-5 closed Mon (except Bank Hol Mons) Christmas Day Boxing Day and Good Fri.
Admission: Free. Group bookings by prior arrangement.
Refreshments: By prior arrangement.
Facilities for the disabled.

Robert Adam - architect

His work can be seen at the following properties included in Historic Houses Castles and Gardens:-

Audley End   *Mellerstain*
Bowood House & Gardens   *Moccas Court*
Culzean Castle   *Newby Hall & Gardens*
Hatchlands Park   *Nostell Priory*
Kedleston Hall   *Osterley Park*
Kenwood, The Iveagh Bequest   *Papplewick Hall*
Killerton   *Saltram House*
Kimbolton Castle   *Syon House*
Luton Hoo

LUTON HOO - WERNER COLLECTION

(The Luton Hoo Foundation)
Luton   **LU1 3TQ**   map **5** S22
Telephone: (01582) 22955
Fax: (01582) 34437

The works of Carl Fabergé, the Russian Court jeweller which are on view at Luton Hoo, are part of the finest private Collection of works of art in Great Britain, which includes continental treasures rarely seen in English Country Houses. There are many paintings, costume and other personal possesions of the Russian Imperial Family Romanov, complemented by the acquisition of memorabilia of Father Gibbes who was tutor to the Tsarevitch. All the Russian Collection has been redesigned and redisplayed in and around the beautiful Chapel - extensively restored to its original decorative splendour, and in 1991, consecrated into the Russian Orthodox Church and dedicated to the memory of Tsar Nicholas II and the Imperial Family. Other treasures in the House are Old Master paintings, magnificent Tapestries, English and French Porcelain, European Ceramics, Furniture, Byzantine and Medieval Ivories, Sculpture, Bronzes and renaissance Jewellery.

Location: Signposted from J10 of M1.
Open: 11 Apr-15 Oct '95 Tues Wed Thurs pre-booked groups only either morning or afternoon by arrangement. Groups on these days will have a guided tour. Fri Sat Sun general public viewing. Gardens & Restaurant open at 12 Wernher Collection at 1.30pm (last entries 5). House *closed* Mon except bank hols when house & garden opens at 10.30.
Admission: Group rates £5 adults, £4.50 sen citizens/students £2.50 children. House & Gardens £5.50 adults £5 sen citizens/students £2 children.
Refreshments: Restaurant.
Disabled facilities. Coaches welcome, picnic area, gift shop. Ample parking.

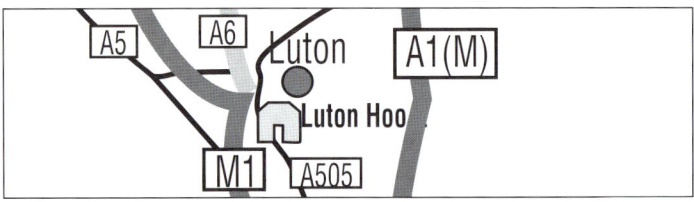

WOBURN ABBEY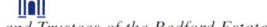

(The Marquess of Tavistock and Trustees of the Bedford Estates)
Woburn   map **5** S21
Telephone: (01525) 290666; Catering (01525) 290662; Antiques Centre (01525) 290350

Home of the Dukes of Bedford for over 350 years, the Abbey contains one of the most important private art collections in the world, including paintings by Canaletto, Van Dyck, Cuyp, Teniers, Rembrandt, Gainsborough, Reynolds, Velazquez and many other famous artists. French and English 18th century furniture, silver and the fabulous Sèvres dinner service presented to the 4th Duke by Louis XV of France. The 3,000 acre Deer Park has lots of wild life, including nine species of deer, roaming freely. One of these, the Père David, descended from the Imperial Herd of China, was saved from extinction at Woburn and is now the largest breeding herd of this species in the world. In 1985 twenty two Père David were given by the Family to the People's Republic of China with the hope that the species may become re-established in its natural habitat. The Marquess of Tavistock visited Beijing (Peking) to release the herd at Nan Haizi, the former Imperial hunting ground outside Beijing (Peking). The tour of the Abbey covers three floors including the Crypt. It is regretted that wheelchairs can only be accommodated in the House by prior arrangement with the Administrator but unfortunately the Crypt area is not accessible. The 40 shop Antiques Centre is probably the most unusual such centre outside London - the shop fronts having been rescued from demolition sites in various parts of Britain. All catering is operated by ourselves with banqueting, conferences, receptions and company days out our speciality, in the beautiful setting of the Sculpture Gallery, overlooking the private gardens. There is a Pottery and summer weekend events are arranged. Extensive picnic areas with ample coach and car parking. Gift shops, Pottery and Camping Equipment Centre.

Location: In Woburn 8½ m NW of Dunstable on A4012. 42 m from London off M1 at junctions 12 or 13.
Station(s): Leighton Buzzard and Bletchley (Euston) and Flitwick (Kings Cross Thameslink). The three local stations are between 6 and 7 miles from Woburn village, which is 1½ m from the Abbey.
Open: HOUSE AND GARDENS Jan 1-Mar 25 Sat & Sun only House 11-4 Park 10.30-3.45. Mar 26-Oct 29 daily House weekdays 11-4 Sun 11-5 Park weekdays 10-4.30 Sun 10-4.45. Last admissions as closing time.
Admission: Including Private Apartments: House £6.50 Chd (12-16) £3, OAPS £5.50 (reduced rates apply when Private Apartments are in use by the Family). Group rates are available. Free car park.
Refreshments: Flying Duchess Pavilion Coffee Shop, Restaurants for pre-booked parties.
Conferences: Facilities available.

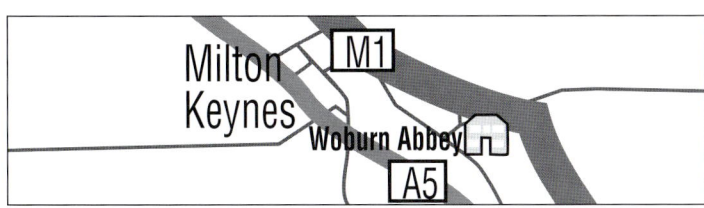

WREST PARK HOUSE AND GARDENS

ENGLISH HERITAGE

Silsoe map **5** S22
Telephone: (01525) 860152

Here is a history of English gardening in the grand manner from 1700-1850, which would not, of course, be complete without some designs by 'Capability' Brown. Every whim of fashion is represented, whether it be for a Chinese bridge, artificial lake, classical temple or rustic ruin. The present house was built about 1839 by the Earl de Grey, whose family had lorded over the Manor of Wrest for 600 years. The State Rooms and gardens are open to the public.

Location: ¾ m (1 km) east of Silsoe.
Open: Apr 1-30 10-6 Sat Sun & Bank Hol only.
Admission: April 1-Sept 30 Adults £2.30 concessions £1.70 children £1.20.
Refreshments: Available.

William Kent (1685 - 1748)
Painter, architect, garden designer

His work can be seen in the following properties included in Historic Houses Castles and Gardens:-

    Chiswick House
    Ditchley Park (decoration of Great
     Hall)
    Euston Hall
    Rousham House
    Stowe (Stowe School)

BERKSHIRE

BASILDON PARK 🌿 The National Trust

Lower Basildon, Reading   **RG8 9NR**   map **3** T20
Telephone: (01734) 843040

Classical house built 1776. Unusual Octagon room; fine plasterwork; important paintings and furniture, Garden and woodland walks.

Location: 7 m NW of Reading between Pangbourne and Streatley on A329. Leave M4 at junction 12.
Station(s): Pangbourne (2½ m); Goring and Streatley (3 m).
Open: 1 Apr-end Oct Wed-Sat 2-6 Sun & Bank Hol Mon 12-6. Grounds open at 12 on Sat. Last adm to house half-hour before closing. Closed (except Bank Hols) Wed following Bank Hols and Good Fri.
Admission: House & Grounds £3.60 Grounds only £1.50 Children half price. Reductions (except Suns and Bank Hol Mons) to House and Grounds for parties of 15 or more (Booking essential). Family ticket house and garden £9. Grounds only £3.50.
Refreshments: Tea-room in house accessible to wheelchairs.
Shop. Dogs in grounds only on leads. House unsuitable for wheelchairs.

DORNEY COURT

(Mr & Mrs Peregrine Palmer)
nr Windsor   **SL4 6QP**   map **3** T19
Telephone: (01628) 604638

'One of the finest Tudor Manor Houses in England' Country Life. A visit to Dorney is a most welcome, refreshing and fascinating experience. Built about 1440 and lived in by the present family for over 400 years, this enchanting, many gabled pink brick and timber house is a joy to behold. The rooms are full of the continuing atmosphere of history: early 15th and 16th century oak, beautiful 17th century lacquer furniture, 18th and 19th century tables, 400 years of family portraits and stained glass and needlework. Charles II came here to seek the charms of Barbara Palmer, Countess of Castlemaine - 'the most intelligent beautiful and influential of ladies'. The 14th century church of St. James next door, is a lovely, cool, cheerful and very English Church.

Location: 2 m W of Eton & Windsor in village of Dorney on B3026. Signposted from M4, exit 7.
Station(s): Burnham (2 m).
Open: Easter weekend Fri-Mon, May Suns & Bank Hol Mons, also June-Sept Sun, Mon & Tues 2-5.30. Last admission and last orders for teas at 5.
Admission: Adults £4 children over 9 £2 10% discount for National Trust and NADFAS members and OAPs. Parties at other times by arrangement.
Refreshments: Home-made cream teas.
Outstanding collection of plants for sale at Bressingham Plant Centre. PYO fruit from June-middle August.

ENGLEFIELD HOUSE GARDEN
Theale, Reading   **RG7 5DU**   map **5** U20
Telephone: (01734) 302504
Fax: (01734) 303226

A seven acre garden, herbacious and rose borders. Fountain, stone balustrade and staircases, woodland and Water Garden, set in Deer Park. Large variety of trees, plants, shrubs, children's garden and plant sales.

Open: Open Mon-Thurs April-Jun inclusive; other months every Mon 10-6.

FROGMORE HOUSE
Windsor   map **3** T19
Telephone: (01753) 831118

One of the least known royal residences Frogmore House is situated within the private Home Park at Windsor Castle. Built in the late 17th century the house is particularly associated with Queen Charlotte and with the Duchess of Kent, Queen Victoria's mother. The house has been extensively restored and is furnished with many of its original contents reflecting the taste and interests of former residents.

Open: During May and Aug and Sept. Telephone above number for details.
Admission: Charge.

MAPLEDURHAM HOUSE AND WATERMILL
See under Oxfordshire

SAVILL GARDEN
(Crown Property)
Windsor Great Park   map **3** T19
Telephone: (01753) 860222

World renowned woodland garden of 35 acres with adjoining area of herbaceous borders, rose gardens, alpine raised beds and an extensive dry garden. The whole garden offering much of great interest and beauty at all seasons.

Location: To be approached from A30 via Wick Road & Wick Lane, Englefield Green.
Station(s): Egham (3 m).
Open: Apr-Sept daily 10-6 Oct-Mar daily 10-4 closed for a short period at Christmas.
Admission: Adults £3.30 OAPs £2.80 parties of 20 and over £2.80 accompanied children (under 16) free.

SWALLOWFIELD PARK
(Country Houses Association)
Swallowfield   **RG7 1TG**   map **12** U21
Telephone: (01734) 883815

Built by the Second Earl of Clarendon in 1678.

Location: In the village of Swallowfield 6 m SE of Reading.
Open: May-September Weds & Thurs 2-5. Last entry 4.00.
Admission: £2.50 Children £1.
Free car park. No dogs admitted.

WELFORD PARK
(Mrs A.C. Puxley)
nr Newbury   **RG16 8HU**   map **3** U20   △
Telephone: (01488) 608203

Queen Anne house with later additions. Attractive gardens and grounds.

Location: 6 m NW of Newbury and 1 m N of Wickham village off B4000.
Station(s): Newbury.
Open: Spring and Summer Bank Hols and Aug 2-27 inclusive from 2.30-5.
Admission: Adults £3 OAPs and under 16s £2.
Interior by prior appointment only.

WINDSOR CASTLE
(Official residence of H.M. The Queen)
Windsor   **SL4 1NJ**   map **3** T19
Telephone: (01753) 831118 (24 hr information line)

Perhaps the largest fortress of its kind in the world, Windsor Castle has belonged to the Sovereigns of England for over 900 years, and is by far, the oldest residence still in regular use. The State Apartments, the most magnificent rooms in the Castle, are open for the majority of the year. The Gallery, which hosts a series of changing exhibitions from the Royal Collection, Queen Mary's Dolls' House and the Exhibition of The Queen's Presents and Royal Carriages are open all year.

Location: 3 m off J6 of M4.
Open: Open all year. *Whilst there is every intention to adhere to the above schedule this cannot be guaranteed as Windsor Castle is always subject to closure, sometimes at short notice.* Enquiries: (01753) 831118.
Admission: Overall charge for the Precincts, The State Apartments, The Gallery, St. George's Chapel and the Albert Memorial Chapel. Separate charge for Queen Mary's Dolls' House and The Exhibition of The Queen's Presents and Royal Carriages. Group rates available. Telephone (01753) 831118 for further information.
Refreshments: Castle Hotel (opposite).

BUCKINGHAMSHIRE

ASCOTT   🌿 The National Trust
Wing, nr Leighton Buzzard   **LU7 0PS**   map **5** T21   △
Telephone: (01296) 688242

Anthony de Rothschild collection of fine pictures. French and English furniture, exceptional Oriental porcelain containing examples of the Ming, K'ang Hsi and Chun ware of the Sung dynasty. Gardens contain unusual trees, flower borders, topiary sundial, naturalised bulbs and water lilies.

Location: ½ m E of Wing; 2 m SW of Leighton Buzzard, on the S side of Aylesbury/Leighton Buzzard Road (A418).
Station(s): Leighton Buzzard (2 m).
Open: HOUSE & GARDENS Apr 5-May 7 Sept 1-30 Tues-Sun 2-6 (open Good Fri but closed Bank Hol Mons). Garden only May 10-Aug 30. Every Wed and last Sun in each month 2-6. Last adm 5.
Admission: House & Gardens £5 Children £2.50 Gardens only £3 Children £1.50. *No reduction for parties which must book.*
Dogs on leads, in car park only. Wheelchair access to ground floor and part of garden only. Enquiries: Estate Manager. NB Owing to large number of visitors, entry is by timed ticket. Occasionally there will be considerable delays in gaining admission to the House.

Thomas Gainsborough (1727-1787)

His paintings can be seen at the following properties included in Historic Houses Castles and Gardens:-

Arundel Castle	*Knowle*
Bowhill	*Parham House &*
Christchurch Mansion	*Gardens*
Dalmeny House	*Petworth House*
Elton Hall	*Shalom Hall*
Gainsborough's House	*Upton House*
Ickworth Park & Garden	*Waddesdon Manor*
Firle Place	*Weston Park*
Kenwood, The Iveagh	*Woburn Abbey*
Bequest	

CHENIES MANOR HOUSE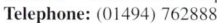
(Lt Col & Mrs MacLeod Matthews)
Chenies   WD3 6ER   map **12** T21 △
Telephone: (01494) 762888

15/16th century Manor House with fortified tower. Original home of the Earls of Bedford, visited by Henry VIII and Elizabeth I. Home of the MacLeod Matthews family. Contains contemporary tapestries and furniture. Hiding places, collection of antique dolls; medieval undercroft and well. Surrounded by beautiful gardens which have featured in many publications - a Tudor sunken garden, a white garden, herbaceous borders, a fountain court, a physic garden containing a very wide selection of medical and culinary herbs, a parterre and two mazes. The kitchen garden is in the Victorian style with unusual vegetables and fruit. Special exhibitions. Flower drying and arrangements. Plants and unique ivy topiary for sale.

Location: Off A404 between Amersham & Rickmansworth (M25 - junction 18).
Station(s): Chorleywood (1½ m).
Open: First week in April to end of Sept Weds and Thurs 2-5. Also open Bank Hol Mons 2-5
Admission: £4 Gardens Only £2 children (under 14) half price. Parties throughout the year by prior arrangement - min charge £50.
Refreshments: Home-made teas. Corporate events welcome.
Free parking. No dogs.

Geoffrey Alan Jellicoe -
contemporary garden architect
and designer

His work can be seen in the following properties
included in Historic Houses Castles and Gardens:-

Hever Castle
RHS Garden Wisley

CHILTERN OPEN AIR MUSEUM
(Chiltern Open Air Museum Ltd)
Newland Park, Gorelands Lane, Chalfont St Giles   HP8 4AD   map **12** T21   ♿
Telephone: (01494) 871117

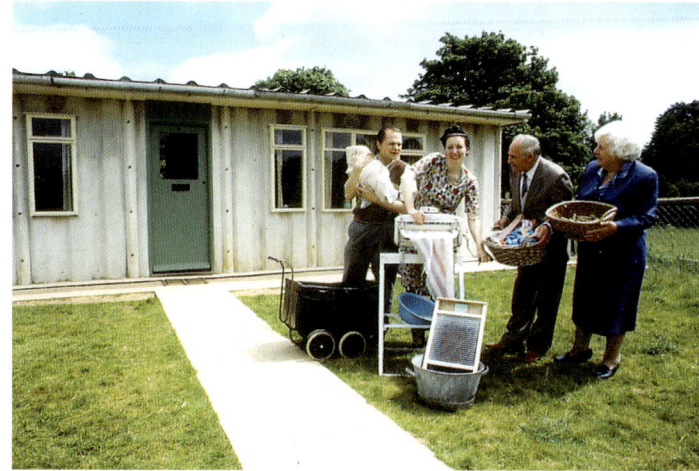

A museum of historic buildings, rescued from demolition, and which reflect the vernacular heritage of the Chilterns region. You can explore barns, granaries, cartsheds and stables, a blacksmith's forge, a toll house, vicarage room, Edwardian cast-iron public conveniences, a pair of 18th century thatched cottages, a 1947 prefabricated bungalow, a reconstruction of an Iron Age House and a 19th century Mission Room - and the collection is growing all the time. Several of the buildings incorporate displays illustrating their original use, or house exhibitions on Chiltern life and landscape. The Museum occupies 45 acres of beautiful parkland and woodland which has an attractive Nature Trail running through it.
Location: At Newland Park, Chalfont St Giles; 4½ m Amersham, 8 m Watford, 6 m Beaconsfield; 2 m A413 at Chalfont St Peter, 4 m from junction 17 on the M25 via Maple Cross and the Chalfonts.
Station(s): Chorleywood.
Open: Apr-Oct Wed-Sun & Bank Hols 2-6. Parties & school parties by arrangement weekdays all year round.
Admission: Adults £3 OAPs £2.50 children under 16yrs £2.50 under 5 free family ticket (2 adults 2 children) £10.
Refreshments: Home-made teas.

CLAYDON HOUSE   🌿 The National Trust
Middle Claydon, nr Buckingham   MK18 2EY   map **5** T21   ♿
Telephone: (01296) 730349/730693

The most perfect expression of Rococo decoration in England, in a series of great rooms with woodcarvings in the Chinese and gothic styles. Relics of the Civil War and a museum with memorabilia of Florence Nightingale and the Verney family.
Location: In the village of Middle Claydon, 13m NW of Aylesbury, 3½ m SW of Winslow. Signposted from A413, A421 and A41.
Open: Apr-end Oct Sat-Wed 1-5 Bank Hol Mons 1-5. Last adm 4.30. *Closed Thurs & Fri (inc Good Fri).*
Admission: £3.60 Children £1.75. Family ticket £9 Parties write to Custodian.
Refreshments: Available at house.
Dogs in park on leads only. Wheelchairs provided (access to ground floor only, half price adm.)

CLIVEDEN   The National Trust
Taplow, Maidenhead (1851)   SL6 OJA   map 12 T21 △
Telephone: (01628) 605069

Gardens contain temples by Giacomo Leoni. Box parterre, fountain, formal walks; amphitheatre, water garden, rose garden, herbaceous borders. Views of Thames.

Location: 3 m upstream from Maidenhead; 2 m N of Taplow on Hedsor Road. Main entrance opposite Feathers Inn.
Station(s): Taplow (2½ m) (not Suns); Maidenhead (4¼ m).
Open: Grounds Mar-end Oct Daily 11-6 or sunset if earlier. Nov and Dec daily 11-4. Closed Jan & Feb. House (3 Rooms Open) Apr-Oct Thurs & Sun 3-6 (last adm 5.30).
Admission: Grounds £4 House £1 extra (timed ticket) Children half price. *Parties must book. Family ticket £10.*
Refreshments: Light lunches, coffee, teas in licensed Conservatory Restaurant Apr-end Oct (Wed-Suns & Bank Hol Mons 11-5).
Events/Exhibitions: For details of centenary events please contact the Property Manager. No dogs in House or in gardens, in specified woodlands only on lead. Shop Apr-end Oct, Weds-Suns (incl Good Fri) & Bank Hol Mons 1-5.30pm. Also pre-Christmas Nov-Dec 17, Weds-Suns 11-4.

COWPER & NEWTON MUSEUM
(Trustees)
Orchard Side, Market Place   MK46 4AJ   map 5 S21
Telephone: (01234) 711516

Personal belongings of eighteenth century poet, William Cowper, and Rev.John Newton, (author of 'Amazing Grace'). Exhibitions of Bobbin Lace. Two gardens, one contains Cowper's Summerhouse.

Location: Market Place, Olney; N of Newport Pagnell via A509.
Station(s): Milton Keynes.
Open: 1st Nov-31 Mar 1-4. 1st Apr-31 Oct 10-1 & 2-5 Tues-Sats. Open Bank Hol Mons. Closed 15 Dec-31 Jan and Good Fri.
Admission: £1.50 adults, £1.00 over 65's 50p children.

HUGHENDEN MANOR   The National Trust
High Wycombe   HP14 4LA   map 12 T21 &
Telephone: (01494) 532580

Home of Benjamin Disraeli, Earl of Beaconsfield (1847-1881). Small formal garden.

Location: 1½ m N of High Wycombe on W side Gt Missenden Road (A4128).
Station(s): High Wycombe (2 m).
Open: House & Garden 4 Mar-26 Mar Sat & Sun only 2-6 1 Apr-1 Oct Weds-Sat 2-6 Sun & Bank Hol Mon 12-6. *Closed* Good Fri. Last Adm 5.30. 4 Oct-30 Oct Wed-Sat 2-5 Sun 12-5 last admissions 4.30 Shop open as House and pre-Christmas Nov to Dec 17 Wed-Sun 11-3. *Parties must book in advance.* Parties Wed-Fri only if booked in advance.
Admission: £3.60 Children half price. Family ticket £9.
Dogs in Park & car park only. Wheelchair provided.

MILTON'S COTTAGE
(Milton Cottage Trust)
Chalfont St Giles   HP8 4JH   map 12 T21 &
Telephone: (01494) 872313

The Cottage where John Milton completed 'Paradise Lost' and wrote 'Paradise Regained', contains many Milton relics and a library including first and early editions. Free car park for visitors. Three museum rooms and charming cottage garden open to the public.

Location: ½ m W of A413; on road to Seer Green and Beaconsfield.
Station(s): Gerrards Cross L.T. to Amersham or Chalfont and Latimer.
Open: Mar-Oct Wed-Sun 10-1 and 2-6 Spring & Summer Bank Hol Mons 10-1 and 2-6 closed Mon and Tues (except Bank Hols) & Jan, Feb, Nov and Dec.
Admission: Adults £2 children (under 15) 60p parties of 20 or more £1.20.
Refreshments: By prior arrangement with Milton's restaurant (opposite).

NETHER WINCHENDEN HOUSE
(Trustees of Will Trust of J.G.C. Spencer Bernard Dec'd)
Aylesbury   HP18 0DY   map 12 T21 △&
Telephone: (01844) 290101

Medieval and Tudor manor house with 18th century Gothic additions. Home of Sir Francis Bernard, Governor of New Jersey and Massachusetts, 1760.

Location: 1 m N of A418 Aylesbury/Thame Road, in village of Lower Winchendon, 6 m SW Aylesbury.
Station(s): Aylesbury (7½ m).
Open: May 1-May 29 and Aug 27 & 28 2.30-5.30. Last party each day at 4.45. Parties at any time of year by written appointment.
Admission: Adults £2.50 children (under 12) and OAPs £1.50 (not weekends or Bank Hols).
Refreshments: By arrangement.
Correspondence to Administrator, R.V. Spencer Bernard Esq.

PRINCES RISBOROUGH MANOR HOUSE
  The National Trust
Princes Risborough   HP17 9AW   map 12 T21 &

17th century red-brick house with Jacobean oak staircase. Opposite church.

Location: Princes Risborough (1 m).
Open: House and garden by written appointment only with tenant Wed 2.30-4.30.
Admission: £1 Children 50p. No reductions for parties.
Principal rooms and staircase shown. No dogs. Wheelchair access.

STOWE LANDSCAPE GARDENS   The National Trust
nr Buckingham   MK18 5EH   map 5 S20
Telephone: (01280) 822850

Splendid landscape gardens with buildings and temples by Vanbrugh, Kent and Gibbs. One of the supreme creations of the Georgian era. (N.B. the main house is in the ownership of Stowe School.)

Location: 3 m NW of Buckingham, via Stowe Avenue off the A422 Buckingham/Banbury Road.
Open: Mar 25-Apr 16 daily 17 Apr-2 July Mon Wed Fri Sun. Jul 3-Sept 3 daily. Sept 4-Oct 29 Mon Wed Fri Sun. Dec 27-Jan 7 daily 10-6 or dusk if earlier. Last adm 1 hour before closing. *Closed* Dec 24, 25 and 26.
Admission: Entry to Gardens £3.80 Family ticket £9.50. The main house belongs to Stowe School and may be open during Stowe School holidays at an additional charge of £2 (inc NT members).
Refreshments: Light refreshments and teas as above 11-5 (11-4 during Dec and Jan).
Dogs on lead only. Batricar available for disabled visitors, telephone Administrator for details.

Gertrude Jekyll
writer and gardener
(1843-1932)

Her designs were used at the following properties included in Historic Houses Castles and Gardens:-

Barrington Court
Castle Drogo
Goddards
Hatchlands Park
Hestercombe House and Gardens
Knebworth
Lindisfarne Castle

A collection of her tools can be found at Guildford Museum

STOWE (STOWE SCHOOL)

Buckingham   **MK18 5EH**   map **12** T21
Telephone: (01280) 813650 house 822850 gardens

Stowe is one of the most majestic English Houses of the eighteenth century. Formerley the home of the dukes of Buckingham it is a house adorned with the traditions of aristocracy and learning. For over one and a half centuries up to the great sale of 1848, the temples and Grenvilles almost continuosly rebuilt and refurbished it in an attempt to match their ever growing ambitions with the latest fashions. Around the mansion is one of Britains moat magnificent landscape gardens now in the ownership of the National Trust.

Location: 4 m N of Buckingham town.
Station(s): Milton Keynes.
Open: House Only Mar 25-11 Apr 5-17 July 4-Sept 1 2-5. **Please note** it may be necessary to close the house for private functions. Please check before visiting. Tel - House (01280) 813650 National Trust Gardens (01280) 822850.
Admission: Adults £2 children £1.
Guide books, postcards, souvenirs and prints available from the Stowe Bookshop situated in the Menagerie on the South Front - opening times 10am-5pm.

WADDESDON MANOR

(Rothschild Waddesdon Ltd/The National Trust)
nr Aylesbury   **HP18 OJH**   map **12** T21   △ &
Telephone: (01296) 651211
Fax: (01296) 651293

Waddesdon Manor was designed by the French architect G.H Destailleur in the 1870s for Baron de Rothschild from the Austrian branch of the family. The Renaissance style château was conceived as a showcase for the Baron's prodigious collection of works of art, which includes French royal furniture, Savonnerie carpets and Sevres porcelain as well as important portraits by Gainsborough and Reynolds and works by Dutch and Flemish masters of the 17th century. The collection on the ground floor was reopened last year following extensive restoration and the newly remodelled Wine Cellars containing an exceptional 'library' of Rothschild vintages, were put on public view for the first time. This year the restoration will be complete with the inauguration of newly created rooms on the first floor. These include a magnificent suite of French 18th century panelled rooms, an exhibition of Sevres porcelain, and the paintings of Leon Bakst showing the Rothschild family in the story of Sleeping Beauty. Restoration work in the Garden has included repairs to the fountains and garden sculpture, reinstatement of the 19th century Parterre and extensive replanting of shrubs and trees.

Location: At W end of Waddeson village; 6 m NW of Aylesbury on Bicester Road (A41).
Station(s): Aylesbury (6 m). Buses: Red Rover 1, 15, 16, from Aylesbury. (Tel: (01296) 28686).
Open: House 6 April to 15 October: Thurs to Sat 1-6; Bank Hol Mon & Good Fri: 11-6 also open Wed 1-6 in July and August. Last admission 5. Grounds, Aviary, Shops, Licensed Restaurant: 1 March to 22 December: Wed to Sun and Bank Hol Mon 11-6. Private tours of the House by special arrangement.
Admission: Grounds, Aviary, Shops, Licensed Restaurant & Parking: £3 children £1.50. House State Reception Rooms: £6 children over 5 only £4.50. First Floor Exhibition Rooms: £6 children over 5 only £4.50. Combined ticket £8 children over 5 £6.50. Additional charge to ~House on Sun, Bank Hol Mon & Good Fri: Adults & children £1.
Dogs not admitted apart from guide dogs.

Lancelot 'Capability' Brown

Born 1716 in Northumberland, Capability Brown began work at the age of 16 in the vegetable gardens of Sir William and Lady Loraine at Kirharle Tower. He left Northumberland in 1739, and records show that he worked at Stowe until 1749. It was at Stowe that Brown began to study architecture, and to submit his own plans. It was also at Stowe that he devised a new method of moving and replanting mature trees.

Brown married Bridget Wayet in 1744 and began work on the estate at Warwick Castle in 1749. He was appointed Master Gardener at Hampton Court in 1764, and planted the Great Vine at Hampton Court in 1768. Blenheim Palace designs are considered amongst Brown's finest work, and the technical achievements were outstanding even for the present day.

Capability Brown died in February 1783 of a massive heart attack. A monument beside the lake at Croome Court was erected which reads "To the memory of Lancelot Brown, who by the powers of his inimitable and creative genius formed this garden scene out of a morass". There is also a portrait of Brown at Burghley.

Capability Brown was involved in the design of grounds at the following properties included in Historic Houses Castles and Gardens:-

Audley End	*Longleat*
Berrington Hall	*Luton Hoo*
Bowood	*Moccas Court*
Burghley House	*Petworth House*
Burton Constable	*Sledmere House*
Charlecote Park	*Stowe (Stowe*
Chilham Castle Gardens	*School)*
(reputed)	*Syon House*
Clandon Park	*Warwick Castle*
Claremont	*Weston Park*
Chillington Hall	*Wimpole Hall*
Corsham Court	*Wrest Park and*
Fawley Court	*Gardens*
Highclere Castle	

WEST WYCOMBE PARK (1750)   The National Trust
West Wycombe   HP14 3AJ   map **12** T21 △
Telephone: (01494) 524411

Palladian house with frescoes and painted ceilings. 18th century landscape garden with lake and various classical temples.

Location: At W end of West Wycombe, S of Oxford Road (A40), 2½ m W High Wycombe.
Station(s): High Wycombe (2½ m).
Open: Grounds only Apr & May Sun & Wed 2-6 and Easter, May and Spring Bank Hols. Sun & Mon 2-6. Closed Good Fri. House and Grounds June July & Aug Sun-Thurs 2-6 (last adm 5.15). Entry to house by timed tickets on weekdays.
Admission: House & Grounds £4 Grounds only £2.50 Children half price. *No reduction for parties.* Family ticket £10.
Dogs in car park only. House unsuitable for wheelchairs.

WINSLOW HALL
(Sir Edward & Lady Tomkins)
Winslow   MK18 3HL   map **5** S21 △
Telephone: (01296) 712323

Built 1698-1702. Almost certainly designed by Sir Christopher Wren. Has survived without major structural alteration and retains most of its original features. Modernized and redecorated by the present owners. Good eighteenth century furniture, mostly English. Some fine pictures, clocks and carpets. Several examples of Chinese art, notably of the Tang period. Beautiful gardens with many unusual trees and shrubs.

Location: At entrance to Winslow on the Aylesbury road (A413).
Station(s): Milton Keynes or Aylesbury (both 10 miles).
Open: Open all Bank Holiday weekends except Christmas 2-5. July and Aug Wed and Thurs 2.30-5.30 or by appointment throughout the year.
Admission: £4.50 Children free.
Refreshments: Catering by arrangement.

CAMBRIDGESHIRE

ANGLESEY ABBEY AND GARDEN   The National Trust
Lode   CB5 9EJ   map **7** S23
Telephone: (01223) 811200

The Abbey, founded in the reign of Henry I, was later converted to an Elizabethan manor. Contains Fairhaven collection of art treasures. About 100 acres of garden including flower borders, trees, avenues, unique garden statuary and a working water mill that grinds corn.

Location: In village of Lode 6 m NE of Cambridge on B1102, signposted off A45.
Station(s): Cambridge (6 m).
Open: House Mar 29-Oct 15 Wed-Sun 1-5 and Bank Hol Mons 1-5. Pre-booked parties of 15 or more (Wed Thurs Fri and Sat only). Garden Mar 29-July 9 Wed-Sun & Bank Hol Mons 11-5.30 July 10-Sept 5 daily 11-5.30. Sept 6-Oct 29 Sat-Wed 11-5.30. Lode Mill Mar 29-Oct 15 Wed-Sun & Bank Hol Mons 1.30-5.15.
Admission: House and Garden £4.80 Sun and Bank Hol Mon £5.80. Pre-booked parties £3.80. Garden £3 Sun & Bank Hol Mon £3.50 children (with adult) half price. Free car park and picnic area.
Refreshments: Restaurant open same days as House 11-5.30 lunches and teas. Table license. And Mon & Tues July 10-Sept 5.
No dogs. Wheelchair access (house difficult); chairs provided.

ELTON HALL
(Mr & Mrs William Proby)
nr Peterborough   PE8 6SH   map **7** R22   △
Telephone: (01832) 280 468
Fax: (01832) 280584

Spanning five centuries, this romantic house has been the home of the Proby family for over 300 years. The house, with its mixture of mediaeval, gothic and classical styles, reflects the family's passion for collecting, and this is shown in the remarkable contents to be seen today - excellent furniture and outstanding paintings by Gainsborough, Reynolds, Constable, Alma Tadema, Millais and other fine artists. There are over 12,000 books, including Henry VIII's prayer book. Wonderful gardens, including restored Rose Garden, new knot and sunken gardens and recently planted Arboretum. Bressingham Plant Centre in walled Kitchen Garden.

Location: On A605, 5 m W of Peterborough.
Open: Bank Hols during Easter May and Aug Sun Mon 2-5 July Weds & Suns 2-5 Aug Wed Thurs Sun 2-5.
Admission: Adults £3.80 children £1.90 private parties by arrangement with House Manager prices on application. Free parking.
Refreshments: Home-made teas. Lunches by arrangement.
Events/Exhibitions: Contact administration.
Conferences: By arrangement. Please apply to office for details.
Souvenirs, Loch Fyne Oyster Bar Restaurant, Bressingham Plant Centre, Garden Shop.

Sir Peter Lely - portrait painter

His paintings can be seen at the following properties included in Historic Houses Castles and Gardens:-

Aynhoe Park	*Kedleston Hall*
Belton House	*Knole*
Breamore House	*Petworth House*
Browsholme Hall	*Ragley Hall*
Dalmeny House	*Rockingham Castle*
Euston Hall	*St Osyth Priory*
Goodwood House	*Stanford Hall*
Gorhambury	*Weston Park*

ISLAND HALL
(Mr Christopher & The Hon Mrs Vane Percy)
Godmanchester   **PE18 8BA**   map **7** S22
Telephone: 0171-491 3724

An important mid 18th century mansion of great charm owned and being restored by an award winning Interior Designer. Lovely rooms with fine period detail and interesting possessions relating to the owners' ancestors since their first occupation of the house in 1800. Tranquil riverside setting with ornamental island forming part of the grounds.

Location: In centre of Godmanchester next to the car park. 1 m S of Huntingdon (A1); 15 m NW of Cambridge (A14).
Station(s): Huntingdon (1 m).
Open: July 2-July 30 Sun only 2.30-4.30. Parties particularly welcome May-Sept by appointment.
Admission: Party rate £2 groups over 40. Adm House and Grounds £2.50 children £1 (grounds only). Grounds only £1.50.
Refreshments: Teas.

KIMBOLTON CASTLE
(Governors of Kimbolton School)
Kimbolton   map **7** S22

Tudor manor house associated with Katherine of Aragon, completely remodelled by Vanbrugh (1708-20); courtyard c. 1694. Fine murals by Pellegrini in chapel, boudoir and on staircase. Gatehouse by Robert Adam. Parkland.

Location: 8 m NW of St Neots on A45; 14 m N of Bedford.
Station(s): St Neots (9 m).
Open: Easter Sun & Mon, Spring Bank Hol Sun & Mon, Summer Bank Hol Sun & Mon also Sun only late July and Aug 2-6.
Admission: Adults £1 children & OAPs 30p.

THE MANOR OR GREEN KNOWE
(Mr and Mrs Peter Boston)
Hemingford Grey   **PE18 9BN**   map **14** T18
Telephone: (01480) 463134

Built about 1130 and recreated by the author Lucy Boston as Green Knowe this is reputedly the oldest continuously inhabited house in the country. It contains Lucy Boston's patchworks. The garden has old roses and topiary.

Open: Year by appointment only.
Admission: £2.50 adults £1.50 children or £1.50 adults and £1 children to garden only.

PECKOVER HOUSE AND GARDEN   The National Trust
North Brink   **PE13 1JR**   map **7** R23   △ &
Telephone: (01945) 583463

Important example of early 18th century domestic architecture. Fine rococo decoration. Interesting Victorian garden contains rare trees, flower borders, roses. Under glass are orange trees. Georgian stables. Restored Reed Barn.

Location: Centre of Wisbech town on N bank of River Nene (B1441).
Station(s): March (9½ m).
Open: House & Gardens: Apr 1-Oct 31 Sun Wed & Bank Hol Mon 2-5.30. Garden also open Mon Tues Sat.
Admission: £2.40 children £1.20. Party rate £1.80. Garden only days £1.
Refreshments: Teas mid-June-mid Sept Sun Wed & Bank Hol Mon.
No dogs. Wheelchairs garden only. Garden Tours contact Head Gardener (01945) 65325.

PRIOR CRAUDEN'S CHAPEL
(The Bursar, The King's School)
The College, Ely   map **7** S23
Telephone: (01353) 662837

Built as a private chapel in 1324/1325 for Prior Crauden, the Prior of the Mediaeval Benedictine Monastery from 1321 to 1341. Recently restored to show glimpses of coloured walls, painted glass and wall paintings.

Location: In the precincts of Ely Cathedral.
Open: Mon-Fri 9-5 excluding statutory and Bank Hols. Key available from Chapter Office in Firmary Lane.
Admission: Free.
Parking in Cathedral Car Park. Not suitable for disabled visitors.

UNIVERSITY BOTANIC GARDEN
(University of Cambridge)
Cory Lodge, Bateman Street, Cambridge   **CB2 1JF**   &   map **5** S23
Telephone: (01223) 336265
Fax: (01223) 336278

Owned by the University of Cambridge. Laid out by Henslow in 1846. Forty acres of outstanding gardens with lake, glasshouses, winter garden, chronological bed and other special features. Incorporates nine National Collections, including Geranium and Fritillaria.

Location: 1½ m south of Cambridge centre. Entrance on Bateman Street.
Station(s): Cambridge Railway Station ½ m (Bateman Street entrance).
Open: Open all year except Christmas Day and Boxing Day 10-6 (summer) 10-5 (autumn & spring) 10-4 (winter).
Admission: Adults under 60 £1.50 adults over 60/children £1 charged weekends and Bank Hols throughout the year and weekdays Mar 1-Oct 31. All parties must be pre-booked. Pre-booked school parties and registered disabled people free. No reductions for parties.
Refreshments: Tea-room and gift shop in Gilmour Building; picnic area.
No dogs except guide dogs for the visually impaired. All parties must pre-book. Guided tours by the Friends of the Garden available by arrangement.

Sir Christopher Wren - architect
(1632-1723)

Fawley Court
Old Royal Observatory
Winslow Hall

WIMPOLE HALL 🌿 The National Trust

Arrington   SG8 0BW   map **7** S22   Ⓢ
Telephone: (01223) 207257

An architecturally refined house of aristocratic proportions, sumptuous 18th and 19th century staterooms, set in a beautifully undulating park devised by the best of the landscape architects.

Location: 8 m SW of Cambridge; signposted off A603 at New Wimpole.
Station(s): Shepreth (5 m) (not Suns); Royston (7 m).
Open: House Garden & Park Mar 25-Nov 5 Tues Wed Thurs Sat Sun 1-5 Bank Hol Sun & Mon 11-5 also Fri 4-25 Aug 1-5.
Admission: £4.50 children £2.25. Pre-booked parties of 15 or more £3.50. Joint ticket for Hall & Farm £6.
Refreshments: Lunches & teas in the Dining Room 12-5. Table license. Light refreshments at stable block 10.30-5.30. Same days as house.
Conferences: Contact Property Manager for progression of events.
Picnic area. Shop. Dogs allowed in park only on leads, Wheelchair access, 3 chairs provided.

CHESHIRE

ADLINGTON HALL

(Mr & Mrs A.S. Barnett Legh)
Macclesfield   SK10 4LF   map **15** Q18   ♿
Telephone: (01625) 829206
Fax: (01625) 828756

Adlington Hall is a Cheshire Manor and has been the home of the Leghs since 1315. The Great Hall was built between 1450 and 1505, the Elizabethan 'Black and White' in 1581 and the Georgian South Front in 1757. The Bernard Smith Organ was installed c 1670. A 'Shell Cottage', Yew Walk and Lime Avenue are features of the gardens. Recently restored follies include a chinese bridge, Temple to Diana and Tig House.

Location: 5 m N of Macclesfield on the Stockport/Macclesfield Road (A523).
Station(s): Adlington (½ m).
Open: Good Fri-end Sept Sun & Bank Hols 2-5.30.
Admission: Hall And Gardens adults £4 children £1.50 *Special parties by arrangement other days (over 25 people £3.50).*
Refreshments: At the Hall.
Gift Shop. Car park free.

ARLEY HALL AND GARDENS

(The Hon Michael and Mrs Flower)
nr Great Budworth and midway between Warrington and Northwich   CW9 6NA   map **15** Q18
Telephone: (01565) 777353
Fax: (01565) 777465

Arley Hall, built about 1840, stands at the centre of an estate which has been owned by the same family for over 500 years. An important example of the early Victorian Jacobean style, it has fine plaster work and oak panelling, a magnificent library, and interesting pictures, furniture and porcelain. There is a private Chapel designed by Anthony Salvin and a fifteenth century cruck barn. The old established gardens overlooking beautiful parkland, and providing great variety of style and design, won the Christies/HHA Garden of the Year Award in 1987. Features include the Double Herbaceous Border established in 1846, a unique avenue of Quercus Ilex clipped to the shape of giant cylinders, a pleached Lime Avenue, fine Yew Hedges, a good collection of Shrub Roses, a Herb Garden and a Woodland Garden which has been developed over the last 20 years with an interesting collection of exotic trees and shrubs including over 200 varieties of Rhododendron.

Location: 5 m N of Northwich; 6 m W of Knutsford; 7 m S of Warrington; 5 m off M6 at junctions 19 & 20; 5 m off M56 at junctions 9 & 10. Nearest main roads A49 and A50.
Open: Apr-Sept incl Tues-Suns & Bank Hol Mons 12-5. Guided Tours and Parties by arrangement.
Admission: GARDENS £2.80 HALL £1.80.
Refreshments: Lunches and light refreshments in converted Tudor barn.
Events/Exhibitions: Antique fairs, Garden Design Show Craft Show Firework & Laser Concert etc.
Conferences: Facilities available. Corporate activities, Product Launches, Filming, weddings, Themed Events, Countryside Days etc.
Shop and Plant Nursery. Craft Worker. Woodland Walk. Facilities for disabled. Dogs allowed in gardens on leads. Picnic area.

BEESTON CASTLE

map **6** Q17

ENGLISH HERITAGE

Telephone: (01829) 260464

Built on an isolated crag, Beeston Castle is visible for miles around. The view across the Cheshire plain extends to the Pennines in the east and westwards to Wales. Begun about 1220 by Ranulf de Blundeville, the castle was further fortified by Edward I. The ditch alone can have been no small task, as it is hewn from the solid rock. There is an exhibition on the history of the castle in the museum.

Location: 2 m (3.2 km) west of Bunbury. 11m (18 km) south east of Chester.
Open: Apr 1-Sept 30 10-6 daily Oct 1-Mar 31 10-4 daily.
Admission: Adults £2.20 concessions £1.70 children £1.10.

CAPESTHORNE

(Mr and Mrs William Bromley-Davenport)
Macclesfield   SK11 9JY   map **6** Q17
Telephone: (01625) 861221
Fax: (O625) 861619

Capesthorne has been the home of the Bromley-Davenport family and their ancestors the Capesthornes and Wards since Domesday times. The family were originally Chief Foresters responsible for the law and order in the King's Forests of Macclesfield and Leek. The family crest, a felon's head with a halter of gold around his neck, denoted the power of life and death without trial or appeal. Later members of this same family were to serve as Speakers to the House of Commons and in the last and present centuries, as Members of Parliament. Recent research has revealed that Francis and William Smith of Warwick were almost certainly the original architects of this Jacobean style house built in 1722. Later alterations were made by Blore and Salvin. Pictures, furniture, Capesthorne collection of vases, family muniments and Americana. The extensive grounds include an arboretum, nature trail and delightful woodland walk. Other amenities include a Touring Caravan Park, fishing and souvenir shop. Capesthorne is available for Corporate entertaining and a brochure outlining the many advantages of using the hall and grounds is available on request. Enquiries to: Administrator, Capesthorne Hall, Macclesfield, Cheshire SK11 9JY. Telephone: Hall (01625) 861221 Caravan Park (01625) 861779. Fax: (01625) 861619.

Location: 7 m S of Wilmslow, on Manchester/London Road (A34); 6½ m N of Congleton, Junction 18 (M6).
Station(s): Chelford (3 m).
Open: PARK, GARDENS AND CHAPEL 12-6 HALL 1.30-3.30. Apr: Sun only May: Sun & Wed June/July: Tues-Thurs & Suns Aug-Sept: Wed & Sun. *Open* All Bank Hols and Easter Tues. Caravan Park open Mar-Oct inc. NB Times of opening may change due to restoration work about to take place in 1995. We strongly advise that you telephone to check details.
Admission: PARK, GARDENS & CHAPEL £2.25 Chd (5-16 years) £1 OAPs £2. PARK, GARDENS, CHAPEL & HALL £4 OAPs £3.50 Chd £1.50 Budget Family ticket £8.50 Visitors £2.50 Chd £1 at the desk in the Hall entrance. Chd under 5 years accompanied by an adult free. Organised parties are welcome on any open day by appointment (please send for booking form and coloured brochure). Special reductions for parties of 20 or more at £3 per person to Hall, Park, Gardens & Chapel. Evening parties are also welcome by appointment. Evening party rate £3.50 per person, Chd £1 minimum number 20. Guided tours 50p. NB Admission charges may change due to restoration work about to take place in 1995. We strongly advise that you telephone to check details.
Refreshments: Bromley Rooms.
Coach and Car Park free. Dogs (exempt from government control regulations) are permitted in the Park area only.

CHOLMONDELEY CASTLE GARDENS
(The Marchioness of Cholmondeley)
Malpas SY14 8AH map **6** Q17
Telephone: (01829) 720383 or 720203

Extensive pleasure gardens dominated by romantic Gothic Castle built in 1801 of local sandstone. Imaginatively laid out with fine trees and water gardens, it has been extensively replanted from the 1960's with rhododendrons, azaleas, cornus, acer and many other acid loving plants. As well as the beautiful water garden, there is a rose and lavender garden and herbaceous borders. Lakeside picnic area, rare breeds of farm animals including Llamas. Ancient private chapel in park.

Location: Off A41 Chester/Whitchurch Road and A49 Whitchurch/Tarporley Road.
Station(s): Crewe.
Open: Gardens & Farm only. Apr 2-Oct 1. Apr: Sun and Bank Holiday Mon only 12-5.30. May-Oct: Wed and Thurs 12-5 Sun and Bank Holiday Mon 12-5.30. Other days by prior arrangement. Enquiries to: The Secretary, Cholmondeley Castle, Malpas, Cheshire. (House not open to public.)
Admission: Adults £2.60 OAPs £1.80 children 75p.
Refreshments: Excellent tea-room open for light lunches.
Gift Shop. Plants for sale.

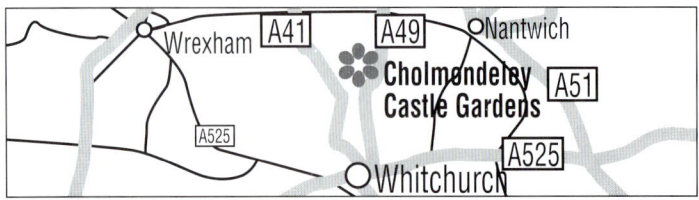

DORFOLD HALL
(R.C. Roundell, Esq)
Nantwich CW5 8LD map **6** Q17 △
Telephone: (01270) 625245
Fax: (01270) 628723

Jacobean country house built 1616. Beautiful plaster ceilings and panelling. Interesting furniture and pictures. Attractive gardens including spectacular sprng garden and newly planted herbaceous borders (1991). Guided tours.

Location: 1 m W of Nantwich on A534 Nantwich/Wrexham Road.
Station(s): Nantwich (1½ m).
Open: Apr-Oct Tues & Bank Hol Mons 2-5. At other times by appointment only.
Admission: Adults £3 children £2.

DUNHAM MASSEY ❧ The National Trust
Altrincham WA14 4SJ map **15** Q18
Telephone: 0161-941 1025

Fine 18th century house with Georgian and Edwardian interiors. Outstanding collection of furniture, paintings and Huguenot silver. Large garden, extensively replanted with shade loving and waterside plants, with attractive woodland. Deer park and water mill.

Location: 3 m SW of Altrincham off A56; junction 19 off M6; junction 7 off M56.
Station(s): Altrincham 3m Hale 3m
Open: 1 Apr-29 Oct House Sat-Wed 12-5 last audio tour 4 last adm 4.30. Garden Apr 1-29 Oct daily 11-5.30. Outside normal hours guided tours of house by arrangement at an extra charge. Shop daily throughout the year 12-5 (or dusk if earlier) closed 25 Dec-5 Jan. Park open until 7.30pm or dusk if earlier.

Admission: House and Garden incl free audio tour £4.50 children £2. House only incl free audio tour £3 children £1.50. Garden only £2.50 children £1. Family ticket incl audio tour £11.
Refreshments: Licensed self-service restaurant for lunches & teas. Open 1 Apr -31 Mar 1995 daily 11-5 or dusk if earlier (lunches 12-2). Closed 25 Dec-5 Jan 1996. Reduced menu weekdays Nov-Mar. Seating for 150. Functions and parties welcome by arrangement. The Piers Davenport Room available for booked parties. All enquiries Tel (0161) 941 2815.
Events/Exhibitions: For details of concerts, walks and other events send sae.
Dogs in park only on lead. Wheelchairs provided: access to shop coffee shop garden and park. Limited access to house. Information from the Property Manager, Dunham Massey Hall, Altrincham, Cheshire. WA14 4SJ.

GAWSWORTH HALL
(Mr & Mrs Timothy Richards)
Macclesfield SK11 9RN map **6** Q18
Telephone: (01260) 223456
Fax: (01260) 223469

Tudor half-timbered manor house with tilting ground. Former home of Mary Fitton, Maid of Honour at the Court of Queen Elizabeth I, and the supposed 'Dark Lady' of Shakespeare's sonnets. Pictures, sculpture and furniture. Open air theatre with covered grandstand - June/July/August. Situated half-way between Macclesfield and Congleton in an idyllic setting close to the lovely medieval church. Open Air Theatre: Shakespeare's Merchant of Venice - June 22-July 1, Gilbert & Sullivan's 'Ruddigore' - July 6-15, Heroic Brass Band Evenings - July 27-29, Plays - July 19-23 and Aug 2-5, also various concerts up to Aug 13. Audience seated in covered stand. Tel: (01260) 223456.

Location: 3 m S of Macclesfield on the A536 (Congleton/Macclesfield Road).
Station(s): Macclesfield.
Open: Apr 8-Oct 8 daily 2-5. Evening parties by arrangement.
Admission: Adults £3.40 children £1.70 groups of 20 or more £2.80.
Refreshments: In the Pavilion.
Events/Exhibitions: Craft Fairs; Spring and Aug Bank Holidays.

HANDFORTH HALL
(Dr & Mrs J.C. Douglas)
Handforth, nr Wilmslow SK9 3AE map **15** Q18

Small 16th century half-timbered manor house. Home of Sir William Brereton, Parliamentary General. Fine Jacobean staircase. Collection of oak furniture. Formal gardens.

Location: ½ m E of Handforth on B5358.
Open: June-Sept by written appointment only.

HARE HILL GARDEN ❧ The National Trust
Over Alderley, nr Macclesfield SK10 4QB map **6** Q18

Walled garden with pergola, rhododendrons and azaleas; parkland.

Location: Between Alderley Edge and Prestbury off B5087 at Greyhound Road. Link path to Alderley Edge 2 m in each direction. Free parking at Alderley Edge.
Station(s): Alderley Edge (3½ m); Prestbury (2½ m).

Open: Mar 29-Oct 29 Wed Thurs Sat Sun and Bank Hol Mons 10-5.30. Special opening for rhododendrons and azaleas May 12-June 2 daily 10-5.30.
Admission: £2.50 Entrance per car £1.50 refundable on entry to the garden. Parties by appointment to the Head Gardener, Garden Lodge, Oak Road, Over Alderley, Macclesfield SK10 4QB. Unsuitable for school parties.
Wheelchair access - some assistance needed. Wheelchair available.

LITTLE MORETON HALL   The National Trust
Congleton   CW12 4SD   map 6 Q18
Telephone: (01260) 272018

Begun in the 15th century, one of the most perfect examples of a timber-framed moated manor house in the country. Remarkable carved gables. Restored 16th century wall paintings are on view. Attractive knot garden.

Location: 4 m SW of Congleton off Newcastle-under-Lyme/Congleton Road (A34).
Station(s): Kidsgrove 3m Congleton 4½ m.
Open: Apr 1-Sept 30 Wed-Sun 12-5.30. Bank Hol Mon 11-5.30 (Closed Good Fri). Oct Sat & Sun 12-5.30 or dusk if earlier last adm 5. Special openings at other times for pre-booked parties. School parties Apr-end Sept Wed-Fri mornings only by prior arrangement with Property Manager (sae please). Optional guided tours most afternoons.
Admission: £3.50 family ticket £8.80. Pre-booked parties £2.80. Joint ticket with Biddulph Grange Garden available £6 family ticket £15.
Refreshments: Light lunches and home-made teas. Limited seating.
Dogs in car park only. Wheelchairs and electric scooter provided. Shop.

LYME PARK   The National Trust
Disley, Stockport   SK12 2NX   map 15 Q18
Telephone: (01663) 762023 Info line (011663) 766492
Fax: (01663) 765035

Home of the Legh family for 600 years - the largest house in Cheshire. Part of the original Elizabethan house survives with 18th and 19th century additions by Giacomo Leoni and Lewis Wyatt. Four centuries of period interiors - Mortlake tapestries, Grinling Gibbons carvings, unique collection of English clocks. Set in extensive historic gardens with orangery by Wyatt, a lake and the 'Dutch' garden. 1,377 acre park, home to red and fallow deer. Magnificent views of Pennine hills and Cheshire plain.

Location: Entrance on A6, 6½ m SE of Stockport, 9m NW of Buxton.
Station(s): Disley ½ m from Park entrance. Bus: Stockport to Park entrance. Park entrance to Hall 1m.
Open: House Apr 1-Oct 31 Sat-Wed 1.30-5 (Bank Hol Mon 11-5). Garden Apr 1-Oct 31 daily 11-5 Nov-Dec 17 Sat & Sun 12-4. Outside normal opening hours guided tours of house and garden by arrangement. Park daily 8-8.30 or dusk if earlier. Dogs under close control in park, no dogs in garden.
Admission: House & Garden £3; children half price; family £7. Garden only £1. Park only £3 per car. (NT members free).
Refreshments: Light lunches and teas in the Servants' Hall Apr 1-Oct 31 Sat-Wed 12-5. Nov-Dec 17 Sat & Sun 12-4.
Disabled access to tea-room and shop; limited access to parts of hall and garden.

NETHER ALDERLEY MILL   The National Trust
Congleton Road, Nether Alderley   map 15 Q18
Telephone: (01625) 523012

15th century corn-mill in use until 1939 and now restored; tandem overshot water wheels. Flour ground occasionally for demonstration.

Location: 1½ m S of Alderley Edge on E side of A34.

Station(s): Alderley Edge (2 m).
Open: 2 Apr-end of May & Oct Wed Sun & Bank Hol Mons 1-4.30. June-Sept Tues-Sun and Bank Hol Mons 1-5. Parties (maximum 20) by prior arrangement tel: (01625) 523012.
Admission: £1.80, Chd 90p.
Correspondence & bookings: 7 Oak Cottages, Styal, Wilmslow SK9 4JQ. Unsuitable for disabled or visually handicapped. No dogs.

PECKFORTON CASTLE
(Graybill Ltd)
Stonehouse Lane , Peckforton   CW6 9TN   map 6 Q17
Telephone: (01829) 260930
Fax: (018290) 261230

The only intact medieval style castle in Britain. Location for "Robin Hood" film 1991.

Location: Off A49 at Beeston Castle 12 m E of Chester.
Station(s): Chester - Crewe
Open: Daily Apr 14-Sept 10 as visitor attraction. Available for private hire.
Events/Exhibitions: Sundays Apr-Sept Medieval Displays. Animatronic figures to assist visitor tour.
Conferences: 275 delegates internal - Marquee unlimited.
Five acres of free parking alongside Castle. Chapel approved for wedding blessings. 4 animatronic figures to assist visitor tour.

PEOVER HALL
(Randle Brooks)
Over Peover, Knutsford   map **6** Q18

An Elizabethan House dating from 1585. Fine Caroline stables. Mainwaring Chapel. 18th century landscaped park. Large garden with Topiary work, also Walled and Herb gardens.

Location: 4 m S of Knutsford off A50 at Whipping Stocks Inn.
Open: Beginning of May-end of Sept (except Bank Holidays).
Admission: House Stables & Gardens Mons 2.30-4.30 adults £2.50 children £1.50 Stables & Gardens Only Thurs 2-5 adults £1.50 children 50p. Enquiries: J.Stocks (01565) 722656.
Refreshments: Teas in the Stables on Mons.

QUARRY BANK MILL   🌿 The National Trust
(The National Trust & Quarry Bank Mill Trust Ltd)
Styal   map **15** Q18   Ⓢ
Telephone: (01625) 527468

Award-winning museum of the cotton textile industry, set in rural park land, with England's largest working waterwheel, producing cloth on historic looms. The Apprentice House recreates the 1830's when it was home to pauper child millworkers, and its unique garden grows rare, historic fruits, vegetables and herbs. Large shop selling goods made from mill-woven cloth and National Trust gifts and books. Licensed restaurant with excellent homecooked menu, also catering for private and business functions. Open all year: 2 miles from Manchester Airport: full details under listing.

Enquiries (01625) 527468

What's On & Information Line (01426) 981359

A National Trust property

Quarry Bank Mill

Kitchen in Apprentice House

Award-winning working museum of the cotton industry housed in a 200-year-old spinning mill. Skilled demonstrators spin and weave cotton which is then made into goods on sale in the Mill Shop. Exhibitions cover the way of life of the Mill Workers, dyeing, finishing and water power. The Mill is powered by a 50 ton, 150 h.p. water-wheel. The restored Apprentice House vividly recreates the life of child workers. The museum is at the heart of a 275 acre country park and the nearby village is largely as it was in the 1850's complete with School, Chapels, Village Green and Pub. Former Museum of the Year and a winner in the 1991 and 1993 Best Attraction in the North West Competition.

Location: 1½ m N of Wilmslow off B5166. 1 m from M56 exit 5. 10 m S of Manchester (log: SJ 35835).
Station(s): Styal (⅓ m); Wilmslow (2 m).
Open: Mill: All year. Apr to Sept daily 11-6. Last admission 4.30. Oct- Mar Tues to Sun 11-5. Last admission 3.30. Pre-booked parties from 9.30 throughout the year (not Sun or Bank Hols) and specified evenings May to Sept. **Apprentice House and Garden:** Mon *closed* except Bank Hol. Tues to Fri during term time open from 2 - Mill closing. During school holidays and weekends open as the Mill. Please note that due to fire and safety regulations a maximum of 30 people can be accommodated in the house at one time. **Shop:** Open as Mill.
Admission: By timed ticket ONLY available from Mill Reception. Members wishing to avoid crowds are advised not to visit on Bank Hols and Sun afternoons in spring and summer.Advance booking essential for all groups of 10 or more, please apply for booking form at least three weeks in advance. Guides, fee per guide per 20 persons, may be booked at the same time.
Refreshments: Available during all Mill opening hours, licensed tearoom/refreshment for morning coffee, home-made soup, hot meals, regional dishes, vegetarian food and teas.
Stocks goods made from cloth woven in Mill. Disabled access: Exterior and special route through part of interior using step-lift. Please telephone for access details and leaflet. Cars may set down passengers in Mill yard, Mill Shop. Specially adapted lavatory for the disabled.

RODE HALL

(Sir Richard Baker Wilbraham, Bt)
Scholar Green   map **6** Q18
Telephone: (01270) 873237

18th century country house with Georgian stable block. Later alterations by L. Wyatt and Darcy Braddell.

Location: 5 m SW of Congleton between A34 & A50.
Station(s): Alsager (2¼ m).
Open: Apr 5-Sept 27 Wed and Bank Hols 2-5.
Admission: House, Garden & Kitchen Garden £3.50 Garden & Kitchen Garden £2.
Refreshments: Bleeding Wolf Restaurant, Scholar Green.

STAPELEY WATER GARDENS LTD

London Road, Stapeley, Nantwich   CW5 7LH   map **6** Q17
Telephone: Gdn Centre (01270) 623868; The Palms (01270) 628628

See under Specialist Growers Section.

TABLEY HOUSE COLLECTION

Victoria University of Manchester
Tabley House, Knutsford   WA16 OHB   map **6** Q18
Telephone: (01565) 750151
Fax: (01565) 653230

Fine Palladian mansion, designed in 1761 by John Carr of York for Sir Peter Byrne Leicester Bt. The State Rooms, including the spectacular Regency Picture Gallery, show furniture by Gillow, Bullock and Chippendale, and paintings by Lely, Turner, Lawrence and other English Masters from the 17th Century to the present day. Also on display is a varied collection including musical instruments and other family memorabilia. The XVIIth Century Chapel adjoins the House.

Location: 2 m W of Knutsford, entrance on A5033 (M6 Junction 19, A556).
Station(s): Knutsford (2 miles).
Open: Apr to end Oct: Thurs, Fri, Sat, Sun and Bank Hols 2-5.(Last entry 4.30). Free car park. Main rooms and the Chapel suitable for the disabled.
Admission: £3.50 child £1.00.
Refreshments: Tea room facilities. All enquiries to The Administrator.

WOODHEY CHAPEL

(The Trustees of Woodhey Chapel)
Faddiley, nr Nantwich   map **6Q17**
Telephone: (01270) 74215

'The Chapel in the Fields.' A small private chapel, recently restored, dating from 1699.

Location: 1 m SW of Faddiley off A534 Nantwich/Wrexham Road.
Open: Apr-Oct Sats & Bank Hol Mons 2-5 at other times by appointment.
Admission: Adults 50p children 25p.

CLEVELAND

ORMESBY HALL   The National Trust

nr Middlesbrough   map **9** O20   △
Telephone: (01642) 324188

Mid-18th century house. Contemporary plasterwork. Small garden.

Location: 3 m SE of Middlesbrough.
Station(s): Marton (1½ m) (not Suns Apr, Sept & Oct).
Open: 1 Apr-31 Oct Wed Thurs Sat Sun Bank Hol Mons & Good Fri 2-5.30. Last adm 5.
Admission: HOUSE & GARDEN £2 Children £1 Family £4Parties £1.70 Child parties 90p. GARDEN £1 Children 50p.
Refreshments: Afternoon teas.
No dogs (except guide dogs). Wheelchair access to ground floor only. Shop and tea-room open as house and some weekends in Nov & Dec.

CORNWALL

ANTONY   The National Trust

Torpoint   PL11 2QA   map **2** W14   △
Telephone: (01752) 812191

The home of Sir. Richard Carew Pole. Built for Sir William Carew 1718-1729. Unaltered early 18th century house, panelled rooms. Fine furniture. Extensive garden and woodland walks.

Location: 5 m W of Plymouth via Torpoint car ferry. 2 m NW of Torpoint, N of A374.
Open: Apr-end of Oct Tues Wed & Thurs also Bank Hol Mons and Suns in June July and Aug 1.30-5.30 (last adm 4.45).
Admission: £3.60 children £1.80. Pre-arranged parties £2.80 children £1.40. Joint garden only ticket with adjoining Antony Woodland Garden (privately owned by the Carew Pole Garden Trust). £2.50 children £1.25 prearranged parties £2. Guided tours.
Refreshments: Tea-room. Lunches available from 12.30 on open days.
No dogs. Unsuitable for wheelchairs. Shop.

ANTONY WOODLAND GARDEN
(Carew Pole Garden Trust)
Torpoint map **2** W14 △
Telephone: (01752) 812364

A woodland garden and natural woods extending to 100 acres in an area designated as one of Outstanding Natural Beauty and a Site of Special Scientific Interest. The Woodland Garden established in the late 18th century with the assistance of Humphry Repton features over 300 types of Camellias and a wide variety of Magnolias, Rhododendrons, Hydrangeas, Azaleas and other flowering shrubs together with many fine species of indigenous and exotic hardwood and softwood trees. Adjoining and contrasting with this long established woodland garden an additional 50 acres of natural woods bordering the River Lynher, featuring a 'Fishful' Pond, many wild flower species and birds make this an area to delight botanists, ornothologists, or those who merely enjoy peaceful woodland walks.

Location: 5 m W of Plymouth via Torpoint Car Ferry. 2 m NW of Torpoint off A374.
Station(s): Plymouth.
Open: Antony Woodland Garden and Woodland Walk Mar 1-Oct 31 Mon-Sat 11-5.30 Sun 11.30-5.30.
Admission: Adults £1.50 children 50p special openings in aid of Charities by arrangement.
Refreshments: Available at adjoining Antony House during its opening times.
Car parking available. No dogs allowed.

CAERHAYS CASTLE GARDENS
St. Austell PL26 6LY map **2** W13 △
Telephone: (01872) 501310
Fax: (01872) 501870

Informal 60 acre woodland garden created by J. C. Williams who sponsored plant hunting expeditions to China at the turn of the century. Noted for Camellias, Magnolias and Rhododendrons.

Location: South coast of Cornwall between Mevagissey and Portloe.
Open: House open Mar 27-May 5 Mon-Fri 2-4 excluding Bank Hols. Gardens Mar 20-May 5 Mon-Fri 11-4.30. Charity events - gardens only Sun Mar 26 Sun Apr 16 Mon May 8 11-4.30.
Admission: House Mar 27-May 5 £3 guided tours only. Gardens Mar 20-May 5 adults £2.50 children £1.50. Combined House/Garden admission £5. Charity events adults £1.50 children free (Gardens only).

Refreshments: Tea-room.
Guided Tours by Head Gardener £3.50 (prior booking). Ample free parking at Beach Car park.

COTEHELE 🌲 The National Trust
St. Dominick PL12 6TA map **2** W14
Telephone: (01579) 50434 Restaurant (01579) 50652

Fine medieval house, the former home of Earls of Mount Edgcumbe. Armour, furniture, tapestries. Terrace garden falling to the sheltered valley, ponds, stream, unusual shrubs. Watermill and Cotehele Quay museum.

Location: On W bank of the Tamar, 1 m W of Calstock by footpath, (6 m by road). 8 m SW of Tavistock; 14 m from Plymouth via Saltash Bridge.
Station(s): Calstock (1½ m).
Open: 1 Apr-Oct 31 Garden Shop and Quay every day 11-5.30. House Mill and Restaurant every day *except Fri* but open Good Fri 1-5.30. 12-5 in Oct closes dusk if earlier. Last adm ½ hr before closing. Nov-Mar Garden open daily during daylight.
Admission: House Gardens Cotehele Mill and Quay £5 children £2.50. Gardens Cotehele Mill and Quay £2.50 children £1.25. *Reduced fee of £4, Chd £2 for pre-booked coach parties. Organisers should book visits & arrange for meals beforehand with the Property Manager.*
Refreshments: Coffee, lunch and tea in Barn (*closed* Fri) and on Quay (open daily) during season.
DOGS IN WOODS ONLY - on lead. Wheelchairs provided; house only accessible. Shop.

GLENDURGAN GARDEN 🌲 The National Trust
Mawnan Smith TR11 5JZ map **2** W12
Telephone: (01326) 250906 (Opening hours only)

A valley garden of great beauty with fine trees and shrubs, overlooking Helford River. Giant's Stride and maze much enjoyed by children.

Location: 4 m SW of Falmouth ½ m SW of Mawnan Smith on road to Helford Passage.
Open: Mar 1-end of Oct Tues-Sat incl (except Good Fri) but open Bank Hol Mons. 10.30-5.30 (last adm 4.30.)
Admission: £2.80 children £1.40. *No reduction for parties.*
Refreshments: Snacks and light refreshments.
No dogs. Unsuitable for wheelchairs.

GODOLPHIN HOUSE

(Mrs. Schofield)
Helston   TR13 9RE   map **2** W12
Telephone: (01736) 762409

A Former home of the Earls of Godolphin and the birthplace of Queen Anne's famous Lord High Treasurer - Sidney, first Earl of Godolphin. Parts of the house are of early Tudor date and additions were made in Elizabethan and Carolean times. The unique front was completed shortly before the Civil War and rests on massive columns of local granite. The fine 'Kings Room' is traditionally said to have been occupied by Charles II (then Prince of Wales) at the time of his escape from Pendennis Castle to the Scilly Islands. Pictures include 'The Godolphin Arabian' by John Wootton. Display of Farm Waggons and Reproduction maps, prints and documents. Five acres of recently identified 17th century gardens, undergoing clearance, £1.

Location: 5 m NW of Helston; between villages of Townshend and Godolphin Cross.
Open: Bank Hol Mons May & June Thurs 2-5. July & Sept Tues 2-5 Thurs 2-5 Aug Tues 2-5 Thurs 10-1 2-5.
Admission: £3 Children 50p and £1. Open at other times for pre-booked parties.
Plants and old roses for sale.

LANHYDROCK   The National Trust

nr Bodmin   PL30 5AD   map **2** W13
Telephone: (01208) 73320   Restaurant (01208) 74331

The great house of Cornwall, with 45 rooms open to the public. 17th century long gallery. Fine plaster ceilings. Family portraits 17th to 20th centuries. The extensive kitchen and servants' quarters (1883)and a newly opened nursery wing are also shown. Formal garden with clipped yews, and parterre, laid out in 1857. Rhododendrons, magnolias, rare trees and shrubs. Woodland garden and parkland setting. 17th century Gatehouse.

Location: 2½ m SE of Bodmin on Bodmin/Lostwithiel Road (B3268).
Station(s): Bodmin Parkway (1¾ m by signposted carriage-drive to house; 3 m by road).
Open: House Garden and Grounds 1 Apr-Oct 31 Daily except Mon when House only is closed (*open* Bank Hol Mons) 11-5.30 (11-5 in Oct). Last adm ½ hr before closing. Nov-end of Mar Garden and Grounds open daily during daylight hours.
Admission: £5.40 children £2.70 Garden only £2.50 children £1.25. Family ticket £13.50 Pre-booked parties £5 children £2.50 *Organisers should book visits and arrange for meals beforehand with The Property Manager.*
Refreshments: Lunches and teas in restaurant at House; snacks in stable block (last adm 5). Dogs in park only on leads. Wheelchairs provided. Shop (also open Nov & Dec).

LONG CROSS VICTORIAN GARDENS

(D.J. Crawford)
Long Cross Victorian Hotel & Gardens, Trelights   map **2** V13
Telephone: (01208) 880243

A late Victorian garden constructed in a maze layout to provide shelter for the borders. The only public garden on the N. Cornwall Coast and is a demonstration of what can be achieved on the coast with salt wind problems. The garden incorporates many granite and water features, as well as a pets corner. Many plants found in the garden can be purchased.

Station(s): Bus service from Wadebridge.
Open: 10.30 until dusk all year.
Admission: £1 children free.
Accommodation: 10 spacious ensuite rooms many with panoramic views of the garden and coastline. Bargain Gardeners breaks in Spring/Autumn.
The gardens contain a Free House Tavern with an exceptional Beer/Tea Garden.

MOUNT EDGCUMBE HOUSE & PARK

(City of Plymouth & Cornwall County Council)
Cremyll, Nr. Plymouth   PL10 1HZ   map **2** W14
Telephone: (01752) 822236
Fax: (01752) 822199

Mount Edgcumbe House, a Tudor mansion restored (after 1941 bombing) by the architect Adrian Gilbert Scott, was the home of the Mount Edgcumbe family for 400 years. The house and furniture have been refurbished to reflect the 18th century. Stretching along 10 miles of spectacular coastline from Plymouth to Whitsand Bay the park contains one of only three Grade I listed gardens in Cornwall. The garden was designed 240 years ago with views, woodland walks, follies, garden buildings and includes formal gardens in English, French and Italian styles and now has New Zealand and American plantations. It holds the National Camellia Collection. In the park are ancient trees, wild fallow deer, and fortifications of Iron age, Tudor and Victorian date.

Location: On Rame Peninsula, 12 m from Torpoint, Cornwall, or by Cremyll (pedestrian) Ferry from Plymouth (Stonehouse) to Park entrance.
Open: Park including Landscaped Park and Formal Gardens open every day all year round Free. House and Earls Garden open Apr 1-Oct 31 11-5 Wed-Sun and Bank Hol Mons.
Admission: Adults £3 children £1.50 concessions £2.20 family (2+2) £7 season ticket £5.50. Advance bookings to the value of £30 or more (20% discount) during normal opening hours only.
Refreshments: Lunches, teas and light refreshments available in the Orangery Restaurant/Cafe, Apr 1 to Oct 31 daily. Reservations and enquiries telephone Plymouth (01752) 822586. Visitor Centre and Shop selling guides and souvenirs open Apr 1 to Oct 31 every day. Gifts produced in Devon and Cornwall a speciality.

PENCARROW

(The Molesworth - St Aubyn Family)
Bodmin   map **2** V13
Telephone: (0120) 884 369

Georgian house and listed gardens, still owned and lived in by the family. A superb collection of 18th century pictures, furniture and porcelain. Mile long drive and Ancient British Encampment. Marked walks through beautiful woodland gardens, past the great granite Victorian Rockery, Italian and American gardens, Lake and Ice House. Approx 50 acres in all. Over 600 different species and hybrid rhododendrons and also an internationally known specimen conifer collection.

Location: 4 m NW of Bodmin off A389 & B3266 at Washaway.
Open: House Tea-rooms and Craft Centre Easter-Oct 15 every day (except Fri and Sat) 1.30-5 (Bank Hol Mon and from 1 June-10 Sept 11am-). Gardens open daily.
Admission: House And Gardens adults £3.50 children £1.50 Gardens Only adults £1.50 children free. Coaches £3 (1994 prices) Guided tours.
Refreshments: Light lunches and cream teas.
Car park and toilet facilities for disabled. Dogs very welcome in grounds. Plant shop. Picnic area. Small children's play area, and pets corner. Self pick soft fruit in season.

PENDENNIS CASTLE

ENGLISH HERITAGE

Falmouth   map **2** W12
Telephone: (01326) 316594

Henry VIII's reply to the Pope's crusade against him was to fortify his coastline. Two castles guarded the Fal Estuary, Pendennis and St Mawes. Built high on a promontory, Pendennis saw action in the Civil War when 'Jack-for-the-King' Arundell held the castle for five terrible months. It continued in military use until 1946. 1588 Gundeck tableau, exhibition, views and refreshments.

Location: Pendennis Head 1 m (1⅔ km) south east of Falmouth.
Open: Apr 1-Sept 30 10-6 daily Oct 1-Mar 31 10-4 daily.
Admission: Adults £2.20 concessions £1.70 children £1.10.

PRIDEAUX PLACE

(The Prideaux-Brune Family)
Padstow   PL28 8RP   map **2** V13
Telephone: (01841) 532411 and 532945

An Elizabethan Mansion set in extensive grounds above the fishing port of Padstow. 20 acres of deer park. Guided tours through this family home include a visit to the Great Chamber with its interesting embossed plaster ceiling dating from 1588, dining room, morning room, drawing room, reading room and library. Newly restored Italian formal garden, woodland walk and childrens 'Treasure Trail'.

Location: 7 m from Wadebridge, 14 m from Newquay.
Open: HOUSE, SHOP, TEAROOM - Easter Sun to 12 October, Sun to Thurs inclusive, 1.30-5. Easter, Spring and Aug Bank Hol Mon from 11. (Closed May 1).
Admission: HOUSE AND GROUNDS £4.00 GROUNDS ONLY £2.00. Special party rates. Open all the year round by appointment.
Concerts and exhibitions throughout the summer. Free parking for cars (not coaches) in grounds. Enquiries to the Administrator, Prideaux Place, Padstow PL28 8RP. Tel (01841) 532945 or 532411.

ST. MAWES CASTLE

map **2** W12
Telephone: (01326) 270526

Shaped like a clover leaf, this small 16th century castle, still intact, nestles among rock plants and tropical shrubs. During the Civil War the Governor capitulated without gunfire or bloodshed, unlike Pendennis on the opposite shore.

Location: St Mawes.
Open: Apr 1-Sept 30 10-6 daily Oct 1-31 10-4 daily Nov 1-Mar 31 Wed-Sun 10-4.
Admission: Adults £1.50 concessions £1.10 children 80p.

ST. MICHAEL'S MOUNT   🌿 The National Trust

Marazion, nr Penzance   TR17 OHT   map **2** W12
Telephone: (01736) 710507

Home of Lord St Levan. Medieval and early 17th century with considerable alterations and additions in 18th and 19th century.

Location: ½ m from the shore at Marazion (A394), connected by causeway. 3 m E Penzance.

Open: 1 Apr-end of Oct Mon-Fri 10.30-5.30 (last adm 4.45). Nov-end of Mar guided tours as tide, weather and circumstances permit. *(NB: ferry boats do not operate a regular service during this period).*
Admission: £3.50 children £1.75 Family ticket £9. Prebooked parties £3.
Shop and restaurant - Apr 1 to end Oct, daily. No dogs. Unsuitable for wheelchairs. NB: Access to the Mount and opening arrangements are liable to interruption in foul weather.

TINTAGEL CASTLE

map **2** V13
Telephone: (01840) 770328

Amazing that anything has survived on this wild, windswept coast. Yet fragments of Earl Reginald's great hall, built about 1145, and Earl Richard's 13th century wall and iron gate still stand in this incomparable landscape. No wonder that King Arthur and his Knights were thought to have dwelt here. Site exhibition.

Location: ½ m (0.8 km) north west of Tintagel.
Open: Apr 1-Sept 30 10-6 daily Oct 1-Mar 31 daily 10-4.
Admission: Adults £2.20 concessions £1.70 children £1.10.

TINTAGEL - THE OLD POST OFFICE

🌿 **The National Trust**
Tintagel   PL34 ODB   map **2** V13 ♿
Telephone: (01840) 770024 (opening hours only)

A miniature 14th century manor house with large hall.

Location: Nos 3 & 4 in the centre of Tintagel.
Open: Apr 1-Oct31 Daily 11-5.30. (11-5 in Oct). Last adm ½ hr before closing.
Admission: £2 children £1 *Pre-booked parties £1.50.*
No dogs. Wheelchair access. Shop.

TREGREHAN

(Mr T.C. Hudson)
Par   PL24 2GT   map **2** W13
Telephone: (01726) 814389 or (01726) 812438

Woodland garden created since early 19th century by Carlyon family concentrating on species from warm-temperate regions. Fine glasshouse range in walled garden. Small nursery, also open by appointment, specialising in wild source material, and camellias bred by the late owner.

Location: 2 m E of St Austell on A390. 1 m W of St. Blazey on A390.
Station(s): Par.
Open: Mid Mar-end of June and Sept 10.30-5 closed Sept 1995.
Admission: Adults £2 children 50p. Guided tours for parties by prior arrangement.
Refreshments: Teas available.
Accommodation: Self catering cottages available.
Parking for cars and coaches. Access for disabled to half garden only. No dogs.

TRELISSICK GARDEN   🌿 The National Trust

nr Truro   TR3 6QL   map **2** W12 ♿
Telephone: (01872) 862090; Restaurant (01872) 863486

Large shrub garden. Beautiful wooded park overlooking the river Fal. Woodland walks. Particularly rich in rhododendrons, camellias and hydrangeas.

Location: 5 m S of Truro on both sides of B3289 overlooking King Harry Ferry.
Open: Gardens only Mar 1-31 Oct Mon-Sat 10.30-5.30 (or sunset if earlier), Sun 12.30-5.30 (or sunset if earlier), 10.30-5 in Mar and Oct. Last adm ½ hr before closing. Entrance on road to King Harry Passage.
Admission: £3.40 children £1.70. *Family ticket £8.50 Pre-booked parties £3.*
Refreshments: In the barn Mon-Sat 10.30-5.30; Sun 12-5.30. (Closed 5 in Mar and Oct). Shop, with special plants section. Art and Craft gallery. Dogs in woodland walk and park only, on leads. Wheelchairs provided.

TRELOWARREN HOUSE & CHAPEL

(Sir John Vyvyan, Bt.)
Mawgan-in-Meneage, Helston   map **2** W12
Telephone: (01326) 221366

Home of the Vyvyan family since 1427 part of the house dates from early Tudor times. The Chapel, part of which is pre-Reformation, and the 17th century part of the house are leased to the Trelowarren Fellowship, an Ecumenical Christian Charity. The Chapel and main rooms containing family portraits are open to the public. Concerts take place, and Sunday Services are held in the Chapel during the holiday season. Exhibitions of paintings.

Location: 6 m S of Helston off B3293 to St Keverne.
Open: House & Chapel open from Apr 5-Oct 4 Weds & Bank Hol Mons always 2.15-4.30. Concerts are held in Chapel and Chapel Services every Sun during the holiday season. Organised tours by arrangement.
Admission: Adults £1.50 children 50p (under 12 years free) including entry to various exhibitions of paintings.
Ground floor only suitable for disabled.

TRENGWAINTON GARDEN   The National Trust

Penzance   **TR20 8RZ**   map **2** W11
Telephone: (01736) 63021

Large shrub and woodland garden. Fine views. A series of walled gardens contain rare sub-tropical plants.

Location: 2 m NW of Penzance ½ m W of Heamoor on Morvah Road (B3312).
Station(s): Penzance (2 m).
Open: Mar 1-end Oct Wed Thur Fri Sat & Bank Hol Mons 10.30-5.30, 10.30-5 in Mar and Oct. Last adm ½ hr before closing.
Admission: £2.60 children £1.30.*No reduction for parties.*
Refreshments: Light refreshments (not NT) available in the farmhouse garden, weather permitting.
No dogs. Wheelchair access. Shop.

TRERICE   The National Trust

nr. Newquay   **TR8 4PG**   map **2** W12
Telephone: (01637) 875404; Restaurant (01637) 879434

A small Elizabethan house, fine furniture, plaster ceilings and fireplaces, in a recently planted garden. A small museum traces the development of the lawn mower.

Location: 3 m SE of Newquay A392 & A3058 (turn right at Kestle Mill).
Station(s): Quintrel Downs (1½ m).
Open: Apr 1-Oct 31 Daily (*except* Tues) 11-5.30 Oct 11-5 Last adm ½ hr before closing.
Admission: £3.60 children £1.80.*Reduced rate of £3 for pre-booked parties.*
Refreshments: In the barn, opening times as for House. *Parties must book.*
No dogs. Wheelchairs available; access to house only. Shop.

TREWITHEN HOUSE AND GARDENS

(A.M.J. Galsworthy)
Probus   **TR2 4DD**   map **2** W13
Telephone: (01726) 882763/882764 (nurseries) (01726) 883794 (garden shop)

'Trewithen' means 'House of the Trees' which truly describes this exceptionally fine early Georgian house in its magnificent setting of wood and parkland. The origins of the house go back to the 17th century but it was the Architect Sir Robert Taylor, aided by Thomas Edwards of Greenwich, who were responsible for the splendid building and interiors we see today. Philip Hawkins bought the property in 1715 and began extensive rebuilding. The house has been lived in and cared for by the same family since that date. The magnificent landscaped gardens have an outstanding collection of magnolias, rhododendron and azaleas which are well known throughout the world. The gardens are particularly spectacular between March and the end of June and again in Autumn, although there is much to see throughout the year. A wide variety of shrubs and plants from the famous nurseries are always on sale. Other attractions include a children's playground and a 25-minute video of the house and gardens. The gardens are one of only two in this county to be awarded 3 stars by the Michelin Guide to the South West.

Location: On A390 between Probus and Grampound, adjoining County Demonstration Gardens.
Open: GARDENS: Open Mar 1-Sept 30 Mon-Sat 10-4.30. Sun Apr-May only. Nurseries: Open throughout the year Mon-Sat 9-4.30.
Admission: Gardens:Adults £2.50 Group adult (over 12) £2.20 children (under 15) £1.50. HOUSE: Guided tours Mon and Tues only Apr-July and Aug Bank Hol Mon (2-4) £3 children (under 15) £1.50. Parties by arrangement please.
Refreshments: Tea shop for light refreshments.

CUMBRIA

ABBOT HALL ART GALLERY & MUSEUM OF LAKELAND LIFE & INDUSTRY

(Lake District Art Gallery & Museum Trust)
Kirkland, Kendal   LA9 5AL   map **9** O17   &
Telephone: (01539) 722464

Impressive Georgian House with works by Ruskin, Constable, Turner; portraits by Romney and Gardner; Lake District landscapes over 250 years; Modern British Art including Sutherland, Piper, Ben Nicholson, Barbara Hepworth, Elizabeth Frink. Furniture by Gillows displayed in recently restored rooms. Lively programme of temporary exhibitions. Access for disabled throughout the Gallery. Adjacent Museum of Lakeland Life recaptures flavour of everyday social and industrial life in the Lakes. Arthur Ransome Room and John Cunliffe Room (Postman Pat). Also visit award-winning Kendal Museum of Natural History and Archaeology on Station Road.

Location: Off Kirkland nr Kendal Parish Church. From M6 exit 36.
Station(s): Oxenholme (1½ m); Kendal (¾ m).
Open: 11 Feb-23 Dec daily 10.30-5. Reduced hours Nov-Mar - please phone.
Admission: Charge; concessions for OAPs/children/students and families.
Refreshments: Coffee Shop.
Events/Exhibitions: Changing exhibitions in 1995; Mar 24-May 14 The Opening of Waterloo Bridge - John Constable, June 20-Sept 4 L. S. Lowry - The Man and His Art, Oct 13-Nov 11 Pop Art Prints.
Conferences: Facilities available.
Disabled access. Free parking.

ACORN BANK GARDEN   🍃 The National Trust
Temple Sowerby, Penrith   map **9** N17
Telephone: (017683) 61893

This 2½ acre garden is protected by fine oaks under which grow a vast display of daffodils. Inside walls are two orchards with medlar, mulberry, cherries, quince and apples. Surrounding the orchards are mixed borders with herbaceous plants and many flowering shrubs and climbing roses. The adjacent herb garden has the largest collection of culinary, medicinal and narcotic herbs in the north. The red sandstone house is let to the Sue Ryder Foundation and is open on application.

Location: Just N of Temple Sowerby, 6 m E of Penrith on A66.
Open: GARDEN ONLY. Apr 1 to Oct 31 - Daily 10-5.30.
Admission: £1.60, Chd 80p. Reduction for pre-arranged parties.
No dogs. Wheelchair access to parts of garden only. Small shop. Plant sales.

"GHOSTS"

Ghosts are in residence at the following properties included in Historic Houses Castles and Gardens:-

Blickling Hall - *Anne Boleyn*

Breamore House - *Haunted picture - if touched, death on the same day*

East Riddleden Hall - *5 ghosts including lady in Grey Hall Lady's Chamber*

Fountains Abbey & Studley Royal - *Choir of monks chanting in Chapel of Nine Altars*

Hinton Ampner - *Nocturnal noises*

Ightham Mote - *Supernatural presence*

Lindisfarne Castle - *Monk, and group of monks on causeway*

Lyme Park - *Unearthly peals of bells and lady in white, funeral procession through park*

Malmesbury House - *Ghost of a cavalier*

Overbecks Museum & Garden - *'Model' ghost in the Children's room (for them to spot)*

Rockingham Castle - *Lady Dedlock*

Rufford Old Hall - *Elizabeth Hesketh*

Scotney Castle Garden - *Man rising from the lake*

Sizergh Castle & Garden - *Poltergeist*

Speke Hall - *Ghost of woman in tapestry room*

Springhill - *Ghost of a woman*

Sudbury Hall - *Lady in Green, seen on stairs*

Tamworth Castle - *Haunted bedroom*

Treasurer's House - *Troop of Roman soldiers marching through the cellar*

Wallington House - *Invisible birds beating against the windows accompanied by heavy breathing*

Washington Old Hall - *Grey lady walking through corridors*

BRANTWOOD

(Brantwood Educational Trust)
Coniston   LA21 8AD   map **9** O16
Telephone: (015394) 41396

The most beautifully situated house in the Lake District with the best lake and mountain views in England. Home of the artist, critic and social reformer John Ruskin from 1872-1900. Splendid collection of Ruskin watercolours. Delightful nature walks around 250 acre estate. Also woodland and lakeshore gardens.

Location: 2½ m from Coniston. Historic House signs at Coniston, Head of Coniston Water & Hawkshead.
Open: Open all year. Mid Mar-mid Nov Daily 11-5.30. Winter season Wed-Sun 11-4.
Admission: House, Exhibitions & Nature Walks £3 Children free. Nature trails only £1 Children free. Free car park.
Refreshments: Licensed restaurant/tea room/coffee; Full meals available.
Steam Yacht Gondola sails regularly from Coniston Pier. Parking for disabled near house. Toilets (incl for disabled). Craft gallery and shop. Also hourly ferry service motor launch 'Ruskin'.

CARLISLE CASTLE

Carlisle   map **9** N17
Telephone: (01228) 591922

Twenty-six years after the Battle of Hastings. Carlisle remained unconquered. In 1092 William II marched north, took the city and ordered the building of a stronghold above the River Eden. Since William's time the castle has survived 800 years of fierce and bloody attacks, extensive rebuilding and continuous military occupation. A massive Norman keep contains an exhibition on the history of the castle. D'Ireby Tower now open to the public, containing furnishings to authentic medieval design, an exhibition and shop. Guided tours are given by a local group of volunteers.

Location: North of town centre.
Open: Apr 1-Sept 30 daily 10-6 open daily Oct 1-Mar 31 (whichever is earlier) daily 10-4.
Admission: Adults £2.20 concessions £1.70 children £1.10.

CASTLETOWN HOUSE

(Giles Mounsey-Heysham, Esq)
Rockcliffe, Carlisle   CA6 4BN   map **9** N17
Telephone: (01228) 74792
Fax: (01228) 74464

Georgian House set in attractive gardens and grounds.

Location: 5 m NW of Carlisle on Solway coast, 1 m W of Rockcliffe village and 2 m W of A74.
Open: HOUSE ONLY by appointment only.

DALEMAIN

(Robert Hasell-McCosh Esq)
nr Penrith   CA11 0HB   map **9** N16
Telephone: (017684) 86450
Fax: (017684) 86223

Mediaeval, Tudor and Georgian house and gardens occupied by the same family for over 300 years. Interesting garden as featured on TV and in various publications. Fine furniture and portraits. Countryside and Agricultural Museum, Westmorland and Cumberland Yeomanry Museum. Fell Pony Museum. Plant Centre, shop, picnic area, playground, ample parking.

Location: 3 m from Penrith on A592. Turn off M6 exit 40 onto A66 (A592) to Ullswater.
Station(s): Penrith.
Open: 9 Apr-8 Oct daily except Fri and Sat 11.15-5.
Admission: Charged. Entry to car park and picnic area, shop, and restaurant free.
Refreshments: Licensed Restaurant. Coffee from 11.15. Bar lunches 12-2.30. Home made teas from 2.30. High teas by arrangement. No dogs please.
Events/Exhibitions: Rainbow Craft Fair July 22nd and 23rd.
Conferences: By arrangement.
Old fashioned Rose Collection on view, and for sale in conjunction with Stydd Nurseries. No dogs please.

DOVE COTTAGE & THE WORDSWORTH MUSEUM

(The Wordsworth Trust)
Grasmere   LA22 9SH   map **9** O17   △ Ⓔ Ⓢ
Telephone: (015394) 35544

Dove Cottage, Wordsworth's home 1799-1808. Visitors are offered guided tours. The garden is oen weather permitting. The award winning Wordsworth Museum houses permanent exhibition and a programme of special exhibitions.

Location: On A591 Kendal-Keswick Road next to Dove Cottage Tea shop.
Station(s): Windermere, bus service 518,555,556,557.
Open: 9.30-5.30. Closed Jan 9-Feb 5 & Dec 24-26 1995.
Admission: Adults £4 children £2 special rates for families & groups - family ticket (1 adult & 1-3 children) £6 (2 adults and 1-3 children) £10 and group rate adults £3.10.
Refreshments: Dove Cottage Tea-rooms serve meals and snacks throughout the day. Groups should book in advance, tea-rooms can take group bookings (pre-arranged) (015394) 35268.

HOLKER HALL AND GARDENS

(Lord and Lady Cavendish)
Cark-in-Cartmel, nr Grange-over-Sands   LA11 7PL   map **6** O11   △ & Ⓔ Ⓢ
Telephone: (015395) 58328
Fax: (015395) 58776

Cumbria's premier Stately home has 25 acres of National Award winning gardens with water features, rare plants and shrubs, 'World Class...not to be missed by foreign visitors' (Good Gardens Guide '94). Also exhibitions, Deer Park, Adventure Playground, Motor Museum. Home of the spectacular Great Garden and Countryside Festival held first weekend in June annually. (Show Office 015395 58838).

Location: ½ m N of Cark-in-Cartmel on B5278 from Haverthwaite; 4 m W Grange-over-Sands.
Open: Apr 2-Oct 31 everyday excluding Sat 10-6 last admissions 4.30.
Admission: ('94) from £3 reduction for groups of 20 or more.
Refreshments: Home made cakes, sandwiches, salads in the Clock Tower Cafe. Dogs on leads in Grounds only. Free parking.

HUTTON-IN-THE-FOREST
(Lord and Lady Inglewood)
Penrith   map **9** N17
Telephone: (017684) 84449

One of the ancient manors in the Forest of Inglewood, and the home of Lord Inglewood's family since the beginning of the 17th century. Built around a medieval pele tower with 17th, 18th and 19th century additions. Fine English furniture and pictures, ceramics and tapestries. The outstanding gardens and grounds include a lovely walled garden established in 1730 which has an every increasing collection of herbaceous plants against a backdrop of wall trained fruit trees and topiary. Also terraces, dovecote, lake and woodland walk through magnificent specimen trees.

Location: 7 m NW of Penrith on B5305 Wigton Road (3 m from M6 exit 41).
Open: House 1-4 Easter Sun and Easter Mon and Thurs, Fri and Sun from Apr 31-Oct 1 with additional Weds in August and Bank Holiday Mons. Gardens and Grounds 11-5 every day except Sat. Private parties by arrangement from Apr 1.
Refreshments: Fresh home-made teas available in the cloisters when house open. Lunch and supper menus available on request.

19/20 IRISH STREET
(Copeland Borough Council)
Whitehaven   map **8** N15   &
Telephone: (01946) 693111 Ext 285

1840-50 Italianate design, possibly by S. Smirke. Stuccoed 3-storey building now occupied by the Council Offices.

Location: In town centre.
Station(s): Whitehaven.
Open: All the year during office hours. For details and appointments telephone Mr J. A. Pomfret.
Refreshments: Hotels and restaurants in town centre.
Ground floor only suitable for disabled.

ISEL HALL
(The Administrator (WA))
Cockermough, Cumbria   CA13 0QG   △   map **9** N16

Pele Town with domesic range, outbuildings and gardens set on north bank of River Derwent. The house is small so groups limited to 30.

Location: 3½ miles N.E. of Cockermouth.
Station(s): Aspatria 9 miles Penrith 32 miles.
Open: Mondays 17 Apr-16 Oct plus Easter Mon 2-4.
Admission: £2.50
No dogs. No photography inside.

LEVENS HALL
(C.H. Bagot, Esq)
Kendal, Cumbria   LA8 0PD   map **9** O17   &
Telephone: (015395) 60321

This magnificent Elizabethan home of the Bagot family, with its famous topiary garden (c.1694) is a must for visitors to the Lake District. The garden is unique in age and appearance, beautifully maintained in it's original design with colourful bedding and herbaceous borders. The house contains a superb collection of Jacobean furniture, fine plaster ceilings, panelling, paintings and needlework, including the earliest English patchwork (c.1708). A collection of working model steam engines shows the development of steam power from 1820 to 1920, with full-sized traction engines in steam on Sundays and Bank Holiday Mondays.

Location: 5 m S of Kendal on the Milnthorpe Road (A6); Exit 36 from M6.
Open: Apr 2-Sept 28 House, Garden, Gift Shop, Tea-rooms, Plant Centre, Play Area and Picnic Area Sun Mon Tues Wed & Thurs 11-5 Steam Collection 2-5 closed Fri & Sat.
Admission: Charge. Group rates for 20 or more.
Refreshments: Home-made light Lunches and teas.
Regret house not suitable for wheelchairs.

MIREHOUSE
(Mr & Mrs Spedding)
Keswick   CA12 4QE   map **9** N16   &
Telephone: (017687) 72287

First built in 1666, Mirehouse has only been sold once in 1688 and remains a welcoming family home: an unusually literary house with an interesting picture collection and live classical piano music. The grounds stretch to Bassenthwaite Lake. French, German and Spanish spoken. Children welcome.

Location: 4½ m N of Keswick on A591 (Keswick to Carlisle Road).
Station(s): Rail: Penrith. Regular bus service past gate.
Open: Apr-Oct Lakeside Walk, Adventure Playgrounds daily 10.30-5.30 House Sun Wed (also Fri in Aug) 2-last entries 4.30. Parties welcome by appointment.
Refreshments: Old Sawmill Tea-room open daily 10.30-5.30; salads & sandwiches made to order, home baking. Parties please book (Tel: Keswick (017687) 74317).

Grinling Gibbons (1648-1721)

Sculptor and wood carver. His work can be seen at the following properties included in Historic Houses Castles and Gardens:-

Blenheim Palace	*Fawley Court*	*Petworth House*
Breamore House	*Kentchurch Court*	*Somerleyton Hall*
Dunham Massey	*Lyme Park*	*Sudbury Hall*

MUNCASTER CASTLE

(Mrs P. Gordon-Duff-Pennington)
Ravenglass   CA18 1RQ   map **9** O16   △ &
Telephone: (01229) 717614
Fax: (01229) 717010

Seat of the Pennington family since the 13th century, this magnificent castle with its famous rhododendron gardens and superb views of Eskdale dates from early 14th century, although the Pele tower is built on Roman foundations. There is an excellent collection of family portraits, tapestry and porcelain, but its outstanding feature is the large collection of 16th and 17th century furniture in beautiful condition. The octagonal library is one of Salvin's finest works and contains over 6,000 books. It is a very special family home. The gardens offer a variety of walks which can all offer some of the finest views in England, including those over the Esk Valley (Ruskin's Gateway to Paradise). The Owl Centre houses a large collection of these mystical creatures and daily at 2.30 (26 Mar-Oct 29) a talk is given on the pioneering work of the Centre. Weather permitting, the birds fly.

Location: 1 m SE of Ravenglass village on A595 (entrance ½ m W of Church).
Station(s): Ravenglass (1 m).
Open: Gardens and Owl Centre daily throughout the year 11-5. Castle Mar 26-Oct 29 Tues-Sun 1-4. Open all Bank Hol Mons.
Admission: Rates available. Admission prices not available at time of going to press. Special party rates available. Write or telephone for Party Bookings and details of events during the season to: Muncaster Castle, Ravenglass, Cumbria. Telephone (01229) 717614; Fax (01229) 717010. SEASON TICKETS AVAILABLE.
Refreshments: Stable Buttery serves light refreshments to full meals 11am to 5pm and is licensed.
Gift shop, owl shop, plant centre, childrens play area, nature trail and wildfowl pond.

NAWORTH CASTLE

(Colleen Hall / owner Philip Howard)
Brampton   map **9** O17
Telephone: (016977) 3229
Fax: (016977) 3679

Location: 12 m E of Carlisle, near Brampton, off the A69 to Newcastle.
Station(s): Brampton Junction 3 m, Carlisle 12 m.
Open: By appointment throughout the year.
Admission: By arrangement.
Refreshments: By arrangement.
Events/Exhibitions: Naworth Spring fair June 4th, 'In the sticks' Property Roadshow 2/3rd Sept.
Accommodation: Six bedrooms.
Conferences: Facilities available including Weddings, Corporate Hospitality, Dinners/Dances, Exhibitions, Shows, Charity Venues, Film Shoots, Conferences, Recitals/Concerts, Product Launches, Outside Events, Country Fairs, Specialist Courses. "The Function Room of the Borders".

Historic border fortress, built by the Dacres in 1335, acquired and renovated by the Howard Family in 1602, now owned by Philip & Elizabeth Howard. A stronghold for the wardens of the West March in the 16th century, an impressive residence for the powerful Earls of Carlisle in the 17th century, and an artistic centre for the pre-Raphaelites in the late 19th century, the Castle features: the Great Hall with Gobelin Tapestries and Heraldic Beasts, Lord William's Tower, the Long Gallery, the Library designed by Philip Webb & Burne-Jones, and the original 14th century dungeons.

Anthony Salvin (1799-1881)
Architect - trained under John Nash

His work can be seen in the following properties included in Historic Houses Castles and Gardens:-

Helmingham Hall Gardens
Muncaster Castle
Petworth House

RYDAL MOUNT
(The Trustees of Rydal Mount)
Ambleside LA22 9LU map **9** O17
Telephone: (015394) 33002

Wordsworth home from 1813-1850. Family portraits and furniture, many of the poet's personal possessions, and first editions of his works. The garden which was designed by Wordsworth has been described as one of the most interesting gardens to be found anywhere in England. Two long terraces, many rare trees and shrubs. Extends to 4½ acres.

Location: Off A591, 1½ m from Ambleside, 2 m from Grasmere.
Open: Mar 1-Oct 31 daily 9.30-5 Nov 1-Mar 1 10-4 (closed Tues in winter). Evening groups by arrangement with curators: Mr & Mrs P. Elkington.
Admission: House & Gardens £2.50 children £1 parties £2.

SIZERGH CASTLE AND GARDEN   The National Trust
Sizergh, Kendal LA8 8AE map **9** O17
Telephone: (015395) 60070

The 14th century Pele tower (the oldest part of the castle) rises to 60 feet, contains some original windows, floors and fireplaces; 15th century Great Hall, extended in later centuries; 16th century wings; fine panelling and ceilings; contents include French and English furniture, china, family portraits. Extensive garden includes two thirds of an acre limestone rock garden, the largest owned by the Trust with large collection of Japanese maples, dwarf conifers, hardy ferns and many perennials and bulbs; water garden; herbaceous borders; wild flower banks; fine autumn colour.

Location: 3½ m S of Kendal NW of interchange A590/A591 interchange; 2 m from Levens Hall.
Open: CASTLE & GARDEN: Apr 2-Oct 31 Sun Mon Tues Wed & Thurs1.30-5.30 (last admission 5). Garden & Shop open from 12.30 same days.
Admission: £3.30 (House and Garden) Children £1.70. GARDEN ONLY £1.70. Parties by arrangement with The Administrator, Sizergh Castle, Tel:(015395) 60070. Please send sae.
Refreshments: Tea-room in basement of Pele tower.
Shop. No dogs. Wheelchairs (one provided) in garden only. Powered mobility vehicle available for disabled.

TOWNEND   The National Trust
Troutbeck LA23 1LB map **9** O17
Telephone: (015394) 32628

17th century Lakeland farmhouse with original furnishings including much wood-carving in traditional style. Home of the Browne family for 300 years, and last remaining glimpse into the old farming way of life.

Location: At S end of Troutbeck village, 3 m SE of Ambleside.
Open: Apr 2-Oct 31 Daily (except Mon & Sat but open Bank Hol Mons) 1-5 or dusk if earlier). Last adm 4.30.
Admission: £2.50 Children £1.30 Family ticket £7. No reductions for parties.
No dogs. No coaches. Unsuitable for wheelchairs.

WORDSWORTH HOUSE   The National Trust
Cockermouth CA13 9RX map **9** N16 △
Telephone: (01900) 824805

North country Georgian House built in 1745, birthplace of the poet Wordsworth, furnished in the style of his time, with some of his belongings. The pleasant garden is referred to in his 'Prelude'. Video displays.

Location: In Main Street.
Open: Apr 3-Oct 31 weekdays. Also Sat 15 and 29 Apr 27 May and all Sats 1 Jul-2 Sept 11-5pm (last admission 4.30). Shop open as house: Mon-Sat 10-5 (incl Sats when house closed). Also Nov 1-Dec 24 Mon-Wed, Fri and Sat 11-4.
Admission: £2.40 Children £1.20 Family ticket £6.50. Reductions for pre-booked parties.
Refreshments: Light refreshments in the old kitchen (licensed).
Events/Exhibitions: Events throughout the season. Please telephone for details.
No dogs. Unsuitable for wheelchairs.

DERBYSHIRE

BAKEWELL OLD HOUSE MUSEUM
(Bakewell & District Historical Society)
Bakewell DE45 1DD map **4** Q19
Telephone: (01629) 813165

An early Tudor house with original wattle & daub screen and open chamber. Costumes and Victorian kitchen, children's toys, craftsmen's tools and lacework.

Location: Above the church in Bakewell. ¼ m from centre.
Open: House Only Apr 1-Oct 31 daily 2-5 parties in morning or evening by appointment (Telephone Bakewell (01629) 813647).
Admission: 1994 rates £1.80 children 80p.

CALKE ABBEY AND PARK   The National Trust
nr Derby map **4** R20
Telephone: (01332) 863822

Baroque mansion built 1701-3. House virtually unaltered since death of last baronet in 1924. Caricature Room, gold and white drawing room, early 18th century Chinese silk state bed. Carriage display in Stable Block. Calke Park is a fine landscaped setting (approx. 750 acres). Park accessible via Ticknall entrance only. (One-way system in operation).

Location: 9m S of Derby on A514 at Ticknall between Swadlincote and Melbourne.
Open: 1 Apr-end Oct Sat-Wed including Bank Hol Mon. *Closed* Good Fri. 1-5.30 (last adm 5).

Lancelot 'Capability' Brown

Born 1716 in Northumberland, Capability Brown began work at the age of 16 in the vegetable gardens of Sir William and Lady Loraine at Kirharle Tower. He left Northumberland in 1739, and records show that he worked at Stowe until 1749. It was at Stowe that Brown began to study architecture, and to submit his own plans. It was also at Stowe that he devised a new method of moving and replanting mature trees.

Brown married Bridget Wayet in 1744 and began work on the estate at Warwick Castle in 1749. He was appointed Master Gardener at Hampton Court in 1764, and planted the Great Vine at Hampton Court in 1768. Blenheim Palace designs are considered amongst Brown's finest work, and the technical achievements were outstanding even for the present day.

Capability Brown died in February 1783 of a massive heart attack. A monument beside the lake at Croome Court was erected which reads "To the memory of Lancelot Brown, who by the powers of his inimitable and creative genius formed this garden scene out of a morass". There is also a portrait of Brown at Burghley.

Capability Brown was involved in the design of grounds at the following properties included in Historic Houses Castles and Gardens:-

Audley End	*Longleat*
Berrington Hall	*Luton Hoo*
Bowood	*Moccas Court*
Burghley House	*Petworth House*
Burton Constable	*Sledmere House*
Charlecote Park	*Stowe (Stowe*
Chilham Castle Gardens	*School)*
(reputed)	*Syon House*
Clandon Park	*Warwick Castle*
Claremont	*Weston Park*
Chillington Hall	*Wimpole Hall*
Corsham Court	*Wrest Park and*
Fawley Court	*Gardens*
Highclere Castle	

Admission: By timed ticket only. Ticket office open at 11am. Visitors are advised that on busy days admission may not be possible. Long distance travellers are advised to contact the Calke office before setting out. Parties **must** book in advance with the Property Manager. £4.50 children £2.20.

Refreshments: Restaurant serving hot and cold lunches 12-2 and teas 2-5 (12-4 Nov/Dec). Shop and information room open same days as house 11-5.30. Also Nov-17 Dec Sat & Sun 12-4.

CHATSWORTH
(Chatsworth House Trust)
Bakewell   DE45 1PP   map **4** Q19
Telephone: (01246) 582204
Fax: (01246) 583536

Built by Talman for 1st Duke of Devonshire between 1687 and 1707. World famous collection of pictures, drawings, books and furniture. Garden with elaborate waterworks surrounded by a 1000 acre park. **House impossible for wheelchairs, but they are most welcome in the garden.**

Location: ½ m E of village of Edensor on A623, 4 m E of Bakewell, 16 m from junction 29, M1. Signposted via Chesterfield.
Open: HOUSE & GARDEN Mar 22-Oct 29 Daily 11-4.30 FARMYARD & ADVENTURE PLAYGROUND Mar 22-Oct 1 Daily 10.30-4.30.
Admission: Charges not available at time of going to press.
Refreshments: Licensed self service restaurant. Coach Drivers' Rest Room.
Gift shops. Baby Room. All details subject to confirmation. Two electric wheelchairs available for use in the Garden only.

EYAM HALL
(R.H.V. Wright)
Eyam   S30 1QW   map **4** Q19   △
Telephone: (01433) 631976
Fax: (01433) 631976

Seventeenth century manor house situated in the famous 'plague village' of Eyam. Built and still occupied by the Wright family. A glimpse of three centuries through the eyes of one family. Great variety of contents, including family portraits, tapestries, clocks, costumes, and toys. Jacobean staircase and spectacular old kitchen.

Location: 100 yds W of church. Eyam is off A623, 12 m W of Chesterfield, 15 m SW of Sheffield.
Open: Sun 2 Apr-Sun 29 Oct Weds, Thurs, Suns and Bank Hol Mons and Bank Hol Tues. (Other Tues for schools only). Opens 11am. Last tour 4.30.
Admission: Adults £3.25 children £2.25 concessions £2.75 family ticket (2 adults + 4 children) £9.50. Advance booking essential for parties, reductions available.
Refreshments: Eyam Hall Buttery: Home-made teas, cakes and light lunches. Open daily except Mons during House opening season plus all Bank Holiday Mons 10.30-5.30. Also open weekends from 4 Mar. Gift shop open same hours as Buttery.
Eyam Hall may be booked outside normal opening hours for private tours and for exclusive conferences, seminars and a wide range of other small events.

CHATSWORTH, DERBYSHIRE
Home of the Duke and Duchess of Devonshire

HADDON HALL
(His Grace the Duke of Rutland)
Bakewell   **DE45 1LA**   map **4** Q19
Telephone: (01629) 812855
Fax: (01629) 814379

HADDON HALL

Estate Office, Haddon Hall, Bakewell, Derbyshire DE45 1LA   Telephone: Backewell (01629) 812855   Fax: (01629) 814379

"GARDEN OF THE YEAR 1994" Christie's/H.H.A. Award

One of our few remaining 12th century manor houses, perfectly preserved. Noted for its tapestries, wood carvings and wall paintings. Standing on a wooded hill overlooking the fast flowing River Wye, Haddon is totally unspoiled. The beautiful terraced gardens dating from the middle ages are famous for roses, old fashioned flowers and herbs. Banqueting and clay pigeon facilities available in Hall and Park. The House is extremely difficult for disabled visitors.

Location: 2 m SE Bakewell & 6½ m N of Matlock on Buxton/Matlock Road (A6).
Open: Apr 1-Sept 30 Mon-Sun 11-5.45 closed Sun in July and Aug except Bank Hol weekends.
Admission: Adults £4.50 children £2.80 party rate £3.50 OAPs £3.50 family ticket £12.50 NB: These prices may vary - please ring to check for details.
Refreshments: Morning coffee, lunches, afternoon teas at Stables Restaurant.

HARDWICK HALL   🍀 **The National Trust**
Nr Chesterfield   map **4** Q20
Telephone: (01246) 850430

Built 1591-1597 by 'Bess of Hardwick'. Notable furniture, needlework, tapestries. Gardens with yew hedges and borders of shrubs and flowers. Extensive collection of herbs. Information Centre in Country Park.

Location: 2 m S of Chesterfield/Mansfield Road (A617) 6½ m NW of Mansfield and 9½ m SE of Chesterfield. Approach from M1 exit 29.
Open: House and Garden 1 Apr-end Oct House Wed Thurs Sat Sun & Bank Hol Mons 12.30-5 (or sunset if earlier). Last adm 4.30. Garden open daily to end Oct 12-5.30. *Closed* Good Friday. Access to Hall may be limited at peak periods.
Admission: House & Garden £5.50 Chd £2.70; Garden only £2, Chd £1.*No reduction for parties (including schools). School parties must book.*
Refreshments: In the Great Kitchen of Hall. Lunches 12-2.15, teas 2.15-4.45 (last orders 15 mins before closing) on days when hall is open.
Car park (gates close 6). Dogs in park only, on leads. Wheelchairs in garden only. *Enquiries to The National Trust, Hardwick Hall, Doe Lea, nr Chesterfield, Derbys S44 5QJ.*

KEDLESTON HALL   🍀 **The National Trust**
Derby   map **4** Q19
Telephone: (01332) 842191

One of the best examples of neo-classical architecture in the country. Robert Adam designed the late 18th century house for Sir Nathaniel Curzon to house his fine collection of furniture, tapestries and portraits. Landscaped park includes further examples of Adam's work.

Location: 4 m NW of Derby on Derby/Hulland Road via the Derby Ring Road Queensway.
Open: House, Park and Gardens 1 Apr-end Oct Sat-Wed including Bank Hol Mons (closed Good Fri). Park and Gardens 11-6. Tea-room 12-5. House and Shop 1-5.30 (last adm 5). Coach parties welcome on days when the property is open, but **must** book well in advance in writing to the Administrator. 1995 events-details from Property Manager.
Admission: £4.20, Chd £2.10.

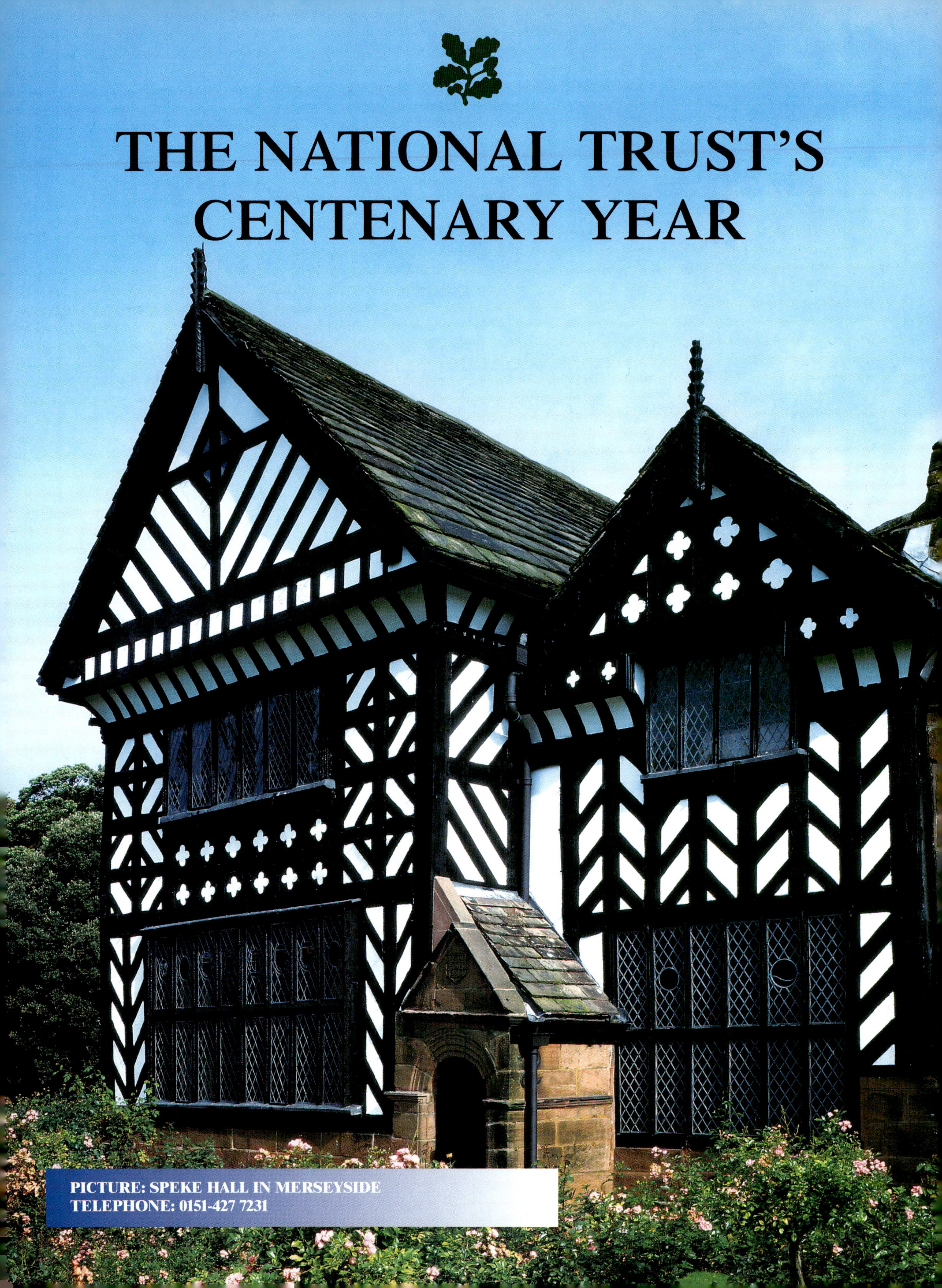

THE NATIONAL TRUST'S CENTENARY YEAR

PEVERIL CASTLE

map **15** Q19
Telephone: (01433) 620613

The castle was built to control Peak Forest, where lead had been mined since pre-historic times. William the Conqueror thought so highly of this metal - and of the silver that could be extracted from it - that he entrusted the forest to one of his most esteemed knights, William Peveril.

Location: In Castleton on A625, 15 m west of Sheffield.
Open: Apr 1-Sept 30 10-6 daily Oct 1-Mar 31 daily 10-4.
Admission: Adults £1.30 concessions £1 children 70p.

SUDBURY HALL AND NATIONAL TRUST MUSEUM OF CHILDHOOD 🍀 The National Trust

nr **Derby**   map **4** Q19   ⓢ
Telephone: (01283) 585305

A 17th century brick built house. Contains plasterwork ceilings. Laguerre murals staircase carved by Pierce and overmantel by Grinling Gibbons. Museum of Childhood.

Location: At Sudbury, 6 m E of Uttoxeter off A50 Road.
Open: 3 May-end of Oct Wed to Sun. 1-5.30 (last adm 5) closed Good Fri. Museum 1-5.30.
Admission: £3.20 children £1.60. Pre-booked parties special rates. Museum £2.20. Joint ticket for Hall and Museum £4.40.
Refreshments: Light lunches & teas in Coach House, same open days as property, 12.30-5.30.
Grounds and tea-room only accessible to disabled visitors. Dogs in car park only, on lead. 1995 events-details available from the Administrator.

WINSTER MARKET HOUSE   🍀 The National Trust

nr **Matlock**   map **4** Q19
Telephone: (0133 529) 245

A stone market house of the late 17th or early 18th century in main street of Winster.

Location: 4 m W of Matlock on S side of B5057.
Open: 1 Apr-end Oct. Daily.
Admission: Free.
Information Room. No dogs. Unsuitable for wheelchairs.

DEVON

A LA RONDE   🍀 The National Trust

Exmouth EX8 5BD   map **3** V16
Telephone: (01395) 265514

A unique 16 sided house built in 1796; fascinating interior decoration including shell encrusted and feather frieze; 18th century contents and collections from European Tour.

Location: 2 m N of Exmouth on A376.
Open: 1 Apr-Oct 31 11-5.30 daily except Fri and Sat. Last adm 5.
Admission: £3.10 children £1.50. No party reduction.
Refreshments: Tea-room.
Shop. Not suitable for coaches or visually handicapped. No dogs.

ARLINGTON COURT   🍀 The National Trust

Barnstaple   map **3** U15   ♿
Telephone: (01271) 850296

Regency house furnished with the collections of the late Miss Rosalie Chichester; including shells, pewter and model ships. Display of horse-drawn vehicles in the stables. Good trees. Victorian formal garden.

Location: 8 m NE of Barnstaple on E side of A39.
Open: Footpaths through park open all year daily during daylight hours. House, Victorian garden, Carriage Collection, Stables, 1 Apr-Oct 31 Daily except Sat (but open Sats of Bank Hol Weekends) 11-5.30. (Last adm half an hour before closing).
Admission: House & Carriage Collection £4.60 children half-price. Family ticket £11. Gardens, Ground & Stables £2.40 children half-price. *Reduced fee of £3.50 for parties of 15 or more on application to the Administrator.* Parties who do not pre-book will be charged full rate.
Refreshments: Licensed restaurant at the House: days and times as for House.
Events/Exhibitions: Carriage driving tuition, Nov-Mar; apply for details to the Administrator.
Shop. Dogs in park only, on leads. Wheelchairs provided. Carriage rides. Party bookings of rides by arrangement.

AVENUE COTTAGE GARDENS

(R.J. Pitts, Esq, R.C.H. Soans, Esq)
Ashprington, Totnes TQ9 7UT   map **3** W15
Telephone: (01803) 732 769

11 acres of garden and woodland walks. Part of 18th century landscape garden under going recreation by Designers/Plantsmen.

Location: 3 m SE of Totnes 300 yds beyond Ashprington Church (Sharpham Drive).
Open: Apr 1-Sept 30 Tues-Sat inclusive 11-5. Parties by arrangement.
Admission: Adults £1 children 25p. Collecting box.
No coaches. Limited access for disabled persons. No wheelchairs available. Dogs on leads only.

BICKLEIGH CASTLE

(Mr O.N. Boxall)
nr **Tiverton EX16 8RP**   map **3** W15   △ Ⓔ Ⓢ
Telephone: (01884) 855363

A Royalist Stronghold with 900 years of history and still lived-in. The 11th c detached Chapel, the Armoury featuring a Civil War display including Cromwellian arms and armour, the Guard Room with Tudor furniture and pictures, the Great Hall, Elizabethan bedroom, and the 17th c farmhouse - all are shown. Museum of 19th c domestic and agricultural objects and toys. Maritime Exhibition showing Bickleigh Castle's connection with the 'Mary Rose' and the 'Titanic'. World War 11 original spy and escape gadgets: picturesque Moated garden, 'Spooky' tower (57 steps). Spinning. Heritage Education Trust Award winner 1983 and 1988. Full of interest for all the family.

Location: 4 m S of Tiverton A396. At Bickleigh Bridge take A3072 and follow signs.
Open: Easter Week (Good Fri-Fri) then Weds, Suns & Bank Hol Mons to late Spring Bank Hol; then to early Oct daily (except Sats) 2-5.30 (last admission 5) *parties of 20 or more by prior appointment (preferably at times other than above) at reduced rates.*
Admission: Adults £3.50 children (5-15) £1.80 family tickets. Free coach & car park.
Refreshments: Devonshire Cream Teas in the thatched Barn.
Souvenir shops. Popular for Wedding Receptions etc. For further details, group booking discounts, and booking of functions, receptions etc throughout the year please telephone the Administrator.

BRADLEY MANOR   🌿 The National Trust
Newton Abbot   TQ12 6BN   map **3** V15
Telephone: (01626) 54513

Small, roughcast 15th century manor house set in woodland and meadows.

Location: W end of town, 7½ m NW of Torquay. On W side of A381.
Open: 1 Apr-end Sept Wed 2-5 also Thurs Apr 6 & 13 Sept 21 and 28. Last admission 4 30.
Admission: £2.60 children half-price. *No reduction for parties.* Parties of 15 or more must book.
No indoor photography. No access for coaches - Lodge gates too narrow. No dogs. Unsuitable for disabled or visually handicapped. No WC.

BUCKLAND ABBEY   🌿 The National Trust
(The National Trust jointly managed with Plymouth County Council)
Yelverton   PL20 6EY   map **2** W14
Telephone: (01822) 853607

13th century Cistercian monastery bought by Sir Richard Grenville in 1541, altered by his grandson Sir Richard Grenville, of the 'Revenge', in 1576. Home of Drake from 1581 and still contains many relics of the great seaman, including Drake's drum. Exhibition to illustrate the Abbey's history. Restored buildings, including the monk's guesthouse and 18th century farm buildings. Great Barn. Craft workshops (variable opening). Introductory video presentation.

Location: 11 m N of Plymouth 6 m S of Tavistock between the Tavistock/Plymouth Road (A386) & River Tavy.
Open: 1 Apr-Oct 31 daily except Thurs 10.30-5.30. Some rooms within the Abbey may be closed during the early part of the season for refurbishment. Last admissions 45 mins before closing time. Nov-Mar 1995 Wed Sat and Sun 2-5 (Wed pre-booked parties only).
Admission: £4 Family ticket £10 Grounds including Great Barn and Craft Workshops £2. Chd half price. Reduced rate for parties £3.20. Parties who do not pre-book will be charged at full rate.
Refreshments: Licensed Restaurant serving home-made lunches, teas and coffee.
Events/Exhibitions: 24/25 June Centenary Craft Fair.
Dogs in designated areas only, on leads. Shop.

Grinling Gibbons (1648-1721)

Sculptor and wood carver. His work can be seen at the following properties included in Historic Houses Castles and Gardens:-

Blenheim Palace   *Lyme Park*
Breamore House   *Petworth House*
Dunham Massey   *Somerleyton Hall*
Fawley Court   *Sudbury Hall*
Kentchurch Court

CADHAY   🏛
(Lady William-Powlett)
Ottery St Mary   EX11 1QT   map **3** V16   △
Telephone: (01404) 812432

Cadhay is approached by an avenue of lime-trees, and stands in a pleasant listed garden, with herbaceous borders and yew hedges, with excellent views over the original mediaeval fish ponds. Cadhay is first mentioned in the reign of Edward I, and was held by a de Cadehaye. The main part of the house was built about 1550 by John Haydon who had married the de Cadhay heiress. He retained the Great Hall of an earlier house, of which the fine timber roof (about 1420) can be seen. An Elizabethan Long Gallery was added by John's successor at the end of the 16th century, thereby forming a unique and lovely courtyard. Some Georgian alterations were made in the mid 18th century. The house is viewed by conducted tour. Photography is permitted outside.

Location: 1 m NW of Ottery St Mary on B3176.
Station(s): Feniton (2½ m) (not Suns).
Open: Spring (May 28 & 29) & Summer (Aug 27 & 28) Bank Hol Suns & Mons, also Tues Wed & Thurs in July & Aug 2-6 (last adm 5.30).
Admission: Adults £3 children £1.50 parties by arrangement.

CASTLE DROGO   🌿 The National Trust
nr Chagford   EX6 6PB   map **2** V15   ⚅
Telephone: (0164 743) 3306

Granite castle designed by Sir Edwin Lutyens, standing at over 900ft overlooking the wooded gorge of the River Teign. Terraced garden and miles of splendid walks.

Location: 4 m NE of Chagford; 6 m S of A30.
Open: 1 Apr-31 Oct Daily except Fri (open Good Fri) *Garden daily* 11-5.30 (last adm 5).
Admission: £4.60 Family ticket £11 Grounds only £2 children half-price.*Reduced rates for parties.* (£3.60) *on application to the Administrator. Parties who do not pre-book will be charged at full rate.*
Refreshments: Coffee, lunches (licensed) & teas at the castle.
No dogs except guide dogs. Wheelchairs provided. Shop and Plant Centre. The restored croquet lawn is open. Equipment for hire from the shop.

COLETON FISHACRE GARDEN   🌿 The National Trust
Coleton   TQ6 0EQ   map **3** W15   ⚅
Telephone: (01803) 752466

20 acre garden in a stream-fed valley. Garden created by Lady Dorothy D'Oyly Carte between 1925 and 1940; planted with wide variety of uncommon trees and exotic shrubs.

Location: 2 m from Kingswear; take Lower Ferry Road, turn off at tollhouse & follow 'Garden Open' signs.
Open: Mar 1-Mar 29 Sun 2-5 Apr 1-Oct 31 Weds Thur Fri & Sun plus Bank Hol Mons 10.30-5.30 . (Last admission ½ hr before closing). Limited wheelchair access.
Admission: £2.80 children half price. Pre-booked parties £2.10.
Refreshments: Light refreshments in kiosk, open as garden weather permitting.
No dogs.

COMPTON CASTLE   🌿 The National Trust
nr Paignton   TQ3 1TA   map **3** W15
Telephone: (01803) 872112

Fortified manor house. Great Hall (restored), Solar, Kitchen, Chapel and rose garden.

Location: 1 m N of Marldon off A381.
Open: 1 Apr-31 Oct Mon Wed & Thur 10-12.15, 2-5 (last adm 30 mins before closing).

Admission: £2.60, Chd half-price. Parties £2 -*organisers should please notify the Secretary.*
Refreshments: At Castle Barton. (Not NT)
No dogs except guide dogs. Additional parking at Castle Barton, opposite entrance.

DARTMOUTH CASTLE

Dartmouth map **3** W15
Telephone: (01803) 833588

Boldly guarding the narrow entrance to the Dart Estuary this castle was among the first in England to be built for artillery. Construction began in 1481 on the site of an earlier castle which was altered and added to over the following centuries. Victorian coastal defence battery with fully equipped guns, a site exhibition and magnificent views can all be seen at the castle.

Location: 1 m (1⅔ km) south east of Dartmouth.
Open: Apr 1-Sept 30 10-6 daily Oct 1-31 10-4 daily Nov 1-Mar 31 Wed-Sun 10-4.
Admission: Adults £2 concessions £1.50 children £1.

ENDSLEIGH HOUSE

(The Endsleigh Charitable Trust)
Milton Abbot, Nr Tavistock PL19 OPQ map **2** V14
Telephone: (01822) 87248
Fax: (01822) 87502

Arboretum, Shell House, Flowering Shrubs, Rock Garden.

Location: 4 m W of Tavistock on B3362.
Open: House and Gardens Apr-Sept weekends 12-4 Tues and Fris by appointment 12-4 Bank Hols 12-4.
Admission: Honesty Box in Aid of Trust.
Refreshments: Lunches and teas at Endsleigh House by appointment. No dogs.
Limited car parking. No coaches. No dogs. Not suitable for the disabled. No wheelchairs

FLETE

(Country Houses Association)
Ermington, Ivybridge PL21 9NZ map **2** W15
Telephone: (01752) 830308

Built around an Elizabethan manor with alterations in 1879 by Norman Shaw.

Location: 11 m E of Plymouth at junction of A379 and B3121.
Station(s): Plymouth (12m), Totnes (14m). Bus Route: No 93 Plymouth-Dartmouth.
Open: May-Sept Weds & Thurs 2-5. Last entry 4.30.
Admission: £2.50 Children £1. Free car park.
No dogs admitted.

FURSDON

(E.D. Fursdon, Esq)
Cadbury, Thorverton, Exeter EX5 5JS map **3** V15 △
Telephone: (01392) 860860

Fursdon is set in a beautiful rural landscape and the Fursdons have lived here for over 700 years. It remains primarily a family home. There is a Regency library, oak screen from the mediaeval hall, family portraits and annual displays from the family costume collection including some fine 18th century examples. Attractive developing garden.

Location: 9 m N of Exeter, 6 m SW of Tiverton; ¾ m off A3072.
Open: Easter Mon-end Sept Thurs and Bank Hol Mon only 2-4.30 Tours at 2.30 and 3.30. Parties over 20 by arrangement please.
Admission: House & Gardens £2.90. Reductions for children under 10 years free.
Refreshments: Home made teas in Coach Hall on open days.

THE GARDEN HOUSE

(The Fortescue Garden Trust)
Buckland Monachorum, Yelverton PL10 7LQ map **2** W14
Telephone: (01822) 854769

Romantic, terraced, walled garden, 2 acres, with mediaeval gatehouse; enhanced by new, excitingly planted 6-acre development. Wide range of herbaceous and woody plants; of interest throughout the opening season.

Location: 1½ m W of Yelverton. Follow signs off A386 Plymouth to Yelverton.
Station(s): Plymouth.
Open: Mar 1-Oct 31 daily 10.30-5 including Bank Holidays.
Admission: Adults £2.75 children 50p OAPs £2.25 parties £2.25 if pre-booked.
Refreshments: Tea-room open 11.30-5 in house.
Plants for sale. Parking for cars. Coaches by arrangement.

HARTLAND ABBEY

(Sir Hugh Stucley, Bt)
Bideford map **2** V13
Telephone: (012374) 41264

Abbey founded in 1157. Dissolved in 1539 and descended to the present day through a series of marriages. Major architectural alterations in 1705 and in 1779. Unique document exhibition dating from 1160 AD. Pictures, furniture and porcelain collected over many generations. Victorian & Edwardian photographic exhibition. Shrub gardens of rhododendrons, azaleas and camellias. Magnificent woodland walk to a remote atlantic cove with spectacular cliff scenery. Set in a designated area of outstanding natural beauty.

Location: NW Devon (Hartland Point); 15 m from Bideford; 5 m approx from A39.
Open: May-Sept incl Wed 2-5.30. July Aug and Sept Sun 2-5.30. Bank Hols (Easter to Summer) Sun & Mon 2-5.30.
Admission: £3.50 Children £1.50. Parties welcomed £3. Shrub garden and grounds only £1.50.
Refreshments: Teas provided at house.
Ample car parking close to house.

HEMERDON HOUSE 🏛

(J.H.G. Woollcombe, Esq)
Plympton map **2** W14 ♿ △
Telephone: (01752) 841410 (office hours);(01752) 337350 (weekend & evenings)
Fax: (01752) 331477

Regency house containing West country paintings and prints, with appropriate furniture and a Library.

Location: 2 m from Plympton.
Station(s): Plymouth.
Open: 30 days including May and August Bank Holidays 2-5.30. For opening dates please contact the Administrator.
Admission: £2.30.

KILLERTON 🌿 The National Trust

nr Exeter EX5 3LE map **3** V16 ♿
Telephone: (01392) 881345

Late 18th century house in a beautiful setting containing the Paulise de Bush Collection of Costume. Lovely throughout the year, with flowers from early spring, and splendid late autumn colours. 19th century Chapel and Ice House. Estate exhibition in Stables. Paths lead up the hill to the Dolbury, an isolated hill with an Iron Age hill fort site.

Location: 7 m NE of Exeter on W side of Exeter - Cullompton road (B3181 - formerly A38); from M5 s'bound exit 28/B3181; from M5 n'bound exit 29 via Broadclyst & B3181.
Open: House Mar 18-Oct 31 Daily except Tues 11-5.30 (last adm ½ hour before closing). Garden and Park all the year 10.30-dusk.
Admission: House and Garden £4.60 (tickets available at Stable Block) children half-price Family ticket £11 Garden only £2.80. *Reduced rates for parties*(£3.50) *on application to the Administrator. Parties who do not pre-book will be charged at full rate.*The Conference Room may be booked for meetings, etc. Applications (in writing) to: The Administrator, Killerton House, Broadclyst, Exeter, Devon.
Refreshments: Licensed restaurant at House, entrance from garden - tickets necessary, available in Stables. Light refreshments and ice cream in Coach House, home baked bread and pastries for sale and to take away.
Events/Exhibitions: 15 & 16 July: Exeter Festival. Open Air concerts. Special costume exhibitions in the house in addition to displays.
Shop, produce shop and plant centre in Stables. Dogs in Park only. Wheelchairs provided. Motorised buggy for disabled visitors to tour the garden.

KNIGHTSHAYES COURT 🌿 The National Trust

nr Tiverton EX16 7RQ map **3** V16 ♿
Telephone: (01884) 254665

One of the finest gardens in Devon with specimen trees, rare shrubs, spring bulbs, summer flowering borders; of interest at all seasons. House by William Burges, begun in 1869, decorated by J D Crace.

Location: 2 m N of Tiverton; turn off A396 (Bampton/Tiverton Road) at Bolham.
Open: 1 Apr-31 Oct Garden daily 11-5.30. House daily except Fri (but open Good Friday) 1.30-5.30 (Last adm 5). *Nov and Dec Sun 2-4 pre-arranged parties only.*
Admission: £4.80 children half-price. Garden & Grounds only £2.80. *Reduced rates for parties* (£3.80) *on application to the Administrator. Parties who do not pre-book will be charged at full rate.*
Refreshments: Licensed restaurant for coffee, lunches and teas. Picnic area in car park.
Shop. Plants available at garden shop. Dogs in park only on leads. Wheelchairs provided.

OVERBECKS MUSEUM & GARDEN 🌿 The National Trust

Sharpitor, Salcombe TQ8 8LW map **2** W15
Telephone: (0154 884) 2893 or (0154 884) 3238

6 acres of garden with rare and tender plants and beautiful views eastwards over Salcombe Bay. Part of house forms museum of local interest and of particular interest to children.

Location: 1½ m SW of Salcombe signposted from Malborough & Salcombe.
Open: Garden open all the year daily 10-8 or sunset if earlier. Museum open 1 Apr-31 Oct daily except Sat 11-5.30. Last adm ½ hour before closing.
Admission: Museum & Garden adults £3.40 children £1.70. Garden only adults £2 children £1. *No reduction for parties.*
Refreshments: Tea-room open same days as museum.
Shop. No dogs in garden (except guide dogs). Reductions for parties except out of hours. Picnics allowed in gardens. Not suitable for coaches or large vehicles.

POWDERHAM CASTLE
(Lord and Lady Courtenay)
nr Exeter   EX6 8JQ   map **3** V16
Telephone: (01626) 890243
Fax: (01626) 890729

Originally built as a medieval castle by Sir Philip Courtenay (1390), the Castle is still lived in by his descendants. The siege of Powderham in the Civil War led to substantial alterations and restoration in the 18th and 19th centuries. A guided tour of the State Rooms brings alive the history of this lived in family home.

Location: 8 m S of Exeter off A379 in Kenton Village.
Station(s): Starcross 1½ m.
Open: Easter-Oct every day except Sat from 10-5.30.
Admission: For details of prices, group booking discounts, private tours and booking of functions, events, receptions etc throughout the year please telephone the General Manager.
Refreshments: Light lunches and cream teas available in the Courtyard. Tea-room.

RHS GARDEN ROSEMOOR
(The Royal Horticultural Society)
Great Torrington, N. Devon   EX38 8PH   map **2** V14   &
Telephone: (01805) 624067
Fax: (01805) 624717

A garden for all seasons. Lying in the wooded valley of the River Torridge, it includes an informal woodland area, mixed borders and intimate gardens close to the 18th century house. Within its original 8 acres, visitors will see a wide range of plants in a variety of beautiful settings and the Society is in the process of expanding the garden from 8 acres to 40. The new areas include 2000 roses in 200 different cultivars, colour theme gardens, herbaceous borders, an ornamental vegetable garden, cottage and herb garden, a foliage and plantsman's garden and a stream and bog garden.

Location: 1 m SE of Great Torrington on B3220 to Exeter.
Open: Garden open all year from 10-6 Apr-Sept. 5pm Mar & Oct 4pm Nov-Feb.'
Admission: Adults £3 children under 6 yrs free children 6-16 £1. Groups of more than 20 £2.50. One person accompanying a blind or disabled person free.
Refreshments: A restaurant provides home-made lunches and Devon Cream teas. Coaches welcome by appointment. Dogs are not admitted (except guide dogs).

SALTRAM HOUSE   🌿 The National Trust
Plymouth   PL7 3UH   map **2** W14   &
Telephone: (01752) 336546

A George II house, built around and incorporating remnants of a late Tudor mansion, in a landscaped park. Two exceptional rooms by Robert Adam. Furniture, pictures, fine plasterwork and woodwork. Great Kitchen. Beautiful garden with Orangery. Octagonal summer-house, rare shrubs and trees. Shop in stables. Art Gallery in Chapel.

Location: 2 m W of Plympton 3½ m E of Plymouth city centre, between A38 & A379 main roads.
Open: 1 Apr-Oct 31. Suns-Thurs. House: 12.30-5.30. Garden, Kitchen, Shop & Art Gallery 10.30-5.30, Last adm 5. The Chapel may be booked for meetings, etc. Applications (in writing) to: The Administrator, Saltram House, Plympton, Plymouth.
Admission: £5, Chd half-price; Garden only £2.20.
Refreshments: Licensed restaurant in House (entrance from Garden). Light refreshments at Coach House near car park during peak periods.
Dogs in designated areas only. Wheelchairs provided.

SAND
(Lt Col P.V. Huyshe)
Sidbury, nr Sidmouth   EX10 0QN   map **3** V16   △
Telephone: (01395) 597230

Lived in Manor house owned by Huyshe family since 1560, rebuilt 1592-4, situated in unspoilt valley. Screens passage, panelling, family documents, heraldry. Also **Sand Lodge** roof structure of late 15th century Hall House. Shady Car Park.

Location: ¾ m NE of Sidbury; 400 yds from A375, Grid ref 146925.
Open: Suns & Mons Apr 16 17 May 7 8 28 29 July 30 31 Aug 27 28 from 2-5.30. Last tour 4.45.
Admission: Adults £2.50 children/students 50p. Sand Lodge and outside of Sand by written appointment £1.
Refreshments: Light teas in house, teas in Sidbury, parking.

SHUTE BARTON   🌿 The National Trust
Shute, nr Axminster   EX13 7PT   map **3** V16
Telephone: (01297) 34692

Manor house, built over three centuries and completed in late 16th century; grey stone with battlemented tower and late Gothic windows; gatehouse. The house is tenanted; there is access to most of interior for conducted visitors.

Location: 3 m SW of Axminster, 2 m N of Colyton on Honiton-Colyton road (B3161) [177(193): SY253974].
Station(s): Axminster 3 m.
Open: 1 Apr-31 Oct Wed & Sat 2-5.30. Last admissions 5 before closing.
Admission: £1.60 pre-booked parties £1.20 children half price.
No dogs except guide dogs. Unsuitable for disabled or visually handicapped. No WC.

TIVERTON CASTLE
(Mr and Mrs A.K. Gordon)
Tiverton   EX16 6RP   map **3** V15
Telephone: (01884) 253200

Historically important mediaeval castle commissioned by Henry I in 1106; magnificent mediaeval gatehouse and tower containing important Civil War armoury, notable clock collection, fine furniture and pictures, New World Tapestry.

Location: Next to St. Peter's Church. The Castle is well signposted in Tiverton.
Station(s): Tiverton Parkway.
Open: Easter Sun-end June, and Sept Suns Thurs and Bank Holiday Mons July Aug Suns to Thurs 2.30-5.30. Open at other times to private parties of more then 12 by prior arrangement.
Admission: Adults £3 children 7-16 £2 children under 7 free. Free parking inside.
Accommodation: 3 superb self-catering holiday apartments inside Castle available weekly, short breaks, or winter lettings. Graded 4 Keys Highly Commended.
Conferences: Castle available for business conferences, wedding receptions, filming or photographic location.
Coach parties by appointment only.

TORRE ABBEY

(Torbay Borough Council)
Torquay TQ2 5JX map **3** W15
Telephone: (01803) 293593

Torbay's most historic building. Founded in 1196 as a monastery and later adapted as a private residence. Contains historic rooms, Cary family chapel, mementoes of crime writer Agatha Christie, and mainly 19th century paintings, sculpture, antiques and Torquay terracotta pottery. Over 20 rooms now open to the public, including the Victorian tea room with its splendid kitchen range. The medieval monastic remains - including the great barn, guest hall, gatehouse, church and undercrofts - are the most complete in Devon and Cornwall. Gardens include tropical palm house, rockeries and spring bulbs. Special 'Quest' leaflet available for children and exhibitions by local artists are held throughout the summer. The enormously popular flower festival takes place in mid September. Rooms may be hired.

Location: On Torquay sea front, behind Torre Abbey sands and next to the Riviera Centre.
Station(s): Torquay (¼ m).
Open: House Apr-Oct daily 9.30-6 (last admissions 5) other times by appointment. Gardens all the year daily.
Admission: (1995 rates) House adults £2.50 students/OAPs £2 children over 8 years £1.50 younger children free family ticket £6.50 (2 adults and up to 3 children). Gardens free.
Refreshments: Victorian tea-room serving refreshments, teas and light lunches.
Events/Exhibitions: Colin T. Johnson 'A Personal View' May 28-July 30; Festival of Flowers Sept 15-18.
Conferences: Facilities available including Christian services, barn dances etc.

TOTNES CASTLE

map **3** W15
Telephone: (01803) 864406

ENGLISH HERITAGE

The Normans also built a stronghold here to overawe the townspeople. But they surrendered without a blow, as they did again in the Civil War. The remains date largely from the 14th century, although the huge earth mound on which the castle rests is Norman.

Location: Totnes.
Open: Apr 1-Sept 30 10-6 daily Oct 1-31 10-4 daily Nov 1-Mar 31 Wed-Sun 10-4.
Admission: Adults £1.50 concessions £1.10 children 80p.

"Playgrounds for the Children"

Belton House
Bowood
Drumlanrig (woodland playground)
Hever Castle
Kelburn (Secret Forest adventure course and stockade)
Longleat
Ragley Hall (adventure wood)
Weston Park
Wilton House

UGBROOKE HOUSE

(Lord Clifford)
Chudleigh TQ13 OAD map **3** V15
Telephone: (01626) 852179
Fax: (01626) 853322

Set in beautiful scenery and quiet parkland in the heart of Devon. The original House and Church built about 1200, redesigned by Robert Adam. Home of the Cliffords of Chudleigh, Ugbrooke contains fine furniture, paintings, beautiful embroideries, porcelain, extremely rare family military collection. Capability Brown landscaped Park with lakes, majestic trees, scenic views to Dartmoor. Guided tours relate stories of Clifford Castles, Shakespeare's 'Black Clifford', Henry II's 'Fair Rosamund' Lady Anne Clifford who defied Cromwell, The Secret Treaty, the Cardinal's daughter, Charles II's Lord High Treasurer Clifford of the CABAL, and many more tales of intrigue, espionage and bravery.

Location: Chudleigh.
Open: July 16-Sept 7 on Sun Tues Wed and Thurs. Grounds 1-5.30. Guided tours of House at 2 and 3.45.
Admission: Adults £4 children (5-16) £2. Groups (over 20) £3.60. Private party tours/functions by arrangement.
Refreshments: Afternoon teas at The Orangery 2-5.

YARDE

(John and Marilyn Ayre)
Malborough, nr Kingsbridge TQ7 3BY map **2** W15
Telephone: (0154 884) 2367

Grade 1 Listed. An outstanding example of the Devon farmstead with a Tudor Bakehouse, Elizabethan Farmhouse and Queen Anne Mansion under restoration. Still a family farm.

Location: On A381 ½ m E of Malborough. 4 m S of Kingsbridge.
Open: Easter-Sept 31 Sun Wed and Fri 2-5.
Admission: Adults £2 children 50p.
Refreshments: Country teas.

DORSET

ATHELHAMPTON HOUSE & GARDENS

(Patrick Cooke)

Athelhampton, Dorchester   DT2 7LG   map 3 V18
Telephone: (01305) 848363

Five centuries of history in a family home built in 1485 on the site of King Athelstan's Palace. Great hall with unique timber roof, oriel window, heraldic glass and linenfold panelling. Other rooms include the Great Chamber, Wine Cellar, Dining Room, Green Parlour, State and Yellow Bedrooms. Surrounded by one of the Great Gardens of England with massive topiary pyramids, pavillions, fountains, rare plants and trees.

Open: 2 Apr-28 Oct 12-5 Tues-Thurs Sun & BHs. July & Aug: also Mon & Fri.

CHETTLE HOUSE

(J.P.C. Bourke)

Chettle, Blandford   DT11 8DB   map 3 V18
Telephone: (01258) 830209
Fax: (01258) 830380

One of the finest examples of a Queen Anne House in the English Baroque style by Thomas Archer. Set in 5 acres of garden with many unusual herbaceous plants and shrubs.

Location: 6 m NE of Blandford on A354 & 1 m W.
Open: Good Fri-8 Oct (except Tues and Sat) 11-5.
Admission: Adults £2 children free.
Refreshments: Many pubs within 2 miles. Picnic area available, teas usually.
Conferences: Available for weddings, filming and corporate hospitality.
Plant Centre with unusual plants for sale. No dogs.

CLOUDS HILL   🍂 The National Trust

nr Wool   BH20 7NQ   map 3 V18

The cottage home of T. E. Lawrence (Lawrence of Arabia) after the first World War; contains his furniture and other relics.

Location: 1 m N of Bovington Camp, ½ m E of Waddock crossroads (B3390), 9 m E of Dorchester.
Open: 2 Apr-29 Oct Wed Thurs Fri Sun & Bank Hol Mons 2-5. (No electric lighting available *closed* dusk if earlier).
Admission: *No reduction for children or parties.* £2.20.
No photography. No dogs. Unsuitable for wheelchairs and coaches. No WCs.

CORFE CASTLE   🍂 The National Trust

nr Wareham   BH20 5ES   map 3 V18
Telephone: (01929) 481294

Ruins of former royal castle, sieged and sleighted by Parliamentary forces in 1646.

Location: In the village of Corfe Castle: on A351 Wareham-Swanage road.
Open: 6 Feb-25 Mar daily 10-4.30. 26 Mar-29 Oct daily 10-5.30. 30 Oct-3 Mar 96 daily 12-3.30. Closed 25 & 26 Dec. Open Good Fri & Bank Hol Mon.
Admission: £3 Children £1.50 Parties £2.50 (children £1.30).
Refreshments: NT tea-room.
Not suitable for wheelchairs. NT Shop and Refreshments. Parking for Castle at Castle View.

CRANBORNE MANOR GARDENS

(The Viscount and Viscountess Cranborne)

Cranborne   BH21 5PP   map 3 V19
Telephone: (01725) 517248
Fax: (01725) 517248

Walled gardens, yew hedges and lawns; wild garden with spring bulbs, herb garden, Jacobean mount garden, flowering cherries and collection of old-fashioned and specie roses. Beautiful and historic gardens laid out in the 17th century by John Tradescant and much embellished and enlarged in the 20th century.

Location: 18 m N of Bournemouth, B3078; 16 m S of Salisbury, A354, B3081.
Open: Garden Centre open Tues-Sat 9-5 Sun 10-5 closed Mon except Bank Holidays. Something for every gardener, but specialising in old-fashioned and specie roses, herbs, ornamental pots and garden furniture. Gardens Only Mar-Sept Wed 9-5 South Court occasionally closed. Free car park.

DEANS COURT

(Sir Michael & Lady Hanham)

Wimborne   map 3 V19   ♿

Thirteen acres of partly wild garden, in a peaceful setting on the River Allen. Specimen trees, monastery fishpond. Peacocks. Herb garden with over 100 varieties. Chemical free herb plants for sale; also kitchen garden produce (also chemical free) as available. Free parking. Wheelchair available.

Location: A few mins walk South from Wimborne Minster & Square.
Station(s): Poole and Bournemouth (30-45 mins. by bus).
Open: Daffodil Weekends with teas Sat & Sun 18/19th & 25/26th Mar. Mar 2-5 Easter Sun 16th Apr 2-6 Bank Hols Suns 2-6 Bank Hol Mons 10-6. Last Sun in Apr, May, July, Aug & Sept 2-6 (includes Bank Hol Weekends) 2-6; Sun Oct 1st 2-6. Wholefood Teas & Morning Coffee. Groups welcome on other days by written arrangement. This can include entry to house and tea or coffee.
Admission: Adults £1.50 children 70p except during Sculpture Exhibition June 13-July 4 10.30-6 daily when admission will be Adults £2 Children, Art Students & groups of 15 or more £1.50 (includes Catalogue). Regret guide dogs only and no unaccompanied children.

EDMONDSHAM HOUSE AND GARDENS

(Mrs J.E. Smith)
Cranborne, nr Wimborne   BH21 5RE   map **3** V19   △ ♿
Telephone: (01725) 517207

A family home since the 16th century, and a fine blend of Tudor and Georgian architecture, with a Victorian stable block and dairy, interesting furniture, lace and other exhibits. The Gardens include an old-fashioned walled garden, cultivated organically, with an excellent display of spring bulbs, shrubs, lawns and herbaceous border.

Location: Between Cranborne and Verwood, off the B3081.
Open: HOUSE AND GARDENS Easter Sun all Bank Hol Mons all Weds in Apr and Oct 2-5. Groups by arrangement at other times. GARDENS Open at all times when the House is open and on all Wed and Suns Apr to Oct 2-5.
Admission: House and Garden £2 children £1. Garden only £1 children 50p.
Refreshments: Teas village hall on house open days. Teas for groups.

FORDE ABBEY AND GARDENS

(Trustees of Forde Abbey)
nr Chard   TA20 4LU   map **3** V17   △ ♿
Telephone: (01460) 220231

Award winning garden 1992. Cistercian monastery, founded 1140. Converted to private house mid 17th c. and unaltered since. Thirty acres of outstanding gardens - trees and shrubs, herbaceous borders, rock garden, bog garden and kitchen garden. Plants on sale.

Location: 1 m E of Chard Junction, 4 m SE of Chard signposted off A30.
Open: Gardens and Nursery open daily throughout the year 10-4.30. House Apr-end Oct Sun Wed & Bank Hol 1-4.30.
Admission: Our charges for 1995: House and Gardens adults £4.50 OAPs £4. Gardens only £3.25 OAPs £2.75.
Refreshments: Undercroft open for light lunches and teas 11-4.30 daily Apr-end of Oct.

HARDY'S COTTAGE   🌿 The National Trust

Higher Bockhampton   DT2 8QJ   map **3** V18   ♿
Telephone: (01305) 262366

Birthplace of Thomas Hardy 1840-1928. A thatched cottage, built by his great-grandfather; little altered.

Location: 3 m NE of Dorchester; ½ m S of Blandford Road (A35).
Station(s): Dorchester South 4 m; Dorchester West 4 m.
Open: Interior by prior appointment with the custodian. Garden daily (except Thurs) from 11-6 or dusk if earlier.
Admission: £2.50 Interior. Garden free.
Approached by 10 mins walk from car park via woods. No dogs. Wheelchairs, garden only. No WCs.

ILSINGTON HOUSE

(Mr & Mrs P. Duff)
Puddletown, Dorchester   map **3** V18
Telephone: (01305) 848454

This family home, set in the picturesque village of Puddletown (Thomas Hardy's Weatherbury). A classical William and Mary mansion built by the 7th Earl of Huntingdon. Home of George III's illegitimate grandson, born to HRH Princess Sophia in 1800, kept a secret until the Royal Scandal of 1829. Ilsington was visited by many members of the Royal Family during George III's reign. Fine furniture and present owners' private collection of pictures and sculpture. A fully guided house tour given. Formal and landscape gardens with probably the longest haha in Dorset.Large collection of beautiful bearded irises and unusual peonies.

Location: 4 m from Dorchester on the A35.
Open: Ilsington House Tours May 1-Sept 29 1995 Wed and Thurs 2-6 last tour 5. Also Sun and Bank Hol Mon in Aug.
Admission: House and Gardens £3.
Refreshments: Lunch, supper or tea for parties by arrangement in the House, teas available in the village.
Conferences: Suitable for small conferences.
Free car parking. Unfortunately not suitable for disabled persons. No dogs. Ideal location for small specialised conferences. Also available for film locations.

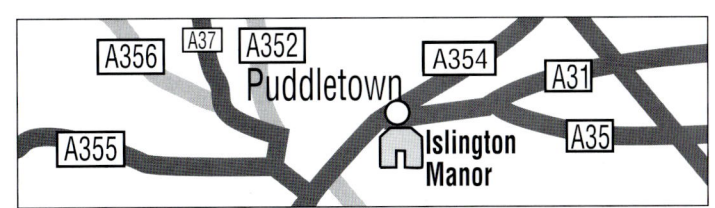

KINGSTON LACY   🍃 The National Trust
nr Wimborne Minster   BH21 4EA   map **3** V18   Ⓢ
Telephone: (01202) 883402

17th century House designed by Sir Roger Pratt but with considerable alterations by Sir Charles Barry in the 19th century. Important Italian and English paintings collected by W. J. Bankes. Collection of Egyptian artefacts. Set in 250 acres of wooded park.

Location: On B3082 - Blandford-Wimborne Road, 1½ m W of Wimborne.
Station(s): Poole 8½ m.
Open: 1 Apr-31 Oct daily except Thurs & Fri. House 12-5.30 (last adm 4.30). Park 11.30-6 or dusk if earlier.
Admission: House Garden & Park £5.50 Children £2.70 Parties £4.80 (children £2.50) Garden & Park only £2.20 children £1.10. Parties by prior appointment with Administrator.
Refreshments: Lunches and cream teas. .
House not suitable for wheelchairs. One wheelchair available for use in Garden. Guide dogs admitted to grounds. Braille guide. Parties by arrangement **only**.Study centre. National Trust Shop and restaurant.

MAPPERTON 
(Montagu family)
Beaminster   DT8 3NR   map **3** V18   △
Telephone: (01308) 862645
Fax: (01308) 863348

Terraced gardens with Italianate fountain court. Modern orangery in classical style, 17th century fish ponds. Tudor manor house, enlarged 1660s. Magnificent walks and views.

Location: 1 m off B3163, 2 m off B3066.
Open: Mar-Oct daily 2-6.
Admission: Adults £2.50 under 18 £1.50 under 5 free. House only open to group tours by appointment, adults £3.50 or £6 for house and gardens.

MAX GATE   🍃 The National Trust
Dorchester   DT1 2AA   map **3** V17
Telephone: (01305) 262538

Poet and novelist Thomas Hardy designed and lived in the house from 1885 until his death in 1928. The house is leased to tenants and contains no Hardy memorabilia. Display in drawing room.

Location: 1 m E of Dorchester.
Station(s): Dorchester 1 m.
Open: Drawing room and garden only. 2 Apr-1 Oct Mon Wed Sun 2-5.
Admission: £2 children £1.

MILTON ABBEY
(The Council of Milton Abbey School Ltd)
Milton Abbas, nr Blandford   DT11 0BP   map **3** V18
Telephone: (01258) 880489 Organising Secretary

A fine Abbey Church (Salisbury Diocese) partially completed 15th century on site of 10th century Abbey. The magnificent Abbot's Hall, completed 1498, with fine hammerbeam roof and carved screen, is incorporated in the Georgian Gothic mansion (now Milton Abbey School). Architect Sir William Chambers with ceilings and decorations by James Wyatt. The ancient St. Catherine's Chapel looks down on this unique group set in secluded valley seven miles SW of Blandford. The little town of Milton, swept away in the late 18th century by the imperious owner of the house, in order to improve his park, was rebuilt as a charming model village nearby.

Location: 7 m SW of Blandford, just N of A354 from Winterborne Whitechurch or Milborne St Andrew.
Open: House and Grounds mid July-end Aug daily 10-6 ABBEY CHURCH Church throughout the year.
Admission: Adults £1.50 children free. ABBEY CHURCH voluntary donations except for above dates.
Refreshments: Abbey Tea-rooms open Easter and main summer season only.
Events/Exhibitions: Easter - Crafts Fair at Milton Abbey. Summer - paint, pigment, canvas and clay including the Eeles Family Pottery.

MINTERNE
(The Lord Digby)
Dorchester   DT2 7AU   map **3** V18
Telephone: (01300) 341370

Important rhododendron and shrub garden, many fine and rare trees, landscaped in the 18th century with lakes, cascades and streams.

Location: On A352 2 m N of Cerne Abbas; 10 m N of Dorchester, 9 m S of Sherborne.
Open: Apr 1-Oct 31 daily 10-7.
Admission: Adults £2 accompanying child free. Free car park.

PRIEST'S HOUSE MUSEUM OF EAST DORSET LIFE AND GARDEN
(Priest's House Museum Trust)
23 High Street, Wimborne Minster   BH21 1HR   map **3** V19   △ Ⓔ Ⓢ
Telephone: (01202) 882533
Fax: (01202) 882533

A fascinating historic town house of medieval origin with many Tudor and Georgian features. Set in an exquisite walled garden, the displays include an 18th century parlour, Victorian stationer's shop and working kitchen plus regular special exhibitions. An award winning museum!

Location: Centre of Wimborne Minster.
Station(s): Poole or Bournemouth.
Open: Apr 1-Oct 28 Mon-Sat 10.30-5. Plus Bank Holiday Suns and every Sun June 4-Sept 24 2-5. Special Christmas exhibition.
Admission: Includes entrance to garden. Group bookings welcome.
Refreshments: Tea-room in summer season and museum gift shop.
Disabled access ground floor and garden only. Free quizzes. Several special events are planned.

PURSE CAUNDLE MANOR
(Michael de Pelet, Esq)
nr Sherborne   DT9 5DY   map **3** V18
Telephone: (01963) 250400

Interesting 15th/16th century Manor House. Lived in as a family home. Great Hall with minstrel gallery; Winter Parlour; Solar with oriel; bedchambers; garden. Not commercialised! Come and visit us.

Location: 4 m E of Sherborne; ¼ m S of A30.
Open: Easter Mon and May-Sept '94 Thurs Sun & Bank Hol Mon 2-5 showing every half hour. Coaches welcomed by appointment.
Admission: Adults £2 children free. Free car park.
Refreshments: Home-made cream teas by prior arrangement at £2 each for coach parties.

SANDFORD ORCAS MANOR HOUSE
(Sir Mervyn Medlycott, Bt)
Sandford Orcas, Sherborne   map **3** V17   △
Telephone: (01963) 220206

Tudor Manor House with gatehouse, fine panelling. furniture, pictures. Terraced gardens, with topiary, and herb garden. Personal conducted tour by owner.

Location: 2½ m N of Sherborne, ent. next to Church.
Open: Easter Mon 10-6 then May-Sept Suns 2-6 & Mons 10-6.
Admission: Adults £2 children £1. Pre-booked parties (of 10 or more) at reduced rates on other days if preferred.

SHERBORNE CASTLE
Sherborne   DT9 3PY   map **3** V18
Telephone: (01935) 813182
Fax: (01935) 816727

Built by Sir Walter Raleigh in 1594. Home of the Digby family since 1617. The House contains fine furniture, porcelain and pictures. Set in 20 acres of lawns and pleasure grounds planned by 'Capability' Brown around the 50 acre lake.

Location: 5 m E of Yeovil off A30 to S.
Station(s): Sherborne.
Open: Easter Sat-end Sept Thurs Sat Sun and Bank Hol Mons. House 1.30-5. Grounds and Tea-room 12-30.
Admission: Charges on request. parties by arrangement.
Refreshments: Tea-room.
Gift Shop. Car parking on site.

WOLFETON HOUSE

(Capt. N.T.L.L. Thimbleby)
Dorchester   DT2 9QN   map **3** V18
Telephone: (01305) 263500

A fine mediaeval and Elizabethan Manor House lying in the water-meadows near the confluence of the rivers Cerne and Frome. It was much embellished around 1580 and has splendid plaster ceilings, fireplaces and panelling of that date. To be seen are the Great Hall, stairs and chamber; parlour; dining room, chapel and cyder house. The mediaeval gatehouse has two unmatched and older towers. There are good pictures and furniture.

Location: 1½ m from Dorchester on Yeovil road (A37); indicated by Historic House signs.
Station(s): Dorchester South and West 1¾ m.
Open: May 1-Sept 30 Tues Thur and Bank Hol Mons 2-6. At other times throughout the year parties by arrangement.
Admission: Charges not available at time of going to press.
Refreshments: Ploughman's lunches, teas and evening meals for parties, by prior arrangement. Cyder for sale.

Sir Peter Lely - portrait painter

His paintings can be seen at the following properties included in Historic Houses Castles and Gardens:-

Aynhoe Park
Belton House
Breamore House
Browsholme Hall
Dalmeny House
Euston Hall
Goodwood House
Gorhambury
Kedleston Hall
Knole
Petworth House
Ragley Hall
Rockingham Castle
St Osyth Priory
Stanford Hall
Weston Park

COUNTY DURHAM

AUCKLAND CASTLE

(The Church Commissioners)
Bishop Auckland   map **9** N19
Telephone: (01388) 601627

Historic home of the Bishops of Durham with parts dating from 12th century. Very fine private Chapel remodelled by Bishop Cosin from 1660. Fourteenth century Hall, gothicised by James Wyatt in 1795. State Rooms include a Gothic Throne Room lined with portraits of past bishops. Also large public park and unusual 18th century deerhouse.

Location: In Bishop Auckland, at the end of Market Place.
Station(s): Bishop Auckland.
Open: Castle and Chapel Bank Hol Mons 2-5 May 2-Sept 17 Tues 10-12 Sun, Wed and Thurs 2-5 Sat in Aug 2-5 Park open during daylight hours throughout the year.
Admission: Adults £2 concessions £1 please contact Warden's office for group bookings at special times throughout the year.

BARNARD CASTLE

Durham   map **9** O19

Telephone: (01833) 38212

Named after it's founder, Bernard de Baliol, the castle overlooks the River Tees from a craggy cliff-top. It's ownership was disputed by the Bishops of Durham, one of whom seized it in 1296. He added a magnificent hall and refortified the castle. Part of the castle has recently been excavated to discover more of it's complex building history.

Location: In Barnard Castle.
Open: Apr 1-Sept 30 10-6 daily Oct 1-31 10-4 daily Nov 1-Mar 31 Wed-Sun 10-4.
Admission: Adults £1.80 concessions £1.40 children 90p.

DURHAM CASTLE

(The University of Durham)
Durham   map **9** N19   △

Durham Castle, the former home of the Prince Bishops of Durham, was founded in the 1070's. Since 1832 it has been the foundation College of the University of Durham. With the Cathedral it is a World Heritage Site. Important features include the Norman Chapel (1072), the Great Hall (1284), the Norman Doorway (1540's). With its 14th century style Keep it is a fine example of a Motte and Bailey Castle. In vacations the Castle is a conference and holiday centre and a prestige venue for banquets etc.

Location: In the centre of the city (adjoining Cathedral).
Station(s): Durham (½ m).
Open: Guided tours only July-Sept 10-12 noon and 2-5pm. Oct-June 2-4pm.
Admission: £1.40 Children 90p Family ticket £3.20.

Robert Adam - architect

His work can be seen at the following properties included in Historic Houses Castles and Gardens:

Audley End
Bowood House & Gardens
Culzean Castle
Hatchlands Park
Kedleston Hall
Kenwood, The Iveagh Bequest
Killerton
Kimbolton Castle
Luton Hoo

Mellerstain
Moccas Court
Newby Hall & Gardens
Nostell Priory
Osterley Park
Papplewick Hall
Saltram House
Syon House

RABY CASTLE
(The Lord Barnard, T.D.)
Staindrop, Darlington   DL2 3AH   map **9** O19   ♿
Telephone: (01833) 660202

Principally 14th century, alterations made 1765 and mid-19th century. The Castle is one of the largest 14th century castles in Britain and was built by the Nevills although one of the towers probably dates back to the 11th century. Interior mainly 18th and 19th century; medieval kitchen and Servants' Hall. Fine pictures of the English, Dutch and Flemish Schools and good period furniture. Collection of horse-drawn carriages and fire engines. Large walled Gardens.

Location: 1 m N of Staindrop village, on the Barnard Castle/Bishop Auckland Road (A688).
Open: Easter weekend (Sat-Wed) closed remainder of Apr then May 1-June 30 Wed & Sun July 1-Sept 30 daily (except Sat) May Spring and Aug Bank Hols Sat-Tues Castle 1-5 Park & Gardens 11-5.30.
Admission: Castle, Park and Gardens £3.50 Senior Citizens £3.20 children £1.50. Park and Gardens only £1 Senior Citizens and children 75p. Separate adm charge for Bulmer's Tower when open. Rates may vary when charity events are held. Special terms for parties over 25 on above days by arrangement (Tel Curator).
Refreshments: Tea at the Stables.
Picnic area.

ROKEBY PARK
nr Barnard Castle   DL12 9RZ   map **9** N19
Telephone: (01833) 637334 - Curator

Palladian House built by Sir Thomas Robinson in 1735. Fine rooms, furniture and pictures (including exceptional collection of 18th century needlework pictures by Anne Morritt). Fine print room.

Location: Between A66 (signposted Barnard Castle and Bowes Museum) and Barnard Castle.
Open: May 8 then each Mon & Tues from May 29-Tues Sept 12 2-5 (last adm 4.30). Parties of 25 or more will also be admitted on other days if a written appointment is made with the Curator.

ESSEX

AUDLEY END HOUSE AND PARK
Saffron Waldron   map **5** S23
Telephone: (01799) 522399

ENGLISH HERITAGE

James I is said to have remarked that Audley End was too large for a king but not for his Lord Treasurer, Sir Thomas Howard, who built it. The house was so large in fact that early in the 18th century about half of it was demolished as being unmanageable, but this still leaves a very substantial mansion. The interior contains rooms decorated by Robert Adam, a magnificent Jacobean Great Hall, a picturesque 'Gothic' chapel and a suite of rooms decorated in the revived Jacobean style of the early 19th century.

Location: ¾ m (1 km) west of Saffron Walden off B1383.
Open: Apr 1-Sept 30 12-6 Wed-Sun (and Bank Hols) Last admission 5.
Admission: House & Grounds adults £5.50 concessions £4.10 children £2.80. Grounds only adults £3 concessions £2.30 children £1.50.
Refreshments: Restaurant.

GOSFIELD HALL
(Country Houses Association)
Halstead   CO9 1SF   map **5** S24
Telephone: (01787) 472914

Very fine Tudor gallery.

Location: 2½ m SW of Halstead on Braintree/Haverhill Road (A1017).
Station(s): Braintree. Bus route 310 Braintree-Halstead.
Open: May-Sept Weds & Thurs 2-5. House tours 2.30 and 3.15.
Admission: £2.50 Children £1. Free car park.
Conferences: By arrangement
No dogs admitted.

HARWICH REDOUBT

(The Harwich Society)
Harwich Harbour, Harwich   CO12 3TE   map **5** T25

Commanding Harwich Harbour this substantial circular fort was built to keep Napoleon out. Now being restored by volunteers of The Harwich Society, with 11 different guns on the battlements and a variety of small museums in the casemates.

Location: Opposite 42A Main Road, Harwich.
Open: Jul and Aug daily 2-5 throughout the year Sun only 10-12 and 2-5 (Excluding 24 and 31 Dec). Parties at any time by arrangement. Annual Fete 29 May 2-5.
Admission: Adults £1 accompanied children free (no unaccompanied children).
Refreshments: Light drinks only.
Not suitable for disabled. Photograph by courtesy of ECC.

INGATESTONE HALL
(Lord Petre)
Ingatestone   CM4 9NR   map **13** T24
Telephone: (01277) 353010
Fax: (01245) 248979

Tudor mansion in 11 acres of grounds, built by Sir William Petre, Secretary of State to four monarchs. The house continues to be the home of his descendants and contains furniture, pictures and memorabilia accumulated over the centuries. The house retains its original form and appearance including two priests' hiding places.

Location: From London end of Ingatestone High Street take Station Lane. House is half a mile beyond the level crossing.

Open: Apr 15-Sept 24 Fri Sat Sun and Bank Holidays. Plus July 12-Aug 31 Wed and Thurs 1-6.
Admission: Adults £3.50 OAPs/students £3 children 5-16 £2 (under 5s free) parties 20 or more 50p per head reduction.
Refreshments: Tea-room.
Car park adjacent to gates. 200m. walk to house. Gift shop. No dogs (except guide dogs). The upper floor and some rooms downstairs are inaccessible to wheelchairs.

LAYER MARNEY TOWER

(Mr Nicholas Charrington)
nr Colchester   CO5 9US   map **13** T24   △ Ⓔ ও
Telephone: (01206) 330784
Fax: (01206) 330784

Lord Marney's 1520 masterpiece is the tallest Tudor gatehouse in the country. Visitors may climb the tower for excellent views of the Essex countryside and the Blackwater estuary, explore the formal gardens and visit the Long Gallery. The adjoining Church has 3 effigy tombs of the Marney's and an original wallpainting of St. Christopher. There is a collection of rare breed farm animals and deer. A Farm walk starts from the Mediaeval Barn. Guided Tours are available by arrangement (minimum number 25 people). The Long Gallery and Carpenters Shop can be hired for Receptions, Banquets and Concerts.

Location: 6 m S of Colchester, signpost off the B1022 Colchester/Maldon Road.
Open: Apr May Jun July Aug and Sept every day except Sat 2-6 Bank Hols 11-6. Parties other days by prior arrangement.
Admission: Adults £3 children £1.50 family ticket £8. Groups of 20 or more people - adults £2.50 children £1.50.
Refreshments: Teas.

THE SIR ALFRED MUNNINGS ART MUSEUM

Castle House, Dedham, Colchester   CO7 6AZ   map **5** T25   ও
Telephone: (01206) 322127

Large collection of paintings and other works by the late Sir Alfred Munnings, KCVO, PRA 1944-1949.

Location: ¾ m Dedham village, 7 m NE Colchester 2 m E of Ipswich Road (A12).
Open: Apr 30-Oct 1 Wed Sun & Bank Hol Mons also Thurs & Sats in Aug 2-5.
Admission: Adults £2 children 25p OAPs £1. Private parties by arrangment. Free car park.

PAYCOCKE'S   ❧ The National Trust

West Street   CO6 1NS   map **5** T24
Telephone: (01376) 561305

Richly ornamented merchant's house, dating from about 1500. Special display of local lace. Delightful garden leading down to small river.

Location: On A120; S side of West St. Coggeshall next to Fleece Inn; 5½ m E of Braintree. *Station(s):* Kelvedon (2½ m).
Open: Mar 26-Oct 29 Tues Thurs Sun and Bank Hol Mons 2-5.30. Last admission 5 pm.
Admission: £1.40 children (accompanied) half-price. *Parties exceeding six should make prior arrangements with the tenant.* No reduction for parties. Joint ticket with Coggeshall Grange barn £2.
No dogs.

RHS GARDEN HYDE HALL

(The Royal Horticultural Society)
Rettendon, Chelmsford   CM3 8ET   map **13** T24   ও
Telephone: (01245) 400256

The most recent addition to the RHS Gardens, Hyde Hall occupies a delightful hilltop site with fine views across the surrounding area. The Garden has been developed over the last 36 years and hosts a wide variety of plants including a large selection of roses. The plantsman's garden extends to 8 acres and includes the national collections of **Malus** and **Viburnum**. Among other features are fine heathers and many willows that have been incorporated for winter colour. Plans are being made to extend the Garden to 50 acres or more. This will include an arboretum, woodlands and meadows sensitively landscaped to nestle in the Essex countryside.

Open: The garden is open on Wed Thurs Sat Sun and Bank Hols from 26 Mar-29 Oct (inclusive) 11-6.
Admission: Adults £2.50 children under 6 years free children 6-16 50p. Groups of more than 20 £2. One person accompanying a blind or disabled visitor free. Dogs are not admitted (except guide dogs).
Refreshments: Light refreshments are available and there are plants for sale during opening hours.

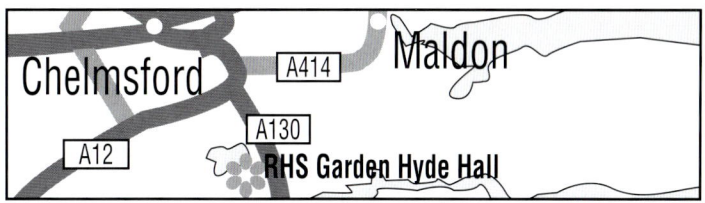

ST. OSYTH PRIORY

(Somerset de Chair)
St.Osyth   map **13** T25
Telephone: (01255) 820492

'Constable Country. Within 12 miles of Dedham and the Stour Valley. The Great gatehouse c 1475, ('unexcelled in any monastic remains in the country',*Country Life*), was built 20 years before Christopher Columbus sailed. A unique group of buildings dating from the 13th, 15th, 16th, 18th and 19th centuries, surrounding a wide quadrangle like an Oxford or Cambridge college. Gardens include Rose garden, Topiary garden, Water garden etc. Peacocks. Art collection in Georgian wing includes world-famous paintings by George Stubbs ARA.

Location: 65 m from London via A12, A120; A133 12 m from Colchester; 8 m from Frinton.
Open: Easter weekend, Then May 1 to Sept 30. Gardens and Ancient Monuments open 10-5. Art Collection 10.30-12.30, 2.30-4.30. Buildings and art collection *closed* Sat although the gardens will remain open. Parties by arrangement.
Admission: £3 children 75p OAPs £2.50. Free car parking.

Refreshments: In village 100 yds from entrance.
Gardens suitable for disabled persons. Gardens overlook but do not include deer park on the estuary of the River Cole. Contact Mrs Colby, Tel (01255) 820242 (9-10 am)

SHALOM HALL

(Lady Phoebe Hillingdon)
Layer Breton, nr Colchester   map **13** T24

19th century house containing a collection of 17th and 18th century French furniture and porcelain and portraits by famous English artists including Thomas Gainsborough, Sir Joshua Reynolds etc.

Location: 7 m SW of Colchester; 2 m from A12.
Open: Aug Mon-Fri 10-1 and 2.30-5.30.
Admission: Free.

GLOUCESTERSHIRE

BARNSLEY HOUSE GARDEN

(Rosemary Verey)
Barnsley, nr Cirencester   GL7 5EE   map **3** T19   ও
Telephone: (01285) 740281
Fax: (01285) 740628

Garden laid out 1770, trees planted 1840. Re-planned 1960. Many spring bulbs. Laburnum avenue (early June). Lime walk, herbaceous and shrub borders. Ground cover. Knot garden. Autumn colour and winter interest. Gothic summerhouse 1770. Classical temple 1780. House 1697 (not open). Vegetable garden laid out as decorative potager.

Location: 4 m NE of Cirencester on Cirencester to Bibury and Burford Road (B4425).
Station(s): Kemble.
Open: Garden Only all the year Mon Wed Thurs Sat 10-6 (or dusk if earlier).
Admission: (Mar-Nov inc) adults £2 OAPs £1 season tickets £4 guided parties entrance plus £50 by R. Verey £25 by another guide. Dec & Jan free.
Refreshments: Morning coffee, lunch, supper and Tea by appointment (0285) 740421. The Village Pub.
Plants and RV books for sale.

BATSFORD ARBORETUM
(The Batsford Foundation)
Moreton-in-Marsh   GL56 9QF   map **3** T19
Telephone: (01608) 650722

Designed and planted as a wild garden, the 50 acres of arboretum contains over 1500 species of trees set in delightful Cotswold countryside. Spring colour is provided by carpets of bulbs, magnificent magnolias and flowering cherries. The large collection of maple and sorbus provide wonderful autumn colour.

Location: 1½ m NW of Moreton-in-Marsh on A44 to Evesham road.
Station(s): Moreton-in-Marsh (1½ m).
Open: GARDEN ONLY: 1 Mar to 5 Nov daily 10-5 .
Admission: Adults £2 OAP's £1.50 Children under 14 free. Groups of 12 or more £1.50 each by prior arrangement.Coach parties welcome, by prior arrangement.
Refreshments: Tea room for coffee, light lunches and teas. Picnic area.

Gertrude Jekyll
writer and gardener
(1843-1932)

Her designs were used at the following properties included in Historic Houses Castles and Gardens:-

Barrington Court
Castle Drogo
Goddards
Hatchlands Park
Hestercombe House and Gardens
Knebworth
Lindisfarne Castle

A collection of her tools can be found at Guildford Museum

BERKELEY CASTLE
(Mr & Mrs R.J. Berkeley)
Gloucestershire   GL13 9BQ   map **14** T18   △
Telephone: (01453) 810332

BERKELEY CASTLE
Gloucestershire

England's most Historic Home and Oldest Inhabited Castle

Completed in 1153 by Lord Maurice Berkeley at the command of Henry II and for nearly 850 years the home of the Berkeley family. 24 generations have gradually transformed a savage Norman fortress into a truly stately home.

The castle is a home and not a museum. Enjoy the castle at leisure or join one of the regular one-hour guided tours covering the dungeon, the cell where Edward II was murdered, the medieval kitchens the magnificent Great Hall and the State Apartments with their fine collections of pictures by primarily English and Dutch masters, tapestries, furniture of an interesting diversity, silver and porcelain.

Splendid Elizabethan Terraced Gardens and sweeping lawns surround the castle, Tropical Butterfly House with hundreds of exotic butterflies in free flight – an oasis of colour and tranquillity.

Facilities include free coach and car parks, picnic lawn and two gift shops. Tea rooms for refreshments, light lunches and afternoon teas.

Opening times and admission charges – see editorial reference. Evening parties by arrangement. Further information from the Custodian, Berkeley Castle, Glos. GL13 9BQ. Telephone 01453-810 332.

Location: Midway between Bristol and Gloucester, just off A38. M5 junctions 13 or 14.
Open: Apr - Daily (exc Mons) 2-5, May to Sept - Tues to Sats 11-5, Suns 2- 5; *closed Mons.* Oct - Suns only 2-4.30, also Bank Hol Mons 11-5. Grounds open same day as House, until 6 pm (5.30 in Oct).
Admission: £4 Children £2 OAPs/Students £3.20 Group rate (parties of 25 or over) £3.50 Children £1.80 OAPs/Students £3.
Refreshments: Light lunches (May to Sept) and teas at Castle.
Evening parties by arrangement. Further information from the Custodian.

BOURTON HOUSE GARDEN
(Mr. & Mrs. Richard Paice)
Bourton on the Hill, Gloucestershire   GL56 9AE   map **3** T19
Telephone: (01386) 700121

An imaginatively planted garden, largely created under the present ownership, enhances a handsome c.18th century Cotswold Manor House (not open). Unusual plants for sale.

Location: 2 m west of Moreton-in-Marsh on A44.
Open: From 25 May-29 Sept Thurs and Fri also Bank Hols Mon May 29 Aug 27 and 28 12 noon-5pm.
Admission: £2.50 children free.
Refreshments: Tea in c.16th century Tithe barn.
For charity in conjunction with village gardens Bank Holiday Sunday May 28 1-6. Entrance £2.50 children free.

CHAVENAGE
(David Lowsley-Williams, Esq)
Tetbury   map **14** T18   △
Telephone: (01666) 502329
Fax: (01453) 836778

Elizabethan House (1576) set in the tranquil Cotswold countryside with Cromwellian associations. 16th and 17th century furniture and tapestries. Personally conducted tours, by the owner or his family.

Location: 2 m N of Tetbury signposted off A46 B4014.
Open: Easter Sun & Mon then May-end Sept Thurs Sun & Bank Hols 2-5.
Admission: Adults £2.50 children half-price. Parties by appointment as above or other dates and times to suit.
Refreshments: Catering for parties by arrangement.
Conferences: Wedding receptions, dinners, corporate hospitality, and film and photograbhic location.

CHEDWORTH ROMAN VILLA   The National Trust
Yanworth, nr Cheltenham   GL54 3LJ   map **3** T19
Telephone: (01242) 890256

One of the best exposed Romano-British villa in Britain. It was built about AD120 and extended and occupied until about AD400. There are good fourth century mosaics in the bath suits and triclinium (dining room). The villa was excavated in 1864, and a museum has a useful range of artefacts.

Location: 3 m NW of Fossebridge on Cirencester-Northleach Road (A429).
Open: Mar-end Oct Tues-Sun & Bank Hol Mon 10-5.30. Last admissions 5. *Open* Good Friday. 1 Nov-3 Dec Wed-Sun 11-4 also Dec 9, 10.
Admission: £2.70 Children £1.35 Family £7.40. Parties by prior written arrangement only. Disabled - all parts accessible but some with difficulty. Disabled WC. Shop open on site - introductory film.

HARDWICKE COURT
(C.G.M. Lloyd-Baker)
nr Gloucester   map **14** T18
Telephone: (01452) 720212

Late Georgian house designed by Robert Smirke, built 1816-1817. Entrance Hall, Drawing Room, Library and Dining Room open.

Location: 5 m S of Gloucester on A38 (between M5 access 12 S only and 13).
Open: Easter Mon-end Sept Mon only 2-4 other times by prior written appointment.
Admission: £1, parking for cars only.
Not suitable for disabled.

HIDCOTE MANOR GARDEN   The National Trust
Hidcote Bartrim, nr Chipping Campden   GL55 6LR   map **3** T19
Telephone: (01386) 438333

One of the most beautiful English gardens.

Location: 4 m NE of Chipping Campden, 1 m E of A46 (re-designated B4632) off B4081.
Open: Apr to end of Oct Daily (except Tue & Fri) 11-7. Last adm 6 or one hour before sunset). Closed Good Fri.
Admission: £5 children £2.50 Family ticket £13.75. *Parties by prior written arrangement only. No party concessions*
Refreshments: Coffee, lunches 11-2. Teas 2.15-5. Light refreshments available in plant sales centre adjacent to car park Apr-30 Sept 10.30-5.45
No dogs. No picnics. Liable to serious overcrowding on Bank Hol weekends and fine Suns. Access: for the less able is limited in parts due to the nature of some informal stone paved paths. Wheelchair access to part of garden only. Wheelchairs available.

HODGES BARN GARDENS
Shipton Moyne, Tetbury   GL8 8PR   map **14** T18
Telephone: (01666) 880202
Fax: (01367) 718096

One of the finest private gardens in England. Spring bulbs, Magnolias and flowering trees are followed by a superb collection of old fashioned and climbing roses with many mixed shrub and herbaceous beds.

Open: Apr 1-Aug 19 Mon Tues Fri 2-5.
Admission: Adults £2.50 children free (groups by appointment).
Refreshments: Teas by appointment. Lunches nearby.

KIFTSGATE COURT
(Mr & Mrs J.G. Chambers)
nr Chipping Campden   map **3** S19

Garden with many unusual shrubs and plants including tree paeonies, abutilons etc, specie and old fashioned roses.

Location: 3 m NE of Chipping Campden.
Open: Gardens only Apr 1-Sept 30 Wed Thurs & Sun 2-6 also Sat in June and July also Bank Hol Mons 2-6 and Sat May 13 & Aug 19 in aid of National Garden Scheme.
Admission: Adults £3 children £1.
Refreshments: Whit Sun to Sept 1.
Coaches by appointment only. *Unusual plants for sale on open days.*

LITTLE DEAN HALL
(D.M. Macer-Wright, Esq)
Littledean, Nr Cinderford   GL14 3NR   map **14** T18
Telephone: (01594) 824213

The Hall reflects 900 years of architectural history with interesting external elevations, 17th century interiors, Civil War connections, displays of archaeological finds and the remains of an ancient hall believed to be Saxon. In the grounds are restored Roman remains identified as a 2nd-3rd c. water shrine, also trees of an exceptional age, an informal water garden.

Location: 12 m W of Gloucester; 2m E of Cinderford; 400 yds from A4151 on Littledean/Newnham-on-Severn Road, turn at King's Head.
Open: GARDENS & HOUSE Apr 1-Oct 31 daily 10.30-5.30.
Admission: Charged
There are ongoing repairs and improvements which may cause changes in advertised details.

LYDNEY PARK GARDENS
(Viscount Bledisloe)
Lydney   GL15 6BU   map **14** T17
Telephone: (01594) 842844 (office)

Extensive Woodland Garden with lakes and a wide selection of rhododendrons and azaleas fine shrubs and trees. Museums and Roman Temple Site. Deer Park (picnics).

Location: ½ m W of Lydney on A48 (Gloucester to Chepstow).
Station(s): Lydney
Open: Easter Sun and Mon. Apr 2-June 5 every Sun Wed and Bank Hol **except Sun May 21** May 29-June 4 every day 11-6 **Coaches and parties** on Open Days and on other days by appointment (minimum 25). Easter-mid June and thereafter to end July for Temple Site and Museum only by appointment.
Admission: Car park and accompanied children free. Adults £2 Wed £1.
Refreshments: Teas in house (house not otherwise open).
Dogs on lead.

THE MANOR
(Mr & Mrs P. R. H. Clifford)
Frampton-on-Severn, Gloucester   map **14** T18
Telephone: (01452) 740698

Medieval/Elizabethan timber-framed Manor House with walled garden. Reputed 12th century birthplace of 'Fair Rosamund' Clifford mistress of King Henry II. 15th century Wool Barn and Granary with dovecote.

Location: 3 miles J 13, M5.
Open: House And Garden open throughout year by written appointment. Garden opens Mons Apr 24-July 10 1995 incl 2-5; also open in aid of Red Cross and NGS.
Admission: House and Garden £2.50 Garden only £1.50.

Do you know what your local museums and art galleries have to offer?

IT'S EASY TO FIND OUT!

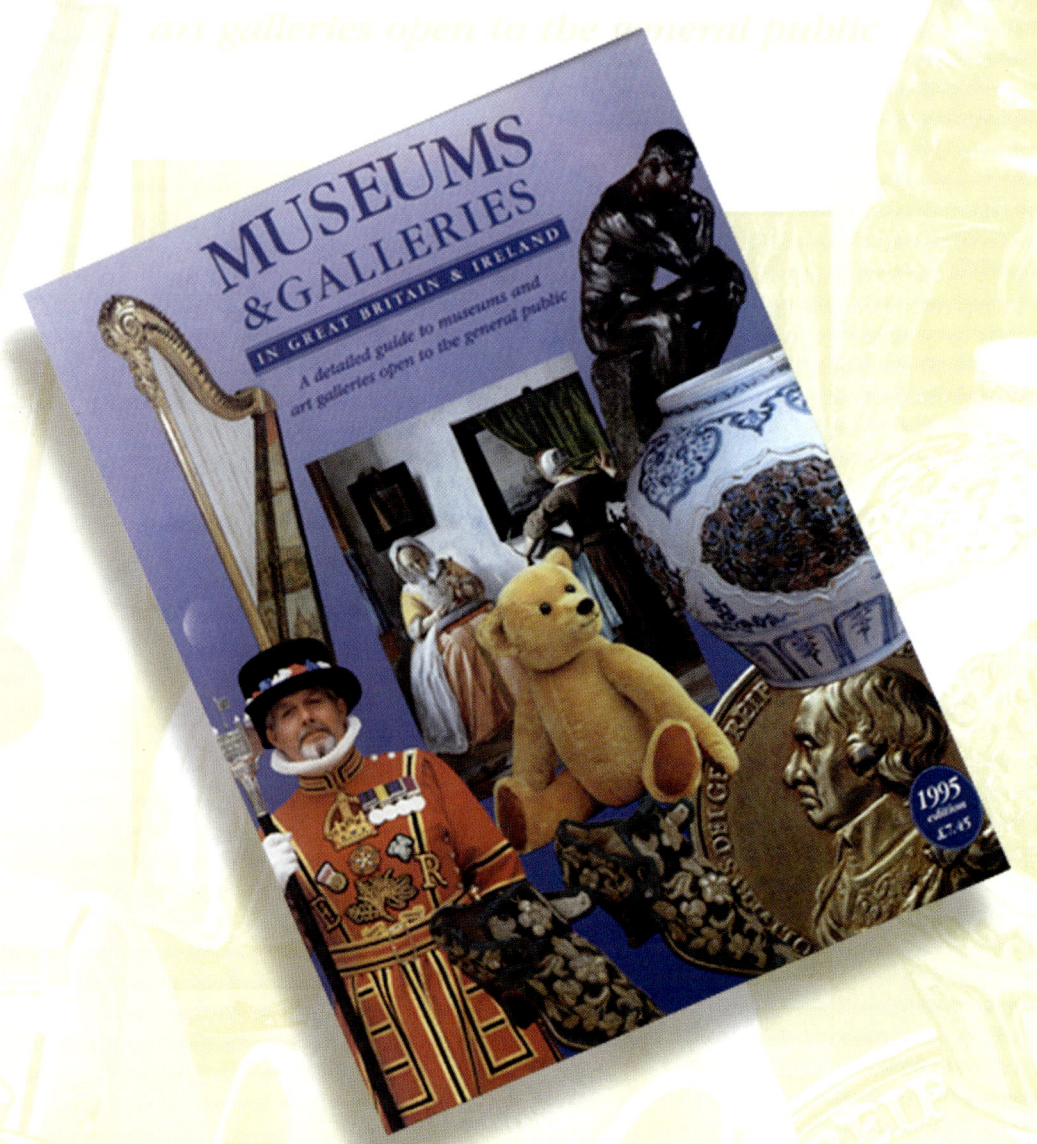

The answers are in Museums & Galleries; the only national guide to over 1,200 museums and art galleries open to the public in Great Britain and Ireland.
Designed to be easy to use, its simple layout allows you to locate the relevant page quickly and easily.

Published by the same company as
Historic Houses Castles & Gardens.
Available in most good bookshops

Price: only £7.45

ISBN: 094 8056 274

MISARDEN PARK GARDENS
(Major M.T.N.H. Wills)
Miserden, Stroud map **14** T18 &
Telephone: (01285) 821303
Fax: (01825) 821530

Spring flowers, shrubs, fine topiary (some designed by Sir Edwin Lutyens) and herbaceous borders within a walled garden, roses and fine specimen trees. 17th century Manor House (not open), standing high overlooking Golden Valley.

Location: Miserden 7 m from Gloucester, Cheltenham, Stroud & Cirencester; 3 m off A417 (signed).
Open: Every Tues, Wed & Thurs from 1 Apr-30 Sept 9.30-4.30. Nurseries adjacent to garden open daily except Mons.
Admission: £2 (includes leaflet) Children (accompanied) free. Reductions for parties (of 20 or more) by appointment.

OWLPEN MANOR
(Mr & Mrs Nicholas Mander)
Uley, nr Dursley GL11 5BZ map **14** T18
Telephone: (01453) 860261
Fax: (01435) 860819

Romantic Tudor manor house in 16th/17th century formal terraced gardens. Picturesque Cotswold manorial group - including Jacobean Court House and Watermill dated 1728 (now holiday cottages), Victorian church and medieval tithe barn - enclosed in its own lovely wooded valley. 'The epitome of romance' (Pevsner). The mellow stone manor dates from 1450-1616, with small improvements of 1719; uninhabited for over 100 years before 1925, when it was restored by Cotswold Arts & Crafts architect, Norman Jewson. Tudor Great Hall and Jacobean Oak Parlour. Contents include unique series of 17th C painted-cloth wall hangings in Queen Margaret of Anjou's bedroom, family and Cotswold Arts & Crafts furniture and pictures, and textiles, wallpaintings and panelling. One of the oldest complete gardens in England, with parterres, topiary yews and mill pond. 'Owlpen, in Gloucestershire - ah, what a dream is there!' Vita Sackville-West.

Location: 3 m E of Dursley off B4066, 1 m E of Uley at Green by Old Crown pub.
Open: Apr 1 to Sept 30 incl 2-5. Tues Thur Suns and Bank Hol Mons Also Wed in July and August. No dogs.
Admission: £3.25 children £1.50. Tours for pre-booked groups of 20 or more.
Refreshments: Light lunches from 12.30 cream teas. Pre-booked evening meals for groups in licensed restaurant in Tithe Barn.
Accommodation: Nine period cottages, including listed buildings, available on the Owlpen Estate.
Conferences: Facilities available including filming and corporate entertaining.

Butterfly Houses

*can be found at the following properties
included in Historic Houses Castles and Gardens:-*

*Berkeley Castle
Elsham Hall - Wild butterfly walkway
Syon House*

PAINSWICK ROCOCO GARDEN
(Painswick Rococo Garden Trust)
Painswick map **3** T18
Telephone: (01452) 813204

This beautiful six acre garden, set in a hidden combe, is a rare and complete survivor of the brief eighteenth century taste for the Rococo in garden design. A restoration programme was begun in October 1984, based on a Thomas Robins painting of 1748, and this is now largely completed. The Garden is a registered charity.

Location: ½ m from Painswick on B4073.
Open: Garden Only: 2nd Wed in Jan-Nov 30 Wed-Sun incl Bank Hols 11-5. Groups by appointment.
Admission: Adults £2.60 OAPs £2.20 children £1.30.
Refreshments: In licensed restaurant, morning coffees and home made light lunches and afternoon teas. Present Collection shop.

RODMARTON MANOR
(Mr & Mrs Simon Biddulph)
Cirencester GL7 6PF map **14** T18
Telephone: (01285) 841253

Rodmarton Manor was one of the last great country houses to be built and is the finest example of the Arts and Craft period. The extensive gardens have many areas of character and beauty.

Location: Off A433 6 m west of Cirencester.
Open: Garden Sats May 13-August 26 2-5 and at other times by appointment. HOUSE guided tours only by prior written appointment.
Admission: House and Garden £4 (minimum group charge £28). Garden £1.50 Sats 2-5 £2 any other time. Please send for full details.

SEZINCOTE
(Mr & Mrs D. Peake)
Moreton-in-Marsh GL56 9AW map **3** T19 △

Oriental water garden by Repton and Daniell with trees of unusual size. House in 'Indian' style inspiration of Royal Pavilion, Brighton.

Location: 1½ m W of Moreton-in-Marsh on A44 to Evesham; turn left by lodge before Bourton-on-the-Hill.
Open: Garden Thurs Fri & Bank Hol Mons 2-6 (or dusk if earlier) throughout year, except Dec. House May June July & Sept Thurs & Fri 2.30-6 parties by appointment. Open in aid of *National Gardens Scheme* Sun July 9 2-6.
Admission: House & Garden £4 Garden only £2.50 children £1.
Refreshments: Hotels & restaurant in Moreton-in-Marsh.
No dogs.

SNOWSHILL MANOR 🌿 The National Trust
nr Broadway WR12 7LU map **3** T19 &
Telephone: (01386) 852410

A Tudor house with c1700 facade; 21 rooms containing interesting collection of craftsmanship, including musical instruments, clocks, toys, bicycles and Japanese armour, with small formal garden.

Location: 3 m SW of Broadway off A44.
Open: Daily except Tues Apr & Oct 1-5 Closed Good Fri. May to end Sept daily except Tues 1-6 Grounds & Visitor facilities open from 12: Last admissions to house & restaurant½ hour before closing. Timed tickets will be issued for the house.
Admission: £5 children £2.50 Family ticket £13.75. Grounds restaurant and shop £2. School Parties by prior written arrangement only.
Refreshments: open for coffees, lunches & teas 12-4.30. Apr & Oct 12-5.30. May-end Sept also 4 Nov-10 Dec Sat & Sun 12.30-4.30.
No coaches. No dogs. Liable to serious overcrowding on Suns and Bank Hol Weekends. Disabled access to visitor facilities but house and grounds unsuitable. Shop.

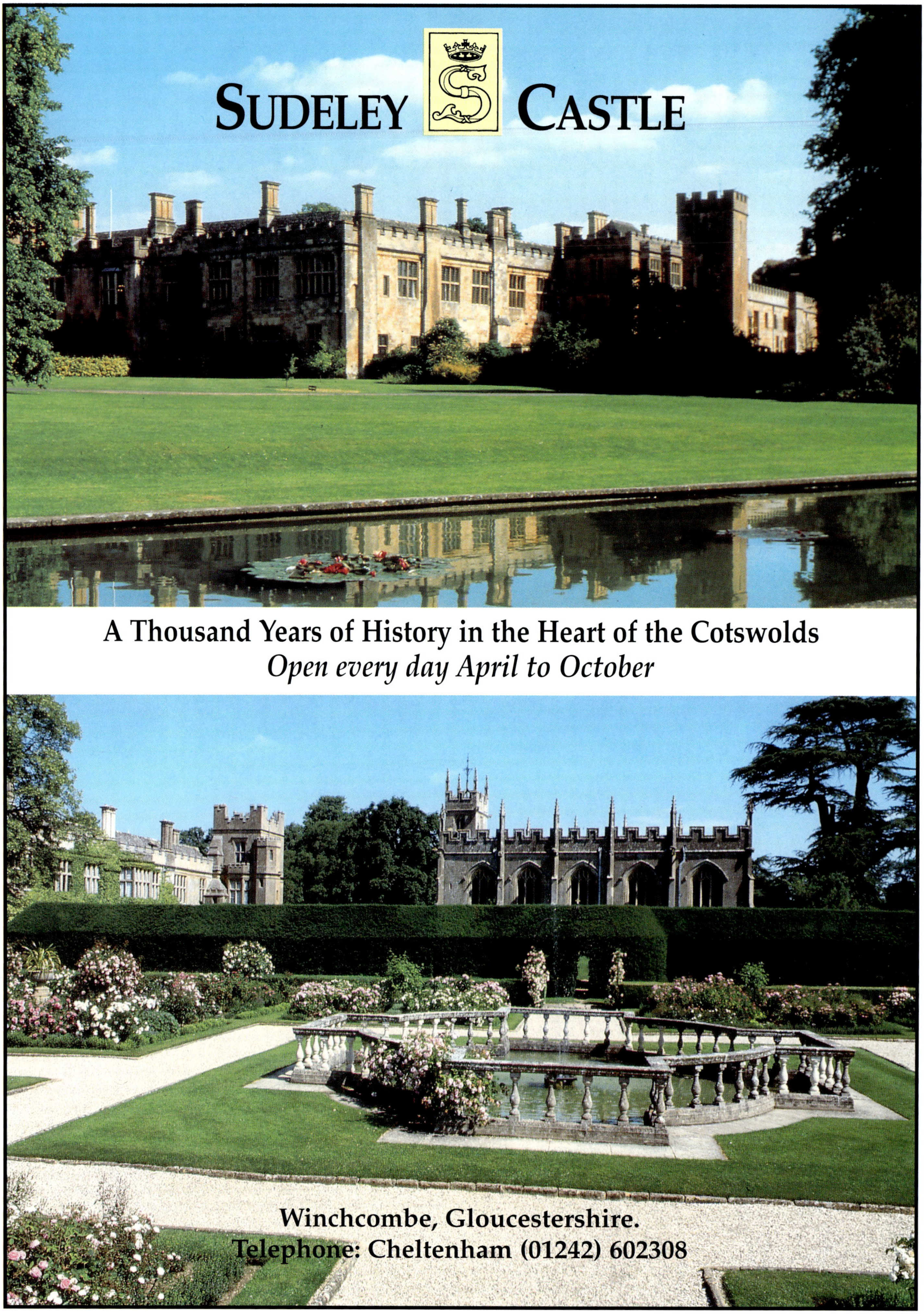
SUDELEY CASTLE
A Thousand Years of History in the Heart of the Cotswolds
Open every day April to October
Winchcombe, Gloucestershire.
Telephone: Cheltenham (01242) 602308

STANWAY HOUSE

(Lord Neidpath)
nr Broadway   GL54 5PQ   map **3** T19
Telephone: (01386) 584469

This jewel of Cotswold Manor houses is very much a home rather than a museum and the centre of a working landed estate which has changed hands once in 1275 years. The mellow Jacobean architecture, the typical squire's family portraits, the exquisite Gatehouse, the old Brewery, mediaeval Tithe Barn, the extensive gardens, arboretum pleasure grounds and formal landscape contribute to the timeless charm of what Arthur Negus considered one of the most beautiful and romantic houses in England.

Location: 1 m off B4632 Cheltenham/Broadway road; on B4077 Toddington/Stow-on-the-Wold road; M5 junction 9.
Open: June-Sept Tues and Thurs 2-5.
Admission: Adults £3 OAPs £2.50 children £1.
Refreshments: Teas in Old Bakehouse in village (Stanton 204).

SUDELEY CASTLE

(Lord and Lady Ashcombe)
Winchcombe   GL54 5JD   map **3** T19   △
Telephone: (01242) 602308
Fax: (01242) 602959

Set against the picturesque splendour of rolling Cotswold Hills, Sudeley Castle is one of England's great historic houses. Sudeley has royal connections stretching back 1000 years. Once the property of King Ethelred the Unready, Sudeley was later the magnificent palace of Queen Katherine Parr who is buried in the Castle Church. Henry VIII, Anne Boleyn, Lady Jane Grey and Elizabeth I stayed at the Castle, Charles I resided here while Prince Rupert established his headquarters during the Civil War. During the Victorian era a sympathetic programme of reconstruction enhanced Sudeley's earlier magnificence. Today the Castle is home to Lord and Lady Ashcombe. Among a wealth of history on show is an impressive collection of art treasures including masterpieces by Turner, Van Dyck and Rubens. Sudeley has eight magnificent gardens, the centrepiece of which is the Queen's garden, famous for its hundreds of varieties of old fashioned roses. There is an exhibition Centre, Picnic Area, Adventure Playground, Castle Shop, Specialist Plant Centre and fully-licensed Restaurant.

Location: 7 m NE of Cheltenham on B4632 (A46). Access A40, A38, A417, M5 (junction 9, Tewkesbury).
Station(s): Cheltenham Spa.
Open: Mar 1-31 Gardens, Plant Centre and Shop 11-4 daily. Restaurant weekends only (weekdays by prior arrangement). Apr 1-Oct 31 Gardens, Church, Exhibition Centre, Shop and Plant Centre 10.30-5.30 daily Restaurant 10.30-5 daily Casle Apartments 11-5 daily. Dec 1-21 Shop and Plant Centre 11-3 daily.
Admission: Adults £4.95 adult party £3.80 adult gardens £3.35 OAPs £4.55 OAP party £3.50 OAP gardens £2.95 children £2.75 child party £2 child gardens £1.60 family £13 family season £36 adult season £19 child season £9.50 garden season £12 adventure play-ground (only) 75p per day.
Refreshments: Fully licensed Restaurant open for morning coffee, lunches and afternoon tea.
Events/Exhibitions: Lace Exhibition: Annual Exhibition of Arts and Crafts.
Accommodation: 16 romantic Cotswold Cottages on Castle Estate.
Conferences: Held in the Castle or in the Chandos Hall Conference Centre (capacity 40) on the Castle Estate.
Private guided tours of Castle Apartments and Gardens by prior arrangement. Schools educational pack available. Corporate Activities, Product Launches, Filming, Wedding Receptions, Business Launches, Exclusive Receptions and Dinners, Medieval Banquets etc.

WESTBURY COURT GARDEN   The National Trust

Westbury-on-Severn   GL14 1PD   map **3** T18   &
Telephone: (01452) 760461

A formal Dutch water-garden with canals and yew hedges, laid out between 1696 and 1705; the earliest of its kind remaining in England.

Location: 9 m SW of Gloucester on A48.
Station(s): Nearest Gloucester, bus from Gloucester Red & White 31 & 73.
Open: Apr to end Oct Wed to Sun & Bank Hol Mons 11-6. *Closed* Good Fri.
Admission: £2.30 children £1.15. Parties by prior written arrangement only. Picnic area. No dogs. Wheelchairs provided.

WHITTINGTON COURT

(Mrs J L Stringer)
Whittington, nr Cheltenham   GL54 4HF   map **3** T19
Telephone: (01242) 820556

Small Elizabethan stone-built manor house with family possessions.

Location: 4½ m E of Cheltenham on A40.
Open: Apr 15-30 Aug 12-28. Daily 2-5.
Admission: £2 OAPs £1.50 Children £1. Open to parties by arrangement.

WOODCHESTER MANSION

(Woodchester Mansion Trust)
Nympsfield   map **3** T18
Telephone: (01453) 860531 (for private bookings and info) or (01453) 750455

Hidden in a secret wooded valley near Stroud is one of the most intriguing houses in the country. Woodchester Mansion was started in 1856 but abandoned, incomplete, in 1870. Designed in the Gothic style by the brilliant young architect, Benjamin Bucknall, it is an unfinished masterpiece of golden Cotswold stone. Like a Victorian building site caught in a timewarp, it offers a unique insight into traditional building techniques. It is now leased by the Woodchester Mansion Trust, whose repair programme includes training courses in stonemasonry and building conservation. Open days and private visits are organised by volunteers from the local community.

Location: By Coaley Peak Picnic Site (parking) on B4066 Stroud-Dursley, ½ m from Nympsfield village.
Open: First weekend in each month from Easter-Oct (Sat/Sun) and Bank Holiday weekends (Sat/Sun/Mon). Gates open 11-4. Regular guided tours. Free minibus service or walk down .75 mile wooded track. Gift shop.
Admission: Adults £3 students £2 children £1. Private visits by arrangement (0453) 860531.
Refreshments: Teas and snacks.
No dogs, please.

HAMPSHIRE

BASING HOUSE

(Hampshire County Council)
Basingstoke   RG24 7HB   map **3** U20
Telephone: (01256) 467294
Fax: (01256) 26283

Basing House ruins were once the country's largest private house, the palace of William Paulet, 1st Marquess of Winchester who was Lord Treasurer of England under three Tudor monarchs. The Civil War brought disaster to Basing which fell to Oliver Cromwell in person after 2.5 years of siege in 1645. The ruins, which cover about 10 acres, contain Norman earthworks, the remains of Tudor kitchens, cellars, towers, a 300 foot long tunnel, a spectacular barn, Civil War defences designed by Inigo Jones and a recently re-created 16/17th century formal garden. Special events in 1995 to commemorate 350th anniversary of the English Civil War Siege.

Location: 2 m from Basingstoke Town Centre & 2 m from Junction 6 of M3.
Open: Apr 1-Oct 1 Wed-Sun and Bank Hols 2-6. Parties any time by prior arrangement.
Admission: £1.50 Children and OAPs 70p.
Refreshments: Meals can be obtained at two public houses near main entrance. Tea-shop usually open on site most Suns.
Car parking. Suitable for disabled persons (please telephone in advance for easier parking).

BEAULIEU
(The Lord Montagu of Beaulieu)
Beaulieu   map **3** V20   Ⓢ
Telephone: (0159) 061 2345

'Beaulieu's Palace House is the ancestral home of the Montagu Family. The house was once the Gatehouse to the Beaulieu Abbey (ruins of which can be seen today along with an Exhibition of Monastic Life) and has many unusual architectural features that make it stand out from other historic houses. Beaulieu is of course famous for its National Motor Museum featuring more than 250 exhibits including motor cars, commercial vehicles and motorcycles. There is 'Wheels' a futuristic ride on space age pods through 100 years of motoring; Monrail and Veterain Bus rides, plus a Driving Simulator and many other rides and drives for the whole family'.

Location: In Beaulieu 7 m SE of Lyndhurst; 14 m S of Southampton; 6 m NE of Lymington.
Station(s): Brockenhurst.
Open: All facilities open throughout the year. Easter to Sept - Daily 10-6; Oct to Easter - Daily 10-5. *Closed Christmas Day.*
Admission: Inclusive charge. Reduced rates for Chd and OAPs. *Parties at special rates.*
Refreshments: Lunches and teas at licensed Brabazon Restaurant.
Events/Exhibitions: A variety of special events is held each year including:- Autojumble, Boat Jumble, Gardening and Countryside Show, Outdoor Symphony Concert, Fireworks Fair and a number of Car Club Rallies. Tel: (01590) 612345 for details.
Conferences: A unique range of facilities is on offer for conference and corporate hospitality including a tiered seating theatre for up to 200 people, the Brabazon Catering Centre which can accomodate up to 300, a 13th century Banqueting Hall, outdoor Exhibition Arena and Rally Field.

Sir Peter Lely - portrait painter

His paintings can be seen at the following properties included in Historic Houses Castles and Gardens:-

Aynhoe Park	*Kedleston Hall*
Belton House	*Knole*
Breamore House	*Petworth House*
Browsholme Hall	*Ragley Hall*
Dalmeny House	*Rockingham Castle*
Euston Hall	*St Osyth Priory*
Goodwood House	*Stanford Hall*
Gorhambury	*Weston Park*

BREAMORE HOUSE

(Sir Westrow Hulse, Bt)

nr Fordingbridge SP6 2DF   map **3** V19   △
Telephone: (01725) 512468

Elizabethan Manor House (1583) with fine collection of paintings, tapestries, furniture. Coutryside Museum takes the visitor back to when a village was self sufficient. Exhibition of Rural Arts and Agricultural machinery. Carriage Museum. 'The Red Rover', and other coaches.

Location: 3 m N of Fordingbridge off the main Bournemouth Road (A338) 8 m S of Salisbury.
Open: Easter Hol Apr - Tues Wed Sun, May June July & Sept - Tues Wed Thurs Sat Sun and all Bank Hols, Aug daily. House 2-5.30 Countryside Museum 1-5.30. Other times by appointment.
Admission: Combined ticket adults £4.50 children £3 reduced rate for parties and OAPs.
Refreshments: Home-made snacks and teas available from midday.

EXBURY GARDENS

(E.L. de Rothschild, Esq)

nr Southampton SO45 1AZ   map **3** V20
Telephone: (01703) 891203
Fax: (01703) 243380

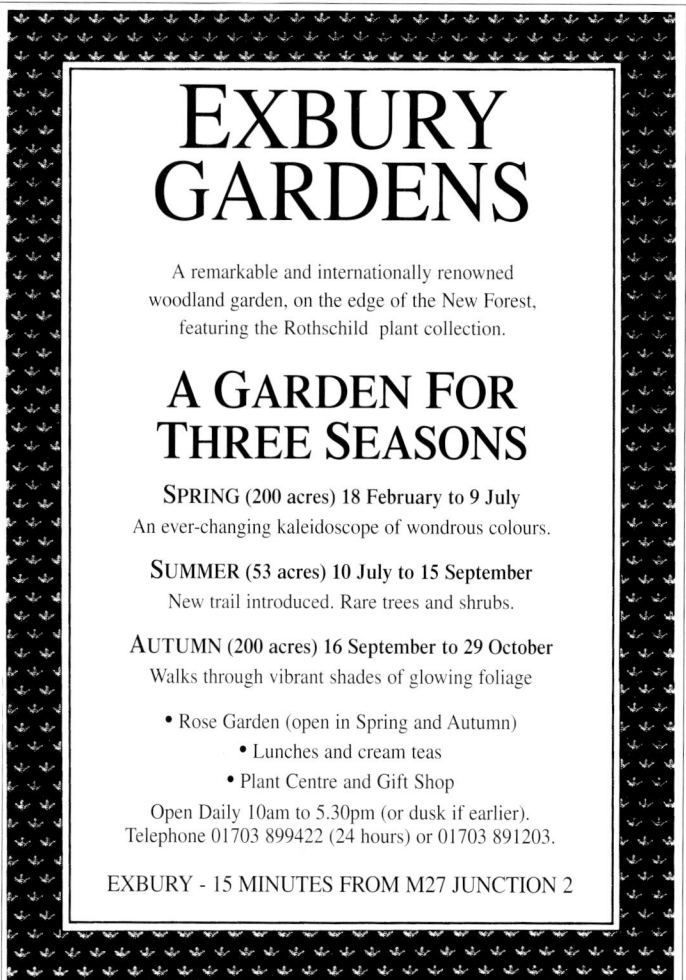

Unique 200 acre woodland garden created by Lionel de Rothschild, with a superb display of rhododendrons, azaleas, camellias, magnolias, other fascinating flora and new plantings. Well stocked Plant Centre and Gift Shop, artist's studio, licensed tea rooms. Dogs welcome on leads.

Location: Exbury village, 15 m SW of Southampton close to New Forest. Turn W off A326 at Dibden Purlieu towards Beaulieu.
Open: Daily 10-5.30pm (dusk if earlier). Gardens: End Feb-Oct. **Plant Centre and Gift Shop** open end Feb-Christmas Eve.
Admission: £4.50 OAPs and parties £4 Chd (10-16) £3.50 for main season, weekends and Bank Holidays. Early and late season discounts.
Refreshments: Licensed refreshments.
Events/Exhibitions: Marquee Hospitality End Apr/Beginning June.
Also ample parking and toilet facilities. Dogs on short leads.

HISTORIC HOUSES
CASTLES & GARDENS

For further details on editorial listings or display advertising contact the

Editor: Deborah Valentine,
Windsor Court, East Grinstead House, East Grinstead, West Sussex RH19 1XA
Tel: (01342) 335794 Fax: (01342) 335720

GILBERT WHITE'S HOUSE & GARDEN AND THE OATES MUSEUM
(Charitable Trust)
The Wakes, High Street   **GU34 3JH**   map **12** U21
Telephone: (01420) 511275

Historic 18th century house & glorious garden, home of famous naturalist REV. GILBERT WHITE, author of 'THE NATURAL HISTORY OF SELBORNE'. Furnished rooms & original manuscript. Also fascinating museum on Frank Oates, Victorian explorer and Capt. Lawrence Oates who accompanied Scott on the ill-fated Antarctic expedition of 1911/1912.

Location: In main high street of Selborne village.
Station(s): Liss or Alton.
Open: 11-5 DAILY from END MAR-END OCT then WEEKENDS ONLY during WINTER. Day, evening & winter opening for groups by arrangement.
Admission: £2.50 OAPs £2 Children £1. Free admission to shop.
Refreshments: Three venues along High Street in village.
Events/Exhibitions: Snowdrop day, Jan/Feb. Unusual Plants Fair 24/25th June. Mulled Wine day, 26th Nov
Excellent gift shop. Plant sales.

HIGHCLERE CASTLE
(The Earl of Carnarvon KCVO, KBE)
nr Newbury   **RG15 9RN**   map **3** U20
Telephone: (01635) 253210

Designed by Charles Barry in the 1830s at the same time as he was building the Houses of Parliament. This soaring pinnacled mansion provided a perfect setting for the 3rd Earl of Carnarvon one of the great hosts of Queen Victoria's reign. The extravagant interiors range from church Gothic through Morrish flamboyance and rococo revival to the solid masculinity on the long Library. Old master paintings mix with portraits by Van Dyck and 18th century painters. Napoleon's desk and chair rescued from St. Helena sits with other 18th century furniture. The 5th Earl of Carnarvon, discovered the Tomb of Tutankhamun with Howard Carter. The castle houses a unique exhibition of some of his discoveries which were only rediscovered in the castle in 1988. The current Earl is the Queen's Horseracing Manager. In 1993 to celebrate his 50th year as a leading owner and breeder "The Lord Carnarvon Racing Exhibition" was opened to the public, and offers a fascinating insight into a racing history that dates back three generations. The magnificent parkland with its massive cedars was designed by Capability Brown. The walled gardens dated from an earlier house at Highclere but the dark yew walks are entirely victorian in character. The glass Orangery and Fernery add an exotic flavour. The Secret Garden has a romance of its own with a beautiful curving lawn surrounded by densely planted herbaceous gardens. A place for poets and romantics.

Location: 4½ m S of Newbury on A34, junction 13 of M4 about 2 m from Newbury. M3. Basingstoke junction about 15 m. Heathrow via M4 1 hour. Rail from London (Paddington station) 1 hour.
Station(s): Newbury
Open: July, Aug, Sept, Wed to Sun, Easter May and Aug Bank Hols Sun and Mon. Grounds and tea rooms 12-5, house 1-6 (last entry 5).
Admission: House and Grounds: Adults £5.00 concessions £4.00 children £3.00. Grounds only: £3.00. Special reductions for parties of 30 or more.
Refreshments: Lunches, teas, ices, soft drinks. Parties by prior arrangement.
Conferences: Business conferences, management training courses, film and photographic location.
Car park and picnic area adjacent to Castle. Suitable for disabled persons on ground floor only. One wheelchair available. Visitors can buy original items in Castle Gift Shop.Qu

THE SIR HAROLD HILLIER GARDENS AND ARBORETUM
(Hampshire County Council)
Ampfield, nr Romsey   **SO51 0QA**   map **5** V20   Ⓔ
Telephone: (01794) 368787
Fax: (01794) 368027

Begun by the famous nurseryman Sir Harold Hillier in 1953, and gifted to Hampshire County Council in 1977, the Gardens and Arboretum now extend to more than 160 acres and contain the largest collection of different hardy plants in the British Isles. With this diversity in plants, the Gardens provide something of interest throughout the seasons, from the magnificent floral displays in spring and the pastel shades of summer, to the riot of autumnal hues in October and the highly-scented winter flowering Witch Hazels.

Location: 3 m north east of Romsey, off A31.
Station(s): Romsey.
Open: Every day Apr-Oct 10.30-6 every day Nov-Mar 10.30-5 (or dusk if earlier). *Closed* Public and Bank Hols over Christmas and New Year.
Admission: Mar-Nov £4 adults £3.50 OAPs £1 children. Dec-Feb £3 adults £2.50 OAPs £1 children.
Refreshments: Teas and light meals at weekends November to March and every day from April to October.
Regret NO DOGS.

HINTON AMPNER   🌱 The National Trust
nr Alresford   **SO24 0LA**   map **3** U20   ♿
Telephone: (01962) 771305

The house was remodelled in the Georgian style in 1936 by Ralph Dutton but decimated by fire in 1960. Rebuilt and re-furnished with fine Regency furniture, pictures and porcelain. The gardens juxtapose formality of design and informality of planting, producing delightful walks and unexpected vistas.

Location: 1 m W of Bramdean Village on A272; 8 m E of Winchester.
Station(s): Alresford 4 m; Winchester 9 m.
Open: Apr 1-end Sept GARDEN Sat Sun Tues and Wed (Closed Good Fri and Easter Mon but open on BH Mons thereafter) 1.30-5.30. HOUSE Tues & Wed only and Sat & Sun in Aug 1.30-5.30 (last adm 5). Car park open at 1.15.
Admission: GARDEN £2.40 HOUSE £1.30 extra. Children half-price. Party reductions by prior booking.
Refreshments: Tearoom same days as garden 2-5. Picnics in car park only.
No dogs. Most of garden accessible by wheelchair.

HOUGHTON LODGE GARDENS

(Captain & Mrs M.W. Busk)
Stockbridge SO20 6LQ map **3** U19 &
Telephone: (01264) 810177 or (01264) 810502
Fax: (01794) 388072

Landscaped pleasure grounds surround unique 18th C 'Cottage Ornee' beside the River Test with lovely views over the tranquil and unspoiled valley. Within the traditional kitchen garden surrounded by rare chalkcob walls is the HAMPSHIRE HYDROPONICUM where flowers, fruits, herbs and vegetables grow WITHOUT SOIL. Believed to be the first Hydroponicum in England primarily intended to delight and inform the visitor. The ease of Hydroponic Gardening (no weeding, or digging, no soil borne pests) makes it an ideal method for the handicapped.

Location: 1½ m S of A30 at Stockbridge on minor road to Houghton village.
Station(s): Winchester, Andover.
Open: Mar-Sept incl 10-5 on Sat and Sun & Bank Holidays house open by appointment. 2-5 on Mon Tues and Fri. Coach tours and parties welcome by prior appointment. Telephone for details.
Refreshments: By appointment.
Free parking.

HURST CASTLE

map **3** V20
Telephone: (01590) 642344

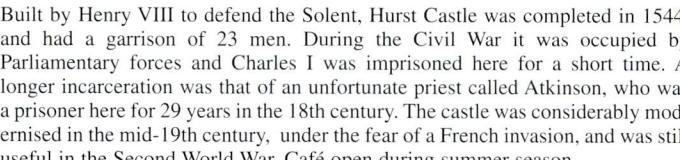

Built by Henry VIII to defend the Solent, Hurst Castle was completed in 1544, and had a garrison of 23 men. During the Civil War it was occupied by Parliamentary forces and Charles I was imprisoned here for a short time. A longer incarceration was that of an unfortunate priest called Atkinson, who was a prisoner here for 29 years in the 18th century. The castle was considerably modernised in the mid-19th century, under the fear of a French invasion, and was still useful in the Second World War. Café open during summer season.

Location: Approach by ferry from Keyhaven.
Open: Apr 1-July 22 10-5.30 (last admission 4.30). July 23-Aug 31 10-6 (last admission 5.15). Sept 1-30 10-5.30 (last admission 4.30).
Admission: Adults £2 concessions £1.50 children £1.
Refreshments: Café open during summer season.

Sir John Van Brugh (1664-1726)

Architect. His work can be seen at the following properties included in historic Houses Castles and Gardens:-

Blenheim Palace
Castle Howard
Claremont
Grimsthorpe Castle
Seaton Delaval Hall

JANE AUSTEN'S HOUSE

(Jane Austen Memorial Trust)
Chawton map **12** U21 &
Telephone: (01420) 83262

Pleasant 17th century village house where Jane Austen lived from 1809 to 1817, and wrote or revised her six great novels. Many interesting mementoes of Jane and her family. Pretty, old fashioned garden, suitable for picnics.

Location: In Chawton, 1 m SW of Alton, sign-posted off roundabout at junction of A31 with A32.
Station(s): Alton (1¾ m).
Open: Daily Apr-Oct; Nov, Dec & Mar: Weds to Suns. Jan & Feb: Sats & Suns only, 11-4.30. *Closed Christmas Day & Boxing Day.*
Admission: Adults £2.00, children (8-18) 50p, groups (15 plus) £1.50.
Refreshments: Available in village.
Bookshop.

MOTTISFONT ABBEY GARDEN The National Trust

Mottisfont SO51 0LP map **3** U19 △ &
Telephone: (01794) 341220

With a tributary of the River Test flowing through, the garden forms a superb setting for a 12th century Augustinian priory, which, after the Dissolution became a house. It contains the spring or 'font' from which the place name is derived, a magnificent collection of trees, and the Trust's unique collection of old roses within walled gardens.

Location: 4½ m NW Romsey ¾ m W of A3057.
Station(s): Mottisfont Dunbridge (¾ m).
Open: GARDEN 19 & 26 Mar 1 Apr-end Oct Sat-Wed 12-6 (or dusk if earlier). June Sat-Thurs 12-8.30. Last admissions one hour before closing. NOTE HOUSE Major restoration work will be taking place until 1996 and the Abbey will be scaffolded so the house itself will be closed to the public until further notice.
Admission: GARDEN £2.50 £3.50 during rose season. No reduction for parties. Coaches please book in advance. Rose season varies according to the weather. Check with the property in June.
Shop; open same time as garden. Dogs in car park only. Wheelchairs and powered buggy available. Special parking area for disabled people for shop and use garden only.

PORTCHESTER CASTLE

map **5** V20
Telephone: (01705) 378291

A Roman fortress, a Norman castle and a Romanesque church share this same site on the north shore of Portsmouth harbour. The outer walls were built in the 3rd century when Britain was the vulnerable north-west frontier of a declining Roman Empire. Today they are among the finest Roman remains in northern Europe. Eight centuries - and very little repair work - later, the walls were sound enough to encompass a royal castle. Portchester was popular with the medieval monarchs but by the 15th century royal money was being spent on Portsmouth instead. The last official use of the castle was as a prison for French seamen during the Napoleonic wars. An exhibition tells the story of Portchester.

Location: South side of Portchester.
Open: Apr 1-Sept 30 10-6 daily Oct 1-Mar 31 daily 10-4.
Admission: Adults £2.50 concessions £1.90 children £1.30.

SANDHAM MEMORIAL CHAPEL   The National Trust

Burghclere, nr Newbury   map **5** U20   ♿
Telephone: (01635) 278394

A small chapel built to house the paintings of the distinguished 1st World War artist Stanley Spencer. The huge canvases which cover the chapel walls depict the lives of the ordinary men Spencer met while working as a hospital orderly at Salonica.

Location: In village of Burghclere 4 m S of Newbury ½ m E of A34.
Station(s): Newbury 4m.
Open: Mar 25-end Oct Wed-Sun 11.30-6. Open Bank Holiday Mons closed Wed after Bank Hol Mon. Nov 1995 and Mar 1996 Sat & Sun only 11.30-4. Dec-Feb by appointment only.
Admission: £1.50 Parties must book. No reduction for parties.
Wheelchair access via two small sets of steps.

STRATFIELD SAYE HOUSE 🏛

(The Duke of Wellington)
Reading   **RG7 2BT**   map **5** U20   ♿
Telephone: (01256) 882882
Fax: (01256) 882345

Homes of the Dukes of Wellington since 1817, Stratfield Saye is a living example of the classic English Country House tradition with the present Duke and Duchess in residence for much of the year. At the same time, the house and exhibition pay tribute to Arthur Wellesley, the first and great Duke - soldier, statesman and victor of the Napoleonic wars. THE HOUSE: Gift of a grateful nation, the house contains a unique collection of paintings, prints, furniture and personal effects belonging to the Great Duke. THE WELLINGTON EXHIBITION: Depicts the life and times of the Great Duke with displays of his maps, weapons, personal effects and clothes of infinite variety. It features his magnificent funeral carriage which celebrates a long and successful military career that culminated in the battle of Waterloo. THE GROUNDS: Include a wildfowl sanctuary, gardens and the grave of Copenhagen, the Dukes's favourite charger that carried him throughout the battle of Waterloo and lived on for many years in retirement at Stratfield Saye. The house and associated Wellington Country Park are situated on the Hampshire/Berkshire borders.

Location: 1 m W of A33 between Reading & Basingstoke (turn off at Wellington Arms Hotel); signposted. Close to M3 & M4.
Open: House and Gardens open daily (except Fri) May 1-last Sun in Sept 11.30-4. Available for private and corporate functions by arrangement with The Wellington Office (Tel 01256 882882). Wellington Country Park (3 m from house) - nature trails, adventure playground, animals, boating, windsurfing, fishing, deer park, miniature railway, National Dairy Museum, Thames Valley Time Trail Mar-Oct daily 10-5 Nov-Feb Sat & Sun only. (Tel 01734 326444).
Admission: Please telephone for charges to House and Park.
Refreshments: Tea and snacks, licensed restaurant.

Thomas Gainsborough (1727-1787)

His paintings can be seen at the following properties included in Historic Houses Castles and Gardens:-

Arundel Castle	*Ickworth Park & Garden*	*Petworth House*
Bowhill	*Firle Place*	*Shalom Hall*
Christchurch Mansion	*Kenwood, The Iveagh*	*Upton House*
Dalmeny House	*Bequest*	*Waddesdon Manor*
Elton Hall	*Knole*	*Weston Park*
Gainsborough's House	*Parham House & Gardens*	*Woburn Abbey*

THE VYNE 🌿 The National Trust

Sherborne St John, nr Basingstoke   **RG26 5DX**   map **5** U20 ♿
Telephone: (01256) 881337

A splendid 16/17th century house set in a peaceful lakeside setting. The distinguished interiors include the Tudor chapel with stunning Renaissance stained glass and the Palladian staircase. Gardens with herbaceous borders; lawns and lake; woodland walks.

Location: 4 m N of Basingstoke between Bramley & Sherborne St John (1½ m from each). *Station(s):* Bramley (2½ m).
Open: 25 Mar-end Sept daily except Mon and Fri (open Good Fri and Bank Hol Mon but closed Tues following). House: 1.30-5.30, Bank Hol Mons 11-5.30. Grounds: 12.30-5.30. Grounds only Oct 12.30-5.30. Last admission 5.
Admission: House and Grounds £4. Grounds only £2 *Children half-price. Reduced rates for pre-booked parties Tues Wed & Thurs only £3.*
Refreshments: Light lunches and teas in the Old Brewhouse, same days as grounds, 25 Mar-end Oct 12.30-2 and 2.30-5.30.
NT Shop. Dogs in car park only. Wheelchair available.

HEREFORD & WORCESTER

ABBERLEY HALL

(Mrs Bishop)
nr Worcester   **WR6 6DD**   map **14** S18
Telephone: (01299) 896634 (office hours only)

Five principal rooms show ornate decoration of mid-Victorian period.

Location: 12 m NW of Worcester on A443.
Open: House only. June 12 July 19-21 and 24-28 July 31-Aug 4 Aug 7-11 14-18 21-25 and 29 1.30-4.
Admission: £1.
Unsuitable for wheelchairs. No dogs.

George Stubbs
Portrait, animal and rural painter

(1724-1806)
Produced his engraved work,
The Anatomy of a Horse, in 1766

His work can be seen in the following properties included in Historic Houses Castles and Gardens:-

Mount Stewart House
St Osyth Priory
Upton House

AVONCROFT MUSEUM OF HISTORIC BUILDINGS

(Council of Management)
Stoke Heath, Bromsgrove   map **14** S18 Ⓢ
Telephone: (01527) 831886 or 831363

An open-air Museum containing buildings of great interest and variety. Exhibits include a working windmill, the magnificent 14th century Guesten Hall Roof from Worcester, a 15th century timber framed house, 1946 prefab: from the 18th century a cockpit theatre, an icehouse, an earth closet and a cider mill, and from the 19th century a toll house and a 3 cell lock-up, and now the National Telephone Kiosk Collection.

Location: At Stoke Heath 2 m S of Bromsgrove off A38 between junctions 4 & 5 of M5 and 3½ m S of M42 junction 1.
Open: Mar and Nov 11-4 (closed Mon and Fri) Apr May Sept and Oct 11-5 (closed Mon) June July & Aug daily 11-5.30. Open Bank Holidays. Closed Dec-Feb.
Admission: Adults £3.50 children £1.75 OAPs £2.80 family ticket (2 adults + 3 children) £9.40 parties at reduced rates by arrangement. Free car park & picnic site.
Refreshments: Available at Museum tea-room. Souvenir and Bookshop.

BERNITHAN COURT 🏛

(Bernithan Court Farm Partnership)
Llangarron   map **3** T17

House 1692: fine staircase, walled gardens.

Location: 1½ m from A40 Ross-Monmouth road.
Open: By prior appointment, Mrs James (01989) 770772. Admission £2.

BERRINGTON HALL 🌿 The National Trust

Leominster   **HR6 0DW**   map **3** S17 △♿
Telephone: (01568) 615721

Built 1778-1781,designed by Henry Holland, the architect of Carlton House. Painted and plaster ceilings. `Capability' Brown laid out the park.
Location: 3 m N Leominster, 7 m S of Ludlow, W of A49.
Station(s): Leominster.

Open: Apr to end of Sept Wed to Suns & Bank Hol Mons 1.30-5.30 (Closed Good Fri). Oct Wed-Sun 1.30-4.30. Grounds & restaurant open from 12.30. Last admission ½ hour before closing. Grounds close 6.30 (Oct 5.30)
Admission: £3.60 Children £1.80 grounds only £1.65. Family ticket £9.90. Parties by prior written arrangement only.
Refreshments: Licensed restaurant in the Servants' Hall, serving homemade lunches and teas. Restaurant 12.30-2 (lunch), 2.30-5.30 (teas) last orders 5. Open same days as house and also Nov 4 to Dec 17, Sats and Suns 12.30-4.30. Park walk open July, August, September & October, same days as house.
No dogs. Wheelchair available. Wheelchair access grounds only. No photography.

BURTON COURT

(Lt-Cmdr & Mrs R.M. Simpson)
Eardisland   HR6 9DN   map 3 S17
Telephone: (01544) 388231

A typical squire's house, built around the surprising survival of a 14th century hall. The East Front re-designed by Sir Clough Williams-Ellis in 1912. An extensive display of European and Oriental costume, natural history specimens, and models including a working model fairground. Pick your own soft fruit in season.
Location: 5 m W of Leominster signposted on A44.
Open: Spring Bank Hol-end Sept Wed Thurs Sat Sun & Bank Hol Mons 2.30-6.
Admission: Adults £2 children £1.50 coach parties £1.50.
Refreshments: Coach parties catered for. Teas.
Accommodation: Holiday flat (first floor) self contained - sleeps 7.
Conferences: Conferences (Oct-Apr only).

CROFT CASTLE   The National Trust

nr Leominster   HR6 9PW   map 3 S17
Telephone: (01568) 780246

Welsh Border castle mentioned in Domesday Book. Inhabited by the Croft family for 900 years. Fine 18th century Gothic interior. Extensive wooded parkland.
Location: 5 m NW of Leominster just N of B4362 signposted from Ludlow/Leominster road (A49), and from A4110 at Mortimers Cross.
Station(s): Leominster.

Open: Apr & Oct Sat & Sun 1.30-4.30 Easter Sat Sun & Mon 1.30-4.30 Closed Good Fri May to end Sept Wed to Sun & Bank Hol Mons 1.30-5.30. Last admission 30 mins before closing.
Admission: £3.10 children £1.55 family ticket £8.50. Parties by prior written arrangement.
Refreshments: Picnics allowed in car park only.
Access for disabled to ground floor and part of grounds. Wheelchair available.

CWMMAU FARMHOUSE, BRILLEY   The National Trust

Brilley   HR3 6JP   map 3 S16
Telephone: (01497) 831251

Early 17th century timber-framed and stone tiled farmhouse.

Location: 4 m SW of Kington between A4111 and A438. Approached by a narrow lane.
Open: Easter May Spring & Summer Bank Hol weekends **only** (Sat Sun & Mon) 2-6. *At other times by prior appointment with the tenant Mr D Joyce.*
Admission: £2, chd £1.*No reduction for parties.*
No dogs. Unsuitable for wheelchairs and coaches.

DINMORE MANOR

(R.G. Murray)
nr Hereford   HR4 8EE   map 3 S17
Telephone: (01432) 830322

Spectacular hillside location. A range of impressive architecture dating from 14th to 20th century. Chapel, Cloisters, Great Hall (Music Room) and extensive roof walk giving panoramic views of the countryside and beautiful gardens below. Large collection of stained glass. Interesting and unusual plants for sale in plant centre.

Location: 6 m N of Hereford on (A49).
Open: All the year daily 9.30-5.30.
Admission: Adults £2.50 children (under 14) free when accompanied.
Refreshments: Available in the Plant Centre most afternoons.

EASTNOR CASTLE

(James and the Hon Sarah Hervey - Bathurst)
nr Ledbury, Hertfordshire   HR8 1RD   map **3** T18
Telephone: (01531) 633160/632302
Fax: (01531) 631776

Splendid Norman Revival Castle built in 1812 in a dramatic setting within the Malvern Hills, Eastnor Castle captures the spirit of medieval chivalry and romance. The lavish interiors, in Italianate, Norman and Gothic style, display a unique collection of armour, tapestries, fine furniture and pictures by Van Dyck, Kneller, Romney, Watts and others. Castellated terraces descend to a lake. There is a renowned arboretum in the pleasure grounds, and a 500 acre park with red deer.

Location: 5 m from M50 (exit 2) 2 m E of Ledbury on Hereford/Tewkesbury Road A438.
Station(s): Ledbury (2 m).
Open: Sun from Easter-end Sept Bank Holiday Mon Sun-Fri during July & Aug 12-5. Group bookings at other times throughout the year by appointment.
Admission: Adults £3.50 children £1.75 reduced rates for parties and for grounds only.
Refreshments: Light lunches and home made cream teas.
Accommodation: Luxury accommodation for select groups.
Conferences: Conference activity days, exclusive 'Land-Rover' off road driving tel. Portcullis Office (01531) 633160.
Dogs on lead allowed.

GOODRICH CASTLE

ENGLISH HERITAGE

map **3** T17
Telephone: (01600) 890538

The castle was built to command the ancient crossing of the Wye by the Gloucester/Caerleon road. Among the extensive remains of the original castle the keep survives, which largely dates from the late 13th century. For almost 300 years from the mid-14th century it was held by the Earls of Shrewsbury.

Location: 3 m (4.8 km) south west of Ross-on-Wye.
Open: Apr 1-Sept 30 10-6 daily Oct 1-Mar 31 daily 10-4.
Admission: Adults £2 concessions £1.50 children £1.

THE GREYFRIARS   🌿 The National Trust

Worcester   WR1 2LZ   map **14** S18   △
Telephone: (01905) 23571

A richly timber-framed house built c. 1480, was rescued from demolition at the time of World War II. Carefully restored and refurbished; interesting textiles and furnishings add character to panelled rooms; an archway leads through to a delightful garden.

Location: In Friar Street, Worcester.
Station(s): Worcester, Foregate Street (½ m).
Open: Apr-end Oct Wed & Thurs and Bank Holiday Mons 2-5.30 Also May 21 11-3. (Last admission 30 minutes before closing). Other times adult parties by written application only.
Admission: £2.10 Children £1 Family ticket £5.70. Parties of children (inc schools) not admitted.
No dogs. Unsuitable for wheelchairs.

HANBURY HALL   🌿 The National Trust

nr Droitwich   map **14** S18   ♿
Telephone: (01527) 821214

William and Mary style red brick house built c. 1700 for a wealthy barrister. Outstanding painted ceilings and staircase by Sir James Thornhill. The Watney Collection of porcelain; Orangery c. 1740. 18th century formal garden reinstatement.

Location: 4½ m E of Droitwich, 1 m N of B4090.
Station(s): Droitwich Spa.
Open: Apr to end Oct Sat Sun and Mon 2-6. Aug also open Tues and Weds 2-6. Last adm 30 mins before closing.
Admission: House & garden £3.70 Children £1.85 Family ticket £10. *Parties by prior written arrangement only.*
Refreshments: Teas in the house.
Shop. No dogs. Wheelchair available.

HARTLEBURY CASTLE

(The Church Commissioners)
nr Kidderminster   DY11 7XX   map **14** S18
Telephone: (01299) 250410

Historic home of the Bishops of Worcester for over 1,000 years. Fortified in 13th century, rebuilt after sacking in the Civil War and Gothicised in 18th century.

State Rooms include medieval Great Hall, Hurd Library and Saloon. Fine plaster-work and remarkable collection of episcopal portraits. Also County Museum in North Wing.

Location: In village of Hartlebury, 5 m S of Kidderminster, 10 m N of Worcester off A449.
Open: State Rooms Easter Mon-Sept 3 first Sun in every month but please telephone to check also Bank Holidays and Tues following Bank Holidays 2-5. Also every Wed Easter during this period 2-4. County Museum Mar-Nov Mon-Thurs 10-5 Fri and Sun 2-5 closed Sat and Good Friday. Open Bank Holidays 10-5.
Admission: State Rooms adults 75p children 25p OAPs 50p guided tours for parties of 30 or more on weekdays by arrangement. County Museum £1.50 OAPs/students/children 75p (1994 prices) family tickets (2 adults and up to 3 children) £4.20. School parties please telephone for information.(Museum tel: (01299) 250416).
Refreshments: Available.
Picnic area.

HARVINGTON HALL

(The Roman Catholic Archdiocese of Birmingham)
nr Kidderminster   DY10 4LR   map **14** S18
Telephone: (01562) 777846 (Trust Office)

Moated medieval and Elizabethan manor-house containing secret hiding-places and rare wall-paintings. Georgian Chapel in garden with 18th century altar, rails and organ.

Location: 3 m SE of Kidderminster, ½ m from the junction of A448 and A450 at Mustow Green.
Station(s): Nearest Kidderminster.
Open: Closed part of 1995 for restoration work, except by special arrangement. Enquiries for re-opening date: (0562) 777846.
Refreshments: When open licensed restaurant.
Events/Exhibitions: Contact Trust Office for details.
Free car parking, picnic area, shop, hospitality suites, gardens.

HELLEN'S

(The Pennington-Mellor-Munthe Trust)
Much Marcle   HR8 2LY   map **3** T17   △
Telephone: (01531) 84668

Built as a stone fortress in 1292 by Mortimer, Earl of March, this manorial house has been lived in since then by descendants of original builder. Visited by Black Prince and Bloody Mary.

Location: In village of Much Marcle on Ledbury/Ross Road. Entrance opp church.
Open: Good Fri-Oct 2 Wed Sat Sun and Bank Hol Mons 2-6 (guided tours 2-5). *Other times by written appointment with the Custodian.*
Admission: Adults £3 children (must be accompanied by an adult) £1.

HOW CAPLE COURT GARDENS

(Mr & Mrs P.L. Lee)
How Caple   HR1 4SX   map **3** T17
Telephone: (01989 86) 626
Fax: (01989 86) 611

11 acres overlooking the River Wye. Formal terraced Edwardian gardens, extensive plantings of mature trees and shrubs, water features and a sunken Florentine garden undergoing restoration. Norman church with 16th century Diptych. Specialist nursery plants and old variety roses for sale.

Location: B4224, Ross on Wye (4½ m) to Hereford (9 m).
Open: Apr 1-Oct 31 Mon-Sat 9-5 May-Oct 31 also Sun 10-5.
Admission: Adults £2.50 children £1.25 parties by apppointment.
Events/Exhibitions: Open air opera Sat June 17. Alan Price concert Fri June 16.
Fabric Shop and Menswear. Car parking. Toilets.

KENTCHURCH COURT

(Mrs JC Lucas-Scudamore)
Hereford   map **3** T17
Telephone: (01981) 240228

Fortified border manor house altered by Nash. Gateway and part of the original 14th century house still survives. Pictures and Grinling Gibbons carving. Owen Glendower's tower.

Location: Off B4347, 3 m SE of Pontrilas; 12 m Monmouth; 14 m Hereford; 14 m Abergavenny, on left bank River Monnow.
Open: May-Sept. *All visitors by appointment.*
Admission: £3, chd £1.50.
Refreshments: At Kentchurch Court by appointment.

KINNERSLEY CASTLE

(Katherina Henning)
Kinnersley   map **3** S17
Telephone: (015446) 407

Medieval Welsh border Castle, reconstructed about 1588. Little changed since then, retaining fine plasterwork and panelling, leaded glass and stone tiled roof. Yew hedges, walled garden and fine trees including probably the largest example of a Ginkgo tree in the United Kingdom. Art and other exhibitions. Still a family home, used out of season for courses and conferences. Early home of the De Kinnardsley and De le Bere families, remodelled by Roger Vaughan and later home of parliamentary General Sir Thomas Morgan.

Location: 4 m W of Weobley on A4112 (Black and White Village Trail).
Open: Dates and times of opening will be available from local tourist information offices (Hereford, Leominster, Hay-on-Wye etc) from Easter 1995 or phone enquiry (01544) 327407. Coach parties by arrangement throughout the year.
Admission: £2 children £1 OAPs/Student/UB40 £1.50 Groups £1.50 (by arrangment throughout the year).
Events/Exhibitions: Traditional French Music festival in Summer and Shakespeare outside performance.
Accommodation: Accommodation for residential groups by arrangement, retreats etc. Plant sales from organic gardens.

LANGSTONE COURT

(R.M.C. Jones Esq.)
Llangarron   HR9 6NR   map **3** T17
Telephone: (01989) 770254

Mostly late 17th century house with older parts. Interesting staircases, panelling and ceilings.

Location: Ross on Wye 5m, Llangarron 1m.
Open: May 3-Aug 3 Wed and Thurs 11-3.
Admission: Free.

LITTLE MALVERN COURT AND GARDENS

(The Trustees of the late T.M. Berington esq.)
nr Great Malvern   WR14 4JN   map **3** S18   △
Telephone: (01684) 892988

14th century Prior's Hall once attached to 12th-century Benedictine Priory, and principal rooms in Victorian addition by Hansom. Family and European paintings and furniture. Collection of 18th and 19th century needlework. Home of the Berington family by descent since the Dissolution. 10 acres of former monastic grounds. Magnificent views, lake, garden rooms, terrace. Wide variety of spring bulbs, old fashioned roses, shrubs and trees.

Location: 3 m S of Great Malvern on Upton-on-Severn Road (A4104).
Open: Apr 19-Jul 20 Wed and Thurs 2.15-5 parties by prior arrangement. Guided tours - last adm 4.30.
Admission: Prices not available at time of going to press.
Refreshments: Home made teas only available for parties by arrangement.
Unsuitable for wheelchairs.

LOWER BROCKHAMPTON   The National Trust
Bringsty   WR6 5UH   map **3** S18
Telephone: (01885) 488099

Small half-timbered manor house c. 1400 with unusual detached 15th century gatehouse and ruins of 12th century chapel.

Location: 2 m E of Bromyard N of A44 Bromyard/Worcester Road. Hall reached by narrow road through 1½ m woods and farmland.
Open: Medieval Hall and Parlour only Apr to end of Sept Wed to Sun & Bank Hol Mons 10-5. *Closed* Good Fri. Oct Wed to Sun 10-4.
Admission: £1.60 Children 80p Family ticket £4.40. Parties by prior written arrangement only.
No dogs. Wheelchair access.

MOCCAS COURT
(Trustees of the Baunton Trust)
Moccas   HR2 9LH   map **3** S17
Telephone: (01981) 500381

'Built by Anthony Keck in 1775 overlooking the River Wye, decoration by Robert Adam including the round room and oval stair. Scene of famous 17th century romance and destination of epic night ride from London. Set in 'Capability' Brown parkland with an attractive walk to The Scar Rapids.'

Location: 10 m E of Hay on Wye and 13 m W of Hereford on the River Wye. 1 m off B4352.
Station(s): Hereford.
Open: House and Gardens Apr-Sept Thurs 2-6.
Admission: £1.95.
Refreshments: Food and drink available at the Red Lion Hotel, Bredwardine, by pre-booking only.
Picnics in garden allowed.

SPETCHLEY PARK
(Mr & Mrs R J Berkeley)
Worcester   WR5 1RS   map **3** S18
Telephone: (01905) 345213/345224

This lovely 30 acre garden is a plantsman's delight, with a large collection of trees, shrubs and plants, many of which are rare or unusual. There is colour and interest throughout the months that the garden is open to visitors. The park contains red and fallow deer.

Location: 3 m E of Worcester on Stratford-upon-Avon Road (A422).
Open: Gardens Apr 1-Sept 30 Tues Wed Thurs Fri 11-5 Sun 2-5 Bank Hol Mons 11-5 closed other Mons and all Sats.
Admission: Adults £2.20 children £1.10 reduced rates for pre-booked parties of 25 or more.
Refreshments: Tea in the garden.
Regret no dogs. House not open.

THE WEIR   The National Trust
Swainshill, nr Hereford   map **3** S17

Delightful riverside garden, particularly spectacular in early spring. Fine views of the river Wye and Black Mountains.

Location: 5 m W of Hereford on A438.
Open: Feb 15-end Oct Wed-Sun & Bank Hol Mon 11-6. (incl Good Fri).
Admission: £1.50. No reductions for parties.
Unsuitable for coaches. No dogs. Unsuitable for wheelchairs or visually handicapped. No WCs.

WITLEY COURT
map **14** S18
Telephone: (01299) 896636

ENGLISH HERITAGE

This is one of the most spectacular country house ruins. Cast in the Victorian Italian style of the 1860s, it is on a huge scale, with a glorious facade. Looking from the house to the gardens, a view enjoyed by Edward VII, who as Prince of Wales often stayed at the house, the scene is dominated by the immense Perseus Fountain.

Location: 10 m NW of Worcester on the A443.
Open: Apr 1-Sept 30 10-6 daily Oct 1-31 10-4 daily Nov 1-Mar 31 Wed-Sun 10-4.
Admission: Adults £1.50 concessions £1.10 children 80p.

WORCESTER CATHEDRAL

(The Dean and Chapter of Worcester)
Worcester map **3** S18 △ &
Telephone: (01905) 28854

Beside the River Severn opposite the Malvern Hills. Built between 1084 and 1375. Norman Crypt and Chapter House. Early English Quire, Perpendicular Tower. Monastic buildings include refectory (now College Hall and open on request during August), cloisters, remains of guesten hall and dormitories. Tombs of King John and Prince Arthur. Cloister herb garden, Elgar memorial window, misericords. Edgar Tower gatehouse.

Location: Centre of Worcester. Main roads Oxford and Stratford to Wales. 3 m junction 7 (M5).
Open: Every day 7.30-6. Choral Evensong daily (except Thurs and school hols).
Admission: No admission charge but donations of £2 accepted. Charges for guided tours £2 adults £1 senior citizens £1 children. Visits Officer (01905) 28854.
Refreshments: Light refreshment in Cloister Tea-Room. Special arrangements made for parties.
Events/Exhibitions: St Wolfstan's Millenium Exhibition 1995 in Chapter House.
No cathedral car parking - City centre parking. Disabled visitors most welcome - some steps, but help and wheelchair available. Information Desk, shop and toilets.

HERTFORDSHIRE

ASHRIDGE

(Governors of Ashridge Management College)
Berkhamsted **HP4 1NS** map **12** T21
Telephone: (01442) 843491

150 acres of both Parkland and intimate smaller gardens. The landscape influenced by Humphrey Repton. Mature trees combined with unique features e.g. Beech Houses with Windows and doors, in a Pink and Grey Garden, Grotto - Ferns planted between Herts Pudding Stone.

Location: 3½ m N of Berkhamsted (A4251), 1 m S of Little Gaddesden.
Open: Gardens open Apr-Oct Sat & Sun 2-6.
Admission: Gardens adults £2 children/OAPs £1.
The House is not open to the public.

CAPEL MANOR

(Capel Manor Charitable Corporation)
nr Enfield **EN1 4RQ** map **12** T22 &
Telephone: 0181-366 4442
Fax: (01992) 717544

Capel Manor is Greater London's only specialist College of Horticulture and Countryside studies with the 30 acres of richly planted and diverse gardens, which surround the Georgian manor, fully open to the public. A comprehensive self-guided tour starts from the new visitor's centre with information boards and free leaflets to help visitors get the most from their visit at all times of the year. There are many 'themed' areas within the garden including for example, historical, modern, rock, and water, a sensory and disabled persons garden, an Italianate maze and Japanese garden. Gardening Which? manage a large site with demonstrations and model gardens and The National Gardening Centre includes more exhibits of gardens and associated products. A small range of rare breeds of farm animals are being introduced around the old stable buildings. Unfortunately, the house is only open for use by Capel Manor students.

Location: 3 mins from M25 junction M25/A10 S and turn right at traffic lights. Nearest station Turkey Street/Liverpool Street line. (Not Sun)
Open: Gardens daily 10-5.30. (Check for winter times)
Admission: Normal rates - adults £3 concessions £2 children £1.50. Please check for dates and charges at special shows. Special rates for coaches, garden tours. All parking free.
Refreshments: Available.
Further details from Capel Manor, Bullsmoor Lane, Enfield, Middlesex EN1 4RQ Tel 0181-366 4442.

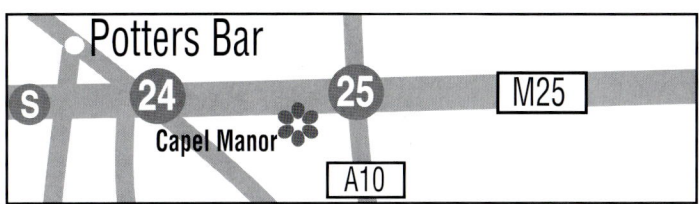

THE GARDENS OF THE ROSE

(Royal National Rose Society)
Chiswell Green, St Albans   AL2 3NR   map **12** T22   &
Telephone: (01727) 850461

The Showgrounds of the R.N.R.S. containing some 30,000 roses of over 1,650 different varieties and many companion plants.

Location: Off B4630 (formerly A412) St Albans/Watford Road.
Station(s): St Alban's City (2 m).
Open: Jun 10-Oct 15 Mon-Sat 9-5 Sun & Bank Hols 10-6.
Admission: £4. Discount for pensioners and disabled. Accompanied children free.
Refreshments: Licensed cafeteria.
Facilities for the disabled.

GORHAMBURY

(The Earl of Verulam)
St Albans   AL3 6AH   map **12** T22   △
Telephone: (01727) 854051
Fax: (01727) 843675

Mansion built 1777-84 in classical style by Sir Robert Taylor. 16th century enamelled glass and historic portraits.

Location: 2 m W of St Albans. Entrance off A4147 at St. Michael's by Roman Theatre.
Station(s): St. Albans.
Open: May-Sept Thurs 2-5. Gardens open with the house.
Admission: Adults £4 children £2.50 OAPs £2. Guided tours only. Parties by prior arrangement Thurs £3.50 other days £5.

HATFIELD HOUSE

(The Marquess of Salisbury)
Hatfield   map **12** T22   △
Telephone: (01707) 262823

This celebrated Jacobean house, which stands in its own great park, was built between 1607 and 1611 by Robert Cecil, 1st Earl of Salisbury and Prime Minister to King James I. It has been the family home of the Cecils ever since. The Staterooms are rich in world-famous paintings, fine furniture, rare tapestries and historic armour. The beautiful stained glass in the chapel is original. Within the delightful gardens stands the surviving wing of the Royal Palace of Hatfield (1497) where

Elizabeth I spent much of her girlhood and held her first Council of State in November 1558. She appointed William Cecil, Lord Burghley as her Chief Minister. Some of her relics can be seen in the house. 25 minutes by regular fast train service from Kings Cross to Hatfield (station faces Park gates). The Moorgate to Hatfield electric train service has direct Underground links; Victoria Line at Highbury, Circle Line at Moorgate, Piccadilly Line at Finsbury Park. Hatfield House Lodge is opposite the station. Further particulars from The Curator, Hatfield House.

Location: In Hatfield, Junction 4 A1(M), 7 m M25.
Station(s): Hatfield (opposite house).
Open: Mar 25-Oct 8 1995. Hatfield House open daily except Mon and Good Fri weekdays from 12 guided tours only (last tour 4). Sun 1.30-5 no guided tours - guides in each room. Also open on Easter, May Day, Spring and Aug Bank Hol Mon 11-5 no guided tours - guides in each room. Park 10.30-8 daily except Good Fri West Gardens 11-6 daily except Good Fri East Gardens 2-5 Mon only (except Bank Hol Mons). Guided Tour (Tues-Sat) takes about 1 hour. LIVING CRAFTS EXHIBITION: May 11-14 10-6; A FESTIVAL OF GARDENING: June 24-25 10-6 10-5.
Admission: Reductions for pre-booked parties of 20 or more. Coach and car park free.
Refreshments: Available in adjacent restaurant - coffee shop. ELIZABETHAN BANQUETING IN THE OLD PALACE THROUGHOUT THE YEAR. Telephone: (01707) 262823 (Curator); Banqueting and Restaurant (01707) 262055/262030. FAX: (01707) 275719.
Dogs not admitted to House or garden.

KNEBWORTH

(The Lord Cobbold)
Knebworth House   map **5** T22
Telephone: (01438) 812661
Fax: (01438) 811908

Home of the Lytton family since 1490. The original Tudor Manor House was transformed 150 years ago with spectacular High Gothic decoration by Victorian novelist and statesman Sir Edward Bulwer-Lytton. There are many beautiful rooms, important portraits and furniture, and a fine collection of manuscripts and letters associated with many famous visitors to the house. Charles Dickens acted here in private theatricals, and Winston Churchill painted at his easel in the superb Jacobean Banqueting Hall. It was the home of Constance Lytton, the suffragette, and Robert Lytton, Viceroy of India. Lord Lytton's Viceroyalty and the great Delhi Durbar of 1877 are commemorated in a fascinating exhibition and audio-visual display. The formal gardens by Sir Edwin Lutyens include a unique pattern Jekyll herb garden - and new for 1995, the reinstated maze. The house stands in a 250 acre country park with herds of Red and Sika deer. For children, hours of pleasure in Fort Knebworth, a large adventure playground with Miniature Railway.

Location: Knebworth 28 m N of central London. Own direct access off the A1 (M) junction 7 (Stevenage South A602) 12 m N of M25.
Station(s): Stevenage (2 m).
Open: PARK AND FORT KNEBWORTH daily Apr 1 and 2 Apr 8-23 inclusive and May 27-Sept 4 inclusive. Plus weekends and Bank Hols from Apr 29-May 21 and weekends only from

Sept 9-Oct 1. (Closed June 30-July 3 inclusive) HOUSE AND GARDENS Open as above except closed Mons. Open Bank Hol Mons. HOURS Park and Fort Knebworth 11-5.30. House and Gardens 12-5.
Admission: HOUSE, GARDENS, PARK, FORT KNEBWORTH £4.50 (not inc. miniature railway) children/sen cits £4. PARK & FORT KNEBWORTH ONLY £3 family ticket (four persons) £10 (no reductions for children/sen cits) Reductions for prebooked parties of 20 or more (Apr 1-Oct 1). Opening times and prices subject to special events. Coach and car park free.
Refreshments: Licensed cafeteria in 16th Century Tithe Barns close to House & Gardens (Tel:(01438) 813825). Oakwood Restaurant in hotel at Park entrance. (Tel:(01438) 742299). Dogs admitted to Park only on leads. Telephone above number for further details.

SCOTT'S GROTTO

(East Hertfordhire District Council)
Ware   SG12 9SQ   map **12** T23
Telephone: (01920) 464131/(01992) 584322

Grotto, summerhouse and garden built 1760-73 by Quaker poet, John Scott. Described by English Heritage as 'one of the finest grottos in England.' Now extensively restored by The Ware Society.

Location: Scott's Road, Ware (off A119 Hertford Road).
Station(s): Ware/Liverpool Street line.
Open: New extended opening times. Every Sat beginning of Apr-Sept and Easter, Spring and Summer Bank Hol Mons 2-4.30.
Admission: Free but donation of £1 requested.
Please park in Amwell End car park by level crossing (300 yds away) and walk up Scott's Road. Advisable to wear flat shoes and bring a torch. Parties by prior arrangement.

WIMPOLE HOME FARM   🌿 The National Trust

Arrington   SG8 0B6   map **5** S22
Telephone: (01223) 207257
Fax: (01223) 207838

An historic farm, faithfully restored by the National Trust, set in 350 acres of beautiful parkland. Approved Rare Breeds Centre. Children's corner. Agricultural museum. Adventure playground. Shop.

Location: 8 m S of Cambridge; signposted off A603 at New Wimpole.
Station(s): Shepreth (5 m); Royston (7 m).
Open: Mar 11-Nov 5 Tues Wed Thurs Sat Sun & Bank Hol Mon 10.30-5. Also open Fri June July Aug. 6 Nov-4 Mar 1996 Sat & Sun 11-4. Closed Christmas.
Admission: £3.75 NT members £1.80 children over 3 £2 parties (pre-booked) £2.50. Joint ticket for Hall and Farm £6.
Refreshments: Lunches & teas at Wimpole Hall. Snacks at Home Farm.
Events/Exhibitions: Lambing weekends 11/12 & 18/19 March 1995. Rare Breeds show and sale 17/18 June. Heavy Horse Show 3 Sept.

HUMBERSIDE

BURNBY HALL GARDENS

(Stewart's Burnby Hall Gardens & Museum Trust)
Pocklington, The Balk   YO4 2QF   map **4** P21   ♿
Telephone: (01759 30) 2068

Large gardens with 2 lakes. Finest display of hardy water lilies in Europe - 80 varieties, **designated National Collection.** Museum housing Stewart Collection - sporting trophies, ethnic material. Picnic area, rose garden. Sales kiosk. Large variety of fish in lakes.

Location: 13 m E of York on A1079.
Open: Sat Apr 8-Sun Oct 8 1995 daily 10-6.
Admission: Adults £2 party rate (over 20) £1.30 children (under 5) free (5-16) 50p OAPs £1.50 party rate (over 20) £1.30.
Refreshments: Teas in the garden.
Free coach and car park. Disabled facilities.

BURTON AGNES HALL

(Preservation Trust Ltd)
nr Bridlington   YO25 0ND   map **4** P22
Telephone: (01262) 490324
Fax: (01262) 490513

The Hall is a magnificent example of late Elizabethan architecture - still lived in by descendants of the family who built it in 1598. There are wonderful carvings, lovely furniture and fine collection of modern French and English paintings of the Impressionist Schools - Renoir, Pissaro, Corot, Utrillo, Gauguin, Augustus John, etc. The recently redeveloped walled garden contains a potager, maze, herbaceous borders, campanula collection, jungle garden and giant games set in coloured gardens. Also woodland gardens and walk, children's corner, Norman manor house, donkey wheel and gift shop.

Location: In village of Burton Agnes, 6 m SW of Bridlington on Driffield/Bridlington Road (A166).
Open: Apr 1-Oct 31 daily 11-5.
Admission: Adults £3.50 OAPs £3 children £2. Group rates on application. Garden only adults £1.80 OAPs £1.50 children 80p. *The management reserves the right to close the house or part thereof without prior notice; adm charges will be adjusted on such days.*
Refreshments: Licensed cafeteria. Teas, light lunches & refreshments.

BURTON CONSTABLE

(Burton Constable Foundation)
nr Hull   HU11 4LN   map **4** P22
Telephone: (01964) 562400
Fax: (01964) 563229

Magnificent Elizabethan House, built c 1570. Outstanding collection of furniture, pictures, eighteenth century scientific instruments and firearms. Eighteenth century additions by James Wyatt, Timothy Lightoler and others. Unusual chapel converted from billiard room and an outstanding Chinese room. Parkland by 'Capability' Brown.

Location: At Burton Constable; 1½ m N of Sproatley; 7½ m NE of Hull (A165); 13 m SE of Beverley (A1035).
Open: Easter Sun-Sept 30 Sun-Thurs incl. and Sat in July-Aug. Grounds and coffee shop open 12 noon. Hall 1-4.15 (last admission).
Admission: Parties anytime by arrangement. Further details write to: the Director, Burton Constable Hall, Nr. Hull HU11 4LN or Tel: (01964) 562400.
Refreshments: Coffee shop.

THE CHARTERHOUSE

(Charterhouse Trustees)
Hull   map **4** P22
Telephone: (01482) 320026

Charterhouse, was founded in 1384 by Michael de la Pole, Earl of Suffolk.

Open: Chapel & Gardens open daily during July and on Good Friday Easter Day Easter Mon Spring and Summer Bank Holidays 10-8.

ELSHAM HALL COUNTRY AND WILDLIFE PARK AND ELSHAM HALL BARN THEATRE

(Capt J Elwes and Robert Elwes)
Brigg   DN20 0QZ   map **4** P22   △ & Ⓔ Ⓢ
Telephone: (01652) 688698
Fax: (01652) 688738

Beautiful lakes and gardens; Miniature zoo; Giant Carp; Falconry Centre; Wild Butterfly walkway; Adventure playground; Garden and Craft Centre; Granary Tea-rooms; Animal farm; Art Gallery; Caravan site; Ten National Awards. Also excellent New Theatre and Conference Facility.

Location: Near Brigg. M180 Jct 5.
Station(s): Elsham or Barnetby.
Open: Times and Prices on application.
Refreshments: Granary Tea-rooms, Ice Cream Parlour, Restaurant.

MAISTER HOUSE The National Trust

Hull   map **4** P22
Telephone: (01482) 324114

Rebuilt 1744 with a superb staircase-hall designed in the Palladian manner.

Location: 160 High Street, Hull.
Station(s): Hull (¾ m).
Open: Staircase and entrance hall only. All the year Mon-Fri 10-4. *Closed Bank Hols.*
Admission: By Guide book 80p.
No dogs. Unsuitable for wheelchairs and parties.

SEWERBY HALL AND GARDENS

(Borough of East Yorkshire)
Bridlington   map **7** O22

Built 1714-20 by John Greame with additions 1808. Sewerby Hall occupies a dramatic setting overlooking Bridlington Bay. The 50 acres of gardens of great beauty and botanical interest include fine old English walled garden and small zoo and aviary. There is also an art gallery and a museum which includes the Amy Johnson Trophy Room dedicated to the pioneer woman aviator.

Location: In Bridlington on the cliffs, 2 m NE from centre of town.
Station(s): Bridlington (2½ m); Bempton (2 m).
Open: Park open all year daily 9-dusk. Art Gallery open March 4-May 2 October 2-December 31 Saturday to Tuesday 11-4. May 6-October 1 10-6 daily.
Admission: From May-Sept (New charges to be agreed).
Refreshments: Traditional tea-room in the Grounds.
Childrens play area.

SLEDMERE HOUSE

(Sir Tatton Sykes, Bart)
Driffield   YO25 0XG   map **7** P21
Telephone: (01377) 236637

A Georgian house begun in 1751 with important additions attributed to Samuel Wyatt in conjunction with Sir Christopher Sykes, containing superb library 100ft long. The entire building was burnt to the ground in 1911 and splendidly restored with an Edwardian feeling for space by York architect Walter Brierley during the first world war. The latter copied Joseph Rose's fine ceilings and inserted a magnificent Turkish room. The House contains much of its original furniture and paintings. An unusual feature is the great organ, which is played daily 2-4. Capability Brown Park. 18th century walled rose garden. Main garden under reconstruction.

Location: 24 m E of York on main York/Bridlington Road; 8 m NW of Driffield at junction of B1251 & B1253.
Open: Apr 14-Sun Oct 1 daily 12-4.30. Closed Mon & Fri but open on Bank Hols.
Admission: £3.25 OAPs £2.75 Children £2. Special rates for booked parties. Gardens and grounds only £1.50 children £1. Private parties arranged by appointment on Wed evenings. Free car and coach parks.
Refreshments: Excellent self service licensed restaurant, Driffield (0377) 236637.
Illustrated brochure from The House Secretary, Sledmere House, Driffield, East Yorkshire.

WILBERFORCE HOUSE
(Hull City Council)
Hull map **4** P22 Ⓢ
Telephone: (01482) 593902
Fax: (01482) 593710

17th century Merchant's house, and adjoining houses, now a local history museum with period furniture. Hull silver, costume, dolls, toys and adjoining chemists' shop. New displays were opened in 1983 to commemorate the 150th Anniversary of the Death of William Wilberforce, the slave emancipator, born in the house in 1759. Secluded gardens.

Location: 25 High Street, Hull.
Station(s): Hull.
Open: All the year weekdays 10-5 Sun 1.30-4.30 closed Good Friday Christmas Day Boxing Day & New Year's Day.
Admission: Free.

ISLE OF WIGHT

BARTON MANOR GARDENS AND VINEYARDS
East Cowes, Isle of Wight PO32 6LB   map **3** V20   &
Telephone: (01983) 292835
Fax: (01983) 293923

Whilst serious state affairs were being conducted at Osborne House - affairs of the heart were being enjoyed at Barton Manor. With much of the original gardens laid out by Edward VII and the farm buildings by Prince Albert, these award winning grounds, once enjoyed and owned by Queen Victoria, are accompanied by many interesting features including the island's largest rose hedge maze, the Dionysus Carving, the National Plant Collections and the vineyard and winery of our internationally acclaimed wines.

Location: Next to Osborne House on the East Cowes Road.
Station(s): Bus numbers 4 & 5.

Open: Apr 1-2nd Sun in Oct 10.30-5.30 daily.
Admission: The Manor is not open to the public - only the grounds and farm buildings. Adults £3.50 OAPs £3 children (accompanied) free. Groups of 15+ £3 per head.
Refreshments: Cafe and tea-rooms serving light refreshments.
Events/Exhibitions: The Exhibition of Banks Florilegium, The memorabilia of music, film and theatre.
Free car and coach parking. Admission includes 2 free wine tastings, souvenir tasting glass and guide leaflet.

CARISBROOKE CASTLE

map **3** V20
Telephone: (01983) 522107

Here are seven acres of castle and earthworks to explore. The oldest parts of the castle are 12th century, but the great mound - 71 steps high - bore a wooden castle before that, and there are fragments of Roman wall at its base. Fortified against the French, then the Spaniards, the castle is best known as the prison of Charles I in 1647/8. A bold escape plan failed when the King became wedged between the bars of the great chamber window. The castle contains the island's museum. A personal stereo guided tour is available.

Location: 1¼ m (2 km) south west of Newport.
Open: Apr 1-Sept30 10-6 daily Oct 1-Mar 31 daily 10-4.
Admission: Adults £3.50 concessions £2.60 children £1.80.

THE NEEDLES OLD BATTERY   The National Trust
West Highdown, Totland Bay   map **3** V19
Telephone: (01983) 754772

A former Palmerstonian fort built in 1862, 77m above sea level; 60m tunnel to spectacular view of the Needles. Exhibition on history of the Needles Headland.

Location: At Needles, Headland. W of Freshwater Bay and Alum Bay.
Open: Mar 30-2 Nov Sun-Thurs (but open Easter week-end and daily in July & Aug) 10.30-5 last admission 4.30. Conducted school and special visits Mar 27-end Oct (but not Aug) by written appointment.
Admission: £2.40 Children half-price. No reductions for parties.
Refreshments: Tea-room open same days as Battery 11-4.30.

NEWTOWN OLD TOWN HALL   The National Trust
Newtown   map **3** V20

18th century building of brick and stone. One of the buildings surviving from the island's former ancient borough.

Location: In Newtown, midway between Newport and Yarmouth.
Open: 27 Mar-30 Oct Mon Wed & Sun 2-5 (also open Good Fri Easter Sat and Tues and Thurs in July and Aug) last adm 4.45. Closed Oct-end March.
Admission: £1.10 Children half-price. No reduction for parties.
No dogs. Unsuitable for wheelchairs.

NUNWELL HOUSE AND GARDENS
(Colonel & Mrs J A Aylmer)
Brading   map **3** V20
Telephone: (01983) 407240

Nunwell with its historic connections with King Charles I is set in beautiful gardens and parkland with channel views. A finely furnished home with Jacobean and Georgian wings. Home Guard museum and family military collection.

Location: 1 m from Brading, turning off A3055; 3 m S of Ryde.
Station(s): Brading.
Open: House and Gardens July 2-Sept 27 Sun 1-5 Mon-Wed 10-5 closed Thurs Fri and Sat.
Admission: Adults £2.80 OAPs £2.30 accompanied children 60p school parties £1.40.
Refreshments: Large parties may book catering in advance. Picnic areas.
Parties welcome at all times if booked. No dogs.

OSBORNE HOUSE

East Cowes   map **3** V20
Telephone: (01983) 200022

This was Queen Victoria's seaside residence built at her own expense, in 1845. The Prince Consort played a prominent part in the design of the house, it was his version of an Italian villa, and the work was carried out by Thomas Cubitt, the famous London builder. The Queen died here in 1901 and her private apartments have been preserved more or less unaltered. Crowded with furniture and bric-a-brac they epitomise the style we call 'Victorian'. Also see the Queen's bathing machine. There is a carriage drawn by horse running from House to the Swiss Cottage Gardens and Museum. This is included in the adm price, see below for details.

Location: 1 m SE of East Cowes.
Station(s): Ferry terminal East Cowes (1 m).
Open: Apr 1-Sept 30 10-6 daily Oct 1-Oct 31 10-5 daily. Last admission to grounds at 4.30.
Admission: House and Grounds adults £5.80 concessions £4.40 children £2.90. Grounds only adults £3 concessions £2.30 children £1.50.

KENT

BELMONT

(Harris (Belmont) Charity)
nr Faversham   ME13 0HH   map **13** U24   △ &
Telephone: (01795) 890202

Belmont was built in the late 18th century to the design of Samuel Wyatt, in a splendid elevated position with commanding views over the attractive and unspoilt countryside. It has been the seat of the Harris family since it was acquired in 1801 by General George Harris, the victor of Seringapatam. The Mansion remains in its original state and contains interesting mementos of the family's connections with India and the finest collection of clocks in any English country house open to the public.

Location: 4 m SSW of Faversham. 1½ m W of A251 follow brown signs from Badlesmere.
Station(s): Faversham.
Open: Easter Sun-end Sept Sat Sun and Bank Hol Mons guided tours 2-5 last adm 4.30. Telephone (01795) 890202 to confirm availability. Groups (minimum 10) by prior arrangement only Tues and Thurs.
Admission: Mansion, Grounds and Clock Museum £4 children £2.50.
Refreshments: Teas in the Stables Tea-room Sat, Sun and Bank Hol Mons. Pre-booked parties by arrangement.
Car parking. Shop.

BLACK CHARLES

(Mr & Mrs Hugh Gamon)
nr Sevenoaks   map **13** U23
Telephone: (01732) 833036

Charming 14th century home of John de Blakecherl and his family. A hall house with beautiful panelling, fireplaces and many other interesting features.

Location: 3 m S of Sevenoaks off A21; 1 m E in the village of Underriver.
Open: Open to groups by appointment (minimum of 10).

BOUGHTON MONCHELSEA PLACE

(Charles W. Gooch)
nr Maidstone   **ME17 4BU**   map **13** U24   △
Telephone: (01622) 743120

Battlemented Elizabethan Manor of Kentish ragstone built in 1567, with interesting Regency alterations. Dramatically situated with breathtaking view over its own landscaped park, in which fallow deer have roamed for at least 300 years, and beyond, to the whole Weald of Kent. The beautiful interior is still that of an intimate and inhabited home to which successive generations have added new treasures. Edwardian ladies bedroom and nursery, dress display and early farm implements. Manor records. Walled flower gardens with interesting plants. Tudor kitchen tearoom. House and Grounds are available for private hire all year. Corporate Days, wedding receptions, private dining, small meetings, Conference and Exhibitions. Clay Shooting, Quad Biking, Pilots etc. Contact (01622) 743120.

Location: On B2163. In village of Boughton Monchelsea 5 m S of Maidstone. Junction 8 off M20. Ten minutes from Leeds Castle.
Open: Good Fri-early Oct Sun & Bank Hols (also Wed during June July & Aug) 2-6.
Admission: House and Grounds adults £3.75 children (under 14) £2.50 students/OAPs/disabled £3. Grounds Only adults £2.75 children (under 14) £1.50 students/OAPs/disabled £2.50. Groups by prior arrangement (20 or more) adults £3.25 children (under 14) £2.25 students/OAPs/disabled £3.25 Grounds only adults £2.25 children (under 14) students/OAPs/disabled £2.25.
Refreshments: Afternoon Teas always available. Lunch or supper for groups can be arranged.
St. Peter's Church, claiming one of the oldest Lych Gates in the country, and is situated next door to the house. Guide Book for church available in Gift Shop at house.

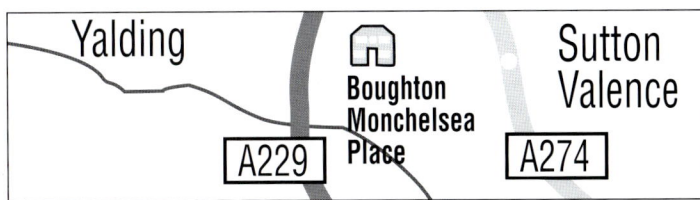

CHARTWELL   The National Trust

Westerham   map **13** U23   &
Telephone: (01732) 866368

The home for many years of Sir Winston Churchill.

Location: 2 m S of Westerham off B2026.
Open: House & garden 1 Apr-end Oct Tue Wed Thur Sat Sun & Bank Hol Mon 11-5.30 (last admission one hr before close). House only Mar & Nov Sat Sun and Wed 11-4.30. (last adm 30 minutes before closing). Closed Good Fri and Tues following Bank Hol.
Admission: House & Garden £4.50 Children £2.25 Garden only £2 Chd £1. House only £2.50 Children £1.25 Studio 50p extra (Children no reduction). Pre-booked parties by arrangement.
Refreshments: Restaurant open from Apr-end Oct 10.30-5 (Mar & Nov 10.30-4) on days when house is open. Self-service, licensed (no spirits).
Events/Exhibitions: Exhibition on Churchill's life during the years he lived at Chartwell. 1940s dance 10th June.
Car park. Lavatory for disabled. Small lift to first floor. Shop.

CHIDDINGSTONE CASTLE
(Trustees of the Denys Eyre Bower Bequest)
nr Edenbridge   TN8 7AD   map **13** U23   ♿ ®
Telephone: (01892) 870347

The dream-child of two romantics. Squire Henry Streatfeild, who c.1805 had his family seat transformed into a fantasy castle, and whose money ran out; and Denys Bower, eccentric and inspired art collector, who never had any money at all. Entranced with the (by then) semi-derelict Castle, he made it his home in 1955. He died in 1977 leaving the Castle and its fascinating contents to the Nation. Untouched by commercialism, lovingly restored and cherished, it remains a home, with its fine furnishings, personal collections of Japanese lacquer and swords, Egyptian antiquities, Stuart and Jacobite relics. Landscaped grounds in course of restoration.

Location: In Chiddingstone village, off the B2027 at Bough Beech about 10 m Sevenoaks, Tonbridge and Tunbridge Wells.
Station(s): Penshurst 2½ miles, Edenbridge 4 miles.
Open: Apr-Oct. Apr May and Oct open Easter holiday public holidays Wed and Sun only June-Sept Tues-Sun and public holidays. Open all year for booked parties and school educational tours (min 20). Fishing in lake in season. Weekdays 2-5.30 Sun and public holidays 11.30-5.30 last admission 5.
Admission: Adults £3.50 children 5-15 (with adult) £1.50 under 5 free. Parties of 20 or more (normal hours) £3 (Special fee at other times). Fishing dawn till dusk £8 one onlooker per fisherman £3.50.
Refreshments: Tea-room serves tea and cakes. Cream teas and light meals for parties by arrangment. Picnics allowed adjacent carpark, not in grounds.
Events/Exhibitions: Festival May 6-8; open air theatre early July; Xmas Fair Sun Dec 3.
Conferences: Gracious functions wing (antique furnishings) based on coachyard for small conferences and special occasions (max 50) with catering. Marquee for larger events and weddings. Details from custodian.
The Trustees reserve the right to close the Castle for special functions.

Sir Joshua Reynolds
Portrait painter (1723-1792)
First President of the Royal Academy, knighted in 1769

His work can be seen in the following properties included in Historic Houses Castles and Gardens:-

Arundel Castle	*Knole*
Dalmeny House (Roseberry Collection of	*Petworth House*
Political Portraits)	*Rockingham Castle*
Elton Hall	*Saltram*
Goodwood House	*Shalom Hall*
Ickworth House, Park & Garden	*Wallington House*
Kenwood, The Iveagh Bequest	*Weston Park*

COBHAM HALL
(Westwood Educational Trust Ltd)
Cobham, nr. Gravesend DA12 3BL   map **13** U23 △
Telephone: (01474) 824319/823371
Fax: (01474) 822995

Cobham Hall is an outstandingly beautiful, red brick mansion in Elizabethan, Jacobean, Carolian and 18th century styles. This former home of the Earls of Darnley is set in 150 acres of parkland. The Gardens, landscaped for the 4th Earl of Darnley by Humphry Repton, are gradually being restored by the Cobham Hall Heritage Trust. Extensive tree planting and clearing have taken place since the hurricanes of the 1980's. The Gothic Dairy and some of the classical garden buildings are being renovated. Charles Dickens used to walk through the grounds from his house in Higham to the Leather Bottle Pub in Cobham Village. Visitors to the house should not miss the many fine 17th century marble fireplaces and the 18th century historic Snetzler organ in the magnificent Gilt Hall. The grounds yield many delights for the lover of nature, especially in Spring, when the gardens and woods are resplendent with displays of Spring bulbs including many rarities. Cobham Hall is now an independent, international boarding and day school for girls aged 11-18 years.

Location: Cobham Hall is adjacent to the A2/M2 between Gravesend and Rochester, 8 miles from Junction 2 on the M25. 27 miles from London.
Station(s): Meopham and Sole Street via London Victoria. Gravesend via London Charing Cross and Waterloo.
Open: Apr most Weds Thurs Suns and Easter Weekend, June 1 and 2, July most Weds Thurs and Suns Aug most Weds Thurs and Suns. Please telephone (01474) 823371 to check opening dates. 2-5 each day. All tours guided.
Admission: Adults £2.50 OAPs and children £2.
Refreshments: Tea, coffee.Lunches and dinner for parties by arrangement.
Events/Exhibitions: Apr 9 National Gardens Scheme Day (House open); Apr 14, 15, 16 and 17 The Medway Craft Fair (House open); May 27 and 28 Kent Festival of Transport; June 1 and 2 Dickens Festival Open House; July 8 and 9 The Game and Countryman Fair; Aug 6 National Gardens Scheme Day; Oct 21 and 22 The Medway Craft Fair (House open).
Accommodation: The House, grounds, accomodation (250 beds) and sports facilities are available for private hire, wedding receptions, business conferences, residential and non-residential courses and film and photographic location.
Conferences: Excellent in-house catering team for private and corporate events (cap. 200). Historical guided tours of the house. Pre-booked guided tours of the garden. Party bookings and coach parties welcomed. Souvenir shop. Ample free parking. For further information contact The Development Director, Sue Anderson, Cobham Hall, Cobham, Kent DA12 3BL. Tel: (01474) 824319. (24hr ansaphone) or (01474) 823371. The Westwood Educational Trust Limited exits to provide high quality education for girls aged 11-18 years at Cobham Hall. Registered Charity No. 313650.

DEAL CASTLE

map **13** U25
Telephone: (01304) 372762

When Henry VIII divorced Catherine of Aragon he defied the Pope and broke with Catholic Europe. Deal and Walmer were built under the threat of a 'crusade' against Henry - an invasion which never came. Deal contains an exhibition on the coastal defences of Henry VIII. At Walmer the atmosphere is country house rather than martial, for this has long been the official residence of the Lords Warden of the Cinque Ports. One of the best remembered is the Duke of Wellington (the original 'Wellington boot' may be seen here), and one of the best loved, Queen Elizabeth the Queen Mother.

Location: Deal Castle is near the town centre.
Open: Apr 1-Sept 30 10-6 daily Oct 1-31 10-4 daily Nov 1-Mar 31 Wed-Sun 10-4.
Admission: Adults £2.50 concessions £1.90 children £1.30.

DODDINGTON PLACE GARDENS
(Mr Richard and The Hon. Mrs Oldfield)
Doddington   ME9 0BB   map **13** U25
Telephone: (01795) 886101

Landscaped gardens in the grounds of a Victorian country house (not open)with good views over surrounding parkland and countryside. Edwardian rock garden and formal garden, rhododendrons and azaleas in a woodland setting, fine trees and yew hedges.

Location: 4 m from A2 and A20. 5 m from Faversham. 6 m from Sittingbourne. 12 m from Canterbury.
Open: 11-6 every Wed and Bank Holiday Mon Easter-end Sept, also Sun in May only 11-6 (In aid of the National Gardens Scheme Sun 7, 14, 21 May) groups also on other days by prior arrangement.
Admission: Adults £2 children 25p group rate £1.50 coaches by prior arrangement only.
Refreshments: Restaurant serving morning coffee, lunches, afternoon teas. Present shop.

DOVER CASTLE
Dover   map **13** U25
Telephone: (01304) 201628

Castle Hill dominates the shortest passage between Britain and the Continent, and has been the scene of military activity from the Iron Age to the present day. Here is extensive proof from every age of man's ingenuity in devising ways to repel invaders. Dover Castle had its narrowest escape in 1216 when in an heroic siege it just managed to hold out against the French. There is much to see, including the Roman lighthouse (now the bell tower of a fine Saxon church) and the great keep itself and a spectacular exhibition 'All the Queen's Men'. The secret war tunnels of the castle are now open to the public. The evacuation of the troops from Dunkirk was planned by Vice-Admiral Ramsay from this once secret base. Entry is by guided tours only.

Location: East side of Dover.
Open: Apr 1-Sept 30 10-6 daily Oct 1-Mar 31 daily 10-4. Last tours begin at 5pm (summer) and 3pm (winter).
Admission: Adults £5.50 concessions £4.10 children £2.80.
Refreshments: In the Keep Yard.

EMMETTS GARDEN   The National Trust
nr Brasted   map **13** U23
Telephone: (01732) 750367 or 750429

Hillside shrub garden 18 acres open to the public. Lovely spring and autumn colours, rock garden, formal garden and roses.

Location: 1½ m S of A25 on Sundridge/Ide Hill Road.
Open: Garden only Mar weekends only Apr-end Oct Wed-Sun Good Fri Bank Hol Mon 1-6. Last adm 5. Pre-booked parties Thurs 11-1.
Admission: £2.50 Children £1.30 Pre-booked parties £2 Children £1 (15 or more).
Refreshments: Tea-room 2-5 Apr-end Oct
Events/Exhibitions: Country fair 19-20 Aug. Jazz Concert 12 Aug.
Dogs admitted on lead. Wheelchair access to level parts of garden only. Small Shop.

FINCHCOCKS

(Mr & Mrs Richard Burnett)
Goudhurst   map **13** U23
Telephone: (01580) 211702

Finchcocks, dated 1725, is a fine example of Georgian baroque architecture, noted for its brickwork, with a front elevation attributed to Thomas Archer. It is set in beautiful gardens and parkland near the village of Goudhurst. The house contains a magnificent collection of historic keyboard instruments which are restored to full playing condition, and provides a unique setting where visitors can hear music performed on the instruments for which it was written. Demonstration tours and music whenever the house is open.

Location: 1½ m W of Goudhurst, 10 m E of Tunbridge Wells off A262.
Open: Easter-end of Sept Suns also Bank Hol Mon & Wed-Sun in Aug: 2-6. Demonstrations & Music on instruments of the collection on Open Days.
Admission: £4.80 children £3.20 Family ticket £12. Garden only £1. Free parking.
Refreshments: Facilities available morning, afternoon & evening.
Events/Exhibitions: Also private visits by appointment with music April to October. Festival: September Festival. Fairs: End of May and 2nd weekend of October. Exhibitions of prints and costumes: 18th century Pleasure Gardens etc.

GODINTON PARK

(Godinton House Preservation Trust, Alan Wyndham Green, Esq)
Ashford   TN23 3BW   map **13** U24

The existing house belongs mostly to Jacobean times though there are records of another house being here in the 15th century. The interior of Godinton contains a wealth of very fine panelling and carving, particularly in the Hall and on the Staircase. The house contains interesting portraits and much fine furniture and china. The gardens were originally laid out in the 18th century and were further extended by Sir Reginald Blomfield with topiary work and formal gardens giving a spacious setting to the house.

Location: 1½ m W of Ashford off Maidstone Road at Potter's Corner (A20).
Station(s): Ashford (2 m).
Open: Easter Sat Sun & Mon then June-Sept Sun & Bank Hols only 2-5.
Admission: House & Gardens £2 children (under 16) 70p Weekdays by appointment only. Parties of 20 or more £1.50.

GOODNESTONE PARK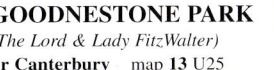

(The Lord & Lady FitzWalter)
nr Canterbury   map **13** U25
Telephone: (01304) 840107

The garden is approximately 14 acres, with many fine trees, a woodland garden and the walled garden with a large collection of old roses and herbaceous plants. Jane Austen was a frequent visitor, her brother Edward having married a daughter of the house.

Location: 8 m SE of Canterbury; 4 m E of A2; ¼ m SE of B2046; S of A257.
Station(s): Adisham (2 m).
Open: GARDEN ONLY **Weekdays** Mar 27-Oct 27 (incl Bank Holidays) Mon-Fri (NOT TUES OR SAT) 11-5. **Suns** Apr 2-Oct 15 12-6.
Admission: £2 OAPs £1.80 Children (under 12) 20p. Wheelchairs £1. Parties (20 or more) £1.80 Guided parties 20 or over £2.20. Guided parties 20 or over for house £1.50.
Refreshments: Teas Apr & May Sun & Wed June July Aug Sun Wed-Fri Pre-booked parties anyday.
Coach parties welcome but please book in advance. Rates on application. *No Dogs Allowed in the Garden.*

Sir Anthony Van Dyck
Portrait and religious painter

Born in Antwerp 1599,
died in London 1641
First visited England in 1620,
knighted by Charles I in 1633

His work can be seen in the following properties included in Historic Houses Castles and Garden:-

Alnwick Castle	*Kingston Lacey*
Arundel Castle	*Petworth House*
Boughton House	*Southside House*
Breamore House	*Sudeley Castle*
Eastnor Castle	*Warwick Castle*
Euston Hall	*Weston Park*
Firle Place	*Wilton House*
Goodwood House	*Woburn Abbey*
Holkham Hall	

GREAT COMP GARDEN

(The Great Comp Charitable Trust)
nr Borough Green   map **12** U23
Telephone: (01732) 882669/886154

This outstanding garden of seven acres has been expertly developed by Mr and Mrs Cameron since 1957 to provide interest throughout the year. In a setting of well maintained lawns the carefully designed layout and good use of plants allows the visitor to wander through areas of different character. Around the 17th century house are formal areas of paving, terraces, old brick walls and hedges. These are surrounded by less formal planting providing winding paths, vistas and woodland glades with occasional ornaments and constructed 'ruins' for additional interest. A wide variety of trees, shrubs, herbaceous plants and heathers offer inspiration and pleasure and include many which are rarely seen. Good Autumn colour. Nursery open daily with wide range of plants from garden for sale. Music festival and other events in July & September. S.A.E. to The Curator Great Comp, Borough Green, Sevenoaks, Kent TN15 8QS.

Location: 2 m E of Borough Green B2016 off A20. First right at Comp crossroads ½ m on left.
Station(s): Borough Green & Wrotham (1½ m).
Open: Garden and Nursery Only Apr 1-Oct 31 daily 11-6. Free parking. Parties by prior arrangement (coaches welcome) guided tours and lectures by arrangement.
Admission: Adults £2.50 children £1 guide book available. Annual tickets £7.50 OAPs £5 annual ticket holders may visit any day Apr-Oct and out of season in Nov Feb and Mar.
Refreshments: Teas on Sun and Bank Hols and for parties by arrangement.
No dogs.

GREAT MAYTHAM HALL
(Country Houses Association)
Rolvenden   **TN17 4NE**   map **13** U24
Telephone: (01580) 241346

Built in 1910 by Sir Edwin Lutyens.

Location: ½ m S of Rolvenden village, on road to Rolvenden Layne.
Station(s): Headcorn (10 m) Staplehurst (10 m).
Open: May-Sept Weds & Thurs 2-5. Last entry 4.30.
Admission: £2.50 Children £1. Free car park.
No dogs admitted.

GROOMBRIDGE PLACE GARDENS AND ENCHANTED FOREST
Groombridge   map **12** U23   ♿
Telephone: (01892) 863999
Fax: (01892) 862813

"The most Romantic Garden in the Kingdom" *164 acres of breathtaking gardens and parkland - the stunning setting for Peter Greenaway's acclaimed film 'The Draughtsman's Contract'. * Fountains, formal gardens, ancient topiary and dramatic views. * Medieval moat and waterlily collection. * Canal boat trips to the Enchanted Forest with its mystical springs * Birds of Prey displays and award winning children's gardens. "Extreme and almost sylvan beauty" Moated Houses, 1910. "The beautiful moat, as still and luminous as quicksilver" Sir Arthur Conan Doyle, The Valley of Fear, 1922. "A mysterious beauty that feeds the imagination" Homes and Gardens, 1994.

Location: On B2110, 1m S of A264. 4m SW of Tunbridge Wells, 9m E of East Grinstead. From London by car 1 hour and 15 minutes.
Station(s): Charing Cross to Tunbridge Wells, 55 minutes.
Open: Daily 1 Apr-17 Dec 10-6. Weekends and Bank Hols 18 Dec-30 March 1996 10-dusk (closed Christmas Day).
Admission: Adults £3.50 Senior Citizens £3 children £2.25 (under 6 free).
For enquiries and event details please contact: The Estate Office, Groombridge Place. Tel: (01892) 863999.

HEVER CASTLE & GARDENS

(Broadland Properties Limited)
nr Edenbridge   TN8 7NG   map **12** U23
Telephone: (01732) 865224
Fax: (01732) 866796

Hever Castle is a romantic 13th century moated castle best known as the childhood home of Anne Boleyn, Henry VIII's second wife and mother of Elizabeth I. At the beginning of this century William Waldorf Astor bought the estate and spent time, money and imagination in restoring the castle and creating one of the most beautiful gardens in England. He filled the castle with wonderful furniture, tapestries, paintings and other works of art and built the unique Italian Garden to display his collection of antique statuary. Today's visitor can wander around this delightfully intimate castle learning about the great love affair between Henry VIII and Anne Boleyn and then enjoy the magnificent grounds which include a maze, topiary, lake and walled rose garden.

Location: Hever Castle is 30 miles from central London and 30 minutes from Gatwick. 3 miles south-east of Edenbridge, Kent, off the B2026. Exit junctions 5 or 6 of the M25 or junction 10 of the M23.
Station(s): Hever Station 1 m, no taxis available. Edenbridge Town Station 3 m, taxis available.
Open: Daily Mar 14-Nov 5 1995 Gardens open 11 Castle 12 noon - last entry 5 and final exit 6 (4 and 5 winter time). Dogs on lead in gardens only. Facilities for disabled. Special pre-booked private tours available all year round. Gift, book and garden shops and an adventure play-ground.
Admission: Family ticket available and discounts for groups of 15 or more.
Refreshments: Two self-service restaurants in grounds (one licensed) serving hot and cold food throughout the day. Picnics welcome. Henry VIII public house opposite the main entrance.
Events/Exhibitions: Miniature model houses exhibition featuring 'Life in English Country Houses through the Ages', extended this year to include the Victorian period. Special events for 1995: Jousting Tournaments, Longbow Archery Demonstrations, Summer Concert Festival and Patchwork & Quilting Exhibition.
Conferences: The Tudor Village adjoining the Castle is available all year round for residential and day conferences, incentive travel, product launches, private dining and receptions.

Grinling Gibbons (1648-1721)

Sculptor and wood carver. His work can be seen at the following properties included in Historic Houses Castles and Gardens:-

Blenheim Palace	*Fawley Court*	*Petworth House*
Breamore House	*Kentchurch Court*	*Somerleyton Hall*
Dunham Massey	*Lyme Park*	*Sudbury Hall*

IGHTHAM MOTE 🌿 The National Trust
Ivy Hatch   map **12** U23
Telephone: (01732) 810378

One of the most complete remaining examples of a medieval moated manor house. Major exhibition of building conservation in action.

Location: 3 m S of Ightham, off A227, 4½ m E of Sevenoaks off A25.
Open: 2 Apr-end Oct Mon Wed Thur Fri 12-5.30 Sun and Bank Hol Mon 11-5.30 (last adm 5) pre-booked guided tours 11-12 weekdays no reduction open Good Fri. NB Property closes 4pm on Sun 16 July and is all day 7 July.
Admission: £4 £3 for Pre-booked parties. (No reduction for pre-booked guided tour.)
Refreshments: Tea pavilion in car park. Open half an hour before house, may close early in bad weather.

Shop open as house. Disabled access to ground floor only. No dogs.

KNOLE 🌿 The National Trust
Sevenoaks   map **12** U23   △
Telephone: (01732) 450608

The largest private house in England, dating mainly from 15th century, with splendid Jacobean interior and fine collection of 17th century furniture.

Location: At the Tonbridge end of Sevenoaks, just E of A225; 25 m from London.
Station(s): Sevenoaks (1½ m).
Open: Apr to end of Oct. Open Wed, Fri, Sat & Sun 11-5 Bank Hol Mon and Good Fri. Thur 2-5 last admission 4. Pre-booked guided tours 10-1 Thurs only, no reductions. Garden - May to Sept: first Wed in each month only.
Admission: Car park £2.50 (NT members free). House: £4 Chd £2. Garden: 50p, chd 30p. Pre-booked parties Wed - Sat (Thurs am pre-booked guided tours, no reductions) £3.
Refreshments: Tea-room open as house.

Shop open as house. Picnics welcome in deer park. No dogs in house.

LEEDS CASTLE
(Leeds Castle Foundation)
nr Maidstone   ME17 1PL   map **13** U24   △ ♿
Telephone: (01622) 765400
Fax: (01622) 735616

Leeds Castle stands as one of the most beautiful and ancient Castles in the Kingdom, rising from its two small islands in the middle of a lake and surrounded by 500 acres of magnificent parkland and gardens. Dating back to the 9th century and rebuilt by the Normans in 1119, Leeds Castle was then a Royal Palace for over three centuries. It now contains a superb collection of mediaeval furnishings, French and English furniture, tapestries and paintings. You can wander down through the Duckery into the Wood Garden, where peacocks and swans roam free. Visit the aviaries with rare tropical birds and the Culpeper Garden full of old fashioned flowers and fragrance. See a fascinating underground grotto at the centre of the maze and visit the greenhouses and vineyard. There's also a museum of Medieval Dog Collars in the 13th century Gate Tower. Or, come and play our 9-hole golf course. Now owned by the Leeds Castle Foundation, a private Charitable Trust, the Castle is also used as a high level residential conference centre.

Location: 4 m E of Maidstone; access on B2163 at junction 8 of the M20 and well signposted.
Station(s): Bearsted (2 m). Inclusive ticket schemes combining admission with rail and coach travel operate all year round on Castle open days from Victoria Station or Charing Cross to Bearsted.
Open: Every day 10-5* Mar-Oct and 10-3* in winter (* last admission to grounds). Closed Christmas Day also 24 June and 1 July before Open Air Concerts and 4 Nov for Fireworks Display (The Trustees reserve the right to close all or parts of the Castle as necessary).
Admission: Fully inclusive Castle and Park adults £7.30 OAPs and students £6.20 children £4.80 disabled visitors £4 family ticket (2 adults and 2 children) £20. Park and attractions £5.50, £4.50, £3.30, £3 and £15 respectively. Significant discounts for groups and school parties. Also a great value Season Pass.

Refreshments: Licenced self-service restaurant in the Fairfax Hall and waitress service in the new Terrace Restaurant provide a full range of hot and cold meals, plus cream teas. Also barbecues and fast food outlets in the Stable Courtyard.
Events/Exhibitions: Sun Jan 1; **New Year's Day Treasure Trail:** Sat Mar 25-Sun Apr 2; **Spring Garden's Week:** Sat Apr 15-Mon 17; **Celebration of Easter:** Sat May 13-Sun 14; **Festival of English Wines:** Sat June 3-Sun 4; **Balloon and Vintage Car Fiesta:** Sat June 24 and Sat July 1; **Annual Open Air Concerts:** Fri Sept 15-Mon 18; **Flower Festival:** Sat Nov 4; **Grand Firework Spectacular:** Wed Nov 1-Sun Dec 24; **Special Christmas Shop:** Throughout Dec; **Christmas at the Castle.**
Conferences: Residential conferences or day meetings in the Castle itself; or in the Culpeper Conference Centre (12-50 delegates). Wide choice of historic venues for special functions. Picnic area. Car park. Fully accessible minibus provides shuttle service to and from car and coach parks, for disabled and elderly visitors. Good facilities for disabled. Regret no dogs. Castle shop, Park shop, book shop, plants for sale from greenhouses.

LULLINGSTONE CASTLE

(Guy Hart Dyke, Esq)
Eynsford   DA14 0JA   map **12** U23   △ &
Telephone: (01322) 862114

Family portraits, armour, Henry VII gatehouse, Church, Herb garden.

Location: In the Darenth valley via Eynsford on A225.
Station(s): Eynsford (½ m).
Open: Castle and Grounds Apr-Sept Sat Sun Bank Hols 2-6 Wed Thur and Fri by arrangement (2-6). Telephone for enquiries or bookings.
Admission: Adults £3.50 children £1.50 OAPs £3. Free car parking.
Refreshments: In the gatehouse tea-rooms.
No dogs.

LULLINGSTONE ROMAN VILLA

ENGLISH HERITAGE

map **12** U23
Telephone: (01322) 863467

The ancient Romans understood the art of gracious living. In this country villa they walked on mosaic floors, dined off fine tableware and commissioned elaborate wall paintings to decorate one of the earliest churches in Britain.

Location: ½ m (0.8 km) south west of Eynsford.
Open: Apr 1-Sept 30 10-6 daily Oct 1-Mar 31 daily 10-4.
Admission: Adults £2 concessions £1.50 children £1. Price includes a Personal Stereo Guided Tour.

LYMPNE CASTLE

(Harry Margary, Esq)
nr Hythe   CT21 4LQ   map **13** U25
Telephone: (01303) 267571

This romantic medieval castle with an earlier Roman, Saxon and Norman history was once owned by the Archdeacons of Canterbury. It was rebuilt about 1360, and restored in 1905, 300 feet above the well known Roman Shore Fort - Stutfall Castle. Four miles from the ancient Cinque Port of Hythe, it commands a tremendous view across Romney Marshes to Fairlight over the great sweep of the coast from Dover to Dungeness and across the sea to France. Terraced gardens with magnificent views out to sea.

Location: 3 m NW of Hythe off B2067, 8 m W of Folkestone.
Station(s): Sandling (2½ m).
Open: Easter-Sept 30 daily 10.30-6 *Parties by appointment* closed occasionally on Sat.
Admission: Adults £2 children 50p.

MARLE PLACE GARDENS

(Mrs Lindel Williams)
Marle Place Road, Brenchley, Tonbridge   TN12 7HS   map **12** U23   △ &
Telephone: (01892) 722304
Fax: (01892) 724099

Marle Place is a romantic privately owned Wealden Garden of 10 acres close to Scotney and Sissinghurst Castles. A plantsmans garden with many interesting trees and shrubs. Featuring a Victorian gazebo and Edwardian rockery (now a herb garden). Walled, fragrant garden and ornamental ponds. Yew hedges and herbaceous border. Architecturally important listed, 17th century house. Unusual plant nursery.

Location: Off the B2162 1 m south of Horsmonden, and 1½ m north west of Lamberhurst, turn west on Marle Place Road for ½ m or follow brown and white tourist signs from Brenchley Village.
Station(s): Paddock Wood B.R. Bus from Tunbridge Wells.
Open: Apr 1-Oct 31 9.30-5.30.
Admission: Adults £2 Groups by arrangement.
Refreshments: Tea-room, self-service tea, coffee & cake.
Coach parties are most welcome, but must be booked in advance. Car parking.

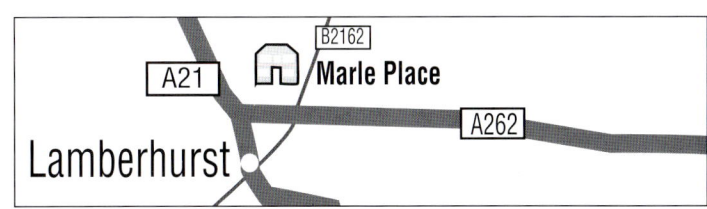

NEW COLLEGE OF COBHAM

(Presidents of the New College of Cobham)
Cobham   map **13** U24   &
Telephone: (01474) 814280

Almshouses based on medieval chantry built 1362, part rebuilt 1598. Originally endowed by Sir John de Cobham and descendants.

Location: 4 m W of Rochester; 4 m SE of Gravesend; 1½ m from junction Shorne-Cobham (A2). In Cobham rear of Church of Mary Magdalene.
Station(s): Sole St (1 m).
Open: Apr-Sept daily (except Thurs) 10-7 Oct-Mar Mon Tues Wed Sat & Sun 10-4.
Refreshments: Afternoon teas by prior arrangement.

OWL HOUSE GARDENS
(Maureen, Marchioness of Dufferin & Ava)
Lamberhurst   map **12** U23

13 acres of romantic gardens surround this 16th century timber framed wool smuggler's cottage. Spring flowers, roses, rare flowering shrubs and ornamental fruit trees. Expansive lawns lead to leafy woodland walks graced by English and Turkish oaks, elm, birch and beech trees. Rhododendrons, azaleas, camellias encircle peaceful informal sunken water gardens.

Location: 8 m SE of Tunbridge Wells; 1 m from Lamberhurst off A21.
Open: GARDENS ONLY. All the year - daily and weekends including all Bank Hol weekends 11-6.
Admission: £3 children £1 (Proceeds towards Lady Dufferin's charity, Maureen's Oast House for Arthritics). Free parking.
Dogs on lead. Coach parties welcome.

"GHOSTS"

Ghosts are in residence at the following properties included in Historic Houses Castles and Gardens:-

Blickling Hall - *Anne Boleyn*

Breamore House - *Haunted picture - if touched, death on the same day*

East Riddleden Hall - *5 ghosts including lady*

in Grey Hall Lady's Chamber

Fountains Abbey & Studley Royal - *Choir of monks chanting in Chapel of Nine Altars*

Hinton Ampner - *Nocturnal noises*

Ightham Mote - *Supernatural presence*

Lindisfarne Castle - *Monk, and group of monks on causeway*

Lyme Park - *Unearthly peals of bells and lady in white, funeral procession through park*

Malmesbury House - *Ghost of a cavalier*

Overbecks Museum & Garden - *'Model' ghost in the Children's room (for them to spot)*

Rockingham Castle - *Lady Dedlock*

Rufford Old Hall - *Elizabeth Hesketh*

Scotney Castle Garden - *Man rising from the lake*

Sizergh Castle & Garden - *Poltergeist*

Speke Hall - *Ghost of woman in tapestry room*

Springhill - *Ghost of a woman*

Sudbury Hall - *Lady in Green, seen on stairs*

Tamworth Castle - *Haunted bedroom*

Treasurer's House - *Troop of Roman soldiers marching through the cellar*

Wallington House - *Invisible birds beating against the windows accompanied by heavy breathing*

Washington Old Hall - *Grey lady walking through corridors*

PATTYNDENNE MANOR

(Mr. & Mrs. D.C. Spearing)
Pattyndenne Manor, Goudhurst   TN17 2QU   map **13** U27
Telephone: (01580) 211361

Imposing domestic house built of oak trees before Columbus discovered America. Features include banqueting hall, dragon beams, upturned oak trees, enormous fireplaces, 13c prison, pleasant gardens. Connected with Henry VIII. Lived in as a family house, furnished, lecture tour by owner.

Location: 1 m south of Goudhurst on W. side of B2079.
Open: Open to groups by appointment (minimum approx. 20). Connoisseur's tour for very small groups also posible.
Admission: £4.
Refreshments: Light refreshments available.

PENSHURST PLACE

(The Rt Hon Viscount De L'Isle, MBE)
Tunbridge Wells   TN11 8DG   map **12** U23   △
Telephone: (01892) 870307
Fax: (01892) 870866

One of England's finest family-owned stately homes with a history going back six and a half centuries. Unique mediaeval Baron's Hall with splendid 60 foot-high chestnut beamed roof, paintings, furniture, and tapestries from 15th, 16th and 17th centuries. Other highlights include Toy Museum, Venture Playground, Nature trail, and magnificent gardens dating back to the 14th century, recently restored to their former glory.

Location: Penshurst, near Tonbridge. From M25, junction 5, follow A21 to Tonbridge, leaving at Tonbridge (North) exit; then follow brown tourist signs to Penshurst Place. From M26 Junction 2a. Follow A25 (Sevenoaks) and the A21 for Tonbridge; further directions as above.
Station(s): Penshurst (2 m). Regular services operate from BR Charing Cross to Hildenborough (4 miles) or Tonbridge (6 miles); then taxi.
Open: Open seven days a week 1 Apr-1 Oct 1995 Grounds 11-6 House 12-5.30 (last entry 5) Weekends in Mar and Oct.
Admission: House and Grounds adults £4.95 concessions £4.50 children (5-16) £2.75 family ticket £13 adult party (20 plus) £4.50 Grounds adults £3.50 concessions £3 children £2.25 Garden Season Ticket £17. Guided tours of the State Rooms are available during the mornings at £4.95 (adults) and £2.50 (children) and must be pre-booked. Garden tours for special interest groups are also available for pre-booked groups (£5.95).
Refreshments: Light luncheons and teas available in Restaurant.
No dogs admitted. Wheelchair visitors welcome. (Disabled access limited by age/architecture of House. For enquiries and group bookings, contact Penshurst Place, Penshurst, Tonbridge, Kent TN11 8DG. (01892) 870307

PORT LYMPNE WILD ANIMAL PARK, MANSION & GARDENS

(John Aspinall, Esq)
Lympne, Hythe   CT21 4PD   map **13** U25
Telephone: (01303) 264647
Fax: (01303) 264944

Built for Sir Philip Sassoon between 1911 and 1915, and described as the 'last historic house to be built this century', Port Lympne encompasses the essence of Roman villas and the English country house. Overlooking the Romney Marsh and Channel and set in 15 acres of terraced gardens. The wonderful Trojan Stairway has 125 steps and the interior of the Mansion features a Moorish Patio, marble columns, an intriguing mosaic hall floor, plus the rare Rex Whistler Tent Room, and the Spencer Roberts Mural Room and other wildlife Exhibitions. The principal architect was Sir Herbert Baker who designed New Delhi. Bought and restored by Mr John Aspinall in 1973, it is now open to the public together with its 300 acre wild animal park which is home to gorillas, lions, tigers, rhinos and many more rare animals. Gift shop. Art Gallery. Picnic areas. Safari trailer, (check for service times).

Location: 3 m W of Hythe; 6 m W of Folkestone; 7 m SE of Ashford exit 11 off M20.
Station(s): Sandling, Ashford, Folkestone.
Open: All the year daily Summer 10-5* Winter 10-one hour before dusk* (*last admissions) closed Christmas Day.
Admission: Reduced prices for OAPs and children 4-14 (3 and under free) special party rates. Free car park.
Refreshments: Licensed restaurant and kiosks in summer.
Events/Exhibitions: A number of special events throughout the year.
Conferences: Catered for.
Some areas not suitable for disabled.

QUEBEC HOUSE   🍂 The National Trust
Westerham   map **12** U23
Telephone: (01959) 562206

Probably early 16th century in origin, now mainly 17th century. Mementoes of General Wolfe, and colourful exhibition about the Battle of Quebec.

Location: At junction of Edenbridge & Sevenoaks Roads (A25 & B2026).
Open: 2 Apr-end Oct Daily (except Thurs & Sat) inc Good Fri and Bank Hol Mon 2-6. Last adm 5.30.
Admission: £2 children £1. *Pre-booked parties £1.50, chd 80p.*
No dogs. Unsuitable for wheelchairs.

QUEX HOUSE, QUEX PARK
(Trustees of the Powell-Cotton Museum)
Birchington   map **13** U25
Telephone: (01843) 42168

Wander through the period rooms of P.H.G. Powell-Cotton's mansion, Quex House, the only stately home in Thanet, with its superb woodcarving and panelling, beautiful plasterwork and an air of mellow maturity. The rooms are arranged much as they were in his lifetime and contain fine 17th and 18th century English furniture and many family treasures. The unique Chinese Imperial porcelain collection, however, has been moved into its own gallery in the Powell-Cotton Museum as have the English and Continental porcelain collections. This purpose-built museum, adjoining the Mansion, now extends to nine large galleries; here Powell-Cotton created huge dioramas showing 500 African and Asian animals, all mounted by Rowland Ward, in scenes re-creating their natural habitats. He assembled the world's finest collection of African ethnography gathered on his 28 expeditions, and displayed it at Quex, together with superb weapons collections, cannon, local archaeological material and outstanding fine arts from many countries of the Orient. Enjoy the Pleasure Gardens and see the Victorian Walled Kitchen Garden presently under restoration.

Location: In Birchington, ½ m S of Birchington Square (signposted). SW of Margate; 13 m E of Canterbury.
Station(s): Birchington (1 m).
Open: Open regularly in summer (times on request) please telephone for brochure.
Admission: Adults £2.50 children/OAPs £1.80 (Summer) adults £2 children/OAPs £1.30 (Winter) Gardens only adults £1 children/OAPs 60p Summer and Winter.
Refreshments: New Restaurant opened Sept 1994.
Ground floor rooms and museum only suitable for disabled. Free car and coach parking. New museum shop in recently completed Visitor Centre. Registered Charity.

HISTORIC HOUSES
CASTLES & GARDENS

For further details on editorial listings or display advertising contact the

Editor: Deborah Valentine,
Windsor Court, East Grinstead House, East Grinstead,
West Sussex   RH19 1XA
Tel: (01342) 335794   Fax: (01342) 335720

RIVERHILL HOUSE
(The Rogers Family)
Sevenoaks   TN15 0RR   map 12 U23   △
Telephone: (01732) 458802/452557

Small Ragstone house built in 1714 and home of the Rogers family since 1840. Panelled rooms, portraits and interesting memorabilia. An historic garden with rare trees and shrubs. Sheltered terraces and rhododendrons and azaleas in woodland setting. Bluebells. Ancient trackway known as 'Harold's Road'.

Location: 2 m S of Sevenoaks on road to Tonbridge (A225).
Station(s): Sevenoaks (2 m).
Open: Garden Apr, May and June **only** every Sun and the Sat and Mon of all Bank Holiday weekends during this period 12-6. Picnics allowed. THE HOUSE is now only open to party bookings and for a limited period when the gardens are at their best. Any day in Apr, May or June except Sun and Bank Holidays.
Admission: Garden adults £2 children 50p Garden and House £3 (a minimum of 20. Adults only).
Refreshments: Home made teas in the old stable from 2.30 on Suns. Special Catering for booked parties - Ploughman's Lunches, teas etc - by arrangement. All enquiries to Mrs Rogers (01732) 458802/452557.
No dogs. Picnics permitted.

ROCHESTER CASTLE
Rochester   map 13 U24
Telephone: (01634) 402276

ENGLISH HERITAGE

Built in the 11th century to guard the point where the Roman road of Watling Street crossed the River Medway, the size and position of this grand Norman bishop's castle, founded on the Roman city wall, eventually made it an important royal stronghold for several hundred years. The keep is truly magnificent - over 100 feet high and with walls 12 feet thick. At the top you will be able to enjoy fine views over the river and surrounding city of Rochester.

Location: By Rochester Bridge (A2).
Open: Apr 1-Sept 30 10-6 daily Oct 1-Mar 31 daily 10-4.
Admission: Adults £2.50 concessions £1.90 children £1.30.

"Playgrounds for the Children"

Belton House
Bowood
Drumlanrig (woodland playground)
Hever Castle
Kelburn (Secret Forest adventure course and stockade)
Longleat
Ragley Hall (adventure wood)
Weston Park
Wilton House

SCOTNEY CASTLE GARDEN   The National Trust
Lamberhurst   map 13 U24   &
Telephone: (01892) 890651

Romantic landscape garden framing moated castle.
Location: 1m SE of Lamberhurst (A21).
Open: Garden 1 Apr-end Oct Wed-Fri 11-6 or sunset if earlier *(closed Good Fri)* Sat & Sun 2-6 or sunset if earlier. Bank Hols and Sun preceeding Bank Hol. Mon 12-6. Old Castle May-Sept 11 days and times as for garden. Last adm one hour before closing.
Admission: £3.20 (pre-booked parties £2 weekdays only) Children £1.60 and £1.
No dogs. Picnic area next to car park. Shop. Wheelchairs available. (Steep entrance to garden).

SISSINGHURST CASTLE GARDEN   The National Trust
Sissinghurst   map 13 U24
Telephone: (01580) 712850

The famous garden created by the late Vita Sackville-West and Sir Harold Nicolson between the surviving parts of an Elizabethan mansion. Exhibition and woodland walks.

Location: 2 m NE of Cranbrook; 1 m E of Sissinghurst village (A262).
Open: Apr-Oct 15 Tues-Fri 1-6.30 Sat Suns & Good Fri 10-5.30. (Last adm 5.) *Closed Mon incl Bank Hol Mons.* Timed tickets in operation. Because of the limited capacity of the garden, visitors may have to wait before admission.
Admission: £5 Children £2.50. Parties by appointment only.
Refreshments: In the Granary Restaurant. Apr-Oct 15 Tues-Fri 12-5.30, Sat & Sun 10-5.30, also Oct 26-Dec 24 Wed-Sat 11-4.
No dogs. No picnics in garden. Admission to wheelchair visitors is restricted to 2 at any one time. Shop, open as restaurant.

SMALLHYTHE PLACE   The National Trust
Tenterden   map 13 U24
Telephone: (01580) 762334

The Ellen Terry Memorial Museum. Half-timbered 16th century yeoman's home. Mementoes of Dame Ellen Terry, Mrs Siddons, etc. Theatre barn open to view most days.

Location: 2½ m S of Tenterden on E side of Rye Road (B2082).
Open: Apr to end of Oct - Daily (except Thurs & Frid) 2-6 or dusk if earlier. Open Good Fri. Last adm half-hour before closing. *Parties should give advance notice - no reduction. Can only take 25 at a time in house.*
Admission: £2.50, Chd £1.30 (Accompanied by an adult).
Refreshments: Tea available at Tenterden.
No dogs. Unsuitable for wheelchairs.

SOUTH FORELAND LIGHTHOUSE   The National Trust
map 13 U25
Telephone: (01892) 890651

Victorian lighthouse on the cliff between Dover and St. Margaret's Bay.

Location: 1½ m SW of St. Margaret's at Cliffe village. Visitors are advised to park in village car park (2 miles).
Open: Apr-end Oct Sat Sun & Bank Hol Mon 2-5.30 (last adm 5).
Admission: £1 Children 50p.

SQUERRYES COURT

(J St A Warde, Esq)
Westerham　TN16 1SJ　map **12** U23
Telephone: (01959) 562345 or 563118
Fax: (01959) 565949

Beautiful manor house built in 1681. Warde family home since 1731 (still lived in today). Important Italian, 18c English and 17c Dutch paintings; furniture, porcelain and tapestries all collected by the family in the 18c Memorabilia of General Wolfe of Quebec. Landscaped garden lovely all seasons. Lake, borders, recently restored formal garden, 18c dovecote.

Location: Western outskirts of Westerham signposted from A25. Junctions 5 & 6 M25 10 mins.
Station(s): Oxted or Sevenoaks.
Open: During Mar Sun only 2-6 Apr 1-Sept 30 Wed Sat Sun and Bank Hol Mons 2-6 (last adm 5.30).
Admission: Adults £3.50 OAPs £3.20 children (14 and under) £1.60 Grounds only £2 OAPs £1.80 children (14 and under) £1. Parties over 20 (any day) by arrangment at reduced rates.
Refreshments: Homemade teas served in Old Library. Catering (light lunches/home made teas) for groups by prior arrangement.
Dogs on leads in grounds only. Free parking at house.

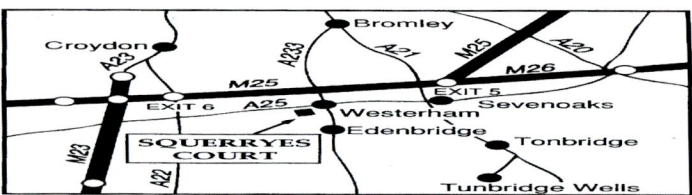

STONEACRE　🍃 The National Trust
Otham　map **13** U24
Telephone: (01622) 862871

A half-timbered small manor house, c. 1480. Small garden.

Location: In Otham, 3 m SE of Maidstone; 1 m S of A20.
Station(s): Bearsted (2 m).
Open: Apr-end Oct Wed & Sat 2-6 (last adm 5).
Admission: £2 Children £1. No reduction for parties.
No dogs. Unsuitable for wheelchairs. Narrow access road.

TONBRIDGE CASTLE
(Owned and Managed by Tonbridge & Malling Borough Council)
Tonbridge　TN9 1BG　map **12** U24　△ Ⓔ
Telephone: (01732) 770929
Fax: (01732) 770449

Reputedly England's finest example of the layout of a Norman Motte and Bailey Castle with 13th century Gatehouse set in landscaped gardens overlooking the River Medway. The site is clearly interpreted for your enjoyment. Superb exhibition in Castle Gatehouse depicting life as it was 700 years ago. Tours are available from the Tourist Information Centre.

Location: In town centre off High Street.
Station(s): Tonbridge (Main line Charing Cross).
Open: Apr-Sept Mon-Sat 9-5 Sun & Bank Hol 10.30-5 Oct-Mar Mon-Fri 9-5 Sat 9-4 Sun 10.30-4 closed Christmas Day and New Year's Day (last tours leave 1 hr before closing time) guided tours by arrangement.
Admission: Adults £2.50 children/OAPs £1.20 family (2 adults+3 children) £6.50 10% discount for groups.
Refreshments: Available nearby.

WALMER CASTLE
ENGLISH HERITAGE
Kingsdown Road, Walmer, Deal　CT14 7LJ　map **13** U25
Telephone: (01304) 364288

One of the coastal castles built by Henry VIII and the official residence of The Lords Warden of The Cinque Ports, including Queen Elizabeth, the Queen Mother and the Duke of Wellington who died at Walmer and whose furnished rooms have been preserved unaltered. (The original 'Wellington Boot' may be seen here).

Location: On coast at Walmer 2 m S of Deal off the Dover/Deal Road.
Station(s): Walmer (1½ m).
Open: Apr 1-Sept 30 10-6 daily Oct 1-31 10-4 daily Nov 1-Mar 31 Wed-Sun 10-4. Closed Jan & Feb, Lord Warden in residence.
Admission: Adults £3.50 concessions £2.60 children £1.80. Price includes a Personal Stereo Guided Tour.

WILLESBOROUGH WINDMILL
(Willesborough Windmill Trust)
Ashford　TN24 0GQ　map **13** U24

Willesborough Windmill, built in 1869, has now been restored as a working smock mill. Visitors can view the turn-of-the-century miller's cottage, enjoy guided tours of the mill which is not suitable for the disabled.

Location: 2 m E of Ashford town centre, just off A292 and approx ¼ m from Junction 10 of the M20.
Open: Easter-Oct 31 Sat Sun and Bank Hols 2-5 (or dusk if earlier).
Admission: Adults £1 children/OAPs 50p. Group rates available on application.
Refreshments: Tea-room and shop in restored barn adjacent to the mill. Light refreshments available. Suitable for disabled.
Limited parking.

LANCASHIRE

ASTLEY HALL

(Chorley Borough Council)

off Hallgate, Astley Park, Chorley   PR7 1NP   map 6 P17
Telephone: (01257) 262166

The Hall dates back to Elizabethan times with major additions in the 1660s and 1880s. Interiors contain elaborate plaster ceilings and fine furniture.

Location: 5 mins SW from J8 of M61, 10 mins SE of J28 and NE of J27 of M6. Follow signs for Chorley and brown tourist signs. 10 mins walk through park from town centre.
Station(s): In town. Bus route near to Hall.
Open: Apr-Oct daily Nov-Mar Fri-Sun. Times to be confirmed.
Admission: Adults £2 concessions £1 family ticket £4.
Refreshments: Adjacent Cafe in park.

BROWSHOLME HALL

nr Clitheroe   BB7 3DE   map 6 P17
Telephone: (01254) 826719
Fax: (01254) 826739

Home of the Parker family, Bowbearers of the Forest of Bowland. Tudor with Elizabethan front, Queen Anne Wing and Regency additions. Portraits furniture and antiquities.

Location: 5 m NW of Clitheroe; off B6243; Bashall Eaves - Whitewell signposted.
Open: 2-5 Easter (Good Friday-Mon) late May Bank Hol weekend, July every Sat, Aug every Sat & Sun and Aug Bank Hol weekend.
Admission: Reductions for booked parties at other times by appointment with A. Parker, Tel. as above.

GAWTHORPE HALL   🌿 The National Trust

Padiham, nr Burnley   BB12 8UA   map 15 P18
Telephone: (01282) 778511

House built in 1600-1605, restored by Sir Charles Barry in 1850's; Barry's designs are re-created in principal rooms. Display of Rachel Kay-Shuttleworth textile collections; private study by arrangement. Major display of late 17th century portraits on loan from the National Portrait Gallery. Estate building, restored, houses a broad programme of craft and management courses.

Location: On E outskirts of Padiham (¾ m drive to house is on N of A671).
Station(s): Station: Rose Grove (2 m).
Open: Apr 1-Oct 29 HALL Tues Wed Thurs Sat & Sun 1-5 last adm 4.15. Open Good Fri & Bank Holiday Mons. GARDEN Open daily all year 10-6.
Admission: House £2.30 Children £1. Reductions for pre-booked parties of 15 or more by prior arrangement.
Refreshments: Refectory in Estate Building open as shop.
Events/Exhibitions: Textile Craft Exhibitions during high season.
No dogs. Access for disabled: Ground floor of Hall. WC.

MARTHOLME

Great Harwood, Blackburn   BB6 7UJ   map 15 P18   △

Screens passage and service wing of medieval manor house altered 1577 with 17th century additions. Gatehouse built 1561, restored 1969.

Open: Exterior Fri & Sat, Interior by appointment only.

RUFFORD OLD HALL   🌿 The National Trust

Rufford, nr Ormskirk   L40 1SG   map 6 P17
Telephone: (01704) 821254

One of the finest 16th century buildings in Lancashire. The Great Hall is remarkable for its ornate hammer-beam roof and unique screen. There are fine collections of 17th century oak furniture, 16th century arms, armour and tapestries.

Location: 7 m N of Ormskirk at N end of Rufford village on E side of A59.
Station(s): Stations: Rufford (½ m) (not Suns); Burscough Bridge (2½ m).
Open: Apr 1-Nov 1 Daily Sat-Wed 1-5. Last adm 4.30. Garden 12-5.30 on same days Sun 1-5.30. Refreshments same days 12-5 Sun 2-5. Shop open 12-4.30 (Sun 2-5).
Admission: £3 Children £1.50. Reduced parties of 15 or more by arrangement.
Refreshments: At the Hall (parties should book).
Events/Exhibitions: Events throughout the season. Please telephone for details.
Access for disabled to garden only. Guide dogs.

STONYHURST COLLEGE

Hurst Green   map 15 P18   △
Telephone: (01254) 826345

The original house, (situated close to the picturesque village of Hurst Green in the beautiful Ribble Valley) dates from the late 16th century. Set in extensive grounds which include ornamental gardens. The College has an impressive approach down a long avenue flanked by man made rectangular ponds constructed in the 17th century. The Parish Church of St. Peters built in 1832, is linked to the main building which is a boys' Catholic boarding school, founded by the Society of Jesus in 1593.

Location: Just off the B6243 (Longridge - Clitheroe) on the outskirts of Hurst Green. 10 m from junction 31 on M6.
Open: House weekly July 25-Aug 28 Tues-Sun only (inc Aug Bank Hol Mon) 1-5 Grounds & Gardens weekly July 8-Aug 28 Tues-Sun only (inc Aug Bank Hol Mon) 1-5.
Admission: House and Grounds £3.50 children (4-14) £2.50 (under 4 free) Senior Citizens £2.50 Grounds only £1.
Refreshments: Refreshments/Gift Shop: Limited facilities for disabled. Coach parties by prior arrangement.
No dogs permitted.

TOWNELEY HALL ART GALLERY & MUSEUM AND MUSEUM OF LOCAL CRAFTS & INDUSTRIES

(Burnley Borough Council)

Burnley   BD11 3RQ   map 15 P18
Telephone: (01282) 424213
Fax: (01282) 36138

The House dates from the 14th century, with 17th and 19th century modifications. The furnished rooms include an Elizabethan Long Gallery, and a fine entrance hall with plasterwork by Vassali completed in 1729. Collections include oak furniture, 18th and 19th century paintings and Zoffany's painting of Charles Towneley. Loan exhibitions are held throughout the summer. There is a Museum of Local Crafts and Industries in the old Bew House, and the Natural History Centre, with an aquarium in the grounds.

Location: ½ m SE of Burnley on the Burnley/Todmorden Road (A671).
Station(s): Burnley Central (1¾ m).
Open: All the year Mon-Fri 10-5 Sun 12-5 closed Sat throughout year and Christmas-New Year.
Admission: Free.
Refreshments: At cafe in grounds.

TURTON TOWER

(Lancashire County Council)

Chapeltown Road, Turton   BL7 OHG   map 15 P18
Telephone: (01204) 852203
Fax: (01204) 853754

Medieaval Tower extended by Tudors, Stuarts and Victorians now displayed as a Country house with period rooms depicting these periods. Collections include a major display of furniture from the Victoria & Albert Museum.

Location: B6391 via A666 and A676.
Station(s): Bromley Cross or Entwistle, Bus GM 563.
Open: May-Sept 1-5 also 10-12 weekdays Mar Apr Oct. Sat-Wed 2-5 Nov and Feb Sun 2-5.
Admission: £1 adults 50p children £2.50 family ticket. Guided Tours out of hours £2 with supper £5 p.h.
Refreshments: Tea-rooms.
Events/Exhibitions: Several Art Exhibitions staged during the season, usually on a contempary crafts or regional design theme.
Wheelchair access to ground floor. Friends, Season ticket holders. Guided tours with catering out of hours.

LEICESTERSHIRE

BELVOIR CASTLE

(His Grace the Duke of Rutland)
nr Grantham   map **7** R21
Telephone: (01476) 870262

Seat of the Dukes of Rutland since Henry VIII's time, and rebuilt by Wyatt in 1816. A castle in the grand style, commanding magnificent views over the Vale of Belvoir. The name dates back to the famous Norman Castle that stood on this site. Many notable art treasures, and interesting military relics. The Statue gardens contain many beautiful 17th century sculptures. Flowers in bloom throughout most of the season. Medieval Jousting Tournaments. Conference and filming facilities. Banquets, school visits, private parties.

Location: 7 m WSW of Grantham, between A607 (to Melton Mowbray) and A52 (to Nottingham).
Open: Apr 1-Oct 1 1995 Tues Wed Thurs Sat 11-5 Sun and Bank Hols 11-6. Other times for groups by appointment.
Admission: Adults £4.25 children £2.65 OAPs £3. All coach tours and excursions £3.25 (coach driver free) parties of 20 or more adults £3 (organiser free) school parties £2.20 (teacher free). On Jousting Tournament days an extra charge of 50p per person will apply. Ticket office and catering facilities in the Castle close approximately 30 mins before the Castle. Guide books are on sale at the ticket office or inside the Castle, or by post (£2.50) incl. post and packing.
We regret that dogs are not permitted (except Guide dogs).

KAYES GARDEN NURSERY

(Mrs Hazel Kaye)
1700 Melton Rd, Rearsby, Leicester   LE7 4YR   map **14** R20
Telephone: (01664) 424578

Hardy herbaceous perennials and good selection of climbers and shrubs. The garden and nursery are in Rearsby, in the Wreake Valley countryside of Leicestershire. Once an orchard, the one acre garden houses an extensive selection of hardy herbaceous plants. Mixed borders and a fine pergola provide year-round interest, while the nursery offers an excellent range of interesting plants.

Location: Just inside Rearsby village, N of Leicester on A607, on L.H. side approaching from Leicester.
Open: Mar-Oct inclusive Wed-Sat 10-5.30 Sun 10-12. Nov to Feb inclusive Fri and Sat 10-4.30. *Closed* Dec 18-Jan 31 inclusive.

Robert Adam - architect

His work can be seen at the following properties included in Historic Houses Castles and Gardens:-

Audley End	*Mellerstain*
Bowood House & Gardens	*Moccas Court*
Culzean Castle	*Newby Hall & Gardens*
Hatchlands Park	*Nostell Priory*
Kedleston Hall	*Osterley Park*
Kenwood, The Iveagh Bequest	*Papplewick Hall*
Killerton	*Saltram House*
Kimbolton Castle	*Syon House*
Luton Hoo	

STANFORD HALL

(The Lady Braye)
Lutterworth   LE17 6DH   map **14** R20   △
Telephone: (01788) 860250
Fax: (01788) 860870

A William and Mary house built in the 1690's containing a fine collection of pictures (including the Stuart Collection), antique furniture and family costumes dating from the early 17th Century. There is a full-size replica of the 1898 Flying Machine of Percy Pilcher who is officially recognised as England's Pioneer Aviator. He experimented at Stanford where he was killed whilst flying in 1899. The Motorcycle Museum contains an outstanding collection of Vintage and historic motorcycles. Walled Rose Garden leading to Old Forge. Nature Trail. Craft Centre most Sundays.

Location: 7½ m NE of Rugby, 3½ m from A5, 6 m from M1 at exit 18, 2 m from M1 at exit 19 (from the North only), 2 m from M6 exit at A14/M1 North junction, 1¼ m from Swinford.
Open: Easter Sat-24 Sept Sats & Suns also Bank Hol Mons & Tues following 2.30-6 (last adm 5.30). NB On Bank Hols and Event Days open 12 noon (House 2.30).
Admission: House and Grounds etc. adults £3.20 children £1.50. Grounds, Rose Garden, Flying Machine, Old Forge, Craft Centre (most Suns) adults £1.80 children 70p. Parties of 20 or more (min £58) adults £2.90 children £1.30. OAPs with a party of 20 or more £2.70. School parties of 20 or more (one teacher adm free) adults £2.90 children £1.30. Prices are subject to increase on some Event Days. Motorcycle Museum adults £1 children 30p.
Refreshments: Home-made teas. Light lunches most Suns. Lunches, Teas, High Teas or Suppers for pre-booked parties any day during season.

LINCOLNSHIRE

AUBOURN HALL

(Sir Henry Nevile)
nr Lincoln   LN5 9DZ   map **7** Q21   △
Telephone: (01522) 788270

Late 16th century house attributed to J. Smythson (Jnr). Important carved staircase and panelled rooms. New rose garden.

Location: In Aubourn village 7 m S of Lincoln.
Open: July and Aug Wed 2-6 also Sun May 21 and June 4 or by appointment.
Admission: Adults £2.50 OAPs £2.

BELTON HOUSE   🌿 The National Trust

nr Grantham   map **7** R21   Ⓢ
Telephone: (01476) 66116

The crowning achievement of Restoration country house architecture, built 1685-88 for Sir John Brownlow, heir to the fortunes of a successful Elizabethan lawyer; alterations by James Wyatt 1777, plasterwork ceilings by Edward Goudge, fine wood carvings of the Grinling Gibbons school. Family portraits, furniture, tapestries, Speaker Cust's silver and silver-gilt, Duke of Windsor memorabilia. Formal gardens, orangery by Jeffrey Wyattville, 17th century stables, magnificent landscape park. Extensive Adventure Playground for children.

Location: 3 m NE of Grantham on A607 Grantham/Lincoln Road; easily accessible from A1.
Open: 1 Apr-end of Oct Wed-Sun & Bank Hol Mons 1-5.30. *Closed* Good Fri. Gardens open 11. Parkland opens daily with free access on foot (may be closed for special events). Last adm 5.
Admission: House £4.30 School parties contact the Property Manager for details. 1995 Events - details from the Administrator.
Refreshments: Counter service licensed restaurant open 12-5 for lunches and teas.

Thomas Gainsborough (1727-1787)

His paintings can be seen at the following properties included in Historic Houses Castles and Gardens:-

Arundel Castle
Bowhill
Christchurch Mansion
Dalmeny House
Elton Hall
Gainsborough's House
Ickworth Park & Garden
Firle Place
Kenwood, The Iveagh Bequest

Knowle
Parham House & Gardens
Petworth House
Shalom Hall
Upton House
Waddesdon Manor
Weston Park
Woburn Abbey

BELVOIR CASTLE

See under Leicestershire.

BURGHLEY HOUSE

(Burghley House Trustees)
Stamford   map **7** R22 △
Telephone: (01780) 52451
Fax: (01780) 480125

The finest example of later Elizabethan architecture in England, built (1565-1587) by William Cecil, the most able and trusted adviser to Queen Elizabeth I. Eighteen magnificent state rooms are open to visitors. Those painted by Antonio Verrio in the late 17th century form one of the greatest decorated suites in England. Burghley is a sumptuous Treasure House and contains one of the finest private collections of 17th century Italian paintings in the world. There are superb collections of English and Continental tapestries and furniture, many of which have been recently conserved. Burghley also houses the earliest inventoried collection of Oriental porcelain in the West. Works of art, silver, marbles and wood-carving fill the state rooms. There is also a special Exhibition which changes annually. The house is surrounded by a large and beautiful deer park, landscaped by 'Capability' Brown in the late 18th century. Car parking and entry to the Park is free.

Location: 1 m SE of Stamford, clearly signposted from the A1 and all approaches.
Station(s): Stamford (1 m), Peterborough (10 m).
Open: Apr 1-Oct 8 daily 11-5 closed Sept 2.
Admission: Adults £5.10 OAPs £4.80 accompanied children free (1 per adult, otherwise £2.50 per child). Party rates available.
Refreshments: Snacks, lunches and teas in the 'Capability' Brown Orangery. Enquiries for bookings party rates & menus tel: (01780) 52451.

DODDINGTON HALL

(Mr & Mrs A. G. Jarvis)
Doddington   map **7** Q21 △ Ⓢ
Telephone: (01522) 694308

One of the Elizabethan gems of England. A romantic house set in 5 acres of superb gardens, with beautiful contents which reflect 400 years of unbroken family occupation. Fine furniture, porcelain, tapestries and pictures, and still very much a family home.

Location: 5 m W of Lincoln on the B1190 & signposted off the A46 Lincoln by-pass.
Open: Gardens: 2-6pm Sundays from 12 March until 30 April and Easter Bank Holiday Monday. House & Garden: 2-6 pm Wednesdays, Sundays and Bank Holiday Mondays May to September inclusive.
Admission: Adults £3.60 Children £1.80 Gardens half price. Family ticket £10.25. Group bookings minimum £72 (20 people).
Refreshments: The Littlehouse Restaurant opens from noon on open days, 'phone (01522) 690980 for bookings.

FULBECK HALL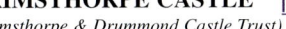
(Mrs M. Fry)
Grantham   NG32 3JW   map **7** Q21   ♿ △
Telephone: (01400) 272205
Fax: (01400) 272205

Home of the Fane family since 1632, with alterations and additions by nearly every generation. Mainly 18th century, older service wing. A friendly, lived-in house where visitors receive a personal welcome from the owners. Links with Wellington and the Raj. HQ of 1st Airbourne Division 1943-45; Arnhem Exhibition in their former Intelligence Room in house. Eleven acre garden contains recent plantings of unusual subjects within the Edwardian design. Plants for sale, nature trail with free leaflet, peacocks, picnic area. Fulbeck Hall (and Fulbeck Manor, see list at back) will open for groups of more than 20 at any time by prior arrangement.

Location: On A607. Lincoln 14 m, Grantham 11 m. 1 m S of A17.
Open: House and Garden Easter May and Aug Bank Hol Mons. Daily from July 2-31 incl, 2-5.
Admission: £3 OAPs £2.50 Children £1. Garden only £1.50 Children £1.
Refreshments: Teas. Special catering of any kind available for groups.
Guided tours for pre-booked groups only.

GRANTHAM HOUSE   ❧ **The National Trust**
Grantham   map **7** R21

Dating from 1380 but extensively altered and added to throughout the centuries. Ground floor only open to the public. The grounds run down to the river.

Location: In Castlegate, immediately E of Grantham Church.
Station(s): Grantham (1 m).
Open: 1 Apr-end of Sept Weds only 2-5 by written appointment only with Maj-Gen Sir Brian Wyldbore-Smith, Grantham House, Castlegate, Grantham NG1 6SS.
Admission: £1.50 children 70p. No reductions for parties.
No dogs. Unsuitable for wheelchairs. No lavatories.

George Stubbs
Portrait, animal and rural painter

(1724-1806)
Produced his engraved work,
The Anatomy of a Horse, in 1766

His work can be seen in the following properties included in Historic Houses Castles and Gardens:-

Mount Stewart House
St Osyth Priory
Upton House

GRIMSTHORPE CASTLE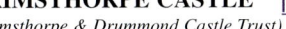
(Grimsthorpe & Drummond Castle Trust)
Bourne   map **7** R22

The home of the Willoughby de Eresby family since 1516. Examples of early 13th century architecture, the Tudor period of the reign of Henry VIII and work by Sir John Vanbrugh. State Rooms and Picture Galleries open to the Public.

Location: 4 m NW of Bourne on A151 Colsterworth/Bourne Road, SE of Grantham.
Open: Sundays, Thursdays and Bank Holidays from Easter Sunday (16 April) until 30 September. Also daily except Fridays and Saturdays in August. Park and Gardens open 11-6. Castle open 2pm (last admission 5).
Admission: Park: Adults £2 concessions £1. Additional separate charge for Castle - Adults £3 concessions £1.50. Combined ticket or Party Rate (20 or more) Adults £4 concessions £2.
Refreshments: The Coach House cafeteria serves home made teas.
Conferences: Conference room available.

GUNBY HALL   ❧ **The National Trust**
Burgh-le-Marsh   map **7** Q23

Built by Sir William Massingberd in 1700. Reynolds' portraits, contemporary wainscoting. Ground floor only open to the public. Walled gardens full of flowers and roses.

Location: 2½ m NW of Burgh-le-Marsh; 7 m W of Skegness on S side of A158.
Open: House & Garden 1 Apr-end of Sept Weds 2-6 Tues Thurs & Fri by prior written appointment only to J. D. Wrisdale, Esq., Gunby Hall, nr Spilsby, Lincs. Gardens only also on Thurs 2-6.
Admission: House & Gardens £3 children £1.50 Garden only £1.80 children 90p. No reduction for parties.
Dogs in garden only, on leads. Wheelchairs in garden only.

MARSTON HALL
(The Rev Henry Thorold, FSA)
Grantham   map **7** R21
Telephone: (01400) 250225

Tudor manor house with Georgian interiors, held by Thorold family since 14th century; interesting pictures and furniture. Romantic garden with long walks and avenues, high hedges enclosing herbaceous borders and vegetables. Gothick gazebo and ancient trees.

Open: Sun June 18 25 July 30 August 13 2-6pm and by appointment.
Admission: House & Garden £2.50.
Refreshments: Home-made teas.

TATTERSHALL CASTLE   ❧ **The National Trust**
Lincoln   map **7** Q22
Telephone: (01526) 342543

The Keep is one of the finest examples of a fortified brick dwelling, although built more for show than defence, c. 1440, for Ralph Cromwell. Museum and shop in Guardhouse.

Location: 12 m NE of Sleaford on Louth Road (A153); 3½ m SE of Woodhall Spa.
Open: 1 Apr-end Oct Sat-Wed & Bank Hol Mons (Closed Good Fri) 10-30-5.30. Nov-17 Dec Sat & Sun only 10-4. Last admissions half hour before closing.
Admission: £2.20 Chd £1.10. Parties of 15 or more - details from Custodian.
Refreshments: Fortescue Arms Hotel, Tattershall.
Dogs in car park only, on leads. Wheelchair access to ground floor of castle, shop and grounds. No wheelchairs available.

WOOLSTHORPE MANOR   🌿 The National Trust

nr Grantham   map **7** R21
Telephone: (01476) 860338

17th century farm house, birthplace of Sir Isaac Newton. Traditionally it was under an apple tree in this garden that Newton was struck with the theory of gravity.

Location: 7 m S of Grantham, ½ m NW of Colsterworth; 1 m W of A1 (not to be confused with Woolsthorpe, nr Belvoir).
Open: 1 Apr-end of Oct Wed-Sun and BH 1-5.30 last adm 5. *Closed Good Fri.*
Admission: £2.30 children £1.10. No reduction for parties.
Wheelchair access to garden & ground floor only. Parking for coaches limited to one at a time - must book. *NB In the interests of preservation numbers admitted to rooms at any time must be limited; liable to affect peak weekends and Bank Hols.*

LONDON (inc Greater London)

THE BLEWCOAT SCHOOL   🌿 The National Trust

Westminster   **SW1H 0PY**   map **12** T22
Telephone: 0171-222 2877

Built in 1709 at the expense of William Green, a local brewer, to provide an education for poor children; in use as a school until 1926, the building was bought by the Trust in 1954; it was restored in 1975 and now houses a National Trust shop and information centre.

Location: No 23 Caxton Street, Westminster, SW1.
Station(s): Victoria ¼ m; Underground St James's Park (Circle and District Lines) less than 100 yards.
Open: All year Mon-Fri 10-5.30. Late night shopping Thurs until 7. Also Sat Dec 2, 9, 16, 11-4.30. *Closed Bank Holiday Mon Dec 25-31 Jan 2 and Good Fri*
Admission: Free.
No Dogs.

BOSTON MANOR

(London Borough of Hounslow)
Brentford   map **12** T22
Telephone: 0181-570 0622

Jacobean house (1622) with elaborate plaster ceiling in the State Room which also contains a fireplace and mantelpiece dating from 1623. Original oak staircase. The house is set in a small park.

Location: In Boston Manor Road. Tube 10 mins walk - Boston Manor - (Piccadilly Line).
Open: May 28-Sept 24 Sun afternoons only 2.30-5.
Admission: Free.

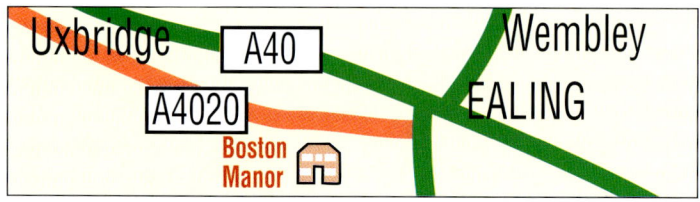

BUCKINGHAM PALACE

(Official residence of Her Majesty The Queen)
London   **SW1A 1AA**   map **12** U22
Telephone: 0171-799 2331

The official London residence of Her Majesty The Queen. Visitors are able to see the State Rooms, open each August and September, The Queen's Gallery and The Royal Mews which are open throughout the year.

Station(s): Victoria (BR) Victoria, Green Park, St. James's Park underground.
Open: Opening times vary according to season. Please telephone 0171-839 1377 for full details.
Admission: 1995 admission charges not available at time of going to press. Telephone 0171-839 1377 for information.
Pre-booking is essential for those visitors with walking difficulties or in wheelchairs for the State Rooms. The Queen's Gallery is not suitable for wheelchairs but The Royal Mews has full access.

BURGH HOUSE

(Burgh House Trust)
Hampstead   **NW3 1LT**   map **12** U22
Telephone: 0171-431 0144

Built 1703. Used for art exhibitions, concerts. Hampstead Museum. Terrace Garden.

Location: New End Sq E of Hampstead Underground Station.
Station(s): Hampstead (Underground). Hampstead Heath (BR North London Link).
Open: Wed-Sun 12-5 Bank Hol Mons 2-5.
Admission: Free.
Refreshments: Coffee, lunches and Teas. Licensed Buttery (for reservations and enquiries about catering for functions at the House Tel: 0171-431 2516).

CAREW MANOR AND DOVECOTE

(London Borough of Sutton)
Church Road, Beddington   **SM6 7NH**   map **12** U22   △
Telephone: 0181-770 4781
Fax: 0181-770 4777

The Grade I listed late-medieval Great Hall, with its arch-braced hammer-beam roof, is now accessible on Suns and Bank Hol Mons from Easter until Nov, together with the restored early 18th century Dovecote, with its 1,288 nesting boxes and potence, which is a scheduled ancient monument. Guided tours available of the Dovecote, the Great Hall and the cellars of the house which contain medieval, Tudor, and later features (cellars accessible on guided tours only). 3pm tours take in the late 14th century Church of St Mary, Beddington, with its Norman font and 15th century Carew Chapel containing important Carew memorials (the Carews of Beddington were lords of the manor for over four hundred years). Carew Manor and Beddington Church stand on the edge of Beddington Park, the landscaped home park of the Carews, through which a Heritage Trail has been established. Guide book, trail leaflet and other publications and souvenirs available.

Location: Church Road, Beddington. Off A232 ¾ m E of junction with A237.
Station(s): WADDON, then bus 407 or 408.
Open: Suns & Bank Hol Mons from Easter to Nov 1 (phone Sutton Heritage Service 0181-773 4555).
Admission: Charge.
Short tours at 2pm and 4pm; Long tour at 3pm.

CARLYLE'S HOUSE   🌿 The National Trust

Chelsea   **SW3 5HL**   map **12** U24
Telephone: 0171-352 7087

Home of Thomas and Jane Carlyle 1834-1881. *Note: Certain rooms have no electric light, visitors wishing to make a close study of the interior should avoid dull days.*

Location: At 24 Cheyne Row, Chelsea SW3 (off Cheyne Walk on Chelsea Embankment).
Station(s): Sloane Sq (Underground 1 m); Victoria (BR 1½ m). South Kensington (Underground 1 m).
Open: 1 Apr-end of Oct Wed-Sun & Bank Hol Mons 11-5. Last adm 4.30. *Closed Good Fri.*
Admission: £2.90 children £1.45. No reductions for parties which should not exceed 20 and must book.
No dogs. Unsuitable for wheelchairs.

CARSHALTON HOUSE

(London Borough of Sutton/Daughters of the Cross)
St. Philomena's School, Pound Street, Carshalton   **SM5 3PN**   map **12** U22   △
Telephone: 0181-770 4781/0181-773 4555
Fax: 0181-770 4777

An important listed building, built by about 1707 around the core of an older house and with grounds laid out originally by Charles Bridgeman, Carshalton House is open on a limited number of occasions each year. Its garden buildings include the unique 18th centurey Water Tower, now in the care of the Carshalton Water Tower Trust. The house contains principal rooms with 18th century decoration, including the 'Adam' or Blue Room and the Painted Parlour (attributed to Robert Robinson). Openings are organised by Sutton Heritage Service in conjunction with the Water Tower Trust and the Daughters of the Cross. Tours of the house and grounds and a programme of short talks on the house and its people are given during the day (included in entrance fee). Refreshments and publications are available. Carshalton House is close to Sutton's Heritage Centre at Honeywood, in the Carshalton conservation area.

Location: Pound Street, Carshalton, at junction with Carshalton Road, on A232.
Station(s): Carshalton (¼ m).
Open: 1995 Mon Apr 17 (Easter Mon) Bank Hol Mon Aug 28 10-5 (last admission 4.15).
Admission: £2.50 adults £1.50 children under 16 yrs.
Refreshments: Sandwiches, tea, coffee and home made cakes available.
For further details telephone Sutton Heritage Service on 0181-770 4781 or 0181-773 4555.

CHAPTER HOUSE AND PYX CHAMBER OF WESTMINSTER ABBEY

ENGLISH HERITAGE

map **12** T22
Telephone: 0171-222 5897

Described as 'incomparable' when it was finished in 1253, with some of the finest of English medieval sculpture, the chapter house was one of the largest in England and could seat 80 monks around its walls. It was converted to a record office in the 16th century, but by 1740 the roof had decayed and been removed. Restoration of the whole building took place in 1865 and again after it was bombed in 1941. The 11th century Pyx Chamber now houses the Abbey Treasures. A joint ticket admits to the Abbey Museum.

Location: East side of the abbey cloister.
Open: Apr 1-Sept 30 10-6 daily Oct 1-Mar 31 daily 10-4.
Admission: Adults £2.50 concessions £1.90 children £1.30.
Liable to be closed at short notice on state occasions.

COLLEGE OF ARMS

(The Corporation of Kings, Heralds & Pursuivants of Arms)
City of London   EC4V 4BT   map **12** T22   △
Telephone: 0171-248 2762
Fax: 0171-248 6448

Mansion built in 1670s to house the English Officers of Arms and their records, and the panelled Earl Marshal's Court.

Location: On N side of Queen Victoria Street; S of St Paul's Cathedral.
Open: Earl Marshal's Court open all the year (except Public holidays & on State & special occasions) Mon-Fri 10-4 group visits (up to 10) by arrangement only. Record Room open for tours (groups of up to 20) by special arrangement in advance with the Officer in Waiting.
Admission: Free (parties by negotiation).
No coaches, parking, indoor photography or dogs. Shop - books, souvenirs.

DE MORGAN FOUNDATION

(De Morgan Foundation)
Old Battersea House, 30 Vicarage Crescent, Battersea   SW11 3LD   map **12** U22
△ &
Telephone: 0181-788 1341

A substantial part of the De Morgan Foundation collection of ceramics by William De Morgan and paintings and drawings by Evelyn De Morgan (nee Pickering), her uncle Roddam Spencer Stanhope, J. M. Strudwick and Cadogan Cowper are displayed in the ground floor rooms of elegantly restored Old Battersea House - a Wren style building which is privately occupied. Works from

the Foundation's collection may also be seen at Cardiff Castle, Cragside (Northumbria), Knightshayes (Tiverton), The St. John portraits are at Lydiard Park, Swindon.

Location: 30 Vicarage Crescent, Battersea.
Station(s): Clapham Junction.
Open: Admission by appointment only usually Wed afternoons. All visits are guided.
Admission: £1 (optional catalogue £1.50) no special reductions. Parties - max 30. (split into two groups of 15).
Refreshments: No catering at house. Many facilities in Battersea/Wandsworth.
Car parking in Vicarage Crescent. Suitable for disabled, (no special facilities for wheelchairs) front steps are the only obstacle. Adm by writing in advance to De Morgan Foundation, 21 St Margaret's Crescent, London SW15 6HL.

FENTON HOUSE   🌿 The National Trust

Hampstead   NW3 6RT   map **12** T22
Telephone: 0171-435 3471

Collection of porcelain, pottery and Benton Fletcher collection of early keyboard musical instruments. Late 17th century house, walled garden.

Location: On W side of Hampstead Grove.
Station(s): Hampstead (Underground 300 yards); Hampstead Heath (BR 1 m).
Open: Mar Sat & Sun only 2-5 Apr-end Oct Sat Suns and Bank Hol Mon 11-5.30; Mon, Tues and Wed 2-5.30. Last adm ½ hour before closing time. *Closed Good Fri.*
Admission: £3.50 Children half-price. No reductions for parties, which must book. Family ticket £9.
No dogs. Suitable for wheelchairs on ground floor only. Opening of house may be delayed due to building work.

GUNNERSBURY PARK MUSEUM

(London Boroughs of Ealing & Hounslow)
Gunnersbury Park   W3 8QL   map **12** T22   &
Telephone: 0181-992 1612
Fax: 0181-752 0686

Large mansion built c.1802 by architect owner Alexander Copland. Fine rooms by Sydney Smirke and painted ceilings by E. T. Parris for N. M. Rothschild c.1836. Now a local history museum which includes Rothschild carriages.

Original Victorian kitchens open summer. Large park with other buildings of interest, and sporting facilities.

Location: Mansion at NE corner of Park; alongside North Circular (A406); N of Great West Road & M4; Kew Bridge 1¼ m; Chiswick Roundabout ½ m. Bus: E3 (daily), 7 (Suns only).
Station(s): Acton Town (Underground ¼ m).
Open: House & Museum Apr-Oct Mon-Fri 1-5 Sat Sun & Bank Hols 1-6 Nov-Mar Mon-Fri 1-4 Sat Sun & Bank Hols 1-4 closed Christmas Eve, Christmas Day, Boxing Day New Years Day & Good Friday. Gardens daily dawn till dusk. Special facilities for school parties by arrangement with Interpretative Officer.
Admission: Free.
Refreshments: Cafeteria in Park (daily, winter weekends according to weather).
Vehicle access Popes Lane (ample car parking). Pedestrians - many entries to Park. Ground floor displays with ramp access, toilets (including disabled-user) nearby in park.

HALL PLACE
(Bexley London Borough Council)
Bourne Road, Bexley   DA5 1PQ   map **12** U23   △
Telephone: (01322) 526574
Fax: (01322) 522921

Historic mansion (1540) with additions c.1640. Museum and other exhibitions. Outstanding Rose, Rock, Herb gardens and Floral bedding displays, Conservatories, Parkland, Topiary.

Location: Near the junction of A2 and A223.
Station(s): Station: Bexley (½ m).
Open: MANSION. Mon-Sat 10-5 (or dusk if earlier) Suns 2-6 (British Summertime only). PARK & GROUNDS. Daily during daylight throughout the year.
Admission: Free.
Refreshments: At cafe & restaurant.

HAM HOUSE   🦡 The National Trust
Ham, Richmond   TW10 7RS   map **12** U22   &
Telephone: 0181-940 1950

Outstanding Stuart house, built about 1610, redecorated and furnished in 1670s in the most up to date style of the time by the Duke and Duchess of Lauderdale; restored 17th century garden in process of restoration. Beautiful setting by the Thames.

Location: On South bank of the river Thames, W of A307 at Petersham.
Station(s): Richmond 2 m by road. Kingston 2 m. Bus: LT 65 Ealing Broadway-Kingston. 371 Richmond-Kingston (both passing BR Richmond and Kingston), 71 also passing BR Surbiton.
Open: House 1 Apr-end Oct Mon-Wed 1-5 Sat 1-5.30 Sun 11.30-5.30 open Good Fri closed Tues following. 4 Nov-17 Dec Sat & Sun 1-4. Last admission half hour before closing. Garden all year daily except Fri 10.30-6 (or dusk if earlier) open Good Fri. *Closed Christmas & New Year*
Admission: Garden free. House £4 children £2 pre booked parties on application.
Refreshments: Orangery Restaurant (licensed) open same days as house, waitress service; lunches from 12.30 Teas 3-5. Garden room counter service only open Apr-end Oct daily except Fri (open Good Fri) 11-5.30.
Disabled visitors may park near entrance. Lavatory for disabled in garden.

Lancelot 'Capability' Brown

Born 1716 in Northumberland, Capability Brown began work at the age of 16 in the vegetable gardens of Sir William and Lady Loraine at Kirharle Tower. He left Northumberland in 1739, and records show that he worked at Stowe until 1749. It was at Stowe that Brown began to study architecture, and to submit his own plans. It was also at Stowe that he devised a new method of moving and replanting mature trees.

Brown married Bridget Wayet in 1744 and began work on the estate at Warwick Castle in 1749. He was appointed Master Gardener at Hampton Court in 1764, and planted the Great Vine at Hampton Court in 1768. Blenheim Palace designs are considered amongst Brown's finest work, and the technical achievements were outstanding even for the present day.

Capability Brown died in February 1783 of a massive heart attack. A monument beside the lake at Croome Court was erected which reads "To the memory of Lancelot Brown, who by the powers of his inimitable and creative genius formed this garden scene out of a morass". There is also a portrait of Brown at Burghley.

Capability Brown was involved in the design of grounds at the following properties included in Historic Houses Castles and Gardens:-

Audley End	*Longleat*
Berrington Hall	*Luton Hoo*
Bowood	*Moccas Court*
Burghley House	*Petworth House*
Burton Constable	*Sledmere House*
Charlecote Park	*Stowe (Stowe*
Chilham Castle Gardens	*School)*
(reputed)	*Syon House*
Clandon Park	*Warwick Castle*
Claremont	*Weston Park*
Chillington Hall	*Wimpole Hall*
Corsham Court	*Wrest Park and*
Fawley Court	*Gardens*
Highclere Castle	

HERITAGE CENTRE
Honeywood Walk, Carshalton, Surrey

The history of the borough and its people plus a changing programme of exhibitions, presented in a 17th cent. listed building. Features include Edwardian Billiard Room & Tudor Gallery. Tearooms and Gift Shop.

LITTLE HOLLAND HOUSE
40 Beeches Avenue, Carshalton, Surrey

The home of Frank Dickinson (1874-1961) follower of the Arts and Crafts Movement, who designed and built the house and its contents himself. Interior listed Grade II* Guide book and other publications on sale.

London Borough of Sutton Heritage Service

For information call 0181-773 4555

CARSHALTON HOUSE
Pound Street, Carshalton, Surrey

Built c.1707 with grounds originally laid out by Charles Bridgeman, the principal rooms contain 18th century decoration. Garden buildings include the unique Water Tower. Publications, souvenirs and home-made refreshments available.

Open Days 1995: Easter Monday 17th April and Bank Hol. Monday 28th August

WHITEHALL
1 Malden Road, Cheam, Surrey

A timber-framed continuous-jettied house built c.1500. Features revealed sections of original fabric plus displays on Cheam Pottery, Nonsuch Palace, Cheam School and timber-framed buildings. Tea Room.

CAREW MANOR & DOVECOTE
Church Road, Beddington, Surrey

Grade I late medieval Great Hall, with hammer-beam roof, and 18th cent. brick Dovecote with 1288 nesting boxes and restored potence (circular ladder). Guided tours include cellars of Manor. Gift Shop.

HERITAGE CENTRE, HONEYWOOD
(London Borough of Sutton)
Honeywood Walk, Carshalton   SM5 3NX   map **12** U22   △
Telephone: 0181-773 4555
Fax: 0181-770 4777

Discover the fascinating history of the area now within the London Borough of Sutton (which includes Beddington, Carshalton, Cheam, Sutton and Wallington). Based in 'Honeywood', a listed building of 17th century origin, with permanent displays plus a changing programme of exhibitions covering many aspects of local life. Areas of particular interest include a magnificent Edwardian billiard room, a Childhood Room full of late Victorian and Edwardian toys and games, a Tudor Gallery and an Art Gallery. A wide range of unusual gifts, souvenirs and local history publications are on sale in the shop. 'Honeywood' overlooks Carshalton's picturesque town ponds, in the heart of a conservation area.

Location: Honeywood Walk, Carshalton. By Carshalton Ponds, opp. the Greyhound Inn. (off A232).
Station(s): Carshalton (¼ m).
Open: Heritage Centre: Wed-Fri 10-5 Sat Sun & Bank Hol Mons 10-5.30. Tea-rooms: Tues-Sun 10-5.15.
Admission: Adults 80p children 40p.
Refreshments: Tea-rooms with separate non-smoking area.
Free entry to the shop and tearooms which serve a tempting array of hot and cold food. Art Gallery and rooms available for hire. Telephone the Heritage Centre on 0181-773-4555 for further information and details of current exhibitions. Display about the Wandle River opening in 1995.

HOGARTH'S HOUSE
(London Borough of Hounslow)
Chiswick   map **12** U22   △
Telephone: 0181-994 6757

Just 50 yards from the busy Hogarth Roundabout lies this charming early 18th century house which was once the country home of William Hogarth, the famous painter and engraver. It is now a gallery where most of his well known engravings are on display. These include: 'Harlot's Progress', 'Rake's Progress', 'Marriage a la mode', and also 'Gin Lane' and 'Beer Street' both of which can be bought at the house, together with books and postcards of Hogarth's works. There is a restoration programme beginning for both the house and garden. In nearby Chiswick Mall are houses of a similar period, and in the graveyard around St. Nicholas' Church, is Hogarth's tomb. World famous Chiswick House is only 10 minutes walk away.

Aviaries and Birds of Prey Centres

can be found at the following properties in

Historic Houses Castles and Gardens:-

Drumlanrig Castle & Country Park
Elsham Hall Country and Wildlife Park
Holdenby House & Gardens
Leeds Castle
Leighton House Museum & Art Gallery
Sewerby Hall & Gardens
Sion Hill Hall
Waddesdon Manor
Muncaster Castle

Location: In Hogarth Lane, Great West Road, Chiswick W4 2QN (200 yards Chiswick House).
Station(s): Chiswick (½ m) (Southern Region); Turnham Green (1 m) (District Line).
Open: Apr-Sept Mon-Sat 11-6 Sun 2-6 Oct-Mar Mon-Sat 11-4 Sun 2-4 closed Tues, Good Friday, first 2 full weeks in Sept, last 3 weeks in Dec & New Year's Day.
Admission: Free. Parties by arrangement.
Parking: Chiswick House car park and in named parking bays in Axis Business Centre - behind house.

KEATS HOUSE

(London Borough of Camden)
Wentworth Place, Keats Grove, Hampstead, NW3 2RR   map **12** T22   △
Telephone: 0171-435 2062
Fax: 0171-431 9293

Keats House was built in 1815-1816 as Wentworth Place, a pair of semi-detached houses. John Keats, the poet, lived here from 1818 to 1820; here he wrote 'Ode to a Nightingale', and met Fanny Brawne, to whom he became engaged. Keats' early death in Italy prevented the marriage. Keats House was completely restored in 1974-1975. It houses letters, books and other personal relics of the poet and his fiancee.

Location: S end of Hampstead Heath nr South End Green.
Station(s): (BR Hampstead Heath). Underground: Belsize Park or Hampstead. Bus: 24, 46, 168, C11, C12 (alight South End Green). 268 (alight Downshire Hill).
Open: All the year Apr 1-Oct Mon-Fri 10-1 and 2-6 Sat 10-1 and 2-5 Sun and Bank Holidays 2-5 Nov-Mar Mon-Fri 1-5 Sat 10-1 and 2-5 Sun 2-5 closed Christmas Eve Christmas Day Boxing Day New Year's Day Good Friday Easter Eve & May 8. Please check times on 0171-435 2062.
Admission: Free.

KENWOOD, THE IVEAGH BEQUEST

Hampstead   map **12** T22
Telephone: 0181-348 1286

Standing in splendid grounds on the edge of Hampstead Heath, Kenwood contains the most important private collection of paintings ever given to the nation. There is a selection of Old Masters among the finest a Self Portrait of Rembrandt and paintings by British artists such as Turner, Reynolds and Gainsborough. The outstanding neoclassical house itself was remodelled by Robert Adam, 1764-73 who created the magnificent Library. Many rooms contain displays of English neoclassical furniture. Outside, the historic landscaped park, with sloping lawns and a lake, form a perfect setting to the lakeside concerts held here in the summer.

Location: Hampstead Lane, NW3.
Station(s): Archway or Golders Green Underground (Northern Line), then Bus 210.
Open: Apr 1-Sept 30 10-6 daily Oct1-Mar 31 daily 10-4.
Admission: Free.
Refreshments: At the Coach House.

LEIGHTON HOUSE MUSEUM AND ART GALLERY

(Royal Borough of Kensington and Chelsea)
12 Holland Park Road   W14 8LZ   map **12** T22
Telephone: 0171-602 3316
Fax: 0171-371 2467

Adjacent to Holland Park in Kensington lies the Artists' Colony, a group of remarkable Studio Houses, built by some of the leading figures of the Victorian Art World. Leighton House Museum was the first of these to be built, and is today a museum of High Victorian art. The opulent fantasy of Frederic Lord Leighton, President of the Royal Academy, the house was designed by George Aitchison. Leighton lived here from 1866 until his death in 1896. His unique collection of Islamic tiles is displayed in the walls of the Arab Hall, and the Victorian interiors, restored to their original splendour, are hung with paintings by Leighton, Millais, Watts, Burne-Jones and others. Sculpture is displayed in the house and garden. The study collection of Leighton drawings may be seen by appointment. Temporary exhibitions of modern and historic art throughout the year.

Location: Kensington.
Station(s): High Street, Kensington.
Open: All year Mon-Sat 11-5.30 (closed Sun & Bank Holidays) Garden Apr-Sept. Parties by arrangement with the Curator. Children under 16 must be accompanied by an adult.
Admission: Free.

LINLEY SAMBOURNE HOUSE
(The Victorian Society)
18 Stafford Terrace   W8 7BH   map **12** U22
Telephone: 0181-994 1019
Fax: 0181-995 4895

The home of Linley Sambourne (1844-1910), chief political cartoonist at 'Punch'. A unique survival of a late Victorian town house. The original decorations and furnishings have been preserved together with many of Sambourne's own cartoons and photographs, as well as works by other artists of the period.
Location: 18 Stafford Terrace, W8 7BH.
Station(s): (Underground) Kensington High Street. Bus: 9, 10, 27, 28, 31, 49, 52, 70 & C1.
Open: 1 Mar-31 Oct Wed 10-4 Sun 2-5 parties at other times by prior arrangement. Apply to The Victorian Society, 1 Priory Gardens, London W4 Telephone: 0181-742 3438.
Admission: £3 Senior Citizens (British) £2.50 under 16 £1.50.

LITTLE HOLLAND HOUSE
(London Borough of Sutton)
40 Beeches Avenue, Carshalton   SM5 3LW   map **12** U22   △
Telephone: 0181-770 4781
Fax: 0181-770 4777

The home of Frank Dickinson (1874-1961), follower of William Morris and the Arts and Crafts movement: artist, designer and craftsman in wood and metal who built the house himself to his own design and in pursuance of his philosophy and theories. Features his interior design, paintings, hand-made furniture and other craft objects.
Location: 40 Beeches Avenue, Carshalton. On B278 (off A232).
Station(s): Few minutes from Carshalton Beeches BR.
Open: First Sun in the month plus Bank Hol Suns & Mons 1.30-5.30. Closed Christmas Eve to Jan 2nd.
Admission: Free.
Further information from Sutton Heritage Service on 0181-770-4781 or 773-4555. Guided tours for groups available outside normal opening hours.

MUSEUM OF FULHAM PALACE
(Fulham Palace Trust)
Bishops Avenue, Fulham, London   SW6 6EA   map **12** U22   △ ♿
Telephone: 0171-736 7181 (General enquiries)/0171-736 3233 (Museum & tours)
Fax: 0171-736 8140

Based in the former residence of the Bishop of London (Tudor with Georgian additions and a Victorian Chapel) the display tells the story of this ancient site. They include paintings, archaeology, garden history, and architecture. The gardens, famous in the 17th century when many American species were introduced to Europe through Fulham Palace, now contain specimen trees and a knot garden of herbs.
Location: In Bishop's Ave, ½ m N of Putney Bridge underground station (District Line).
Open: Grounds, Botanic Garden and herb collection open daily during daylight hours. Museum Mar-Oct Wed-Sun 2-5 and BH Mons, Nov-Feb Thurs-Sun 1-4.
Admission: Grounds and Botanic Garden Free. Museum 50p concessions 25p children free. Tour of 4 rooms and gardens every second Sun throughout the year at 2 costing £2. Private tours at other times by arrangement (£4 per head incl. tea). School visits including sessions with replica costume by appointment.
Refreshments: Tea available on tour days or by arrangement.
Events/Exhibitions: Lectures, concerts and exhibitions (ring for details).
Audio tour available including versions for visually impaired and people with learning difficulties. Quizzes and trails for children.

MUSEUM OF GARDEN HISTORY
(The Tradescant Trust (Registered Charity No 273436)
Lambeth   map **12** U22
Telephone: 0171-261 1891
Fax: 0171-401 8869

Fascinating permanent exhibition of the history of gardens, collection of ancient tools, re-creation of 17th century garden displaying flowers and shrubs of the period, the seeds of which may be purchased in the Garden Shop. Also tombs of the Tradescants and Captain Bligh of the 'Bounty'. Lectures, courses, concerts, fairs and art exhibitions are held regularly throughout the year. Knowledgeable staff; a shop selling books and gifts; light refreshments all combine to make a visit both pleasurable and worthwhile.
Location: Lambeth Palace Road.

Station(s): Waterloo or Victoria, then 507 Red Arrow bus, alight Lambeth Palace.
Open: Mon-Fri 10.30-4 Sun 10.30-5. *Closed Sat. Closed from second Sun in Dec to first Sun in Mar.*
Admission: Free. Donation requested.
Refreshments: Tea, coffee, light lunches; parties catered for but prior booking essential. Literature sent on request with SAE.

THE OCTAGON, ORLEANS HOUSE GALLERY

(London Borough of Richmond upon Thames)
Riverside Twickenham, Middlesex   TW1 3DJ   map **12** U22   ♿
Telephone: 0181-892 0221
Fax: 0181-744 0501

The magnificent Octagon built by James Gibbs in c.1720 for James Johnston, Joint Secretary of State for Scotland under William III. An outstanding example of baroque architecture. The adjacent wing has been converted into an art gallery which shows temporary exhibitions and the whole is situated in an attractive woodland garden.
Location: Access from Richmond Road (A305).
Station(s): St Margaret's (½ m); Twickenham (½ m); Richmond (underground 2 m)
Open: Tues-Sat 1-5.30 (Oct-Mar 1-4.30) Sun 2-5.30 (Oct-Mar 2-4.30) Easter, Spring and Summer Bank Hols 2-5.30. Closed Christmas Day, Christmas Eve, Boxing Day. Other times by appointment.
Admission: Free. Parking also free.
Disabled access to Octagon: W.

OLD ROYAL OBSERVATORY

(National Maritime Museum)
Greenwich   SE10   map **12** U23
Telephone: 0181-858 4422
Fax: 0181-312 6632

Following a major restoration and reinterpretation the Old Royal Observatory re-opened in March 1993. It includes Flamsteed House, designed by Sir Christopher Wren, the Meridian Building and the Greenwich Planetarium.
Location: In Greenwich Park, N side of Blackheath off A2.
Station(s): Maze Hill (short walk).
Open: Mon-Sat 10-5 Sun 12-5. *Closed Dec 24/25/26.*
Admission: Combined ticket to three attractions adult £4.95 OAPS/students £3,95 children £2.95.
Refreshments: In Park cafeteria and museum main buildings.
Partial wheelchair access.

Butterfly Houses

*can be found at the following properties includ-
ed in Historic Houses Castles and Gardens:-*

*Berkeley Castle
Elsham Hall - Wild butterfly walkway
Syon House*

OSTERLEY PARK   🌳 The National Trust

Isleworth, Middlesex   TW7 4RB   map **12** U22   △ ♿
Telephone: 0181-560 3918

Elizabethan mansion transformed by Robert Adam 1760-80; with Adam decorations and furniture; 140 acres of parkland.
Location: ¼ m E of Osterley Underground station (Piccadilly Line) and ½ m W of Gillette Corner, access from Thornbury Road, N side of Great West Road (A4).
Station(s): Syon Lane (1¾ m); Underground: Osterley (¾ m). Bus: LT 91 Hounslow-Wandsworth (½ m)
Open: House 1 Apr-end Oct Wed-Sat 1-5 Sun and Bank Holiday Mon 11-5. House closed Good Fri. Last admission 4.30. Park and Pleasure grounds all year 9-7.30 or sunset if earlier. Car park closed Dec 25, 26. Shop open as house and pre-Christmas Nov-Dec 17 Wed-Sun 12-4.
Admission: £3.60 Family ticket £9. Parties must book, rates on application to Administrator. Park free. Car park 250 yds £1.50. Guided tours may be arranged in advance with the Administrator.
Refreshments: Teas and light lunches in stables, Weds to Sun and Bank Holiday Mon, Mar to end Oct 12-5. Also open Good Friday.
Park suitable for disabled. Lavatory for disabled. Dogs in park only; On leads except in certain areas as specified at the property.

PITSHANGER MANOR MUSEUM

(London Borough of Ealing)
Mattock Lane, Ealing   W5 56Q   map **12** T22
Telephone: 0181-567 1227 or 0181-579 2424 ext 42683
Fax: 0181-567 0595

Set in an attractive park, Pitshanger Manor was built 1800-04 by the architect Sir John Soane (1753-1837) as his family home. The house incorporates a wing of the late 1760s by George Dance. The interiors are being restored. A Victorian room holds a changing and extensive display of Martinware pottery including a unique chimney-piece of 1891. Exhibitions and cultural events are held regularly.
Location: 3 mins from Ealing Broadway Tube Station (Central and District Lines). On the A3001 (Ealing Green). No parking.
Open: Tues-Sat 10-5. *Closed Sun & Mon.* (but open Sun afternoons in July and Aug). *Also closed Christmas, Easter and New Year.* All rooms are open to the public after 1pm. *Please enquire in advance as to which rooms are open in the mornings.*
Admission: Free. Parties by arrangement in advance.
Refreshments: Tea and coffee vending machine.
Limited disabled access - further details available on request.

THE QUEEN'S HOUSE
(National Maritime Museum)
Greenwich   SE10   map **12** U23
Telephone: 0181-858 4422
Fax: 0181-312 6632

THE QUEENS HOUSE
GREENWICH
A Royal Palace by the Thames

Visit the House of Delights designed by Inigo Jones for the wife of Charles I. Admire the sumptuous Royal Apartments that recreate the original seventeenth century splendour, and learn the fascinating history of the House in the special display in the vaulted brick basement. A combined ticket allows you to visit the Old Royal Observatory and National Maritime Museum which are nearby

ADMISSION – SEE EDITORIAL REFERENCE

Royal Palace designed by Inigo Jones for Anne of Denmark, wife of James I, and Henrietta Maria, wife of Charles I. Now restored to its former 17th century glory, after a £5M refurbishment. Highlights include the sumptuous Royal Apartments and the Great Hall, a perfect 40ft cube. The vaulted brick basement houses a display on the history of the house, and the treasury, showing the NMM's richest trophies, swords and ornamental silver.

Location: Greenwich, London.
Station(s): Maze Hill (BR); Island Gardens (Docklands Light Railway); River Cruises.
Open: Mon-Sats 10-5 Suns 12-5 . *Closed* Christmas Eve & Day, Boxing Day also 4-31 January 1995.
Admission: Combined 3 attraction ticket adults £4.95 OAPs/Students £3.95 children £2.95.
Refreshments: Licensed restaurant.
Conferences: Small conferences & functions by arrangement.
Wheelchair access to ground floor and basement. Wheelchairs available.

Giovanni Antonio Canale
- known as Canaletto
Born in Venice 1697, died 1768
Lived in England 1746 - 1755

His work can be seen in the following properties included in Historic Houses Castles and Gardens:-

Alnwick Castle
Bowhill
Goodwood House
Upton House

ROYAL BOTANIC GARDENS, KEW
Kew, Richmond   TW9 3AB   map **12** U22
Telephone: 0181-940 1171
Fax: 0181-332 5197

Few attractions offer the variety and spectacle of Kew Gardens, 300 acres - six of them under glass - containing a collection of plants unique in the world. Rhododendrons from the Himilayas, roses from Europe and the Far East, brilliant formal flower beds, a wild woodland covered in bluebells. At every season of the year, Kew presents a lasting memory. the extensive, world famous glass houses mean that even in the winter a visit is full of fascination. The Princess of Wales Conservatory contains ten climatic zones under one roof - from steamy rain forest with wild orchids, to arid desert with giant cacti. Many new features have been added to Kew in the past five years: a twenty minute multi-media display in the Sir Joseph Banks Building, the Marine display of plants from the sea, swamp and river estuary under the Palm House, and the Victoria Gate visitor centre which contains a splendid shop, and where hour-long tours of the Garden are available.

Location: South circular (A205) car and coach parking. Underground Kew Gardens. British Rail Kew Bridge.
Open: Gardens open everyday except Christmas and New Years day 9.30-sunset. Galleries and Glass Houses open 9.30.
Admission: Adults £4 children/OAPs/concessions £2 family ticket (2+4) £10.
Refreshments: Refreshment Pavilion (open Apr-Oct), Orangery Restaurant (open all year), Picnic Box (open Apr-Oct), Kew Bakery (open Apr-Oct). Tel: 0181-332 5157
Easy access for disabled, W.C., wheelchairs available. Guided tours (Victoria Gate Visitor Centre) 11 and 2. Educational visits including topic days Tel: 0181-940 1171. Enquiry Unit: address as above Tel: 0181-940 1171.

ROYAL INSTITUTE OF BRITISH ARCHITECTS: DRAWINGS COLLECTION AND HEINZ GALLERY
(Royal Institute of British Architects)
London   W1   map **12** T22
Telephone: 0171-580 5533
Fax: 0171-486 3797

Changing architectural exhibitions throughout most of the year.
Location: 21 Portman Square W1H 9HF.
Open: Weekdays 11-5 Sats 10-1 Study room open weekdays by appointment only.
Admission: Free (exhibitions).
Unsuitable for disabled persons. No car parking.

RSA (THE ROYAL SOCIETY FOR THE ENCOURAGEMENT OF ARTS, MANUFACTURES AND COMMERCE)
8 John Adam Street, London   WC2N 6EZ   map **12** T22
Telephone: 0171-930 5115
Fax: 0171-839 5805

Founded in 1754, the RSA moved to its bespoke house, designed and built by Robert Adam, in 1774. The most interesting features of the Society's premises are its Great Room, a lecture hall, capacity 200, with murals by James Barry, and the recently restored vaults.

Location: 8 John Adam Street, London WC2N 6EZ.
Station(s): Charing Cross, Embankment.
Open: Mon-Fri 10-1 visitors who wish to see any of the Society's rooms are requested to telephone Susan Bennett in advance in order to avoid disappointment if the rooms are in use and therefore inaccessible.
Admission: Free.

ST. JOHN'S GATE

(The Order of St. John)
Clerkenwell   EC1M 4DA   map **12** T22   △
Telephone: 0171-253 6644, Ext 27/28
Fax: 0171-490 8835

Headquarters of the Order in England, the 16th century gatehouse contains the most comprehensive collection of items relating to the Order of St John outside Malta. Together with the nearby Priory Church and 12th century Crypt it now forms the headquarters of the modern Order of St. John, whose charitable foundations include St. John Ambulance and the Ophthalmic Hospital in Jerusalem. The collection includes Maltese silver, Furniture, paintings, coins and pharmacy jars.

Location: In St John's Lane, EC1M 4DA.
Station(s): (Underground) Farringdon, Barbican.
Open: Mon-Fr 10-5 Sat 10-4. Tours of the building including the Grand Priory Church and Norman crypt on Tues Fri and Sat 11 & 2.30.

SIR JOHN SOANE'S MUSEUM

(Trustees of Sir John Soane's Museum)
13 Lincoln's Inn Fields   WC2A 3BP   map **12** T22
Telephone: 0171-405 2107; Information line 0171-430 0175

Built by Sir John Soane, RA, in 1812-13 as his private residence. Contains his collection of antiquities and works of art.

Station(s): Holborn Tube.
Open: Tues-Sat 10-5 (lecture tours Sat 2.30 maximum 22 people. No groups). Groups welcome at other times but must book in advance. Late evening opening on the first Tues of each month 6-9. Also library and architectural drawings collection access by appointment. Closed Bank Holidays.
Admission: Free.
Events/Exhibitions: Beginning in April 1995.

SOUTHSIDE HOUSE

(The Pennington-Mellor-Munthe Charity Trust)
Wimbledon Common   SW19 4RJ   map **12** U22   △
Telephone: 0181-947 2491 or 0181-946 7643

Built by Robert Pennington as a safe retreat for his family after his little son died in the London Plague in 1665. Still lived in by his descendants today. Much

original furnishing remains. Family portraits by Van Dyke & Hogarth. Personal possessions of Ann Boleyn - whose sister married into this family - are shown. Also a bedroom prepared for the Prince of Wales in 1750 and gifts to John Pennington - the family 'Scarlet Pimpernel' - by those he helped to escape from the guillotine - including a pearl necklace which fell from Marie Antoinette when her head was cut off. Also the Dining Room where Admiral Lord Nelson dined with Sir William and Lady Hamilton and the Music Room where she performed her 'attitudes'. In 1907 the heiress of this house, Hilda Pennington Mellor married Axel Munthe the Swedish Doctor and Philanthropist who wrote part of his 'Story of San Michele' here.

Location: On S side of Wimbledon Common (B281), opposite The Crooked Billet Inn.
Station(s): Wimbledon (British Rail & Underground) 1 m. Buses: No 93, alight Rose & Crown Inn, Wimbledon High Street - six minutes walk along Southside of Common to Crooked Billet Inn and Southside House.
Open: From Oct 1-May 31. Guided tours only on Tues, Thurs, Sat & Bank Holiday Mons *(Closed Christmas)* on the hour from 2-5 (last admission), lasting approximately 1 hr. Other times by special agreement with Administrator. Organised school groups accompanied by responsible teachers free by appointment in writing.
Admission: Adults £5 (children accompanied by adult £2).

SPENCER HOUSE

27 St.James's Place, London   SW1A 1NR   map **12** T22
Telephone: 0171-409 0526

Spencer House, built 1756-66 for the first Earl Spencer, an ancestor of HRH The Princess of Wales, is London's finest surviving 18th century townhouse. This magnificent private palace, overlooking Green Park, has regained the full splendour of its 18th century appearance after a painstaking ten-year restoration. Eight state rooms are open to the public for viewing on Sundays and are available for private and corporate entertaining during the rest of the week.

Location: 27 St.James's Place, London SW1A 1NR.
Station(s): Green Park.
Open: Every Sun (except during Jan and Aug) from 11.30-4.45. Tours last approx. 1 hr. Tickets available at door from 10.30 on day, however, advance reservation recommended for both individuals and groups (Tel 0171-499 8620 Tues-Fri 10-1).
Admission: Adults £6 concessions £5 (students/Friends of the Royal Academy/Tate and V&A all with cards/children 10-16; under 10 not admitted). Prices valid until end March 1995. Accessible for wheelchair users.

William Kent (1685 - 1748)
Painter, architect, garden designer

His work can be seen in the following properties included in Historic Houses Castles and Gardens:-

> *Chiswick House*
> *Ditchley Park (decoration of Great*
>   *Hall)*
> *Euston Hall*
> *Rousham House*
> *Stowe (Stowe School)*

STRAWBERRY HILL

St. Mary's University College
Waldegrave Road, Twickenham   TW1 4SX   map **12** U22
Telephone: (0181) 744 1932
Fax: (0181) 744 1947

Horace Walpole bought Strawberry Hill in 1749 and converted the modest house into his own vision of a 'gothic' fantasy. It is widely regarded as the first substantial building of the gothic revival and as such is internationally known and admired. A century later, Lady Frances Waldegrave added a magnificent wing to Walpole's original structure. It is only recently that Strawberry Hill is open more widely to the public for guided tours by professional trained guides.

Location: Twickenham.
Station(s): Strawberry Hill BR, No. 33 bus.
Open: Sun pm's May-mid Oct 2-3.30 for guided tours otherwise by pre-arrangement.
Admission: £3.50 per person.
Refreshments: Strawberry cream teas available on request for pre-booked tours.
Tours can be arranged for groups of 10+ people any day throughout the year Sun-Fri by telephoning the Conference Office. Not suitable for children under 12 years.

SUTTON HOUSE   🍃 The National Trust

2 & 4 Homerton High Street, Hackney   E9 6JQ   map **12** T22
Telephone: 0181-986 2264

In London's East End; a rare example of a Tudor red-brick house, built in 1535 by Sir Rafe Sadleir, Principal Secretary of State for Henry VIII, with 18th century alterations and later additions. The recent restoration has revealed many 16th century details which are displayed even in rooms of later periods. Notable features include original linenfold panelling and 17th century wall paintings. The Edwardian chapel contains an audio-visual presentation and there is a craft workshop in the Old Tudor Kitchen.

Location: At the corner of Isabella Road and Homerton High Street. *Station(s):* Hackney Central ¼ m; Hackney Downs ½ m. Frequent local bus services (tel: 0171-222 1234).
Open: 1 Feb to 26 Nov & 4 Feb 1996 onwards: Wed, Sun & BH Mon Mon 11.30-5.30 (closed Good Fri). Last admissions 5. Also open Wed and Fri evenings during July 7-9.30.
Admission: Adults £1.60. Group visits by prior arrangement. Guided tours available. Rates on application. Public car park in Morning Lane and St.John's Churchyard ¼ m.
Refreshments: Cafe bar open all year except 24 Dec to 17 Jan, Wed-Sun 11.30-5.30. Wed and Fri evenings 7-9.30.
Events/Exhibitions: For full programme of concerts, exhibitions, fairs, lectures, Children's Day on 4 June and other events, please contact Project Manager on 0181-986 2264.
Ground floor only accessible to wheelchairs. No lift. WC. Braille guide. Baby changing facilities. Family trails.

SYON HOUSE

(His Grace the Duke of Northumberland)
Brentford   **TW8 8JF**   map **12** U22   △
Telephone: 0181-560 0881
Fax: 0181-568 0936

Noted for its magnificent Adam interior and furnishings, famous picture collection, and historical associations dating back to 1415, 'Capability' Brown landscape.

Location: On N bank of Thames between Brentford & Isleworth.
Station(s): Gunnersbury (District line), Kew Bridge (BR). Buses 237, 267.
Open: For charges and times of entry please telephone 0181-560 0881.
Refreshments: Cafeteria and coffee shop. Telephone 0181-568 0778/9.

SYON PARK GARDENS

(His Grace the Duke of Northumberland)
Brentford   **TW8 8JF**   map **12** U22
Telephone: (0181) 560 0881
Fax: (0181) 568 0936

Includes the Great Conservatory by Charles Fowler and Miniature Steam Railway (operates weekends and Bank Holiday Mondays April to October and other times by arrangement). Within the Estate is the Garden Centre, The Butterfly House, Brit Koi Aquatic Centre, Art Centre, Needlecraft Centre, Gift Shop, Wholefood Shop. Pet care centre and pine furniture / Gift shop.

Location: On N bank of Thames between Brentford & Isleworth.
Station(s): Waterloo to Kew Bridge, nearest tube Gunnersbury. Buses: 267 or 237 to Brentlea.
Open: All the year daily 10-6 or dusk. Last adm 1 hour before closing. *Closed Christmas Day & Boxing Day.* Adm charges not available at time of going to press. Free car park. Telephone (0181)560 0881. London Butterfly House opening times & adm charges Telephone (0181)560 7272.
Admission: For admission charges telephone 0181 560 0881.
Refreshments: Cafeteria and coffee shop. Telephone 0181 568 0778/9. Enquiries to Administrator, Syon Park.

THE TRAVELLERS CLUB
Pall Mall   **SW1Y 5EP**   map **12** T22   △
Telephone: 0171-930 8688 (by prior appointment)

Built in 1829-33 by Sir Charles Barry.

Location: 106 Pall Mall.
Station(s): Piccadilly Circus Underground.
Open: By prior appointment Mon-Fri only from 10-12 and 3-5.30 weekends by negotiation. Closed Bank Hols, Aug and Christmas.
Admission: £6.
Refreshments: Included.

WHITEHALL
(London Borough of Sutton)
1 Malden Road, Cheam   **SM3 8QD**   map **12** U22   △
Telephone: 0181-643 1236
Fax: 0181-770 4777

A unique timber-framed house built c 1500. A feature is the revealed sections of original fabric. Displays include medieval Cheam pottery; Nonsuch Palace; timber-framed buildings and Cheam School. Changing exhibitions and a variety of events and fairs throughout the year.

Location: On A2043 just N of junction with A232.
Station(s): Cheam (¼ m).
Open: Apr-Sept Tues-Fri,Sun 2-5.30 Sat 10-5.30 Oct-Mar Wed Thurs Sun 2-5.30 Sat 10-5.30. Also open Bank Hol Mons 2-5.30. *Closed Dec 24-Jan 2 inclusive* Further information from Sutton Heritage Service on 0181-770 4781. Party bookings, guided tours by prior arrangement.
Admission: 1995 prices adults 80p children 40p.
Refreshments: Tea-room with home made cakes.
Conferences: Facilities available.
Gift Shop. Rooms and Exhibition space available for hire.

GREATER MANCHESTER

DUNHAM MASSEY 🌳 The National Trust
See under Cheshire.

SMITHILLS HALL
(Bolton Metropolitan Borough)
Bolton   map **15** P18
Telephone: (01204) 841265

One of the oldest manor houses in Lancashire, a house has stood on this site since the 14th century. The oldest part of Smithills, the Great Hall, has an open timber roof. Smithills has grown piece by piece over the centuries and such irregularly planned buildings, with the cluster of gables at the west end, give the hall its present day picturesque effect. Furnished in the styles of the 16th and 17th centuries. Withdrawing room contains linenfold panelling. Grounds contain a nature trail.

Location: Off Smithills Dean Road; 1½ m NW of town centre off A58 (Moss Bank Way); signposted.
Station(s): Bolton.
Open: Apr-Sept Tues-Sat 11-5 Sun 2-5. *Closed* Mons except BHs. Oct-Mar *Closed* to general public. Open to pre-booked educational parties and to evening party tours.
Admission: Adults £1.55 concessions 75p groups £1.05.

MERSEYSIDE

CROXTETH HALL & COUNTRY PARK
(Liverpool City Council)
Liverpool   **L12 0HB**   map **6** Q17   △ Ⓔ Ⓢ
Telephone: 0151-228 5311
Fax: 0151-228 2817

500 acre Country Park centred on the ancestral home of the Molyneux family, Earls of Sefton. Hall rooms with character figures on the theme of an Edwardian houseparty. Victorian Home Farm and Walled Garden both with quality interpretive displays; superb collection of farm animals (Approved Rare Breeds Centre). Miniature Railway. Special events and attractions most weekends. Picnic areas and adventure playground.

Location: 5 m NE of Liverpool City Centre; Signposted from A580 & A5088 (ring road).
Open: Parkland open daily throughout the year, adm free. Hall, Farm & Garden open 11-5 daily in main season, please telephone to check exact dates.
Admission: (Inclusive) Hall, Farm and Gardens £3.00 Children/OAPs £1.50. Reduced rates for parties. Free car parking.
Refreshments: 'The Old Riding School' cafe during season.
Wheelchair access to Farm, Garden and Cafe but to ground floor only in Hall. Leisure Services Directorate, Liverpool City Council.

MEOLS HALL
(R.F. Hesketh, Esq)
Southport   **PR9 7LZ**   map **6** P17
Telephone: (01704) 29826
Fax: (01704) 29826

A 17th century house, with subsequent additions, containing an interesting collection of pictures, furniture, china etc.

Location: 1 m N of Southport; 16 m SW of Preston; 20 m N of Liverpool; near A565 & A570.
Station(s): Southport
Open: All of Aug 2-5.
Admission: £3 children £1 those under 10 accompanied by adult free.
Refreshments: Available in local village 200 yds.
Events/Exhibitions: Maybe available 1995/6.

Sir Peter Lely - portrait painter

His paintings can be seen at the following properties included in Historic Houses Castles and Gardens:-

Aynhoe Park	*Euston Hall*	*Ragley Hall*
Belton House	*Goodwood House*	*Rockingham Castle*
Breamore House	*Gorhambury*	*St Osyth Priory*
Browsholme Hall	*Kedleston Hall*	*Stanford Hall*
Dalmeny House	*Knole*	*Weston Park*
	Petworth House	

SPEKE HALL 🌿 The National Trust
The Walk, Liverpool   L24 IXD   map **6** Q17
Telephone: 0151-427 9860

Richly half-timbered Elizabethan house around a courtyard; features include Great Hall, Priest holes, Jacobean plasterwork and Victorian restoration and decoration. Attractive gardens and extensive woodlands.

Location: On N bank of Mersey. 1 m off A561 on W side of Liverpool Airport. Follow airport signs from M62; M56 junction 12.
Station(s): Garston (2 m); Hunts Cross (2 m).
Open: Apr 1-Oct 29 daily except Mon but open Bank Holiday Mons 1-5.30. *(Closed Good Fri)*. Nov 4-Dec 17 Sat & Sun 12-4.30. Garden Apr 1-Oct 29 open as house Nov-Mar 1996 daily except Mon 12-4. (Closed Good Fri 24,25,26,31 Dec & 1 Jan)
Admission: £3.60 Family ticket £9. Garden only £1. Discount for pre-booked parties. Guided tours and school visits by prior arrangement with Property Manager.
Refreshments: Tea-room open same days as house from 12: light lunches 12-2. Shop open as house.

NORFOLK

BLICKLING HALL 🌿 The National Trust
Blickling   NR11 6NF   map **4** R25   ♿
Telephone: (01263) 733084
Fax: (01263) 734924

Great Jacobean house, altered 1765-70. State rooms include Peter the Great Room with fine Russian tapestry, Long Gallery with exceptional ceiling and State bedroom. The Formal Garden design dates from 1729. Temple and Orangery, park and lake.

Location: 1½ m NW of Aylsham on N side of B1354 (which is 15 m N of Norwich on A140).
Open: Hall Mar 25-Nov 5 *(Closed* Good Friday) Tues Wed Fri Sat Sun and Bank Hol Mon 1-5. Garden as Hall but open 11am. Daily in July & Aug.

Admission: House and Garden: £4.90,Sun & Bank Hol Mon £5.50. Chd (with adult) £2.45.Sun & Bank Hol Mon £2.75.Pre booked parties £3.90 Sun & Bank Hol Mon £4.50. Garden only: £2.50, Chd £1.20. Free car park.
Refreshments: Teas, coffee and lunches 11-5. *(Parties by arrangement;* table license). Picnic area in walled orchard. Restaurant, shop and garden open daily in July & Aug. Plant centre in orchard. Buckinghamshire Arms Inn open all year. NB Free access to the South Front, shop and restaurant when Hall is open.
Shop. Dogs in park and picnic area only, on leads. Wheelchair access - 2 provided. Lift to first floor. Sympathetic hearing scheme. Events. Leaflet on request.

CASTLE RISING CASTLE   ENGLISH HERITAGE
map **4** R23

Telephone: (01553) 631330

The long and distinguished history of Castle Rising began in 1138. It was then that William de Albini started to build a grand castle to mark the upturn in his fortunes which followed his marriage to Henry I's widow. Later owners were no less notable and included Isabella 'The She-Wolf of France', wife of Edward II, the Black Prince, Prince Hal and the Howard Dukes of Norfolk. The 12th century keep, reached through a handsome decorated doorway is the finest part of the castle. Outside, there is a gatehouse of the same date and the remains of a church.

Location: 4 m (6.4 km) north of King's Lynn.
Open: Apr 1-Sept 30 10-6 daily Oct 1-31 10-4 daily Nov 1-Mar 31 Wed-Sun 10-4.
Admission: Adults £1.30 concessions £1 children 70p.

FELBRIGG HALL 🌿 The National Trust
Felbrigg   NR11 8PR   map **4** R25   ♿
Telephone: (01263) 837444 Restaurant:(01263) 838237

17th century country house with Georgian interiors set in a fine wooded park. Important 18th century Library and Orangery, Traditional walled garden. Woodland and Lakeside walks. Recently opened. Additional 11 rooms on show including Domestic Wing and Morning Room.

Location: 2 m SW of Cromer on S side of A148.
Station(s): Cromer (2¼ m).
Open: Hall & Gardens Mar 25-Nov 5 Mon Wed Thurs Sat and Sun 1-5. Bank Hol Suns and Mons 11-5. Gardens 11-5.
Admission: £4.60 children (with adult) £2.30. Gardens only £1.80. Pre-booked parties of 15 or more £3.40.
Refreshments: 11-5.15, coffee, lunches, teas in the Park restaurant. Note: Free access to restaurant, shop, park and picnic area.
Events/Exhibitions: Coast and Country Fair. Events leaflet on request.
Shop. No dogs. Wheelchair access, 2 provided. Picnic area. Family woodland trail. Sympathetic hearing scheme.

GRIME'S GRAVES   ENGLISH HERITAGE
map **4** S24
Telephone: (01842) 810656

This is an intricate network of pits and shafts sunk by our neolithic ancestors some 4000 years ago. The purpose of all this industriousness was to find flints for the world's first farmers - flints to make axes to fell trees so that the cleared ground could be sown with seed. Between 700 and 800 pits were dug, some of them to a depth of 30 or 40ft (9-12m). Two of the 16 excavated shafts have been left open; they give an idea of those early miners' working conditions.

Location: 2¾ m (4.4 km) north east of Brandon.
Open: Apr 1-Sept 30 10-6 daily Oct 1-31 10-4 daily Nov 1-Mar 31 Wed-Sun 10-4.
Admission: Adults £1.30 concessions £1 children 70p.

HOLKHAM HALL
(The Earl of Leicester)
Wells   NR23 1AB   map **4** R24
Telephone: (01328) 710227
Fax: (01328) 711707

ENJOY 300 YEARS OF HISTORY IN A DAY

Holkham Hall is one of Britain's most majestic Stately homes, situated in a 3,000 acre deer park on the beautiful north Norfolk coast. This classic 18th Century Palladian style mansion is part of a great agricultural estate, and is a living treasure house of artistic and architectural history.

Attractions include: Holkham Hall, Bygones Museum, Pottery, Garden Centre, Gift Shop, Art Gallery, Tea Rooms, Deer Park, Lake and Beach.

OPENING TIMES & ADMISSION CHARGES

Daily (except Fridays & Saturdays) from 29th May to 29th September, 1.30pm-5.00pm. Also Easter, May, Spring & Summer Bank Holiday Sundays & Mondays, 11.30am-5.00pm. Last admission 4.40pm.

Hall & Park: Adults £3.00   Children £1.50
Bygones: Adults £3.00   Children £1.50
All inclusive: Adults £5.00   Children £2.50
10% reduction on pre-paid parties of 20 or more

Holkham Hall, Wells-next-the-Sea, Norfolk, NR23 1AB. Tel. (01328) 710227

Fine Palladian mansion. Pictures, Tapestries, Statuary, Furnishings. Bygones Museum.

Location: 2m W of Wells; S off the Wells/Hunstanton Road (A149).
Open: Daily (except Fri/Sat) May 28-Sept 28 1.30-5 also Easter, May, Spring and Summer Bank Holiday Sun and Mon 11.30-5 (last adm 4.40).
Admission: Adults £3 children (5-15) £1.50. Bygones adults £3 children £1.50. All inclusive adults £5 children £2.50. Reductions on pre-paid parties of 20 or more.
Refreshments: Served in tea-rooms.

MANNINGTON GARDENS AND COUNTRYSIDE
(Lord and Lady Walpole)
Saxthorpe, Norfolk   map **4** R25   △
Telephone: (01263) 584175
Fax: (01263) 761214

15th century moated house and Saxon church ruin set in attractive gardens. Outstanding rose gardens. Extensive walks and trails around the estate.

Location: 2 m N of Saxthorpe, nr B1149; 18 m NW of Norwich. 9 m from coast.
Open: Garden Apr-Oct Sun 12-5 Also June-Aug Wed Thurs and Fri 11-5.
Admission: Adults £2.50 children (accompanied children under 16) free OAPs/students £2. House open by prior appointment only.
Refreshments: Coffee, salad lunches and home-made teas.

NORWICH CASTLE MUSEUM
(Norfolk Museum Service)
Norwich   NR1 3JU   map **4** R25
Telephone: (01603) 223624
Fax: (01603) 765651

Norfolk Museums Service

The stone Keep of Norwich Castle was built about 1090 and is one of the most important buildings of its kind in Europe. Once a royal castle, then a prison, it is among the best museums in East Anglia. The museum houses one of the country's finest regional collections of natural history, archaeology and art including Norwich School paintings and the world's largest collection of British cermaic teapots. Guided tours of battements and dungeons.

Open: Monday-Saturday 10-5; Sunday 2-5 (Closed Good Friday, Christmas period).
Admission: Adult £2.20 child £1.00 concessions £1.50.
Refreshments: Available.
Events/Exhibitions: Various.

OXBURGH HALL   The National Trust
Oxborough   PE33 9PS   map **4** R24   &
Telephone: (0136 621) 258

Late 15th century moated house. Outstanding gatehouse tower. Needlework by Mary Queen of Scots. Unique French parterre laid out circa 1845. Woodland walks and traditional herbaceous garden. Chapel with fine altar piece.

Location: 7 m SW of Swaffham on S side of Stoke Ferry Road.
Open: House Mar 25-Nov 5 Sat-Wed 1-5. Garden: 12-5.30. Bank Hol Mons 11-5.
Admission: £3.80 children (with adult) £1.90. Pre-booked parties of 15 or more £2.80. Garden only £2.
Refreshments: In Old Kitchen. Light lunches and teas 12-5.
Events/Exhibitions: Childrens Fun Festival in August. Events leaflet on request. Shop. No dogs. Wheelchair access, 2 provided.

RAVENINGHAM HALL GARDENS
(Sir Nicholas Bacon, Bt)
Norwich   NR14 6NS   map **4** R26
Telephone: (01508) 548222
Fax: (01508) 548958

An extensive garden laid out at the turn of the century surrounding original Georgian house. In the last thirty years a large number of new areas have been designed and brought into cultivation, many in the traditional style, with plantings of unusual shrubs, herbaceous plants and roses. An Arboretum planted in March 1990 contains many unusual trees. In recent years an important and extensive Nursery and Plant Centre has developed, to include many rare and exotic plants that can be seen in the garden. (Catalogue 3 x first class stamps). Also Victorian Conservatory and walled vegetable garden. The house is not open to the public.

Location: 4 m from Beccles off the B1136 between Beccles and Loddon.
Open: Plant Centre Mon-Fri 9-5 all year Sat 9-5 and Sun 2-5. Mid-Mar to mid-Sept. Garden Sun and Bank Hol Mon 2-5 Wed 1-4 Mar 19-Sept 17.
Admission: £2 Children free in aid of local charities. Free car park.
Refreshments: Home-made teas served when gardens open.

WALSINGHAM ABBEY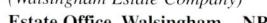

(Walsingham Estate Company)
Estate Office, Walsingham   NR22 6BP   map **4** S26   &
Telephone: (01328) 820259
Fax: (01328) 820098

The grounds contain the remains of the Augustinian Priory founded in 1153 on a site next to the Holy House, the Shrine of our Lady built in 1061.

Location: On B1105 between Wells and Fakenham.
Open: 2-5 Apr May June July & Sept Wed Sat & Sun, Aug Mon Wed Fri Sat & Sun. Also all Bank Holidays from Easter-Sept. Usual office hours through Estate office (01328) 820259.
Admission: Adults £1 children under 16 and OAP's 50p. parties over 100 by arrangement. Walsingham is a picturesque village containing fine examples of 15th-18th century architecture with half timbered houses and medieval pump house. Ruins of Franciscan Friary, court house museum, Anglican shrine, R.C. Slipper Chapel. Guided tours, accommodation and catering available.

WOLTERTON PARK

(Lord and Lady Walpole)
Erpingham   map **4** S25   △
Telephone: (01263) 584175

Extensive historic park with lake.

Location: Nr Erpingham, signposted from A140 Norwich to Cromer road.
Open: Park open all year daily 9-5 or dusk if earlier.
Admission: £2 per car. See local press for details of special events and garden and Hall tours.

NORTHAMPTONSHIRE

AYNHOE PARK

(Country Houses Association)
Aynho   OX17 3BQ   map **5** S20
Telephone: (01869) 810636

17th century mansion. Alteration by Soane.

Location: Junction 10 M40 then 3 m west on B4100.
Station(s): Banbury (7½ m), Bicester (8 m).
Open: May-Sept Weds & Thurs 2-5. Last entry 4.30.
Admission: £2.50 Children £1. Free car park. No dogs admitted.

"GHOSTS"

Ghosts are in residence at the following properties included in Historic Houses Castles and Gardens:-

Blickling Hall - *Anne Boleyn*

Breamore House - *Haunted picture - if touched, death on the same day*

East Riddleden Hall - *5 ghosts including lady in Grey Hall Lady's Chamber*

Fountains Abbey & Studley Royal - *Choir of monks chanting in Chapel of Nine Altars*

Hinton Ampner - *Nocturnal noises*

Ightham Mote - *Supernatural presence*

Lindisfarne Castle - *Monk, and group of monks on causeway*

Lyme Park - *Unearthly peals of bells and lady in white, funeral procession through park*

Malmesbury House - *Ghost of a cavalier*

Overbecks Museum & Garden - *'Model' ghost in the Children's room (for them to spot)*

Rockingham Castle - *Lady Dedlock*

Rufford Old Hall - *Elizabeth Hesketh*

Scotney Castle Garden - *Man rising from the lake*

Sizergh Castle & Garden - *Poltergeist*

Speke Hall - *Ghost of woman in tapestry room*

Springhill - *Ghost of a woman*

Sudbury Hall - *Lady in Green, seen on stairs*

Tamworth Castle - *Haunted bedroom*

Treasurer's House - *Troop of Roman soldiers marching through the cellar*

Wallington House - *Invisible birds beating against the windows accompanied by heavy breathing*

Washington Old Hall - *Grey lady walking through corridors*

BOUGHTON HOUSE

(His Grace the Duke of Buccleuch & Queensberry, KT. and The Living Landscape Trust)
Kettering   map **4** S21   △ ⅊ Ⓢ
Telephone: (01536) 515731
Fax: (01536) 417255

Northamptonshire Home of The Duke of Buccleuch and Queensberry K.T., and his Montagu ancestors since 1528. A 500 year old Tudor monastic building gradually enlarged around 7 courtyards until the French style addition of 1695. Outstanding collection of 17/18th century French and English furniture, tapestries, 16th century carpets, porcelain, painted ceilings - notable works by El Greco, Murillo, Caracci and 40 Van Dyck sketches - celebrated Armoury and Ceremonial Coach. Exhibition and lecture rooms in Stable block with audio/visual facilities. Beautiful parkland with historic avenues and lakes - picnic area - gift shop - exciting adventure woodland play area - garden centre - tea-room. Boughton House is administered by The Living Landscape Trust, which was created by the present Duke of Buccleuch to show the relationship between the historic Boughton House and its surrounding, traditional, but modern run, working estate. For details of our specialist one, three and five day Fine Art Courses run in conjunction with Sotheby's and our Schools Education Facilities (Sandford Award Winner 1988 and 1993), please telephone The Living Landscape Trust at Kettering (01536) 515731. BOUGHTON HOUSE 'The English Versailles'.

Location: 3 m N of Kettering on A43 at Geddington; 75 m N of London by A1 or M1, on northern spur from A14.
Open: House and grounds Aug 1-Sept 1 daily grounds 1-5 House 2-5 (last entry 4.30) staterooms strictly by prior booking. Grounds May 1-Oct 1 daily except Fri 1-5. Garden Centre open daily throughout year Adventure play area and tea-rooms open 1-5 at weekends and public holidays May-Sept and daily throughout Aug (at other times by appointment). Museum and educational groups welcome by appointment at other times.
Admission: House and grounds adults £4 OAPs/students £3. Grounds adults £1.50 OAPs/students £1.
Refreshments: Tea-rooms, weekends, public holidays and daily in August.

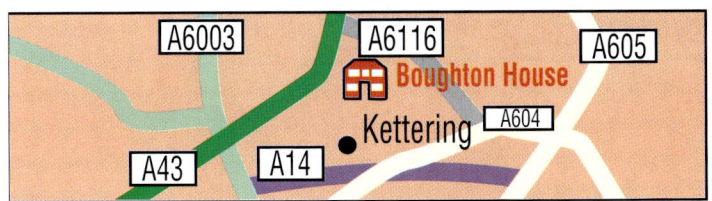

CANONS ASHBY HOUSE   The National Trust
Canons Ashby   map **5** S20
Telephone: (01327) 860044

The home of the Dryden family since the 16th century; a manor house c. 1580 and altered for the last time in 1710; Elizabethan wall paintings and outstanding Jacobean plasterwork; formal garden with terraces, walls and gate piers of 1710: medieval Priory Church, privately owned since the Reformation. 70 acre park.

Location: Easy access from either M40 junction 11 or M1 junction 16. From M1 signposted from A5 2 m S of Weedon crossroads, along unclassified road (13 m) to Banbury. From M40 at Banbury take A422 exit, then left along unclassified road.
Open: 1 Apr-end of Oct Sat-Wed incl Bank Hol Mons 1-5.30. *Closed Good Friday.*
Admission: £3.20 Chd £1.60. Parking for cars and coaches which must pre-book (discount for parties).
Refreshments: Light lunches 12-2, afternoon teas in Brewhouse same days as house. Party bookings by prior arrangement.
Dogs on leads, in Home Paddock only. 1995 events - details from the Administrator.

COTON MANOR GARDEN
(Mr & Mrs Ian Pasley-Tyler)
Nr Guilsborough   **NN6 8RQ**   map **4** S20
Telephone: (01604) 740219
Fax: (01604) 740838

An outstanding old English Garden set in Northamptonshire countryside and imaginatively laid out on different levels. Old hedges, herbaceous borders, lawns and water gardens lend it a special charm and character enhanced by flamingoes, cranes and waterfowl roaming at large. Recently featured in RHS magazine 'The Garden'.

Location: 10 m N of Northampton & 11 m SE of Rugby. Follow tourist signs on A428 and A50.
Open: Easter-end of Sept daily Weds-Sun and Bank Hol Mons 12-6.
Admission: £2.70 OAPs £2.20 Children £1.
Refreshments: Restaurant serving home-made lunches and teas.
Unusual plants for sale, propagated from the garden.

Sir John Van Brugh (1664-1726)

Architect. His work can be seen at the following properties included in historic Houses Castles and Gardens:-

Blenheim Palace
Castle Howard
Claremont
Grimsthorpe Castle
Seaton Delaval Hall

COTTESBROOKE HALL AND GARDENS
(Captain & Mrs John Macdonald-Buchanan)
nr Northampton   map **4** S21   △
Telephone: (01604) 505808
Fax: (01604) 505619

Architecturally magnificent Queen Anne house commenced in 1702. Renowned picture collection, particularly of sporting and equestrian subjects. Fine English and Continental furniture and porcelain. Main vista aligned on celebrated 7th century Saxon church at Brixworth. House reputed to be the pattern for Jane Austen's 'Mansfield Park'. Notable gardens of great variety including fine old cedars and specimen trees, herbaceous borders, water and wild gardens.

Location: 10 m N of Northampton (A14 - A1/M1 Link Road) nr Creaton on A50, nr Brixworth on A508.
Open: Thurs from Apr 20-Sept 28 Easter Mon, May day, Spring Bank Holiday, Aug Bank Holiday 2-5.30. Last adm 5.
Admission: Adults £3.50. Gardens only £2.50. Children half-price.
Refreshments: In the Old Laundry 2.30-5.
Parties accommodated by appointment on other days. Car parking. Gardens but not house suitable for disabled. No dogs.

Lancelot 'Capability' Brown

Born 1716 in Northumberland, Capability Brown began work at the age of 16 in the vegetable gardens of Sir William and Lady Loraine at Kirharle Tower. He left Northumberland in 1739, and records show that he worked at Stowe until 1749. It was at Stowe that Brown began to study architecture, and to submit his own plans. It was also at Stowe that he devised a new method of moving and replanting mature trees.

Brown married Bridget Wayet in 1744 and began work on the estate at Warwick Castle in 1749. He was appointed Master Gardener at Hampton Court in 1764, and planted the Great Vine at Hampton Court in 1768. Blenheim Palace designs are considered amongst Brown's finest work, and the technical achievements were outstanding even for the present day.

Capability Brown died in February 1783 of a massive heart attack. A monument beside the lake at Croome Court was erected which reads "To the memory of Lancelot Brown, who by the powers of his inimitable and creative genius formed this garden scene out of a morass". There is also a portrait of Brown at Burghley.

Capability Brown was involved in the design of grounds at the following properties included in Historic Houses Castles and Gardens:-

Audley End	*Longleat*
Berrington Hall	*Luton Hoo*
Bowood	*Moccas Court*
Burghley House	*Petworth House*
Burton Constable	*Sledmere House*
Charlecote Park	*Stowe (Stowe*
Chilham Castle Gardens	*School)*
(reputed)	*Syon House*
Clandon Park	*Warwick Castle*
Claremont	*Weston Park*
Chillington Hall	*Wimpole Hall*
Corsham Court	*Wrest Park and*
Fawley Court	*Gardens*
Highclere Castle	

HOLDENBY HOUSE AND GARDENS

(Owners Mr & Mrs Lowther - Administration Barbara Brooker)
Northampton NN6 8DJ map **14** S20 Ⓢ
Telephone: (01604) 770074
Fax: (01604) 770962

Once the largest house in Elizabethan England, Holdenby secured its place in history when it became the prison of Charles I during the Civil War. Today Holdenby's Falconry Centre and collection of rare farm animals complement the beauty and history of the grounds with their Elizabethan and fragrant borders. As buzzards and other birds of prey capture the attention in the sky above, an authentic armoury and reconstructed 17th century homestead add historical interest on the ground. And for the children, a 'cuddle farm' and play area ensure an enjoyable day. The house, with its collection of rare pianos, is open Bank Hol Mons (except May Day) and by appointment. The major event in 1995 will be a reconstruction of the Battle of Naseby by The Sealed Knot on 17 and 18 June.

Location: 7 m NW of Northampton, off A428 & A50; approx 7 m from M1 exit 15a, 16 or 18.
Station(s): Northampton.
Open: Apr-end Sept GARDENS Sun 2-6 Bank Hol Suns and Mons 1-6 Thurs in July & Aug 1-5 Weekdays enter through the Falconry Centre. HOUSE Bank Hol Mons (except May Day) 1-6. *HOUSE Open by arrangement to pre-booked parties Mon-Fri.*
Admission: GARDEN £2.75 Children £1.75 OAPs £2.25 HOUSE & GARDENS £3.75 Children £2 Enquire for special rates for school parties and business conferences throughout the year.
Refreshments: Home-made teas in Victorian Kitchen.
Events/Exhibitions: A major muster of the Sealed Knot will re-enact the famous Battle of Naseby on 17 and 18 June, 1-6 pm.
Accommodation: A range of good quality accommodation is available locally.
Conferences: Holdenby is well known for its use as a corporate hospitality and conference venue. Open year round.
Souvenir shop selling Holdenby branded goods and craft items.

LAMPORT HALL AND GARDENS

(Lamport Hall Trust)
Northampton   NN6 9HD   map **4** S21   Ⓢ
Telephone: (01604) 686272
Fax: (01604) 686224

Lamport Hall was the home of the Isham family from 1560 to 1976. The South West front is a rare example of the work of John Webb, pupil and son-in-law of Inigo Jones and was built in 1655 (during the Commonwealth) with wings added in 1732 and 1740. High Room with plaster ceiling by John Woolston, an outstanding library, and thirteen other fine rooms containing the Ishams' collections of superb paintings, furniture and china. The Hall is set in spacious wooded parkland with tranquil gardens including a remarkable rock garden. Teas in Victorian dining room. Now run by the Lamport Hall Trust, school visits, group and private bookings are especially encouraged and a programme of fairs, music, art and craft events is put on throughout the season - details from the Director.

Location: 8 m N of Northampton on A508 to Market Harborough. M1 J15/16/18/20.
Station(s): Northampton.
Open: Easter-Oct 1 every Sun and Bank Holiday Mon 2.15-5.15 (Aug every day with one tour at 4.30 or 5) Oct 28-29 2.15-5.15 Dec 2-3 tour at 2.15.
Admission: Prices to be confirmed.
Refreshments: Home-made teas at the house.
Events/Exhibitions: Most months through the year, telephone for free brochure.
Conferences: The Hall and Grounds are available for conferences and corporate hospitality throughout the year.
Dogs on leads in picnic area only.

LYVEDEN NEW BIELD   🌿 The National Trust

Oundle   map **4** S21
Telephone: (01832) 205358

The shell of an unusual Renaissance building erected about 1600 by Sir Thomas Tresham to symbolize the Passion. He died before the building could be completed and his son was then imprisoned in connection with the Gunpowder Plot. A viewing platform allows visitors to look from the East Window.

Location: 4 m SW of Oundle via A427. 3 m E of Brigstock (A6116) (½ m walk from roadside parking).
Open: All the year - Daily. *Property approached via two fields. Parties by arrangement with Custodian, Lyveden New Bield Cottage, nr Oundle, Northants. No parking for coaches but they may drop & return to pick up passengers.*
Admission: £1.20, Child 60p.
Dogs admitted on leads. Unsuitable for disabled or visually handicapped. No WCs

THE MENAGERIE, HORTON

(Gervase Jackson-Stops and Ian Kirby)
Horton, Northampton NN7 2BX   map **4** S21

A garden in the making, designed by Ian Kirby, and surrounding a folly built by Thomas Wright of Durham for the 2nd Earl of Halifax, c1754-57. Spiral mount, lime and hornbeam allees, formal ponds with fountains and wetlands, thatched arbours in the classical and gothic styles. Plant sales.

Location: 6 m S of Northampton and 1 m S of Horton on B526 turn left immediately after lay-by.
Open: April-end Sept. Garden only Thurs 10-4. House Garden and Shell Grotto open to groups of 20 or more by appointment at other times.
Admission: Garden adults £2.50 children £1.

THE PREBENDAL MANOR HOUSE

Nassington   map **4** R22   △
Telephone: (01780) 782575

Probably the earliest surviving Manor in Northamptonshire, dating from the early 13th century. The present stone manor overlays one of the royal manors of the Danish King Cnut who once ruled England. The existing stone manor is of significant architectural and historical interest and forms the focus of a group of stone buildings which include a fine 16th century Dovecote. The Museum in the Tithe barn depicting medieval life in the manor is an added attraction.

Location: 6 m N of Oundle. A605-C14, 7 m S of Stamford. A1 to Wansford C14. 9 m E of Peterborough. A47-C14.
Open: Wed and Sun 2-5.30 from June-Aug 31 Easter Mon 2-5.30 Bank Hol Mons 2-5.30 closed Christmas.
Admission: Adults/OAPs £3 children £1.50 parties by arrangement. Free car parking Tel (01780) 782575.
Refreshments: Teas.
Not suitable for disabled.

PRIEST'S HOUSE The National Trust

Easton-on-the-Hill map **4** R21
Telephone: (01780) 62506

Pre-Reformation priest's house given to the National Trust by The Peterborough Society. Contains a small museum of village bygones.

Location: 2 m SW of Stamford off A43.
Station(s): Stamford (2 m).
Open: Access only by prior appointment with Mr. R. Chapman, Glebe Cottage, 45 West St., Easton-on-the-Hill, nr Stamford, PE9 3LS.
Admission: Free.
No dogs. Unsuitable for disabled or visually handicapped and coaches.

ROCKINGHAM CASTLE

(Commander Michael Saunders Watson)
nr Corby map **4** R21   △ Ⓔ Ⓢ
Telephone: (01536) 770240
Fax: (01536) 771692

Built by William the Conqueror, used by the early Kings of England until the 16th century when granted to Edward Watson whose family live there today. The house itself is memorable, representing a procession of periods. The dominant influence is Tudor within the Norman walls, but most centuries have left their mark in the form of architecture, furniture or works of art. There is a fine collection of English 18th, 19th and 20th century paintings. Dickens a frequent visitor used the Castle as a model for Chesney Wold in Bleak House. The Castle stands in 12 acres of formal and wild gardens. Special exhibition: 450 Years a Royal Castle, 450 Years a Family Home.

Location: 2 m N of Corby; 9 m from Market Harborough; 14 m from Stamford on A427; 8 m from Kettering on A6003.
Open: Easter Sun-Sept 30 Sun & Thurs also Bank Hol Mons & Tues following and Tues during Aug 1.30-5.30. Any other day by previous appointment for parties. Grounds open 1.30 Sun and Bank Hol Mon.
Admission: Adults £3.80 OAPs £3.20 children £2.30. Gardens only £2.30 (variable for special events) family ticket (2+2) £10.
Refreshments: Teas: home-made at Castle.

SOUTHWICK HALL

(Christopher Capron, Esq)
nr Oundle map **4** R22
Telephone: (01832) 274064

A family home since 1300, retaining medieval building dating from 1300, with Tudor re-building and 18th century additions. Exhibitions:- Victorian and Edwardian life; collections of agricultural and carpentry tools, named bricks and local archaeological finds and fossils.

Location: 3 m N of Oundle 4 m E of Bulwick.
Open: Bank Holidays, Sun & Mon (Apr 16 17 May 7 8 28 29 Aug 27 28) Wed May 3-Aug 30 2-5. Parties at other times (Easter-Aug) by arrangement with Secretary at Southwick Hall, Peterborough PE8 5BL.
Admission: Adults £2.50 OAPs £1.80 children £1.50.
Refreshments: Teas available.

STOKE PARK PAVILIONS

(A.S. Chancellor, Esq)
Towcester map **5** S21   ♿

Two pavilions and colonnade. Built in 1630 by Inigo Jones.

Location: Stoke Bruerne village; 7 m S of Northampton just W of Stony/Northampton Road A508.
Open: June July & Aug Sat Sun & Bank Hols 2-6. *Exterior only on view.*
Admission: £1. Car park free.

Gertrude Jekyll writer and gardener (1843-1932)

Her designs were used at the following properties included in Historic Houses Castles and Gardens:-

Barrington Court
Castle Drogo
Goddards
Hatchlands Park
Hestercombe House and Gardens
Knebworth
Lindisfarne Castle

A collection of her tools can be found at Guildford Museum

SULGRAVE MANOR

(The Sulgrave Manor Board)
Banbury   OX17 2SD   map **5** S20   △
Telephone: (01295) 760205

A delightful 16th Century Manor House presenting a typical wealthy man's home and gardens in Elizabethan times. Restored with scholarly care and attention to detail.

"A perfect illustration of how a house should be shown to the public"
– Nigel Nicholson, Great Houses of Britain

Opening Times 1995

All groups and individuals are taken around the Manor House in regularly organised conducted tours.

Weekdays – every day except Wednesdays. 1st April-31st October 2.00-5.30pm Mornings by appointment only. Bank holidays & the month of August 10.30am-1.00pm 2.00pm-5.30pm
December 27th, 28th & 29th 10.30am-1.00pm 2.00-4.30pm

Weekends – April-October 10.30am-1.00pm 2.00pm-5.30pm. March, November & December 10.30am-1.00pm 2.00-4.30pm. Note: Last admissions 1 hour before closing times

All special event days 10.30am-5.30pm

Open by appointment only

Weekdays in February, March, November and December

Morning and evening guided tours for pre-booked parties are available throughout year year.

Closed – Christmas Day, Boxing Day and the whole of January.

Free Car Parking. All individuals and parties are taken round the house on regularly conducted tours.

Dogs allowed in grounds on lead

Historic Gardens • Loft Museum •
Brew House Tea and Coffee Shop •
Audio Visual Display • Brass Rubbing Centre •
Picnic Area • Gift Shop • Restaurant

SULGRAVE MANOR, NR. BANBURY,
OXON OX17 2SD. TELEPHONE: (01295) 760205

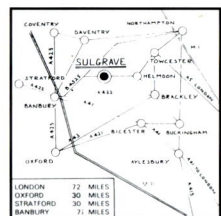

The Washington ownership dates from 1539 when Lawrence Washington purchased the land upon the Dissolution by Henry VIII, of St. Andrew's Priory, Northampton. The House was completed in 1558 (the year Elizabeth I came to the throne of England) and was lived in by descendants of the Washington family for 120 years. Today it is an excellent example of a small Manor House, typical of a wealthy man's home and gardens in Elizabethan times, restored and refurbished with scholarly care and attention to detail which makes a visit both a delight and an education. Sulgrave Manor has been open to the public since 1921 when it was established as a 'Token of Friendship' between the people of Britain and the United States. It is now held in trust for the peoples of both nations, the trustee being the Sulgrave Manor Board which includes the American Ambassador in London and the British Ambassador in Washington. Endowed by the National Society of Colonial Dames of America.

Location: Sulgrave Village is off Banbury/Northampton Road (B4525); 5 m from Banbury junction of M40, 12 m from Northampton junction of M1. 7 m NE of Banbury; 28 m SE of Stratford-upon-Avon; 30 m N of Oxford; 70 m NW of London.

Open: Weekdays open every day except Weds. 1 Apr-31 Oct 2-5.30 (mornings by appointment only) Bank Hols and Aug 10.30-1 and 2-5.30 Dec 27 28 29 10.30-1 and 2-4.30. Weekends Apr-Oct 10.30-1 and 2-5.30 Mar Nov and Dec 10.30-1 and 2-4.30 (last admission 1 hour before closing times). All special event days 10.30-5.30. Open by appointment only weekdays in Feb Mar Nov and Dec and morning and evening guided tours for pre-booked parties are available throughout the year. Closed Christmas Day Boxing Day and Jan. All groups and individuals are taken round the Manor House in regularly organised conducted tours.

Admission: Adults £3 children £1.50 family ticket £9 group rate for Pre-booked Parties of 12 or more.

Refreshments: At Thatched House Hotel opposite, Tel Sulgrave (01295) 760232. Light refreshments in Brewhouse.

Events/Exhibitions: We have a wide range of Special Events throughout the year. Period re-enactments, living histories, needlework festivals, country fairs, chamber music concerts and outdoor theatre productions. Please send for a special leaflet for full details.

NORTHUMBERLAND

ALNWICK CASTLE

(His Grace the Duke of Northumberland)
Alnwick   map **9** M19
Telephone: (01665) 510777
Fax: (01665) 510876

Described by the Victorians as 'The Windsor of the North', Alnwick Castle is the main seat of the Duke of Northumberland whose family, the Percys, have lived here since 1309. This border stronghold has survived many battles, but now peacefully dominates the picturesque market town of Alnwick, overlooking landscape designed by Capability Brown. The stern, medieval exterior belies the treasure house within, furnished in palatial Renaissance style, with paintings by Titian, Van Dyck and Canaletto, fine furniture and an exquisite collection of Meissen china. The Regiment Museum of Royal Northumberland Fusiliers is housed in the Abbot's Tower of the Castle, while the Postern Tower contains a collection of early British and Roman relics. Other attractions include the Percy State Coach, the dungeon, the gun terrace and the grounds, which offer peaceful walks and superb views over the surrounding countryside.

Location: Just off the town centre on the northern side of Alnwick.

Open: Daily Easter-mid Oct 11-5 (last admission 4.30).

Admission: Address: Estate Office, Alnwick Castle, Alnwick, Northumberland NE66 1NQ. Free parking for cars and coaches.

Refreshments: Tea-room serving home-made fare.

Gift Shop. Special party rates. Guide service if required. Enquiries to the Administrator, Alnwick Castle, Alnwick, Northumberland, NE66 1NQ. Tel (01665) 510777 Mon-Fri and weekends only during season only. (01665) 603942.

BAMBURGH CASTLE

(Lady Armstrong)
Bamburgh   ME69 7DF   map **9** L19   △
Telephone: (01668) 214208
Fax: (01669) 21236

BAMBURGH CASTLE

AND ARMSTRONG MUSEUM, The home of Lady Armstrong
The Norman Keep has stood for eight centuries and its setting upon The Crag, which is referred to as a Royal Centre by A.D. 547, is certainly one of the most dramatic of all Castles in Britain.
Featuring:
● Magnificent Seascapes including Holy Island and the Farne Islands, and Landscapes extending to the Cheviot Hills.
● Public Rooms with exhibition of porcelain, china, paintings, furniture and items of interest.
● The Armoury, including loan collections from H.M. Tower of London, The John George Joicey Museum, Newcastle-upon-Tyne, and others.
● Fine Paintings including some from the Duke of Cambridge's collection.
Open to the Public from Maundy Thursday to the last Sunday in October.
Concessionary Rates for parties in or out of Season – Restaurant – Tea Room in the Castle Clock Tower
Operators — All at one stop. Tour. Food. Cloakrooms. Free Coach Parking at Entrance to Walled Castle.
CUSTODIAN – TEL: BAMBURGH (01668) 214208

Fine 12th century Norman Keep with its setting upon The Crag, and referred to as a Royal Centre by AD 547, is certainly one of the most dramatic of all Castles in Britain. Remainder of the Castle considerably restored. Magnificent seascapes including Holy Island and the Farne Islands, the landscapes extending to the Cheviot Hills. Public rooms with exhibition of porcelain, china, paintings, furniture and items of interest. The Armoury includes loan collections from HM Tower of London, The John George Joicey Museum, Newcastle upon Tyne and others. Fine paintings, including some from the Duke of Cambridge's collection.

Location: Coastal - 16 m N of Alnwick 6 m from Belford; 3 m from Seahouses.
Open: Easter-last Sun of Oct daily (incl Suns) open at 12 noon parties may be booked out of normal hours. For closing times enquire The Custodian.
Admission: Adults £2.50 children £1.20.
Refreshments: Clock Tower tea-rooms.

BELSAY HALL CASTLE AND GARDENS

map **9** M19
Telephone: (0166 181) 636

19th-century Neo-Classical mansion lies at the entrance to 30 acres of exciting gardens, which in turn lead on to the 14th-century castle and ruined manor. Important collections of rare and exotic flowering trees grow in the meandering, deep ravines of the 'picturesque' Quarry Gardens. Massed plantings of rhododendrons. Large heather garden. Spring bulbs. Exhibition of Belsay's architectural and landscape history in stable block.

Location: 14 m (22.4 km) north west of Newcastle upon Tyne.
Open: Apr 1-Sept 30 10-6 daily Oct 1-Mar 31 daily 10-4 daily.
Admission: Adults £2.60 concessions £2 children £1.30.

BERWICK UPON TWEED BARRACKS

map **9** L18
Telephone: (01289) 304493

The barracks were designed in 1717 to accommodate 36 officers and 600 men, first being occupied in 1721. The buildings consist of three blocks of accommodation around a square, the fourth side having a splendidly decorated gatehouse. The barracks' new exhibition, the award winning 'Beat of Drum' traces the history of the British infantryman from 1660 to the end of the 19th century. The regimental museum of the King's Own Scottish Borderers and Borough Museum of Berwick on Tweed are also housed here.

Location: On the Parade, off Church St, Berwick town centre.
Open: Apr 1-Sept 30 10-6 daily Oct 1-31 10-4 daily Nov 1-Mar 31 10-4 Wed-Sun.
Admission: Adults £2.20 concessions £1.70 children £1.10.

CHERRYBURN   The National Trust
Mickley   NE43 7DB   map **9** N19
Telephone: (01661) 843276

Birthplace of Northumbria's greatest artist, wood engraver and naturalist, Thomas Bewick, in 1753. His birthplace is restored. The museum explores his famous works and life and in the occasional demonstrations of hand printing from wood blocks in the printing house. Farmyard Animals; Picnic Area, garden.

Location: 11 m W of Newcastle on A695 (200 yards signed from Mickley Square).
Open: Apr 1-end Oct daily except Tues & Wed 1-5.30. Last adm 5. Pre-booked coach parties Mon Thurs and Fri mornings.
Admission: £2.50 No party rate.
Wheelchair access and WC.

CHESTER'S ROMAN FORT AND MUSEUM
ENGLISH HERITAGE
map **9** M18
Telephone: (01434) 681379

An impressive bath-house, buildings of great interest inside the fort, the remains of the bridge carrying Hadrian's Wall across the Tyne, a museum full of Roman inscriptions and sculptures, all set in one of the most beautiful valleys in Northumberland - these are among the attractions of Chesters, once garrisoned by a regiment of Roman cavalry.

Location: ½ m (0.8 km) south west of Chollerford.
Open: Apr 1-Sept 30 10-6 daily Oct 1-Mar 31 10-4 daily.
Admission: Adults £2.20 concessions £1.70 children £1.10.

CORBRIDGE ROMAN SITE
ENGLISH HERITAGE
map **9** N18
Telephone: (01434) 632349

For nearly a century this was the site of a sequence of Roman forts, since Corbridge was an important junction of roads to Scotland, York and Carlisle. It developed into a prosperous town and supply base for Hadrian's Wall, with shops, temples, houses, granaries and an elaborate fountain. Among the rich collection of finds in the museum is a remarkable fountainhead - the Corbridge Lion.

Location: ½ m (0.8 km) north west of Corbridge.
Open: Apr 1-Sept 30 10-6 daily Oct 1-31 10-4 daily Nov 1-Mar 31 Wed-Sun 10-4.
Admission: Adults £2.20 concessions £1.70 children £1.10.

Humphrey Repton (1752-1815)

Artist and garden designer

His work can be seen at the following properties included in Historic Houses Castles and Gardens:-

Corsham Court

Uppark

Sezincote

CRAGSIDE HOUSE, GARDEN AND GROUNDS
  The National Trust
Rothbury   NE65 7PX   map **9** M19
Telephone: (01669) 620333/620266

The House was designed by Richard Norman Shaw for the first Lord Armstrong and built between 1864-95. It contains much of its original furniture and Pre-Raphaelite paintings. It was the first house in the world to be lit by electricity generated by water power. The Grounds are famous for their rhododendrons, magnificent trees and the beauty of the lakes. The Armstrong Energy Centre displays the past and future stories of 'energy' and the 'Power Circuit Walk' includes restored hydraulic and hydroelectric machinery. Formal garden with Orchard House, Rose loggia and Ferneries.

Location: ½ m E of Rothbury; 30 m N of Newcastle-upon-Tyne. Entrance off Rothbury/Alnwick Road B6341; 1 m N of Rothbury at Debdon Burn Gate.
Open: House Apr 1-end Oct daily except Mon (open Bank Holiday Mons) 1-5.30. Last adm 4.45. Grounds Apr 1 end Oct daily except Mon (open Bank Holiday Mon) 10.30-7. 4 Nov-17 Dec Tues, Sat & Sun 10.30-4. Visitor Centre 1 Apr -end Oct Daily except Mon (open Bank Hol Mons) 10.30-5.30. 4 Nov - 17 Dec Tues Sat & Sun 12-4pm.
Admission: House, Garden, Grounds, Museum and Power circuit: £5.50 Parties £5.20 Garden and Grounds £3.50 Parties £3.20 *Parties are by prior arrangement only with the Property Manager.* Family ticket (House Gardens and Grounds 2 adults and 2 children) £14.
Refreshments: Restaurant in Visitor Centre. Telephone Rothbury (01669) 620134.
Fishing: adapted fishing pier Tumbleton lake. Armstrong Energy Centre & Shop in visitor centre. Dogs in Grounds only. Wheelchair access to House - lift available (wheelchairs provided). Wheelchair pathway, adapted picnic tables and parking. Toilets for disabled. Nelly's Moss Lake. Braille Guide.

DUNSTANBURGH CASTLE
ENGLISH HERITAGE
map **9** M19
Telephone: (0166576) 231

Isolated and unspoilt, the ruins stand on a large, rocky cliff top rising steeply from the sea. Begun by Thomas, Earl of Lancaster, in 1313, the castle was attacked by the Scots and besieged during the Wars of the Roses. The keep gatehouse is still impressive and the south wall an enduring memorial to the workmanship of Earl Thomas's masons.

Location: 8 m (13 km) north east of Alnwick.
Open: Apr 1-Sept 30 10-6 daily Oct 1-31 10-4 daily Nov 1-Mar 31 Wed-Sun 10-4.
Admission: Adults £1.30 concessions £1 children 70p.

HOUSESTEADS ROMAN FORT
ENGLISH HERITAGE
map **9** N18
Telephone: (01434) 344363

This is the best-preserved Roman troop-base on Hadrian's Wall. In the museum, a model shows the layout of barracks, headquarters buildings, commandant's house and granaries. Also displayed are relics from the fort and the settlement that grew up outside the walls in the 3rd and 4th centuries.

Location: 2¾ m (4.4 km) north east of Bardon Mill.
Open: Apr 1-Sept 30 10-6 daily Oct 1-Mar 31 daily 10-4.
Admission: Adults £2.30 concessions £1.70 children £1.20.

HOWICK HALL GARDENS

(Howick Trustees Ltd)
Alnwick WE66 3LB   map **9** M19
Telephone: (01665) 577 285
Fax: (01665) 577 285

Extensive grounds including a natural woodland garden in addition to the formal gardens surrounding the Hall.

Location: 6 m NE of Alnwick, nr Howick village.
Open: Apr-Oct daily 1-6.
Admission: £1.50 (OAPs 75p).

KIRKLEY HALL GARDENS

(Dr R. McParlin)
Ponteland NE20 OAQ   map **9** M19
Telephone: (01661) 860808
Fax: (01661) 860047

Prestigious gardens, Greenhouses, Plantsman's paradise, All plants labelled, Plant sales, Sculptures, Conducted tours (prior arrangement).

Location: 3 m N of Ponteland off A696.
Open: Every day throughout the year 10-5.
Admission: £1.50 per person £3 per family parties of 20 or more (prior notice) £1.20 per person. Group guided tours (min no 13 prior notice) £2.50 per person. Free parking.
Refreshments: Available.
No dogs.

LINDISFARNE CASTLE  The National Trust

Holy Island TD15 2SH   map **9** L19
Telephone: (01289) 89244

Built about 1550. Sympathetically restored as a comfortable house by Lutyens in 1903.

Location: 5 m E of Beal across causeway.
Open: Apr 1-end Oct Daily (closed Fri open Good Fri) 1-5.30 Last adm 5. Please check tide times as castle times do not always coincide with tide.
Admission: £3.60. No party rate.
No dogs in Castle. Unsuitable for wheelchairs.

LINDISFARNE PRIORY

map **9** L19
Telephone: (01289) 89200

ENGLISH HERITAGE

Roofless and ruined, the priory is still supremely beautiful, its graceful arches and decorated doorways commemorating the craftsmanship of their Norman builders. This has been sacred soil since 634 when the missionary Bishop Aidan was sent from Iona, to spread Christianity through northern England. New visitor centre with atmospheric exhibition and shop.

Location: On Holy Island, which can be reached at low tide across a causeway. Tide tables are posted at each end of the causeway.
Open: Apr 1-Sept 30 10-6 daily Oct 1-Mar 31 10-4 daily.
Admission: Adults £2.30 concessions £1.70 children £1.20.

PRESTON TOWER

(Major T.H. Baker-Cresswell)
Chathill   map **9** L19

One of the few survivors of 78 Pele Towers listed in 1415. The tunnel vaulted rooms remain unaltered and provide a realistic picture of the grim way of life under the constant threat of 'Border Reivers'. Two rooms are furnished in contemporary style and there are displays of historic and local information.

Location: 7 m N of Alnwick; 1 m E from A1. Follow Historic Property signs.
Open: All year Daily during daylight hours.
Admission: £1 children/OAPs 50p. Free car park.
No dogs (except those left in car).

SEATON DELAVAL HALL

(The Lord Hastings)
Seaton Sluice, Whitley Bay   map **9** M19
Telephone: 0191-237 3040/1493

Palladian House designed by Sir John Vanbrugh for Admiral George Delaval 1718-1728.

Open: May-Sept Wed Sun and Bank Holidays 2-6.
Admission: £2 Children 50p.
Refreshments: Tea-room.

WALLINGTON HOUSE, WALLED GARDEN AND GROUNDS
 The National Trust

Cambo NE61 4AR   map **9** M19
Telephone: (01670) 774283 (House)

Built 1688, altered 18th century. Central Hall added in 19th century, decorated by William Bell Scott, Ruskin and others. Fine porcelain, furniture and pictures in series of rooms including a late Victorian nursery and dolls' houses. Coach display in West Coach House. Woodlands, lakes, walled terraced garden and conservatory with magnificent fuchsias.

Location: Access from N, 12 m W of Morpeth on B6343. Access from S, A696 from Newcastle; 6 m NW of Belsay B6342 to Cambo.
Open: HOUSE Apr 1 end Oct daily 1-5.30. Last adm 5. *Closed* Tues. WALLED GARDEN Open all year daily. Apr 1-30 Sept 10.30-7 Oct 10.30-6 Nov-Mar 10.30-4 (or dusk if earlier). GROUNDS: All year during daylight hours.
Admission: House Walled Garden and Grounds £4.60 Grounds only £2.30. Party rate House Walled Garden and Grounds £4.10 Walled Garden and Grounds only £1.80.
Refreshments: Available at Clock Tower Restaurant. Telephone (01670) 774274.
No dogs in house; on leads in walled garden. Shop and Information Centre. Wheelchairs provided. *Parties by prior arrangement with the Administrator.*

WARKWORTH CASTLE AND HERMITAGE

map **9** M19
Telephone: (01665) 711423

ENGLISH HERITAGE

From 1332 the history of Warkworth was the history of the Percy family. In 1399 this became the history of England, when the third Percy lord of Warkworth and his son Harry Hotspur put Henry IV on the throne. Three scenes from Shakespeare's Henry IV Part 1 are set at Warkworth. Norman in origin, the castle has some very fine medieval masonry. Part of the keep was restored and made habitable in the 19th century. The hermitage and chapel of Holy Trinity is situated in a peaceful, retired place, overshadowed and surrounded by trees upon the left bank of the River Coquet half a mile above the castle.

Location: 7½ m (12 km) south of Alnwick.
Open: Apr 1-Sept 30 10-6 daily Oct 1-31 10-4 daily Nov 1-Mar 31 10-4 Wed-Sun.
Admission: Adults £2 concessions £1.50 children £1.

NOTTINGHAMSHIRE

CARLTON HALL

(Trustees of G H Vere-Laurie dec'd)
Carlton-on-Trent, Newark NG23 6NW   map **7** Q21 △

George III house built c.1765 by Joseph Pocklington of Newark, banker, 1736-1817. Beautiful drawing room. Magnificent ancient cedar in grounds. Stables attributed to Carr of York.

Location: 7 m N of Newark just off A1.
Station(s): Newark.
Open: Any day. Telephone (01636) 821421. Written confirmation required.
Admission: House and Garden £3 minimum charge per head per party of 10 min.
Conferences: By arrangement.

CLUMBER PARK The National Trust

nr Worksop   map **7** Q20   ♿
Telephone: (01909) 476653

4,000 acre landscaped park with lake and woods. Classical bridge, temples, lawned Lincoln Terrace and pleasure grounds. Walled kitchen garden and tools exhibition.

Location: Clumber Park 4½ m SE of Worksop; 6½ m SW of East Retford.
Open: Open daily all year. The Estate Office, Clumber Park, Worksop, Notts S80 3AZ.
Admission: Vehicle parking charges.
Refreshments: Cafeteria open all year daily. Licensed restaurant for lunches daily, evening meals available for pre-booked parties. Telephone: (01909) 484122.
Events/Exhibitions: 1995 Events: Clumber Park Horse Trials 6/7 May; Clumber Show 18 June; Open Air Concerts 8 July & 5 August.
Dogs admitted. Cycle hire. Fishing bank. Wheelchairs, Batricar available for disabled visitors (contact Visitor Liaison Officer). Shop open daily 10.30-6.00 (5.00 in winter).

NEWARK TOWN HALL

(Newark Town Council)
Newark   NG24 1DU   map **7** Q21   △ ♿
Telephone: (01636) 640100
Fax: (01636) 640967

One of the finest Georgian Town Halls in the country, the building has recently been refurbished in sympathy with John Carr's original concept. On display is the Town's collection of Civic Plate, silver dating generally from the 17th and 18th century, including the 'Newark Monteith' and the Newark Siege Pieces. Other items of interest are some early historical records and various paintings including a collection by the artist Joseph Paul.

Location: Market Place, Newark; located on A1 and A46.
Station(s): Newark Castle; Northgate (½ m).
Open: All the year Mon-Fri 10-12 2-4. Open at other times for groups by appointment. *Closed* Sat Sun Bank Hol Mons and Tues following and Christmas week.
Admission: Free.

PAPPLEWICK HALL

(Dr R.B. Godwin-Austen)
Near Nottingham   NG15 8FE   map **7** Q20   △
Telephone: (0115) 9633491

Fine Adam house built 1784 with lovely plasterwork ceilings. Park and woodland garden, particularly known for its rhododendrons.

Location: 6 m N Nottingham off A60. 2 m from exit 27 M1.
Open: By appointment only, all year.
Accommodation: Country House hospitality, full breakfast and dinner, prices on request.

THRUMPTON HALL

(Mrs George Seymour)
Nottingham   NG11 0AX   map **7** Q20   △ ♿
Telephone: (0115) 9830333

Fine Jacobean house, built 1607, incorporating earlier manor house. Priest's hiding hole, magnificent Charles II carved staircase carved and panelled saloon and other fine rooms containing beautiful 17th and 18th century furniture and many fine portraits. Large lawns separated from landscaped park by ha-ha and by lake. This house retains the atmosphere of a home, being lived in by owners who will show parties around.

Location: 7 m S of Nottingham; 3 m E of M1 at junction 24; 1 m from A453.
Open: By appointment for parties of 20 or more persons. Open all year including evenings.
Admission: House and Gardens £3 children £1.50. Minimum charge of £60.
Refreshments: By prior arrangement.
Events/Exhibitions: To be arranged.

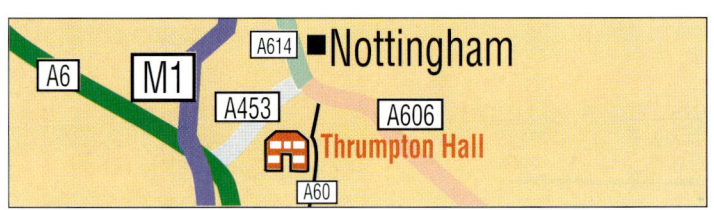

OXFORDSHIRE

ARDINGTON HOUSE

(Mrs Desmond Baring)
nr Wantage   OX12 8QA   map **5** T20   △ Ⓔ
Telephone: (01235) 833244

Early 18th century of grey brick with red brick facings. Hall with Imperial staircase, panelled dining room with painted ceiling. Attractive Stable Yard.

Location: 12 m S of Oxford; 12 m N of Newbury; 2½ m E of Wantage.
Station(s): Didcot (8 m).
Open: May-Sept Mons & all Bank Hols 2.30-4.30 parties of 10 or more welcomed any day by appointment.
Admission: House & Grounds £2.
Refreshments: Coffee & Teas by arrangement.

ASHDOWN HOUSE The National Trust
nr Lambourn   RG16 7RE   map **5** T19   △

17th century house built by 1st Lord Craven and by him 'consecrated' to Elizabeth, Queen of Bohemia; great staircase rising from hall to attic; portraits of the Winter Queen's family; access to roof, fine views; box parterre and lawns. Avenues and woodland walks.

Location: 2¼ m S of Ashbury; 3½ m N of Lambourn on W side of B4000.
Open: Hall, stairway & roof only (fine views). Apr-end Oct Weds & Sats 2-6. Guided tours only at 2.15 3.15 4.15 and 5.15 from front door. *Closed* Easter and Bank Hols. **Woodlands** open all year Sat-Thurs dawn to dusk.
Admission: Grounds, hall, stairway & roof £2 Children half-price. Woodlands free. No reduction for parties (which should pre-book in writing).
No dogs allowed in house or grounds. Wheelchair access to garden only. No WCs.

BLENHEIM PALACE

(His Grace the Duke of Marlborough)
Woodstock   OX20 1PX   map **5** T20   △ ⓢ
Telephone: (01993) 811325 (24 hr information)
Fax: (01993) 813527

Blenheim Palace is the home of the Dukes of Marlborough and the birthplace of Sir Winston Churchill. It was built for John Churchill, 1st Duke of Marlborough, by Sir John Vanbrugh and was a gift from a munificent sovereign, Queen Anne, and a grateful nation to the victor of the Battle of Blenheim, 1704. The Palace, which is in the Baroque style, is set in 2100 acres of parkland landscaped by 'Capability' Brown who also created Blenheim's lake and significantly altered the original gardens of Henry Wise. Close to Oxford and next to the historic town of Woodstock, the Palace is easily accessible by car, train and coach. An inclusive ticket covers the Palace tour, Park, Gardens, Butterfly House, Motor Launch, Train, Adventure Play Area, Nature Trail and car parking. The Marlborough Maze and Rowing Boat Hire (on Queen Pool) are optional. 1995 events include the annual Charity Cricket Match on Spring Bank Holiday Sunday, the International Horse Trials on 14th, 15th, 16th and 17th September, Craft Fairs on the May Day and August Bank Holiday weekends and various other events which will be publicised in the local press. For further details apply to Administrator's Office, Blenheim Palace, Woodstock, Oxon. OX20 1PX.

Location: SW end of Woodstock which lies 8 m N of Oxford (A44).
Open: Mid Mar-Oct 31 daily 10.30-5.30 (last adm 4.45).
Admission: Charges not available at time of going to press.
Refreshments: Licensed Restaurant & Self Service Cafeteria at the Palace. Self Service Cafeteria at Pleasure Gardens.
Education Service. A Sandford award holder since 1982.
The right to close the Palace or Park without notice is reserved.

Grinling Gibbons (1648-1721)

Sculptor and wood carver. His work can be seen at the following properties included in Historic Houses Castles and Gardens:-

Blenheim Palace	*Lyme Park*
Breamore House	*Petworth House*
Dunham Massey	*Somerleyton Hall*
Fawley Court	*Sudbury Hall*
Kentchurch Court	

BROUGHTON CASTLE

(The Lord Saye & Sele)
Banbury   OX15 5EB   map **5** S20
Telephone: (01295) 262624

Broughton Castle is essentially a family home lived in by Lord and Lady Saye and Sele and their family. The original medieval Manor House, of which much remains today was built about 1300 by Sir John de Broughton. It stands on an island site surrounded by a 3 acre moat. The Castle was greatly enlarged between 1550 and 1600, at which time it was embellished with magnificent plaster ceilings, splendid panelling and fine fireplaces. In the 17th century, William 8th Lord Saye and Sele, played a leading role in national affairs. He opposed Charles I's efforts to rule without Parliament and Broughton became a secret meeting place for the King's opponents. During the Civil War, William raised a regiment and he and his 4 sons all fought at the nearby Battle of Edgehill. After the battle, the Castle was beseiged and captured. Arms and armour from the Civil War and other periods are displayed in the Great Hall. Visitors may also see the Gatehouse, Garden and Park together with the nearby 14th century Church of St. Mary in which there are many family tombs, memorials and hatchments. The garden consists of mixed herbaceous and shrub borders containing many old roses. In addition, there is a formal walled garden with beds of roses surrounded by box hedging and lined by more mixed borders.

Location: 2 m SW of Banbury on the Shipston-on-Stour Road (B4035).
Station(s): Banbury.
Open: Mid May-mid Sept Weds & Suns 2-5 also Thurs in July & Aug 2-5 Bank Hol Suns & Bank Hol Mons including Easter 2-5.
Admission: Adults £3.50 OAPs/students £3 children £1.50 (1995). Groups on other days throughout the year by appointment (reduced rates).
Refreshments: Buffet teas on open days; by arrangement for groups.
Conferences: Some of the Park is available for private hire.
Castle and Gardens available for product launches, film and T.V. location work.

BUSCOT OLD PARSONAGE   The National Trust
Buscot, Faringdon   SN7 8DQ   map **5** T19   △

Built in 1703 of Cotswold stone and stone tiles. On the banks of the Thames. Small garden.

Location: 2 m SE of Lechlade; 4 m NW of Faringdon on A417.
Open: Apr-end Oct Weds 2-6 by appointment in writing with the tenant.
Admission: £1. *No parties.*
No dogs,no WCs. Unsuitable for wheelchairs.

BUSCOT PARK   The National Trust
nr Faringdon   SN7 8BU   map **5** T19   △
Telephone: (01367) 242094 (not weekends)

Built 1780. Fine paintings and furniture. Burne-Jones room. Attractive garden walks, lake. Administered for the National Trust by Lord Faringdon.

Location: 3 m NW Faringdon on Lechlade/Faringdon road (A417).
Open: Apr-end Sept (incl Good Fri Easter Sat & Sun) Wed Thurs Fri and every 2nd and 4th Sat and immediately following Sun 2-6 i.e. Apr 8-9 15-16 22-23 May 13-14 27-28 June 10-11 24-25 July 8-9 22-23 Aug 12-13 26-27 Sept 9-10 23-24. Timed entry to house if crowding occurs.
Admission: House and Grounds £4 Chd £2 Grounds only £3 Chd £1.50.
Refreshments: Tea-room. Lunches for coach parties only (10-50) by appointment with housekeeper.
No dogs. No indoor photography. Unsuitable for wheelchairs.

DITCHLEY PARK

(Ditchley Foundation)
Enstone   OX7 4ER   map **5** T20   △
Telephone: (01608) 677346
Fax: (01608) 677399

Third in size and date of the great 18th century houses of Oxfordshire, Ditchley is famous for its splendid interior decorations (William Kent and Henry Flitcroft). For three and half centuries the home of the Lee family and their descendants - Ditchley was frequently visited at weekends by Sir Winston Churchill during World War II. It has now been restored, furnished and equipped as a conference centre devoted to the study of issues of concern to the people on both sides of the Atlantic.

Location: 1½ m W of A44 at Kiddington; 2 m from Charlbury (B4437).
Station(s): Charlbury (2 m).
Open: Visits by prior arrangement with the Bursar, Mon. Tues and Thurs afternoons only. Closed July-mid Sept.

FAWLEY COURT - MARIAN FATHERS HISTORIC HOUSE & MUSEUM

(Marian Fathers)
Henley-on-Thames   **RG9 3AE**   map **12** T21

Designed by Sir Christopher Wren, Fawley Court was built in 1684 for Colonel William Freeman as a family residence. The Mansion House, decorated by Grinling Gibbons and later by James Wyatt, is situated in a beautiful park designed by Lancelot 'Capability' Brown. The Museum consists of a library, various documents of the Polish kings, a very rare and well preserved collection of historical sabres and many memorable military objects of the Polish Army. There are classical sculptures, and paintings from Renaissance and later times. Fawley Court also serves nowadays as a seat of religious community, and from 1953 has been cared for, maintained and restored by the Congregation of Marian Fathers.

Location: 1 m N of Henley-on-Thames via A4155 to Marlow.
Station(s): Henley-on-Thames (1½ m).
Open: Mar-Oct Wed Thurs Sun 2-5 closed Easter and Whitsuntide weeks. Nov and Feb open to groups by pre-booked appointment.
Admission: Adults £3 OAPs £2 children £1.
Refreshments: Tea, coffee & home-made cakes available.
Car park. No dogs.

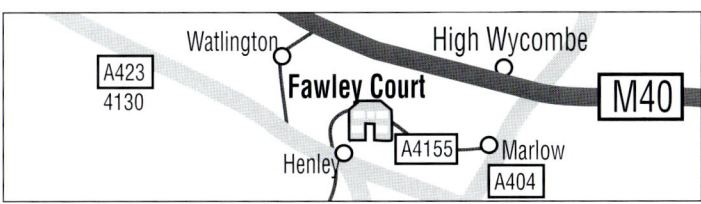

THE GREAT BARN   The National Trust
Great Coxwell   map **5** S19

13th century, stone built, stone tiled roof, exceptionally interesting timber roof construction. Magnificent proportions.

Location: 2 m SW of Faringdon between A420 & B4019.
Open: All year daily at reasonable hours. Dogs on leads admitted. Wheelchair access.
Admission: 50p.

GREYS COURT   The National Trust
Henley-on-Thames   **RG9 4PG**   map **12** T21
Telephone: (01491) 628529

Jacobean house with Georgian and 19th century additions set amid the remains of the courtyard walls and towers of a 14th century fortified house; beautiful gardens; Tudor donkey wheel well-house; Archbishop's Maze, ice house.

Location: At Rotherfield Greys 3 m W of Henley-on-Thames E of B481.
Open: House Apr-end Sept Mon Wed Fri 2-6. Garden Apr-end of Sept Mon-Wed Fri and Sat 2-6. *Closed* Good Fri. Last admissions half-hour before closing.
Admission: House and Garden £4 Garden only £3 Children half-price. Parties must book in advance. No reduction for parties. Family tickets £10 and £7.50.
Refreshments: Teas, Apr to end Sept - Mons, Weds, Fris & Sats 2.30-5.15, also for booked parties at other times by arrangement.
Dogs in car park only. No picnics in grounds.

KINGSTON BAGPUIZE HOUSE

(Lady Tweedsmuir)
Kingston Bagpuize   OX13 5AX   map **5** T20   △ ⅙ (garden only)
Telephone: (01865) 820259

A superb Charles II manor house surrounded by parkland, a large garden and attractive 17th century stable buildings. The house has a magnificent cantilevered staircase and well-proportioned panelled rooms with fine furniture and pictures. The large and interesting garden contains beautiful trees, lawns, a woodland garden, herbaceous and shrub borders and many lovely bulbs.

Location: 5½ m W of Abingdon (A415 near A420 interchange).
Station(s): Oxford or Didcot.
Open: Apr-Sept Suns and Bank Holiday Mons 2.30-5.30 (last adm 5).
Admission: House and Garden adults £3 OAPs £2.50 children £2. Garden only £1. (children under 5 free adm to Garden, not admitted to House). Groups welcome by written appointment on week days only. Group rates on request.
Refreshments: Teas.
Wheelchairs garden only. No dogs. Small gift shop. Car parking.

KINGSTONE LISLE PARK

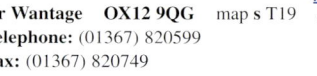

Nr Wantage   OX12 9QG   map **s** T19   △
Telephone: (01367) 820599
Fax: (01367) 820749

Kingstone Lisle is a sensational Palladian House, home of the Lonsdale Family. The house is set in 140 acres of parkland. Superb views are enjoyed up to the Lambourn Downs where the Roman Ridgeway marks the southern boundary. Three spring fed lakes beside the house complete this very attractive landscape. The house built in 1677, is on the site of a fortified castle which burnt down in 1620 (the original 12th century church is all that remains). The nearby blowing stone which according to legend was blown by King Alfred to muster his armies on the downs is still in the village and can be blown by visitors during daylight hours. The hall is in the style of Sir John Soane and there is a strong impression of entering an Italian Palazzo with beautiful ornate plaster ceilings, colomns and figurines. By complete contrast the inner hall becomes the classical English country house, the most exciting feature being the Flying Staircase winding its way up, totally unsupported. A fine collection of art, furniture, clocks, glass and needlework together with the architecture inspire visitors with admiration for the craftsmanship that has existed in Britain over the centuries. **Gardens** Twelve acres of gardens include a shrubbery, pleached limes, an avenue leading up to an ornamental pond and a replica of Queen Mary's rose garden in Regents Park.

Location: 5 m W of Wantage
Station(s): Didcot 13 m
Open: 17 Apr 8 May 29 May 28 Aug 2-5.
Admission: £5 per adult children free.
Refreshments: Teas available.
Events/Exhibitions: Family funday for charity on 29 May 11-5.
Accommodation: Strictly by prior arrangement.

Sir Peter Lely - portrait painter

His paintings can be seen at the following properties included in Historic Houses Castles and Gardens:-

Aynhoe Park	*Kedleston Hall*
Belton House	*Knole*
Breamore House	*Petworth House*
Browsholme Hall	*Ragley Hall*
Dalmeny House	*Rockingham Castle*
Euston Hall	*St Osyth Priory*
Goodwood House	*Stanford Hall*
Gorhambury	*Weston Park*

MAPLEDURHAM HOUSE AND WATERMILL

(J J Eyston and Lady Anne Eyston)
Mapledurham RG4 7TR   map **5** U20 △
Telephone: (01734) 723350
Fax: (01734) 724016

Late 16th century Elizabethan home of the Blount family. Original plaster ceilings, great oak staircase, fine collection of paintings and private chapel in Strawberry Hill Gothic added in 1797. Interesting literary connections with Alexander Pope, John Galsworthy's Forsyte Saga and Kenneth Graham's Wind in the Willows. Unique setting in grounds running down to the Thames. The 15th century Watermill is fully restored and producing flour and bran which are sold in the gift shop. Film set for "Eagle has Landed" and "Class Act".

Location: 4 m NW of Reading on North Bank of Thames. Signed off A4074.
Open: Sat Sun and Bank Hols 12.30-5. Midweek parties by arrangement.
Admission: House & Mill £4 House only £3 Mill £2.50. Children under 14 half price. Weekend parties £3.80.
Refreshments: Tea-rooms serving cream teas.
Events/Exhibitions: By arrangement.
Accommodation: Eleven self catering holiday cottages.
Conferences: By arrangement. Wedding receptions by arrangement.
Car parking and picnic area.

Sir Joshua Reynolds
Portrait painter (1723-1792)
First President of the Royal Academy, knighted in 1769

His work can be seen in the following properties included in Historic Houses Castles and Gardens:-

Arundel Castle
Dalmeny House (Roseberry Collection of
Political Portraits)
Elton Hall
Goodwood House
Ickworth House, Park & Garden
Kenwood, The Iveagh Bequest

Knole
Petworth House
Rockingham Castle
Saltram
Shalom Hall
Wallington House
Weston Park

MILTON MANOR HOUSE

(Anthony Mockler-Barrett, Esq)

nr Abingdon   map **5** T20   △ &
Telephone: (01235) 831871
Fax: (01235) 831287

Mellow restoration house, near Oxford, with Georgian wings, traditionally designed by Inigo Jones. Very much a family home, seat of the Barrett family for six generations. Exquisite Roman Catholic chapel where Mass is still celebrated. 'Like all the best things in England', wrote the late Poet Laureate John Betjeman (a family friend), 'This is hidden. Milton village street is true Berkshire. The Manor House is splendid. Inside are handsome rooms and an exciting contrast - a Chapel and Library in Strawberry Hill Gothick. Do go and see it.' Walled garden (fruit, veg and flowers for sale), Stables, Dovecoat, Doves, Llamas, Pygmy goats, Shetland ponies, Rare-breed pigs and other animals to see. Fine mature trees and a (rather overgrown) woodland walk. Headquarters of the 'Back to Berkshire Campaign,' and host to the annual 'Authors' Book Fair.' 'A perfect gem of an historic house - the interior is a delight,' says Elisabeth de Stroumillo, writing in the Daily Telegraph. 'Milton Manor is not to be missed.' 'We were overwhelmed at Blenheim, we relaxed at Milton' said an American visitor. Most people agree.

Location: 9 m S of Oxford. A34 leading S towards Newbury and the M4. Turning off signposted Milton. Village 1/2 m. Entrance gates by church. 3 m S of Abingdon. 1 m from Sutton Courteney on B4016 1 ½ hr from London via M4 or M40.
Station(s): Didcot (2 m).
Open: Every Sun from Easter-end Sept [the Season]. All Bank Hol Sats & Mons (beginning with Easter Sat) during the Season. Open every day in Aug [the high Season] *except* Mons. Times of opening 12-5. The house is only open for guided tours which will take place at 12, 2.30 & 3.30. *Dogs not admitted (except in picnic/parking area).*
Admission: House and gardens £3. Gardens only £1.50. Chd half-price. Groups (min 20) always welcome by appointment at any time.
Refreshments: Home-made snacks and teas in the old kitchens, where the famous teapot collection of Mrs Marjorie Mockler, the present owner's late mother, is on show. Light suppers and lunches can be arranged for groups. *Weddings and other special events can be booked.*
Free parking (except for Special Events).

NUFFIELD PLACE

(Nuffield College, Friends of Nuffield Place)

Nettlebed   map **5** T20
Telephone: (01491) 641224

The home from 1933-1963 of Lord Nuffield, founder of Morris Motors, Nuffield Place is a rare survival of a complete upper-middle class home of the 1930s. Built in 1914, the house was enlarged in 1933 for Lord Nuffield. Several rooms are still decorated in the '30s style, and all rooms contain furnishings acquired by Lord and Lady Nuffield when they took up residence. Clocks, rugs and some tapestries are of fine quality. Some of the furniture is antique but much was custom made by Cecil A. Halliday of Oxford, and is of skilled craftsmanship. The gardens, with mature trees, stone walls and rockery, were laid out during and just after the First World War. Lady Nuffield's Wolseley car is also on display.

Location: Approximately 7 m from Henley-on-Thames, just off A4130 formerly A423 to Oxford.
Open: May-Sept every 2nd and 4th Sun 2-5.
Admission: Adults £2.50 concessions £1.50 children 50p. Parties by arrangement. Tel: (0491) 825556.
Refreshments: Home-made teas.
Ground floor and garden suitable for disabled, but no disabled lavatory.

ROUSHAM HOUSE

(C Cottrell-Dormer, Esq)
Steeple Aston   map **5** T20   △
Telephone: (01869) 347110 or (01860) 360407

Rousham House was built by Sir Robert Dormer in 1635 and the shooting holes were put in the doors while it was a Royalist garrison in the Civil War. Sir Robert's successors were Masters of Ceremonies at Court during eight reigns and employed Court artists and architects to embellish Rousham. The house stands above the River Cherwell one mile from Hopcrofts Holt, near the road from Chipping Norton to Bicester. It contains 150 portraits and other pictures and much fine contemporary furniture. Rooms were decorated by William Kent (1738) and Roberts of Oxford (1765). The garden is Kent's only surviving landscape design with classic buildings, cascades, statues and vistas in thirty acres of hanging woods above the Cherwell. Wonderful herbaceous borders, pigeon house and small parterre. Fine herd of rare Long-Horn cattle in the park. Wear sensible shoes and bring a picnic, and Rousham is yours for the day.

Location: 12 m N of Oxford east of A4260 south of B4030.
Station(s): Heyford (1 m).
Open: Apr-Sept inclusive Wed Sun & Bank Hols 2-4.30. Gardens only every day all year 10-4.30. No children under 15. No dogs. Groups by arrangement on other days.
Admission: House adults £2.50. Garden £2.50.

"GHOSTS"

Ghosts are in residence at the following properties included in Historic Houses Castles and Gardens:-

Blickling Hall - *Anne Boleyn*

Breamore House - *Haunted picture - if touched, death on the same day*

East Riddleden Hall - *5 ghosts including lady*

in Grey Hall Lady's Chamber

Fountains Abbey & Studley Royal - *Choir of monks chanting in Chapel of Nine Altars*

Hinton Ampner - *Nocturnal noises*

Ightham Mote - *Supernatural presence*

Lindisfarne Castle - *Monk, and group of monks on causeway*

Lyme Park - *Unearthly peals of bells and lady in white, funeral procession through park*

Malmesbury House - *Ghost of a cavalier*

Overbecks Museum & Garden - *'Model' ghost in the Children's room (for them to spot)*

Rockingham Castle - *Lady Dedlock*

Rufford Old Hall - *Elizabeth Hesketh*

Scotney Castle Garden - *Man rising from the lake*

Sizergh Castle & Garden - *Poltergeist*

Speke Hall - *Ghost of woman in tapestry room*

Springhill - *Ghost of a woman*

Sudbury Hall - *Lady in Green, seen on stairs*

Tamworth Castle - *Haunted bedroom*

Treasurer's House - *Troop of Roman soldiers marching through the cellar*

Wallington House - *Invisible birds beating against the windows accompanied by heavy breathing*

Washington Old Hall - *Grey lady walking through corridors*

STANTON HARCOURT MANOR
(Mr Crispin & The Hon Mrs Gascoigne)
Stanton Harcourt   map **5** T20   &
Telephone: (01865) 881928

Unique medieval buildings in tranquil surroundings - Old Kitchen, Pope's Tower and Domestic Chapel. House maintained as family home, contains fine collection of pictures, furniture, silver and porcelain. 12 acres of Garden with Great Fish Pond and Stew Ponds.

Location: 9 m W of Oxford; 5 m SE of Witney; on B4449, between Eynsham & Standlake.
Open: Apr 16 17 27 30 May 1 7 8 11 14 25 28 29 June 8 11 22 25 July 6 9 20 23 Aug 10 13 24 27 28 Sept 7 10 21 24 open 2-6 pm.
Admission: House and Gardens adults £3 children (12 and under)/OAPs £2. Coaches by prior arrangement. Gardens only adults £1.50 children (12 and under)/OAPs £1.
Refreshments: Teas on Suns and Bank Hols in aid of Parish Church.
Disabled visitors welcome. Home container-grown shrubs and pot plants for sale.

Butterfly Houses

can be found at the following properties included in Historic Houses Castles and Gardens:-

Berkeley Castle
Elsham Hall - Wild butterfly walkway
Syon House

Lancelot 'Capability' Brown

Born 1716 in Northumberland, Capability Brown began work at the age of 16 in the vegetable gardens of Sir William and Lady Loraine at Kirharle Tower. He left Northumberland in 1739, and records show that he worked at Stowe until 1749. It was at Stowe that Brown began to study architecture, and to submit his own plans. It was also at Stowe that he devised a new method of moving and replanting mature trees.

Brown married Bridget Wayet in 1744 and began work on the estate at Warwick Castle in 1749. He was appointed Master Gardener at Hampton Court in 1764, and planted the Great Vine at Hampton Court in 1768. Blenheim Palace designs are considered amongst Brown's finest work, and the technical achievements were outstanding even for the present day.

Capability Brown died in February 1783 of a massive heart attack. A monument beside the lake at Croome Court was erected which reads "To the memory of Lancelot Brown, who by the powers of his inimitable and creative genius formed this garden scene out of a morass". There is also a portrait of Brown at Burghley.

Capability Brown was involved in the design of grounds at the following properties included in Historic Houses Castles and Gardens:-

Audley End	*Longleat*
Berrington Hall	*Luton Hoo*
Bowood	*Moccas Court*
Burghley House	*Petworth House*
Burton Constable	*Sledmere House*
Charlecote Park	*Stowe (Stowe*
Chilham Castle Gardens	*School)*
(reputed)	*Syon House*
Clandon Park	*Warwick Castle*
Claremont	*Weston Park*
Chillington Hall	*Wimpole Hall*
Corsham Court	*Wrest Park and*
Fawley Court	*Gardens*
Highclere Castle	

STONOR PARK

(Lord & Lady Camoys)
nr Henley-on-Thames   RG9 6HF   map **12** T21
Telephone: (01491) 638587
Fax: (01491) 638587

Ancient home of Lord and Lady Camoys and the Stonor family for over eight hundred years, and centre of Catholicism throughout the Recusancy Period, with its own medieval Chapel where mass is still celebrated today. Sanctuary for St. Edmund Campion in 1581. An exhibition features his life and work. The house is of considerable architectural interest, built over many centuries from c.1190, and the site of prehistoric stone circle, now recreated within the grounds. A family home containing fine family portraits and rare items of furniture, paintings, drawings, tapestries, sculptures and bronzes from Britain, Europe and America. Peaceful hillside gardens with magnificent roses and ornamental ponds. Now featuring exhibition of stone sculpture from Zimbabwe. Souvenir gift shop and afternoon tearoom serving home-made cakes. Parties welcome, lunches available by prior arrangement.

Location: On B480; 5 m N of Henley-on-Thames, 5 m S of Watlington.
Station(s): Henley-on-Thames.
Open: Apr open Suns and Bank Hol Mons only, May June and Sept open Weds, Suns and Bank Hol Mons, Jul open Weds, Thurs, Suns, Aug open Weds, Thurs, Sats, Suns and Bank Hol Mons 2-5.30 (Bank Hol Mons 12.30-5.30). Last adm 5. Parties by prior arrangement any Tues, Wed or Thur (morning, afternoon or evening with supper) and Sun (afternoon only).
Admission: Adults £4 children (under 14 with adult) free Gardens and Chapel only £2. Party rates on application. Discount for NT and English Heritage members, HHA members free on production of card.
Refreshments: Tea-room. Group lunches and suppers by arrangement.

WALLINGFORD CASTLE GARDENS

Castle Street, Wallingford   map **5** T20

These Gardens are situated on part of the site of Wallingford Castle, which was built by William the Conqueror and demolished by Oliver Cromwell in 1652. The remains of St Nicholas Priory are a feature of the Gardens, which is a haven of beauty and tranquillity.

Open: Apr-Oct 10-6 Nov-Mar 10-3.
Admission: Free.

George Stubbs
Portrait, animal and rural painter

(1724-1806)
Produced his engraved work,
The Anatomy of a Horse, in 1766

His work can be seen in the following properties included in Historic Houses Castles and Gardens:-

Mount Stewart House
St Osyth Priory
Upton House

WATERPERRY GARDENS
nr Wheatley   map **5** T20
Telephone: (01844) 339226/339254

WATERPERRY GARDENS
Nr. WHEATLEY, OXFORDSHIRE

The peaceful gardens at Waterperry feature a magnificent herbaceous border, shrub and heather borders, alpine and rock gardens, and a new formal garden. Together with stately trees, a river to walk by and a quiet Saxon Church to visit – all set in 83 acres of unspoilt Oxfordshire – the long established herbaceous and alpine nurseries provide year round interest. For the experienced gardener, the novice, or those who have no garden of their own here is a chance to share, enjoy and admire the order and beauty of careful cultivation.

Garden Shop and Plant Centre with exceptionally wide range of plants, shrubs and fruit produced in the nurseries for sale. Expert care and training is shown in all stages of development. Pots, tubs and sundries also available.

A new art and crafts gallery exhibiting and selling quality ceramics, glass and jewellery etc.

The Teashop provides a delicious selection of home-made food, tea, coffee, fruit juices, etc. Light lunches, morning coffee, teas with scones and cream, cakes, etc. Wine licence.

Open all year from 10am. Closed for Christmas and New Year Holidays. Open only to visitors to ART IN ACTION between 13th and 16th July.

Enquiries Telephone: (01844) 339226/339254

ADMISSION SEE EDITORIAL REFERENCE 20 & 23.

Spacious and peaceful ornamental gardens of 6 acres. Church of Saxon origin and historical interest in grounds with famous old glass, brasses and woodwork. Many interesting plants. Shrub, Herbaceous and Alpine Nurseries.

Location: 2½ m from A40, turn off at Wheatley. 50 m from London, 9 m from Oxford. 62 m Birmingham M40, junction 8. Well signposted locally with Tourist Board Rose' symbol.
Open: All the year. Daily Mar-Oct 10-5.30 (weekdays) 10-6 (weekends) Nov-Feb 10-5 (Tea-shop closes 30 mins earlier) closed for Christmas and New Year Hols. Open only to visitors to ART IN ACTION (enquiries 0171-381 3192) July 13-16. Parties and coaches at all times by appointment only. High quality Plant Centre and Garden Shop, telephone: (01844) 339226 In aid of National Gardens' Scheme & Gardeners' Sun June 11 & Aug 13.
Admission: Ornamental Gardens & Nurseries Mar-Oct £2.20 Nov-Feb 75p.
Refreshments: Tea-shop for morning coffee, light lunches and teas. Wine licence. Tel (01844) 338087.
A new **Art and Crafts Gallery** exhibiting and selling quality ceramics, glass and jewellery etc. Tel (01844) 338085.

SHROPSHIRE

ADCOTE
(Adcote School Educational Trust Ltd)
Little Ness, nr Shrewsbury   SY4 2JY   map **6** R17
Telephone: (01939) 260202
Fax: (01939) 261300

'Adcote is the most controlled, coherent and masterly of the big country houses designed by Norman Shaw' (Mark Girouard, 'Country Life' Oct 1970).

Location: 7 m NW of Shrewsbury off A5.
Open: Apr 24-July 14 (except May 27-31 inclusive) 2-5 re-open Sept 11-Oct 20 all other times by appointment.
Admission: Free but the Governors reserve the right to make a charge.

ATTINGHAM PARK   The National Trust
nr Shrewsbury   SY4 4TP   map **6** R17   ♿
Telephone: (01743) 709203
Fax: (01743) 709352

Designed in 1785 by George Steuart for the 1st Lord Berwick. Elegant classical interior decoration. Famous painted boudoir. Nash Picture Gallery. Fine collection of Regency Silver. Park landscape designed by Humphry Repton, 1797. Extensive deer park.

Location: At Atcham; 4 m SE of Shrewsbury, on N side of Telford Road B4380 (from M54 B5061, then B4380).
Station(s): Shrewsbury 5 m.
Open: Apr 1-Sept 27 Sat-Wed 1.30-5, (Bank Hol Mons 11-5). Oct Sat & Sun 1.30-5. Last adm 4.30. Shop open as house. Pre-booked parties, including evening opening, by arrangement. Deer park and grounds open daily (except Christmas Day) dawn to dusk.
Admission: House & Grounds £3.50 children £1.75 Family ticket £8.70. Deer Park & Grounds £1.40.
Refreshments: Light lunches 12.30-2.30 and home-made teas 2.30-5 Bank Holiday Mon 11-5. Licensed. Lunches and suppers at other times for pre-booked parties.
Dogs in grounds only (Not in deer park). Wheelchairs available. Electric mobility vehicle available for use in grounds. Shop. Mother and Baby room.

BENTHALL HALL   The National Trust
Broseley   TF12 5RX   map **6** R17
Telephone: (01952) 882159

16th century stone house with mullioned windows. Interior improved in 17th century. Fine oak staircase and plaster ceilings. Family collections of furniture and paintings. Carefully restored plantsman's garden.

Location: 1 m NW of Broseley; 4 m NE of Much Wenlock; 6 m S of Wellington, (B4375).
Station(s): Telford Central 7½ m.
Open: Apr 2-27 Sept Wed Sun and Bank Hol Mons 1.30-5.30 (last adm 5). House visits and garden visits at other times for groups by appointment Tues and Wed a.m.
Admission: £3 Garden only £2. Reduced rates for booked parties. Coaches by appointment.
Refreshments: Dudmaston (NT) 20 mins drive from Benthall catering for groups by arrangement. No picnics in garden.
No dogs. Wheelchair access.

CARDING MILL VALLEY & LONG MYND
   The National Trust
Church Stretton   SY6 6JG   map **6** R17
Telephone: (01694) 722631

Chalet Pavilion in the magnificent scenery of Carding Mill Valley.

Location: 15 m S of Shrewsbury; W of Church Stretton Valley & A49.
Station(s): Church Stretton (1 m).
Open: Moorland open all year. Chalet Pavilion Information Centre, Shop & Cafe 1 Apr-end June and Sept Tues-Fri 11-5 Sat Sun and Bank Hol Mons 10.30-5. July-end Aug daily 10.30-5. Oct Sat and Sun 11-5 or dusk if earlier. Booked parties at other times by arrangement.
Admission: Car park charge £1.50 per car £10 per coach (coaches must book).
Refreshments: Snacks, light lunches, teas, etc at Chalet Pavilion.
Dogs allowed if kept under control on moorland; not admitted to Chalet Pavilion.

CASTLE GATES LIBRARY
Shrewsbury   SY1 2AS   map **6** R17
Telephone: (01743) 241487
Fax: (01743) 368576

Former premises of Shrewsbury Grammar School, from 16th and 17th centuries. Now used as a public library. Also houses Shropshire's Local Studies Library. Granted a Civic Trust award for a recent restoration scheme.

Open: Public part of the building Mon-Fri 9-5 (Thurs a.m. only) Sat 9-4 Private areas by prior appointment only.

DUDMASTON   The National Trust
Quatt, Bridgnorth   WV15 6QN   map **14** S18   ♿
Telephone: (01746) 780866

Late 17th century house; collections of Dutch flower paintings, modern art, botanical paintings and family history. Extensive grounds, woodlands and lakeside garden. Estate walks open all year.

Location: 4 m SE of Bridgnorth on A442.
Station(s): Bridgnorth (Severn Valley Railway) 4 m Kidderminster 10 m.
Open: Mar 29-Oct 1 Wed & Sun 2-5.30 (last adm 5). Special opening for pre-booked parties Thur 2-5.30.
Admission: House and Garden £3.50 Family £8. Garden only £2.50. Parties must book in advance.
Refreshments: 1-5.30 (light lunches 1-2). Light lunches for booked parties by arrangement on Wed & Thurs.
Dogs in Dingle, Park and Estate only, on leads. Shop. Electric mobility vehicle available for use in garden.

HAWKSTONE HALL AND GARDENS

(The Redemptorists)
Weston-U-Redcastle, SY4 5LG   map **6** R17   ⅖
Telephone: (01630) 685242
Fax: (01630) 685565

Grade 1 Georgian Mansion and Gardens set in spacious parkland. From 1556 to 1906 Hawkstone was the seat of the distinguished HILL family of Shropshire. The principal rooms include the Venetian Saloon, the Ballroom, the Drawing Room and the Winter Garden. The Gardens comprise terraces and lawns, rose garden, lily pool and extensive woodland with a magnificent collection of trees.

Location: Entrance at MARCHAMLEY, on A442, 2 m N of HODNET.
Open: 5-31 Aug 2-5pm.
Admission: £2.50 adults £1 children (House and Gardens). Pre-booked groups welcome.
Refreshments: Home made teas.

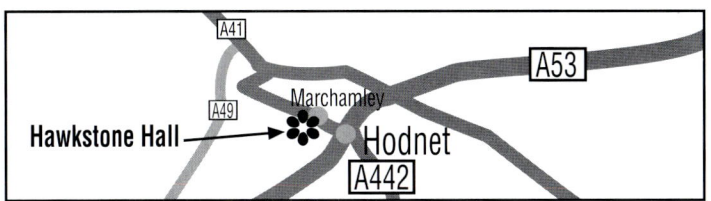

Aviaries and Birds of Prey Centres
can be found at the following properties in Historic Houses Castles and Gardens:-

Drumlanrig Castle & Country Park
Elsham Hall Country and Wildlife Park
Holdenby House & Gardens
Leeds Castle
Leighton House Museum & Art Gallery
Sewerby Hall & Gardens
Sion Hill Hall
Waddesdon Manor
Muncaster Castle

HAWKSTONE PARK

(Hawkstone Park Leisure Ltd)
Weston-under-Redcastle   SY4 5UY   map **6** R17
Telephone: (01939) 200300/200611
Fax: (01939) 200311

A woodland fantasy of castle, caves and cliffs. Open to the public for the first time in over 100 years. The ideal out for young and old - It's a magical world of mystery and intrigue - a legend reborn! Originally one of the most visited landscapes in Britain, Hawkstone once more reveals its many secrets and myths. This is the only Grade I landscape in Shropshire and ranks in the same category as Blenheim Palace in Oxfordshire. The Park is full of attractions, surprises and features. You can for example tread the stone steps so timeless they might have been carved by the Incas. You can see dramatic cliffs and rocks, towers, monuments, tunnels, passageways, precipitous rock paths, rustic sofas, romantic secret valleys. This is an experience not to be missed of both history, make believe, fear and awe. Location for BBC T.V. 'Chronicles of Narnia' and 'One Foot in the Past'. One admission price covers entrance to entire park including The White Tower, Monument, Swiss Bridge, Gingerbread Hall, Arches, Hermit's Cave, Grottos, Rhododendron Jungle, picnic areas, interpretation centre, cafeteria, gift shop, free car park and coach park. Please remember to bring sensible shoes. Park not suitable for frail or disabled.

Location: 10 m N of Shrewsbury off A49 or A53. 3 m from village of Hodnet.
Station(s): Wem/Prees/Crewe.
Open: Apr 1-Oct 31 every day 10-6.
Admission: Adults £4 children £2 family £11 (2+3) OAPs/students £3. 50p off above prices for parties of 10+ booking and paying in advance. Large free car and coach park.
Refreshments: Tea-room. Restaurant at hotel adjacent.
Events/Exhibitions: Most Bank Holidays have Treasure Trails or Craft Fayres.
Accommodation: Country House hotel set in 400 acres Grade I landscape.
Conferences: Facilities available.
Two 18-hole golf courses and Academy course and practice ground. Video analysis room, golf school, restaurants, bars.

HODNET HALL GARDENS

(Mr & the Hon Mrs Heber-Percy)
nr Market Drayton   TF9 3NN   map **6** R17   &
Telephone: (01630) 685202

From the glorious daffodils of Spring to the magnificent roses of Summer, each season brings fresh delights to these award winning gardens. Over 60 acres of magnificent forest trees, sweeping lawns and tranquil pools ensure plentiful wildlife and brilliant natural colour within this beautiful setting.

Location: 12 m NE of Shrewsbury; 5½ m SW of Market Drayton, at junction of A53 to A442; M6 18½ m (junction 15) leading to A53 or M54 (junction 3).
Open: Apr 1-Sept 30 Tues-Sat 2-5 (closed Mons) Suns & Bank Holiday Mons 12-5.30.
Admission: Adults £2.60 OAPs £2.10 children £1 (1994 prices). Reduced rates for organised parties of 25 or over. Season tickets on application. Free car and coach park.
Refreshments: Tea-rooms open daily 2-5 Sun and Bank Holiday Mons 12-5.30. *Parties to pre-book (menu on request). Gift shop, kitchen garden sales.*
Dogs allowed but must be kept on leads.

LUDFORD HOUSE

(Mr D.F.A. Nicholson)
Ludlow   SY8 1PJ   map **6** S17
Telephone: (01584) 872542
Fax: (01584) 875662

House dating back to 12th century.

Location: ½ m S of Ludlow, B4361 road.
Station(s): Ludlow.
Open: Grounds and exterior by written permission, with limited inspection of interior.
Admission: £3.
Refreshments: Hotels and Restaurants in Ludlow available.
Unsuitable for disabled.

LUDLOW CASTLE

(The Trustees of the Powis Castle Estate)
Castle Square, Ludlow   map **6** R17
Telephone: (01584) 873947 - Custodian or (01584) 873355 - Castle Ticket Office

Originally a Norman Castle of which the remains include the round nave of a Chapel with fine Norman doorways. Then a fortified Royal Palace and headquarters of the Council of the Marches. An unusually complete range of medieval buildings still stands. Visitors can enjoy the large open space of the outer bailey, gift shop and exhibition gallery. Audio tape guides available.

Location: Castle Square, Ludlow.
Open: Daily Feb 1-Apr 30 10.30-4, May 1-Sept 30 10.30-5, Oct 1-Dec 24 10.30-4. Closed January.
Admission: Adults £2.50, children £1.50, OAPs £2, family ticket £7.50, discounts for school parties by arrangement with the Custodian.
Refreshments: In Castle Square.
Public car park off Castle Square. Suitable for disabled with assistance.

MAWLEY HALL

Cleobury Mortimer   map **14** S18

18th century house attributed to Francis Smith. Fine plasterwork and panelling.

Location: 1 m S of Cleobury Mortimer (A4117); 7 m W of Bewdley.
Open: Apr 18 to July 19th Tues & Wed 2.30-5. Visitors must give advance notice to Mrs R Sharpe, 43 Dover Street, London W1X 3RE. Tel (0171) 495 6702.
Admission: £3.

MOAT HOUSE

(Mr & Mrs C. P. Richards)
Longnor, nr Shrewsbury   SY5 7PP   map **6** R17   △
Telephone: (01743) 718434
Fax: (01743) 718434

Fine example of a timber framed manor house of c1463. The hall exhibiting unique timber work and wooden masks, Surrounded by its moat of c1250.

Location: 8 m S of Shrewsbury E off A49 through village left into lane.
Open: Apr-Sept Thurs & Spring & Summer Bank Hols 2.30-5 other times by arrangement for parties of 20 plus.
Admission: £2.
Accommodation: Available for six, dinner if pre-booked, licensed, brochure available.
No dogs. Not suitable for disabled.

SHIPTON HALL

ENGLISH HERITAGE

(J.N.R.N. Bishop, Esq)
Much Wenlock   TF13 6JZ   map **6** R17 △
Telephone: (0174 636) 225

Delightful Elizabethan stone manor c.1587 with Georgian additions. Interesting Roccoco and Gothic plasterwork by T. F. Pritchard. Georgian stable block containing working pottery. Stone walled garden, medieval dovecote, and Parish Church dating from late Saxon period.

Location: In Shipton; 6 m SW of Much Wenlock junction B4376 & B4368.
Open: Easter-end Sept Thurs Bank Holiday Suns and Mons (except Christmas and New Year) 2.30-5.30 also by appointment for parties of 20 or more any time of year.
Admission: House and Garden £2.50 children £1.50 special rate for parties.
Refreshments: Teas/buffets by prior arrangement.

STOKESAY CASTLE

ENGLISH HERITAGE

Craven Arms   map **6** R17
Telephone: (01588) 672544

A rare and wonderfully preserved example of a 13th century fortified manor house situated in peaceful countryside. The castle now stands in a picturesque group with its own splendid timber-framed Jacobean gatehouse and the parish church.

Location: 8 m from Ludlow; ¾ m S of Craven Arms on 3rd class Road off A49.
Station(s): Craven Arms (1 m).
Open: Apr 1-Sept 30 daily 10-6 Oct1-Mar 31 Wed-Sun 10-4.
Admission: Adults £2.50 concessions £1.90 children £1.30. Party bookings in advance.

UPTON CRESSETT HALL

(William Cash, Esq)
Bridgnorth   map **14** R18
Telephone: (0174 631) 307

Elizabethan Manor House and magnificent Gatehouse in beautiful countryside by Norman church. Unusually fine medieval timber work and interesting brick and plaster work; 14th century Great Hall.

Location: 4 m W of Bridgnorth; 18 m SE of Shrewsbury off A458.
Open: May-Sept Thurs 2.30-5. Parties at other times throughout the year by appointment.
Admission: Adults £2.50 children £1.
Accommodation: Self catering accommodation available in Gatehouse.

WALCOT HALL

(C.R.W. Parish)
Lydbury North, Nr Bishops Castle   SY7 8AZ   map **6** R17
Telephone: 0171-581 2782
Fax: 0171-589 0195

Built by Sir William Chambers for Lord Clive of India. This Georgian House possesses a free-standing and recently restored Ballroom, stable yard with matching clock towers, extensive walled garden, in addition to its icehouse, meat safe and dovecote. There is a fine arboretum, noted for its rhododendrons and azaleas and specimen trees.

Location: 3 m E of Bishop's Castle, on B4385, ½ m outside Lydbury North.
Station(s): Craven Arms.
Open: Bank Hols Sun & Mon (except Christmas and New Year) May Sun Wed & Fri Jun Wed & Fri Jul & Aug Sun Sept Wed 2.15-4.30. Groups of 10 or more and other times, by appointment.
Admission: Adults £2.50 children (under 15) free.
Refreshments: Powis Arms; teas when available.
Accommodation: Holiday accommodation; 3 flats and Ground Floor Wing available all year.
Conferences: Magnificent ballroom: Weddings; Anniversaries; Celebrations; Conferences, with Estate suitable for Film and Photographic Locations etc. Suitable for disabled.

WENLOCK PRIORY

ENGLISH HERITAGE

Much Wenlock   map **6** R17
Telephone: (01952) 727466

The long history of Wenlock stretches back to the 7th century, although nothing visible remains of the religious house founded by St Milburge. After the Norman Conquest, a Cluniac priory was established, which came to be regarded as alien during the Hundred Years' War with France. Decorative arcading from the 12th century chapter house survives and some unusual features in the later, rebuilt church.

Location: In Much Wenlock.
Open: Apr 1-Sept 30 10-6 daily Oct 1-31 10-4 daily Nov 1-Mar 31 Wed-Sun 10-4.
Admission: Adults £2 concessions £1.50 children £1. Price includes a Personal Stereo Guided Tour.

WESTON PARK

(Weston Park Foundation)
nr Shifnal   TF11 8LE   map **14** R18   &
Telephone: (01952) 850207
Fax: (01952) 850430

Built 1671 and designed by Lady Wilbraham, contains a superb collection of antiques and paintings including works by Van Dyck, Lely and Gainsborough. Set in 1000 acres of classic 'Capability' Brown Parkland and formal gardens including restored Rose Garden, Italian Broderie. Fine Arboretum. Miniature Railway, Woodland Adventure Playground, Museum and Pets Corner. Horse Trials, Classical Concerts and other special events throughout the Summer. Conferences and private events all year.

Location: Entrance from A5 at Weston-under-Lizard, 6 m W of Junction 12, M6 (Gailey); 3 m N of Junction 3, M54 (Tong).
Station(s): Wolverhampton or Stafford.
Open: Easter-Sept (please enquire for dates and times) daily in Aug Park 11-7 (last adm 5) House 1-5 (last adm 4.30).
Admission: House, Park and Gardens adults £4.50 children £3 OAPs £3.75 Park and Gardens adults £3 children £2 OAPs £2.50 (1994) special rates for pre-booked parties and school visits. Entry charges may be adjusted on certain days for special events. Free coach/car parking.
Refreshments: Traditional country cooking in The Old Stables Tea-rooms and Licensed Bar. Restaurant service for pre-booked parties. Gourmet Dinners in the House on selected dates. Private functions incl. residential dinners and wedding receptions by arrangement. Dogs (on leads) welcome in Park.

WILDERHOPE MANOR    The National Trust

Longville   TF13 6EG   map **6** R17   &
Telephone: (01694) 771363

Elizabethan manor house with 17th century plaster ceilings,remarkable wooden spiral stairs and unique bow rack. House now run as a Youth Hostel.

Location: 7 m SW of Much Wenlock; ½ m S of B4371.
Station(s): Church Stretton 8 m.
Open: Apr 1-end of Sept: Weds & Sats 2-4.30; Oct to Mar: Sats only 2-4.30.
Admission: £1, Chd 50p.*No reduction for parties.*
Dogs around Manor on leads.

WROXETER (VIROCONIUM) ROMAN CITY

ENGLISH HERITAGE

map **6** R17
Telephone: (01743) 761330

Viroconium was the fourth largest city in Roman Britain and the largest to escape modern development. Deep beneath the exposed walls of the market-hall excavations are revealing a legionary fortress of the first century; while nearby the timber buildings of later settlers are being examined. The most impressive feature is the huge wall dividing the exercise yard from the baths.

Location: 5½ m (8.8 km) south east of Shrewsbury.
Open: Apr 1-Sept 30 10-6 daily Oct 1-31 10-4 daily Nov 1-Mar 31 10-4 Wed-Sun.
Admission: Adults £2 concessions £1.50 children £1.

SOMERSET

BARFORD PARK

(Mr & Mrs Michael Stancomb)
Enmore   TA5 1AG   map **3** U16
Telephone: (01278) 671269

Set in a large garden and looking out across a ha-ha to a park dotted with fine trees, it presents a scene of peaceful domesticity, a miniature country seat on a scale appropriate today. The well proportioned rooms, with contemporary furniture, are all in daily family use. The walled flower garden is in full view from the house, and the woodland and water gardens and archery glade with their handsome trees form a perfect setting for the stone and red-brick Queen Anne building.

Location: 5 m W of Bridgwater.
Open: May-Sept by appointment.
Admission: Charges not available at the time of going to press.
Teas and Buffet Luncheons for groups, by arrangement.

BARRINGTON COURT   The National Trust

Nr Ilminster   TA19 0NQ   map **3** V17
Telephone: (01460) 241938

Beautiful garden influenced by Gertrude Jekyll and laid out in a series of rooms. Tudor manor house restored in 1920s by the Lyle family. Now sub-let to Stuart Interiors, the furniture reproducers.

Location: In Barrington village, 5 m NE of Ilminster on B3168 visitors approaching from A303 follow signs for Ilminster town centre. (193: ST397182).
Station(s): Crewkerne 7 m.
Open: Barrington Court Garden 1 Apr-1 Oct Daily except Fri 11-5.30. Last admission 5pm. Court House 5 Apr-27 Sept Wed only 11-5.30.
Admission: Garden £3.10 Children £1.50 Parties £2.60 (children £1.20). Court House additional charge £1 Children 50p.
Refreshments: Licensed restaurant open same days as Garden.
Garden suitable for wheelchairs. No dogs. National Trust shop.

THE BISHOP'S PALACE

(The Church Commissioners)
Wells   BA5 2PD   map **14** U17
Telephone: (01749) 678691 The Manager; The Henderson Rooms

The fortified and moated mediaeval Palace unites the early 13th century first floor hall (known as The Henderson Rooms), the late 13th century Chapel and the now ruined Great Hall also the 15th century wing which is today the private residence of the Bishop of Bath and Wells. The extensive grounds, where rise the springs that give Wells its name, are a beautiful setting for borders of herbaceous plants, roses, shrubs, mature trees and the Jubilee Arboretum. The Moat is home to a collection of waterfowl and swans.

Location: City of Wells: enter from the Market Place through the Bishop's Eye or from the Cathedral Cloisters, over the Drawbridge.
Station(s): Bath, Bristol.
Open: The Henderson Rooms, Bishop's Chapel and Grounds Apr 1-Oct 31 on Sun 2-6 Tues Thurs Bank Holiday Mons and daily in Aug 10-6 also for exhibitions as advertised. As this is a private house The Trustees reserve the right to alter these times on rare occasions.
Admission: As advertised - guided and educational tours by arrangement with the Manager.
Refreshments: A limited restaurant service is available in the Undercroft unless prior bookings made.
Conferences: Conferences and special events by arrangement with the Manager.

COLERIDGE COTTAGE   The National Trust

Nether Stowey, nr Bridgwater   TA5 1NQ   map **3** U16
Telephone: (01278) 732662

Home of S T Coleridge from 1797-1800, where he wrote 'The Ancient Mariner'.

Location: At W end of village on S side of A39; 8 m W of Bridgwater.
Station(s): Bridgwater 8 m.
Open: Parlour and Reading Room only 2 Apr-3 Oct Tues-Thurs and Sun 2-5.
Admission: £1.50 Children 80p. No reduction for parties. Parties must book beforehand.
Adm in winter by written application to the tenant.
Refreshments: In village.
No dogs. Unsuitable for wheelchairs and coaches.

COMBE SYDENHAM COUNTRY PARK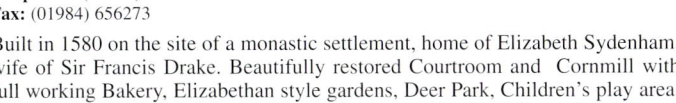
Monksilver, Taunton   TA4 4JG   map **3** U16   Ⓢ
Telephone: (01984) 656284
Fax: (01984) 656273

Built in 1580 on the site of a monastic settlement, home of Elizabeth Sydenham, wife of Sir Francis Drake. Beautifully restored Courtroom and Cornmill with full working Bakery, Elizabethan style gardens, Deer Park, Children's play area. Woodland Walks with Alice Trail and The Ancient Trail of Trees. Trout Farm, beginners fly fishing school.

Location: 5 m N of Wiveliscombe; 3 m S of Watchet on B3188.
Open: Apr-Oct Park/Shop Sun-Fri 10-5. Farmshop sells smoked trout/pate, venison and freshly baked bread, also open Sat am. West wing of House Mon-Fri 1.30-4 evening tours of Private Rooms and supper by arrangement.
Admission: Adults £4 children £1.50. Free car/coach parking.
Refreshments: Country Park produce used for lunches, snacks and teas.

CROWE HALL
(Mr John Barratt)
Widcombe, Bath   BA2 6AR   map **3** V16
Telephone: (01225) 310322

Elegant George V classical Bath villa, retaining grandiose mid-Victorian portico and great hall. Fine 18th century and Regency furniture; interesting old paintings and china. 10 acres of romantic gardens cascading down hillside. Terraces, Victorian grotto, ancient trees.

Location: Approx ¼ m on right up Widcombe Hill. 1 m from Guildhall.
Open: Gardens only Suns Apr 23 and June 18 *for NGS*, Also Suns Mar 26 May 14 & 28 June 16. House and Gardens by appointment. Groups welcome.
Admission: Gardens only £1.50, House and Gardens £3.00.
Refreshments: Teas on opening days and by appointment.

DODINGTON HALL
(Lady Gass, occupiers Mr and Mrs P Quinn).
nr. Nether Stowey, Bridgwater   map **3** U16
Telephone: (01278) 741400

Small Tudor Manor House on the lower slopes of the Quantock Hills. Great hall with oak roof. Carved stone fireplace. Semi-formal garden with roses and shrubs.

Location: ½ m from A39. 11 m from Bridgwater; 7 m from Williton.
Open: Bank Hol Mon, May 29, Sat & Sun 3-25 June incl. & Sat 1 July 2-5. Donations for Charity.
Parking for 15 cars. Regret unsuitable for disabled.

DUNSTER CASTLE   🌿 The National Trust
Dunster, nr.Minehead   TA24 6SL   map **3** U16
Telephone: (01643) 821314

Castle dating from 13th century, remodelled by Anthony Salvin in 19th century. Fine 17th century staircase and plaster ceilings. Terraced Gardens.

Location: In Dunster, 3 m SE of Minehead on A39.
Station(s): Dunster (West Somerset Railway) (1 m).
Open: Castle 1 Apr-1 Oct Sat-Wed 11-5 Oct 2-Oct 31 Sat-Wed 11-4. Garden and Park Feb 1-Dec 10 daily. Feb Mar Oct Nov Dec 11-4 Apr-Sept 11-5.
Admission: Castle garden and park £4.80 Children (under 16) £2.40. Parties by prior arrangement. Garden and park only £2.70 Children (under 16) £1.30.
Refreshments: In village (not N.T.).
Ten minute steep climb from NT car park. No dogs in garden, in park area on leads. Volunteer driven multi seater and self drive Batricar available from car park. Children's guidebook. Exploration trail for grounds. Study centre. Areas of the house can be visited by wheelchair, and assistance given if needed. National Trust Shop.

GAULDEN MANOR
(Mr & Mrs James Le Gendre Starkie)
Tolland, nr Taunton   TA4 3PN   map **3** U16   △ &
Telephone: (019847) 213

Small historic red sandstone Manor House of great charm. A real lived-in home. Past Somerset seat of the Turberville family, immortalised by Thomas Hardy. Great Hall has magnificent plaster ceiling and oak screen to room known as the Chapel. Fine antique furniture. Interesting grounds include bog garden with primulas and other moisture loving plants. Herb garden.

Location: 9 m NW of Taunton; 1 m E of Tolland Church. Gaulden Manor signposted from A358 Taunton/Williton Rd just N of Bishops Lydeard and from B3188 Wivelscombe/Watchet Rd (cars only). Nearest village Lydeard St Lawrence (1½ m).
Open: May 7-Sept 3 Sun & Thurs also Easter Sun and Mon and all Bank Hols 2-5.30 (last adm 5).
Admission: House and Garden adults £3 children (under 14) £1.50. Garden only £1.50 parties on other days by prior arrangement mornings, afternoons or evenings & out of season.
Refreshments: Teas in Garden Tea-room.
Shop - books, rare and unusual plants.

HATCH COURT
(Dr and Mrs Robin Odgers)
Hatch Beauchamp, Taunton   TA3 6AA   map **3** V17   △ &
Telephone: (01823) 480120
Fax: (01823) 480058

1750 Palladian mansion, a lived in family home with good furniture, pictures and porcelain. Deer Park and gardens with a fine restored walled kitchen garden.

Location: 6 m SE of Taunton off A358.
Station(s): Taunton.
Open: House June 15-Sept 14 Thurs and August Bank Holiday Mon 2.30-5.30. Garden May 2-Sept 28 Tues Wed Thurs and Bank Holiday Mon May 8, 29 and Aug 28 2.30-5.30
Admission: House £3 Garden £1.50. Groups at other times by prior arrangement.
Refreshments: Home made teas Thurs only. Full catering by arrangement.
Conferences: Full day time conference facilities.
No coaches. Organised parties by prior appointment at all times (unless open as above).

HESTERCOMBE HOUSE GARDENS
(Somerset County Council Fire Brigade)
Hestercombe House, Cheddon Fitzpaine   TA2 8LQ   map **3** U16
Telephone: (01823) 337222

A unique Edwardian garden designed by Sir Edwin Lutyen and Gertrude Jekyll. Restored to its former glory using the original Jekyllian planting schemes.

Location: 4 m north of Taunton, close to Cheddon Fitzpaine village.
Station(s): Taunton.
Open: All year Mon-Fri 9-5 May 1-Sept 31 Sat and Sun 2-5.
Admission: Adults £2 OAPs £1.50 children free. Parties by arrangement.

KENTSFORD HOUSE
(Mrs Wyndham. Occupier: Mr H Dibble)
Watchet   map **3** U16

House open **only** by written appointment with Mr H. Dibble.

Open: Gardens Tues and Bank Hols Mar 14-Aug 29.
Admission: Donations towards renovation of fabric.

LYTES CARY MANOR   🌿 The National Trust
nr Ilchester   A11 7HU   map **3** U17

Medieval manor house with chapel; fine furnishings; formal garden.

Location: On W side of Fosse Way (A37); 2½ m N of Ilchester signposted on bypass (A303).
Open: 1 Apr-28 Oct Mon Wed & Sat 2-6 or dusk if earlier (last adm 5.30).
Admission: £3.70 Children £1.90.
Refreshments: National Trust Shop at Montacute.
No dogs. NB Coaches strictly by appointment only, large coaches cannot pass gate piers, so must stop in narrow road, ¼ m walk.

MILTON LODGE GARDENS
(Mr & Mrs David Tudway Quilter)
Wells   map **14** U17
Telephone: (01749) 672168

'The great glory of the gardens of Milton Lodge is their position high up on the slopes of the Mendip Hills to the north of Wells...with broad panoramas of Wells Cathedral and the Vale of Avalon.' *Lanning Roper.* Mature alkaline terraced garden of great charm dating from 1909. Replanned 1962 with mixed shrubs and herbaceous plants, old fashioned roses and ground cover; numerous climbers; old established yew hedges. Fine trees in garden and in separate 7 acre arboretum on opposite side of Old Bristol Road.

Location: ½ m N of Wells. From A39 Bristol-Wells turn N up Old Bristol Road; free car park first gate on left.
Open: Garden and Arboretum Only Easter-end Oct daily (except Sat) 2-6 parties and coaches by prior arrangement.
Admission: Adults £2 children (under 14) free. Open on certain Suns in aid of National Gardens Scheme.
Refreshments: Teas available Suns and Bank Hols Apr-Sept.
No dogs.

MONTACUTE HOUSE   🌿 The National Trust
Yeovil   TA15 6XP   map **3** U17
Telephone: (01935) 823289

Magnificent Elizabethan house of Ham Hill stone begun in the 1590s by Sir Edward Phelips. Fine heraldic glass, tapestries, panelling and furniture. National

Portrait Gallery Exhibitions of Elizabethan and Jacobean portraits. Fine formal garden and park.

Location: In Montacute village 4 m W of Yeovil on S side of A3088; 3 m E of A303. *Station(s):* Yeovil Pen Mill 5½ m; Yeovil Junction 7 m.
Open: House 1 Apr-30 Oct Daily (except Tues) 12-5.30. *Closed* Good Fri. Last adm 5 (or sunset if earlier). *Parties by written appointment with the Property Manager.* Garden & Park 1 Apr-Mar 1996 Daily (except Tues) 11.30-5.30 or dusk if earlier.
Admission: House Garden and Park £4.80 Children £2.50 Pre-booked Parties 15 or more £4.40 Children £2.20. Gardens and Park only Apr 1-end Oct £2.70 Children £1.20. From Nov-Apr £1.30.
Refreshments: Light lunches & teas. *Parties catered for by arrangement with the Restaurant Manager.*
National Trust Shop.

ORCHARD WYNDHAM
(Mrs Wyndham)
Williton, nr Taunton   TA4 4HH   map **3** U16
Telephone: (01984) 632309

Modest English Manor House. Family home for 700 years encapsulating continuous building and alteration between 14th and 20th centuries.

Location: 1 m from A39 at Williton.
Open: House and Gardens guided tours only Aug 1995 Tues & Weds 2-5 (Last tour begins at 4). *(Property undergoing restoration, please telephone (01984) 632309 before planning a visit).* Limited parking, no coaches - narrow access road. Maximum of 15 people in house at any one time. No dogs. Not suitable for wheelchairs.
Admission: Adults £3 children under 12 £1.

STOKE-SUB-HAMDON PRIORY   🌿 The National Trust
nr Montacute   TA4 6QP   map **3** V17   ♿

Complex of buildings begun in 14th century for the priests of the chantry chapel of St Nicholas (destroyed).

Location: Between A303 & A3088; 2 m W of Montacute between Yeovil & Ilminster.
Open: All the year Daily 10-6 (or sunset if earlier). *Great Hall only open to the public.*
Admission: Free.
No dogs.

TINTINHULL HOUSE GARDEN   🌿 The National Trust
nr. Yeovil   BA22 9PZ   map **3** V17   △ ♿
Telephone: (01935) 822545

Beautiful 20th century formal garden surrounding 17th century house (house not open).

Location: 5 m NW of Yeovil; ½ m S of A303 on outskirts Tintinhull village.
Station(s): Yeovil Pen Mill 5½ m; Yeovil Junction 7 m.
Open: Wed Thurs Fri Sat & Sun also Bank Hol Mons 12-6 (last adm 5.30). 1 Apr-2 Oct.
Admission: £3.50 children £1.60 *No reductions for parties.*
Coach parties by written arrangement with the tenant. No dogs. Wheelchairs provided.

Gertrude Jekyll
writer and gardener
(1843-1932)

Her designs were used at the following properties included in Historic Houses Castles and Gardens:-

Barrington Court
Castle Drogo
Goddards
Hatchlands Park
Hestercombe House and Gardens
Knebworth
Lindisfarne Castle

A collection of her tools can be found at Guildford Museum

STAFFORDSHIRE

ALTON CASTLE
(Monumental Trust)
Alton   ST10 4TT   map **7** Q19
Telephone: (01538) 703300

Alton Castle

A great stronghold since Saxon Times, with massive rock-cut fosse and tower built by Bertram de Verdun circa 1175, Alton Castle eventually passed to the mighty warrior John Talbot, First Earl of Shrewsbury in the early 15th century. Ruined by bombardment in the Civil War, the 16th Earl - in 1844 - commissioned the architect A W N Pugin to rebuild the Castle. Pugin produced a highly evocative building growing out of the remains of the original walls. Work stopped abruptly on the deaths of both the Earl and Pugin in 1852, before their dream was quite finished. Now the subject of a major rennovation and completion project (see article in the introductory pages), the Castle is open for the first time in 1995. Imaginative *Time Machine* audio tours conduct the visitor through over 900 years of history. There is also a limited number of guest suites available in the Castle, and it makes an ideal place to stay whilst visiting the popular Alton Towers attraction nearby.

Location: In the village of Alton. Follow signs to Alton towers from M1 or M6, then find Castle signs at Alton.
Open: <u>Summer</u> Good Fri-end of Sept 11-6 daily last admission 5.30. <u>Winter</u> Oct 1-Maundy Thurs daily (except Dec 24 25 and 26) 1-5 last admission 4.30. Open all year round for group, educational and evening 'Candlelit Tours'. PLEASE NOTE THAT THE CASTLE OPENS ON MAY 1st (1995 ONLY).
Admission: Daytime tours adult £3.25 child (5-16) £1.95 concession (OAP/student/UB40) £2.75 family (2+2) £7.75. Evening 'Candlelit Tours' adult £3.75 child £2.40 (Tour free with 'Wars of the Roses' Feast). Open all year round. Christmas Candlelit Tours every evening Nov 15-Dec 23 (includes mince pies & hot punch) adult £5.25 child £3.30. Coach parties welcome 10% discount for parties of 20+ visitors.
Refreshments: Teas and Sunday lunches all through the year. 'Wars of the Roses Feasts' with pre-booking.
Accommodation: Stay in the most romantic Castle in England! There are a limited number of Guest Suites available, most with additional children's bedroom. Two tower bedrooms. All bedrooms have bathrooms and supper is available in the Castle.
Conferences: The Castle's 'Moot Hall' is an ideal conference centre. Other facilities available include receptions, children's parties and weddings all available by prior booking. Weddings may be solemnised in the castle's beautiful chapel. Full facilities for receptions and a honeymoon suite with four poster bed.
Full educational programme to National Curriculum standards available. 1995 events in the Castle and Castle Park: please write or telephone for details. Full wheelchair access for the disabled with special audio-tour. No dogs except on a lead in car park only. Riverside picnic permits available at Castle. PLEASE NOTE BECAUSE IT IS THE CASTLE'S OPENING YEAR, SOME SERVICES WILL BE INTRODUCED DURING THE SEASON.

ANCIENT HIGH HOUSE
Stafford   map **14** R18

The Ancient High House is the largest timber-framed town house in England, and was built in 1595 by John Dorrington. It has been in the hands of several famous Staffordshire families, inlcuding the Sneyds and Dyotts, and has enjoyed a long and varied history. It has recently been restored to its Elizabethan splendour and houses a permanent collection in period room settings. A special feature of interest is the collection of rare 18th and 19th century wallpapers, found during the restoration. The house also has an exhibition area, along with a video theatre and souvenir shop. The Staffordshire Yeomanry Museum is the latest additional attraction housed on the top floor. Tourist Information Centre on the ground floor.

Location: M6 Off junction 13 - A449 to Stafford and M6 junction 14 - A5013 to Stafford.
Open: House and Tourist Information: Mon to Fri 9-5; Sat Apr to Oct: 10-4. Nov to Mar: 10-3.
Admission: £1.40, Chd/OAPs 80p, reduced rate for parties.
Tourist Information Centre: Mon to Fri 9-5; Oct to Mar: Sat 10-3. Apr to Sept: 10-4. Contact: The Heritage Manager (01785) 223181 ext 352, or (01785) 40204. No car park.

BIDDULPH GRANGE GARDEN   🍃 The National Trust
Biddulph, Stoke-on-Trent **ST8 7SD** map **7** Q18
Telephone: (01782) 517999

An exciting and rare survival of a high Victorian garden, acquired by the National Trust in 1988. The garden has undergone an extensive restoration project, which will continue for a number of years. Conceived by James Bateman, the 15 acres are divided into a number of smaller gardens which were designed to house specimens from his extensive and wide-ranging plant collection. An Egyptian Court, Chinese Pagoda, Bridge, Joss House and Pinetum, together with many other settings, all combine to make the garden a miniature tour of the world. *Please note that at weekends and Bank Hols in the high season the garden and tea-room can be very crowded.*

Location: ½ m N of Biddulph, 3½ m SE of Congleton, 7 m N of Stoke-on-Trent. Access from A527 (Tunstall/Congleton). Entrance on Grange Road.
Station(s): Kidsgrove 8 m Congleton, 2½ m. Stoke-on-Trent 7 m.
Open: Apr 1-Oct 29 Wed-Fri 12-6 (last adm 5.30 or dusk if earlier). Sat, Sun and Bank Holiday Mon 11-6. *Closed Good Friday.* Pre-booked guided tours at 10, Wed, Thurs, Fri £5 (inc NT members); Nov 4 to Dec 17: Sat and Sun 12-4.

Admission: 1 Apr-29 Oct £3.90 Children half-price Family ticket £9.75. 4 Nov-17 Dec £2 Family £5 Joint ticket with Little Moreton Hall available mani season only£6 Family £15.Free parking (car park 50 yds).
Refreshments: Coffee, light lunches and teas. Tea-room and shop open same time as garden. Picnics in car park only.
Access for disabled visitors is extremely difficult; unsuitable for wheelchairs. Please contact Head Gardener for details.

CHILLINGTON HALL
(Mr & Mrs Peter Giffard)
nr Wolverhampton **WV8 1RE** map **14** R18 △
Telephone: (01902) 850236

Georgian house. Part 1724 (Francis Smith); part 1785 (Sir John Soane). Fine saloon. The lake in the Park is believed to be the largest ever created by 'Capability' Brown. The bridges by Brown and Paine, and the Grecian and Roman Temples, together with the eyecatching Sham House, as well as many fine trees and plantations add great interest to the four mile walk around the lake. Dogs welcome in grounds if kept on lead.

Location: 4 m SW of A5 at Gailey; 2 m Brewood; 8 m NW of Wolverhampton; 14 m S of Stafford. Best approach is from A449 (Junction 12, M6, Junction 2, M54) through Coven and follow signposts towards Codsall (no entry at Codsall Wood).
Open: June-Sept 14 Thurs (also Suns in Aug) 2.30-5.30 open Easter Sun & Suns preceding May and late Spring Bank Holidays 2.30-5.30. Parties of at least 15 other days by arrangement.
Admission: Adults £2.50 (Grounds only £1.25) children half-price.

DOROTHY CLIVE GARDEN
(Willoughbridge Garden Trust)
Willoughbridge, Nr. Market Drayton **TF9 4EU** map **7** R18 ♿
Telephone: (01630) 647237

8 acre woodland and rhododendron garden; shrub roses, water garden and a large scree in a fine landscape setting. Good herbaceous plantings are a summer feature: autumn colour. Spectacular waterfall, many interesting and less usual plants. Fine views.

Location: On A51 road midway between Nantwich and Stone and 3 m South of Bridgemere Garden World.
Open: Garden only Apr-Oct daily 10-5.30.
Admission: Adults £2.60 children £1.
Refreshments: Attractive tea-room and lawn open daily. Home baking.
Large car park.

Lancelot 'Capability' Brown

Born 1716 in Northumberland, Capability Brown began work at the age of 16 in the vegetable gardens of Sir William and Lady Loraine at Kirharle Tower. He left Northumberland in 1739, and records show that he worked at Stowe until 1749. It was at Stowe that Brown began to study architecture, and to submit his own plans. It was also at Stowe that he devised a new method of moving and replanting mature trees.

Brown married Bridget Wayet in 1744 and began work on the estate at Warwick Castle in 1749. He was appointed Master Gardener at Hampton Court in 1764, and planted the Great Vine at Hampton Court in 1768. Blenheim Palace designs are considered amongst Brown's finest work, and the technical achievements were outstanding even for the present day.

Capability Brown died in February 1783 of a massive heart attack. A monument beside the lake at Croome Court was erected which reads "To the memory of Lancelot Brown, who by the powers of his inimitable and creative genius formed this garden scene out of a morass". There is also a portrait of Brown at Burghley.

Capability Brown was involved in the design of grounds at the following properties included in Historic Houses Castles and Gardens:-

Audley End	*Longleat*
Berrington Hall	*Luton Hoo*
Bowood	*Moccas Court*
Burghley House	*Petworth House*
Burton Constable	*Sledmere House*
Charlecote Park	*Stowe (Stowe*
Chilham Castle Gardens	*School)*
(reputed)	*Syon House*
Clandon Park	*Warwick Castle*
Claremont	*Weston Park*
Chillington Hall	*Wimpole Hall*
Corsham Court	*Wrest Park and*
Fawley Court	*Gardens*
Highclere Castle	

FORD GREEN HALL
(Stoke on Trent City Council)
Ford Green Road, Smallthorne   ST6 1NG   map 7 Q18
Telephone: (01782) 534771
Fax: (01782) 205033

A timber-framed farmhouse built for the Ford family in 1624, with eighteenth century brick additions. The house is furnished according to inventories of the 17th and 18th century to give a flavour of the domestic life of the Ford family. Regular performances of Early Music and other events; guided tours available.

Location: Smallthorne on B5051 Burslem-Endon Road.
Station(s): Nearest Stoke-on-Trent.
Open: Sunday-Thursday 1-5pm. Closed 25 December - 1 January.
Admission: Free.
Refreshments: Small tea-room.
Events/Exhibitions: Early music second Sun of each month. Wide variety of other events held throughout the year.
Small parties by prior arrangement.

MOSELEY OLD HALL   🍀 The National Trust
Moseley Old Hall Lane, Fordhouses   WV10 7HY   map 14 R18   △ ♿ Ⓢ
Telephone: (01902) 782808

A 17th century formal garden surrounds this mainly Elizabethan house where Charles II hid after the battle of Worcester.

Location: 4 m N of Wolverhampton mid-way between A449 & A460 Roads. Off M6 at Shareshill then via A460. Traffic from S via. M6 and M54 take junction 1 to Wolverhampton and Moseley is signposted after ½ m. Coaches via. A460 to avoid low bridge.
Station(s): Wolverhampton 4 m.
Open: Apr 1-Oct 29 Wed Sat Sun & Bank Hol Mons (and Tues in July & Aug) 2-5.30. Bank Hol Mon 11-5. Pre-booked parties at other times including evening tours. Shop as Hall also open Nov 5-Dec 17. Sun only 2-4.30.
Admission: £3.30 Children half-price. Family ticket £8.00.
Refreshments: Tea-room in 18th century barn. Teas as house 2-5.30; Light lunches BH Mon, also Sun July & Aug from 12.30. Christmas Shop and tea-room open Nov 5-Dec 17 Sun only 2-4.30. Other times for parties by prior arrangement. Licensed.
Educational facilities. Wheelchair access ground floor only.

"Playgrounds for the Children"

Belton House
Bowood
Drumlanrig (woodland playground)
Hever Castle
Kelburn (Secret Forest adventure course and stockade)
Longleat
Ragley Hall (adventure wood)
Weston Park
Wilton House

SHUGBOROUGH 🌿 The National Trust

(Administered by Staffordshire County Council)
Stafford   **ST17 0XB**   map **14** R18   △ ㊓ Ⓔ Ⓢ
Telephone: (01889) 881388
Fax: (01889) 881323

Seat of the Earls of Lichfield. Architecture by James Stuart and Samuel Wyatt. Rococo plasterwork by Vassalli. Extensive parkland with neo-classical monuments. Beautiful formal gardens. Edwardian terraces and rose-garden. Guided garden and woodland walks. Working rare breeds farm. Restored Mill. Restored Victorian servants working areas.

Location: 6 m E of Stafford on A513, entrance at Milford common 10 mins drive from M6, junction 13.
Station(s): Stafford.
Open: House, Servants' Quarters, Farm with Working Kitchens, Laundry and Corn Mill. Grade I Historic Garden Mar 25-Oct 27 daily inc. Bank Holiday Mons 11-5 site open all year round to pre-booked parties only from 10.30. The estate offers a superb range of tours and packages for schools and adult groups.
Admission: House £3.50 (reduced rate £2) Servants Quarters £3.50 (reduced rate £2) Farm £3.50 (reduced rate £2) all-in ticket (House Servants' Quarters and Farm) £7.50 (reduced rate £5) family all-in ticket (2 adults and 2 reduced rates) £15 coach parties all-in ticket £5 or £2 per site (prices subject to change). Reduced rates available for children, OAPs and registered unemployed children under 5 free. *NT members free entry to house, reduced rate to Servants' Quarters and Farm.* Party bookings for guided tours. Specialist tours and demonstrations available. School parties guided tour £1.50 per head per site (all 3 sites inc. of guide - £4.50). Working School demonstrations Oct-Easter £2.50 per head, per demo. When Special Events are held charges may vary.
Refreshments: Tea-rooms restaurant.
Events/Exhibitions: Full programme of events available throughout the year. 'Lichfield at Home' Exhibition Mar-Oct in the Mansion.
Accommodation: Details of Group accomodation can be obtained from the Booking Officer.
Conferences: Rooms available for hire throughout the year. Contact: Mrs Anne Wood, Promotion and Events Manager for details.
Guide Dogs admitted to House and Servants' Quarters. Site access for parking, picnic area, gardens, monuments and woodland trails £1.50 per vehicle. Coaches free. National Trust shop and toilets.

STAFFORD CASTLE

(Stafford Borough Council)
Stafford   map **14** R18

Impresssive site of Norman keep and medieval castle, subsequently destroyed during the Civil War. Rebuilt in part during the 19th century, later largely demolished. Visitor centre and Herb Garden.

Location: Off the A518 south west of Stafford.
Open: Visitor Centre 10am-5pm Nov-Mar 10am-4pm. Closed Monday except Bank Holidays.
Admission: Visitor Centre Adult £1.15 child/concessions 60p. Reduced rate for parties.

TAMWORTH CASTLE

(Tamworth Borough Council)
The Holloway, Tamworth   B79 7LR   map **14** R19
Telephone: (01827) 63563
Fax: (01827) 52769

Tamworth's sandstone castle is one of the few remaining shell-keeps in the country. Occupied at various periods between Norman and Victoran times, the castle's room settings include the Tudor chapel & great hall. Jacobean state apartments and the Victorian suite. Norman exhibition, dungeon, haunted bedroom plus local history collections and audio visual.

Location: In Tamworth; 15 m NE of Birmingham.
Station(s): Tamworth (¾ m).
Open: All the year weekdays 10-5.30 Suns 2-5.30 (Last adm 4.30) open Bank Hols. Closed Christmas Day & Boxing Day.
Admission: Adults £3 concessions £1.50 family ticket £7.50.

IZAAK WALTON COTTAGE

(Staffordshire Borough Council)
Shallowford, nr. Stafford   map **7** R18

Cottage bequeathed to Stafford by Izaak Walton. Now houses a fishing museum with attractive gardens and picnic orchard.

Location: Shallowford, off the A5013 - 5 m north of Stafford.
Open: Apr-Oct 11am-4.30pm. Nov-Mar 11am-4pm. Closed Dec-Feb.
Admission: Adult £1.15 child/concessions 60p. Reduced rate for parties.

WHITMORE HALL

(Mr R.G.D. Cavenagh-Mainwaring)
Whitmore, nr Newcastle-under-Lyme   map **7** R18
Telephone: (01782) 680478

Carolinian Manor House, owner's family home for over 800 years. Family portraits dating back to 1624. Outstanding Tudor Stable Block.

Location: 4 m from Newcastle-under-Lyme on the A53 Road to Market Drayton.
Open: Open 2-5.30 every Tues & Weds May-Aug inclusive (last tour 5).
Admission: Adults £2 *no reduction for parties* free car parking.
Refreshments: Mainwaring Arms Inn, Whitmore & also at Whitmore Art Gallery & Tearooms, Whitmore.
Not suitable for disabled. No wheelchairs available.

SUFFOLK

BLAKENHAM WOODLAND GARDEN

(Lord Blakenham)
Little Blakenham, nr Ipswich   map **5** S24

5 acre woodland garden with many rare trees and shrubs. Especially lovely in the spring with daffodils, bluebells, camellias, magnolias and cornus followed by roses in the early summer.

Location: 4 m NW of Ipswich. The garden is signposted from Little Blakenham which is 1 m off the B1113.
Open: 1 Mar-30 June every day except Sat 1-5.
Admission: £1. Free car park.
No dogs.

CHRISTCHURCH MANSION

(The Borough of Ipswich)
Christchurch Park, Ipswich   map **5** S25 △
Telephone: (01473) 253246/213761
Fax: (01473) 281274

A fine Tudor house set in beautiful parkland. Period rooms furnished in styles from 16th to 19th century; outstanding collections of china, clocks and furniture. Paintings by Gainsborough, Constable and other Suffolk artists. Attached Wolsey Art Gallery shows lively temporary exhibition programme.

Location: In Christchurch Park, near centre of Ipswich.
Station(s): Ipswich (1¼ m).
Open: All the year Tues-Sat 10-5 (dusk in winter) Sun 2.30-4.30 (dusk in winter). Open Bank Hol Mons. Closed Dec 24 25 26 Jan 1 2 and Good Friday.
Admission: Free.

EUSTON HALL
(The Duke and Duchess of Grafton)
Thetford   map **5** T25
Telephone: (01842) 766366

Euston Hall - Home of the Duke and Duchess of Grafton. The 18th century house contains a famous collection of paintings including works by Stubbs, Van Dyck, Lely and Kneller. The pleasure grounds were laid out by John Evelyn and William Kent. 17th century parish church in Wren style, Watermill. Teas and Craft Shop in Old Kitchen. Picnic area.

Location: A1088; 3 m S Thetford.
Open: June 1-Sept 28 Thurs only 2.30-5 also Sun June 25 & Sept 3 2.30-5.
Admission: Adults £2.50 children 50p OAPs £2. Parties of 12 or more £2 per head.
Refreshments: Teas in Old Kitchen. Craft shop. Picnic area.

FRAMLINGHAM CASTLE
map **5** S25
Telephone: (01728) 724189

ENGLISH HERITAGE

The present massive walls and their 13 towers were built by Roger Bigod, second Earl of Norfolk, on a site given to his father by Henry I. The ornamental brick chimneys were added in Tudor times when the arch of the entrance gateway was rebuilt. In 1636 the castle passed to Pembroke College, Cambridge, and in later years the great hall was converted to a poor-house and many of the buildings inside the walls were demolished. It was here, in 1553, that Mary Tudor learned she had become Queen of England.

Location: North side of Framlingham.
Open: Apr 1-Sept 30 10-6 daily Oct 1-Mar 31 10-4 daily.
Admission: Adults £2 concessions £1.50 children £1.

GAINSBOROUGH'S HOUSE
(Gainsborough's House Society)
Sudbury   CO10 6EU   map **4** S24
Telephone: (01787) 372958

Gainsborough's House is the birthplace of Thomas Gainsborough RA (1727-88). The Georgian-fronted town house, with an attractive walled garden, displays more of the artist's work than any other gallery. The collection is shown together

with eighteenth-century furniture and memorabilia. Commitment to contemporary art is reflected in a varied programme of exhibitions throughout the year. These include fine art, craft, photography, printmaking, sculpture and highlights in particular the work of East Anglian artists.

Location: 46 Gainsborough Street, Sudbury.
Station(s): Sudbury (¼ m).
Open: Open all the year. Easter-Oct Tues-Sat 10-5 Sun & Bank Hol Mons 2-5 Nov-Maundy Thurs Tues-Sat 10-4 Sun and Bank Hol Mon 2-4 closed Mon Good Fri & between Christmas & New Year.
Admission: Adults £2.50 OAPs £2 students/children £1.25.

GUILDHALL OF CORPUS CHRISTI   The National Trust
Market Place, Lavenham   CO10 9QZ   map **5** T25
Telephone: (01787) 247646

Early 16th century timber-framed Tudor building; originally hall of Guild of Corpus Christi. Display of local history, industry and farming including a unique exhibition of 700 years of the woollen cloth trade. Delightful walled garden which houses restored Parish Lock Up and Mortuary. Shop.

Location: Market Place Lavenham, Sudbury.
Open: Mar 25-Nov 5 daily 11-5. *closed* Good Friday.
Admission: £2.50 children *first two free, then* 60p. Parties £2.10. Please book with sae to Administrator. School parties 50p by prior arrangement. Children free during school summer holidays.
Refreshments: Coffee, light lunches and teas.
Events/Exhibitions: May Fortnight.

HAUGHLEY PARK
(Executor of A. J. Williams)
nr Stowmarket   IP14 3JY   map **4** S24   △ &
Telephone: (01359) 240205

Jacobean manor house. Gardens and woods, fine trees and shrubs.

Location: 4 m W of Stowmarket signed on A14 (previous A45) nr Wetherden (not Haughley).
Open: May-Sept Tues 3-6.
Admission: Adults £2 children £1.

HELMINGHAM HALL GARDENS
(The Lord & Lady Tollemache)
Ipswich   IP14 6EF   map **5** S25
Telephone: (01473) 890363

The Hall, which was completed in 1510, has been the home of the Tollemache family from that date to the present day. It is one of the finest houses of the Tudor period, surrounded by a wide moat with drawbridges raised every night. There are two superb gardens which extend to several acres all set in 400 acres of ancient park containing herds of Red and Fallow deer and Highland Cattle. The main garden is surrounded by its own moat and 1740 wall, with wide herbaceous borders and planted tunnels intersecting an immaculate kitchen garden; the second is a very special rose garden enclosed within high yew hedges with a herb and Knot garden containing plants grown in England before 1750. English Heritage Grade I Garden.

Location: 9 m N of Ipswich on B1077.
Open: Gardens Only: Apr 30-Sept 10 Suns only 2-6 Wed 2-6 for group bookings which must be pre-booked 30+ people *House not open to the public*.
Admission: Adults £2.80 children (15 and under) £1.50 OAPs £2.60 groups £2.30.
Refreshments: In the Coach House Tea-rooms. Cream teas.
Safari rides. Gift shop. Home-grown plants and produce for sale.

ICKWORTH HOUSE, PARK & GARDEN
The National Trust
The Rotunda, Horringer   **IP29 5AE**   map **5** S24
Telephone: (01284) 735270

The house, begun c. 1794, was not completed until 1830. Contents of this architectural curiosity include late Regency and 18th century French furniture, magnificent silver, pictures. Formal gardens, herbaceous borders, orangery. Extensive waymarked park walks.

Location: 3 m SW of Bury St Edmunds on W side of A143.
Open: House & Garden Mar 25-Nov 5 Tues Wed Fri Sat and Sun 1-5. Open Bank Hol Mons: 1-5. Garden open all year 10-4 daily. Park open daily 7-7.
Admission: £4.30 children £2. Access to Park, Garden, Restaurant and Shop £1.50 children 50p. Prebooked parties £3.50.
Refreshments: Lunch & tea in old Servants' Hall. Table license, restaurant opens 12 noon on House open days.
Events/Exhibitions: Craft Exhibition in Garden Apr-Sept Other events leaflet on request.
Dogs in park only, on leads. Wheelchair access, one provided. Shop.

IPSWICH MUSEUM
(*Ipswich Borough Council*)
Ipswich   IP1 3QH   map **5** S25
Telephone: (01473) 213761/2
Fax: (01473) 281274

Geology and natural history of Suffolk; Mankind galleries covering Africa, Asia, America and the Pacific. 'Romans in Suffolk' gallery showing local archaeology. Temporary exhibitions in attached gallery.

Location: High Street, in town centre.
Station(s): Ipswich.
Open: Tues-Sat 10-5 closed Dec 24 25 26 Jan 1 2 closed Bank Holidays. Temporary exhibition programme.
Admission: Free.

KENTWELL HALL
(*J. Patrick Phillips, QC*)
Long Melford   CO10 9BA   map **5** S24
Telephone: (01787) 310207

Kentwell is the subject of a unique long term project to restore the House and its once fine gardens. As well as being a family home it also has a rare feeling of the 16th century with the service areas, Great Kitchen, Bakery, Dairy, Forge etc - always fully equipped 16th century style. The gardens are intimate, yet spacious with a fine moated walled garden including a herb garden and potager. Kentwell is also home to the Award Winning Re-Creations of Tudor Domestic Life when visitors meet numerous 'Tudors' with dress, speech, activities & locations appropriate for the 16th century. These take place on selected week-ends between April & September.

Location: Entrance on W of A134, N of Green in Long Melford; 3 m N of Sudbury.
Station(s): Sudbury (4 m).
Open: House Open 12-5 Apr 2-June 11 Suns + April 14-21, May 6-8 & May 27-June 2; June 18-July 16. Open only for Re-Creation (see below); July 19-Sep 24 daily; October Suns only. Re-Creations Open: 11-6 Easter (Apr 14-17) May Day w/e (May 6-8) Spring BH w/e (May 27-29), Great Annual Re-Creation June 18-July 16 Sats Sun & Fri July 14 only (11-5); Lammas (Aug 5 & 6); Michaelmas (Sep 23 & 24)
Admission: House £4.50 adults £2.75 children £3.75 OAPs. Garden & Farm only: £2.50 adult, £1.75 child, £2.25 OAP. Special prices apply for Re-Creations. (Children charged from 5 to 15 3rd & 4th children in family free).
Refreshments: Lunches and teas available.
No dogs beyond Avenue.

MELFORD HALL   The National Trust
Long Melford   CO10 9AH   map **5** S24
Telephone: (01787) 880286

Built between 1554 and 1578 by Sir William Cordell, contains fine pictures, furniture and Chinese porcelain. Interesting garden and gazebo. Beatrix Potter display.

Location: In Long Melford on E side of A134; 3 m N of Sudbury.
Open: Principal Rooms & Gardens Apr Sat and Sun. May 1-Sept 30 Wed Thur Sat Sun and all Bank Hol Mons 2-5.30. Oct Sat and Sun 2-5.30. Last admission 5pm.
Admission: £2.70 children (with adult) £1.30. Pre-booked parties of 15 or more £2.30 Wed & Thur only.
Refreshments: In Long Melford.
No dogs. Wheelchair access, one provided.

ORFORD CASTLE
map **5** S26
Telephone: (0139) 445 0472

ENGLISH HERITAGE

No sooner had Henry II built this castle on the Suffolk coast than rebellion broke out (in 1173). The castle's powerful presence helped to uphold the King's authority and it continued to be an important royal residence for more than 100 years. In 1280 it was granted to the Earl of Norfolk for his lifetime, and from then on it remained in private hands. The design was very advanced for its time, and the keep, much of which remains, is unique in England. The outer wall of the castle, the last section of which collapsed in 1841, was punctuated by rectangular towers, an innovation that provided excellent cover for the defenders.

Location: In Orford.
Open: Apr 1-Sept 30 10-6 daily Oct 1-Mar 31 10-4 daily.
Admission: Adults £2 concessions £1.50 children £1.

OTLEY HALL

(Mr J G and Baroness Anne)
Otley, nr Ipswich IP6 9PA   map **5** S25 △
Telephone: (01473) 890264
Fax: (01473) 890803

Stunning 15th century Moated Hall (Grade 1) set in gardens and grounds of 10 acres, frequently described as 'one of England's loveliest houses'. Voted Oct 1994 by the AA as one of Britain's top 20 historic houses. Rich in history and architectural detail. Features of particular note are richly carved beams, herringbone brickwork, pargetting, linenfold and fresco-work. Otley Hall was built by the Gosnold family in around 1450 and was their home for 250 years. Some of the famous names and events connected with both the Gosnolds and the Hall are the Royal households of Elizabeth I, James I and Charles I; the Civil War (Colonel Robert Gosnold - Seige of Carlisle); the Virginia colonisation of 1607 - Bartholomew Gosnold, who settled and named Cape Cod and Martha's (Gosnold) Vineyard, and later founded Jamestown; Lady Jane Grey; Shakespeare. The Gardens are formal and informal, including part of a fascinating and historically important design by Francis Inigo Thomas (1866-1950) with canal mount, nutteries, croquet lawn, rose garden and moat walk.

Location: From A14 take Norwich/Diss junction (A140) and then follow B1078 to T-junction and follow sign for Otley (approx. 7 miles from Ipswich).
Open: General Public Open Days 1995: 16/17 Apr 28/29 May and 27/28 Aug 2-6.
Admission: Adults £4 children £2.50.
Refreshments: Cream teas on Open Days. Otley Hall is also open by appointment to groups for private guided tours throughout the year when Lunches or Afternoon Teas can be arranged in advance. Party bookings and coach parties welcomed.
Accommodation: The Hall, grounds and accommodation are available for private hire.
Conferences: Wedding receptions, corporate entertaining, film and photographic location. For further information please contact The Secretary, Otley Hall, Otley, Suffolk, IP6 9PA. Tel. (01473) 890264. Fax. (01473) 890803.

SOMERLEYTON HALL

(The Lord & Lady Somerleyton)
nr Lowestoft   map **4** S26   ♿

Somerleyton Hall is a perfect example of a House built to show off the wealth of the new Victorian aristocracy. The house was remodelled from a modest 17th century Manor House by the rich railwayman Sir Morton Peco. When he was declared bankrupt in 1863 his concoction of real brick white stone and lavish interiors was sold to another hugely successful businessman, carpet manufacturer Sir Francis Crossley. The present owner, Lord Somerleyton, is his great grandson. No expense was spared in the building or the fittings. Stone was brought from Caen and Aubigny and the magnificent carved stonework created by John Thomas (who worked on the Houses of Parliament) has been recently fully restored. In the State Rooms there are paintings by Landseer, Wright of Derby and Stanfield, together with fine wood carvings by Willcox of Warwick and from the earlier house, Grinling Gibbons. The Oak Rooms retains its carved oak panelling and Stuart atmosphere, the rest is lavishly Victorian. Grandest of all is the Ballroom with its crimson damask walls reflected in rows of long white and gilt mirrors. Somerleyton's 12 acre gardens are justly renowned. The 1846 yew hedge maze is one of the few surviving Victorian mazes in Britain. The stable tower clock by Vuilliamy made in 1847 is the original model for a great clock to serve as the Tower Clock in the new Houses of Parliament, now world famous as Big Ben. Colour is added to the gardens by rhododendrons, azaleas and a long pergola trailing mauve, pink and white whisteria. Special features include a sunken garden; the Loggia Tea Room; glasshouses by Sir Joseph Paxton; an aviary; fine statuary.

Location: 5 m NW Lowestoft off B1074; 7 m Yarmouth (A143).
Station(s): Somerleyton (1½ m).
Open: House, Maze and Gardens, Easter Sun to and including October 1 Thursday, Sundays and Bank Holidays, with the additions of Tuesday and Wednesday in July and August. House open 2-5. Gardens 12.30-5. The house and gardens are available for guided tours for private parties or school groups. Details on application.
Admission: Adults £3.75 OAP £3.25 Children £1.75 Family ticket (2+2) £10.50. Group rates on application.
Refreshments: Luncheon and Teas in the loggia from 12.30.
Conferences: Suitable for conferences.
Suitable for receptions, fashion shows, archery, clay pigeon shooting, equestrian events, garden parties, shows, rallies, filming, wedding receptions. Details on request. Free car parking, sorry no dogs. Facilities for the disabled.

WINGFIELD OLD COLLEGE

(Ian Chance, Esq)
nr Eye IP21 5RA map **5** S25 △
Telephone: (01379) 384505

Founded in 1362 on the 13th century site of the Manor House by Sir John de Wingfield, a close friend of the Black Prince. Surrendered to Henry VIII in 1542 and seized by Cromwell's Parliament in 1649. Magnificent Medieval Great Hall. Mixed period interiors with 18th century neo-classical facade. Walled gardens and Topiary. Teas. Celebrated Arts and Music Season. Adjacent church with tombs of College founder and Benefactors, The Earls and Dukes of Suffolk.

Location: Signposted off B1118; 7 m SE of Diss.
Open: Easter Sat-Sept 25 Sats Suns & Bank Hols 2-6.
Admission: Adults £2.50 children £1.
Refreshments: Home-made teas.

SURREY

ALBURY PARK

(Country Houses Association)
Albury, Guildford GU5 9BB map **12** U22
Telephone: (01483) 202964

Country mansion by Pugin.

Location: 1½ m E of Albury off A25 Guildford to Dorking road.
Station(s): Stations: Chilworth (2 m); Gomshall (2 m); Clandon (3 m). Bus Route: Tillingbourne No 25 Guildford-Cranleigh
Open: May-Sept Weds & Thurs 2-5. Last entry 4.30.
Admission: £2.50 Children £1. Free car park.
No dogs admitted.

CLANDON PARK 🍃 The National Trust

nr Guildford GU4 7RQ map **12** U22 &
Telephone: (01483) 222482

An unusual Palladian house by Venetian architect Giacomo Leoni. Attracts visitors from all over the world to view the magnificent collection of porcelain and the John Fowler decorative scheme. Garden with parterre, grotto and Maori house.

Location: At West Clandon 3 m E Guildford on A247; S of A3 & N of A246.
Station(s): Clandon (1 m).
Open: 1 Apr-29 Oct daily except Thurs and Fri 1.30-5.30 (but open Good Fri) last adm 5. Open Bank Hol Mons 11-5.30. Parties & guided tours by arrangement with the Administrator *no reduced rate at weekends and Bank Hols.*
Admission: £4 Children half-price Family ticket £10. Parties (Mon-Wed only) £3.50.
Refreshments: Licensed Restaurant in house; lunches from 12.30 & teas 3.15-5.30. Limited advance booking available Tel (01483) 222502. Also open every weekend in March and pre-Christmas.
Shop. Picnic area. No dogs except on leads in car park and picnic area. Wheelchairs provided.

CLAREMONT

(The Claremont Fan Court Foundation Ltd)
Esher KT10 9LY map **12** U22
Telephone: (01372) 467841

Excellent example of Palladian style; built 1772 by 'Capability' Brown for Clive of India; Henry Holland and John Soane responsible for the interior decoration. It is now a co-educational school run by Christian Scientists.

Location: ½ m SW from Esher on Esher/Cobham Road A307.
Open: Feb-Nov first complete weekend (Sat and Sun) in each month 2-5.
Admission: Adults £2 children/OAPs £1 reduced rates for parties.
Souvenirs.

CLAREMONT LANDSCAPE GARDEN

The National Trust

Esher KT10 9JG map **12** U22 ♿

Telephone: (01372) 469421

One of the earliest surviving English landscape gardens, restored by the NT to its former glory. Features include a lake, island with pavilion, grotto, turf amphitheatre, view points and avenues. *House not National Trust property.*

Location: .5 SE of Esher on E side of A307. NB: no access from A3 by-pass.
Station(s): Esher (2 m) (not Suns); Hersham (2 m); Claygate (2 m).
Open: All year Jan-end Mar daily (except Mons) 10-5 or sunset if earlier. April-end Oct Mon-Fri 10-6 Sat Sun and BH Mons 10-7. 12-16 July garden closes at 4. Nov-end Mar 1996 daily except Mon 10-5 or sunset if earlier. Last admission half hour before closing. Closed 25 Dec and 1 Jan. No coaches on Sunday.
Admission: Sun and Bank Hols £2.60 Mon-Sat £1.80 (Children half-price). Parties by prior booking. Tel (01372) 469421. No reduction for parties.
Refreshments: Tea-room open Jan 14-end Mar Sat and Sun 11-4.30 Apr-end Oct daily (except Mons) 11-5.30 Nov-Dec 10 daily (except Mons) 11-4. 13 Jan-end Mar 1996 Sat-Sun 11-4.30. Open Bank Hol Mons.
Events/Exhibitions: Phone for details.
Wheelchairs provided. Dogs allowed on leads Nov to Mar but **not** admitted Apr to end Oct. Braille guide available. Shop open as Tea-room.

CROSSWATER FARM

(Mr & Mrs E. G. Millais)

Crosswater Lane, Churt, Farnham GU10 2JN map **12** U21

Telephone: (01252) 792698

Fax: (01252) 792526

6-acre woodland garden surrounded by acres of National Trust property. Plantsman's collection of Rhododendrons and Azaleas including many rare species collected in the Himalayas, and hybrids raised by the owners. Pond, stream and companion plantings. Plants for sale from adjoining Rhododendron nursery. (See Millais Nurseries entry in Garden Specialists section).

Location: Farnham/Haslemere 6 m. From A287 turn East into Jumps Road ½ m north of Churt village centre. After ¼ m, turn left into Crosswater Lane, and follow Nursery signs.
Open: May 1-June 3 daily 10-5. In aid of the *National Gardens Scheme* on May 27 28 29.
Admission: Adults £1.50 children free.
Refreshments: Teas available on NGS days.
No dogs.

FARNHAM CASTLE

(The Church Commissioners)

Farnham map **12** U21 △

Bishop's Palace built in Norman times by Henry of Blois, with Tudor and Jacobean additions. Formerly the seat of the Bishops of Winchester. Fine Great Hall re-modelled at the Restoration. Features include the Renaissance brickwork of Waynefleter's tower, and the 17th century chapel.

Location: ½ m N of Town Centre on A287.
Station(s): Farnham.
Open: All year round/Weds 2-4 parties at other times by arrangement. All visitors given guided tours. Centrally heated in winter.
Admission: Adults £1.20 OAPs/children/students 60p reductions for parties.
Centrally heated in winter. Not readily accessible by wheelchairs.

GODDARDS

(The Lutyens Trust)

Abinger Common, Dorking RH5 6TH map **12** U22

Telephone: (01306) 730487

Edwardian country house by Sir Edwin Lutyens, with Gertrude Jekyll garden, in beautiful setting on slopes of Leith Hill. Given in 1991 to The Lutyens Trust by the family whose home it was for 38 years.

Location: 4½ m SW of Dorking in Abinger Common.
Station(s): Dorking.
Open: By telephone appointment Apr-Oct.
Refreshments: Morning coffee, afternoon tea - functions and receptions by arrangement with the Administrator.
Conferences: Day conferences only.

GREATHED MANOR

(Country Houses Association)

Lingfield RH7 6PA map **12** U23

Telephone: (01342) 832577

Victorian Manor house.

Location: 2½ m SE of Lingfield on B2028 Edenbridge road, take Ford Manor road beside Plough Inn, Dormansland for final 1 m.
Station(s): Dormans (1½ m); Lingfield (1½ m). Bus Route: No. 429 to Plough Inn, Dormansland.
Open: May-Sept Weds & Thurs 2-5. Last entry 4.30.
Admission: £2.50 Children £1. Free car park.
No dogs admitted.

"GHOSTS"

Ghosts are in residence at the following properties included in Historic Houses Castles and Gardens:-

Blickling Hall - *Anne Boleyn*

Breamore House - *Haunted picture - if touched, death on the same day*

East Riddleden Hall - *5 ghosts including lady*

in Grey Hall Lady's Chamber

Fountains Abbey & Studley Royal - *Choir of monks chanting in Chapel of Nine Altars*

Hinton Ampner - *Nocturnal noises*

Ightham Mote - *Supernatural presence*

Lindisfarne Castle - *Monk, and group of monks on causeway*

Lyme Park - *Unearthly peals of bells and lady in white, funeral procession through park*

Malmesbury House - *Ghost of a cavalier*

Overbecks Museum & Garden - *'Model' ghost in the Children's room (for them to spot)*

Rockingham Castle - *Lady Dedlock*

Rufford Old Hall - *Elizabeth Hesketh*

Scotney Castle Garden - *Man rising from the lake*

Sizergh Castle & Garden - *Poltergeist*

Speke Hall - *Ghost of woman in tapestry room*

Springhill - *Ghost of a woman*

Sudbury Hall - *Lady in Green, seen on stairs*

Tamworth Castle - *Haunted bedroom*

Treasurer's House - *Troop of Roman soldiers marching through the cellar*

Wallington House - *Invisible birds beating against the windows accompanied by heavy breathing*

Washington Old Hall - *Grey lady walking through corridors*

GUILDFORD HOUSE
(Guildford Borough Council)
155, High Street, Guildford   GU1 3AJ   map **12** U21
Telephone: (01483) 444740
Fax: (01483) 444742

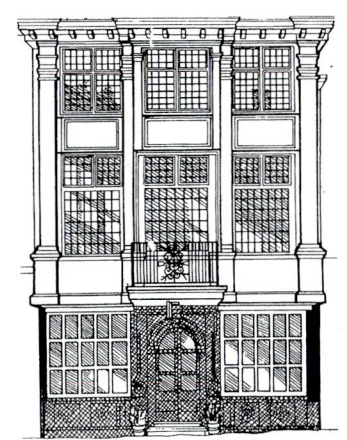

GUILDFORD HOUSE

Guildford House Gallery

155 High Street,
Guildford GU1 3AJ

Telephone:
01483 444740

Newly restored 17th century town house. Original fine carved staircase, plaster ceilings and wrought iron window fittings. Temporary exhibitions include historical and modern paintings of local and national importance, photography and craftwork.

Location: Centre of Guildford on High Street.
Station(s): Guildford ½ m.
Open: Tues-Sat 10-4.45 *Closed* Bank Hols.
Admission: Free.
Refreshments: Tea-room in old kitchen.
Events/Exhibitions: Temporary exhibitions and selections from the Borough's Collection - including pastel portraits by John Russell RA (1745-1806) Leaflets available.
Public car park nearby, none on site. Gallery shop with publications, cards and craftwork.

HATCHLANDS PARK   🍃 **The National Trust**
East Clandon   GU4 7RT   map **12** U22
Telephone: (01483) 222482

Hatchlands is an 18th century house with rich and inviting interiors. It houses the Cobbe Collection of early keyboard instruments, paintings and furniture. Garden by Gertrude Jekyll and new walks have opened in the Repton parkland.

Location: E of East Clandon on N side of Leatherhead/Guildford Road (A246).
Station(s): Clandon (2½ m), Horsley (3 m).
Open: 2 Apr-Oct 31 Tue Wed Thur Sun and Bank Hol Mons but also open Fri in Aug 2-5.30. Last admission 5. Park walks open 12.30-6.
Admission: £4 Children half-price Family ticket £10. Pre-booked parties £3.50. Park walks and grounds only £1.50.
Refreshments: Licensed restaurant lunches from 12.30 and home-made teas 3-5pm, same days as house. Tel. (01483) 211120.
Events/Exhibitions: Please telephone for details.
Dogs permitted on leads in car park only. Wheelchair access to ground floor and part of the garden. Shop.

LITTLE HOLLAND HOUSE

(London Borough of Sutton)
Carshalton - See under Greater London.

LOSELEY HOUSE

(Mr and Mrs James More-Molyneux)
Guildford   GU3 1HS   map **12** U21   △ &
Telephone: (01483) 304440

The Elizabethan country house with the friendly atmosphere. Built of stone from Waverley Abbey in a glorious parkland setting by an ancestor of the present owner and occupier. Queen Elizabeth I stayed here three times, James I once. Queen Mary visited in 1932. Panelling from Henry VIII's Nonsuch Palace. Fine ceilings, unique carved chalk chimney piece, inlaid cabinets, tapestries, needlework, but Loseley is a home, not a museum. Moat walk. Rose garden and herb Garden. Farm tours. Licensed Restaurant housed in the 17th century Tithe Barn except on Saturdays when it will be in our permanent marquee. Morning coffee, lunches and teas. Shop selling Loseley ice cream, yoghurt and cream as well as Loseley bakery products and gifts.

Location: 2½ m SW of Guildford (take B3000 off A3 through Compton); 1½ m N of Godalming (off A3100).
Station(s): Farncombe (2 m).
Open: May 3-Sept 30 Wed Thurs Fri Sat also Bank Hol Mon 8 & 29 May 28 Aug 2-5. Farm Tours Wed-Sat at other times booked parties only.
Admission: £3.50 Children £2 Parties of 20 and over £2.75 per person. School parties £1.50 per child. Gardens and grounds £1.50 Children 50p. Parties of 20 or more £1.20 per person.
Refreshments: Catering by Alexander Catering (est 1960). Professional Caterers provide morning coffee, home-made lunches and teas in Tithe Barn (except on Sat when Restaurant is in Marquee). Open May 3- Sept 30 Wed, Thurs, Fri, Sat also Bank Hol Mon 8 May 29 May and 28 Aug.
Events/Exhibitions: Craft Fair 2/4 June, Performing Arts Open Air Concert 8 July, Queen Elizabeth's Foundation Classic Car Show 5/6 Aug.
Conferences: Facilities available.
Tithe Barn Restaurant and Farm Shop open same days as House 11-5. Tithe Barn available for hire for weddings company days, fun days, product launches and conferences.

THE OLD PALACE

(The Whitgift Foundation)
Old Palace Road, Croydon   map **12** U22   △
Telephone: 0181-668 3349 or 0181-688 2414

Seat of Archbishops of Canterbury since 871. 15th century Banqueting Hall and Guardroom, Tudor Chapel, Norman undercroft.

Location: In central Croydon. Adjacent to Parish Church.
Station(s): East Croydon or West Croydon (few mins walk).
Open: Doors open at 2pm. Conducted Tours only (last tour commences 2.30) Tues Apr 18-Sat Apr 22, Mon May 29-Fri Jun 2, Mon Jul 10-Sat Jul 15, Mon Jul 17-Sat Jul 22.
Admission: Adults £4 children/OAPs £3 family £10. This includes afternoon tea served in the undercroft.
Car park. Souvenir shop. Parties catered for, apply 0181-668 3349 or 0181-688 2414. Unsuitable for wheelchairs.

PAINSHILL PARK
(Painshill Park Trust)
Portsmouth Road, Cobham   KT11 1JE   map **12** U22   △ &
Telephone: (01932) 868113 ansafone (01932) 864674
Fax: (01932) 868001

Painshill, contemporary with Stourhead & Stowe, is one of Europe's finest landscape gardens. It was created by The Hon Charles Hamilton, plantsman, painter, and brilliantly gifted designer, between 1738 and 1773. He transformed barren heathland into ornamental pleasure grounds and parkland of dramatic beauty and contrasting scenery, dominated by a 14 acre meandering lake fed from the river by an immense waterwheel. Garden buildings and features adorn the Park amongst magnificent shrubberies typical of the period: an extraordinary grotto, a Gothic temple, a ruined abbey, a chinese bridge, a castellated tower, a turkish tent, a mausoleum, and a working vineyard. Well maintained for 200 years in private ownership the Park was neglected after 1948 and sank into dereliction. In 1981 the Painshill Park Trust, a registered charity was formed to restore the gardens to their original splendour, raising the extensive funds needed for such an ambitious project. The Trust has made enormous progress and this masterpiece is re-emerging from the wilderness.

Location: W of Cobham on A245. 200 yards E of A3/A245 roundabout.
Station(s): Cobham.
Open: Apr 9-Oct 15 (Suns only) 11-5 (gates close 6). Pre-booked parties (min. 10) any day except Suns. Please ring (01932) 868113 for more information. Wide ranging Education programme - school parties welcomed, holiday activities organised and childrens parties catered for by arrangement with Painshill Park Education Trust, (01932) 866743. Full opening is excepted during 1995. Telephone ansaphone (01932) 864674 to confirm opening arrangements.
Admission: Adults £3.50 OAPs/students/UB40s £3 children 5-16 £2.50 groups £2.80.
Refreshments: Light refreshments available.
Much of park accessible for disabled (wheelchairs available). Limited facilities and parking. No dogs please.

POLESDEN LACEY   🌿 The National Trust
nr Dorking   RH5 6BD   map **12** U22   &
Telephone: (01372) 458203 or 452048

Originally a Regency villa altered in Edwardian period. The Queen Mother honeymooned here in the 1920s. First-rate collection of pictures, tapestries and furniture. 18th century garden set in magnificent North Downs countryside. Rose garden and a croquet lawn, with croquet equipment available for hire.

Location: 5 m NW of Dorking, reached via Great Bookham (A246) & then signed on road leading S (1½ m).
Station(s): Boxhill or Bookham (both 2½ m).
Open: Mar Sat and Suns 1.30-4.30 Mar 30-end of Oct Wed-Sun including Good Friday 1.30-5.30. Last adm half hour before closing. Open Bank Hol Mons and preceding Suns 11-5.30. Grounds open daily all year 11-6 or dusk if earlier.
Admission: £2.50 HOUSE £3 extra Children half-price. *Party reductions on Wed Thurs and Fri only by prior arrangement with the Administrator.* £4.50.
Refreshments: Licensed Restaurant in courtyard. Jan 14-end Mar: (light refreshments). Sats and Suns only 11-4.30. Mar 30-end Oct Weds-Suns and Bank Hol Mons 11-5.30. Nov-Dec 17 Wed-Sun 11-4.30. Special times before Christmas. Tel (01372) 456190.
Events/Exhibitions: Please telephone for details.
Wheelchairs admitted and provided. Shop open: 14 Jan-end of Mar: Sat & Sun only from Jan 14, 11-4.30. Apr to end Oct: Wed to Sun and BH Mon 11-6.00. Open Mon and Tues in July and Aug. Nov to Dec 17 Wed-Sun 11-4.30. (Tel (01372) 457230.

PYRFORD COURT   🏛
Pyrford Common Road, Pyrford, nr Woking   GU22 8UB   map **12** U21
Telephone: (01483) 765880
Fax: (01483) 740938

Twenty acres of wild and formal gardens, azaleas, wisteria, rhododendrons, pink marble fountain, venetian bridge, and views to North Downs.

Location: 2 m E of Woking, M25 (exit 10) on to A3 towards Guildford, off to Ripley, turn right in centre of Ripley to B367 - Newark Lane, signposted Pyrford. 1¾ m on left Jct Pyrford Common Road and Upshott Lane.
Station(s): Woking
Open: Sat & Sun May 13 and 14 2-6 Sun Oct 15 12-4 and by appointment. Open in aid of *National Gardens Scheme and Age Concern.* For details of operas and concerts please phone.
Admission: £2.50 Children 80p to gardens on above dates.
Refreshments: Teas.
Parking, suitable for wheelchairs, dogs on lead. Toilet facilities.

RHS GARDEN WISLEY
(The Royal Horticultural Society)
Wisley, Woking   GU23 6QB   map **12** U22   &
Telephone: (01483) 224234

British gardening at its best in all its aspects. 250 acres of glorious garden. The Alpine Meadow, carpeted with wild daffodils in spring, Battleston Hill, brilliant with rhododendrons in early summer, the Heathers and autumnal tints together with the glasshouses, trials and model gardens are all features for which the garden is famous. But what makes **Wisley** unique is that it is not just beautiful to look at. As the showpiece of the Royal Horticultural Society, the Garden is a source of practical advice and a model of good horticulture to hundreds of thousands of visitors every year. It is probably the only garden in the world to give such a complete picture of different gardening styles and techniques.

Location: Wisley is just off M25 Junction 10, on A3. London 22 m Guildford 7m.
Open: The garden is open to the public Mon-Sat throughout the year (except Christmas Day) from 10-sunset (or 7pm during the summer). Sundays RHS Members only.
Admission: Adults £4.70 children under 6 yrs free children 6-16 £1.75. Groups of more than 20 Mon-Sat £3.75. Tickets for group visits must be obtained in advance of visit. RHS Members free. One person accompanying a blind or disabled person free.
Refreshments: Wisley's Terrace Restaurant and Conservatory Café inside the Garden are open throughout the year.
Dogs not admitted (except guide dogs). Information centre. Shop and Plant sales centre.

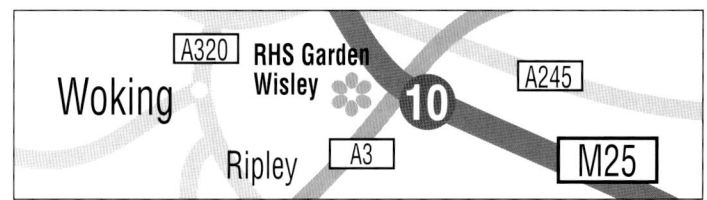

WHITEHALL
Cheam - See under Greater London.

WINKWORTH ARBORETUM   🌿 The National Trust
Hascombe Road, nr Godalming   GU8 4AD   map **12** U21   &
Telephone: (01483) 208477

99 acres of trees and shrubs, world-renown for spectacular displays of Spring and Autumn colour. Two lakes and wonderful views.

Location: 2 m SE of Godalming on E side of B2130.
Station(s): Godalming (2 m).
Open: All year during daylight hours.
Admission: £2, Chd half-price. No reduction for parties.*Coach parties by prior appointment in writing to* Head of Arboretum, Winkworth Arboretum, nr Godalming.
Refreshments: Apr 1-Nov 14 daily 11-5.30 (weather permitting) for light lunches and teas. Also open weekends in Mar and Mid Nov-Xmas. Bookings with Concessionaire, Winkworth Arboretum (0483) 208265 when tea-room open.
Dogs must be kept under control. Limited wheelchair access.

EAST SUSSEX

ALFRISTON CLERGY HOUSE   The National Trust
Alfriston, nr Seaford   map **12** V23
Telephone: (01323) 870001

Picturesque thatched medieval hall house bought in 1896, the first building acquired by the Trust. Cottage garden.

Location: 4 m NE of Seaford just E of B2108; adjoining The Tye & St Andrew's Church.
Station(s): Berwick (2½ m).
Open: Apr to end Oct - Daily 10.30-5 (or sunset if earlier). Last admission half-hour before closing.
Admission: £2, Chd £1, Pre-booked parties £1.50, Chd 80p.
Shop (open until Christmas). No dogs. Unsuitable for wheelchairs. Parking and lavatories in village car park.

BATEMAN'S   The National Trust
Burwash   map **12** V23 △
Telephone: (01435) 882302

Built 1634. Rudyard Kipling lived here. Water-mill restored by the National Trust. Attractive garden, yew hedges, lawns, daffodils and wild garden.

Location: ½ m S of Burwash on the Lewes/Etchingham Road (A265).
Open: Apr to end of Oct - Daily (except Thurs & Fri but open Good Fri) 11-5.30. Last adm 4.30.
Admission: House Mill & Garden Adults £4 Children £2. Pre-booked parties £3 Children £1.50.
Refreshments: Tea room: coffees, light lunches and teas, open as House.
Events/Exhibitions: Orchestral Concert with fireworks 5 Aug.
No dogs. Shop.

BATTLE ABBEY

Battle   map **13** V24
Telephone: (01424) 773792

The Battle of Hastings, 1066 - the best-known date in English history. Battle Abbey was built by William the Conqueror as a thanksgiving for his victory, with the high altar on the spot where King Harold died. The church has yet to be fully excavated, but visitors may walk over the battlefield, and see the remains of many of the domestic buildings of the monastery and see an audio-visual show. An exhibition is open in the newly restored 14th century gatehouse re-creating the history of this famous monument. A Personal Stereo Guided Tour is available.

Location: Battle.
Open: Apr 1-Sept 30 10-6 daily Oct 1-Mar 31 daily 10-4.
Admission: Adults £3.20 concessions £2.40 children £1.60.

BENTLEY HOUSE & GARDENS
Halland **BN8 5AF**   map **12** V23 &
Telephone: (01825) 840573
Fax: (01825) 840573

Bentley House dates back to Tudor times and was built on land granted to James Gage by the Archbishop of Canterbury with the permission of Henry VIII. The family of Lord Gage was linked with Bentley from that time until 1904. The estate was purchased by Gerald Askew in 1937, and during the 1960's he and his wife, Mary, added two large double height Palladian rooms to the original farmhouse. The architect who advised them was Raymond Erith, who had previously worked on 10 Downing Street. The drawing room in the East wing contains mid 18th century Chinese wallpaper and gilt furniture, and the Bird room in the West wing contains a collection of wildfowl paintings by Philip Rickman. The Gardens at Bentley have been created as a series of 'rooms' divided by Yew hedges, one room leading into the next, specialising in many old fashioned roses including the Bourbons, the Gallicas and the Damask. Nearby six stone sphinxes stand along a broad grass walk where daffodils bloom in spring.

Location: 7 m NE of Lewes signposted on A22, A26 & B2192.
Open: Summer open daily 21 Mar-31 Oct 10.30-4.30 (last admissions) 5pm in July and Aug House opens 12 noon daily from 1 Apr. Winter open weekends only 10.30-4 (last admissions). House closed all winter, Estate throughout Dec & Jan.

Admission: Adults £3.80 OAPs £2.90 Children (4-15) £2.20 Family ticket (2 adults+4 children) £10.50. Special rates for disabled (wheelchairs available). Parties of 11 or more - 10% discount. Adm price allows entry to House, Garden and Grounds, Wildfowl reserve, Motor Museum, Woodland Walk, Animal section, Children's adventure play area, Picnic area, Tearoom, Gift Shop and Education Centre with audio/visual.
Refreshments: Tea-Rooms on site (licensed).
Ample free parking. Dogs allowed in this area only. Special arrangements can be for parties outside normal hours. Please contact the Manager for details (01825) 840573.

BRICKWALL HOUSE AND GARDENS
(Frewen Educational Trust)
Northiam, Rye   TN31 6NL   map **13** V24   △ க
Telephone: (01797) 252494 or Curator (01797) 223329
Fax: (01737) 252567

BODIAM CASTLE   🌼 The National Trust
nr Robertsbridge   map **13** V24   க
Telephone: (01580) 830436
Fax: (01580) 830436

Built 1385-9, one of the best preserved examples of medieval moated architecture.
Location: 3 m S of Hawkhurst; 2m E of A21.
Open: 18 Feb-end Oct daily 10-6 or dusk if earlier. Nov-2 Jan Tues-Sun 10-dusk (closed Christmas holiday) open New Years Day.
Admission: £2.50 Children £1.30 *Parties of 15 or more by prior arrangement.* £2 Children £1. Car park 50p.
Refreshments: Restaurant as Castle from April closes half hour before castle.
Events/Exhibitions: Medieval Spring Fair 29/30 April Jazz concert 24 June.
Museum. Audio visual. Shop. Dogs admitted in grounds only. Wheelchair access.

Home of the Frewen family since 1666. 17th century drawing room, superb plaster ceilings and family portraits. Grand staircase. The grounds contain a formal wall garden, topiary and an arboretum.
Location: 7m NW of Rye on B2088.
Open: Apr-Sept Sats and Bank Hol Mons 2-5 open at other times by prior arrangement with the curator.
Admission: £2.

Sir Peter Lely - portrait painter

His paintings can be seen at the following properties included in Historic Houses Castles and Gardens:-

Aynhoe Park	*Kedleston Hall*
Belton House	*Knole*
Breamore House	*Petworth House*
Browsholme Hall	*Ragley Hall*
Dalmeny House	*Rockingham Castle*
Euston Hall	*St Osyth Priory*
Goodwood House	*Stanford Hall*
Gorhambury	*Weston Park*

CHARLESTON FARMHOUSE
(The Charleston Trust)
Firle, nr Lewes   map **12** V23   △
Telephone: (01323) 811265 (Visitor information) (01323) 811626 (Administration)
Fax: (01323) 811628

17/18th century farmhouse, the home of Vanessa and Clive Bell and Duncan Grant from 1916 until Grant's death in 1978. Virginia and Leonard Woolf 'discovered' Charleston in 1916, when her sister Vanessa was looking for a house in the country, 'If you lived there, you could make it absolutely divine' Virginia wrote prophetically. Vanessa Bell's household at Charleston was an unconventional and creative one, and was to become the focal point for a group of artists and intellectuals later to be known as 'Bloomsbury'. Walls, furniture and ceramics were decorated by the artists with their own designs, influenced by Italian fresco painting and post-impressionism. The walled garden has been restored as it was in its heyday, showing an artist's use of colour, shapes and textures.

Location: 6 m E of Lewes, on A27, between Firle and Selmeston.
Station(s): Lewes 6 m; Berwick 3 m.
Open: Apr 1-Oct 29 Off-peak period Apr 1-July 16 Sept 13-Oct 29 Wed Thur Fri Sat (guided tours) and Sun and Bank Hol Mon (unguided) 2-6 (last adm 5). Fridays are on a Connoisseur basis only (see below). Kitchen open Thurs and Fri only. Also open Nov-Christmas weekends only mini tours 2-4pm (£2.50 per head) and Xmas shopping 2-5pm. Peak period July 19-Sept 10. As for off-peak but Fridays are not connoisseur days. Kitchen open Thurs only. Also open 11-2 (shop and gardens from 11, 'accompanied' tours from 11.45) every open day except Sun and Bank Hol Mon.
Admission: Adults £4.50 children £3 Connoisseur Days £6. Students/OAPs/UB40 concessions midweek throughout the season also W/E Apr May Oct.
Refreshments: Sats thoughout season. Also Weds, Thurs, Fris in peak period.
Numbers in the House will be limited. No dogs. Coaches by prior appointment only. Contact Charleston Office at Farmhouse.

Lancelot 'Capability' Brown

Born 1716 in Northumberland, Capability Brown began work at the age of 16 in the vegetable gardens of Sir William and Lady Loraine at Kirharle Tower. He left Northumberland in 1739, and records show that he worked at Stowe until 1749. It was at Stowe that Brown began to study architecture, and to submit his own plans. It was also at Stowe that he devised a new method of moving and replanting mature trees.

Brown married Bridget Wayet in 1744 and began work on the estate at Warwick Castle in 1749. He was appointed Master Gardener at Hampton Court in 1764, and planted the Great Vine at Hampton Court in 1768. Blenheim Palace designs are considered amongst Brown's finest work, and the technical achievements were outstanding even for the present day.

Capability Brown died in February 1783 of a massive heart attack. A monument beside the lake at Croome Court was erected which reads "To the memory of Lancelot Brown, who by the powers of his inimitable and creative genius formed this garden scene out of a morass". There is also a portrait of Brown at Burghley.

Capability Brown was involved in the design of grounds at the following properties included in Historic Houses Castles and Gardens:-

Audley End	*Longleat*
Berrington Hall	*Luton Hoo*
Bowood	*Moccas Court*
Burghley House	*Petworth House*
Burton Constable	*Sledmere House*
Charlecote Park	*Stowe (Stowe*
Chilham Castle Gardens	*School)*
(reputed)	*Syon House*
Clandon Park	*Warwick Castle*
Claremont	*Weston Park*
Chillington Hall	*Wimpole Hall*
Corsham Court	*Wrest Park and*
Fawley Court	*Gardens*
Highclere Castle	

FIRLE PLACE

(Viscount Gage)

nr Lewes   BN8 6LP   map **12** V23   △
Telephone: (01273) 858335

Home of the Gage family since the 15th century, the original Tudor house was largely altered about 1730. The House contains a magnificent collection of European and British Old Masters. The pictures are further enhanced with French and English furniture by famous craftsmen. There is also a quantity of Sèvres porcelain of the finest quality. These are largely derived from the Cowper collection, and can be seen in a spacious family setting. A Connoisseurs house. There are items of particular interest to visitors from the USA through General Gage, Commander-in-Chief of the British Forces at the beginning of the War of Independence, and his wife Margaret Kemble of New Jersey. The House is set in parkland under the South Downs, 55 miles from London by road. Hourly rail service Victoria to Lewes, takes 65 minutes, thence by taxi (5 miles).

Location: 5 m SE of Lewes on the Lewes/Eastbourne Road (A27).
Station(s): Lewes (5 m, taxis available).
Open: May-Sept Wed Thurs & Sun also Easter, May, Spring & Summer Bank Hol Suns & Mons 2-last tickets at 5. First Wed in month longer unguided Connoisseurs' tour of House. Exclusive Private Viewing Groups 25+ by arrangement.
Admission: Pre-booked group parties of 25 on Open Days (except first Wed in month) at reduced rate. Special exclusive viewings at other times of year for private parties over 25 by arrangement.*Party bookings in writing to Showing Secretary, Firle Place, nr Lewes, East Sussex BN8 6LP (01273) 858335.*
Refreshments: Licensed cold buffet luncheons 12-2 Sussex cream teas from 3, only on house open days. (Bookings (01273) 858307).
Shop and contemporary pictures exhibition. Car park adjacent to house.

GLYNDE PLACE

(Viscount & Viscountess Hampden)

nr Lewes   BN8 6SX   map **12** V23   △
Telephone: (01273) 858224
Fax: (01273) 858224

Set below an escarpment of the ancient hill-fort of Mount Caburn, Glynde Place is a magnificent example of Elizabethan architecture and is the manor house of an estate which has been in the same family since the 12th century. Built in 1579 of Sussex flint and Caen stone around a courtyard the house commands fine views towards Pevensey marshes and the South Downs. Amongst the collections of four hundred years of family living can be seen a fine collection of 17th century portraits of the Trevors, an early 18th century set of embroidery and a Victorian silver garniture given to Mr Speaker Brand, a room in whose memory has been especially created. The house is still the family home of the Brands and can be enjoyed as such.

Location: In Glynde village 4 m SE of Lewes on A27.
Station(s): Within easy walking distance of Glynde Station with hourly services to Eastbourne and Brighton with connecting services from London at Lewes.
Open: May-Sept Wed & Thurs and Sun of each month. Open Easter Day and Easter Mon and Bank Hols. Guided tours for parties (25 or more) can be booked either on a regular open day (£2.50 per person) or a non-open day when tour will be guided by owner (£5 per person) by telephoning Lord Hampden on (01273) 858224 (daytime) or by writing to him.
Admission: House adults £3 children free if accompanied by adult. Free parking.
Refreshments: Sussex cream teas in Georgian Stable Block. Parties to book in advance (as above).
Events/Exhibitions: Exhibition of paintings and prints in Tea-room for sale.
Conferences: House can be hired for weddings and parties. (Contact Lord Hampden).

GREAT DIXTER
Northiam   **TN31 6PH**   map **12** V24 △
Telephone: (01797) 252878

A beautiful example of a 15th century half-timbered manor house with a Great Hall of unique construction in a truly 'English' garden setting. Restorations and the addition of a smaller 16th century hall house were carried out by Sir Edwin Lutyens who also designed the gardens. Yew hedges, topiary and garden buildings create a delightful setting for flower borders. These contain a rich diversity of plants of horticultural interest. Naturalised daffodils and fritillaries; paeonies; primulas, fuchsias, clematis, herbaceous and bedding plants informally arranged.

Location: ½ m N of Northiam; 8 m NW of Rye; 12 m N of Hastings. Just off A28.
Open: Apr 1-Oct 15 daily except Mon (but open all Bank Hol Mons) open 2-last adm at 5. Gardens open at 11 on May 27/28/29. Sun in July & Aug, also Aug 28.
Admission: House and Gardens adults £3.50 children 50p. Gardens only adults £2.50 children 25p concessions to OAPs and NT members on Fri - House and Gardens ask for details. No dogs.

KIDBROOKE PARK WITH REPTON GROUNDS
(The Council of Michael Hall School)
Forest Row   map **12** U13
Telephone: (01342) 822275
Fax: (01342) 826004

Sandstone house and stables built in 1730s with later alterations.

Location: 1 m SW of Forest Row, off A22, 4 m S of East Grinstead.
Open: Spring Bank Hol Mon (May 30) then Aug-Daily (inc Bank Hol Mon) 11- 6.
Admission: Apply for admission to the Bursar.

LAMB HOUSE   🍃 The National Trust
Rye   map **13** V24
Telephone: (01892) 890651

Georgian house with garden. Home of Henry James from 1898 to 1916. Pretty garden. Also home of E.F.Benson.

Location: In West Street facing W end of church.
Station(s): Rye (½ m).
Open: House (Hall & 3 rooms only) & Garden. Apr-end of Oct Wed & Sat 2- 6 (last admission 5.30).
Admission: £2. No reduction for children or parties. No dogs. Unsuitable for wheelchairs. No lavatories.

MONKS HOUSE   🍃 The National Trust
Rodmell   map **12** V23
Telephone: (01892) 890651

A small village house and garden. The home of Virginia and Leonard Woolf from 1919 until his death in 1969. House administered and largely maintained by tenants.

Location: 3 m SE of Lewes, in Rodmell village.
Station(s): Southease (1 m).
Open: Apr to end Oct - Weds & Sats 2-5.30 (last adm 5.00).
Admission: £2. No reduction for chd or parties. No dogs. Unsuitable for wheelchairs. Max. of 15 people in house at any one time. Narrow access road. Car park 50 yds.

MOORLANDS
(Dr and Mrs Steven Smith)
Crowborough   map **12** U23
Telephone: (01892) 652474

Three acres set in lush valley adjoining Ashdown Forest; water garden with ponds and streams; herbaceous border, primulas, rhododendrons, azaleas and many unusual trees and shrubs; good autumn colour.

Location: Friar's Gate. 2 m N of Crowborough. Approach via B2188 at Friar's Gate - take L fork signposted 'Crowborough Narrow Road', entrance 100 yards on left. From Crowborough crossroads take St. Johns Road to Friar's Gate.
Open: Suns May 7 and 28 and June 4 and July 23 (National Garden Scheme) 2-6. Also by appointment only Apr 1-Oct. *In aid of National Gardens Scheme.* Open every Wed Apr-Oct 11-5.
Admission: £2 OAPs £1.50 children free.
Refreshments: Teas in garden on open days; and for parties by prior arrangement. Unsuitable for disabled persons. Limited free parking.

PASHLEY MANOR GARDENS
(Mr & Mrs J.A. Sellick)
Ticehurst, Wadhurst   **TN5 7HE**   map **12** U23
Telephone: (01580) 200692
Fax: (01580) 200102

Pashley Manor Gardens, surrounding the Grade 1 Tudor timber-framed ironmaster's house dating from 1550 with a Queen Anne rear elevation of 1720, stands in a well timbered park with magnificent views across to Brightling Beacon. The 8 acres of formal garden, dating from the 18th century, were created in true English romantic style and are planted with many ancient trees and fine shrubs. New plantings over the past decade give additional interest and subtle colouring throughout the year. All is enhanced by waterfalls, ponds and a moat which encircled the original house built in 1262. The delightful view, peaceful environment and the sound of running water makes this garden very worthwhile visiting.

Location: Between Ticehurst and A21 on B2099. Wadhurst 5 m.
Open: Gardens Only Apr 15-Sept 30 Tues Wed Thurs Sat and all Bank Hols 11-5.
Admission: Adults £3 OAPs £2.50. Coaches by appointment only.
Refreshments: Teas/coffee, light lunches in fine weather 11-5.
Events/Exhibitions: April 29 Plant Fair, May 5-8 Whichford Pottery Exhibition, May 11-16 Tulip Festival; June 8-11 Rose Festival; Aug 20 Plant Fair.
Coach and car park. Unsuitable for wheelchairs. No dogs. Plants for sale.

PEVENSEY CASTLE
ENGLISH HERITAGE

Pevensey   map **12** V23
Telephone: (01323) 762604

The walls that enclose this 10-acre site are from the 4th century Roman fort, Anderida. The inner castle, with its great keep, is medieval. With the fall of France in 1940, Pevensey was put into service again, after centuries of neglect. A Personal Stereo Guided Tour is available.

Location: Pevensey.
Open: Apr 1-Sept 30 10-6 daily Oct 1-31 10-4 daily Nov 1-Mar 31 Wed-Sun 10-4.
Admission: Adults £2 concessions £1.50 children £1.

PRESTON MANOR

(Borough of Brighton)
Brighton   map **12** V22
Telephone: (01273) 603005
Fax: (01273) 779108

A Georgian house built in 1738 and added to in 1905; the house of the Stanford family for nearly 150 years. The house is fully furnished and illustrates the way of life of a rich gentry family and their servants. Includes Servants Quarters and Edwardian Day Nursery, toy collection and attic rooms. Delightful grounds with walled garden and pets' cemetery.

Location: On main Brighton to London Road at Preston Park.
Station(s): Preston Park.
Open: All the year Mon 1-5 (Bank Hols 10-5) Tues-Sat 10-5 Sun 2-5 closed Good Fri Christmas & Boxing Day.
Admission: Charged. Reduced rates for parties, families, children and OAPs. Garden free. Parties by arrangement. Available for evening hire.

ROYAL PAVILION

Brighton   map **12** V22   &
Telephone: (01273) 603005

Spectacular seaside palace of the Prince Regent, transformed by John Nash (1815-1822) into one of the most dazzlingly exotic buildings in Europe. Interiors furnished in the Chinese style, extensive structural and interior restoration programme now complete. New: The Yellow Bow Rooms - bedroom suites of the Dukes of York and Clarence now open to the public. Gardens restored to original Regency design and planting scheme. Pavilion shop.

Location: In centre of Brighton (Old Steine).
Station(s): Brighton (¾ m).
Open: All the year daily 10-5 (June-Sept 10-6) closed Christmas Day & Boxing Day.
Admission: Charged. Reduced rates for parties, families, children and OAPs.
Refreshments: Tea-room with balcony overlooking the gardens.
Conferences: State rooms available for evening hire plus daytime meeting space.
Ground floor accessible for the disabled.

SHEFFIELD PARK GARDEN  The National Trust

nr Uckfield   map **12** U23
Telephone: (01825) 790231

100 acre garden with series of lakes linked by cascades; great variety of unusual shrubs.

Location: Midway between East Grinstead & Lewes on E side of A275; 5 m NW of Uckfield.
Open: Mar Sat and Sun only 11-4. Apr-5 Nov Tues-Sun and BH Mon 11-6 or sunset if earlier. Nov 8-Dec 16 Wed-Sat 11-4. Last admission one hour before close.
Admission: May & Oct £4 Children £2. Mar Apr & Jun-Sept Nov & Dec £3.70 Children £1.80. Pre-booked parties £3. *No reduction for parties on Sat Sun & Bank Hols.*
Refreshments: Tea-room (not NT) next to car park.
No dogs. Shop. Wheelchairs available.

WEST SUSSEX

ARUNDEL CASTLE

(Arundel Castle Trustees Ltd)
Arundel   map **12** V21   &
Telephone: (01903) 883136

BORDE HILL GARDEN

(Borde Hill Garden Ltd)
Haywards Heath   RH16 1XP   map **12** U22   &
Telephone: (01444) 450326
Fax: (01444) 440427

Large garden with woods and parkland of exceptional beauty. Rare trees and shrubs, herbaceous borders and fine views. Woodland Walk, water feature, picnic area by lake.

Location: 1½ m N of Haywards Heath on Balcombe Road. Brighton 17 m; Gatwick 10 m.
Station(s): Haywards Heath 1½ m.
Open: Daily Mar 18-Oct 1 10-6.
Admission: Adults £3.50 OAPs £3 children £1.50 family ticket £7.50 parties £3. Parkland admission £1 per person (not available during special events).
Refreshments: Licensed - morning coffee, lunches, cream teas and dinner; parties by arrangement.
Events/Exhibitions: Ring for details.
Conferences: Ring (01444) 441102 for details.
Children's Adventure Playground and trout fishing.

CHICHESTER CATHEDRAL

(The Dean & Chapter of Chichester)
West Street, Chichester   PO19 1PX   map **12** V21
Telephone: (01243) 782595
Fax: (01243) 536190

In the heart of the city, this fine Cathedral has been a centre of Christian worship and community life for 900 years and is the site of the Shrine of St Richard of Chichester. Its treasures range from Romanesque stone carvings to 20th century works of art by Sutherland, Feibusch, Procktor, Chagall, Skelton, Piper, and Ursula Benker-Schirmer. Treasury.

Location: Centre of city; British Rail; A27, A286.
Open: All year 7.30-7 (5 in winter except for those attending Evensong). Choral Evensong daily (except Wed) during term time and occasionally visiting choirs at other times. Ministry of welcome operates. Guided tours must be booked.
Admission: Free: suggested donations adults £1 children 20p.
Refreshments: Refectory off Cathedral Cloisters with lavatory facilities (including those for the disabled). Medieval Vicars' Hall (by prior arrangement).
Conferences: Meeting room available in the Vicar's Hall (for 100 people max).
Wheelchair access (one wheelchair available on application to Vergers). Loop system in the Cathedral. Touch and hearing centre for the blind and a braille guide. Guide dogs only. Gift shops in the Bell Tower and at 23 South Street. Parking in city car and coach parks.

DANNY

(Country Houses Association)
Hurstpierpoint   BN6 9BB   map **12** V22
Telephone: (01273) 833000

Elizabethan E-shaped house, dating from 1593.

Location: Between Hassocks and Hurstpierpoint (B2116) - off New Way Lane.
Station(s): Hassocks (1 m).
Open: May-Sept Weds & Thurs 2-5. Last entry 4.30.
Admission: £2.50 Children £1. Free car park.
No dogs admitted.

DENMANS GARDEN

(Mr John Brookes)
Denmans Lane, Fontwell, nr Arundel   BN18 0SU   map **12** V21   &
Telephone: (01243) 542808
Fax: (01243) 544064

Unique 20th Century Garden artistically planted forming vistas with emphasis on colours, shapes and textures for all year interest; areas of glass areas for tender and rare species. John Brookes school of garden design in the Clock House where seminars available.

Location: Between Arundel and Chichester; turn off A27 into Denmans Lane (W of Fontwell racecourse).
Station(s): Barnham (2 m).
Open: Open daily throughout the year including all Bank Holidays except Christmas Day and Boxing Day 9-5. Coaches by appointment.
Admission: Adults £2.50 children £1.50 OAPs £2.25. Groups of 15 or more £1.95.
Refreshments: Restaurant and shop open 10-5.
Plant centre. The Country Shop. No dogs. National Gardens Scheme.

GOODWOOD HOUSE

(Duke of Richmond)
Chichester   PO18 0PX   map **12** V21
Telephone: (01243) 774107
Fax: (01243) 774313

Bought by the first Duke of Richmond (son of King Charles II and a French female spy!) and home of the Dukes of Richmond ever since, Goodwood House is filled with the treasures collected by all ten Dukes. They include Canaletto's first London paintings, tapestries, family portraits by Van Dyck, Kneller, Lely, Reynolds, etc; French commodes(!) and a collection of Sèvres porcelain bought by the Third Duke when (a very bad) British Ambassador at Versailles. There are royal relics, Napoleonic booty and the bits and pieces inevitable when a family has stayed put for 300 years. Chambers, then Wyatt, enlarged the House to hold these Collections. Country Park for picnics near the Racecourse on crest of South Downs. Pleasure flights available from the Goodwood Aerodrome together with flying instruction to top standards. Festival of Speed in June. Glorious Goodwood Racecourse for 20 summer racedays.

Location: 3½ m NE of Chichester, approach roads A283 & A286, A27. Aerodrome 1 m from House.
Station(s): Chichester.
Open: 2-5 Easter Sun & Mon then Sun & Mon to 25 Sept (except 23/24 April 14/15 May 18/19/25/26 June and event days; prospective visitors should check these dates before setting out) also Tues Wed & Thurs in Aug.
Admission: Large free car park for visitors to House during open hours; For all information and group rates contact the House Secretary. Goodwood House, Chichester, West Sussex PO18 0PX.
Refreshments: Teas in one of the State Rooms for pre-booked parties (min 15); unbooked teas for individuals and families on days when no evening function, or tea and biscuits at The Goodwood Park Hotel Golf and Country Club at the Park Gate (east). Weddings and Functions throughout the year.
House suitable for wheelchairs (no steps); a wheelchair is available.

HAMMERWOOD PARK

(David Pinnegar, Esq)
nr East Grinstead   RH19 3QE   map **12** V23   △ &
Telephone: (01342) 850594
Fax: (01342) 850864

HAMMERWOOD PARK is said by visitors to be the most interesting house in
Sussex. Built in 1792, the house was the first work of **Latrobe**, the architect of
The White House and The Capitol, Washington D.C., U.S.A. Set in
Reptonesque parkland on the edge of the Ashdown Forest, the house is an early
example of Greek Revival. In 1982 David Pinnegar purchased the house as a near
ruin from the pop-group Led Zeppelin. Award winning restoration works have
been completed and one of the most ambitious *trompe-l'oeil* decoration schemes
of this century has recently been painted in the staircase hall. Just one room
remains spectacularly derelict. Various collections include photographica, musical instruments, and a copy of the **Elgin Marbles.** Guided tours by the owner and
his family, luscious cream teas and musical evenings bring the house to life.

Location: 3½ m E of East Grinstead on A264 Tunbridge Wells; 1 m W of Holtye.
Station(s): East Grinstead
Open: Easter Mon-end Sept Wed Sat & Bank Hol Mons 2-5.30. Guided tour starts just after
2. Coaches (21 seats or more) by appointment. School groups welcome.
Admission: £3.50 Children £1.50.
Refreshments: Luscious cream teas in the Elgin Room.

HIGH BEECHES GARDENS

(High Beeches Gardens Conservation Trust. Reg. non profit making Charity)
Handcross   RH17 6HQ   map **12** U22   △
Telephone: (01444) 400589

Twenty acres of enchanting landscaped woodland and water gardens, with
Magnolias, Camellias, Rhododendrons, and Azaleas in Spring. In Autumn this is
one of the most brilliant gardens for leaf colour. Gentians and Asiatic Primulas
are naturalised, with Royal Fern and Gunnera in the Water Gardens. There are
four acres of Wildflower Meadows, with cowslips and many Orchids.

Location: 1 m E of A23 at Handcross, on B2110.
Open: Gardens Only Mar 17 18 19 24 25 and 26 Apr May June Sept and Oct daily 1-5
closed Wed. Coaches by appointment at all times please.

Admission: Adults £3.00 per person accompanied children free £4.50 per person for guided
groups by appointment on any day at any time.
Refreshments: Teas on Sundays in Apr, May & Oct and on Event Days. Light lunches or
teas by appointment for Groups.
Events/Exhibitions: All open 10-5. Homemade Refreshments all day. Plants for sale.
Daffodil Day - Apr 16; Bluebell Day - Apr 30; Azalea Day - May 28; Autumn Splendour -
Oct 15. Covered Bazaar, in aid of Heatherley Cheshire Home.
Sadly, gardens not suitable for wheelchairs. Regret no dogs in gardens.

LEONARDSLEE GARDENS

(The Loder Family)
Horsham   RH13 6PP   map **12** U22
Telephone: (01403) 891212

One of the most beautiful gardens in the country. Fantastic setting of natural valley with 6 lakes. Famous for camellias & magnolias in April, glorious rhododendrons and azaleas in May, tranquil Summer foliage; brilliant Autumn tints.
Rock garden, Bonsai exhibition, Alpine house. Wallabies, Deer parks. Souvenirs
& plants for sale.

Location: In Lower Beeding at junction of A279 & A281: 5 m SE of Horsham or 3 m SW
of Handcross at bottom of M23.
Open: Apr 1-Oct 31 every day 10-6 (In May 10-8).
Admission: May adults £4 children £2 Apr & June-Oct adults £3 children £2.
Refreshments: Licensed Restaurant and Tea-room.
No dogs please.

NEWTIMBER PLACE

(Andrew Clay esq)
Newtimber   BN6 9BU   map **12** V22   △
Telephone: (01273) 833104

Moated house - Etruscan style wall paintings.

Location: Off A281 between Poynings and Pyecombe.
Open: May-Aug incl Thurs 2.30-5 by appointment. Parties at other times by arrangement.
Admission: £2.

NYMANS GARDEN   The National Trust
Handcross, nr Haywards Heath   RH17 6EB   map **12** U22
Telephone: (01444) 400321 or 400002

One of the great gardens of the Sussex Weald; rare and beautiful plants, shrubs and trees from all over the world; azaleas, rhododendrons, eucyphias, hydrangeas, magnolias, camellias and roses; walled garden, hidden sunken garden, pinetum, laurel walk; romantic ruins.

Location: At Handcross just off London/Brighton M23/A23.
Station(s): Crawley 5½ m, Haywards Heath 6 m.
Open: Mar-end Oct Daily (except Mons & Tues) and open BH Mons; Wed-Fri 11-6 Sat/Sun 11-7 or sunset if earlier. Last adm 1 hour before closing.
Admission: £3.80 Children half-price. Parties of 15 or more £3 by prior arrangement with Administrator. Special joint party ticket which includes entry to Standen £5.50 available Wed-Fri.
Refreshments: Light lunches and teas in licensed tea-room. Open all year, Wed-Sun 11-5. Dogs in car park only. Wheelchair available. Braille Guide. Shop and exhibition.

PALLANT HOUSE
9 North Pallant, Chichester   PO19 1TJ   map **12** V21
Telephone: (01243) 774557

Meticulously restored Queen Anne Townhouse with eight rooms decorated and furnished in styles from early Georgian to late Victorian. Also important displays of Bow Porcelain (1747-1775) and Modern British Art (1920-1980).

Location: Chichester City centre.
Open: All year Tues-Sat 10-5.30 (last admissions 4.30).
Admission: Adults £2.50 students/Over 60s £1.70.

George Stubbs
Portrait, animal and rural painter

(1724-1806)
Produced his engraved work,
The Anatomy of a Horse, in 1766

His work can be seen in the following properties included in Historic Houses Castles and Gardens:-

Mount Stewart House
St Osyth Priory
Upton House

PARHAM HOUSE AND GARDENS
(Parham Park Ltd. - Reg. Charity No. 276673)
Pulborough   RH20 4HS   map **12** V22
Telephone: (01903) 744888
Fax: (01903) 746557

As seen in BBC TV's 'Keeping Up Appearances'. Beautiful Elizabethan House with important collection of Elizabethan and Stuart portraits, furniture, carpets, tapestries and needlework. The flowers for the arrangements in the rooms on view to visitors are grown in the 11-acre gardens, which include a four-acre walled garden with potager and herb garden.

Location: A283 Storrington-Pulborough road.
Station(s): Pulborough (Victoria line).
Open: Wed Thurs Sun and Bank Hol Mon. Afternoons from Easter Sun-first Sun in Oct Gardens 1-6 House 2-6 (last adm 5).
Admission: House and Gardens adults £4.25 OAPs £3.75 children £2.50 Gardens only adults/OAPs £3 children £1.50 Group rates for both guided (Wed & Thurs mornings only) and unguided visits available on application to The Administrator.
Refreshments: Self service teas in Big Kitchen, some outside seating.
Events/Exhibitions: Parham House Garden Weekend - 15 & 16 July '95.
Church, shop, plant sales (until the end of August). Picnic area close to large car park and House. Access for disabled to garden (House by special arrangement only); 2 wheelchairs available.

PETWORTH HOUSE   🌿 The National Trust

Petworth   GU28 0AE   map **12** V23 ♿
Telephone: (01798) 342207

Magnificent late 17th century house set in beautiful Capability Brown deer park. Recently restored rooms are North Gallery, Square Dining Room and old kitchens. Stunning carved room by Grinling Gibbons.

Location: In centre of Petworth 5½ m E of Midhurst.
Station(s): Pulborough 5 m.
Open: 1 Apr-end Oct daily except Mon and Fri. Open Good Fri and Bank Hol Mon 1-5.30 last adm 5. Pleasure grounds and car park 12.30-6. Deer Park open daily all year 8-sunset *closed* June 23-25 from 12 noon. Car park for visitors to House during open hours, 800 yds. Car park for Park only on A283, 1½ m N of Petworth.
Admission: £4 Children half-price Family ticket £10 Pre-booked parties of 15 or more £3.50. Deer park free.
Refreshments: Light lunches and teas in licensed restaurant 12.30-5 (last orders 4.30) same days as house and 19 & 26 Mar 2-5. Shop 1-5.
Dogs under control in the park - no dogs in house or Pleasure Grounds. Shop. Wheelchairs provided. No prams or pushchairs in showrooms. Braille guide. Children's quiz.

SACKVILLE COLLEGE

(Patron Earl De La Warr)
East Grinstead   RH19 3AZ   map **12** U22   △
Telephone: (01342) 323279/326561

Jacobean Almshouses founded in 1609 and still in use. Common Room, Dining Hall, Chapel and Study. Original furniture.

Location: High Street, East Grinstead off A22.
Station(s): East Grinstead.
Open: June and July Wed-Sat 2-5 Aug each day 2-5.
Admission: Adults £1.25 children 65p parties by arrangement Apr-Oct.
Refreshments: Teas to order for parties.

Giovanni Antonio Canale
- known as Canaletto
Born in Venice 1697, died 1768
Lived in England 1746 - 1755

His work can be seen in the following properties included in Historic Houses Castles and Gardens:-

> *Alnwick Castle*
> *Bowhill*
> *Goodwood House*
> *Upton House*

SAINT HILL MANOR

Saint Hill, East Grinstead   RH19 4JY   map **12** U22   △ ♿ 📷
Telephone: (01342) 326711

Fine Sussex sandstone house built in 1792 and situated near the breathtaking Ashdown Forest. Saint Hill Manor's final owner, acclaimed author and humanitarian, L. Ron Hubbard lived here for many years with his family. Under his direction extensive renovations were carried out uncovering exquisite period features hidden for over a century. Fine wood panelling, marble fireplaces, Georgian windows and plasterwork ceilings have been expertly restored to their original beauty. Outstanding features of this lovely house include a complete library of Mr. Hubbard's works, elegant Wintergarden, and the delightful Monkey Room housing John Spencer Churchill's 100 feet mural depicting many famous characters as monkeys, including his uncle Sir Winston Churchill. 59 acres of landscaped gardens, lake and woodlands.

Location: 2 miles SW of East Grinstead on Saint Hill Road off A22.
Station(s): East Grinstead
Open: Open all year. Daily tours 2pm-5pm or by appointment.
Admission: Free
Refreshments: Tea room serving light refreshments.
Events/Exhibitions: Summer concerts on the terrace. Annual European Arts Festival and musical evenings throughout the year.
Parking for cars and coaches.

ST. MARY'S HOUSE AND GARDENS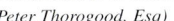
(Peter Thorogood, Esq)
Bramber, nr Steyning   BN44 3WE   map **12** V22
Telephone: (01903) 816205

Famous historic house in the downland village of Bramber. Built in 1740 by William Waynflete, Bishop of Winchester, founder of Magdalen College, Oxford. Classified (Grade 1) as 'the best example of late 15th Century timber-framing in Sussex'. Fine panelled rooms including the unique Trompe l'oeil 'Painted Room', decorated for the visit of Elizabeth I. The 'Kings Room' has connections with Charles II's escape to France in 1651. Rare 16th century painted wall leather. English furniture, ceramics, manuscripts and fine English costume -doll collection. The library houses important private collection of works by Victorian poet and artist Thomas Hood. Still a lived in family home, St. Mary's was awarded the 'Warmest Welcome' Commendation by the S.E. Tourist Board. **GARDENS** Charming gardens with amusing topiary as seen on BBC TV. Features include an exceptional example of the Living Fossil Tree, Ginkgo Biloba, a magnificently tall Magnolia Grandiflora, and the mysterious ivy-clad Monk's Walk.

Location: 10 m NW of Brighton in village of Bramber off A283.
Station(s): Shoreham-by-Sea (4 m). Trains from London (Victoria).
Open: Easter Sun-last Sun in Sept Sun & Mon including Bank Hol Mons 2-6. Also Tues Wed Thurs in August 2-6. **Coach party bookings** daily morning or afternoon by prior arrangement from Apr-Oct.
Admission: £3.50 OAPs £3.20 children £2. Reduced rates for parties £3 (25 or over). Free coach and car parking in grounds.
Refreshments: Homemade afternoon tea in the Music Room. Catering for parties by arrangement. Seating for up to 60.

STANDEN   🍃 The National Trust
East Grinstead   RH19 4NE   map **12** U22
Telephone: (01342) 323029

A family 'Arts and Crafts' inspired house and garden built 100 years ago. Wonderful collection of William Morris interiors - wallpapers, textiles, period furniture and paintings. The gardens have fine views across the Medway Valley.

Location: 2 m S of East Grinstead signposted from the Turners Hill road (B2110).
Station(s): East Grinstead (2 m).
Open: March 18/19 & 25/26 1.30-4.30 last admission 4pm. Apr 1-end Oct Wed-Sun (incl Good Fri) 1.30-5.30 (last adm 5). Open Bank Holiday Mons. Access may be restricted at busy times. Pre-booked parties Wed Thurs & Fri only telephone Administrator.
Admission: House and Garden £4 Sat Sun Good Fri & Bank Hol Mon £4.80. Garden only £2.50 and £3.00 respectively. Children half price Parties £3.50. Special joint party ticket which includes entry to Nymans Garden £5.50 available Wed-Fri.
Refreshments: Light lunches and teas served from 12.30-5.00. March 1.30-4 (teas only).
Events/Exhibitions: Please phone for details.
Dogs admitted to car park & woodland walks only. Wheelchairs provided; disabled drivers may park near house with prior permission from Administrator. Shop. *No pushchairs or back-packs in house.*

WAKEHURST PLACE GARDEN   🍃 The National Trust
(Administered by Royal Botanic Gardens, Kew)
Ardingly, nr Haywards Heath   RH17 6TN   map **12** U22   ♿
Telephone: (01444) 892701 or (0181) 332 5066

A wealth of exotic plant species including many fine specimens of trees and shrubs. Picturesque watercourse linking several ponds and lakes. Heath garden and rock walk.

Location: 1½ m NW of Ardingly on B2028.
Station(s): Haywards Heath 6 m. East Grinstead 6½ m.
Open: All the year Daily Nov-end Jan 10-4 Feb & Oct 10-5 Mar 10-6 Apr-end of Sept 10-7. Last adm ½ hour before closing. *Closed Christmas Day & New Year's Day.* Opening times may be subject to alteration. Please telephone 0181 332 5066 or 01444 892701 for up to date information.

Admission: £4 Children (16 and under) £1.50. Reduced rates for Students/OAPs £2 Pre-booked parties but prices may be subject to alteration. *Visitors should check with Wakehurst Place for 1995 prices.*
Refreshments: Self service restaurant (not NT) open daily all year.
No dogs except guide dogs. Wheelchairs provided. Exhibition in Mansion. Book shop open (not NT).

THE WEALD AND DOWNLAND OPEN AIR MUSEUM
Singleton, nr Chichester   map **12** V21   △
Telephone: (01243) 811348

The Museum is rescuing and re-erecting historic Buildings from South-East England. The Collection illustrates the history of vernacular architecture in the Weald and Downland area. Exhibits include a Medieval Farmstead, Garden and History of Farming Exhibition centred on Bayleaf Farmhouse (above) Timber-framed Houses, a Tudor Market Hall, a 16th century Treadwheel. Farm Buildings include two 18th century Barns and a Granary, a Blacksmith's Forge, Plumber's and Carpenter's Workshops, a Village School and a History of Brickwork Exhibition. A 'Hands On' gallery explores building materials and techniques.

Location: 6 m N of Chichester on A286 just S of Singleton.
Open: Mar 1-Oct 31 daily 11-5 Nov 1-Feb 28 Wed Sat and Sun only 11-4 Dec 26-Jan 1 daily 11-4.
Admission: Charged. Parties by arrangement (group rates available).
Refreshments: Light refreshments during main season.

WEST DEAN GARDENS
(The Edward James Foundation)
nr Chichester   PO18 0QZ   map **12** V21   ♿
Telephone: (01243) 811303

Extensive downland garden with 300' pergola, water garden, herbaceous borders, 3 acre working walled kitchen garden with recently restored Victorian glasshouses, 13 in total, and Mower museum. Circuit walk (2¼ miles) through parkland and the 45 acre St. Roches Arboretum. House not open.

Location: 6 m N of Chichester on A286, nr Weald & Downland Open Air Museum.
Open: Apr-Oct incl. daily 11-5 (last adm 4.30) parties by arrangement.
Admission: Adults £3 OAPs £2.50 children £1.50 pre-booked parties 20+ £2.50 per person.
Refreshments: Available.
Coach and car parking. Sorry no dogs.

TYNE & WEAR

GIBSIDE   The National Trust
Gibside   NE16 6BG   map 9 N19
Telephone: (01207) 542255

Gibside is one of the finest 18th century designed landscapes in the north of England. The chapel was built to James Paine's design soon after 1760. Outstanding example of Georgian architecture approached along a terrace with an oak avenue. Walk along River Derwent through woodland.

Location: 6 m SW of Gateshead; 20 m NW of Durham between Rowlands Gill and Burnopfield.
Open: Apr 1-end Oct daily except Mon (open Bank Hol Mons) 11-5. Last admission 4.30.
Admission: Chapel & Grounds £2.80 Children half-price. Pre-booked parties £2.50.
Refreshments: Tea-room.
Shop, picnic area, circular walk.

SOUTER LIGHTHOUSE   The National Trust
Whitburn   SR6 7NH   map 9 N20
Telephone: 0191-529 3161

Shore based lighthouse and associated buildings, built in 1871 - the first to be powered by an alternative electric current.

Location: 2½ m S of South Shields on A183, 5m N of Sunderland.
Open: 1-30 Apr & 1-29 Oct Sat Sun & Wed. Good Fri & Easter Mon 11-5. Last admission 4.30. 1 May-30 Sept daily except Fri weekdays 10.30-4.30 last admission 4. Sat & Sun 11-5 last admission 4.30.
Admission: £2.30 Children half-price. Pre-booked parties £1.70.
Refreshments: Restaurant.
Shop, picnic area.

TYNEMOUTH CASTLE AND PRIORY
map 9 M20
ENGLISH HERITAGE

Telephone: 0191-257 1090

Two saints were buried within the walls of this Benedictine priory, established in the 11th century on the site of an earlier abandoned monastery. Two walls of the presbytery still tower to their full height and the 15th century chantry chapel has a splendid collection of roof bosses. A fortified gatehouse was added during the Border wars, which persuaded Henry VIII to retain the priory as a royal castle after the Dissolution. The headland remained in use for coastal defence until 1956, one restored battery is open to the public.

Location: Tynemouth.
Open: Apr 1-Sept 30 10-6 daily Oct 1-31 10-4 daily Nov 1-Mar 31 10-4 Wed-Sun.
Admission: Adults £1.30 concessions £1 children 70p.

WASHINGTON OLD HALL   The National Trust
Washington   NE38 7LE   map 9 N20
Telephone: 0191-416 6879

Jacobean manor house incorporating portions of 12th century house of the Washington family.

Location: In Washington on E side of Ave; 5 m W of Sunderland (2 m from A1); S of Tyne Tunnel, follow signs for Washington New Town District 4 & then village.
Open: Apr 1-end Oct daily (closed Fri & Sat but open Good Fri) 11-5 (last adm 4.30).
Admission: £2.30 Children half-price. *Parties of 15 or more £1.80 each by prior arrangement only with Property Manager.*
Refreshments: Tea, coffee and cake available during opening hours.
Conferences: Facilities available for weddings and meetings, apply to Property Manager.
Shop. Dogs in garden only, on leads. Wheelchair access.

WARWICKSHIRE

ARBURY HALL
(The Rt Hon the Viscount Daventry)
Nuneaton   CV10 7PT   map **14** R20   △ &
Telephone: (01203) 382804
Fax: (01203) 641147

16th century Elizabethan House, gothicized late 18th century, pictures, period furniture etc. Park and landscape gardens. Arbury has been the home of the Newdegate family since the 16th century. For a country house the Gothic architecture is unique, the original Elizabethan house being Gothicised by Sir Roger Newdigate between 1750 and 1800, under the direction of Sanderson Miller, Henry Keene, and Couchman of Warwick. Beautiful plaster ceilings, pictures and fine specimens of period furniture, china and glass. Fine stable block with central doorway by Wren. Arbury Hall is situated in very large grounds and is about 1½ miles from any main road. Excellent carriage drives lined with trees. George Eliot's 'Cheveral Manor'.

Location: 2 m SW of Nuneaton off B4102.
Station(s): Nuneaton.
Open: Easter Sun-end Sept. Hall Sun & Bank Hol Mon 2-5.30 Gardens Sun & Mon 2-6 (last adm. 5). Arbury is an ideal venue for Corporate hospitality functions, promotions and as a film location etc. and the Dining Room is also available for exclusive luncheon and dinner functions. Wheelchair access ground floor only.
Admission: Hall and Gardens adults £3.50 children £2 Gardens adults £2 children £1 organised parties most days (25 or over) special terms by prior arrangement with Administrator. School parties also welcome. Free car park.
Refreshments: Available on all open days. Set meals arranged for parties.
Events/Exhibitions: Craft Fairs held twice a year. Motor Transport Spectacular in early summer.
Conferences: Suitable for small conferences with capacity of 50 for seated meals and 120 for buffets. Marquees can also be provided for larger meetings.

BADDESLEY CLINTON   🌿 The National Trust
Rising Lane, Lapworth, Knowle   B93 0DQ   map **14** S19   &
Telephone: (01564) 783294

A romantically sited medieval moated manor house, with 120 acres, dating back to the 14th century and little changed since 1634.

Location: ¾ m W of A4141 Warwick to Birmingham Road, nr Chadwick End; 7½ m NW of Warwick; 15 m SE of Birmingham.
Station(s): Lapworth (2 m) (not Suns).

Open: Mar 4 to end of Sept Wed to Sun & Bank Hol Mon 2-6. *Closed Good Fri* Grounds and shop open from 12.30. Oct Wed to Suns 12.30-4.30. Mar 6 Wed to Sun 2-6. Last admissions 30 mins before closing. Coach parties (not Sun) by prior arrangement. Timed tickets issued to control numbers in house.
Admission: £4.20 Children £2.10 grounds only £2.10. Family tickets £11.60.
Refreshments: Lunches and teas in licensed restaurant from 12.30-5.30 same days as house. Closed 2-2.30 (Oct 4.30). Also open Nov 1 to Dec 17 Wed to Sun 12.30-4.30.
No prams, pushchairs or back carriers in the house. No dogs. Wheelchair available. Shop. Restaurant.

CHARLECOTE PARK   The National Trust
Warwick   CV35 9ER   map **14** S19   △ &

Telephone: (01789) 470277

Originally built by the Lucy family, 1550s. Refurbished 1830s in Elizabethan Revival style. 'Capability' Brown Deer park.

Location: 5 m E of Stratford-upon-Avon on the N side of B4086.

Station(s): Leamington Spa No 18 bus.

Open: Apr to end Oct Fri to Tues 11-6 House closed 1-2.(*Closed* Good Friday. Last admission to house 5. Parties (including schools) by prior arrangement only. Evening guided tours for pre-booked parties Mons, May to Sept 7.30-9.30.

Admission: £4 Children £2 Family ticket £11 Full price for evening visits (incl. NT members). Group rate & introductory talk available weekdays only.

Refreshments: Morning coffee, lunches, afternoon teas in the Orangery Restaurant (Licensed) 11-5.30. Picnics in Deer park only.

No dogs. Wheelchairs provided. Shop.

"GHOSTS"

Ghosts are in residence at the following properties included in Historic Houses Castles and Gardens:-

Blickling Hall - *Anne Boleyn*

Breamore House - *Haunted picture - if touched, death on the same day*

East Riddleden Hall - *5 ghosts including lady*

in Grey Hall Lady's Chamber

Fountains Abbey & Studley Royal - *Choir of monks chanting in Chapel of Nine Altars*

Hinton Ampner - *Nocturnal noises*

Ightham Mote - *Supernatural presence*

Lindisfarne Castle - *Monk, and group of monks on causeway*

Lyme Park - *Unearthly peals of bells and lady in white, funeral procession through park*

Malmesbury House - *Ghost of a cavalier*

Overbecks Museum & Garden - *'Model' ghost in the Children's room (for them to spot)*

Rockingham Castle - *Lady Dedlock*

Rufford Old Hall - *Elizabeth Hesketh*

Scotney Castle Garden - *Man rising from the lake*

Sizergh Castle & Garden - *Poltergeist*

Speke Hall - *Ghost of woman in tapestry room*

Springhill - *Ghost of a woman*

Sudbury Hall - *Lady in Green, seen on stairs*

Tamworth Castle - *Haunted bedroom*

Treasurer's House - *Troop of Roman soldiers marching through the cellar*

Wallington House - *Invisible birds beating against the windows accompanied by heavy breathing*

Washington Old Hall - *Grey lady walking through corridors*

COUGHTON COURT   The National Trust

(Mrs Clare Throckmorton)
Alcester   B49 5JA   map **14** S19
Telephone: (01789) 400777 (01789) 762435 (visitor information)
Fax: (01789) 765544

Coughton Court has been the home of the Throckmortons since the fifteenth century and the family still live there today. The magnificent Tudor gatehouse was built around 1530 with the north and south wings completed ten or twenty years later. The gables and the first story of these wings are of typical mid-sixteenth century half-timber work. Of particular interest to visitors is the Throckmorton family history from Tudor times to the present generation. On view are family portraits through the centuries, together with furniture, porcelain, tapestries and other family memorabilia and recent photographs. A strong Roman Catholic theme runs through the family history as the Throckmortons have maintained their Catholic religion until the present day. The house has a strong connection with the Gunpowder Plot and also suffered damage during the Civil War. The house stands in 25 acres of gardens and grounds which also contain two churches and a lake. A new formal garden was constructed in 1992 with designs based on an Elizabethan knot garden in the courtyard. Further extensive gardens development plus new orchard and bog garden taking place 1995. Visitors can also enjoy a specially created walk beside the River Arrow, returning to the house alongside the lake. Exhibitions of Gunpowder Plot and Childrens Clothes.

Location: 2 m N of Alcester on A435.
Station(s): Redditch.
Open: Apr Sat Sun 12-5 Easter Sat-Wed 12-5 (All Bank Hol Mons incl. Easter Mon 12-5 (closed Good Fri May) end Sept daily (except Thurs & Fri) 12-5 Oct Sat Sun 12-5. Last admissions to house 30 mins before closing. Evening Guided tours for pre-booked parties Mon-Wed Garden tours by appointment. Grounds open same days as house but 11-5.30 (5 in Oct).
Admission: Adults £4.50 children £2.25 family ticket £12 Grounds only £2.50. Parties by prior written arrangement no party rate or membership concessions for out-of-hours visits.
Refreshments: Restaurant open 11.30-5.30 for coffee, lunches and teas (licensed).
Events/Exhibitions: Gunpowder Plot Exhibition, Childrens' Clothes (open all season).Entrance included in admission.
Shop and plant centre. Limited access for wheelchairs in house. Riverside walk and new garden suitable for wheelchairs. Dogs on leads and picnics in car park only. House, grounds, shop and restaurant managed by the family.

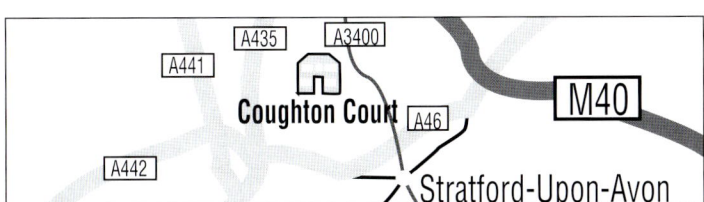

FARNBOROUGH HALL   The National Trust

nr Banbury   OX17 1DU   map 7 S20
Telephone: (01295) 690202

Home of the Holbech family since 1684 reconstructed in early 18th century. The house incorporates fine plasterwork and ancient sculpture. e mile terrace walk feature temples and obelisk.

Location: 6 m N of Banbury; ½ m W of A423.
Open: House, grounds and terrace walk Apr to end of Sept Wed and Sat 2-6. Also May 7 & 8 2-6. Terrace Walk only Thurs & Fri 2-6. Last adm 5.30.
Admission: House, grounds and terrace walk £2.70 Garden and terrace walk £1.50. Terrace walk only Thurs & Fri £1. Children half-price. *No reductions for parties.* Parties by prior written arrangement only.
Dogs in grounds only, on leads. No indoor photography. Farnborough Hall is occupied and administered by Mr. & Mrs. G Holbech.

HALL'S CROFT

Stratford-upon-Avon   map 14 S19   △ &
Telephone: (01789) 292107

A fine Tudor house complete with period furniture and walled garden, where Shakespeare's daughter Susanna and Dr. John Hall lived.

Location: Old Town.

Open: Mar 20-Oct 19 Mon-Sat 9.30-5 Sun 10-5 Jan 1-Mar 19 and Oct 20-Dec 31 Mon-Sat 10-4 Sun 10.30-4.
Admission: (1995 prices) adult £1.90 child 90p.
Refreshments: Tea-room/restaurant open daily and bookings can be taken for small parties. Tel: (01789) 297848.

ANNE HATHAWAY'S COTTAGE

Stratford-upon-Avon   map 14 S19   △
Telephone: (01789) 292100

The picturesque thatched home of Anne Hathaway before her marriage to Shakespeare. Attractive garden and orchard, Shakespeare Tree Garden and pleasant walks.

Location: Shottery (1¼ m).
Open: Mar 20-Oct 19 Mon-Sat 9-5.30 Sun 9.30-5.30 Jan 1-Mar 19 and Oct 20-Dec 31 Mon-Sat 9.30-4 Sun 10-4.
Admission: (1995 prices) adult £2.30 child £1.10. **Free coach park.**
Refreshments: On site including lovely tea-garden in summer. Thatch Restaurant caters for coach parties by prior arrangement (01789) 293122.

HONINGTON HALL

(B. Wiggin, Esq)
Shipston-on-Stour   CV36 5AA   map 7 S19   △
Telephone: (01608) 661434

Originally built by the Parker family in 1680. Contains fine 18th century plasterwork.

Location: 10 m S of Stratford-on-Avon; ½ m E of A3400.
Open: June July Aug Weds & Bank Hol Mons 2.30-5. Parties at other times by appointment.
Admission: Adults £2.75 children £1.

KENILWORTH CASTLE

map 14 S19
Telephone: (01926) 52078

One of the grandest ruins in England, this castle was made famous by Sir Walter Scott. Gone now is the great lake that once surrounded it, but still standing is the huge Noman keep with walls nearly 20ft (6m) thick in places. Inside the encircling walls built by King John are the remains of John of Gaunt's chapel and great hall, the Earl of Leicester's stables and gatehouse. The most splendid royal occasion took place in 1575 when Queen Elizabeth I was entertained lavishly by the Earl with music and dancing, fireworks and hunting, for 19 days.

Location: West side of Kenilworth.
Open: Apr 1-Sept 30 10-6 daily Oct 1-Mar 31 daily 10-4.
Admission: Adults £2 concessions £1.50 children £1.

Gertrude Jekyll
writer and gardener
(1843-1932)

Her designs were used at the following properties included in Historic Houses Castles and Gardens:-

> *Barrington Court*
> *Castle Drogo*
> *Goddards*
> *Hatchlands Park*
> *Hestercombe House and*
> *Gardens*
> *Knebworth*
> *Lindisfarne Castle*

A collection of her tools can be found at Guildford Museum

Sir Edwin Landseer Lutyens

Architect

His work can be seen at the following properties included in Historic Houses Castles and Gardens:-

> *Castle Drogo*
> *Goddards*
> *Great Dixter*
> *Great Maytham Hall*
> *Hestercombe House and*
> *Gardens*
> *Knebworth*
> *Lindisfarne Castle*

LORD LEYCESTER HOSPITAL

(The Governors of Lord Leycester Hospital)
High Street, Warwick CV34 4BH   map **14** S19 △
Telephone: (01926) 492797

In 1100 the chapel of St. James was built over the West Gate of Warwick and became the centre for the Guilds established by Royal Charter in 1383. In 1571 Robert Dudley, Earl of Leycester, founded his Hospital for twelve 'poor' persons in the buildings of the Guilds, which had been dispersed in 1546. The Hospital has been run ever since for retired or disabled ex-Servicemen and their wives. The buildings have been restored to their original condition including the Great Hall of King James, the Guildhall (museum), the Chaplain's Hall (Queen's Own Hussars Regimental Museum) and the Brethren's Kitchen.

Location: W gate of Warwick (A46).
Station(s): Warwick (¾ m).
Open: All the year Tues-Sun 10-5 (summer) 10-4 (winter). Last admission 15 mins earlier. *Closed Mon, Good Fri & Christmas Day.*
Admission: £2.25 Children (under 14) £1 OAPs/Students £1.50. Free car park.
Refreshments: (Easter-Oct) morning coffee, light lunches, afternoon teas.
Conferences: Great Hall available including facilities for receptions, concerts, corporate entertainment, dinners, luncheons.

MARY ARDEN'S HOUSE AND THE SHAKESPEARE COUNTRYSIDE MUSEUM

Stratford-upon-Avon   map **14** S19 △ &
Telephone: (01789) 293455

The Tudor farmhouse where Shakespeare's mother lived as a child, with a museum of farming and country life incorporating the Victorian Glebe Farm. Interesting dovecote, Rural Crafts, Falconry displays all day. Field walk. Rare breeds. Picnic area.

Location: Wilmcote (3½ m).
Open: Mar 20-Oct 19 Mon-Sat 9.30-5 Sun 10-5 Jan 1-Mar 19 and Oct 20-Dec 31 Mon-Sat 10-4 Sun 10.30-4.
Admission: (1995 prices) adult £3.20 child £1.40. **Also, at this property only: family ticket £8 (2 adults + 2/3 children).**
Refreshments: On site. Bookings can be taken for group catering (01789) 298574.

NEW PLACE/NASH'S HOUSE

Stratford-upon-Avon   map **14** S19 △ &
Telephone: (01789) 292325

Foundations of Shakespeare's last home, preserved in an Elizabethan style knott garden setting with Nash's House adjoining which is furnished in period style.

Location: Chapel Street.
Open: Mar 20-Oct 19 Mon-Sat 9.30-5 Sun 10-5 Jan 1-Mar 19 and Oct 20-Dec 31 Mon-Sat 10-4 Sun 10.30-4.
Admission: (1995 prices) adult £1.90 child 90p.

PACKWOOD HOUSE 🍃 The National Trust

Lapworth B94 6AT   map **14** S19
Telephone: (01564) 782024

Elizabethan house with mid 17th century additions. Tapestry, needlework, Carolean formal garden, and yew garden of c. 1650 representing the Sermon on the Mount.

Location: 2 m SE of Hockley Heath (which is on A3400) 11 m SE of Birmingham.
Station(s): Lapworth (1½ m); Dorridge (2 m).
Open: Apr to end of Sept Wed to Sun & Bank Hol Mons 2-6. *Closed* Good Fri. Oct Wed to Suns 12.30-4.30. Last adm 30 minutes before closing.
Admission: £3.50 Children £1.75 Family tickets £9.60. Gardens only £2. Parties by prior written arrangement only.
Refreshments: Picnics welcome in car park and avenue opposite main gate.
Shop. No dogs. No prams in House. Wheelchair access to part of garden and ground floor. No sharp heeled shoes. No large bags.

RAGLEY HALL
(The Earl and Countess of Yarmouth)
Alcester　B49 5NJ　map **14** S19　△ &
Telephone: (01789) 762090
Fax: (01789) 764791

Built in 1680. Superb baroque plasterwork, fine paintings, china, furniture and works of art including the mural 'The Temptation'. Gardens, park and lake. Woodland trails, lakeside picnic areas. Superb Adventure Wood play-ground and maze for children.

Location: 2 m SW of Alcester on Birmingham/Alcester/Evesham Road (A435); 8 m from Stratford-upon-Avon; 20 m from Birmingham.
Open: Apr 1-Oct 1 Park & Gardens open daily 10-6 (except Mon & Fri but open Bank Holiday Mons) House open daily except Mon and Fri 11-5 (open Bank Holiday Monday) Park open every day July & Aug.
Admission: House, Gardens & Park (includes Adventure Wood and Woodland Trails) £4.50 OAPs/group rate adults £4 children £3.50. Free car park.
Refreshments: Licensed Cafe1teria open daily except Mon and Fri, please telephone for group reservations. Refreshments available in park. **Advance Bookings:** (at any time of the year). Coach parties welcome by arrangement. Lunches and teas - parties please write for menus. Private dinner parties for any number up to 150 can be arranged. For further information please contact: The Business Manager, Ragley Hall, Alcester,Warwickshire B49 5NJ. Telephone: Alcester (01789) 762090.
Conferences: Available for non-residential conferences and dinners. Activity days. Photographic locations.
Dogs welcome on leads in Park and on Woodland Trails, not in House, Gardens or Adventure Wood.

SHAKESPEARE'S BIRTHPLACE
Stratford-upon-Avon　map **14** S19　△ &
Telephone: (01789) 204016

The half-timbered house where Shakespeare was born, containing many rare Shakespearian exhibits.

Location: Henley Street.
Open: Mar 20-Oct 19 Mon-Sat 9-5.30 Sun 9.30-5.30 Jan 1-Mar 19 and Oct 20-Dec 31 Mon-Sat 9.30-4 Sun 10-4.
Admission: (1995 prices) incl. Exhibition adult £2.75 child £1.30. Free Coach Terminal.
Refreshments: Shakespeare Coffee House opposite and many other options.

THE SHAKESPEARIAN PROPERTIES
Stratford-upon-Avon   map 14 S19

THE SHAKESPEARIAN PROPERTIES
STRATFORD-UPON-AVON

Besides the world-famous attractions of Shakespeare's Birthplace and Anne Hathaway's Cottage there are three other houses associated with William Shakespeare and his family.

Mary Arden's House and the Shakespeare Country Museum, Wilmcote. Tudor farmstead home of Shakespeare's mother plus turn-of-the-century Glebe Farmhouse. Exhibits illustrating country life over 400 years. Gypsy caravans, dovecote, rare breeds, field walk, and falconry displays all day. Refreshments and picnic area. Ideally allow 2 hours.

Hall's Croft. A delightful Elizabethan town house, once the home or Dr. Hall, Shakespeare's physician son-in-law. Exceptional furniture and paintings. 17th century-style doctor's dispensary and exhibition about medical life in Shakespeare's time. Lovely secluded garden. Tea Room/restaurant.

New Place/Nash's House

The site and grounds of Shakespeare's last home, with colourful Elizabethan-style knott garden, provides a quiet oasis in the heart of Stratford. Nash's House adjoining the site contains fine Tudor furniture.

Single admission fees available but particularly good value offered by 3-Property Town Heritage Trail or 5-Property Inclusive Tickets

Open Daily all year round
except on the mornings of Good Friday, and 1st January, and all day on Christmas Eve, Christmas Day, and Boxing Day. For those needing transport there is a regular guided bus tour service connecting the town properties with Anne Hathaway's Cottage and Mary Arden's House.

See editorial for opening times and admission fees.

Presented by The Shakespeare Birthplace Trust which is a registered charity incorporated by Act of Parliament to promote appreciation of William Shakespeare's life and works and to maintain the Shakespearian properties.

Admission: Visits to several of the properties: *Special ticket for all 3 in-town properties with self-guiding leaflet for the Town Heritage Trial.* Price: adults £5.50 children £2.50 Senior citizens/students £5 family £14. *For admission to all five Shakepearian Properties, inclusive tickets with descriptive leaflet are available at each property.* Adults £8 children £3.60 Senior citizens/students £7 family £21. There are special rates for Students and school groups. Enquiries: Shakespeare Centre Stratford-upon-Avon CV37 6QW Tel: (01789) 204061 Fax: (01789) 296083.

UPTON HOUSE   🌿 **The National Trust**
Banbury   OX15 6HT   map 7 S20   ♿
Telephone: (01295) 670266

17th century house remodelled 1927-29 containing one of the National Trust's finest collections of paintings and porcelain. Tapestries and 18th century furniture. Beautiful terraced garden descending to lakes and bog garden in deep valley.

Location: 1 m S of Edge Hill; 7 m NW of Banbury on the Stratford Road (A422).
Station(s): Banbury, 7 miles.
Open: 1 Apr-31 Oct Sat-Wed (inc BH Mon) 2-6. Closed Good Fri. Last admission 5.30.*Note: Entry to the House, tea-room and shop is by timed tickets at peak times on Suns and Bank Hols, therefore delays are possible.* Motorized buggy with driver available for access to/from lower garden, manned by volunteers of the Banbury NT Association.
Admission: £4.60 Children £2.30 Family ticket £12.60 Garden only £2.30.
Refreshments: Tea-room in House.
No indoor photography. Wheelchair available. Wheelchair access ground floor only. Shop.

WARWICK CASTLE
(Warwick Castle Ltd)
Warwick CV34 4QU map **14** S19 △
Telephone: (01926) 408000
Fax: (01926) 401692

Situated on the banks of the River Avon, Warwick Castle is the epitome of a Mediaeval fortress and is renowned as the finest Mediaeval Castle in England. 'Kingmaker-A preparation for battle' is a dramatic new attraction housed in the Castle's 14th century undercroft. Portraying life in the year 1471 as Warwick the Kingmaker prepares his men for battle, swords are sharpened, armour polished and cannons are prepared as the household makes ready. Visitors can experience the sights, sounds and smells and are able to touch everything they see within this attraction. 'A Royal Weekend Party' captures the Victorian period of the Castle's history. Over 30 wax portraits recreate an actual event in 1898 with guests including a young Winston churchill and the future Edward VII. The Great Hall, Armoury and State Rooms contain an outstanding collection of arms, armour, pictures and furniture. The Towers, Ramparts and Dungeon are testimony to the Castle's rich and varied history.

Location: In the centre of Warwick, only 8 m from Stratford-upon-Avon and 1½ hours journey from London.
Station(s): Warwick (½ m); Leamington Spa (2 m).
Open: Every day (except Christmas Day) 10-6 (1 Apr-28 Oct) 10-5 (29 Oct-31 Mar).
Admission: (From March 1995) Adults £8.25 Children (4-16 yrs incl.) £4.95 Seniors £5.95 Students £6.25.
Refreshments: 2 Restaurants, 1 Cafe, Picnic areas.

Thomas Gainsborough (1727-1787)

His paintings can be seen at the following properties included in Historic Houses Castles and Gardens:-

Arundel Castle	*Knowle*
Bowhill	*Parham House &*
Christchurch Mansion	*Gardens*
Dalmeny House	*Petworth House*
Elton Hall	*Shalom Hall*
Gainsborough's House	*Upton House*
Ickworth Park & Garden	*Waddesdon Manor*
Firle Place	*Weston Park*
Kenwood, The Iveagh	*Woburn Abbey*
Bequest	

WEST MIDLANDS

ASTON HALL
(Birmingham City Council)
Birmingham map **14** R19 △
Telephone: 0121-327 0062

A fine Jacobean house built 1618-1635 it was home to the Holte family for 200 years. Many of the rooms are furnished as period settings and decorated with outstanding Jacobean plasterwork and panelling. A great staircase with elaborate oak balustrade leads up through the formal state rooms to the impressive Long Gallery with oak panelling and elaborate chimneypiece of stone and alabaster. There are many events throughout the season and the successful bi-ennial Candlelight evenings during the winter show the hall as it would have been 300 years ago. A branch of Birmingham Museums and Arts.

Location: 2½ m from centre of city.
Station(s): Aston (¾ m).
Open: Daily from late March to late October.
Admission: Free. School parties can arrange to visit throughout the year.
Free parking for cars and coaches next to the Albert Road entrance.

BLAKESLEY HALL
(Birmingham City Council)
Birmingham map **14** R19
Telephone: (0121) 783 2193

A timber-framed yeoman's farmhouse c.1590 carefully furnished to an inventory of the period. Built for Richard Smallbroke, a leading merchant in late 16th century Birmingham, with original wall paintings and diminutive Long Gallery. Also contains displays of building methods and 17th century pottery from a single excavation. In walking distance of Yardley Village (medieval church, trust school, Georgian cottages). Pre-booked parties by arrangement. Summer events. Admission is free. A branch of Birmingham Museums and Arts.

Location: 3 m from city centre; entrance in Blakesley Road.
Station(s): Stechford (¾ m); Birmingham New Street. Buses: 16 & 17, 11 on Outer Circle.
Open: Late Mar-end Oct 1993 - Daily 2-5.
Admission: Free. School parties can arrange to visit throughout the year.

Lancelot 'Capability' Brown

Born 1716 in Northumberland, Capability Brown began work at the age of 16 in the vegetable gardens of Sir William and Lady Loraine at Kirharle Tower. He left Northumberland in 1739, and records show that he worked at Stowe until 1749. It was at Stowe that Brown began to study architecture, and to submit his own plans. It was also at Stowe that he devised a new method of moving and replanting mature trees.

Brown married Bridget Wayet in 1744 and began work on the estate at Warwick Castle in 1749. He was appointed Master Gardener at Hampton Court in 1764, and planted the Great Vine at Hampton Court in 1768. Blenheim Palace designs are considered amongst Brown's finest work, and the technical achievements were outstanding even for the present day.

Capability Brown died in February 1783 of a massive heart attack. A monument beside the lake at Croome Court was erected which reads "To the memory of Lancelot Brown, who by the powers of his inimitable and creative genius formed this garden scene out of a morass". There is also a portrait of Brown at Burghley.

Capability Brown was involved in the design of grounds at the following properties included in Historic Houses Castles and Gardens:-

Audley End	*Longleat*
Berrington Hall	*Luton Hoo*
Bowood	*Moccas Court*
Burghley House	*Petworth House*
Burton Constable	*Sledmere House*
Charlecote Park	*Stowe (Stowe*
Chilham Castle Gardens	*School)*
(reputed)	*Syon House*
Clandon Park	*Warwick Castle*
Claremont	*Weston Park*
Chillington Hall	*Wimpole Hall*
Corsham Court	*Wrest Park and*
Fawley Court	*Gardens*
Highclere Castle	

CASTLE BROMWICH HALL GARDENS
Birmingham   map **14** S19   ♿
Telephone: 0121-749 4100

CASTLE BROMWICH HALL GARDENS

An 18th Century, 10–Acre Garden being expertly restored to its former glory using plants, shrubs, trees and architectural features of that age.

A guided tour of these historic gardens is of equal interest to the lay person, the garden lover or expert. Enjoy the peace and tranquility of the walled garden on the edge of a busy city. Open daily April to September (except Fridays, or by arrangement) at the heart of Castle Bromwich village. All the usual visitors facilities.

Tel: 0121–749 4100

Castle Bromwich Hall Gardens Trust, Chester Road, Castle Bromwich, Birmingham B36 9BT

A vision of England more than 250 years ago. The ongoing restoration, started nine years ago, now provides visitors, academics and horticulturists the opportunity of seeing a unique collection of historic plants, shrubs, medicinal and culinary herbs and a fascinating plant collection. The Gardens are a cultural gem and an example of the Formal English Garden of the 18th century.

Location: 4m E of Birmingham 1m from exit 5 of the M6 (exit Northbound only).
Open: Mainly Apr-Sept (others by arrangement) Mon-Thur 1.30-4.30 *closed* Fri. Sat Sun Public Holidays 2-6. Guided tours Wed Sat Sun.
Admission: £2 Concessions for seniors and children.
Refreshments: Coffee shop, but also light meals by arrangement.
Gift shop.

Giovanni Antonio Canale - known as Canaletto Born in Venice 1697, died 1768 Lived in England 1746 - 1755

His work can be seen in the following properties included in Historic Houses Castles and Gardens:-

> *Alnwick Castle*
> *Bowhill*
> *Goodwood House*
> *Upton House*

HAGLEY HALL

(The Viscount & Viscountess Cobham)
nr Stourbridge DY9 9LG map **14** S18 △
Telephone: (01562) 882408
Fax: (01562) 882632

The last of the great Palladian Houses, designed by Sanderson Miller and completed in 1760. The House contains the finest example of Rococo plasterwork by Francesco Vassali, and a unique collection of 18th century furniture and family portraits including works by Van Dyck, Reynolds and Lely. Teas in the House. Receptions and private dinner parties by arrangement throughout the year.

Location: Just off A456 Birmingham to Kidderminster; 12 m from Birmingham within easy reach M5 (exit 3 or 4), M6 or M42.
Station(s): Hagley (1 m) (not Suns); Stourbridge Junction (2 m).
Open: Jan 16-Mar 9 daily except Sats closed Feb 9 and 10. Thereafter open only Apr 14-21 May 28-June 1 Aug 27-29 2-5.
Admission: Open for pre-booked parties by arrangement. For further details, please telephone (01562) 882408.
Refreshments: Tea available in the House.
Conferences: Specialists in corporate entertaining.

WIGHTWICK MANOR   The National Trust
Wightwick Bank, Wolverhampton WV6 8EE map **14** R18 △ &
Telephone: (01902) 761108
Fax: (01902) 764663

Strongly influenced by William Morris, the interiors of this late 19th century house include Morris wallpapers and fabrics, Kempe glass, de Morgan ware and a connoisseurs' collection of pre-Raphaelite paintings. Victorian/Edwardian gardens, terraces & pools.

Location: 3 m W of Wolverhampton, up Wightwick Bank (A454).
Station(s): Wolverhampton 3 m.
Open: House Mar 1-Dec 31 and Mar 96 Thur and Sat 2.30-5.30 also open Bank Hol Sat Sun and Mon 2.30-5.30 (Ground floor only, no guided tours). Admission to house by timed ticket. Open for pre-booked parties Wed & Thurs and special evening tours. School visits on Wed & Thurs, contact Administrator for details. Owing to the fragile nature of their contents and the requirements of conservation, some rooms cannot always be shown. Tours of the house will vary, therefore, during the year. Garden Wed & Thurs 11-6 Sat Bank Hol Sun & Bank Hol Mon 1-6 other days by appointment.
Admission: £4.50 Chd half price. Students £2.25 Gardens only £2. *Parties must book in advance (no reductions).*
Dogs in garden only, on leads.

WILTSHIRE

AVEBURY MANOR & GARDEN   The National Trust
nr Marlborough SN8 1RF map **3** U19
Telephone: (01672) 539388

A regularly altered house of monastic origin, the present buildings date from the early 16th century, with notable Queen Anne alterations and Edwardian renovation by Colonel Jenner. The topiary and flower gardens contain medieval walls, ancient box and numerous compartments.

Location: 6 m west of Marlborough.
Station(s): Pewsey 10 m. Swindon 11 m.
Open: Parts of the house are open subject to restoration work, please telephone (01672) 539388 (answer phone) to check opening times. Garden 1 Apr-31 Oct daily except Mon & Thurs 11-5.30. Last adm 5.
Admission: Garden £2.20 children £1.40. Parties £2 children £1.20.
Refreshments: Lunches and teas at Stones Restaurant and Red Lion Inn (not NT) NT shop in village.

*Sir Christopher Wren - architect
(1632-1723)*

*Fawley Court
Old Royal Observatory
Winslow Hall*

BOWOOD HOUSE & GARDENS
(The Earl and Countess of Shelburne)
Calne   map **3** U19   &
Telephone: (01249) 812102

Outstanding example of 18th century architecture, set in one of the most beautiful parks in the country, landscaped by 'Capability' Brown and not altered since his time. On display in the House is a remarkable collection of family heirlooms built up over 250 years, including Victoriana, Indiana, silver, porcelain, fine paintings and watercolours. Interesting rooms include Robert Adam's famous Library, Dr. Joseph Priestley's Laboratory where he discovered oxygen gas, and the Chapel. The 100 acre park contains many exotic trees, a 40 acre lake, Cascade, Grotto, caves and a Doric Temple, arboretum, pinetum, rose garden and Italian garden. For children, a massive Adventure Playground. For six weeks during May and June a separate garden of 50 acres features spectacular rhododendron walks.Garden centre open throughout the year.

Location: 2½ m W of Calne; 5 m SE of Chippenham. Immediately off A4 at Derry Hill village between Calne and Chippenham.
Open: House, Gardens & Grounds. Apr 1-Oct 29 - Daily incl Bank Hols 11-6. Rhododendron Walks (entrance off A342 at Kennels Lodge) six weeks during May and June (depending on season) 11-6.
Admission: Free car park. £4.50 OAPs £4 children £2.30. Party rates (20 and over) £4.15 OAPs £3.50 children £2.05. (1994 prices shown please telephone for 1995.)
Refreshments: Licensed restaurant & Garden Tea-room. **Advance Bookings:** Coach parties welcome by arrangement. Lunches and Teas - please write for party menus and further information: The Estate Office, Bowood Estate, Calne, Wiltshire SN11 0LZ.
No dogs.

BROADLEAS GARDENS (CHARITABLE TRUST)
(Lady Anne Cowdray)
Devizes   **SN10 5JQ**   map **14** U18
Telephone: (01380) 722035

A delightful garden with rare and unusual plants and trees, many Rhododendrons, Azaleas and Magnolias with interesting perennials and ground cover.

Location: 1½ m SW of Devizes on A360.
Open: Apr 1-Oct 31 Sun Wed & Thurs 2-6.
Admission: Adults £2 children (under 12) £1. Discount for parties.
Refreshments: Home-made teas on Sundays - also by prior arrangement.
Plants propagated for sale.

CHARLTON PARK HOUSE
(The Earl of Suffolk and Berkshire)
Malmesbury   map **14** U18

Jacobean/Georgian mansion, built for the Earls of Suffolk, 1607, altered by Matthew Brettingham the Younger, c. 1770.

Location: 1½ m NE Malmesbury. Entry only by signed entrance on A429, Malmesbury/Cirencester Road. No access from Charlton village.
Open: May-Oct Mon & Thurs 2-4 viewing of Great Hall, Staircase and saloon.
Admission: Adults £1 children/OAPs 50p.
Car parking limited. Unsuitable for wheelchairs. No dogs. No picnicking.

CORSHAM COURT
Mr. & Mrs. H. Wallace (Curators)
Corsham   **SN13 OBZ**   map **14** T18   &
Telephone: (01249) 701610
Fax: c/o (01249) 444556

Elizabethan (1582) and Georgian (1760-70) house, fine 18th century furniture. British, Spanish, Italian and Flemish Old Masters. Park and gardens laid out by 'Capability' Brown and Humphrey Repton. Contains one of the oldest and most distinguished collections of Old Masters and furniture.

Location: In Corsham 4 m W of Chippenham off the Bath Road (A4).
Open: Staterooms Jan 1-Nov 30 Daily except Mon and Fri 2-4.30. From Good Fri-Sept 30 2-6 (including Fri and Bank Hols) *Closed* Dec. Last adm 30 minutes before closing time. Other times by appointment. Parties welcome.
Admission: (incl gardens) £3.50 Children £2 Senior Citizens (U.K.only) £3. Parties of 20 or more by arrangement. Gardens only £1.50. £2 Children £1 Senior Citizens (U.K. only).
Refreshments: Audrey's Tea-room Tel: (01249) 714931.

THE COURTS GARDEN   🌿 The National Trust
Holt   **BA14 6RR**   map **14** U18   &
Telephone: (01225) 782340

7 acre garden of mystery - of interest to amateur and botanist. Borders, lily pond and arboretum carpeted with wild flowers.

Location: 2½ m E of Bradford-on-Avon on S side of B3107; 3 m N of Trowbridge.
Station(s): Bradford-on-Avon (2½ m). Trowbridge 3 m.
Open: GARDEN ONLY 2 Apr-31 Oct Daily except Sat 2-5. House not open.
Admission: £2.80 children £1.40. Other times by appointment please telephone the Head Gardener.
No dogs. Wheelchair access. No WCs.

GREAT CHALFIELD MANOR   🌿 The National Trust
nr Melksham   **SN12 8NJ**   map **14** U18

15th century moated manor house restored in the 20th century. Set across a moat between Parish Church and stables.

Location: 2½ m NE Bradford-on-Avon via B3109, signposted in Holt village.
Station(s): Bradford-on-Avon 3 m.
Open: 4 Apr-31 Oct Tues-Thurs. Guided tours only starting at 12.15 2.15 3 3.45 & 4.30. *Closed*Public Hols.
Admission: £3.50. Historical & other Societies by written arrangement. No reductions for parties or children.
Refreshments: Bradford-on-Avon; Melksham.
No dogs. Unsuitable for wheelchairs. No WCs.

HAMPTWORTH LODGE

(Mr N. Anderson)
Landford, Salisbury SP5 2EA map **3** V19
Telephone: (01794) 390215
Fax: (01794) 390700

Rebuilt Jacobean Manor, with period furniture.

Location: 10 m SE of Salisbury, on the C44 road linking Downton on A338, Salisbury-Bournemouth to Landford on A36, Salisbury-Southampton.
Open: House and garden daily except Suns 1 Apr-4 May 1995 2.15-5. Conducted parties only 2.30 and 3.45. Coaches by appointment only 1 Apr-30 Sept. By appointment all year, 18 hole golf course (01794) 390155, Riding (01794) 390118.
Admission: £3 under 11 free. No special arrangements for parties, but about 15 is the maximum.
Refreshments: Downton, Salisbury; nil in house.
Car parking: disabled ground floor only.

LACOCK ABBEY   The National Trust

nr Chippenham   SN15 2LG   map **14** U18
Telephone: (01249) 730227

13th century abbey converted into a house in 1540, with 18th century Gothick alterations. 19th century home of William Fox-Talbot, inventor of photography. The medieval cloisters, the brewery and the house are open to the public. Fine trees and spring flowers and rose garden.

Location: In the village of Lacock; 3 m N of Melksham; 3 m S of Chippenham just E of A350.
Station(s): Chippenham 3½ m.
Open: House 1 Apr-30 Oct daily (except Tues) 1-5.30. Cloisters and Grounds Daily 12-5.30 (last adm 5). *Closed* Good Fri.
Admission: House Grounds and Cloisters £4.20 Children £2.20 Parties (15 or more) £3.70 Children party £1.90 per person. Cloisters and Grounds only £2.10 Children £1.
Refreshments: In village (not NT).
Wheelchairs available at Museum. NT shop in village.

Grinling Gibbons (1648-1721)

Sculptor and wood carver. His work can be seen at the following properties included in Historic Houses Castles and Gardens:-

Blenheim Palace   *Lyme Park*
Breamore House   *Petworth House*
Dunham Massey   *Somerleyton Hall*
Fawley Court   *Sudbury Hall*
Kentchurch Court

LONGLEAT HOUSE

(The Marquess of Bath)
Warminster   map **3** U18
Telephone: (01985) 844400
Fax: (01985) 844885

Longleat House, built by Sir John Thynne in 1580, and still owned and lived in by the same family, was the first truly magnificent Elizabethan House to be built. Longleat was also the first Stately Home to be opened to the public in 1949. Throughout its existence, ancestors have commissioned alterations within the House; ceilings by Italian craftsmen, rooms and corridors by Wyatville, additional libraries to house the vast collection of rare books and of course, the beautiful parkland landscaped by 'Capability' Brown. In 1966 the late Lord Bath established the first drive through wild animal reserve outside Africa. It remains the model for safari parks throughout the world. Many other attractions have since been opened, making Longleat a full day's entertainment for all the family. Attractions include Victorian Kitchens, Henry, Lord Bath's Bygones, Dolls Houses, Lord Bath's Murals, Dr Who Exhibition, Butterfly Garden, Railway, World's Largest Maze, Pets Corner, Safari Boats, Historic Vehicle Exhibition, Adventure Castle for children and the Life and Times of Henry Lord Bath an exhibition of memorabilia on Edward VIII, Churchill and Hitler.

Open: Longleat House open all year (days and times may vary) please telephone before setting out. 13 Mar-29 Oct 10-6 remainder of year 10-4 Safari Park every day from Mar-Oct 10-6 (Last cars admitted 5.30 or sunset if earlier). All other attractions Apr-Sept 11-6 dates and times may vary - please telephone before your journey.
Admission: Pre-booked School Parties and Tours of Safari Park and House welcome. Reduced rates for Party Bookings in advance. Helicopter landing facilities provided advance notice needed.
Refreshments: At the Cellar Cafe in the old vaults of Longleat House.
Specialist Tours and Seminars on request. Language tours also available.

LUCKINGTON COURT

(The Hon Mrs Trevor Horn)
Luckington   SN14 6PQ   map **14** T18
Telephone: (01666) 840205

Mainly Queen Anne with magnificent group of ancient buildings. Beautiful mainly formal garden with fine collection of ornamental trees and shrubs.

Location: 6 m W of Malmesbury on B4040 Bristol Road.
Open: All the Year Weds 2-6. Open Sun May 14 2.30-6.*Collection box for National Gardens' Scheme.* Inside view by appointment 3 weeks in advance.
Admission: Outside only 50p. Inside £1.
Refreshments: Teas in garden or house (in aid of Luckington Parish Church). May 14 1995 only.

LYDIARD PARK
(Borough of Thamesdown)

Lydiard Park, Lydiard Tregoze, Swindon   SN5 9PA   map **3** T19   △ & Ⓔ
Telephone: (01793) 770401

Once dilapidated and now fully restored ancestral home of the St.John family, remodelled in the Georgian classical style in 1743 and set in attractive country parkland. Fine furniture, family portraits (16th - 19th century), beautiful plaster-work, original wallpaper, fascinating painted glass window and room devoted to artistic works of Lady Diana Spencer, 2nd Viscountess Bolingbroke incl large scale decorative panels. Adjacent church of St.Mary's houses exceptional St.John family monuments.

Location: 5 m W of Swindon just N of Junction 16 M4; signposted Lydiard Park.
Open: Weekdays and Sat 10-1 and 2-5.30 Suns 2-5.30 (Early closing 4 Nov-Feb incl.).
Admission: Adults 60p children 25p car parking charge 60p (2 hrs) £1 (day). Coach parking. Wheelchair access. Gift shop. Teachers resource pack, group guided tours by appointment, adventure playgrounds. Visitors centre in grounds houses cafe and toilet facilites.

MALMESBURY HOUSE 🏛

The Close, Salisbury   SP1 1EB   map **3** U19   ▯ △
Telephone: (01722) 327027
Fax: (01722) 411265

Malmsbury House was originally a 13th century canonry. It was enlarged in the 14th century and was leased to the Harris family in 1660 whose descendant became the first Earl of Malmsbury. The west facade was added by Wren, to accommodate rooms displaying magnificent rococo plaster work. Among the many illustrious visitors to the house, the most important were King Charles II and the composer Handel who used the chapel above the St. Ann Gate for recitals. Francis Webb, a direct Ancestor of Queen Elizabeth II lived here in the 1770's. The house is now the residence of Mr. & Mrs. John Cordle.

Station(s): Salisbury B R and bus station.
Open: Oct 1-Mar 31 by appointment only.
Admission: £4 per person weekdays £5 per person during weekends (children half price).
Refreshments: Self service cafeteria in garden orangery in summer season.
Events/Exhibitions: Throughout the year in Cathedral.
Conferences: At former Theological College in the Close.
Malmesbury House is a family home, in residence. Guided tours only. Parties welcome. Car parking available in close. Hotels within 2 mins.

MOMPESSON HOUSE  The National Trust

Salisbury   SP1 2EL   map 3 U19
Telephone: (01722) 335659

Fine Queen Anne town house, furnished as the home of a Georgian gentleman; walled garden. Art exhibition throughout the season.

Location: In Cathedral Close on N side of Choristers' Green.
Station(s): Salisbury ½ m.
Open: 1 Apr-31 Oct daily except Thurs & Fri 12-5.30. Last adm 5.
Admission: £3 children £1.50 parties £2.70.
Refreshments: Teas in Garden Room 12-5.
No dogs. Visitors sitting room.

OLD SARUM

map **3** U19
Telephone: (01722) 335398

ENGLISH HERITAGE

On the summit of a hill north of Salisbury, huge ramparts and earth mounds are silhouetted against the skyline. Ancient Britons fortified the hill-top which was later inhabited by Romans, Saxons and Normans. Parts of an 11th century castle remain and the foundations of two successive cathedrals are marked on the grass.

Location: 2 m (3.2 km) north of Salisbury.
Open: Apr 1-Sept 30 10-6 daily Oct 1-Mar 31 10-4 daily.
Admission: Adults £1.50 concessions £1.10 children 80p.

OLD WARDOUR CASTLE

map **3** U18
Telephone: (01747) 870487

ENGLISH HERITAGE

The ruins stand in a romantic lakeside setting as a result of landscaping and planting in the 18th century. French in style and designed more for living than defence, the castle was built in 1393 by the fifth Lord Lovel, a campaigner in France. It was badly damaged in the Civil War and never repaired. The 18th century Banqueting House contains a small display about the 'Capability' Brown landscape.

Location: 2 m (3.2 km) south of Tisbury.
Open: Apr 1-Sept 30 10-6 daily Oct 1-31 10-4 daily Nov 1-Mar 31 Wed-Sun 10-4.
Admission: Adults £1.50 concessions £1.10 children 80p.

PHILIPPS HOUSE  The National Trust

Dinton   SP3 5HJ   map 3 U19
Telephone: (01722) 716208

Classical house completed in 1816 by Sir Jeffry Wyattville for the Wyndham family.

Location: 9 m W of Salisbury; on N side of B3089.
Open: By prior written appointment only with the YWCA Warden.
Admission: £1.50 *No reduction for parties or children.* House leased to YWCA for residential conferences.
No dogs.

PYTHOUSE

(Country Houses Association)
Tisbury   SP3 6PB   map 3 U18
Telephone: (01747) 870210

Palladian style Georgian mansion.

Location: 2½ m W of Tisbury; 4½ m N of Shaftesbury.
Station(s): Tisbury (2½ m).
Open: May-Sept Weds & Thurs 2-5. Last entry 4.30.
Admission: £2.50 Children £1. Free car park.
No dogs admitted.

SHELDON MANOR

(Antony Gibbs ESQ Owner, Mrs Martin Gibbs Administration)
Chippenham   SN14 0RG   map 14 U18
Telephone: (01249) 653120

Plantagenet Manor House, lived in as a family home for 700 years. There has been a house here since early Plantagenet times. The present Great Porch and Parvise above, dating from 1282, were built by Sir Geoffrey Gascelyn, Lord of the Manor and Hundred of Chippenham and were 700 years old in 1982. Sheldon is the sole survivor of a vanished medieval village. Succeeding generations and other families, notably the Hungerfords, have added to the beautiful house, its forecourt and surrounding buildings. All the house is lived in and it is shown by the family. There are good collections of early oak furniture, Nailsea glass, porcelain and Persian saddlebags. There are beautiful informal terraced gardens with ancient yew trees, water, interesting trees and shrubs and a connoisseur collection of old fashioned roses. The Elaborinth, a maze of edible plants, in late summer. Home-made lunches and cream teas served in the Barn or on the lawn. Visitors to Sheldon have found the food 'a major consideration'. 'In nominating an eating place with an intimate atmosphere, I could do no better than to recommend Sheldon'. Hugh Montgomery-Massingberd, Weekend Telegraph, July 11th, 1987. 'It was worth the whole trip for this.' - American visitor 1992. National Winner of the first Historic House Awards, given by the AA and the National Pensions Institute, in co-operation with the Historic Houses Association, for the privately-owned house open to the public which has best preserved its integrity and the character and furniture while remaining a lived-in family home. "National winner of the first Historic House Awards, given by the AA and the National Pensions Institute, in co-operation with the Historic Houses Association, for the privately owned historic house open to the public which has best preserved its integrity and the character of its architecture and furniture while remaining a lived-in family home".

Location: 1½ m W of Chippenham, signposted from A420; eastbound traffic also signposted from A4, E of Corsham (2½ m). M4 exit 17 4 m.
Station(s): Chippenham (2½ m).
Open: Open Easter Sun and Easter Mon then every Sun Thurs and Bank Hol to Oct 1 1995 12.30-6. House opens 2.
Refreshments: Home-made lunches & cream teas. Coaches welcome by appointment.
Conferences: Sheldon is delighted to host small conferences and corporate entertaining. Sheldon has made a speciality of wedding receptions.
Most of the property suitable for wheelchairs.

STONEHENGE

map **3** U19
Telephone: (01980) 624714

ENGLISH HERITAGE

Built between 3100 and 1100 BC, this is Britain's most famous ancient monument and one of the world's most astonishing engineering feats. Many of the stones, some weighing 4 tons each, were brought from the Preseli Mountains in Wales to Salisbury Plain, there to be erected by human muscle power.

Location: 2 m (3.2 km) west of Amesbury.
Open: Apr 1-May 31 9.30-6 June 1-30 9.30-7 Sept 1-Oct 8 9.30-6 Oct 9-15 9.30-5 Oct 16-Mar 31 9.30-4.
Refreshments: Available.
Admission: Adults £3 concessions £2.30 children £1.50.

Ghosts are in residence at the following properties included in Historic Houses Castles and Gardens:-

Blickling Hall - *Anne Boleyn*

Breamore House - *Haunted picture - if touched, death on the same day*

East Riddleden Hall - *5 ghosts including lady*

in Grey Hall Lady's Chamber

Fountains Abbey & Studley Royal - *Choir of monks chanting in Chapel of Nine Altars*

Hinton Ampner - *Nocturnal noises*

Ightham Mote - *Supernatural presence*

Lindisfarne Castle - *Monk, and group of monks on causeway*

Lyme Park - *Unearthly peals of bells and lady in white, funeral procession through park*

Malmesbury House - *Ghost of a cavalier*

Overbecks Museum & Garden - *'Model' ghost in the Children's room (for them to spot)*

Rockingham Castle - *Lady Dedlock*

Rufford Old Hall - *Elizabeth Hesketh*

Scotney Castle Garden - *Man rising from the lake*

Sizergh Castle & Garden - *Poltergeist*

Speke Hall - *Ghost of woman in tapestry room*

Springhill - *Ghost of a woman*

Sudbury Hall - *Lady in Green, seen on stairs*

Tamworth Castle - *Haunted bedroom*

Treasurer's House - *Troop of Roman soldiers marching through the cellar*

Wallington House - *Invisible birds beating against the windows accompanied by heavy breathing*

Washington Old Hall - *Grey lady walking through corridors*

STOURHEAD 🌿 **The National Trust**
Stourton, nr Mere   BA12 6QH   map **3** U18   △ &

Telephone: (01747) 841152

The world famous garden was laid out 1741-80; its lakes, temples and rare trees forming a landscape of breath-taking beauty throughout the year. Palladian House designed in 1721 by Colen Campbell. Furniture by Thomas Chippendale the Younger.

Location: 3 m NW of Mere (A303) in the village of Stourton off the Frome/Mere Road (B3092).
Station(s): Gillingham 6½ m; Bruton 7 m.
Open: Garden all year daily 9-7 or sunset if earlier (except June 17, July 19-22 when garden closes at 5). House 1 Apr-31 Oct daily except Thur & Fri 12-5.30 or dusk if earlier. Last adm 5. Other times by written arrangement with the House Manager.
Admission: House £4.20 Children £2.20 Parties by prior written appointment only. Garden Mar-Oct £4.20 Children £2.20 Parties £3.60 Family £10 Nov-end Feb £3.20 Children £1.50 Family £8.
Refreshments: National Trust Shop. Village Hall Restaurant (01747) 840161.
Events/Exhibitions: Exhibition in visitor reception building in main car park.
Accommodation: Accommodation, Spread Eagle Inn at Garden entrance, (01747) 840587. Wheelchair provided - access to gardens only. Batricar. No dogs in garden except on leads from Nov-end Feb only. In woods throughout the year. Reception Building, exhibition, parent's room. NT shop.

Butterfly Houses

can be found at the following properties included in Historic Houses Castles and Gardens:-

Berkeley Castle
Elsham Hall - Wild butterfly walkway
Syon House

WESTWOOD MANOR 🌿 **The National Trust**
nr Bradford-on-Avon   BA15 2AF   map **14** U18   △

Telephone: (01225) 863374

15th century stone manor house altered in the late 16th century. Fine furnishings.Gardens of clipped yew. Administered for the National Trust by a tenant.

Location: 1½ m. SW of Bradford-on-Avon in Westwood Village, beside church.
Station(s): Avoncliff (1 m); Bradford-on-Avon 1½ m.
Open: 2 Apr-1 Oct Sun Tues Wed 2-5.*Other times parties of up to 20 by written application to the tenant.*
Admission: £3.30 No reduction for parties or children.
No dogs. Unsuitable for wheelchairs. No WCs.

WILTON HOUSE

(The Earl of Pembroke)
Salisbury   **SP2 OBJ**   map **3** U19   △
Telephone: (01722) 743115
Fax: (01722) 744447

The 17 minute film narrated by Anna Massey provides a dynamic introduction to the Earls of Pembroke and the 450 year history of the Estate. The Tudor origins of the House can still be seen in the tower which survived the 1647 fire and is now incorporated within the splendid 17th Century House, based on designs by Inigo Jones. Perhaps most famous of the State Rooms are the Single and Double Cube Rooms, with their fabulous painted ceilings. With early 19th Century additions by James Wyatt, Wilton House, over looking the majestic Palladian Bridge across the river Nadder provides a fascinating record of British history. Wilton House boasts, what is reputed to be, one of the best private art collections in Britain, with original paintings by Van Dyck, Reynolds, Breughel and Rubens amongst the 230 works of art on public show. Step back in time in the re-constructed Tudor Kitchen and the Estate's Victorian Laundry (in use until 1969). Relax in the 21 acres of landscaped parkland, including the walled rose garden with its Pergola, the water garden and, especially for children the massive adventure playground.

Location: Wilton 3 m W of Salisbury on A30.
Station(s): Salisbury.
Open: Apr 11-Oct 29 1995 7 days a week 11-6 (last admission 5).
Admission: Adults £5.75 OAPs £4.75 Children (aged 5-15) £3.75 under 5 FOC. All day family ticket (2+2) £15.25. Discounts for pre-booked parties and/or Grounds' admission only.
Refreshments: Licensed self-service restaurant.
Events/Exhibitions: Events calender available.
Conferences: Corporate hospitality facilities available for up to 120 guests.

NORTH YORKSHIRE

ALLERTON PARK

(The Gerald Arthur Rolph Foundation for Historic Preservation and Education)
nr Knaresborough   map **7** O20
Telephone: (01423) 330927

The grandest of the surviving Gothic revival stately homes. Its Great Hall and Dining Room are considered amongst the finest carved wood rooms in England. Allerton Park is the ancestral home of Lord Mowbray (c. 1283), Segrave (c. 1283) and Stourton (c. 1448), the premier Baron in England. House designed by George Martin, some interior rooms by Benjamin Baud. Temple of Victory built by Frederick, Duke of York (brother to King George IV) in 18th century. The setting for Sherlock Holmes film 'The Sign of Four'. Private collection of mechanical music machines and luxury antique motor cars. World War II museum dedicated to Number 6 Group (RCAF).

Location: 14½ m W of York; ¼ m E of A1 on York Road (A59); 4½ m W of Knaresborough, 6 m N of Wetherby; 7 m S of Boroughbridge; 14 m N of Leeds.
Open: Easter Sun-end Sept Sun and Bank Hol Mons 1-6 last house tour 5. Other days by appointment for parties of 25 or more and events. Enquiries to: Mr. Farr, Administrator, Allerton Park, nr. Knaresborough, N. Yorkshire HG5 0SE. Tel: (01423) 330927.
Admission: House Grounds and Car Museum £3 Students/OAPs/accompanied Children (under 16) £2. Parties (25 and over) £2.50. School groups £2. Free car parking.
No dogs, except guide dogs for the blind.

ASKE HALL

(The Marquess and Marchioness of Zetland)
Aske, Rickmond   **DL10 5HJ**   map **7** O19
Telephone: (01748) 823222

Continuously the seat of the Dundas family since the house and estate were purchased by Sir Lawrence Dundas in 1762. Fine collection of pictures, furniture and porcelain, much of which was acquired by Sir Lawrence himself.

Location: 2 m east of Richmond on the Gilling West Road (B6274).
Open: For parties of 15 or more by written appointment only. Week days only.
Admission: Adults £3.50 children £1.50.
Refreshments: At the hall by appointment.

BENINGBROUGH HALL

The National Trust

nr York map **7** O20 △ ♿
Telephone: (01904) 470666

This handsome Georgian house has been completely restored and in the principal rooms are 100 famous portraits on loan from the National Portrait Gallery. Victorian laundry, potting shed and exhibitions. Garden and wilderness play area.

Location: 8 m NW of York; 3 m W of Shipton (A19); 2 m SE Linton-on-Ouse; follow signposted route.
Open: 1 Apr-31 Oct Mon Tues Wed Sat Sun & Good Fri also Fri in July and Aug. House 11-5 (last adm 4.30) Grounds shop and restaurant 11-5.30 (last adm 5).
Admission: HOUSE GARDEN & EXHIBITION £4.50 Children £2.30 Family £9 Parties £3.60 Child parties £1.80. GARDEN & EXHIBITION £3 Children £1.50 Family £6 (Family ticket 2 adults 3 children).
Refreshments: The Restaurant serves home-made hot & cold lunches, teas, special suppers. Wheelchair access. Picnic area. Kiosk. Special functions catered for, details from the Administrator.
No dogs. Wheelchairs provided. Baby changing facilities.

BOLTON ABBEY ESTATE

(Trustees of the Chatsworth Settlement)
Bolton Abbey, Skipton BD23 6EX map **7** O19 △ ♿
Telephone: (01756) 710533
Fax: (01756) 710535

Location: On B6160 north from the roundabout junction with the A59 Skipton to Harrogate Road, 23 m from Leeds.
Station(s): Skipton and Ilkley.
Open: Open all year.
Admission: £2.50 car park charge £1.50 car park charge for disabled. No charge for coaches.
Refreshments: Restaurant and two tea-rooms.
Accommodation: Farmhouse bed & breakfast; self catering cottage; hotel.
Conferences: Available at the Devonshire Arms Country House Hotel.

BROCKFIELD HALL

(Lord & Lady Martin Fitzalan Howard)
Warthill, York YO3 9XJ map **7** O21
Telephone: (01904) 489298

Small country house designed 1804 by Peter Atkinson. Dramatic round Hall and Staircase.

Location: 5m E of York off A166 or A64.
Open: Aug 1-31 1995 1-4 except Mon (Other times by appointment) tel: (01904) 489298.
Admission: Adults £2.50 children £1.

CASTLE HOWARD

(The Hon. Simon Howard)
York   **YO6 7DA**   map **7** O21
Telephone: (01653) 648333
Fax: (01653) 648462

Designed by Vanbrugh 1699-1726 for the 3rd Earl of Carlisle, assisted by Hawksmoor, who designed the Mausoleum. Has been open to the public since the day it was built. Impressive Great Hall and many other magnificent rooms filled with fine collections of pictures, statuary and furniture. Interesting rooms include The Castle Howard Bedroom, Lady Georgiana's Bedroom and Dressing Room, The Antique Passage, The Music Room, The Tapestry Room, The Museum Room, The Long Gallery, and the Chapel. Beautiful park and grounds with nature walks, rose gardens in season, Ray Wood, superb Atlas fountain, Temple of The Four Winds. Lakeside Adventure Playground for children. Plant Centre. Boat trips on the lake in Victorian style launch in season, (weather permitting). Stable courtyard catering and shopping facilities.

Location: 15 m NE of York; 3 m off A64; 6 m W of Malton; 38 m Leeds; 36 m Harrogate; 22 m Scarborough; 50 m Hull.
Open: Daily Mar 17-Oct 29. House open from 11. Plant centre, rose gardens, grounds and cafeteria open from 10. Last admissions 4.30.
Admission: £6 children £3 OAPs £5 special terms for booked parties.
Refreshments: Cafeteria. Licensed restaurant available for booked parties.

CLIFFORD'S TOWER

York   map **7** O20
Telephone: (01904) 646940

York Castle, like the city itself, has had a long and turbulent history. Clifford's Tower was built on an earlier motte (or mound) in the 13th century. The tower is named after a Lancastrian leader from the Wars of the Roses, Sir Robert Clifford, who was defeated in 1322, and his body hung in chains from the tower.

Location: Near Castle Museum.
Open: Apr 1-Sept 30 10-6 daily Oct 1-Mar 31 daily 10-4.
Admission: Adults £1.50 concessions £1.10 children 80p.

CONSTABLE BURTON HALL

(M. C. A. Wyvill, Esq)
Leyburn   **DL8 5LJ**   map **7** O19
Telephone: (01677) 450428
Fax: (01677) 450626

Extensive borders, interesting alpines, large informal garden. John Carr house completed in 1768.

Location: On A684, between Leyburn (3 m) & Bedale; A1 (7 m).
Open: Gardens May 1-Oct 1 daily 9-6 House opening dates not available at time of going to press.
Admission: Garden £1 (collecting box) House charges not available at time of going to press. Party rates by arrangement.

DUNCOMBE PARK

(The Rt Hon Lord Feversham)
Helmsley, York   YO6 5EB   map **7** O20
Telephone: (01439) 770213
Fax: (01439) 771114

Helmsley - North Yorkshire

Award winning home of Lord and Lady Feversham.
Originally built 1713, recently restored to a family home.
Unique 18th Century landscape gardens. Visitor Centre.
Country Walks, Playground. Licenced Tea Room.

Further information: Tel: 01439 770213

Year round programme of events and exhibitions

Admission: see editorial

Home of the Duncombes for 300 years; 60 years a school, now restored to family home and opened to public for first time in 1990. Fine 19th century interiors, family pictures, English and Continental furniture. Unique early 18th century landscape garden with lawns, temples, tree-lined terraces, woodland and riverside walks in National Nature Reserve.

Location: 3 mins from Helmsley market square.
Open: Easter weekend Apr 14-18 Apr/Oct Wed & Sun 11-5 May/June Wed-Sun 11-5 July/Aug/Sept daily 11-5.
Admission: Adults £4.50 children (10-16) £2.50 OAPs £3.75. Gardens and Park adults £2.75 children £1. Parkland only £1.
Refreshments: Restaurant/coffee shop.
Gift shop, children's playground, car park. Winner BTA Come to Britain Award.

FAIRFAX HOUSE

(York Civic Trust)
Castlegate, York   map **7** P20
Telephone: (01904) 655543

An 18th century house designed by John Carr of York and described as a classic architectural masterpiece of its age. Certainly one of the finest townhouses in England and saved from near collapse by the York Civic Trust who restored it to its former glory during 1982/84. In addition to the superbly decorated plasterwork, wood and wrought iron, the house is now home for an outstanding collection of 18th century Furniture, and Clocks, formed by the late Noel Terry. Described by Christie's as one of the finest private collections of this century, it enhances and complements the house and helps to create a very special 'lived in' feeling. The gift of the entire collection by Noel Terry's Trustees to the Civic Trust has enabled it to fill the house with appropriate pieces of the period and has provided the basis for what can now be considered a fully furnished Georgian Townhouse.

Location: Centre of York, follow signs for Castle Area and Jorvik Centre.
Open: Feb 20-Jan 6 Mon-Thurs and Sat 11-5 Sun 1.30-5 (last admission 4.30) closed Fri except during Aug. Special evening tours, connoisseur visits and receptions welcomed by arrangement with the Director.
Admission: Adults £3 OAPs/students £2.50 children £1.50 adult parties (pre-booked 15 or more) £2.50 children £1.25
Events/Exhibitions: Chocolate, Coffee and Tea Drinking in 18th Century England Exhibition runs Sept 1-Nov 21 1995.
Public car park within 50 yds. Suitable for disabled persons only with assistance (by telephoning beforehand staff can be available to help). A small gift shop offers selected antiques, publications and gifts. Opening times are the same as the house.

HISTORIC HOUSES
CASTLES & GARDENS

For further details on editorial listings or display advertising contact the

Editor: Deborah Valentine,
Windsor Court, East Grinstead House, East Grinstead,
West Sussex RH19 1XA
Tel: (01342) 335794   Fax: (01342) 335720

FOUNTAINS ABBEY & STUDLEY ROYAL
The National Trust
Ripon   HG4 3DY   map **7** O19
Telephone: (01765) 601002/608888
Fax: (01765) 608889

Extensive ruins of Cistercian Abbey. Ornamental water gardens laid out by John Aislabie, 1720. 400 acre deer park with fine Burges church. Awarded World Heritage status in 1987, visitor centre.

Location: 2 m W of Ripon; 9 m W of Harrogate; NW of A61.
Station(s): Harrogate.
Open: Deer Park open all year during daylight hours. Abbey and Garden open daily except 24 & 25 Dec and Friday in Jan Nov & Dec. Jan-Mar 10-5pm Apr-Sept 10-7pm Oct to Dec 10-5 or dusk if earlier. Last admission 1 hr before closing.
Admission: Deer Park Free. Fountains Hall Free. Abbey & Gardens Adults £4 children £2 Family £8 Group (min of 15) £3.50 Children £1.70. Free car parking at Visitor Centre Car Park. Studley Park £2.
Refreshments: Fully licensed restaurant lunches, sandwiches, soup and cakes etc. Visitor Centre Restaurant Daily Jan-Mar, Oct-Dec 10-5 Apr-Sept 10-6. Studley Royal Tea-room daily Apr-Aug and some weekends in winter.
Events/Exhibitions: Many open air concerts and Shakespeare plays during the season. Corporate hospitality, private parties and special events can be organised.
Conferences: Facilities available.
Wheelchair access. Picnics can be taken anywhere on Estate. Dogs on leads only. Visitor Centre shop: open daily.

GEORGIAN THEATRE ROYAL
(The Georgian Theatre (Richmond) Trust Ltd)
Richmond   DL10 4DW   map **7** O19
Telephone: (01748) 823710
Fax: (01748) 823710

18th century Georgian Theatre.

Location: Victoria Road, Richmond.
Station(s): Darlington.
Open: Mar 31-Oct 31 (Museum) Mar-Dec (Theatre).
Admission: £1 (performance prices £12-£3).
Refreshments: Coffee-Bar (June-Sept).

HELMSLEY CASTLE
map **7** O20
Telephone: (01439) 70442

Even in its ruined state, Helmsley Castle is spectacular. Begun by Walter Espec shortly after the Norman Conquest, the huge earthworks - now softened to green valleys - are all that remain of this early castle. The oldest stonework is 12th century. Like many English castles, Helmsley rendered indefensible during the Civil War, when it belonged to the notorious George Villiers, Duke of Buckingham. It was abandoned as a great house when its owners built nearby Duncombe Park. The 17th century domestic buildings contains an exhibition about the castle.

Location: Helmsley.
Open: Apr 1-Sept 30 10-6 daily Oct 1-31 10-4 daily Nov 1-Mar 31 Wed-Sun 10-4.
Admission: Adults £2 concessions £1.50 children £1.

HOVINGHAM HALL
(Sir Marcus & Lady Worsley)
York   YO6 4LU   map **7** O21
Telephone: (01653) 628206
Fax: (01653) 628668

Palladian House designed c. 1760 by Thomas Worsley to his own designs. Unique entry by huge Riding School. Visitors see family portraits and rooms in everyday use; also the extensive garden with magnificent yew hedges and dovecot and the private cricket ground, said to be the oldest in England.

Location: 20 m N of York on Malton/Helmsley Road (B1257).
Open: Open for parties of 15 or more **by written appointment only** Apr 4-Sept 28 1995 Tues Wed & Thurs 11-7.
Admission: Adults £2.50 children £1.25.
Refreshments: At the Hall by arrangement. Meals at The Worsley Arms, Hovingham.
Conferences: Facilities for up to 140.

MARKENFIELD HALL
(The Lord Grantley, MC)
Ripon   HG4 3AD   map **7** O19

Fine example of English manor house 14th, 15th & 16th century buildings surrounded by moat.

Location: 3 m S of Ripon off the Ripon/Harrogate Road (A61). Access is up a road marked Public Bridleway Hell Wath Lane'.
Open: Apr-Oct Mon 10-12.30 and 2.15-5. Exterior only outside courtyard and moat all other days in May times as above.
Admission: Adults £1 children (accompanied by adult) free. Exterior and outside courtyard free.

MIDDLEHAM CASTLE
map **7** O19
Telephone: (01969) 23899

The great days of Middleham were in the 14th and 15th centuries, when it was the stronghold of the mighty Neville family. After the death of Richard Neville - 'Warwick the Kingmaker' - in 1471, the castle was forfeited to the Crown and was the childhood home of Richard III. The dominant feature of the castle is the great keep, one of the largest in England. A replica of the famous Middleham jewel is on display.

Location: 2 m (3.2 km) south of Leyburn.
Open: Apr 1-Sept 30 10-6 daily Oct 1-31 10-4 daily Nov 1-Mar 31 Wed-Sun 10-4.
Admission: Adults £1.50 concessions £1.10 children 80p.

MOUNT GRACE PRIORY
map **7** O20
Telephone: (01609) 883494

These 14th century ruins provide a rare opportunity to study the plan of a Carthusian monastery, or 'charterhouse'. The Carthusian monks lived like hermits - in seclusion not only from the world, but from each other. They met together only in chapel, and for religious feasts. Every monk had his own cell - 21 in all - a tiny two-storey house with its own garden and workshop. And each cell had running water - a remarkable luxury in the Middle Ages. A fully restored cell with hand-carved furniture and exhibition gives a fascinating insight into the lives of the monks.

Location: 7 m (11⅓ km) north east of Northallerton.
Open: Apr 1-Sept 30 10-6 daily Oct 1-31 10-4 daily Nov 1-Mar 31 Wed-Sun 10-4. Last admission summer season 5.30, winter season 3.30.
Admission: Adults £2.20 concessions £1.70 children £1.10.

NEWBURGH PRIORY
(Sir George Wombwell, Bt)
Coxwold   Y6 4AS   map **7** O20
Telephone: (01347) 868435

One of the North's most interesting Historic Houses. Originally built in 1145 with alterations in 1568 and 1720-1760, the Priory has been the home of one family and its descendants since 1538. The house contains the tomb of Oliver

Cromwell (his third daughter, Mary, was married to Viscount Fauconberg - owner 1647-1700). In the grounds there is a really beautiful Water Garden full of rare alpines, plants and rhododendrons. Afternoon tea is served in the original kitchen.

Location: 5 m from Easingwold off A19, 9 m from Thirsk.
Open: GROUNDS AND HOUSE Apr 2-June 28 Suns and Weds Easter Mon and Aug Bank Hol Mons HOUSE OPEN 2.30-4.45 GROUNDS 2-6 *Other days for parties of 25 or more by appointment with the Administrator.*
Admission: House and Grounds £3 Children £1 Grounds only £1.50 Children free.
Refreshments: In the Old Priory Kitchens.

NEWBY HALL & GARDENS

(R.E.J. Compton, Esq)
Ripon   HG4 5AE   map **7** O20   ⅃
Telephone: (01423) 322583
Fax: (01423) 324452

The family home of Mr and Mrs Robin Compton is one of Yorkshire's renowned Adam houses. It is set amidst 25 acres of award-winning gardens full of rare and beautiful plants. Famous double herbaceous borders with formal compartmented gardens including species rose garden, water and rock gardens, the Autumn garden and the tranquility of Sylvia's garden - truly a 'Garden for all Seasons'. Also holds National Collection of genus CORNUS. The contents of the house are superb and include an unique Gobelins Tapestry Room, a gallery of classical statuary and some of Chippendale's finest furniture. Other attractions are railway rides beside the river, adventure gardens for children, a woodland discovery walk, Newby shop and plants stall, and picnic area. Coach and car park free.

Location: 4m SE of Ripon on Boroughbridge Road (B6265). 3m W of A1; 14m Harrogate; 20m York; 35m Leeds; 32m Skipton.
Open: Apr 1-Sept 30 daily except Mons (but open Bank Holidays) from 11 and House open from 12. Full visitor information from the Administrator, The Estate Office, Newby Hall, Ripon HG4 5AE.
Admission: Please telephone for details.
Refreshments: Lunches & teas in the licensed Garden Restaurant.
Events/Exhibitions: Craft Fair June 10/11 Sept 16/17, Northern Country Fair June 18, Historic Vehicle Rally July 16.

NORTON CONYERS

(Sir James Graham, Bt)
Ripon   HG4 5EH   map **7** O19   △ ⅃
Telephone: (01765) 640601/640333 (house & garden).

Visited by Charlotte Brontë in 1839, Norton Conyers is an original of 'Thornfield Hall' in 'Jane Eyre', and a family legend was an inspiration for the mad Mrs Rochester. The building is late medieval with Stuart and Georgian additions. Family pictures, furniture, ceramics and costumes. The friendly atmosphere, resulting from over 370 years of occupation by the same family, has been noticed by many visitors. The 18th century walled garden, with Orangery and herbaceous borders, is 100 yards from the house. Pick your own fruit: intending pickers are advised to check beforehand.

Location: 4 m NW of Ripon nr Wath. 3 m from A1; turn off at the Baldersby Flyover, take A61 to Ripon, turn right to Melmerby.
Station(s): None.
Open: House open Bank Hols Sun and Mon, Sun 28 May-10 Sept, daily 24-29 July 2-5. Garden the same,
Admission: £2.95, children (10-16) £2.50, OAPs £2.00. Prices for parties of 20 or more: on application. Garden free; donations are welcome.
Refreshments: Teas and light refreshments for booked parties. Teas served at charity openings of garden.
Dogs in grounds and garden only, (except guide dogs) and must be on a lead. Visitors are requested not to wear high-heeled shoes in the house. Photography by owner's written permission only.

NUNNINGTON HALL 🌿 The National Trust
nr Helmsley   map **7** O21
Telephone: (01439) 748283

16th century manor house with fine panelled hall and staircase. Carlisle Collection of Miniature Rooms on display.

Location: In Ryedale; 4½ m SE of Helmsley; 1½ m N of B1257.
Open: 1 Apr-31 Oct Tues Wed Thurs Sat Sun & Good Fri 2-6. Bank Hols 12-6. July and Aug also Fri 2-6 Sat & Sun 12-6. Last adm 5. School Parties on weekdays by arrangement with the Administrator.
Admission: HOUSE & GARDEN £3.50 Children £1.50 Family £7 Parties £3 Child parties £1.30 GARDEN: £1 Children free.
Refreshments: Afternoon teas available at all times when house is open 2-5.30 in indoor tea-rooms or tea garden. Lunches July & Aug.
Shop open as house. Access to Ground floor and tea-room only for wheelchairs. Lavatory for disabled at rear of house. Access to main gardens via ramp. Guide dogs permitted. Dogs in car park only. Baby changing facilities.

PICKERING CASTLE
map **7** O21
Telephone: (01751) 474989

Most of the medieval kings visited Pickering Castle. They came to hunt deer and wild boar in the neighbouring forest. It was a sport of which they were inordinately fond, and the royal forests were zealously guarded. Romantics may like to speculate as to why Rosamund's Tower has been linked with 'Fair Rosamund', mistress of Henry II. They should, however, be aware that the tower was built in 1323, a century after the lady died.

Location: Pickering.
Open: Apr 1-Sept 30 10-6 daily Oct 1-31 10-4 daily Nov 1-Mar 31 Wed-Sun 10-4.
Admission: Adults £2 concessions £1.50 children £1.

RICHMOND CASTLE
map **7** O19
Telephone: (01748) 822493

Surrounded on three sides by high moorland, Richmond Castle is in a strongly defensible position. However, the castle has seen little active service, which accounts for the remarkable amount of early Norman stonework that has survived. Built by Alan the Red, shortly after 1066, the castle went with the title 'Duke of Richmond' and has had many royal and powerful owners. The 100 foot high keep provides fine views over the ruins and surrounding countryside.

Location: Richmond.
Open: Apr 1-Sept 30 10-6 daily Oct 1-Mar 31 Wed-Sun 10-4.
Admission: Adults £1.80 concessions £1.40 children 90p.

RIEVAULX ABBEY
map **7** O20
Telephone: (0143) 96 228

The fluctuating fortunes of the abbey may be read from the ruins. Within two decades of its foundation in 1131, Rievaulx - the first Cistercian monastery in the north - was vast, with 140 monks and 500 lay brothers. A costly building programme followed, and it is little wonder that by the 13th century the monastery was heavily in debt, and buildings were being reduced in size. By the Dissolution in the 16th century, there were only 22 monks. The church is a beautiful example of early English Gothic. New visitor centre with exhibition and shop.

Location: 3 m (4.8 km) north west of Helmsley.
Open: Apr 1-Sept 30 10-6 daily Oct 1-Mar 31 daily 10-4.
Admission: Adults £2.40 concessions £1.80 children £1.20.

RIEVAULX TERRACE 🌿 The National Trust
Helmsley   map **7** O20 ♿
Telephone: (01439) 798340

Beautiful half mile long grass terrace with views of Rievaulx Abbey. Two 18th century Temples and permanent exhibition.

Location: 2½ m NW of Helmsley on Stokesley Road (B1257).
Open: 1 Apr-31 Oct Daily 10.30-6 (or dusk if earlier). Ionic Temple closed 1-2. Last adm 5.
Admission: £2.50 Children £1 Family £5 Parties £1,80 child parties 80p.
Refreshments: Teas available at Nunnington Hall, 7 m E.
All dogs on leads. Battery operated 'Runabout' available.

Sir Anthony Van Dyck
Portrait and religious painter

Born in Antwerp 1599, died in London 1641
First visited England in 1620, knighted by Charles I in 1633

His work can be seen in the following properties included in Historic Houses Castles and Garden:-

Alnwick Castle
Arundel Castle
Boughton House
Breamore House
Eastnor Castle
Euston Hall
Firle Place
Goodwood House
Holkham Hall
Kingston Lacey
Petworth House
Southside House
Sudeley Castle
Warwick Castle
Weston Park
Wilton House
Woburn Abbey

RIPLEY CASTLE

(Sir Thomas Ingilby, Bt)
Ripley   **HG3 3AY**   map **7** O19
Telephone: (01423) 770152
Fax: (01423) 771745

Ripley Castle and Gardens

Home of the Ingilby Family for over 650 years, the castle is situated ten minutes north of Harrogate, in the centre of one of England's most beautiful and historic estate villages. The castle itself overlooks a seventeen acre lake and deer park; the setting is wonderful. The rooms are packed with anecdote, humour and items of fascination, and the knight's chamber in the 1555 tower remains one of the most startlingly complete medieval rooms in the country, complete with waggon roof ceiling, ancient panelling. Royal Greenwich armour and secret priest's hiding hole.

The extensive walled gardens contain the national hyacinth collection and a magnificent assortment of tropical and semi tropical plants in the greenhouse.

There is also a lovely walk through deer park. The village is quite unique and well worth a visit, and the four star **Boar's Head Hotel** with its first class restaurant and bar makes an excellent base for touring Yorkshire's stately homes, almost all of which are within one hour's drive.

OPENING TIMES: April, May and October: Sats & Suns 11.30-4.30 (Also Good Friday and Bank Holidays 11.00-4.30). **June and September** Thurs, Fri, Sat & Sun 11.30-4.30. **July and August** Daily 11.30-4.30. **Booked Parties**: Groups of 15+ can visit the Castle and Gardens on any day throughout the year, (except Christmas day) by prior arrangement. 10.30-7.30. **Gardens**: March, Thurs, Fri. Sat & Sun. 11.00-4.00. Apr to Oct., Daily. 11.00-5.00. Nov to Dec 23rd. Daily 11.00-3.30.

Has been the home of the Ingilby family since early 14th century. Priests secret hiding place and Civil War armour. Fine furnishing, Anecdotal History. Extensive gardens. National Hyacinth and tropical plant collections, parkland walk.

Location: In Ripley 3½ m N Harrogate; 7½ m from Ripon.
Station(s): Harrogate (4 m)
Open: Castle and Gardens Apr May and Oct Sat & Sun 11.30-4.30 (also Good Friday and Bank Holidays 11-4.30) June and Sept Thurs Fri Sat & Sun 11.30-4.30 July and Aug daily 11.30-4.30. Parties of more than 15 people can arrange to visit the Castle and Gardens on any day of the year (except Christmas day) by arrangementment 10.30-7.30. Gardens only Mar Thurs Fri Sat Sun 11-4 Apr- Oct daily 11-5 Nov-Dec 23 daily 11-3.
Admission: Castle & Gardens adults £3.75 parties over 25 people £3 OAPs £3 children (under 16 yrs) £2 parties over 25 children (under 16 yrs) £1.75. Gardens only adults £2.25 parties over 25 people £1.75 OAPs £1.75 children (under 16 yrs) £1 parties over 25 children (under 16 yrs) £1 family ticket (2 adults 2 children) £9.50 each additional child (under 16 yrs) £1.75. Garden Season Ticket £15.
Refreshments: Licensed restaurant and public bar (The Boar's Head Hotel) in village: Tearoom in castle courtyard, serving teas and refreshments. Party catering by arrangement.
Events/Exhibitions: Spring Flower Festival Apr 22-May 6; Homes and Gardens Magazine Grand Summer Fair June 8-11; Performing Arts Viennese Concert and Fireworks Aug 6.
Accommodation: 25 deluxe bedrooms at the Estate owned by the Boar's Head Hotel, 100 yards from the Castle in Ripley village. The Hotel is rated RAC★★★★.
Conferences: Facilities for meetings up to 75 Theatre style. Dinners up to 66 in Castle, up to 800 in marquee adjacent to Castle. Weddings, activity days and launches/promotions catered for at Castle.

SCARBOROUGH CASTLE

Scarborough   map **7** O22
Telephone: (01723) 372451

Standing on the massive headland between the North and South Bays, the castle commands magnificent views. There was a prehistoric settlement here, and a Roman signal station, but the first mention of the castle is in the 12th century, when it was seized by Henry II. During the Civil War the castle was besieged and changed hands several times. A hundred years later it was still in use to detain political prisoners - notably George Fox, founder of the Society of Friends (Quakers).

Location: East of town centre.
Open: Apr 1-Sept 30 10-6 daily Oct 1-Mar 31 daily 10-4.
Admission: Adults £1.50 concessions £1.10 children 80p.

SHANDY HALL

(The Laurence Sterne Trust)
Coxwold   **YO6 4AD**   map **7** O20
Telephone: (01347) 868465

Here in 1760-67 the witty and eccentric parson Laurence Sterne wrote *Tristram Shandy* and *A Sentimental Journey,* 'novels that jump clean out of the 18th century into the 20th', influencing Dickens, Goethe, Tolstoy, Balzac, Proust, Melville, Joyce, Virginia Woolf, and other great writers. Shandy Hall was built as a timber-framed open-hall in the mid-15th century, modernised in the 17th, curiously added to by Sterne in the 18th. It survives much as he knew it, almost as full of surprises and odd digressions as his novels, most of which he wrote in his little book-lined study. Not a museum but a lived-in house where you are sure of a personal welcome. Surrounded by a walled garden full of old-fashioned roses and cottage-garden plants. Also one acre wild garden in old quarry.

Location: 20 m from York via A19; 6 m from A19 at Easingwold; 8 m from Thirsk; 13 m from A1 at Dishforth.
Open: June-Sept Wed 2-4.30 Suns 2.30-4.30 any other day or time all year by appointment with Hon Curators. Gardens open everyday May-Sept 11-4.30 except Sat.
Admission: Adults £2.50 children (accompanied) half-price. Garden only £1.50.
Refreshments: Close by in village.
Events/Exhibitions: Paintings by local artists June-Sept.
Book and handicrafts shop. Unusual plants for sale.

Aviaries and Birds of Prey Centres

can be found at the following properties in Historic Houses Castles and Gardens

Drumlanrig Castle & Country Park
Elsham Hall Country and Wildlife Park
Holdenby House & Gardens

Leeds Castle
Leighton House Museum & Art Gallery
Sewerby Hall & Gardens

Sion Hill Hall
Waddesdon Manor
Muncaster Castle

SION HILL HALL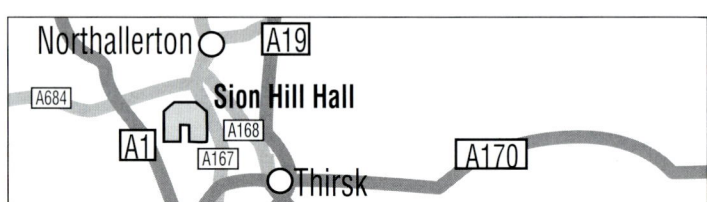

(The H W Mawer Trust. Reg.d Charity No.502772)
Kirby Wiske, nr Thirsk   YO7 4EU   map 7 020   △ &

Telephone: (01845) 587206
Fax: (01845) 587486

Charming Edwardian Country Mansion designed for the Stancliffe family by Walter Brierley - the 'Lutyens of the North'. One of the last country houses built before the Great War and designated by the RIBA as being of outstanding architectural merit. This award winning mansion now houses the Mawer Antique Collection of furniture, porcelain, paintings and clocks - probably the best collection in the North; and extensive Period Costume displays. Birds of Prey and Conservation Centre in the Victorian walled garden.

Location: Off A617; 6 m S of Northallerton, 4 m W of Thirsk, 8 m E of Al via A61.
Station(s): Thirsk or Northallerton.
Open: Mar 26-end Oct. Hall open Wed-Sun 12.30-4.30 Birds of Prey Tues-Sun 10.30-5.30. Open Bank Hol Mons. Groups by arrangement at any time Jan-Nov.
Admission: Hall adults £3.50 concessions £3 children £1.50 group reductions. Birds of Prey additional charge.
Refreshments: Granary Tea-room 10.30-5.30. Visitor Centre/Shop 10.30-5.30.

SKIPTON CASTLE
Skipton   map 7 P18   △
Telephone: (01756) 792442

This is one of the best preserved mediaeval castles in England, Over 900 years old and fully roofed. Explore this massive fortress and discover Lady Anne Clifford's famous yew in the beautiful Conduit Court.

Location: Head of High Street.
Station(s): (½ m). Bus Station: (town centre).
Open: Every day from 10 Sunday 2. Last admission 6 Oct-Feb 4pm. *Closed* Christmas Day.
Admission: Adults £3.20 Over 60's £2.70 with illustrated tour sheet. Under 18's £1.60 with tour sheet and badge. Under 5's free! with badge. School parties £1.60 per head (teachers free) Large coach and car park off nearby High Street.

STOCKELD PARK

(Mr and Mrs P.G.F. Grant)
Wetherby   LS22 4AH   map **7** P20   △
Telephone: (01937) 586101
Fax: (01937) 580084

This small country mansion is set amidst an extensive rural estate of farms, wood and parklands on the edge of the Vale of York and is one of the finest examples of the work of the celebrated architect James Paine and a splendid example of the Palladian style. Stockeld Park was built for the Middleton family during the period 1758-63 and purchased in 1885 by Robert John Foster. Mr Foster was the great grandson of John Foster who founded John Foster & Son based at the Black Dyke Mills. Visitors have an opportunity to see the house as it is lived in at present, together with furniture and pictures collected by the Foster family over many years.

Location: 2 m N of Wetherby; 7 m SE of Harrogate on A661.
Station(s): Nearest Harrogate then direct bus route approx. 7 m.
Open: Thurs only Apr 6-Oct 12 1995 incl. 2-5 (other times by appointment in writing to the Estate Office or tel: (01937) 586101).
Admission: Adults £2 children £1 OAPs £1.50.
Conferences: Film and photographic location - contact Estate office for further information.

THORP PERROW ARBORETUM

(Sir John Ropner)
nr Snape   map **7** 019

Thorp Perrow, the country home of Sir John Ropner, contains a magnificent arboretum - a collection of over 1,000 varieties of trees and shrubs, including some of the largest and rarest in England. It has rapidly become a popular attraction in the area and can be enjoyed by all members of the family, who may wander amidst these 85 acres of landscaped grounds. Lake, grassy glades, tree trails and woodland walks. Thousands of daffodils in Spring, summer wild flowers and glorious autumn colour. Nature trail, children's mystery trail. Tea-room and information centre. Plant centre. Electric wheelchair available.

Location: on Well to Ripon Road, south of Bedale. O.S. map ref: SE258851. 4 m from Leeming Bar on A1.
Open: All year dawn-dusk. Guided tours available tel:(01677) 425323.
Admission: Adults £2.75 children/OAPs £1.50 free car and coach park.
Refreshments: Tea-room.
Picnic area. Toilets. Dogs permitted on leads.

TREASURER'S HOUSE   🍂 The National Trust

York   map **7** P20
Telephone: (01904) 624247

Large 17th century house of great interest. Fine furniture and paintings. Exhibition.

Location: Behind York Minster.
Station(s): York (½ m).
Open: 1 Apr-31 Oct daily 10.30-5 last adm 4.30. Guided tours by arrangement.
Admission: £3 Children £1.50 Family £6 Parties £2.50 Child parties £1.20.
Refreshments: Available in licensed tea-rooms serving morning coffee, light lunches, teas. Open for pre-booked parties during and outside normal opening hours and for private functions. Tel: York (01904) 646757.
Conferences: Facilities available for private functions.
Wheelchair access - part of ground floor only. No car parking facilities. Dogs not allowed, except for guide dogs. Baby changing facilities. Tea-room open as house.

WHITBY ABBEY

map **7** O21
Telephone: (01947) 603568

ENGLISH HERITAGE

Founded in 657 and presided over by the Abbess Hilda, Whitby was a double monastery for both men and women - a feature of the Anglo-Saxon church. This early history has been chronicled by the Venerable Bede, who tells us that here the poet Caedmon lived and worked. Destroyed by invading Danes in 867, the monastery was refounded after the Norman Conquest, but its exposed cliff-top site continued to invite attack by sea pirates. The building remains are from the later Benedictine monastery.

Location: Whitby.
Open: Apr 1-Sept 30 10-6 daily Oct 1-Mar 31 daily 10-4.
Admission: Adults £1.50 concessions £1.10 children 80p.

SOUTH YORKSHIRE

BISHOPS' HOUSE

(Sheffield City Museums)
Meersbrook Park, Norton Lees Lane, Sheffield   S8 9BE   map **15** Q20
Telephone: (0114) 2557701

Beautiful Tudor timber framed house with furnished rooms and permanent displays about life in Tudor and Stuart times. Exciting programme of temporary exhibitions and events.

Location: 2 m south of Sheffield on A61.
Open: Wed-Sat 10-4.30 Sun 11-4.30 open Bank Holidays.
Admission: Nominal charge.

BRODSWORTH HALL

Brodsworth map **15** P20
Telephone: (01302) 722598

ENGLISH HERITAGE

The most complete example of a Victorian country house in England. A unique insight into a vanished way of life. But, as well as being an irreplacable document of High Victorian art and social history, Brodsworth is also an enchanting place, splendidly set in its Park and Garden.

Location: Brodsworth, S. Yorkshire.
Open: July 6-Oct 15 1-6 Tues-Sun & Bank Hol Mons. Gardens open at 12 Last admission 5.
Admission: Adults £4 concessions £3 children £2. 15% discount for groups of 11 or more.

CANNON HALL

(Barnsley Metropolitan Borough Council)
Cawthorne map **15** P19
Telephone: (01226) 790270

18th century house by Carr of York. Collections of fine furniture, paintings, glassware, pewter and pottery. Also the Regimental Museum of the 13th/18th Royal Hussars. 70 acres of parkland.

Location: 5 m W of Barnsley on A635; 1 m NW of Cawthorne.
Open: All the year Tues-Sat 10.30-5 closed Mon (Open Bank Hol Mons) Suns 12-5 closed Dec 25-Jan 1 (incl.) also closed Good Friday.
Admission: Free.

SHEFFIELD BOTANIC GARDENS

(Sheffield City Council)
Meersbrook Park, Brook Road, Sheffield S8 9FL map **15** Q20
Telephone: (0114) 2500500
Fax: (0114) 2552375
Open: Daily except Christmas day, Boxing day and New Years day.
Admission: Free.
Refreshments: Available for pre-arranged guided tours.
Events/Exhibitions: Aproximately 150 events/lectures held by the Friends of the Botanical Gardens and special horticultural societies.
Conferences: Room for 100 people in the classroom and 50 in the new demonstration greenhouse.
On street at Clarkehouse or Thompson Road Entrances.

WEST YORKSHIRE

BAGSHAW MUSEUM

(Kirklees Metro Council)
Wilton Park, Batley map **15** P19
Telephone: (01924) 472514

Victorian gothic mansion, fine panelled interior, Egyptian displays.

Open: Mon-Fri 11-5 Sat-Sun 12-5.
Admission: Free.

BRAMHAM PARK

(Mr & Mrs George Lane Fox)
Wetherby   LS23 6ND map **15** P20
Telephone: (01937) 844265

The house was created during the first half of the 18th century and affords a rare opportunity to enjoy a beautiful Queen Anne mansion containing fine furniture, pictures and porcelain - set in magnificent grounds with ornamental ponds, cascades, tall beech hedges and loggias of various shapes - unique in the British Isles for its grand vistas design stretching out into woodlands of cedar, copper beech, lime and Spanish chestnut interspersed with wild rhododendron thickets.

Location: 5 m S of Wetherby on the Great North Road (A1).
Open: Grounds Only Easter weekend May Day Weekend Spring Bank Hol weekend House & Grounds June 18-Sept 3 (incl. Bank Holiday Mon) Sun Tues Wed & Thurs also Bank Hol Mon 1.15-5.30 last adm 5. 'Bramham Horse Trials' June 8-11 1995.
Admission: For charges and concessionary rates contact The Estate Office, Bramham Park, Wetherby, W. Yorks LS23 6ND Tel: (0937) 844265.
Refreshments: Picnics in grounds permitted.
The Red Lion in Bramham village offers bar meals and traditional Sunday lunches.

DEWSBURY MUSEUM

(Kirklees Metropolitan Council)
Crow West Park, Dewsbury map **15** P19
Telephone: (01924) 468171

Refurnished mansion house, childhood displays, 1940s schoolroom.

Open: Mon-Fri 11-5 Sat-Sun 12-5.
Admission: Free.

EAST RIDDLESDEN HALL    The National Trust

Keighley   map **15** P19   ♿
Telephone: (01535) 607075

17th century manor house. Magnificent tithe barn. Small formal garden.

Location: 1 m NE of Keighley on S side of A650, on N bank of Aire.
Station(s): Keighley (1½ m).
Open: 1 Apr-31 Oct Sat-Wed also Good Fri. and Fri in July and Aug 12.00-5. Last adm 4.30.
Admission: £3 Children £1.50 Family £6 Parties £2.50 Child parties £1.25.
Refreshments: Afternoon teas and refreshments in Bothy tea-room adjacent to house (on first floor) special arrangements for disabled visitors contact Administrator.
Dogs with the exception of guide dogs, allowed in grounds only and must be on a lead. Only ground floor and garden accessible for disabled visitors. Braille guide. Baby changing facilities. Shop and tea-room open as house.

HAREWOOD HOUSE AND BIRD GARDEN

(The Earl of Harewood)
Leeds   **LS17 9LQ**   map **15** P19   Ⓢ
Telephone: (0113) 2886331/263225
Fax: (0113) 2886467

Harewood House, home of the Earl and Countess of Harewood, was designed for the Lascelles family by John Carr in 1759. The magnificent interior, created by Robert Adam, has superb ceilings and plasterwork and contains a fine collection of English and Italian paintings, Chippendale furniture and Sevres and Chinese porcelain. New for 1995 is a dedicated Watercolour Gallery. In the grounds, landscaped by 'Capability' Brown, are lakeside and woodland walks, an internationally-renowned Bird Garden with 120 species, many endangered, and an outstanding Adventure Playground. Sir Charles Barry's parterre design on the Terrace has been

continued over...

HAREWOOD HOUSE AND BIRD GARDEN - *continued*

restored to its original condition of intricate patterns made with box, bedding plants and white chippings. The Earl of Harewood is the son of the late Princess Mary, daughter of King George V, and is a cousin of Queen Elizabeth II. Princess Mary lived at Harewood for many years and some of her pictures and possessions are on display in her rooms.

Location: 7 m S of Harrogate; 8 m N of Leeds on Leeds/Harrogate road; Junction A61/659 at Harewood village; 5 m from A1 at Wetherby 22m from York. No. 36 bus from Leeds or Harrogate.
Station(s): Leeds.
Open: House, Grounds, Bird Garden and all Facilities Mar 25-Oct 31 daily. Gates open 10 House open 11. Concession rates for Coach parties, school parties welcome at all times.
Admission: Charges and details of Special Event Admissions - including Car Rallies and Leeds Championship Dog Show available from Gerald Long, Visitors Information, Estate Office, Harewood, Leeds LS17 9LQ.
Refreshments: Cafeteria; Courtyard Suite; State Dining Room (private functions-max 50).
Conferences: Courtyard Functions Suite for Conferences/Product launches all year.

LEDSTON HALL
(G.H.H. Wheler, Esq)
nr Castleford   WF10 2BB   map **15** P20

17th century mansion with some earlier work.

Location: 2 m N of Castleford off A656.
Station(s): Castleford (2¾ m).
Open: Exterior only May June July and Aug Mon-Fri 9-4. Other days by appointment.
Refreshments: Chequers Inn, Ledsham (1 m).

LOTHERTON HALL
(Leeds City Council)
Aberford   LS25 3EB   map **15** P20
Telephone: (0113) 281 3259
Fax: (0113) 260 2285

Lotherton Hall was built round an earlier house dating from the mid-eighteenth century. The extensions to the east were completed in 1896 and those to the west in 1903. The Hall, with its art collection, park and gardens, was given to the City of Leeds by Sir Alvary and Lady Gascoigne in 1968 and opened as a country house museum in 1969. The Gascoigne collection, which contains pictures, furniture, silver and porcelain of the 17th and 18th centuries, as well as works of a later period, includes a magnificent portrait of Sir Thomas Gascoigne by Pompeo Batoni and an impressive group of silver race cups ranging in date from 1776 to 1842. The first floor and costume galleries were opened in 1970 and the oriental gallery in 1975. There is also a Museum shop and audio visual room.

Location: 1 m E of A1 at Aberford on the Towton Road (B1217).
Open: All the year Tues-Sun 10.30-5.30 (or dusk if earlier) closed Mon except Bank Hol Mons.
Admission: Adults £2 children 50p OAPs/students £1 season ticket £4.75 (includes Temple Newsam, see below) pre-booked coach parties £1 Tel: (0113) 813259.
Refreshments: Cafe.

NOSTELL PRIORY   The National Trust
Wakefield   map **15** P20
Telephone: (01924) 863892

Built for Sir Rowland Winn by Paine; a wing added in 1766 by Robert Adam. State rooms contain pictures and famous Chippendale furniture made especially for the house.

Location: 6 m SE of Wakefield, on N side of A638.
Station(s): Fitzwilliam (1½ m).
Open: 1 Apr-31 Oct Apr May June Sept & Oct Sat 12-5 Sun 11-5 July & Aug to 10 Sept Daily (except Fri) 12-5 Sun 11-5. Bank Hols 11-5, not Good Fri. Guided tours on weekdays only (last tour 4).
Admission: HOUSE & GROUNDS £3.50 Children £1.80 Family £7 Parties £3 Child parties £1.50. GROUNDS £2.20 Children £1.10 Family £4.40. Free parking. Pre-booked parties welcome outside normal published opening times. However, on these occasions, a charge will be made to National Trust members.
Refreshments: Lunches and afternoon teas available in stable tea-rooms (not NT).
Dogs in grounds on leads, not in house (except guide dogs). Lift available for disabled.

OAKWELL HALL
(Kirklees Metropolitan Council)
Birstall   WF19 9LG   map **15** P19
Telephone: (01924) 474926
Fax: (01924) 420536

Historic house, 17th century furnishings, country park, visitor centre.

Open: Mon-Fri 11-5 Sat-Sun 12-5.
Admission: Charges between 1 Mar-31 Oct. Please phone for details.
Refreshments: Oak Tree Cafe, light refreshments, restricted opening in winter.
Events/Exhibitions: Year round programme. Telephone for leaflet.
Conferences: Restored Oakwell barn and classroom available.

RED HOUSE

(Kirklees Metropolitan Council)
Gomersal, Cleckheaton   map **15** P19
Telephone: (01274) 872165

1830s period home, strong Bronte connections. Shop, exhibitions, garden.

Open: Mon-Fri 11-5 Sat-Sun 12-5.
Admission: Free.

SHIBDEN HALL

(Calderdale Metropolitan Borough Council)
Halifax   HG3 6XG   map **15** P19   △ &
Telephone: (01422) 352246 or (01422) 321455
Fax: (01422) 348440

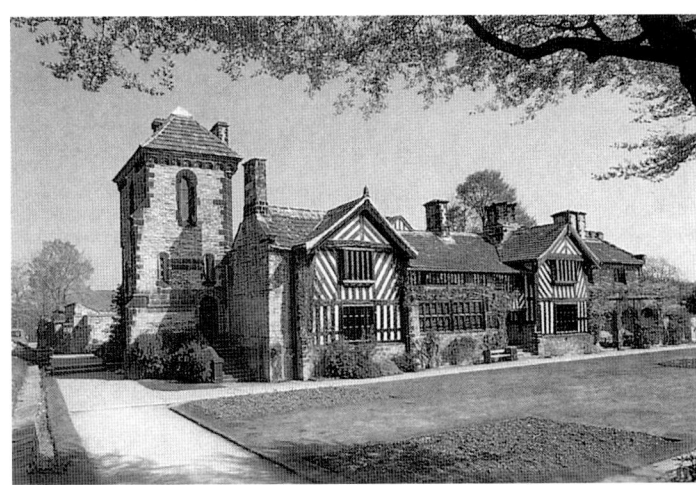

An early 15th century half-timbered house with later additions, furnished with 17th to 19th century material. The 17th century barn and outbuildings are equipped with early agricultural implements and craft workshops. The museum is set in a large park and surrounded by terrace gardens. Cafe facilities.

Location: 1½ m SE of Halifax on the Halifax/Hipperholme Road (A58).
Station(s): Halifax.
Open: Mar-Nov Mons-Sats 10-5 Suns 12-5 please telephone for winter opening.
Admission: Adults £1.50 children/OAPs 75p family ticket £4.50. Conducted tours after normal hours (Fee payable).
Refreshments: At the Hall.
Ground floor access for disabled.

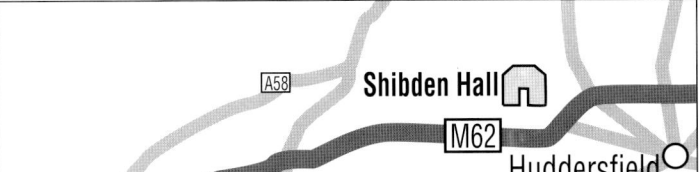

TEMPLE NEWSAM HOUSE

(Leeds City Council)
Leeds   LS15 0AE   map **15** P20
Telephone: (0113) 264 7321
Fax: (0113) 260 2285

The Temple Newsam estate belonged to the Knights Templar and later passed to the D'Arcy family who retained it until 1537. The house was the birthplace of Lord Darnley and a centre of English and Scottish intrique during the reign of Elizabeth I. It was later acquired by Sir Arthur Ingram, whose descendants became Viscounts Irwin. It was eventually inherited by the late Lord Halifax who sold it to Leeds Corporation in 1922. The house has many fine features of 16th and 17th century date, as well as a magnificent suite of Georgian rooms, and contains some superb furniture, silver, ceramics and a fine collection of pictures. There is also a Museum shop in the house.

Location: 5 m E of Leeds; 1 m S of A63 (nr junction with A641).
Station(s): Cross Gates (1¾ m).
Open: All the year Tues-Sun 10.30-5.30 (or dusk if earlier) closed Mons except Bank Hol Mons.
Admission: Adults £2 children 50p OAPs/students £1 season tickets £4.75 (includes Lotherton Hall, see above) pre-booked coach parties £1 Tel: (0113) 264 7321.
Refreshments: Tea-room.

TOLSON MEMORIAL MUSEUM

(Kirklees Metropolitan Council)
Ravensknowle Park, Huddersfield   HD5 8DJ   map **15** P19
Telephone: (01484) 541455

Victorian mansion, local natural history, archaeology and social history.

Open: Mon-Fri 11-5 Sat-Sun 12-5.
Admission: Free.

WALES

CLWYD

BODELWYDDAN CASTLE
(Bodelwyddan Castle Trust)
Bodelwyddan, St Asaph   LL18 5YA   map **6** Q16
Telephone: (01745) 584060
Fax: (01745) 584563

Bodelwyddan Castle has been authentically restored as a Victorian Country House and contains a major collection of portraits and photography from the National Portrait Gallery. The collection includes works by many eminent Victorian Portraitists such as G. F. Watts, William Holman Hunt, John Singer Sargeant, Sir Edwin Landseer and Sir Thomas Lawrence. The portraits are complemented by furniture from the Victoria & Albert Museum and sculptures from the Royal Academy. An exhibition of Victorian Amusements and inventions features parlour games, puzzles and optical illusions - an extravaganza of Victorian fun, games and hands-on experience of the 19th century! The Castle is set in rolling parkland and gardens against the impressive backdrop of the Clwydian Hills. A programme of events takes place throughout the year. Winner of the Museum of the Year Award. Free audio guide and quiz sheet.

Location: Just off the A55 near St. Asaph (opposite the Marble Church).
Open: Apr 8-June 30 and Sept 8-Oct 31 daily except Fri 10*-5 July 1-Sept 7 daily 10*-5 Nov 1-Mar 30 1996 daily except Mon and Fri 11-4. Last admission 1 hour before closing. *Castle galleries open at 10.30.
Admission: Castle and Grounds adults £4 OAPs/unemployed £3.50 children/students/disabled £2.50 family (2+2) £10. Grounds only adults £1.50 OAPs/unemployed £1.50 children/students/disabled £1.50 family (2+2) £5.
Refreshments: Victorian Tea-room. Full catering service at the Warner Hotel on site.
Events/Exhibitions: Programme of temporary exhibitions, concerts and events throughout the year.
Suitable for disabled persons (wheelchairs available). Giftshop. Picnic Area. Woodland Walk. Maze and Aviary.

Butterfly Houses

can be found at the following properties included in Historic Houses Castles and Gardens:-

Berkeley Castle
Elsham Hall - Wild butterflywalkway
Syon House

CHIRK CASTLE   🌿 The National Trust
nr Wrexham   LL14 5AF   map **6** R16
Telephone: (01691) 777701

Built 1310; a unique example of a border castle of Edward I's time, continuously inhabited. Interesting portraits, tapestries etc. Gardens. Celebrates 700th anniversary this year.

Location: ½ m from Chirk (on A5 trunk road) then 1½ m private driveway; 20 m NW of Shrewsbury 7 m SE of Llangollen.
Station(s): Chirk (2 m).
Open: 2 Apr-29 Sept daily except Mon and Sat but open BH Mon July and Aug open daily except Sat. 1 Oct-29 Oct open Sat & Sun. Castle 12-5 Gardens 11-6. Last admissions 4.30.
Admission: Adults £4 children £2. Pre-booked parties of 20 or more £3.20. Family ticket (max 2 adults 2 children) £10. Connoisseurs' Tours, Tues mornings by prior arrangement only for parties of min. 20.
Refreshments: Tea-rooms (light lunches & teas).
No dogs. Limited access for wheelchairs.

ERDDIG   🌿 The National Trust
nr Wrexham   LL13 0YT   map **6** Q16   Ⓔ
Telephone: (01978) 313333

Late 17th century house with 18th century additions and containing much of the original furniture, set in a garden restored to 18th century formal design and containing varieties of fruit known to have been grown there during that period. Range of domestic outbuildings include laundry, bakehouse, sawmill and smithy, all in working order; fine walks in extensive woods and parkland.

Location: 2 m S of Wrexham off A525 or A483.
Station(s): Wrexham Central (1¾ m); Wrexham General (2½ m), includes 1 m driveway to House. Crosville bus service Number 37 direct to House from Wrexham.
Open: 14 Apr (Good Fri)-1 Oct daily except Thur and Fri House 12-5 Gardens 11-6 Last admission 4. 2 Oct-29 Oct Whole house Sat and Sun only, below stairs only Mon Tues and Wed House 12-4 Gardens 11-5 Last admission 3.
Admission: Ticket for below stairs gardens and outbuildings only Adults £3.20 children £1.60 Family (max 2 adults, 2 children) £8 pre-booked group £2.50. All-inclusive ticket (includes Downstairs all inclusive ticket) Adult £5 children £2.50 pre-booked group £4. NB Mid week discount Mon Tues Wed (except BH Mon) in July and August.
Refreshments: Morning coffee. Light lunches & teas.

EWLOE CASTLE
(Cadw: Welsh Historic Monuments)
nr Hawarden   map **6** Q16

Native Welsh castle with typical round and aspidal towers.

Open: All times.
Admission: Free.

GYRN CASTLE
(Sir Geoffrey Bates, BT, MC)
Llanasa, Holywell   map **6** Q16
Telephone: (01745) 853500

Dating, in part, from 1700; castellated 1820. Large picture gallery, panelled entrance hall. Pleasant woodland walks and fantastic views to Mersey and Lake District.

Location: 26 m W of Chester (off A55); 4 m SE of Prestatyn.
Open: All the year-by appointment.
Admission: £3, parties welcome.
Refreshments: By arrangement.

PLAS NEWYDD AND THE LADIES OF LLANGOLLEN
(Glyndŵr District Council)
Llangollen　LL20 8AW　map **6** R16
Telephone: (01978) 861314
Fax: (01691) 773595

Plas Newydd was the home of Lady Eleanor Butler and Miss Sarah Ponsonby, the 'Ladies of Llangollen' from 1780-1831. They eloped from Kilkenny, Ireland before settling in the enchanted spot of Llangollen. They became the centre of a personality cult which still draws visitors today as strongly as it did during the Regency period. The house retains some of the Gothic elements that they introduced, the gardens also possess the peace and tranquility that they sought.

Station(s): Nearest station Ruabon 7 miles
Open: 1 Apr-31 Oct Mon-Sun 10-5.
Admission: Adults £1.80 children 90p (1995 prices). Limited car parking.

VALLE CRUCIS ABBEY
(Cadw: Welsh Historic Monuments)
Llangollen　LL20 8DD　map **6** R16
Telephone: (01978) 860326

Lovely ruins of a 13th century Abbey set beside the Eglwyseg stream.

Open: Mar 28-Oct 22 daily 9.30-6.30 Oct 23-Mar 26 weekdays 9.30-4 Sun 2-4.
Admission: Adults £1.50 reduced £1 family £4.

DYFED

CAREW CASTLE & TIDAL MILL
(Pembrokeshire Coast National Park)
Carew, Tenby　map **2** T13
Telephone: (01646) 651782
Fax: (01646) 651782

A magnificent Norman Castle - later Elizabethan residence. Royal links with Henry Tudor, setting for Great Tournament of 1507. The Mill is only restored tidal mill in Wales. Automatic talking points explaining milling process. Special exhibition, 'The Story of Milling'.

Location: 4 m east of Pembroke.
Station(s): Rail - Pembroke. Bus - Haverfordwest.
Open: Every day Easter-end Oct.
Admission: Entrance Carew Castle or Tidal Mill £1.50 dual ticket £2 children/OAPs special rate. School parties for both £1.20 per pupil. Teachers free.

CARREG CENNEN CASTLE
(Cadw: Welsh Historic Monuments)
Trapp　SA19 6UA　map **2** T14
Telephone: (01558) 822291

A 13th century castle dramatically perched on a limestone precipice.

Open: Mar 28-Oct 22 daily 9.30-6.30 Oct 23 -Mar 26 daily 9.30-4.
Admission: Adults £2 reduced £1.50 family ticket £6.

CILGERRAN CASTLE
(Cadw: Welsh Historic Monuments)
Cilgerran　SA43 2SF　map **2** S13
Telephone: (01239) 615007

Picturesque remains that date essentially from the early 13th century.

Open: Mar 28-Oct 22 daily 9.30-6.30 Oct 23-Mar 26 weekdays 9.30-4 Sun 2-4.
Admission: Adults £1.50 reduced £1 family ticket £4.

COLBY WOODLAND GARDEN 🍂 The National Trust
Amroth　SA67 8PP　map **2** T13
Telephone: (01558) 822800/(01834) 811885

An attractive woodland garden. The early 19th century house is not open. There are walks through secluded valleys along open and wooded pathways, one of which links the property with the nearby coastal resort of Amroth.

Location: NE of Tenby off A477; E of junction A477/A478.
Station(s): Kilgetty (2½ m).
Open: 1 Apr-3 Nov daily 10-5. Walled Garden 1 Apr-30 Oct 11-5.
Admission: Adults £2.60 Children £1.10 Adult groups £2.10 Child/School Groups 90p. 1 child (16 and under) free per 1 paying adult during period 25 July-4 September.
Refreshments: Morning coffee, light refreshments and tea daily 10-5.
Mr. & Mrs. A. Scourfield Lewis allow access to walled garden 1 Apr-30 Oct 11-5. Shop, plant sales, gallery, open as property.

DINEFWR PARK 🍂 The National Trust
Llandeilo　SA19 6RT　map **2** T14
Telephone: (01558) 823902
Fax: (01558) 822036

A Victorian-Gothic mansion with an 18th century landscaped park. Part of the ground floor is accessible (no contents inside house, which is under repair) and a minor exhibition and video explains the history of Dinefwr. There is a rear Victorian garden, and an ancient deer park with White Park cattle. Access to the outside of Dinefwr Castle and Llandysfeisant Church (owned by Dyfed Wildlife Trust). Also, footpaths through parts of 400 acre estate and outstanding views of the Towy Valley.

Location: A40 nr Llandeilo.
Open: 1 Apr-1 Oct daily 10.30-5. The park is open during the winter in daylight hours.
Admission: Adults £1.70 Children 90p Adult group £1.30 Child group 70p Last admission one hour before closing. 1 child (16 and under) free per 1 paying adult during period 25 July-4 Sept.
Refreshments: Cafeteria and WCs in car park.

KIDWELLY CASTLE
(Cadw: Welsh Historic Monuments)
Kidwelly　SA17 5BQ　map **2** T14
Telephone: (01554) 890104

An outstanding example of late 13th century castle design.

Open: Mar 28-Oct 22 daily 9.30-6.30 Oct 23-Mar 26 Please phone for times.
Admission: Adults £2 reduced £1.50 family £6.

LAMPHEY BISHOP'S PALACE
(Cadw: Welsh Historic Monuments)
Lamphey　SA71 5NT　map **2** T13
Telephone: (01646) 672224

Substantial remains of the medieval Bishops of St David's residence.

Open: May 1-Sept 30 10-5. Otherwise open at all times.
Admission: Adults £1.50 Reduced £1.

LLAWHADEN CASTLE
(Cadw: Welsh Historic Monuments)
Llawhaden　map **2** T13
Telephone: (01437) 541201

A fortified palace at the centre of a manorial estate belonging to the Bishops of St Davids.

Open: Mar 28-Oct 22 9.30-6.30 daily Oct 23-Mar 26 weekdays 9.30-4 Sun 2-4.

PICTON CASTLE

(The Picton Castle Trust)
Haverfordwest   SA62 4AS   map **2** T13   △
Telephone: (01437) 751326

A scheduled ancient monument, but also a beautiful home, occupied continuously since the 15th century by the Philipps family who are still in residence.

Location: 4 m SE of Haverfordwest S of A40 via the Rhos.
Station(s): Haverfordwest.
Open: Castle open Easter Sun & Mon and following Bank Hols also every Sun & Thurs mid July-mid Sept 2-5. Grounds Apr 1-Sept 30 daily 10.30-5 except Mon. Graham Sutherland Gallery (tel: (01437) 751296) Apr 1-Sept 30 daily 10.30-12.30 and 1.30-5 except Mon but open Bank Hol Mons. Dates and times of opening under review.
Admission: Grounds £2 Castle and Grounds £3 children and OAPs half-price (Subject to review). Free car park.
Refreshments: Restaurant *Closed* Mon.
Craft Shop. Garden shop.Closed Monday.

ST. DAVIDS BISHOP'S PALACE

(Cadw: Welsh Historic Monuments)
St Davids   SA62 6PE   map **2** T12
Telephone: (01437) 720517

A most impressive medieval Bishop's Palace within the Cathedral Close.

Open: Mar 28-Oct 22 daily 9.30-6.30 Oct 23-Mar 26 weekdays 9.30-4 Sun 2-4.
Admission: Adults £1.50 reduced £1 family ticket £4.

STRATA FLORIDA ABBEY

(Cadw: Welsh Historic Monuments)
Strata Florida   SY25 6BT   map **2** S15
Telephone: (01974) 831261

The ruins of this Cistercian abbey (1164) stand in a lovely valley.

Open: May 1-Sept 30 daily 9.30-6.30 otherwise open at all times.
Admission: Adults £1.50 reduced £1 Family ticket £4.

TALLEY ABBEY

(Cadw: Welsh Historic Monuments)
Talley   map **2** T14
Telephone: (01558) 685444

A 13th century monastic site founded for the Premonstratensian Order.

Open: Mar 28-Oct 22 daily 9.30-6.30 Oct 23-Mar 26 weekdays 9.30-4 Sun 2-4.
Admission: Adults £1 reduced 60p.

TUDOR MERCHANT'S HOUSE   The National Trust

Tenby   map **2** T13
Telephone: (01834) 842279

An example of a merchant's house of the 15th century.

Location: Quay Hill, Tenby.
Station(s): Tenby (8 mins walk) (not Suns, except June-Aug).
Open: 2 Apr-31 Oct Mon-Fri 10.30-5.30 Sun 1.30-5.30. Closed Sat.
Admission: Adults £1.60 Children 80p   Adult group £1.30 Child/school group 60p. One child (16 and under) free per 1 paying adult during period 25 July-4 Sept.

MID GLAMORGAN

CAERPHILLY CASTLE

(Cadw: Welsh Historic Monuments)
Caerphilly   CF8 1JL   map **14** T16
Telephone: (01222) 883143

One of the largest medieval castles, water defences of 30 acres

Open: Mar 28-Oct 22 daily 9.30-6.30 Oct 23-Mar 26 Please phone for times.
Admission: Adults £2 reduced £1.50 family (2 adults & 3 children) £6.

COITY CASTLE

(Cadw: Welsh Historic Monuments)
Coity   map **3** T15
Telephone: (01656) 652021

An early Norman stronghold. In the Owain Glyndwr Uprising, the castle withstood a siege by the Welsh.

Open: Open at all times. (Key keeper arrangement).

LLANCAIACH FAWR

(Rhymney Valley District Council)
Treharris   map **14** T16
Telephone: (01443) 412248

Llancaiach Fawr is an award-winning Living History Museum set in this beautifully restored semi-fortified Manor House. Built in the 1530's by the Prichard family the house came to the centre of public interest during the Civil War period when the master of Llancaiach Fawr dramatically changed his allegiance from Royalist to Parliamentarian. Today the house is furnished as it was when King Charles visited in 1645. Costumed stewards, taking on the roles of servants from the gentry household of Colonel Prichard, guide visitors around with fascinating tales of 17th century life. Visitors can try out the furniture, dress in period costume or even take a turn in the stocks! The period gardens have also been recreated whilst an excellent Visitor Centre provides an insight into the history of the house through exhibition and audio visual displays. Other visitor centre facilities include gift shop, restaurant, teaching room. There is disabled access to all Visitor Centre facilites, the garden and ground floor of the house itself. Wales Tourist Board 'Best New Tourist Attraction 1992.' British Tourist Authority 'Come To Britain Special Award Winner 1991.'

Location: Thirty minutes north of Cardiff (M4 Jtn 32) just off the A470 at Nelson on the B4254.
Station(s): Ystrad Mynach (3 miles - bus connects).
Open: All year except Dec 25, 26, Jan 1. Mon to Fri 10-5.00, Sat and Sun 10-6.00. Last admission 1½ hours before closing.
Admission: Charged. Ample free car and coach parking.
Refreshments: In Conservatory Cafe. Serves 17th century 'dish of the day' as well as more contemporary cuisine. Ghost Tours, Murder Mysteries and 17th Century Evenings in the manor.

SOUTH GLAMORGAN

CASTELL COCH
(Cadw: Welsh Historic Monuments)
Tongwynlais, nr Cardiff CF4 7JS map **14** T16
Telephone: (01222) 810101

This late 19th century castle - a combination of Victorian Gothic fantasy and timeless fairytale - peeps unexpectedly through the trees on the north hills of Cardiff.

Open: Mar 28-Oct 22 daily 9.30-6.30 Oct 23-Mar25 Please phone for times.
Admission: Adults £2 reduced £1.50 family (2 adults & 3 children) £6.

WEST GLAMORGAN

NEATH ABBEY
(Cadw: Welsh Historic Monuments)
Neath SA10 7DW map **2** T15
Telephone: (01792) 812387

Originally founded 1130, the abbey was absorbed into the Cistercian order in 1147.

Open: All times.

WEOBLEY CASTLE
(Cadw: Welsh Historic Monuments)
Llanrhidian, nr. Swansea SA3 1HB map **2** T14
Telephone: (01792) 390012

Picturesque fortified late medieval manor house.

Open: Mar 28-Oct 22 daily 9.30-6.30 Oct 23-Mar 26 week days 9.30-4 Sun 2-4.
Admission: Adults £1.50 reduced £1 family ticket £4.

GWENT

CAERLEON ROMAN FORTRESS
(Cadw: Welsh Historic Monuments)
Caerleon NP6 1AY map **14** T17
Telephone: (01633) 422518

Impressive remains of baths, amphitheatre, barracks and fortress wall.

Open: Mar 28-Oct 22 daily 9.30-6.30 Oct 23-Mar 26 Please phone for details.
Admission: Adults £1.50 reduced £1 family ticket £4.

CHEPSTOW CASTLE
(Cadw: Welsh Historic Monuments)
Chepstow NP6 5EZ map **14** T17
Telephone: (01291) 624065

This strategic fortress is one of the earliest stone built castles.

Open: Mar 28-Oct 22, daily 9.30-6.30 Oct 23-Mar 26 Phone for opening times.
Admission: Adults £2.90 reduced £1.50 family (2 adults 3 children) £8.

PENHOW CASTLE
(Stephen Weeks, Esq)
nr Newport NP6 3AD map **14** T17 △ Ⓔ Ⓢ
Telephone: (01633) 400800
Fax: (01633) 400990

Three Sandford Awards. Penhow Castle is Wales' Oldest Lived-in Castle, and was the first home in Britain of the illustrious Seymour family, ancestors of Queen Jane Seymour, King Edward VI and the Dukes of Somerset. This most enchanting Knight's Border Castle has been substantially restored since 1973 by the present owner. Visitors explore the many period rooms guided by the acclaimed 'Time Machine' Walkman Tours included in the admission price. Visitors discover at their own pace the only restored Norman Bedchamber in Wales, the splendid view from atop the Keep Tower's battlements, 15th century Great Hall with its minstrels' gallery, Tudor Moat Room and excavated moat, elegant Charles II panelled Dining Room, 18th century kitchen, cosy Victorian Housekeeper's room and more. The Castle holds several awards for its fine restoration, entertaining Tours and imaginative educational activities.

Location: On A48, midway between Chepstow and Newport. M4 junctions 22 or 24.
Station(s): Newport.
Open: Good Fri-end of Sept Wed-Sun inclusive and Bank Holidays Aug open daily 10-last adm 5.15. Winter opening Wed only 10-4 and selected Sun afternoons 1-4. Open all year round for group bookings, Evening Candlelit Tours and Educational Visits. Christmas Candlelit Tours Nov 15-Jan 5.
Admission: Adults £3.15 children £1.85 family (2+2) £8.15. Price includes choice of TIME MACHINE Walkman Tours.
Refreshments: Tea-bar at tour point.
Events/Exhibitions: Have the Castle to yourselves! Groups of 10+ can book an atmospheric Evening Candlelit Tour at any time of the year, possibly with light refreshment. Seasonal party evenings for the Christmas Tour see the Castle traditionally decorated, with carols and customs, log fires and holly, mince pies and hot punch. Remember Christmas past, today!
Accommodation: Bed & Breakfast in a distinctive 17th century guest room with genuine Edwin Lutyens bed; private bathroom. Free castle tour.
Conferences: 12th century Keep Room seats 14 for dinner in the oldest Dining Room still in regular use in the whole of Britain!

RAGLAN CASTLE
(Cadw: Welsh Historic Monuments)
Raglan NP5 2BT map **14** T17
Telephone: (01291) 690228

A 15th century castle with its tower, the 'Yellow Tower of Gwent'.

Open: Mar 28-Oct 22 daily 9.30-6.30 Oct 23-Mar 26 Phone for opening times.
Admission: Adults £2 reduced £1.50 family (up to 2 adults 3 children) £6.

TINTERN ABBEY
(Cadw: Welsh Historic Monuments)
Tintern NP6 6SE map **14** T17
Telephone: (01291) 689251

Impressive ruins of Cistercian abbey 1131 set in the Wye valley.

Open: Mar 28-Oct 22 daily 9.30-6.30 Oct 23-Mar 26 Please phone for times.
Admission: Adults £2 reduced £1.30 family (2 adults 3 children) £6.

TREDEGAR HOUSE
(Newport Borough Council)
Newport   map **14** T17   △
Telephone: (01633) 815880

One wing of the 16th century house survives, but Tredegar House owes its character to lavish 17th century rebuilding in brick. Ancestral home of the Morgan family, Lords of Tredegar. The 90 acre park includes gardens, lake, adventure play farm, carriage rides and craft workshops.

Location: SW of Newport; signposted from M4 junction 28, A48.
Station(s): Newport (2¾ m).
Open: Park open daily 6.15-Sunset. House and Attractions open Good Fri-Sept Wed-Sun and Public Hols and Tues school hols and weekends in Oct. House Tours every ½ hour from 11.30-4. House open at other times by appointment.
Admission: House and Walled Gardens adults £3.60 children/OAPs £2.80 family £9 coach and school parties welcome if booked in advance.
Refreshments: Lunch and teas at the Brewhouse Tea-room. Supper tours by arrangement.
Events/Exhibitions: Concerts and special events inside the House. Open air theatre, festivals and shows in the Park.
Conferences: Conference and meeting facilities, also wedding receptions and private functions by arrangement.

WHITE CASTLE
(Cadw: Welsh Historic Monuments)
Llantilio Crossenny   NP7 8UD   map **3** T17
Telephone: (0160085) 380

Imposing moated remains of 12th century castle by Henry II.

Open: Mar 28Oct 22 daily 9.30-6.30 Oct 23-Mar 26 open at all times.
Admission: Adults £1.50 reduced £1.
Refreshments: Abergavenny.

GWYNEDD

ABERCONWY HOUSE 🌿 The National Trust
Conwy   LL32 8AY   map **6** Q15
Telephone: (01492) 592246

Town house that dates from 14th century. Furnished rooms and an audio-visual presentation show daily life from different periods in its history.

Location: In the town at junction of Castle Street & High Street.
Station(s): Conwy 300 yds.
Open: 31 Mar-30 Oct daily except Tues 10-5. Last admission 4.30.
Admission: Adults £1.80 children 90p family (max 2 adults 2 children) £4.50. Pre-booked group visits £1.60.
Shop. Open all year daily 9.30-5.30. Closed Sundays Nov-Mar.

BODNANT GARDEN 🌿 The National Trust
Tal-y-Cafn   LL28 5RE   map **6** Q15   &
Telephone: (01492) 650460

Begun in 1875 by Henry Pochin. Amongst the finest gardens in the country. Magnificent collections of rhododendrons, camellias, magnolias and conifers.

Location: 8 m S of Llandudno & Colwyn Bay on A470; Entrance along Eglwysbach Road. Sign posted from A55 North Wales coastal route.
Station(s): Tal-y-Cafn (1½ m).
Open: 18 Mar-31 Oct daily 10-5. Last admission 4.30.
Admission: Adults £3.90 children £1.95 pre-booked parties of 20 or more £3.50.
Refreshments: Pavilion in car park.
No dogs (except guide dogs for the blind) Wheelchairs provided but garden is steep and difficult. Braille guide.

BEAUMARIS CASTLE
(WORLD HERITAGE LISTED SITE)
(Cadw: Welsh Historic Monuments)
Beaumaris, Anglesey   LL58 8AP   map **6** Q14
Telephone: (01248) 810361

The last and largest of the castles built by King Edward I.

Open: Mar 28-Oct 22 daily 9.30-6.30 Oct 23-Mar 26 Please phone for times.
Admission: Adults £1.50 reduced £1 family £4.

CAERNARFON CASTLE
(WORLD HERITAGE LISTED SITE)
(Cadw: Welsh Historic Monuments)
Caernarfon   LL55 2AY   map **6** Q14
Telephone: (01286) 677617

Mighty medieval fortress built by King Edward I.

Open: Mar 28-Oct 22 daily 9.30-6.30 Oct 23-Mar 26 Please phone for times.
Admission: Adults £3.50 reduced £2.50 family (2 adults & 3 children) £10.

COCHWILLAN OLD HALL
(R.C.H. Douglas Pennant, Esq)
Talybont, Bangor LL57 3AZ map **6** Q14
Telephone: (01248) 364608

Fine example of medieval architecture (restored 1971).

Location: 3½ m Bangor; 1 m Talybont village off A55.
Open: Open by appointment.

CONWY CASTLE (WORLD HERITAGE LISTED SITE)
(Cadw: Welsh Historic Monuments)
Conwy LL32 8AY map **6** Q156
Telephone: (01492) 592358

Imposing medieval fortress built between 1283 and 1289.

Open: Mar 28-Oct 22 daily 9.30-6.30 Oct 23-Mar 26 Please phone for times.
Admission: Adults £2.90 reduced £1.50 family £8 (2 adults & 3 children).

CRICCIETH CASTLE
(Cadw: Welsh Historic Monuments)
Criccieth LL52 0DP map **6** R14
Telephone: (01766) 522227

Castle (1230) perched in a commanding position above Tremadog Bay.

Open: Mar 28-Oct 22 daily 9.30-6.30 Oct 23-Mar 26 weekdays 9.30-4 Suns 2-4.
Admission: Adults £2 reduced £1.50 family (2 adults & 3 children) £6.

CYMER ABBEY
(Cadw: Welsh Historic Monuments)
Dolgellau map **6** R15
Telephone: (01341) 422854

Substantial remains of Cistercian abbey founded in 1199.

Open: Mar 28-Oct 22 daily 9.30-6.30 Oct 25-Mar 26 weekdays 9.30-4 Sun 2-4.
Admission: Adults £1 reduced 60p.

GWYDIR UCHAF CHAPEL
(Cadw: Welsh Historic Monuments)
Llanrwst map **6** Q15
Telephone: (01492) 640978

A 17th century chapel with elaborately painted ceilings and walls.

Location: On Forestry Commission land ½ m SW of Llanrwst. B5106, then minor road, then forest road.
Station(s): Llanrwst ½ m.
Open: Mon-Fri 8.30-4.00 weekends closed.
Admission: Adults £1.00 reduced 60p.
Refreshments: Llanrwst.

HARLECH CASTLE (WORLD HERITAGE LISTED SITE)
(Cadw: Welsh Historic Monuments)
Harlech LL46 2YH map **6** R14
Telephone: (01766) 780552

This magnificent castle was built by King Edward I in 1283.

Open: Mar 28-Oct 22 daily 9.30-6.30 Oct 23-Mar 26 Please phone for times.
Admission: Adults £2.90 reduced £1.80 family (2 adults & 3 children) £8.

Giovanni Antonio Canale
- known as Canaletto
Born in Venice 1697, died 1768
Lived in England 1746 - 1755

His work can be seen in the following properties included in Historic Houses Castles and Gardens:-

Alnwick Castle
Bowhill
Goodwood House
Upton House

PENRHYN CASTLE 🍀 The National Trust
Bangor LL57 4HN map **6** Q14 Ⓔ
Telephone: (01248) 353084 Information line (01248) 371337

The 19th century Castle is a unique and outstanding example of neo-Norman architecture. The garden and grounds have exotic and rare trees and shrubs. There is an Industrial Railway Museum. Victorian formal garden. Superb views of mountains and Menai Strait. Audio tour.

Location: 1 m E of Bangor, on A5122.
Station(s): Bangor (3 m).
Open: 29 Mar-29 Oct daily except Tues. Castle 12-5 (11-5 in July & Aug) grounds 11-6. Last admission 4.30 (last audio tour 4).
Admission: Adult £4.40 children £2.20 booked parties of 20 or more £3.50. Family ticket £11 (max 2 adults 2 children). Audio tour for adults and children in Welsh and English. School and youth groups by arrangement.
Refreshments: Light lunches & teas at Castle.
Dogs in grounds only on lead. Access to all ground floor rooms for disabled. Wheelchair available. Braille Guide. Golf buggy (prior Booking required).

PLAS BRONDANW GARDENS
nr Penrhyndeudraeth map **6** R14
Telephone: (01766) 771136

Created by Sir Clough Williams-Ellis, architect of Portmeirion, below his ancestral home. Italian inspired gardens with spectacular mountain views, topiary and folly tower.

Location: 2 m N of Penrhyndeudraeth. ¼ m off the A4085 on Croesor Road.
Open: Open all year daily 9-5.
Admission: Adults £1.50 children 25p.

PLAS NEWYDD 🍀 The National Trust
Isle of Anglesey LL61 6EQ map **6** Q14
Telephone: (01248) 714795

18th century house by James Wyatt in unspoilt position adjacent to Menai Strait. Magnificent views to Snowdonia. Fine spring garden. Rex Whistler exhibition and mural painting. Military museum.

Location: 1 m SW of Llanfairpwll on A4080 to Brynsiencyn; turn off A5 to Llanfairpwll at W end of Britannia Bridge.
Station(s): Llanfairpwll (1¾ m).
Open: 31 Mar-29 Sept daily except Sat. 1 Oct-29 Oct Fri and Sun only. House 12-5 Garden 11-5 Last admission 4.30.
Admission: Adults £3.80 children £1.90 Family (max 2 adults 2 children) £9.50. Pre-booked parties of 20 or more £3.
Refreshments: Tea-rooms (light lunches & teas).
Rhododendron Garden open April-early June only. No dogs. Ground floor accessible for disabled. Wheelchair available. Shop, tea-room and WC easy access. Braille Guide.

TŶ MAWR WYBRNANT 🍀 The National Trust
nr Penmachno LL25 0HJ map **6** Q15
Telephone: (01690) 760213

The birthplace of Bishop William Morgan. (c. 1545-1604), the first translator of the whole Bible into Welsh.

Location: At the head of the little valley of Wybrnant, 3½ m SW of Betws-y-Coed; 2 m NW of Penmachno.
Open: 1 Apr-1 Oct Thurs-Sun 12-5. 6-29 Oct Thurs Fri & Sun 12-4.
Admission: No access for coaches. Adult £1.50 children 75p Family (max 2 adults 2 children) £3.75. Pre-booked groups £1.20.
No coaches.

TY'N Y COED 🌿 The National Trust
nr Penmachno LL24 OPS map **6** Q15
Telephone: (01690) 760229

A small holding with 19th century farmhouse and outbuildings. The house is approached through fields of nature and conservation interest.

Location: 1½ m S of Betws-y-Coed on the A5. NT car park approached via Penmachno Woollen Mills' car park.
Open: 2 Apr-1 Oct Thurs Fri and Sun 12-5. 6-29 Oct Thurs Fri & Sat 12-4.
Admission: £1.50 Children 75p Family ticket (max 2 adults 2 children) £3.75 Pre-booked groups £1.20.

POWYS

GREGYNOG
(The University of Wales)
Newtown map **6** R16 △ &
Telephone: (01686) 650224
Fax: (01686) 650656

A Victorian mansion, in 750 acres of wooded parkland with extensive gardens, including one of the most striking displays of rhododendrons in Wales; the Western red cedar 'Zebrina' is probably the biggest tree of this variety in the U.K. Many walks in the grounds. The Hall has an exceptionally fine carved parlour dating to 1636, retained when the old hall was rebuilt in the 1840s. The works of art still remaining from the collections of the Davies sisters include two Rodin bronzes. On show also are books by the Gregynog Press, one of the best-known private presses of the 1920s and 30s, and by the present Gwasg Gregynog, where fine printing is still carried on. This is a working Press and visitors can only be accepted occasionally by prior appointment. Accommodation is sometimes available in the Hall, depending on the nature and size of the resident conference. Since 1963, The Hall has operated as an intercollegiate course and conference centre for the various colleges and institutions of the University of Wales. During the last week in June, an important annual Music Festival is held here.

Location: Near the village of Tregynon, 5 m N of Newtown, off B4389.
Station(s): Newtown
Open: Gardens always open. Hall Jun 1-Sept 30 Mon-Sat. Guided tours at 11 and 3. Hall and Gardens may very exceptionally have to be closed for a day.
Admission: £2 Guided tour to include morning coffee or afternoon tea. Children (under 15) half-price. Parties by arrangement. Free car parking.
Suitable for disabled persons (no wheelchairs provided).

POWIS CASTLE 🌿 The National Trust
Welshpool SY21 8RF map **6** R16 &
Telephone: (01938) 554336

The medieval stronghold of the Welsh princes of Upper Powys, the home of the Herbert family since 1587. Clive of India Museum. Fine plaster work, murals, furniture, paintings and tapestry. Historic terraced garden; herbaceous borders, rare trees and shrubs.

Location: 1 m S of Welshpool off A483; Pedestrian access from High Street (A490);
Station(s): Welshpool (1¼ m); Welshpool Raven Square (1¼ m).
Open: 1 Apr-30 June & 1 Sept-29 Oct daily except Mon and Tues. July and Aug daily except Mon but open Bank Hol Mon. Castle and Clive Museum 12-5 Garden 11-6. Last admission 30 minutes prior yo closing in all cases. Winter opening Sun only until Christmas tea-room and shop 2-4.
Admission: Garden Adults £3.80 chidren £1.90 family max 2 adults 2 children £9.50. Parties £3. All in ticket (incl. Castle, Museum and Garden) Adults £5.80 children £2.90 family £14.50. Parties for Castle, Museum and Garden £5.40.
Refreshments: Tea-rooms (light lunches & teas).
Shop and plant sales. No dogs. Castle not accessible for wheelchair users. Access to tea-room, shop and parts of garden only.

TRETOWER COURT & CASTLE
(Cadw: Welsh Historic Monuments)
Crickhowell NP8 2RF map **3** T16
Telephone: (01874) 730279

One of the finest medieval houses in Wales. The castle is located across an open meadow to the rear. Audio-cassette tour and 'medieval' garden.

Open: Mar 28-Oct 22 daily 9.30-6.30. Oct 23-Mar 26 weekdays 9.30-4 Sun 2-4.
Admission: Adults £2 reduced £1.50 family (2 adults & 3 children) £6.

IRELAND

BANTRY HOUSE
(Mr & Mrs Egerton Shelswell-White)
Bantry, Co Cork   map **16** T4
Telephone: (027) 50047

Partly-Georgian mansion standing at edge of Bantry Bay, with beautiful views. Seat of family of White, formerly Earls of Bantry. Unique collection of tapestries, furniture etc. Terraces and Statuary in the Italian style in grounds.

Location: In outskirts of Bantry (½ m); 56 m SW of Cork.
Open: Open all year-Daily 9-6 *(open until 8 on most summer evenings).*
Admission: House & Grounds £3.00, Children (up to 14) accompanied by parents, free, OAPs/Students £1.75. Parties (20 or more) £2.25.
Refreshments: Tea room. Bed and Breakfast.
Events/Exhibitions: 1796 Bantry French Armada - (permanent exhibition).
Accommodation: Bed and Breakfast and dinner. Nine rooms en suite.
Conferences: Facilities available.
Craft shop.

Lancelot 'Capability' Brown

Born 1716 in Northumberland, Capability Brown began work at the age of 16 in the vegetable gardens of Sir William and Lady Loraine at Kirharle Tower. He left Northumberland in 1739, and records show that he worked at Stowe until 1749. It was at Stowe that Brown began to study architecture, and to submit his own plans. It was also at Stowe that he devised a new method of moving and replanting mature trees.

Brown married Bridget Wayet in 1744 and began work on the estate at Warwick Castle in 1749. He was appointed Master Gardener at Hampton Court in 1764, and planted the Great Vine at Hampton Court in 1768. Blenheim Palace designs are considered amongst Brown's finest work, and the technical achievements were outstanding even for the present day.

Capability Brown died in February 1783 of a massive heart attack. A monument beside the lake at Croome Court was erected which reads "To the memory of Lancelot Brown, who by the powers of his inimitable and creative genius formed this garden scene out of a morass". There is also a portrait of Brown at Burghley.

Capability Brown was involved in the design of grounds at the following properties included in Historic Houses Castles and Gardens:-

Audley End	*Claremont*	*Petworth House*
Berrington Hall	*Chillington Hall*	*Sledmere House*
Bowood	*Corsham Court*	*Stowe (Stowe School)*
Burghley House	*Fawley Court*	*Syon House*
Burton Constable	*Highclere Castle*	*Warwick Castle*
Charlecote Park	*Longleat*	*Weston Park*
Chilham Castle Gardens (reputed)	*Luton Hoo*	*Wimpole Hall*
Clandon Park	*Moccas Court*	*Wrest Park and Gardens*

BLARNEY CASTLE AND BLARNEY HOUSE

(Sir Richard La T. Colthurst, Bart)
Blarney, Co Cork   map **16** T5   &
Telephone: (021) 385252
Fax: (021) 381578

Blarney Castle and Rock Close. Situated 5 miles from Cork City, the Castle is famous for its Stone which has the traditional power of conferring eloquence on all who kiss it. The word 'Blarney' has found its way into the English language and has been described as conferring upon anyone who kisses it 'a cajoling tongue and the art of flattery, or of telling lies with unblushing effrontery'. The battlements crowning the fine intact keep are typically Irish in form and set in the walls below the battlements is the Stone. To kiss it one has to lean backwards out from the parapet walk. Adjacent to the Castle is the Rock Close, said to have Druidic connections and containing the gardens laid out by the Jefferyes family in 1759 and now containing many old specimens and much new planting of shrubs, trees and beds, amongst the fine old limestone rocks scattered in 25 acres.
Blarney House & Gardens: 200 yards from the Castle is Blarney House and Gardens, a fine Scottish Baronial type house, with distinguished corner turrets and bartizans with conical roofs and now restored inside with fine rooms and stairwell. Outside, the formal gardens and fine view of Blarney Lake together with the walk down to it and between the House and the Castle a large area of new planting, with shrubs, trees, beds and walks.

Location: 7 m from Cork City. 9 m from Cork Airport; 9 m from Ringaskiddy Port.
Open: Blarney Castle & Rock Close: Mon-Sat May 9-6 June July Aug 9-7 Sept 9-6 Oct-Apr 9-5 (or sunset). Sun Summer 9.30-5.30 Winter 9.30-5.30 (or sunset). **Blarney House & Gardens:** June-mid Sept Mon-Sat only 12-6. (Last adm 30 mins before stated closing times.)
Admission: Blarney Castle and Rock Close: IR £3 children IR £1 OAPs/Students IR £2.
Blarney House & Gardens: IR £2.50 childrenIR £1 OAPs/Students IR £2.
Refreshments: Sweet and soft drink kiosk; three hotels, three public houses; tea houses. Car and coach parking.

CASTLETOWN HOUSE

(Office of Public Works)
Celbridge, Co Kildare   map **16** Q9
Telephone: (01) 628 8252
Fax: (01) 627 1811

Begun c.1722, Ireland's largest and finest Georgian country house.

Location: 12 m W of Dublin. Bus 67/67A to the gates.
Open: Open throughout the year. Summer every day winter Suns and Bank Hols. Telephone for times.
Admission: Adults £2.50 OAPs £1.75 Children/Students £1 Family £6.
Refreshments: Coffee shop.

CRAGGAUNOWEN - THE LIVING PAST

(The Hunt Museums Trust)
Kilmurry, Sixmilebridge, Co Clare   map **16** R5

Craggaunowen, "Where Celtic Life is brought to life," is pleasantly situated in the wooded farmland of County Clare. The site consists of a mediaeval Tower House containing a display of furniture and art objects, including some rare Irish pieces. There are two iron-age dwellings - a lake dwelling and a ring fort - and the leather boat 'Brendan' sailed by Tim Severin from Ireland to Newfoundland. In the summer months displays and experiments are conducted on the techniques associated with milling, pottery making and weaving in the iron age.

Location: 3½ m E of Quin, 6 m N of Sixmilebridge. 15 m NW of Limerick.
Open: 10.00-18.00 daily mid Mar-Oct.
Admission: £3.50 Senior Citizens £2.75 Family ticket £9.50. Group rates available.
Refreshments: Tea, scones, porter cake available in tea-room.
Events/Exhibitions: 'Living Past Experience' dramatised images of Ancient Ireland, mid May to mid Sept.

DUBLIN WRITERS MUSEUM

(Esther O' Hanlon, Curator)
18 Parnell Square, Dublin 1.   map **16** Q10
Telephone: (01) 8722077
Fax: (01) 8722231

The Dublin Writers Museum is located in a splendidly restored 18th century house. It uniquely represents that great body of Irish writers - in prose, poetry and drama - which has contributed so much to world literature over the years.

Location: City centre - 5 mins walk from Tourist Information Office in O'Connell Street.
Open: Jan-Dec Mon-Sat 10-5 Sun & Public Hols 11.30-6. June-Aug Mon-Fri 10-7 Sat 10-5 Sun & Public Hols 11.30-6.
Admission: Adults £2.60 Concessions & under 18 yrs £2 Children (3-11 yrs) £1.10 Family Ticket £7. Group rates Adults £2.20 Concessions & under 18 yrs £1.70 Children (3-11 yrs) 80p.

DUNKATHEL

Dunkathel, Glanmire   map **16** T6
Telephone: (021) 821014/821767
Fax: (021) 821023

DUNKATHEL is a fine late eighteenth century neo-classical mansion, built on high ground overlooking the beautiful Lee estuary, 3 miles/5½ km east of Cork city. The architect is thought to have been Hargreave, a pupil of Sardinian architect Davis Ducart. Built c 1790 Dunkathel has a finely proportioned interior with simple plasterwork, Adam chimney-pieces and a particularly elegant bifurcating staircase of Bath stone. In the hall stands a rare late nineteenth century orchestrion by Imhoff & Muckle which may be played on request. The house contains a unique collection of Victorian watercolours by Beatrice Gubbins, a former owner of the house. Dunkathel House is well known for its charming interior, the hall retains its 19th century decoration with marbled walls representing Siena and the ceiling depicting a skye scene.

Location: 3 m E of Cork.
Open: May 1-Oct 15. Wed-Sun 2-6.
Refreshments: By arrangement.

FERNHILL GARDEN 
(Mrs Sally Walker)
Sandyford, Co Dublin   map **16** Q10
Telephone: (01) 2956000

A Garden for all seasons, 200 years old in Robinsonian style with over 4,000 species and varieties of trees, shrubs and plants. Dogs not allowed.

Location: Sandyford, Co. Dublin.
Open: Tues-Sat 11-5 Sun 2-6 Mar-Nov inclusive.
Admission: Adults £2.50 OAPs £1.50 children £1.

THE GEORGE BERNARD SHAW BIRTHPLACE
33 Synge Street, Dublin 8   map **16** Q10
Telephone: (01) 4750854 (May-Oct) / 8722077
Fax: (01) 8722231

The famous playwright, essayist and Nobel prize winner for literature George Bernard Shaw, was born in the house on 26 July 1856. The terraced House built in 1838 is furnished with authentic victorian furniture and laid out in such a way to suggest the family have literally gone out for the day themselves, leaving their home to be enjoyed by visitors.

Location: City centre.
Open: May-Oct Mon-Sat 10-5 Sun and Public Hols 11.30-6.
Admission: Adults £2 Concessions & under 18yrs £1.60 Children (3-11 yrs) £1.10 Family ticket £5.80. Group rates Adults £1.60 Concessions & under 18yrs £1.30 Children (3-11 yrs) 80p.

GLIN CASTLE
(The Knight of Glin and Madam Fitz-Gerald)
Glin   map **16** R4   △ &
Telephone: (068) 34173/34112
Fax: (068) 34364

A Georgian Gothic castle with a series of battlemented folly lodges on lands held by the Knights of Glin for over 700 years. The interiors possess elaborate neo-classical plaster ceilings, a flying grand staircase and a notable collection of 18th century Irish mahogany furniture, family portraits and Irish landscapes. Formal gardens and walled kitchen garden.

Location: Situated on the N69 9km W of Foynes & 5km E of Tarbert Car ferry.
Open: May & June and other times by appointment. Tours, meals etc. can be arranged in the Castle. Please contact The Administrator, Mrs O'Sullivan (068) 36230.
Admission: £3 Group rate £2 Students £1.
Accommodation: Overnight stays arranged. Castle can be rented.
Conferences: Facilities for small groups.

JAPANESE GARDENS
(Irish National Stud)
Tully   map **16** Q9
Telephone: (045) 21617
Fax: (045) 22129

Created between 1906-1910, the Japanese Gardens symbolise the Life of Man from the Cave of Birth to the Gateway to Eternity. Special features include the Tea House, Bridge of Life and some very old bonsai trees.

Location: Co. Kildare 1 m from Kildare Town and 5 m from Newbridge.
Open: 17 Mar-31 Oct EVERYDAY 9.30-6.
Admission: Adults £4 Students/OAPs £3 Children under 12 years £2. Family 2 adults and 4 children under 12 years £10. Please note that it is one ticket for both the Irish National Stud and Japanese Gardens.
Refreshments: Tea, coffee, soup, salads, sandwiches etc. Groups can be catered for with some notice.
The path of life in the Japanese Gardens is unsuitable for disabled. The Irish National Stud is very suitable for disabled.

JOHNSTOWN CASTLE DEMESNE
(Teagasc Soils and Environment Centre)
Wexford   map **16** S10   △

Grounds and gardens only. 50 acres of well laid out grounds, with artificial lakes and fine collection of ornamental trees and shrubs. Agricultural museum.

Location: 5 m SW of Wexford.
Open: All the year - Daily 9-5. Guidebook available at Castle. Although the grounds will continue to be open throughout the year, an admission charge will apply only from Apr 29-Oct 1 1995.
Admission: Car (and passengers) £2.50 coach (large) £17 coach (small) £9. Adults (pedestrians/cyclists) £1.50. Wedding parties for photography £17.
Refreshments: Coffee shop during July & Aug at museum.

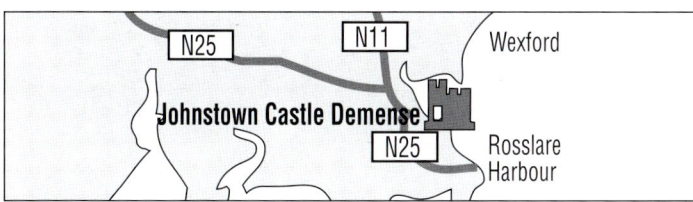

THE JAMES JOYCE TOWER
(Dublin Tourism)
Sandycove   map **16** Q10
Telephone: (01) 2809265/28722077

The Joyce Tower is a Martello tower, one of 26 built around Dublin in 1804 as defence against Napoleon. It has thick granite walls and a gun platform on the top. The building was lived in by James Joyce in 1904 and is described in his novel *Ulysses*. It now houses the James Joyce Museum and a modern exhibition hall has been added at ground floor level. The living-room upstairs, described in *Ulysses*, has recently been reconstructed.

Location: Sandycove Point on seafront 1 mile from Dun Laoghaire.
Station(s): Rail: Sandycove. Bus: No.8 to Sandycove.
Open: April-October Mon-Sat 10-1,2-5: Suns and Public Holidays 2-6.
Admission: Adults 18+ £2.00 concessions £1.60 Children (3-11) £1.10. Special reductions on application. 20+ rates on application.

KYLEMORE ABBEY
Kylemore, Connemara   map **16** P3
Telephone: (095) 41146, or shops (095) 41113
Fax: (095) 41123

The only home of the Benedictine Nuns in Ireland. The Castle was acquired by the Nuns in 1920, and a precious heirloom was preserved, both for and on behalf of the people of Ireland, and visitors from all over the world. Built by Mr Mitchell Henry, MP for County Galway, and a native of Manchester. The Abbey is set amidst the lakes and mountains of Connemara in an area of outstanding beauty.

Location: Connemara, Co Galway.
Station(s): Galway.
Open: Easter-Halloween.
Admission: Adults £1.50 Families £3 Students-Senior Citizens £1.
Refreshments: Full self-service restaurant.
Events/Exhibitions: Visitors centre, history panels, exhibits, 17 min video of the history. Craftshop.

LISMORE CASTLE GARDENS

(Trustees of the Lismore Estates)
Lismore, Co Waterford   map **16** S7
Telephone: (058) 54424
Fax: (058) 54896

Beautifully situated walled and woodland gardens, containing a fine collection of camellias, magnolias and other shrubs. There is a remarkable yew walk.

Location: In town of Lismore; 45 m W of Waterford; 35 m NE of Cork.
Open: Open daily from the end of Apr-mid Sept.
Admission: Adults £2.50 children (under 16) £1.50 Reduced rates for groups of more than 20 - adults £2.25 children £1.30.

MALAHIDE CASTLE

(Maria Morgan, Curator)
Malahide, Co Dublin   map **16** Q10
Telephone: (01) 8462184/8462516
Fax: (01) 8462537

One of Ireland's oldest and most historic castles containing a unique collection of Irish period furniture and Irish historical portraits, most of which are on permanent loan from the National Gallery of Ireland. In the adjacent gardens there are in excess of 5000 species and varieties of shrubs.

Location: 8 m from centre of Dublin.
Station(s): Malahide.
Open: Jan-Dec Mon-Fri 10-5. Nov-Mar Sat Sun and Public Hols 2-5. Apr-Oct Sat 11-6 Sun and Public Hols 11.30-6. Closed for tours 12.45-2 everyday.
Admission: £2.75 OAPs/Students (12-17 yrs) £2.15 children (3-11 yrs) £1.40. Family ticket (2 adults 3/4 children) £7.50. Group rates: Adults £2.35 OAPs/Students (12-17 yrs) £1.90 Children £1.30.
Refreshments: Restaurant - waitress and self service.
Private banquets in 15th century Great hall. Craft shop. Coach and public car park. Fry Model Railway is located in the grounds of Malahide Castle -special combined ticket available for Castle and Model Railway.

MUCKROSS HOUSE, GARDENS AND TRADITIONAL FARMS

Killarney, Co Kerry   map **16** T4
Telephone: (064) 31440
Fax: (064) 33926

Muckross House is a 19th century manor house, beautifully situated close to Muckross Lake, second largest of Killarney's three lakes. The house has many items of historic interest including locally carved period furniture, prints, maps and items which illustrate a traditional way of life of the people of Kerry. Skilled craftworkers at Muckross House carry on some of the traditional crafts of Kerry as their predecessors did in bygone days. The gardens, informal in design, are noted for their fine collection of rhododendrons and azaleas, extensive water gardens and an outstanding rock garden on natural limestone. New in 1992 a 70 acre outdoor portrayal of rural life in Kerry in the 1930's complete with working period farms and crafts.

Location: 3½ m from Killarney on the Kenmare road.
Open: Daily all year 9-5.30 During July and Aug 9-7pm.
Admission: IR £3 Children IR £1.25 Group rates for 20 plus IR £2 Family ticket IR £7.50 Ditto for Muckross Traditional Farms. Discount for joint ticket. Gardens free. Free car park and coach parking.
Refreshments: Restaurant located in the old coach-house, serving teas, coffees, soup, sandwiches, pastries, hot and cold lunches. Wine licence.

NATIONAL BOTANIC GARDENS

(Office of Public Works)
Glasnevin, Dublin 9   map **16** Q10
Telephone: (01) 8374388
Fax: (01) 8360080

Founded 1795. 47 acres in extent containing 20,000 different living plant species and varieties. Trees, flowering shrubs and herbaceous plants. Conservatories. Herbarium, 500,000 specimens.

Location: 2 m city centre.
Open: All the year daily (except Christmas Day) weekdays 9-6 (summer) 10-4.30 (winter) Sun 11-6 (summer) 11-4.30 (winter). Conservatories Mon-Fri 9-12.45 and 2.15-5 (summer) 10-12.45 and 2.15-4.15 (winter) Sat 9-12.15 and 2.15-5.45 (summer) 10-12.15 and 2.15-4.15 Thurs 3.15 (winter) Sun 2-5.45 (summer) 2-4.15 (winter).
Admission: Free.

NEWBRIDGE HOUSE & TRADITIONAL FARM

Donabate, Co Dublin   map **16** Q10
Telephone: (01) 8436534/5
Fax: (01) 8462537

Splendid 18th century manor residence containing a very fine collection of period furniture and paintings. Traditional working farm with farm machinery, farm animals, newborn chicks and daily life on the farm.

Location: 12 m from N Dublin city.
Station(s): Donabate.
Open: Apr-Sept (incl) Tues-Fri 10-5 Sats 11-6 Sun & Public Hols 2-6. Oct-Mar (incl) Sat Sun & Public Hols 2-5.
Admission: Adults £2.50 Concessions & under 18 yrs £2.15 Children (3-11 yrs) £1.35 Family ticket £6.95. Group rates Adults £2.25 Concessions & under 18 yrs £1.95 Children (3-11 yrs) £1.25.
Coach, Bus, Car parking.

POWERSCOURT GARDENS & WATERFALL

Enniskerry, Co Wicklow   map **16** Q10
Telephone: (01) 2867676/7/8
Fax: (01) 2863561

Powerscourt is owned by the Slazenger family and has been welcoming visitors for more than 50 years. Powerscourt is a magnificent example of an artistocratic garden laid out with taste and imagination. The breathtaking location nestling under the Great Sugar Loaf mountain, the beauty of its Italian and Japanese Gardens, the splendid statuary and the incomparable iron work make it a fairytale demesne. The Waterfall is 398 feet high, and is the highest in Ireland. Restaurant, souvenir gift and craft shop and children's play areas, garden centre and house-plant shop.

Location: ¼ m Enniskerry, 12 m S of Dublin, just off N11.
Open: Gardens mid Mar-Oct 31 Daily 9.30-5.30. Waterfall open all year 9.30-7, 10.30 to dusk in winter. Guided tours for specialist groups on request.
Admission: Gardens £2.80 Student/OAPs £2.30 Children £1.70 Waterfall £1.50 Student/OAPs £1 Children 80p. Group reductions, season tickets.
Refreshments: Gardens: small tea-room (50 people) serving cakes, teas etc. Waterfall: Teas, light lunches available in high season.
Wheelchair available. Disabled Toilet. Limited access for wheelchairs.

STROKESTOWN PARK HOUSE

Strokestown, Co Roscommon   map **16** P6
Telephone: (078) 33013
Fax: (078) 33712

Ancestral home of the Pakenham Mahon family. Although now owned by a local company, Westward Garage, the Palladian style house is complete with its original contents and includes fine examples of 18th and 19th century interiors. The stable yards of the house have been converted into Ireland's only museum to commemorate the Great Irish Famine of the 1840's. The restored walled garden will open to the public in 1995.

TULLYNALLY CASTLE

(Thomas & Valerie Palceham)
Castlepollard, Co Westmeath   map **16** P8   △ &
Telephone: (044) 61159 or (044) 61289
Fax: (044) 61856

Home of the Pakenhams (later Earls of Longford) since the 17th century; the original house is now incorporated in a huge rambling Gothick castle. Approximately 30 acres of woodland and walled gardens are also open to the public.

Open: House open mid June-mid Aug 2-6 (Pre-booked groups admitted at other times). Gardens open May-Sept 2-6.
Admission: HOUSE AND GARDENS: £3.50 children £2 Groups £2.50. GARDENS ONLY: £2 children 50p.
Refreshments: Tea-room open mid June-mid Aug.

NORTHERN IRELAND

ARDRESS HOUSE   🌿 The National Trust
Co Armagh   map **16** O9   △ ♿
Telephone: (01762) 851236

17th century country house with fine plasterwork. Small garden, agricultural display in farmyard. Woodland play area.

Location: 7 m W of Portadown on Portadown/Moy Road (B28); 2 m from Loughgall intersection on M1.
Open: Apr weekends and Good Fri-Easter Tues Apr 14-18 May-June weekends and Bank Hols only July-Aug daily except Tues Sept weekends only 2-6. (Picnic area available from 12 noon.) Farmyard open May June & Sept weekdays 12-4.
Admission: House, Grounds and Farmyard £2 Children £1 groups £1.60 after hours £2.80.
Refreshments: Picnickers welcome.
Wheelchairs admitted. Picnic areas.

THE ARGORY   🌿 The National Trust
Co Armagh   map **16** O9   △ ♿
Telephone: (01868) 84753

295 acre estate with neo-classical house, built c. 1820.

Location: 4 m from Moy on Derrycaw Road; 3 m from Coalisland intersection.
Open: Easter (Apr 14-18) Apr May June weekends and Bank Hols only July and Aug daily exc Tues 2-6 (open from 1 on Bank Hols). Last adm 5.15.
Admission: House and grounds £2.20 Children £1.10 groups £1.60 (after hours) £2.80. Car park £1.
Refreshments: Shop/tea-room open as house 2-6; Bank Holidays 1-6; weekdays July & Aug 3-5.
Wheelchairs provided - access to ground floor only. Dogs in grounds only on leads.

Aviaries and Birds of Prey Centres
can be found at the following properties in Historic Houses Castles and Gardens

Drumlanrig Castle & Country Park
Elsham Hall Country and Wildlife Park
Holdenby House & Gardens
Leeds Castle
Leighton House Museum & Art Gallery
Sewerby Hall & Gardens
Sion Hill Hall
Waddesdon Manor
Muncaster Castle

CASTLE COOLE   🌿 The National Trust
Co Fermanagh   **BT74**   map **16** O7
Telephone: (01365) 322690

Magnificent 18th century mansion by James Wyatt with plasterwork by Joseph Rose.

Location: 1½ m SE of Enniskillen on Belfast/Enniskillen Road (A4).
Open: The estate is open from dawn to dusk from Apr 1-Sept 30. House Easter (Apr 14-18) Apr May weekends and Bank Hols June July & Aug daily exc Thurs Sept weekends only 1-6.
Admission: House and Grounds £2.50 Children £1.25 groups £2 (after hours £3). Estate parking £1.50.
Refreshments: Shop and tea-room in reception area open as house 1.30-5.30.

CASTLE WARD   🌿 The National Trust
Co Down   **BT30 7LS**   map **16** O11   △ ♿ Ⓢ
Telephone: (01396) 881204
Fax: (01396) 881729

Built by the first Lord Bangor in 1765 in a beautiful setting. Laundry museum. Strangford Lough Wildlife Centre in converted barn on edge of shore.

Location: 7 m NE of Downpatrick; 1½ m W of Strangford village (A25).
Open: Apr weekends and Good Fri-Sun after Easter (Apr 14-23) May-Aug daily (including Bank Hols) except Thurs 1-6. Sept-Oct weekends only. Estate and grounds open all year dawn to dusk daily. Shop and Restaurant open as house weekends and Bank Holidays 1-6 weekdays 1-5. Strangford Lough Wildlife Centre weekends and Good Fri-Sun after Easter Apr May June Sept weekends and Bank Holidays only July and Aug daily except Thurs 2-6.
Admission: House £2.60 Children £1.30 Groups £2 (after hours £3). Estate £3.50 per car Nov to end Mar £1.75 per car. Coaches Booked groups to house no charge others £10. Horses using bridlepath £5 per single horsebox.
Refreshments: Shop & tea-room open same days as house weekends and Bank Hols 1-6, weekdays 1-5.

DOWNHILL 🌿 The National Trust
Londonderry   map **16** M9 ♿
Telephone: (01265) 848728

Built by the Earl of Bristol, Bishop of Derry, in 1783 with Mussenden Temple, the Bishop's Gate, the Black Glen and the Bishop's Fish Pond.

Location: 5 m W of Coleraine on Coleraine/Downhill Road (A2).
Station(s): Castlerock.
Open: Temple Apr weekends and Good Fri-Easter Tues (Apr 14-18) May June Sat Sun and Bank Hols only July and Aug daily. Sept weekends only 12-6.
Admission: Grounds free Glen open free at all times.
Dogs admitted. Wheelchair access.

FLORENCE COURT 🌿 The National Trust
Co Fermanagh   map **16** 07   △♿
Telephone: (01365) 348249 or 348788 (shop)

Important 18th century house built by John Cole. Excellent rococo plasterwork. Pleasure Gardens with working sawmill, ice house, waymarked walks.

Location: 8 m SW of Enniskillen via A4 and A32; 1 m W of Florence Court village.
Open: House Apr weekends and Good Fri-Easter Tues (Apr 14-18) May weekends and Bank Hols June July and Aug daily except Tues Sept weekends only 1-6. Grounds open all year round 10-one hour before dusk.
Admission: House £2.50 Children £1.25 Groups £2. After hours £3. Estate parking £1.50.
Refreshments: Tea-room and shop open as house.
Dogs in pleasure gardens only on leads. Wheelchair access - ground floor only.

GRAY'S PRINTING PRESS 🌿 The National Trust
Strabane, Co Tyrone   BT82 8AU   map **16** N8
Telephone: (01504) 884094

The shop was in existence in 18th century. It has close links with Scots-Irish tradition in America. Audio visual show tells story of printing.

Location: In Main Street, Strabane.
Open: Apr-Sept daily 2-5.30 except Thur Sun and Bank Hols. At other times by prior arrangement. Shop (not N.T.) all year daily except Thur Sun and public hols 9-1 and 2-5.30.
Admission: £1.40 Children 70p. Groups £1 (after hours £1.80).

HEZLETT HOUSE 🌿 The National Trust
Co Londonderry   BT51 4RE   map **16** M9   △
Telephone: (01265) 848567

Thatched cottage of particular importance because of the unusual cruck/truss construction of the roof.

Location: 4 m W of Coleraine on Coleraine/Downhill Coast Road (A2).
Open: Apr weekends and Good Fri-Easter Tues (Apr 14-18) May June weekends and Bank Hols only July and Aug daily except Tues. Sept weekends only 1-6.
Admission: £1.50 Children 75p Groups £1 (after hours £1.90).
Unsuitable for wheelchairs. No dogs.

MOUNT STEWART HOUSE, GARDEN AND TEMPLE
🌿 **The National Trust**
Co Down   BT22 2AD   map **16** N11   △♿
Telephone: (012477) 88387/88487

Interesting house with important associations with Lord Castlereagh. Gardens designed by Lady Edith, Marchioness of Londonderry. Fine topiary work, flowering shrubs and rhododendrons. Temple of the Winds, modelled on that at Athens, built 1783.

Location: On E shore of Strangford Lough; 5 m SE of Newtownards; 15 m E of Belfast (A20).
Open: Apr weekends and Good Fri-Sun after Easter (Apr 14-23). May-Sept daily except Tues 1-6. Oct weekends only 1-6. Garden Apr 1-end Sept daily. Oct weekends only 10.30-6. Temple of the Winds closed for repairs throughout 1995 season. Shop and tea-room Apr weekends and Apr 14-23 May-Sept daily except Tues 1.30-5.30 Oct weekends only 1.30-5.30.
Admission: House Garden and Temple £3.30 Children £1.65 groups £2.60 (after hours £4.30). Garden and Temple £2.70 Children £1.35, groups £2 (after hours £3.70).
Refreshments: Tea-room.
Wheelchairs provided, also electric wheelchair. Booked parties by arrangement throughout the season.

ROWALLANE GARDEN 🌿 The National Trust
Saintfield, Co Down   map **16** 011   ♿
Telephone: (01238) 510131

Beautiful gardens containing large collection of plants, chiefly trees and shrubs. Of particular interest in spring and autumn.

Location: 11 m SE of Belfast; 1 m S of Saintfield on the W of the Downpatrick Road (A7).
Open: Apr 1-end Oct Mon-Fri 10.30-6. Sat and Sun 2-6. Nov-end Mar 10.30-5 Mon-Fri. *Closed* Dec 25 and 26 Jan 1.
Admission: Easter-end Oct £2.50 Children £1.25 Parties £1.60 (after hours £2.80). Nov-end Mar £1.40 Groups 80p.
Refreshments: Tea-room Apr weekends and Good Fri-Easter Tues (Apr 14-18) May-Aug daily 2-6. Sept weekends only.
Dogs admitted on leads, to indicated areas. Wheelchair access (1 provided).

SPRINGHILL   The National Trust
Moneymore, Co Londonderry   **BT45 7NQ**   map **16** N9   △ &
Telephone: (016487) 48210

House dating from 17th century. Magnificent oak staircase and interesting furniture & paintings. Costume museum. Cottar's kitchen.

Location: On Moneymore/Coagh Road (1 m from Moneymore).
Open: Apr weekends and Good Fri-Easter Tues (Apr 14-18) May June weekends and Bank Hols only July and Aug daily except Thurs. Sept weekends only 2-6.
Admission: House £2.20 Children £1.10 Groups £1.60 (after hours £2.80).
Refreshments: Shop and tea-room open as house.

WELLBROOK BEETLING MILL   The National Trust
Cookstown, Co Tyrone   map **16** N9
Telephone: (016487) 51735

A water-powered mill built in 18th century with 19th century modifications. Final process in the manufacture of linen.

Location: 3 m from Cookstown on Cookstown/Omagh Road.
Open: Apr weekends and Good Fri-Easter Tues (Apr 14-18) May June weekends and Bank Hols. July and Aug daily except Tues 2-6. Sept weekends only.
Admission: £1.40 Children 70p Groups £1 (after hours £1.80).
Unsuitable for wheelchairs.

SCOTLAND

BORDERS

NATIONAL TRUST FOR SCOTLAND

Last admissions to most NTS properties are 45 minutes before the advertised closing times. Other than guide-dogs for the blind and deaf, dogs are not generally permitted inside Trust buildings, walled and enclosed gardens or in the immediate area beside buildings which are open to the public. At a number of properties, special 'dog walks' are signposted.

ABBOTSFORD HOUSE
(Mrs P. Maxwell-Scott)
Melrose   **TD6 9BQ**   map **9** L17   & △
Telephone: (01896) 752043

The home of Sir Walter Scott, containing many historical relics collected by him.

Location: 3 m W of Melrose just S of A72; 5 m E of Selkirk.
Station(s): No railway.
Open: 3rd Mon of Mar-Oct 31 daily 10-5 Sun 2-5.
Admission: Adults £3 Children £1.50 Party rates Adults £2.20 Children £1.10.
Refreshments: Tea-shop.
Cars with wheelchairs or disabled enter by private entrance. Gift Shop.

AYTON CASTLE
Eyemouth   **TD14 5RD**   map **9** L18
Telephone: (0189 07) 81212
Fax: (0189 07) 81550

Victorian castle in red sandstone.

Location: 7 m N of Berwick-upon-Tweed on A1.
Open: May-Sept Sun 2-5 or by appointment.
Admission: Adults £2 children (under 15) free.

BOWHILL
(His Grace the Duke of Buccleuch & Queensberry KT)
nr Selkirk   **TD7 5ET**   map **9** L17   △ & Ⓔ Ⓢ
Telephone: (01750) 20732
Fax: (01750) 22172

Border home of the Scotts of Buccleuch. Famous paintings include 8 Guardis, Canaletto's Whitehall, Claudes, Gainsboroughs, Reynolds and Raeburns. Superb furniture and porcelain. Monmouth, Sir Walter Scott and Queen Victoria relics. For details of our specialist art courses, please tel: Buccleuch Heritage Trust Selkirk (01750) 20732. Restored Victorian kitchen. Audio-Visual programme. Lecture Theatre. Exciting Adventure Woodland Play Area. Walks to historic Newark Castle and by lochs and rivers along nature trails.

Location: 3 m W of Selkirk on A708 Moffat-St. Mary's Loch road. Edinburgh, Carlisle, Newcastle approx 1½ hours by road.
Open: House open July 1-July 31 daily 1-4.30. Country Park (includes Adventure Woodland Play Area and Nature Trails) Apr 30-late summer Bank Hol (UK) inclusive daily except Fri 12-5 (last entry 45 mins before closing time). Open by appointment at additional times for museums and specialist or educational groups. Mountain bike hire (01721) 22515.
Admission: House and Grounds £4 parties over 20 £3.50 OAPs £3.50 Grounds only £1 (Wheelchair users and children under 5 free). Free car and coach parking.
Refreshments: Gift shop and licensed tea-room.
BOWHILL LITTLE THEATRE a lively centre for the performing arts. To join mailing list please write to the Administrator.

FLOORS CASTLE, KELSO
(The Duke of Roxburghe)
Roxburghe Estates Office, Kelso   **TD5 7SF**   map **9** L18
Telephone: (01573) 223333
Fax: (01573) 226056

Scotland's largest inhabited castle; built in 1721 by William Adam and remodelled by Playfair; outstanding collection of French furniture, stunning tapestries and works of art. Beautiful Chinese and European porcelain and a unique Victorian collection of birds.

Location: N of Kelso.
Station(s): Berwick-on-Tweed.
Open: Easter weekend late Apr-end Oct Sun-Thurs except July and Aug when it is open daily. In Oct Sun & Wed.
Admission: Adults £3.80 OAPs £3 children (5-16) £1.90 family ticket £10 party rates on request.
Refreshments: Restaurant and coffee shop.
Accommodation: Accommodation at nearby Sunlaws House Hotel.
Conferences: Facilities available including dinners, receptions, product launches and outdoor events.
Free parking, walled garden, woodland walks and garden centre.

THE HIRSEL GROUNDS & DUNDOCK WOOD
(Lord Home of The Hirsel, KT)
Coldstream   **TD12 4LP**   map **9** L18   &
Telephone: (01890) 882834/882965
Fax: (01890) 882834

Snowdrops, aconites and daffodils in Spring in grounds. Fantastic rhododendrons and azaleas May/June Dundock wood and grounds. Herbaceous borders and roses in summer. Marvellous Autumn colouring. Picnic areas. Parking. Playground. Homestead museum, Craft Centre and workshops.

Location: W of Coldstream on A697.
Open: Grounds all reasonable daylight hours throughout the year. Crafts & Museum 10-5 weekdays 12-5 weekends.
Admission: Parking charge.
Refreshments: In main season.
Events/Exhibitions: Craft Fairs May and November.

MANDERSTON
(Lord and Lady Palmer)
Duns, Berwickshire   **TD11 3PP**   map **9** L18
Telephone: (01361) 883450
Fax: (01361) 882010

The swan-song of the great classical house. Georgian in its taste but with all the elaborate domestic arrangements designed for Edwardian convenience and comfort. Superb classical yet luxurious rooms and the only silver staircase in the world, in a house on which the architect was ordered to spare no expense. The

199

The National Trust for Scotland

over

100

beautiful

places

for

WELCOME!

All that we do, we do for you

to

visit

CASTLES
GREAT HOUSES
MUSEUMS
LITTLE HOUSES
HISTORIC PLACES
MOUNTAINS
WILD PLACES
GARDENS
PARKLANDS
EXHIBITIONS
RESTAURANTS
GIFT SHOPS

Telephone 031 226 5922
Fax 031 243 9302

Culzean Castle and Country Park, Strathclyde - 12 miles south of Ayr on the A719, 4 miles west of Maybole off the A77

extensive 'downstairs' domestic quarters are equally some of the grandest of their type. Biscuit Tin Museum. Outside, the grandeur is continued. See the most splendid stables and picturesque marble dairy. 56 acres of formal woodland garden and lakeside walks.

Location: 2 m E of Duns on A6105; 14 m W of Berwick upon Tweed.
Open: May 11-Sept 28 Sun & Thurs only + Bank Hol Mons 29 May and 28 Aug. Parties at any time of year by arrangement.
Admission: Charges not available at time of going to press.
Refreshments: Tea-room, Cream Teas.
Gift Shop.

MELLERSTAIN
(The Mellerstain Trust)
Gordon, Berwickshire TD3 6LG   map **9** L17
Telephone: (01573) 410225

Scotland's famous Adam mansion. Beautifully decorated and furnished interiors. Terraced gardens and lake. Gift shop.

Location: 9 m NE of Melrose; 7 m NW of Kelso; 37 m SE of Edinburgh.
Open: Easter weekend (Apr 14-17) then May June and Sept Wed Fri and Sun only 12.30-5 July and Aug daily except Sat 12.30-5 (last adm 4.30). Groups at other times by arrangement.
Admission: Charges not available at time of going to press *special terms for organised parties by appointment, apply Curator* Free parking.
Refreshments: Tea rooms.
Events/Exhibitions: May 28 - RNLI fete June 4 - Vintage Car Rally; July 22-24 - Craft Festival; Permanent Exhibition - Antique Dolls and Toys.

MERTOUN GARDENS
(His Grace the Duke of Sutherland)
St Boswells, Roxburghshire TD6 0EA   map **9** L17
Telephone: (01835) 823236

20 acres of beautiful grounds with delightful walks and river views. Fine trees, herbaceous plants and flowering shrubs. Walled garden and well-preserved circular dovecot.

Location: 2 m NE of St Boswells on the B6404.
Open: Garden only Sat and Sun and Mon on Public Holidays only Apr-Sept 2-6 (last entry 5.30) parties by arrangement.
Admission: Adults £1 children 50p.
Refreshments: Dryburgh Abbey Hotel, Buccleuch Arms Hotel, St Boswells.
No dogs. Car parking.

PAXTON HOUSE
(The Paxton Trust)
Paxton, nr Berwick-upon-Tweed TD15 1SZ   map **9** L18 ♿ △
Telephone: (01289) 386291
Fax: (01289) 386660

Scotland's most perfect Palladian country mansion. Built for a daughter of Frederick The Great. Designed by the Adam family and furnished by Chippendale and Trotter. Restored Regency picture gallery (outstation of National Galleries of Scotland). Gardens. Riverside Walks. Adventure Playground. Tearoom. Gift Shop.

Location: 5 m from Berwick-upon-Tweed on B6461.
Open: Daily Good Fri-Oct 31. House noon-5 Grounds 10-5 last tour of house 4.15.
Admission: £3.50 grounds only £1.50 family ticket £10. Parties catered for.
Refreshments: Morning coffee, light lunches, afternoon teas, Licensed.
Car parking. Suitable for disabled persons. No wheelchairs available.

PRIORWOOD GARDEN
(The National Trust for Scotland)
Melrose   map **9** L17
Telephone: (01896) 822493

Garden featuring flowers suitable for drying. Shop and Trust visitor centre.

Location: In Melrose.
Open: 1 Apr-24 Dec, Mon-Sat 10-5.30, Sun 1.30-5.30.
Admission: £1.00. Groups should pre-book.

ROBERT SMAIL'S PRINTING WORKS
(The National Trust for Scotland)
Tweeddale   map **15** L16
Telephone: (01896) 830206

The buildings contain vintage working machinery, including a 100-year-old printing press which was originally driven by water wheels. The Victorian office is on display complete with its acid-etched plate-glass windows and examples of historic items printed in the works.

Location: In Innerleithen High Street, 30 m S of Edinburgh.
Open: 14 Apr-22 Oct Mon-Sat 10-1 and 2-5. Sun 2-5.
Admission: £2 children £1.50 adult parties £1.60 schools 80p. Groups should pre-book.

THIRLESTANE CASTLE
(Thirlestane Castle Trust)
Lauder, Berwickshire TD2 6RU   map **9** L17
Telephone: (01578) 722430
Fax: (01578) 722761

Described as one of the oldest and finest Castles in Scotland, Thirlestane has its roots in an original 13th century fort overlooking the Leader Valley. The main keep was built in 1590 by the Maitland family who have lived in the Castle for over 400 years; it was extended in 1670 and again in 1840. The Restoration Period plasterwork ceilings are considered to be the finest in existence. The family nurseries now house a large collection of historic toys and children are encouraged to dress up. Visitors see the old kitchens, pantries and laundries as well as the Country Life Exhibitions portraying day to day life in the Borders through the centuries. Grounds, picnic tables, woodland walk, gift shop and tea room.

Location: 28 m S of Edinburgh off A68 - follow signs on all main approach roads.
Open: Easter 12-19 Apr incl. May June and Sept Mon Wed Thurs and Sun only. July and Aug daily except Sat Castle 2-5 (last adm 4.30) Grounds 12-6.
Admission: £3.50 party rate £3 family ticket (parents and own children only) £9 booked party tours at other times by arrangement. Free car park.
Refreshments: Tea-room.

TRAQUAIR
(C. Maxwell Stuart of Traquair)
Innerleithen EH44 6PW   map **15** L16 △
Telephone: (01896) 830323
Fax: (01896) 830639

A house full of beauty, romance and mystery. Rich in associations with Mary Queen of Scots, the Jacobites and Catholic persecution. Priest's room with secret stairs. The world-famous Traquair House Ale is brewed in the 18th-century brewhouse. Extensive grounds, craft workshops and maze.

Location: 1 m from Innerleithen; 6 m from Peebles; 29 m from Edinburgh at junction of B709 & B7062 (40 minutes by road from Edinburgh Airport, 1½ hours from Glasgow).
Open: Apr 15-Sept 30 daily 12.30-5.30 (July and Aug 10.30-5.30) Oct Fri-Sun 2-5. Last adm 5. Grounds May-Sept 10.30-5.30.
Admission: Adults £3.75 children £1.75 OAPs £3.20 family £10.
Refreshments: Home cooking at the 1745 Cottage Tea Room from 12 pm.
Events/Exhibitions: New High Gallery in House with rotating exhibitions.
Accommodation: 2 rooms B&B and Holiday flat to rent.
Conferences: Suitable for small conferences, meetings, lunches and dinners.
Gift Shop, Antique Shop. Traquair Fair 5th & 6th August. Sheep and Wool Day Sun 30th July. Needlework Weekend 16th & 17th September.

CENTRAL

CALLENDAR HOUSE
(Falkirk District Council)
Callendar Park, Falkirk FK1 1YR   map **15** L15 ♿ 🏠
Telephone: (01324) 612134

CALLENDAR HOUSE

Imposing mansion within attractive parkland with a 900 year history. Facilities include a working kitchen of 1825 where costumed interpreters carry out daily chores including cooking based on 1820's recipes. Exhibition area, "Story of Callendar House" plus two temporary galleries, with regularly changing exhibitions. There is also a history research centre, gift shop and Georgian tea-shop at the Stables.

Location: To the east of Falkirk Town Centre on Callendar Road (A803).
Open: Jan-Dec Mon-Sat 10-5 Apr-Sept Sun 2-5 open all Public Hols.
Admission: Adults £1.60 children and OAPs 80p.

SCOTLAND'S BORDER

HERITAGE

TRAQUAIR · NEAR PEEBLES
OLDEST INHABITED HOUSE IN SCOTLAND

BOWHILL · NEAR SELKIRK
INTERNATIONALLY RENOWNED ART COLLECTION

ABBOTSFORD · NEAR MELROSE

HOME OF SIR WALTER SCOTT

THIRLESTANE CASTLE · LAUDER

UNSURPASSED 17TH CENTURY CEILINGS

FLOORS CASTLE · KELSO
SCOTLAND'S LARGEST INHABITED CASTLE

PAXTON HOUSE · NEAR BERWICK UPON TWEED
BUILT FOR A KING'S DAUGHTER

*S*pectacular Houses, Castles, Parks and Gardens, all within a 50 mile radius in one of the most scenic areas of Scotland.

THE HIRSEL · COLDSTREAM

COUNTRY PARK, MUSEUM AND CRAFTS

MELLERSTAIN · NEAR GORDON

SCOTLAND'S FINEST ADAM MANSION

MANDERSTON · DUNS

THE SWAN-SONG OF THE GREAT CLASSICAL HOUSE

Please send me more information, including details of the 10% saving with a Scotland's Border Heritage Pass.

NAME ....

ADDRESS ....

....

.... POSTCODE ....

Return to SBTB, 70 High Street, Selkirk TD7 4DD Telephone: 0750 20555

Ghosts are in residence at the following properties included in Historic Houses Castles and Gardens:-

Blickling Hall - *Anne Boleyn*

Breamore House - *Haunted picture - if touched, death on the same day*

East Riddleden Hall - *5 ghosts including lady*

in Grey Hall Lady's Chamber

Fountains Abbey & Studley Royal - *Choir of monks chanting in Chapel of Nine Altars*

Hinton Ampner - *Nocturnal noises*

Ightham Mote - *Supernatural presence*

Lindisfarne Castle - *Monk, and group of monks on causeway*

Lyme Park - *Unearthly peals of bells and lady in white, funeral procession through park*

Malmesbury House - *Ghost of a cavalier*

Overbecks Museum & Garden - *'Model' ghost in the Children's room (for them to spot)*

Rockingham Castle - *Lady Dedlock*

Rufford Old Hall - *Elizabeth Hesketh*

Scotney Castle Garden - *Man rising from the lake*

Sizergh Castle & Garden - *Poltergeist*

Speke Hall - *Ghost of woman in tapestry room*

Springhill - *Ghost of a woman*

Sudbury Hall - *Lady in Green, seen on stairs*

Tamworth Castle - *Haunted bedroom*

Treasurer's House - *Troop of Roman soldiers marching through the cellar*

Wallington House - *Invisible birds beating against the windows accompanied by heavy breathing*

Washington Old Hall - *Grey lady walking through corridors*

DUMFRIES & GALLOWAY

BROUGHTON HOUSE
(Managed by The National Trust for Scotland)
High Street, Kirkcudbright DG6 4JX map **8** N14
Telephone: (01557) 330877

Home of the artist E.A. Hornel (1864-1933), one of the 'Glasgow Boys' group, who lived here from 1901 to 1933. House contains a fine collection of his paintings and has an outstanding town garden whose design incorporates Japanese elements. Also collection of samplers.

Location: Near town centre.
Open: (1995) 1 Apr-22 Oct daily 1-5.30, last admission 4.45.
Admission: Adults £2 concessions £1.

CARLYLE'S BIRTHPLACE
(The National Trust for Scotland)
Ecclefechan map **8** L13
Telephone: (01576) 300666

Thomas Carlyle was born here in 1795. Mementoes and MSS.

Location: 5 m SE of Lockerbie on the Lockerbie/Carlisle Road (A74).
Open: 14 Apr-30 Sep, daily 1-30-5.30; 1 to 22 Oct Sat/Sun 1.30-5.30.
Admission: £1.50 Children 80p adult parties £1.20 school parties 60p. Groups should pre-book.
Refreshments: Ecclefechan Hotel.

CASTLE KENNEDY GARDENS
(The Earl and Countess of Stair)
Stranraer DG9 8BX map **8** M13
Telephone: (01776) 702024
Fax: (01776) 706248

World famous gardens, set in 75 acres of landscaped terraces and mounds between two lochs. Outstanding displays of Rhododendrons, Azaleas, Embothriums, Eucryphia. Surrounded by breathtaking scenery. Many original specimens from Hooker expeditions. Also only known Monkey Puzzle avenue. Plant Centre selling plants produced from garden stock.

Location: 5 m E of Stranraer on A75 opposite Castle Kennedy village.
Open: Easter to Sept - Daily 10-5.
Admission: Charged. Disabled free. Reduction for groups over 20.
Refreshments: Light refreshments only. Hotels Eynhallow, Castle Kennedy & Stranraer.

CRAIGDARROCH HOUSE
(J. H. A. Sykes)
Moniaive DG3 4JB map **8** M15
Telephone: (0184) 82202

William Adam house built for Annie Laurie.

Location: 2 miles west of Moniaive on B729.
Open: All July 1995 2-4.
Admission: £2.
Please note: no public conveniences.

DRUMLANRIG CASTLE GARDENS AND COUNTRY PARK

(Home of the Duke of Buccleuch & Queensberry KT)
nr Thornhill   map **8** M13   △ ⅻ Ⓢ
Telephone: (01848) 330248 and (01848) 331682 (24 hr answering service). Country Park: (01848) 331555

'1680/90' pink sandstone castle with outstanding art treasures - Leonardo, Rembrandt, Holbein - '300 year old silver chandelier' & 'Louis XIV' furniture, Bonnie Prince Charlie's relics. Extensive grounds and woodland includes gardens, exciting adventure woodland play area, nature trails and picnic sites. Tearoom and giftshop. Working craft studios, lecture room and cycle hire. Bird of Prey Centre.

Location: 18 m N of Dumfries; 3 m N of Thornhill off A76; 16 m from A74 at Elvanfoot; approx 1½ hrs by road from Edinburgh, Glasgow & Carlisle.
Open: Sat 29 Apr-Mon 28 Aug inc Sat Sun and Bank Holidays 11-5, weekdays until 16 June 1-5, weekdays from 17 June-end of season 11-5 (last entry to Castle 4.15). Castle closed Thurs and open by appointment at additional times (mornings, not Thurs) during season for schools and specialist groups. 'Country park open until Saturday 16 September'.
Admission: Prices not available at time of going to press.
Refreshments: Lunches, Afternoon Teas and snacks at above times.

RAMMERSCALES

(M A Macdonald, Esq)
Lockerbie   map **8** M16
Telephone: (0138) 781 0229

Georgian manor house dated 1760 set on high ground with fine views over Annandale. Pleasant policies and a typical walled garden of the period. There are Jacobite relics and links with Flora Macdonald retained in the family. There is also a collection of works by modern artists.

Location: 5 m W of Lockerbie (M6/A74); 2½ m S of Lochmaben on B7020.
Open: 2-5 every day in Aug except Sats.
Admission: £2.50.

THREAVE GARDEN

(The National Trust for Scotland)
nr Castle Douglas   map **8** N15   ⅻ
Telephone: (01556) 502575

The Trust's School of Horticulture. Gardens now among the major tourist attractions of SW Scotland. Visitor centre. Magnificent springtime display of some 200 varieties of daffodil, Trust shop, Restaurant, Exhibition. Ramp into garden for wheelchairs.

Location: 1 m W of Castle Douglas off A75.
Open: All year daily 9.30-Sunset. Visitor Centre, Exhibition and Shop 1 Apr-22 Oct daily 9.30-5.30.
Admission: £3.50 Children £1.80 Adult parties £2.80 Schools £1.40 Children (under 5 years) free. OAPs/Students (on production of their cards) half-price. Groups should pre-book.
Refreshments: Restaurant daily 10-5.

FIFE

BALCARRES

(Balcarres Trust)
Colinsburgh   map **9** K17
Telephone: (01333) 340206

16th century house with 19th century additions by Burn and Bryce. Woodland and terraced garden.

Location: ½ m N of Colinsburgh.
Open: Woodlands and Lower Garden Feb 13-Mar 1 Apr 3-June 24 (daily except Suns) West Garden June 12-24 (Daily except Suns) 2-5 *House not open except by written appointment* and Apr 24-May 10 (except Suns).
Admission: Gardens Only Adults £2.50 OAPs/children £1.50 House £4. Car park. Suitable for disabled persons, no wheelchairs provided.

CULROSS PALACE, TOWN HOUSE & STUDY

(The National Trust for Scotland)
Culross   map **15** K15
Telephone: (01383) 880359

Outstanding survival of Scottish 17th century burgh architecture carefully restored to 20th century living standards. Induction loop for the hard of hearing.

Location: 12 m W of Forth Road Bridge, off A985.
Open: Palace 14 Apr-30 Sept daily 11-5.30 1-22 Oct Sat/Sun 11-5. Town house and study dates as above 1.30-5.
Admission: £3.50 children £1.80 adult parties £2.80 school parties £1.40. Groups must pre-book.
Refreshments: Tea-room.

FALKLAND PALACE & GARDEN

(Her Majesty the Queen. Hereditary Constable, Capt & Keeper: Ninian Crichton Stuart. Deputy Keeper: The National Trust for Scotland)
Fife   map **9** K16
Telephone: (01337) 857397

Attractive 16th century Royal Palace, favourite retreat of Stuart kings and queens. Gardens now laid out to the original Royal plans. Town Hall, Visitor Centre, Exhibition and Shop. Original Royal Tennis court built in 1539. Ramp into garden for wheelchairs.

Location: In Falkland, 11 m N of Kirkcaldy on A912.
Open: 1 Apr-22 Oct, Mon-Sat 11-5.30, Sun 1.30-5.30.
Admission: Palace and Garden, adults £4 children £2 adult parties £3.20 school parties £1.60. Grounds only, adults £2 children £1. Groups must pre-book.
Refreshments: Bruce Arms, Falkland.
Visitor centre and Trust shop. Display in Town Hall: Apr 1 - Oct 31, 11-5. Sun 2-5 (last adm 4.30).

HILL OF TARVIT

(The National Trust for Scotland)
nr Cupar   map **9** K17
Telephone: (01334) 653127

Mansion house remodelled 1906. Collection of furniture, tapestries, porcelain and paintings. Gardens.

Location: 2½ m SW of Cupar A916.
Station(s): Cupar (2½ m).
Open: 14 Apr-22 Oct daily 1.30-5.30 Garden and Grounds all year daily 9.30-sunset.
Admission: House and Gardens adults £3 children £1.50 adult parties £2.40 school parties £1.20. Gardens only £1. Groups should pre-book.

KELLIE CASTLE AND GARDEN

(The National Trust for Scotland)
Fife   map **9** K17   &
Telephone: (01333) 720271

Fine example of 16th-17th century domestic architecture of Lowland Scotland. Victorian walled garden with wheelchair access. Nursery, video, adventure playground, picnic area, shop.

Location: 3 m NNW of Pittenweem on B9171.
Open: 14 Apr-22 Oct daily 1.30-5.30. Garden and grounds all year daily 9.30-sunset.
Admission: Castle and Gardens £3 adults £1.50 children. Adult parties £2.40 school parties £1.20. Gardens only adults £1. Groups must pre-book.
Refreshments: Tea-room.
Gardens only suitable for the disabled. A/V presentation with induction loop for the hard of hearing.

GRAMPIAN

ARBUTHNOTT HOUSE AND GARDEN

(The Viscount of Arbuthnott)
Arbuthnott House, Laurencekirk   map **11** H18
Telephone: (01561) 361226
Fax: (01561) 320476

Arbuthnott family home for 800 years. Formal 17th century garden on unusually steep slope with grass terraces, herbaceous borders and shrubs.

Location: On B967 between A90 and A92 25 mile south of Aberdeen.
Open: Gardens open all year 9-5. House open on selected days May-Sept. Telephone or fax for further information.
Admission: House £2 Gardens £1.50 concessions to OAPs/children/parties.
Refreshments: Available at Grassic Gibbon Centre in village.

BRAEMAR CASTLE

(Captain A A C Farquharson of Invercauld Trusts)
Braemar, Aberdeenshire   **AB35 5XR**   map **11** H16   △
Telephone: (013397) 41219
Fax: (013397) 41252

Built in 1628 by the Earl of Mar. Attacked and burned by the celebrated Black Colonel (John Farquharson of Inverey) in 1689. Repaired by the government and garrisoned with English troops after the rising of 1745. Later transformed by the Farquharsons of Invercauld, who had purchased it in 1732, into a fully furnished private residence of unusual charm. L-plan castle of fairy tale proportions, with round central tower and spiral stair. Barrel-vaulted ceilings, massive iron 'Yett', and underground pit (prison). Remarkable star-shaped defensive curtain wall. Much valuable furniture, paintings and items of Scottish historical interest.

Location: ½ m NE of Braemar on A93.
Open: Easter-late Oct daily 10-6 except Fri.
Admission: Adults £1.90 children 90p special rates for groups and OAPs. Free car and bus park.
Refreshments: In Braemar.

BRODIE CASTLE
(The National Trust for Scotland)
nr Nairn Moray   map **11** G15
Telephone: (01309) 641371

Ancient seat of the Brodies, burned in 1645 and largely rebuilt, with 17th/19th century additions. Fine furniture, porcelain and paintings. Audio-taped guide for the blind.

Location: Off A96 between Nairn & Forres.
Open: 14 Apr-30 Sept Mon-Sat 11-5.30, Sun 1.30-5.30; 1 to 22 Oct, Sat 11-5.30 Sun 1.30-5.30. Grounds, all year, daily 9.30-sunset.
Admission: £3.50 children £1.80 adult parties £2.80 school parties £1.40. Gardens only £1. Parties should pre-book.
Refreshments: Tea-room.

CASTLE FRASER
(The National Trust for Scotland)
Sauchen   map **11** H18
Telephone: (01330) 833463

One of the most spectacular of the Castles of Mar. Z-plan castle begun in 1575 and completed in 1636. Formal garden.

Location: Off A944 4 m N of Dunecht. 16 m W of Aberdeen.
Open: 14 Apr-30 June and 1-30 Sept daily 1.30-5.30 1 July-31 Aug daily 11-5.30 1-22 Oct Sat/Sun 1.30-5.30. Garden and Grounds all year daily 9.30 to sunset.
Admission: £3.50 children £1.80 adult parties £2.80 school parties £1.40 Garden and Grounds £1 Children 50p. Groups should prebook.
Refreshments: Tea-room
Picnic area, childrens' adventure playground.

CRAIGSTON CASTLE
(Bruce Urquhart of Craigston)
Turriff   map **11** G18
Telephone: (01888) 551228

Early 17 th century, unfortified castle with Adam wings and an 18th century library.

Open: By written appointment only.

CRATHES CASTLE & GARDEN
(The National Trust for Scotland)
Banchory   map **11** H18
Telephone: (01330) 844525
Fax: (01330) 844797

Fine 16th century baronial castle. Remarkable early painted ceilings. Beautiful gardens provide a wonderful display all year. Great yew hedges from 1702. Children's adventure playground.

Location: 3 m E of Banchory on A93; 15 m W of Aberdeen.
Open: 1 Apr-22 Oct daily 11-5.30. Garden and Grounds all year, daily 9.30-sunset.
Admission: Combined ticket £4 Children £2 adult parties £3.20 School parties £1.60. Grounds only Adults £1.50 Children 80p. Groups should pre -book.
Refreshments: Shop and licensed Restaurant.

DRUM CASTLE
(The National Trust for Scotland)
nr Aberdeen   map **11** H18
Telephone: (01330) 811204

The oldest part of the historic Castle, the great square tower - one of the three oldest tower houses in Scotland - dates from the late 13th century. Charming mansion added in 1619. Garden of historic roses.

Location: 10 m W of Aberdeen, off A93.
Open: 14 Apr-30 June and 1-30 Sept daily 1.30-5.30 1 Jul-31 Aug daily 11-5.30 1-22 Oct 1.30-5.30 Sat/Sun. Grounds all year daily 9.30-sunset.
Admission: House and Garden £3.50 children £1.80. Adult parties £2.80 school parties £1.40. Gardens only £1.50 children 80p.
Refreshments: Tea-room.

DRUMMUIR CASTLE & WALLED GARDEN
(L.A. Gordon-Duff)
Drummuir   AB55 3JE   map **11** G16
Telephone: (01542) 810300
Fax: (01542) 810280

Built in 1848 by a Duff and home of the Duff family since then. 60ft high Lantern Tower. Castellated Victorian Gothic style with fine plasterwork, and interesting family portraits, artifacts and other paintings.

Location: Half way between Keith and Dufftown (5 m) off B9014.
Station(s): Keith.
Open: Tours at 2 and 3 on Aug 27 Sept 2 and 3 and Sept 9-30.
Admission: OAPs/children £1.50 others £2 special reductions negotiated with parties.
Refreshments: At Mill of Towie 3 m away.
Free car park.

FASQUE

(The Gladstone Family)
Fettercairn   AB30 1DJ   map **11** H17
Telephone: (01561) 340202 or (01561) 340569
Fax: (01561) 340325

1809 Home of the Gladstone family with a full complement of furnishings and domestic articles little changed for 160 years. A wonderful example of 'Upstairs-Downstairs' family life. Deer Park. Church. Picnic Site.

Location: 1 m N of Fettercairn on the B974 Cairn O Mount pass road; 34 m Aberdeen and Dundee; 17 m Stonehaven; 12 m Montrose; 18 m Banchory. Part of The Victorian Heritage Trail.
Open: House open May 1-Sept 30 every day 11-5.30 with last entry at 5.
Admission: Adults £3 OAPs £2.50 children £1. Parties welcome. Morning and evening opening for parties by arrangement.
Refreshments: By arrangement.
Events/Exhibitions: Various.
Welcome. Available for all functions - Entrance Hall, Dining Room, Drawing Room and Library available.

FYVIE CASTLE

(The National Trust for Scotland)
Fyvie   map **11** H18
Telephone: (01651) 891266

The oldest part of the castle dates from the 13th century and its five great towers are the monuments to the five families who owned the castle. The building contains the finest wheel stair in Scotland and a magnificent collection of paintings.

Location: Off A947, 8 m SE of Turriff, 25 m NW of Aberdeen.
Open: 1 Apr-30 Jun and 1-30 Sep daily 1.30-5.30 1 Jul-31 Aug daily 11-5.30 1-22 Oct Sat/Sun 1.30-5.30. Grounds all year daily 9.30-sunset.
Admission: £3.50, children £1.80. Adult parties £2.80 school parties £1.40. Groups must pre-book.
Refreshments: Tea-room.
Permanent exhibition - Castles of Mar.

HADDO HOUSE

(The National Trust for Scotland)
nr Methlick   map **11** H18   △ &
Telephone: (01651) 851440

Georgian house designed in 1731 by William Adam. Home of the Gordons of Haddo for over 500 years. Terraced gardens.

Location: 4 m N of Pitmedden; 19 m N of Aberdeen (A981 & B999).
Open: 14 Apr-30 Jun and 1-30 Sep daily 1.30-5.30 1 July-31 Aug daily 11-5.30 1-22 Oct Sat/Sun 1.30-5.30. Garden and Country Park all year daily 9.30-sunset.
Admission: £3.50 children £1.80 adult parties £2.80 school parties £1.40. Garden and Grounds £1.00. Groups must prebook.
Refreshments: Restaurant open daily 11-5.30.
Wheelchair access.

LEITH HALL AND GARDEN

(The National Trust for Scotland)
Kennethmont   map **11** H18   &
Telephone: (0146 43) 216

Home of the Leith family from 1650. Jacobite relics, and major exhibition of family's military collection. Charming garden.

Location: 1 m W of Kennethmont on B9002; 34 m NW of Aberdeen.
Open: 14 Apr-1 Oct daily 1.30-5.30. Garden and Grounds all year daily 9.30-sunset.
Admission: House and Garden £3 children £1.50 adult parties £2.40 school parties £1.20. Garden and Grounds £1 children 50p. Groups must pre-book.
Refreshments: Tea-room.
Picnic area.

PITMEDDEN GARDEN

(The National Trust for Scotland)
Udny   map **11** H18   &
Telephone: (01651) 842352

Reconstructed 17th century garden with floral designs, fountains and sundials. Display on the evolution of the formal garden. Museum of Farming Life.

Location: 14 m N of Aberdeen on A920.
Open: 28 Apr-1 Oct daily 10-5.30.
Admission: Garden and Museum adults £3 children £1.50 adult parties £2.40 school parties £1.20. Groups must pre-book.
Refreshments: Tea-room.
No dogs in garden please.

HIGHLANDS

CAWDOR CASTLE

(Countess Cawdor)
nr Inverness   IV12 5RD   map **11** G15
Telephone: (01667) 404615
Fax: (01667) 404674

The 14th century Keep, fortified in the 15th century and impressive additions, mainly 17th century, form a massive fortress. Gardens, nature trails and splendid grounds. Shakespearian memories of Macbeth. The most romantic castle in the Highlands.

Location: S of Nairn on B9090 between Inverness and Nairn.
Open: May 1-Oct 1 daily 10-5.30 (last adm 5).
Admission: Adults £4.50 children (aged 5-15) £2.50 OAPs and disabled £3.50 parties of 20 or more adults £4 and 20 or more children (aged 5-15) £1.90 family ticket (2 adults and up to 5 children) £12.50. Gardens, grounds and nature trail only £2.50. Blind people, no charge.
Refreshments: Licensed restaurant (self-service); Snack bar.
Gift shop. Book shop. Wool shop. Picnic area.9-hole golf course. Nature Trails. No dogs allowed in Castle or Grounds.

THE DOUNE OF ROTHIEMURCHUS

Inverness-shire   PH22 1QH   map **11** H15
Telephone: (01479) 810858

The family home of the Grants of Rothiemurchus was nearly lost as a ruin and has been under an abmitious repair programme since 1975. This exciting project may be visited on selected Mondays throughout the year. Book with the Visitor Centre for a longer 2 hour 'Highland Lady Tour' which explores the haunts of Elizabeth Grant of Rothiemurchus, born 1797 author of 'Memoirs of a Highland Lady', who vividly described The Doune and it's surroundings from the memories of her childhood. Rothiemurchus also has a full programme of walks and tours which provide a fascinating experience of it's most famous native Caledonian pinewoods, Loch an Eilein with it's island castle, Highland farming and the Cairngorms. Fishing, Clay Pigeon shooting and 4x4 Off Road Driving can also be experienced on the estate. Coaches are welcome by appointment.

Location: Inverness-shire.
Open: From May until August The Doune Grounds may be visited on Mondays between 10-12.30 and 2-4.30 and on the first Monday of the month in winter.
Admission: Doune Grounds £1 per person. Guided Highland Lady Tour £5 per person with a minimum charge of £20. Booking is essential.

DUNROBIN CASTLE

(The Sutherland Trust)
Golspie, Sutherland   KW10 6SF   map **11** G15
Telephone: (01408) 633177/633268
Fax: (01408) 633800 - Office; (01408) 634081 - Castle

One of Scotland's oldest inhabited houses. Historic home of the Sutherland family. Furniture, paintings and china. Exhibits of local and general interest. Victorian Museum in grounds. Magnificent formal gardens.

Location: ½ m NE of Golspie on A9.
Station(s): Dunrobin Castle Station (200 metres).
Open: 14-17 Apr and 1 May-15 Oct Mon-Sat 10.30-5.30 Sun 1-5.30 (last admission 5) closes 1hr earlier during Easter, May & Oct.
Admission: Adults £3.70 party rates £3.50 OAPs £2.30 children £1.90 party rates £1.80 family tickets £9.40 open all year round for pre-booked groups.
Refreshments: Tea-room.
Events/Exhibitions: Aug 20 - Vintage Car Rally.

DUNVEGAN CASTLE

(John MacLeod of MacLeod)
Isle of Skye   map **10** H9   △
Telephone: (01470) 521206
Fax: (01470) 521205

Dating from the 13th century and continuously inhabited by the Chiefs of MacLeod. Fairy flag. Licensed restaurant; two craft and souvenir shops; castle water garden; audio-visual theatre; clan exhibition; items belonging to Bonnie Prince Charlie; loch boat trips; famous seal colony; pedigree highland cattle fold.

Location: Dunvegan village (1 m); 23 m W of Portree on the Isle of Skye.
Open: Mon 20 Mar-Tues 31 Oct Mon-Sat 10-5.30. Last admission 5. Sun gardens craft shop and restaurant open all day 10-5.30. Castle open 1-5.30. Last admission 5pm.
Admission: Adults £4 Children £2.20 parties OAPs students £3.60. Gardens only Adults £2.50 Children £1.50.
Loch cruises aboard the motor vessel "Macleod of Macleod" seats 35 passengers - Department of Marine Transport Licensed - Fully insured. Also visit our exclusive woolen shop "The St Kilda Connection".

EILEAN DONAN CASTLE
(Conchra Charitable Trust)
Wester Ross   map **10** H12   △
Telephone: (0159 985) 202

13th century Castle. Jacobite relics - mostly with Clan connections.
Location: In Dornie, Kyle of Lochalsh; 8 m E of Kyle on A87.
Station(s): Kyle or Lochalsh.
Open: Easter-Sept 30 daily (inc Suns) 10-6.
Admission: £1.50.

INVEREWE GARDEN
(The National Trust for Scotland)
Poolewe, Wester Ross   map **10** G11   ♿
Telephone: (01445) 781200
Fax: (01445) 781497

Remarkable garden created by the late Osgood Mackenzie. Rare and sub-tropical plants.
Location: 7 m from Gairloch; 85 m W of Inverness, A832.
Open: Garden 1 Apr-22 Oct 9.30-9, 23 Oct-31 Mar 9.30-5.30. Visitor Centre and Shop, 1 Apr to 22 Oct daily 9.30-5.30.
Admission: £3.50 children £1.80 adult parties £2.80 school parties £1.40. Groups should prebook.
Refreshments: (Licensed) restaurant open during same period, *open at 10 and closes at 5.00.*
Ranger Naturalist Service. For disabled: Half garden, greenhouse, toilets, wheelchair available. Guided walks with gardener Apr 1-Oct 22. Mon-Fri at 1.30pm.

HUGH MILLER'S COTTAGE
(The National Trust for Scotland)
Cromarty   map **11** G4
Telephone: (01381) 600245

Birthplace (10 Oct 1802) of Hugh Miller, stonemason, eminent geologist, editor and writer. Furnished thatched cottage built c 1711 for his grandfather contains an interesting exhibition on his life and work. Captioned video programme. Cottage garden.
Location: In Cromarty 22 m from Invernes A832.
Open: 28 Apr-1 Oct daily 10-1 and 2-5.30 Sun 2-5.30.
Admission: £1.50 children 80p.

LOTHIAN

ARNISTON HOUSE
(Mrs A. Dundas-Bekker)
Gorebridge, Midlothian   EH23 4RY   map **15** L16
Telephone: (01875) 830238
Fax: (01875) 830573

William Adam house commissioned by the Dundases in 1726. The family have owned Arniston since 1571 and still live there. Set in acres of outstanding Adam landscaping with views to the Moorfoot hills much loved by Sir Walter Scott it was the hunting ground of King David in the 1100's. The Dundases rose to great legal heights in the 18th century and boast two Lord Presidents of the Court of Session, and Henry Dudas, 1st Viscount Melville, was Cabinet Minister and close friend of Sir William Pitt. Arniston contains portraits of the generations of the family from the 16th century up to the present day by artists including Ramsay and Raeburn. Also are fine examples of Adam architecture, stucco work, furniture and other fascinating contents. Arniston has been beset by dry rot problems and has been involved , grant aided by 'Historic Scotland', in an extensive restoration programme over the years which still continues. 1994-95 the John Adam dining room, gutted in 1957, is being reinstated.
Location: On B6372 between Gorebridge and Temple 1 mile from A7 and half an hour's drive from Edinburgh's city centre.
Open: July-14 Sept 1995. Sun Tuesand Thurs from 2-5. Guided tours. Pre-arranged groups welcome throughout the year.
Admission: £3. Grounds free
Refreshments: Home baked teas.

ARTHUR LODGE
(S.Roland Friden)
60 Dalkeith Road, Edinburgh   EH16 5AD   map **15** L16
Telephone: 0131-667 5163

A Neo Grecian dream of a country gentleman's residence in Town (Thomas Hamilton 1827). Set in a beautiful garden and imaginatively restored and decorated, an exquisite and surprising private residence.
Open: June-July Wed and Sat Aug-Sept Wed only. Tours 2.15 3.15 and 4.15 or by appointment.
Admission: £2.50 concessions £1.50.

DALKEITH COUNTRY PARK
(Duke of Buccleuch and Queensberry KT)
Dalkeith   EH22 2NA   map **15** L16
Telephone: (0131) 663 5684 / 665 3277

Magnificent former home of the Dukes of Buccleuch. 800 acres of parkland dominated by Dalkeith Palace, the last remaining Dutch influenced Palladian house in the area. Extensive parkland first enclosed as deer parks by Charles I in 1637 still retain many fascinating features. Traces of a former lime avenue, manmade caves and tunnels, an amphitheatre and woodland walks can still be seen, reflecting the former glory of Dalkeith Park. The remains of the 12-sided conservatory of 1832 dominates what would have been an elaborate parterre designed by William Gilpin. The Victorian ice house is open for special guided tours with a ranger. Plunge into pitch darkness in this perfectly preserved building. Children thrill to our exciting woodland adventure play area including aerial ropeways, highlevel walkways, giant slides, wildwest fort and entertainment for all ages. Ancient scottish farm animals, events and Clydesdale horses all go toward making Dalkeith a place not to miss. A ranger service operates at Dalkeith to help people enjoy the beauties of the countryside and the work of a country estate. Guided walks, talks and special school activities are available year round by arrangement.

Location: Off Dalkeith High Street A68.
Station(s): Edinburgh Railway / Dalkeith Bus.
Open: Apr 1-Oct 31. 10-6.
Admission: 1995 all entrants £1.50. Family tickets and group discounts on request.
Refreshments: New restaurant.
Events/Exhibitions: See annual programme.

DALMENY HOUSE
(The Earl of Rosebery)
South Queensferry   EH30 9TQ   map **15** L16
Telephone: 0131-331 1888
Fax: 0131-331 1788

Family home of the Earls of Rosebery, magnificently set in beautiful parkland on the shores of the Firth of Forth, 7m from the centre of Edinburgh. Scotland's first Gothic Revival house, designed in 1814 by William Wilkins. Rothschild Collection of 18th century French furniture and decorative art. Portraits by Reynolds, Gainsborough, Raeburn and Lawrence. Goya tapestries. Napoleonic Collection assembled by Prime Minister, the 5th Earl. Woodland garden with superb rhododendrons and azaleas.

Location: 3 m E of South Queensferry; 7 m W of Edinburgh off A90.
Open: May-Sept incl Sun 1-5.30 Mon 12-5.30 Tues 12-5.30. Special parties also welcome at other times by arrangement with Administrator.
Admission: Adults £3.40 students £2.70 children 10-16 years £1.80 (under 10 years free). Groups (min 20) £2.70.
Refreshments: Light lunches and home-made teas.
Events/Exhibitions: Fashion shows, product launches, shows, filming, shooting and small meetings.
Public Transport: From St. Andrew Sq Bus Station to Chapel Gate (1 m from house). Disabled facilities available.

THE GEORGIAN HOUSE
(The National Trust for Scotland)
No. 7 Charlotte Square, Edinburgh   EH2 4DR   map **15** L16
Telephone: 0131-225 2160

The north side of Charlotte Square is classed as Robert Adam's masterpiece of urban architecture. The main floors of No. 7 are open as a typical Georgian House. Audio-visual shows. Shop.

Location: In Edinburgh city centre.
Open: Apr 1-Oct 22 Mon-Sat 10-5 Sun 2-5.
Admission: £3.50 children £1.80 adult parties £2.80 school parties £1.40. Groups must pre-book.

GLADSTONE'S LAND
(The National Trust for Scotland)
Edinburgh   map **15** L16
Telephone: 0131-226 5856

Built 1620 and shortly afterwards occupied by Thomas Gledstanes. Remarkable painted wooden ceilings; furnished as a typical 'Old Town' house of the period. Shop.

Location: 477B Lawnmarket, Edinburgh.
Open: Apr 1-Oct 22 Mon-Sat 10-5 Sun 2-5.
Admission: £2.50 children £1.30 adult parties £2 school parties £1. Groups must pre-book.

GOSFORD HOUSE

(Lord Wemyss' Trust)
East Lothian   EH32 0PX   map **9** L17
Telephone: (01875) 870201
Fax: (01875) 870620

Robert Adam Mansion, central block surviving; striking maritime situation. Original wings demolished early 19th Century; replaced 1890 (William Young, Architect); South wing contains celebrated Marble Hall, fine collection of paintings etc. Part of Adam block burnt 1940, re-roofed 1987. Policies laid out with ornamental water. Grey Lag Geese and other wildfowl breeding.

Location: On A198 between Aberlady & Longniddry; NW of Haddington.
Station(s): Longniddry (2½ m).
Open: June and July Wed Sat and Sun 2-5.
Admission: Adults £1 children 50p OAPs 75p.
Refreshments: Hotels in Aberlady.
Wemyss & March Estates, Longniddry, East Lothian EH32 OPY.

THE HOUSE OF THE BINNS

(The National Trust for Scotland)
by Linlithgow   map **15** L15   △
Telephone: (0150 683) 4255

Historic home of the Dalyells. Fine plaster ceilings. Interesting pictures. Panoramic viewpoint.

Location: 3½ m E of Linlithgow off A904.
Open: 29 Apr-1 Oct daily except Fri 1.30-5.30. Parkland all year daily 10-7.
Admission: £3 children £1.50 adult parties £2.40 school parties £1.20.

INVERESK LODGE GARDEN

(The National Trust for Scotland)
Inveresk   map **15** L16
Telephone: 0131-665 1855

New garden, with large selection of plants.

Location: In Inveresk village; 6 m E of Edinburgh off A1.
Open: 1 Apr-30 Sept Mon-Fri 10-4.30 Sat/Sun 2-5 1 Oct-31 Mar Mon-Fri 10-4.30 Sun 2-5.
Admission: £1 Honesty Box. Groups must pre-book.

LAURISTON CASTLE
(City of Edinburgh District Council)
Edinburgh   map **15** L16 △

A late 16th century tower – house with extensive 19th century additions. It has a fine Edwardian interior containing 18th and 19th century furniture, impressive collections of Derbyshire Blue John, Crossley wool mosaics and objets d'art. Visitors are taken on a guided tour lasting approximately 40 minutes. There is a free car park. Opening hours - April to October, Daily (except Friday) 11am - 1pm, 2 - 5pm, Nov-March, Sat & Suns only 2 - 4pm (last tour starts 40 minutes before closing. Telephone 0131 336 2060.

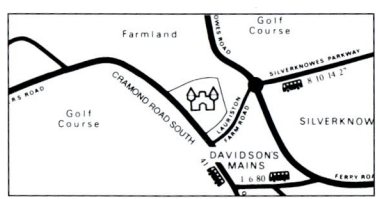

Admission Charges Adults: £2.00 Children, UB40's, Benefit recipients and Leisure Access card holders: £1.00.
Free admission to the Castle grounds.

Bus no 41 from George Street to Lauriston Castle gates, and Bus no 40 from the Mound, Princes Street to Davidson Mains.

A beautifully furnished Edwardian home, associated with John Law (1671-1729), founder of first bank in France.
Location: Cramond Road South, Davidsons Mains, 4½ m from GPO, Edinburgh.
Open: Castle all year Apr-Oct daily (except Fri) 11-1 and 2-5 Nov-Mar Sat and Sun only 2-4 guided tours only (last tour 40 mins before closing time) Grounds daily 9-dusk.
Admission: Adults £2 children £1.

William Kent (1685 - 1748)
Painter, architect, garden designer

His work can be seen in the following properties included in Historic Houses Castles and Gardens:-

Chiswick House
Ditchley Park (decoration of Great Hall)
Euston Hall
Rousham House
Stowe (Stowe School)

LENNOXLOVE
(His Grace the Duke of Hamilton)
Haddington EH41 4NZ map **9** L17
Telephone: (01620) 823720
Fax: (01620) 825112

Lennoxlove, home of the Duke of Hamilton, is a house with a three-fold interest; its historic architecture, the association of its proprietors with the Royal House of Stewart and the famous Hamilton Palace collection of works of art, including the Casket, ring and Death Mask of Mary Queen of Scots. Formerly Lethington Tower, ancient home of the Maitlands. The Lime Avenue, known as Politician's Walk, was laid out by William Maitland, Secretary of State to Mary Queen of Scots.

Location: 1½ m S of Haddington on B6369; 18 m E of Edinburgh off A1.
Open: Easter weekend then May-Sept Wed Sat & Sun 2-5 at other times by appointment (minimum charge £30); apply to Estate Office, Lennoxlove, Haddington (01620 823720).
Admission: Adults £3 children £1.50 pre-booked parties (15 or more - minimum charge £30) £2 children £1 price includes guided tour of House, entry to gardens and parking.
Refreshments: Tea-room.
Conferences: Select business conferences, residential or non-residential, and film and photograph location, etc. For further information contact The Factor, Lennoxlove, Haddington. East Lothian EH41 4NZ (Tel. 01620 822156, Fax 01620 825112).

MALLENY GARDEN
(The National Trust for Scotland)
Balerno map **15** L16
Telephone: 0131-449 2283

A delightfully personal garden with a particularly good collection of shrub roses. National Bonsai Collection for Scotland.

Location: In Balerno, off A70.
Open: All year daily 9.30-sunset.
Admission: £1 Honesty box.
No dogs in garden please.

PALACE OF HOLYROODHOUSE
(The official residence of HM The Queen in Scotland)
Edinburgh EH8 8DX map **15** L16
Telephone: 0131-556 7371

The ridge, known as the Royal Mile, that slopes downwards from Edinburgh Castle, comes to a majestic conclusion at Holyroodhouse, where Palace and Abbey stand against the spectacular backdrop of Salisbury Crag. Throughout history, Holyrood has been the scene of turbulent and extraordinary events, yet the Palace retains a modern appeal appropriate to a Royal residence still in regular use.

Location: Central Edinburgh.
Open: Open all year (except when Her Majesty The Queen is in residence). *Closed. The Palace and Abbey may sometimes be closed at short notice.* **Enquiries:** Telephone 0131-556 1096.
Admission: Charge. Group rates available.

PRESTON MILL
(The National Trust for Scotland)
East Linton map **9** L17
Telephone: (01620) 860426

The oldest mill (16th century) of its kind still working and only survivor of many on the banks of the Tyne. Popular with artists. Renovated machinery.

Location: 5½ m W of Dunbar, off A1.
Open: 14 Apr-30 Sep Mon-Sat 11-1 and 2-5.30 Sun 1.30-5.30 1-22 Oct Sat/Sun 1.30-4.
Admission: £1.50 children 80p adult parties £1.20 school parties £1.60. Groups must pre-book.

PRESTONHALL

(Major J.H. Callander (WA))
Pathhead map **9** L17

Built in 1791, in 70 acres of parkland with fine architecture and interiors.

Location: Within ½ hour of Edinburgh.
Open: House open by appointment only.
Accommodation: There is limited accommodation available.
Conferences: Prestonhall is ideally situated for Corporate Entertainment and Conferences for up to 40.

STEVENSON HOUSE

(Trustees of the Brown Dunlop Country Houses Trust)
Haddington **EH41 4PU** map **9** L16
Telephone: (01620) 823376 Mrs J.C.H Dunlop

A family home for four centuries, of charm and interest and dating from the 13th century when it belonged to the Cistercian Nunnery at Haddington, but partially destroyed on several occasions, and finally made uninhabitable in 1544. Restored about 1560 and the present house dates mainly from this period, with later additions in the 18th century. Fine furniture, pictures etc.

Location: 20 m approx from Edinburgh; 1½ m approx from A1; 2 m approx from Haddington. (See Historic House direction signs on A1 in Haddington.)
Open: July-mid-Aug Thur Sat & Sun 2-5. Guided tours take at least 1-1½ hours 3 pm. Other times by arrangement only. GARDENS House and Walled Kitchen Garden are open daily Apr-Oct.
Admission: £2 OAPs £1.50 Children under 14 £1. Special arrangement parties welcome. GARDENS 50p only payable into Box on House Garden entrance gate.
Refreshments: Appointment parties morning coffee etc at Stevenson. Nearest hotels and restaurants are in Haddington, i.e. 2 m from Stevenson.
Car parking. Suitable for wheelchairs in garden only.

ORKNEY ISLANDS

BALFOUR CASTLE

Shapinsay, Orkney Islands **KW17 2DY** map **11** D17
Telephone: (01856) 711282
Fax: (01856) 711283

Balfour Castle was built in 1848

Open: On Suns & Weds May-Sept. Guided tours of the walled garden and Castle by members of the resident family.

STRATHCLYDE

ARDUAINE GARDEN

(The National Trust for Scotland)
Argyll map **8** K11
Telephone: (01852) 200366

Outstanding 18 acre garden on a promontory bounded by Loch Melfort and the Sound of Jura. Nationally noted for rhododendrons and azalea specied, magnolias and other rare trees and shrubs.

Location: A816, 20 m S of Oban and 17 m N of Lochgilphead.
Open: All year daily 9.30-sunset. Reception Centre 1 Apr-31 Oct daily 11-5.30.
Admission: £2, children £1 (under 5 free) adult parties £1.60 school parties 80p. Groups should pre-book.

BACHELORS' CLUB

(The National Trust for Scotland)
Tarbolton map **8** L13
Telephone: (01292) 541940

17th century thatched house where Burns and his friends formed their club in 1780. Period furnishings.

Location: In Tarbolton village 7½ m NE of Ayr (off A758).
Open: 14 Apr-30 Sep daily 1.30-5.30 1-22 Oct Sat/Sun 1.30-5.30.
Admission: £1.50 children 80p adult parties £1.20 school parties 60p. Groups must pre-book.

BLAIRQUHAN CASTLE AND GARDENS

(James Hunter Blair)
Straiton, Maybole, Ayrshire **KA19 7LZ** map **8** M13
Telephone: (0165 57) 239
Fax: (0165 57) 278

Magnificent Regency castellated mansion approached by a 3m private drive beside the river Girvan. Walled gardens and pinetum. Picture gallery.

Location: 14m S of Ayr off A77. Entrance Lodge is on B7045 ½ m S of Kirkmichael.
Open: July 16-Aug 13 *not Mons.*

Admission: £3 Children £2 OAPs £2. Parties by arrangement at any time of year.
Refreshments: Tea in castle.
Car parking. Wheelchairs - around gardens and principal floor of the castle.

BRODICK CASTLE, GARDEN AND COUNTRY PARK

(The National Trust for Scotland)
Isle of Arran   map **8** M13
Telephone: (01770) 302202
Fax: (01770) 302312

Historic home of the Dukes of Hamilton. The castle dates in part from the 13th century. Paintings, furniture, objet d'art. Formal and woodland gardens, noted for rhododendrons. Country park.

Location: 1½ m N of Brodick pierhead on the Isle of Arran.
Station(s): Ardrossan Harbour and Claonaig in Kintyre (& hence by Caledonian MacBrayne ferry). Ferry enquiries to Caledonian MacBrayne. Tel. Gourock (01475) 33755.
Open: Castle 14 Apr-30 Sep daily 11.30-5 1-22 Oct Sat/Sun 11.30-5. Reception Centre and Shop dates as Castle 10-5. Garden and Country Park, all year daily 9.30-sunset
Admission: House and Garden £4 children £2 adult parties £3.20 school parties £1.60. Garden only adults £2 children £1. Groups should pre-book.
Refreshments: RESTAURANT. (Self-service in Castle). Dates as Castle, Mons to Sats 10-5.

CULZEAN CASTLE, GARDEN AND COUNTRY PARK

(The National Trust for Scotland)
Maybole   map **8** M13   △ ⅓ Ⓢ
Telephone: (016556) 274
Fax: (016556) 615

One of the finest Adam houses in Scotland. Spacious policies and gardens. Adventure playground.

Location: 12 m SW of Ayr just off A719.
Open: Castle, Visitor Centre and Shops 1 Apr-22 Oct daily 10.30-5.30. Country Park, all year daily 9.30-sunset.
Admission: Country Park: adults £3 children/OAPs £1.50. Castle: adults £3.50 children\OAPs £1.80. Combined tickets adults £5.50 children\OAPs £3. Party Rate £4.50. School Coaches £20. Groups should pre-book.
Refreshments: Licensed restaurant. Open 10.30-5.30.

DUART CASTLE

(Sir Lachlan MacLean)
Isle of Mull, Argyll   **PA64 6AP**   map **8** K11   △
Telephone: (01680) 812309

Duart Castle is built on a cliff dominating the Sound of Mull. Home of the Chief of Clan Maclean. Panoramic views from 13th Century Keep built by 5th Chief Lachlan Lubanach. Dungeons and exhibitions.

Open: May-Mid Oct daily 10.30-6.
Admission: Adults £3 OAPs £2 children £1.50 family ticket £7.50.
Refreshments: Tea-room with home baking. Shop.

FINLAYSTONE HOUSE AND GARDENS

(Mr G MacMillan)
Langbank   **PA14 6TJ**   map **8** L13
Telephone: House (01475) 540285 Ranger Service (01475) 540505

Formerly home of fifteen Earls of Glencairn; now the home of the chief of Clan MacMillan. Exhibitions of international dolls, flower books, Victoriana, and Celtic art. Beautiful Gardens, Woodlands, with picnic/play areas. Ranger service. Visitor centre. Clan Centre. Tea-room in re-designed walled garden.

Location: On A8 between Langbank & Port Glasgow; 10 minutes W of Glasgow Airport. On S bank of the Clyde.
Station(s): Langbank (1¼ m).
Open: Beautiful gardens and woods open all the year (House Apr-Aug Suns 2.30-4.30 and by appointment any time).
Admission: Adults £1.50 children £1. Pre-booked groups welcome. House adults £1.40 children 90p.
Refreshments: Summer 11-5 daily and Winter weekends.

GREENBANK GARDEN

(The National Trust for Scotland)
Glasgow   map **15** L14   ⅓
Telephone: 0141-639 3281

Walled garden, woodland walk and policies. Wide range of plants, flowers and shrubs. Regular garden walks and events. Best seen Apr-Oct. Attractive series of gardens, extending to 2½ acres, surrounding Georgian house (not open to the public). Special garden and greenhouse for the disabled, together with special gardening tools.

Location: Flenders Road, near Clarkston Toll.
Station(s): Clarkston (1¼ m).
Open: Garden all year daily 9.30-sunset.
Admission: £2 children (accompanied by adult) £1 adult parties £1.60 school parties 80p. children (under 5) free OAPs/students (on production of their cards) half-price. Groups must pre-book.

THE HILL HOUSE

(The National Trust for Scotland)
Helensburgh   map **8** K13
Telephone: (01436) 673900

Overlooking the estuary of the River Clyde the house is considered to be the finest example of the domestic architecture of Charles Rennie Mackintosh. Commissioned in 1902 and completed in 1904 for the Glasgow publisher Walter W Blackie. Special display about Charles Rennie Mackintosh.

Location: In Upper Colquhoun Street, Helensburgh; NW of Glasgow via A814.
Open: Apr 1-Dec 23 daily 1.30-5.30.
Admission: £3 children £1.50 adult parties £2.40 school parties £1.20. Groups must pre-book.
Refreshments: Tea-room open 1.30-4.30 Apr-Oct only.

HUTCHESONS' HALL

(The National Trust for Scotland)
Glasgow   map **15** L14
Telephone: 0141-552 8391
Fax: 0141-562 7031

Described as one of the most elegant buildings in Glasgow's city centre, the Hall was built in 1802-5 to a design by David Hamilton.

Location: 158 Ingram Street, nr SE corner of George Square.
Open: Hall viewing subject to functions. Visitor Centre and Function Hall all year Mon-Fri 9.30-5 Sat 10-4. Closed 24 Dec 95-10 Jan 96.
Admission: Free. Groups must pre-book.
Shop: Mons to Sats 10-4.

INVERARAY CASTLE

(The Trustees of the 10th Duke of Argyll)
Inveraray   PA32 8XE   map **8** K12   △ ら
Telephone: (01499) 302203
Fax: (01499) 302421

Since the early 15th century Inveraray has been the Headquarters of the Clan Campbell. The present Castle was built in the third quarter of the 18th century by Roger Morris and Robert Mylne. The Great Hall and Armoury, the State Rooms, Tapestries, Pictures and 18th century Furniture and old kitchen are shown.

Location: ¾ m NE of Inveraray on Loch Fyne 58 m NW of Glasgow.
Open: First Sat in Apr-second Sun in Oct. Apr-June Sept & Oct daily (except Fri) 10-1 and 2-5.30 Sun 1-5.30 July & Aug daily 10-5.30 Sun 1-5.30 (Last admission 12.30 & 5). Gardens open by appointment, woodland walk open all year. Craft shop. *Enquiries:* The Factor, Dept HH, Cherry Park, Inveraray, Argyll. Telephone: (01499) 302203.
Refreshments: Tea-room.

Sir Peter Lely - portrait painter

His paintings can be seen at the following properties included in Historic Houses Castles and Gardens:-

Aynhoe Park
Belton House
Breamore House
Browsholme Hall
Dalmeny House
Euston Hall
Goodwood House
Gorhambury

Kedleston Hall
Knole
Petworth House
Ragley Hall
Rockingham Castle
St Osyth Priory
Stanford Hall
Weston Park

KELBURN CASTLE AND COUNTRY CENTRE

(The Home and Park of the Earls of Glasgow on the Firth of Clyde)
Largs KA29 0BE   map **8** L13
Telephone: (01475) 568685
Fax: (01475) 568121

Kelburn Castle

Kelburn Country Centre

Situated on the scenic North Ayrshire coast, Kelburn has been the home of the Boyle family for over 800 years and the seat of the Earls of Glasgow since the creation of the title in 1703. Kelburn Glen is one of the most romantic in Scotland, with woodland walks on each side of the Kel Burn which drops 700ft by way of many waterfalls and deep gorges. Featured gardens at Kelburn are the Plaisance, a formal walled garden dominated by two magnificent 1000 year old Yew trees and planted with exotic shrubs and varieties of rhododendron, and the Children's Garden, a small formal garden planted in 1760 by the 3rd Earl. A Robert Adam monument, erected in 1775, can be seen in the Glen and there is a Sundial dating 1707. Kelburn's Monterey Pine is the oldest and tallest in Scotland, and an unusual Weeping Larch with a double-headed canopy is a spectacular attraction. Kelburn Castle is the family home of the 10th Earl and Countess of Glasgow. Its striking architectural design features an early 13th century Norman Keep, with extensions dating from 1581, 1700 and 1879 reflecting the different styles and needs of the times. Although only open to the public in July and August, the Castle makes an impressive background to Kelburn's many walks and views. Kelburn Country Centre offers much more than spectacular scenery and lovely walks. Kelburn's colourful history is re-told in The Kelburn Story Cartoon Exhibition, there is a family Museum, Horse Riding, Adventure Play Areas, Commando Assault Course, Soft Play Room, Pets Corner, Nature Centre, Activity Workshop, Information office, Gift Shop, Ranger Service. Kelburn's newest attraction, 'The Secret Forest' features The Maze of the Green Man , The Gingerbread House, The Castle With No Entrance, The Chinese Pavilion, A Mysterious Grotto and Crocodile Swamp.

Location: On the A78 between Largs and Fairlie in Ayrshire.
Station(s): Largs (2 m) free minibus service at 11.45 am and 1.45 pm (weekends only Apr-June; daily July and Aug).
Open: Kelburn Country Centre open daily 10-6 Easter-and Oct. Grounds only end Oct-Easter. Kelburn Castle open afternoons in July and Aug (to be confirmed).
Admission: Kelburn Country Centre adults £3.50 children/OAPs/concessions £2. Groups (12 +) adults £2 children/OAPs/concessions £1.50.
Refreshments: Licensed cafe, lunches, snacks, ice cream parlour, picnic areas. Fully open from Easter-end Oct.
Country Centre: Dogs admitted on leads.

MOUNT STUART HOUSE AND GARDENS

(The Mount Stuart Trust)
Rothesay, Isle of Bute PA20 9LR   map **8** L12
Telephone: (01700) 503877
Fax: (01700) 505313

Open to the public for the first time in 1995: ancestral home of the Marquesses of Bute; one of Britain's most spectacular High Victorian Gothic houses; fabulous interiors, art collection and architectural detail; extensive grounds with lovely woodland and shoreline walks; exotic gardens, Victorian kitchen garden; mature Victorian Pinetum.

Location: 5½ m south of Rothesay pierhead on Isle of Bute.
Station(s): Glasgow Airport: 50 mins drive/train to Wemyss Bay. Rail Stations: Glasgow Central and Wemyss Bay (British Rail: (0141) 204 2844). Frequent ferry service from Wemyss Bay (Caledonian MacBrayne: (01475) 650 100). Bus service from Rothesay Pier (Stagecoach Western Scottish: (01700) 502076).
Open: June-end Sept 12.00-17.00 (16.30 last admission). Mon, Wed, Fri, Sat & Sun. Gardens open 11.00-17.00 (16.30 last admission).
Admission: House and garden: Adult £5, Child £2.50, Family £14. Garden only: Adult £3, Child £2, family £8. Concessions and group rates given.
Pre-booked house/gardens/ranger guided tours available on application.

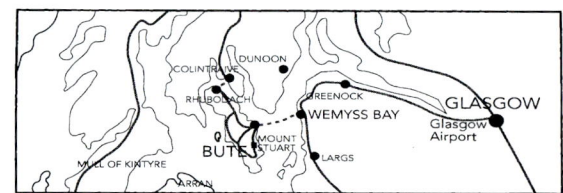

POLLOK HOUSE & PARK

(City of Glasgow District Council)
Glasgow map **15** L14 ♿
Telephone: (0141) 632 0274
Fax: (0141) 649 0823

Built 1747-52, additions by Sir Rowand Anderson 1890-1908. Contains Stirling Maxwell collection of Spanish and other European paintings; displays of furniture, ceramics, glass and silver. Nearby in Pollok Park is the Burrell Collection. Opening times as Pollok House.

Location: 3½ m from City Centre.
Station(s): Pollokshaws West (1 m).
Open: All the year Mons-Sats 10-5 Suns 11-5. *Closed December 25, 26 and 27 & New Year's Day.*
Admission: Free.
Refreshments: Tea-room (reservations Tel: 0141-649 7547).

SORN CASTLE

Sorn, Mauchline map **8** M14
Telephone: (01505) 612124 (Cluttons)

Dating from the 14th century in impressive setting on sandstone cliff over the River Ayr with attractive woodland walks.

Location: 4 m E of Mauchline on B743.
Open: Jul 22-Aug 19 2-5 or by appointment. Grounds Apr 1-Oct 30.
Admission: £3.50.

SOUTER JOHNNIE'S COTTAGE

(The National Trust for Scotland)
Kirkoswald map **8** M13
Telephone: (016556) 671

Thatched home of the original Souter in Burns', 'Tam o' Shanter', Burns' relics. Life-sized stone figures of the Souter, Tam, the Innkeeper and his wife, in restored ale house in the cottage garden.

Location: In Kirkoswald village 4 m W of Maybole on A77.
Station(s): Maybole.
Open: 14 Apr-30 Sep daily 1.30-5.30 1-22 Oct Sat/Sun 1.30-5.30.
Admission: £1.50 children 80p adult parties £1.20 school parties 60p. Groups must pre-book.

THE TENEMENT HOUSE

(The National Trust for Scotland)
Glasgow map **15** L14
Telephone: 0141-333 0183

A restored first floor flat in a Victorian tenement building, built 1892, presents a picture of social significance. A second flat on the ground floor provides reception, interpretative and educational facilities.

Location: No 145 Buccleuch Street, Garnethill (N of Charing Cross).
Open: 1 Mar-22 Oct daily 1.30-5.
Admission: £2 children £1 adult parties £1.60 school parties 80p. Groups must book.

TOROSAY CASTLE AND GARDENS

(Mr Christopher James)
Craignure, Isle of Mull **PA65 6AY** map **8** J11
Telephone: (01680) 812421
Fax: (01680) 812470

Early Victorian house by David Bryce, still a family home, surrounded by 12 acres of terraced and contrasting informal gardens, all offset by dramatic West Highland scenery.

Location: 1½ m SE of Craignure by A849, by Forest Walk or by N.G. Steam Railway.
Open: Castle mid Apr-mid Oct 10.30-5.30 (last adm 5). Gardens Summer 9-7 Winter sunrise to sunset. Parties at other times to Castle by appointment only.
Admission: Castle £3.50 also concession rates. Garden only adults £1.50 children (5-16)/OAPs/students £1 (honesty box when castle closed). Free car park.
Refreshments: Home baked teas in Castle.
Dogs on lead in Gardens only. Gardens and tearoom only suitable for wheelchairs. Local Craft Shop.

WEAVER'S COTTAGE

(The National Trust for Scotland)
Kilbarchan map **15** L13
Telephone: (01505) 705588

Typical cottage of 18th century handloom weaver: looms, weaving equipment, domestic utensils. (Weaving demonstrations check for times).

Location: In Kilbarchan village; 12 m SW of Glasgow off A737.
Station(s): Johnstone (2½ m).
Open: 14 Apr-30 Sept daily 1.30-5.30 1-22 Oct Sat/Sun 1.30-5.30.
Admission: £1.50 children 80p adult parties £1.20 school parties 60p. Groups must pre-book.
Video programme.

TAYSIDE

ANGUS FOLK MUSEUM

(The National Trust for Scotland)
Glamis map **9** J16
Telephone: (01307) 840288

Row of 19th century cottages with stone-slabbed roofs, restored by the Trust. Adapted to display the Angus Folk Collection, one of the finest in the country. In agricultural annexe are farming implements and the Bothy Exhibition incl. taped recordings.

Location: In Glamis village; 12 m N of Dundee A94.
Open: 14 Apr-2 Oct daily 11-5 3-22 Oct Sat/Sun 11-5.
Admission: £2 children £1 adult parties £1.60 school parties 80p. Groups must pre-book.

BARRIE'S BIRTHPLACE

(The National Trust for Scotland)
Kirriemuir map **9** J16
Telephone: (01575) 572646

Contains mementoes of Sir James Barrie. Exhibition features Peter Pan and other works of Barrie.

Location: No 9 Brechin Road, in Kirriemuir.
Open: 14 Apr-30 Sept Mon-Sat 11-5.30 Sun 1.30-5.30 1-22 Oct Sat 11-5.30 Sun 1.30-5.30.
Admission: £1.50 children 80p adult parties £1.20 school parties 60p.
Refreshments: Airlie Arms Hotel.

BARRY MILL

(The National Trust for Scotland)
Carnoustie map **9** J17
Telephone: (01241) 56761

This 18th century meal mill works on a demonstration basis. Displays highlight the important place the mill held in the community.

Location: 2 m NW of Carnoustie.
Open: 14 Apr-30 Sept daily 11-5.00 1 to 22 Oct Sat/Sun 11-5.00.
Admission: £1.50 children 80p adult parties £1.20 school parties 60p. Groups must pre-book.

BRANKLYN GARDEN

(The National Trust for Scotland)
Perth   map **9** K16
Telephone: (01738) 625535

One of the finest gardens of its size in Britain (2 acres).

Location: In Perth on Dundee Road (A85).
Open: Mar 1-Oct 31: daily 9.30-sunset.
Admission: £2 children £1 adult parties 1.60 school parties 80p. Groups should pre-book.

DRUMMOND CASTLE GARDENS

(Grimsthorpe & Drummond Castle Trust Ltd)
Muthill, Crieff   PH5 2AA   map **8** K15
Telephone: (01764) 681257
Fax: (01764) 681550

The gardens of Drummond Castle first laid out in the early 17th century by John Drummond, 2nd Earl of Perth, are said to be among the finest formal gardens in Europe. A spectacular view can be obtained from the upper terrace, overlooking a magnificent example of an early Victorian Parterre in the form of a St. Andrew's cross. The multi faceted sundial by John Mylne, Master Mason to Charles 1 has been the centre piece since 1630.

Location: Entrance 2 m south of Crieff on Muthill Road A822.
Open: Daily 2-6 (last admission 5) May-Oct.
Admission: Adults £3 OAPs £2 children £1.50.
Coach parties by prior arrangement.

CASTLE MENZIES

(Menzies Charitable Trust)
Weem   PH15 2JD   map **8** J15
Telephone: (01887) 820982

Magnificant example of a 16th century fortified house, seat of the Chiefs of Clan Menzies, situated in the beautiful valley of the Tay. It was involved in the turbulent history of the Central Highlands and here 'Bonnie Prince Charlie' rested on his way to Culloden in 1746.

Location: 1½ m from Aberfeldy on B846.
Open: Apr-mid Oct weekdays 10.30-5 Suns 2-5.
Admission: Adults £2.50 children £1 OAPs £2 family concessions. Reductions for parties by prior arrangement.
Refreshments: Tea-room.

Gertrude Jekyll
writer and gardener
(1843-1932)

Her designs were used at the following properties included in Historic Houses Castles and Gardens:-

Barrington Court
Castle Drogo
Goddards
Hatchlands Park
Hestercombe House and Gardens
Knebworth
Lindisfarne Castle

A collection of her tools can be found at Guildford Museum

GLAMIS CASTLE
(The Earl of Strathmore and Kinghorne)
Glamis DD8 1RT   map **9** J16   △
Telephone: (01307) 840393/242
Fax: (01307) 840257

Family home of the Earls of Strathmore and Kinghorne and a royal residence since 1372. Childhood home of H.M. Queen Elizabeth The Queen Mother and birthplace of H.R.H. The Princess Margaret. Legendary setting of Shakespeare's play 'Macbeth'. Five-storey L shaped tower block dating from 15th century, remodelled 1606, containing magnificent rooms with wide range of historic pictures, furniture, porcelain etc.

Location: Glamis.
Open: Apr 1-Oct 30 daily 10.30-5.30 (last admission 4.45).
Admission: Adults £4.50 OAPs £3.50 children 5-16 £2.40 party rates £4.10 OAPs £3.10 children 5-16 £2.10 family ticket £13 Grounds only £2.20 children £1.10.
Refreshments: Licensed Restaurant at the Castle.
Ample bus and car parking. Picnic area, Shops, Garden and Nature Trail. Further details available from The Administrator, Tel: (01307) 840393/242. Fax: (01307) 840257.

George Stubbs
Portrait, animal and rural painter

(1724-1806)
Produced his engraved work,
The Anatomy of a Horse, in 1766

His work can be seen in the following
properties included in Historic Houses Castles
and Gardens:-

Mount Stewart House
St Osyth Priory
Upton House

HOUSE OF DUN
(The National Trust for Scotland)
nr Montrose   map **9** J17
Telephone: (01674) 810264

Palladian house overlooking the Montrose Basin, built in 1730 for David Erskine, Lord Dun, to designs by William Adam. Exuberant plasterwork in the saloon.

Location: 4 m W of Montrose.
Open: 14 Apr-30 June 1-30 Sept daily 1.30-5.30 1 July-31 August daily 11-5.30. 1-22 Oct Sat/Sun 1.30-5.30.
Admission: £3 children £1.50 adult parties £2.40 school parties £1.20. Groups must pre-book.
Refreshments: Restaurant open at 12. Dates as above.

MONZIE CASTLE
Crieff, Perthshire PH7 4HD   map **8** K15
Telephone: (01764) 653110

Built in 1791. Destroyed by fire in 1908. Rebuilt and furnished by Sir Robert Lorimer.

Location: 2 miles north east of Crieff.
Open: May 29-June 18 1995 inclusive 2-5. By appointment anytime.
Admission: Adults £3 children £1 groups £2.50.

SCONE PALACE

(Rt Hon the Earl of Mansfield)
Perth   PH2 6BD   map **9** K16
Telephone: (01738) 552300

This medieval palace was Gothicised for the third Earl of Mansfield in the early 19th century. Superb collections of French furniture, china, ivories, clocks, Vernis Martin vases and objets d'art. Magnificent trees.

Location: 2 m NE of Perth on the Braemar Road (A93).
Station(s): Perth (2½ m).
Open: Good Fri-mid Oct Mon-Sun 9.30-5.
Admission: Palace and Grounds: adults £4.50 party rate £4 OAPs £3.70 party rate £3.40 children £2.50 party rate £2.25 family ticket £13 Grounds only: adults £2.25 children £1.25. Free car park.
Refreshments: Coffee shop. Old Kitchen Restaurant (licensed). Home baking. State Room dinners.
Shops. Picnic park. Playground.

STOBHALL

(Earl of Perth)
Guildtown, Perth   map **9** J16

Gardens and Policies, Chapel with 17th century painted ceiling.

Location: 8 m north of Perth on A93.
Open: Mid May-mid June 1-5.
Admission: Adults £2 children £1.

The Garden Specialists

in Great Britain and Ireland

A selection of nurseries specialising in rare or uncommon plants

♿ Denotes the major part of the property is suitable for wheelchairs

---

ARCHITECTURAL PLANTS

(Angus White)
Cooks Farm, Nuthurst, Horsham, West Sussex   RH13 6LH
Telephone: (01403) 891772
Fax: (01403) 891056

Hardy Exotics - evergreen trees and shrubs with big, spiky and frondy leaves, including conservatory plants. Many extremely rare. Please send for free catalogue.

Location: Behind Black Horse pub in Nuthurst, 5 m S of Horsham, West Sussex.
Station(s): Horsham.
Open: Mons-Sats 9-5.

BODIAM NURSERY

(Richard Biggs)
Ockham House, Bodiam, Robertsbridge, East Sussex   TN32 5RA
Telephone: (01580) 830811/830649

Set beside fine old oasthouse and Queen Anne house in unspoilt countryside. Spectacular view of Bodiam Castle just across the River Rother. Enormous selection of heathers (over 200), Acers, shrubs (over 700), climbers, conifers, alpine and herbaceous plants, many unusual, propagated and grown here. Sizes from tinies for the economy minded to specimens for 'instant gardening'. Acres of plants in pots.

Location: 11 m from Hastings, 3 m from Hurst Green which is on the A21. Follow signs for Bodiam Castle. Nursery is just across the river valley from the Castle.
Station(s): Etchingham (5 m).
Open: Every day 9-7 (sunset in winter).

BODNANT GARDEN NURSERY LTD

Tal Y Cafn, nr Colwyn Bay, Clwyd   LL28 5RE   ♿
Telephone: (01492) 650460
Fax: (01492) 650448

Bodnant Garden Nursery is famous for its unusual trees and shrubs. We propagate over 800 species and varieties of flowering and foliage shrubs, including rhododendrons, azaleas, magnolias and camellias. The many thousands of plants produced in our own propagation units by experienced staff are available to purchase, either by personal selection or our efficient mail order service.

Location: 8 m S of Llandudno and Colwyn Bay on the A470, just off the A55 Coastal Expressway.
Open: Daily (excl. Christmas Day) 9.30-5.
Admission: Free.
Refreshments: Morning coffee, light lunches and afternoon teas are available Apr-Sept. Car parking. Ramps for disabled.

J.W. BOYCE

(Mr Roger Morley)
Bush Pasture, Fordham, Ely, Cambridgeshire   CB7 5JU
Telephone: (01638) 721158

Specialists in garden seeds for over 80 years. Specialising in the production of pansy seed and plants. Also over 1000 items of seed which includes a wide range of separate colours for cut flowers, bedding and drying. Also old and unusual vegetables. Seed list free on request: Telephone above number, or write to J. W. Boyce, Bush Pasture, Carter Street, Ely, Cambs CB7 5JU.

BURNCOOSE NURSERIES AND GARDEN

(C H Williams)
Gwennap, Redruth, Cornwall   TR16 6BJ   ♿
Telephone: (01209) 861112
Fax: (01209) 860011

The Nurseries are set in the 30-acre woodland gardens of Burncoose. Some 12 acres are laid out for nursery stock production of over 2000 varieties of ornamental trees, shrubs and herbaceous plants. Specialities include camellias, azaleas, magnolias, rhododendrons and conservatory plants. The nurseries are widely known for rarities, and for unusual plants. Full mail order catalogue £1 (posted).

Location: 2 m SE of Redruth on the main A393 Redruth to Falmouth road between the villages of Lanner and Ponsanooth.
Station(s): Redruth.
Open: Mon-Sat 9-5 Sun 11-5 Gardens and tea-rooms open all year.
Admission: Nurseries free Gardens £1.
Refreshments: Light refreshments in tea-rooms.

DEACONS NURSERY (H.H.)

(Grahame and Brian Deacon - Partners)
Moor View, Godshill, Isle of Wight   PO38 3HW
Telephone: (01983) 840750/(01983) 522243

Specialist national fruit tree growers. Trees and bushes sent anywhere so send NOW for FREE catalogue. Over 250 varieties of apples on various types of rootstocks from M27 (4ft), M26 (8ft), to M25 (18ft). Plus Pears, Peaches, Nectarines, Plums, Gages, Cherry, soft fruits and an unusual selection of Family Trees. Many special offers. Catalogue always available, 30p stamp please.

Location: Godshill - a picturesque village visited by all. Deacons Nursery is in Moor View off School Crescent (behind the only school).
Open: Summer Mon-Fri 8-4 winter Mon-Fri 8-5 Sat 8-1.

FAMILY TREES

PO Box 3, Botley, Hampshire   SO3 2EA
Telephone: (01329) 834812

Fruit for the connoisseur in wide variety. Trained tree specialists; also ornamental trees and old roses; hedgerow and woodland trees. Free mail order catalogues (and nursery location) from Family Trees, PO Box 3, Botley, Hampshire SO3 2EA.

Location: See map in free catalogue.
Station(s): Botley 2½ m.
Open: Mid Oct-mid Apr Wed and Sat 9.30-12.30.
Admission: No charge.

HADDONSTONE SHOW GARDEN

The Forge House, Church Lane, East Haddon, Northampton   NN6 8DB   ♿
Telephone: (01604) 770711

See Haddonstone's classic garden ornaments in the beautiful setting of the walled manor gardens - including urns, troughs, fountains, statuary, bird baths, sundials and balustrading. Featured on BBC Gardeners World, the garden is on different levels with shrub roses, ground cover plants, conifers, clematis and climbers.

Location: 7 miles NW of Northampton off A428.
Open: Mon-Fri 9-5.30 closed weekends, Bank Holidays and Christmas.
Admission: Free.
Groups must apply in writing for permission to visit.

THE HERB AND HEATHER CENTRE
West Haddlesey, nr Selby, North Yorkshire   YO8 8QA
Telephone: (01757) 228279

The nursery has herb, heather and conifer display gardens, and specialises in herbs and heathers.

Location: 6 m S of Selby off A19.
Open: Daily 9.30-5.30 (dusk in Winter).
Refreshments: Herb shop and tea-room.
New Water Garden. Parking, WC.

THE HERB FARM AND SAXON MAZE
Sonning Common, Reading   RG4 9NJ
Telephone: (01734) 724220

Specialist herb nursery with herb garden filled with culinary, medical and aromatic plants. Restored 18th century timber frame barn houses, a unique shop filled with all manner af things herbal (from toothpastes to table mats)! Also visit the Saxon maze, a Beech hedge maze planted in 1991. An intriguing puzzle for all the family.

Location: 4 m N of Reading on B481.
Station(s): Reading.
Open: Every day except Mon 10-5 also open on Bank Hol Mons.
Admission: Free. 60p for maze. Parties by arrangement.
Refreshments: Coffee shop.

LANGLEY BOXWOOD NURSERY
(Mrs Elizabeth Braimbridge)
Rake, nr Liss, Hampshire   GU33 7JL &
Telephone: (01730) 894467
Fax: (01730) 894703

This small nursery in a beautiful setting specialises in box-growing, offering a chance to see together a unique range of old and new varieties, hedging, topiary, specimens and rarities. Some taxus also. Descriptive list available (4 x 1st class stamps).

Location: On B2070 (old A3) 3 m S of Liphook.
Open: Notify by telephone first.

MILLAIS NURSERIES
(David Millais)
Crosswater Farm, Churt, Farnham, Surrey   GU10 2JN
Telephone: (01252) 792698
Fax: (01252) 792526

MILLAIS NURSERIES RHODODENDRONS

Specialist growers of 600 varieties of choice hybrids and rare species. One of the widest selection of Rhododendrons and Azaleas in the World!

Crosswater Farm, Churt, Farnham, Surrey, GU10 2JN
Tel: (01252) 792698 Fax: (01252) 792526

Growers of one of the finest ranges of Rhododendrons and Azaleas in the country, including many rare species from the Himalayas, and a good selection of new American hybrids. Specialist advice. Mail Order Catalogue available £1. Display garden also open (see Crosswater Farm).

Location: Farnham/Haslemere 6 m. From A287 turn E into Jumps Road ½ m N of Churt village centre. After ¼ m, turn into Crosswater Lane, and follow Nursery signs.
Open: Tues-Fri 10-5 Sat Oct Nov Mar Apr and daily in May.

PERHILL NURSERIES
(Baker Straw Partnership)
Worcester Road, Great Witley, Worcestershire   WR6 6JT &
Telephone: (01299) 896329
Fax: (01299) 896990

Specialist growers of 2,000 varieties of alpines, herbs and border perennials. Many rare and unusual. Specialities include penstemons, salvias, osteospermums, dianthus, alpine phlox, alliums, campanulas, thymes, helianthemums, diascias, lavenders, artemesias, digitals and scented geraniums.

Location: 10 m NW of Worcester on main Tenbury Wells Road (A443).
Open: Every day Feb 1-Oct 15 9-6 closed Oct 16-Jan 31 except by appointment.

PERRYHILL NURSERIES
(Mrs S M Gemmell)
Hartfield, East Sussex   TN7 4JP
Telephone: (01892) 770377
Fax: (01892) 770929

The Plant Centre for the discerning gardener, with the widest range of plants in the South East of England. Old fashioned and shrub roses a speciality, also herbaceous plants. Trees, shrubs, rhododendrons, alpines, fruit trees and bushes, bedding plants in season. No mail order. Catalogues £1.65 inc. postage.

Location: 1 m N of Hartfield on B2026.
Open: Mar-Oct 9-5 Nov-Feb 9-4.30 seven days a week.

SAMARÈS HERBS-A-PLENTY
(Richard Adams)
Samarès Manor, St. Clement, Jersey   JE2 6QW & △
Telephone: (01534) 870551
Fax: (01534) 68949

Specialist Herb and Hardy Perennial Nursery situated in the grounds of Samarès Manor. Extensive range of culinary, fragrant and medicinal herbs including many variegated and ornamental forms. Specialist range of hardy perennials including plants for shade, ground cover and wet conditions. Availability list on request. Herb shop, craft centre, farm animals, herb gardens, tours of Manor.

Location: 2 m E of St. Helier on the St. Clements Inner Road.
Open: Daily 10-5 Apr-Oct.
Admission: Charge for gardens. No charge for Nursery.
Refreshments: Tea garden and restaurant.

SEAFORDE NURSERY AND BUTTERFLY HOUSE
(Patrick Forde)
Seaforde, Downpatrick, Down   &
Telephone: (01396) 811225
Fax: (01396) 811370

Over 600 trees and shrubs, container grown. Many Camellias and Rhododendrons. National collections of E. ucryphius. Tropical Butterfly House with hundreds of free flying butterflies. Also open beautiful gardens and maze.

Location: On A24 Ballynahinch to Newcastle Road.
Open: Easter to end Sept: Mon to Sat 10-5; Sun 2-6. Nursery only: Sept to Easter, 10-5.
Refreshments: Tea rooms.

STAPELEY WATER GARDENS
Stapeley, Nantwich, Cheshire
Telephone: (01270) 628628

Home of The National Collection of Nymphaea (water lilies) with over 350 varieties. The World's Largest Water Garden Centre with over 3 acres of display gardens, aquatic plants, pools and fountains. Expert advice and ideas. The Palms Tropical Oasis - a 1d acre pavilion: home to piranhas, parrots, monkeys and exotic plants. Plus the Stapeley Yesteryear Museum rouses restored memorabilia.

Location: 1 m S of Nantwich on the A51 to Stone, signposted from Jct 16 on the M6.
Open: Open every day except Christmas Day.
Admission: YES. SPECIAL GROUP RATES.
Refreshments: Excellent restaurant, cafeteria and snack bar are available.
Disabled catered for. No dogs please.

TREHANE CAMELLIA NURSERY
(Miss Jennifer Trehane)
Stapehill Road, Hampreston, nr Wimborne, Dorset   BH21 7NE
Telephone: (01202) 873490
Fax: (01202) 873490

Britain's leading Camellia Specialists:- Scented Sasanquas, rare Species from China and Japan, huge Reticulatas, extra hardy Williamsii varieties, specially selected free-flowering Japonicas. Also Evergreen Azaleas, Pieris, Magnolias, Blueberries. All sizes. Visitors most welcome. Mail Order and Export. Catalogue/Handbook £1.50.

Open: All year weekdays 9-4 and weekends Mar-Oct 10-4.30 closed over the Christmas/New Year.
Information and display greenhouse. Woodland Garden. Lecture/demonstrations available for groups.

Lancelot 'Capability' Brown

Born 1716 in Northumberland, Capability Brown began work at the age of 16 in the vegetable gardens of Sir William and Lady Loraine at Kirharle Tower. He left Northumberland in 1739, and records show that he worked at Stowe until 1749. It was at Stowe that Brown began to study architecture, and to submit his own plans. It was also at Stowe that he devised a new method of moving and replanting mature trees.

Brown married Bridget Wayet in 1744 and began work on the estate at Warwick Castle in 1749. He was appointed Master Gardener at Hampton Court in 1764, and planted the Great Vine at Hampton Court in 1768. Blenheim Palace designs are considered amongst Brown's finest work, and the technical achievements were outstanding even for the present day.

Capability Brown died in February 1783 of a massive heart attack. A monument beside the lake at Croome Court was erected which reads "To the memory of Lancelot Brown, who by the powers of his inimitable and creative genius formed this garden scene out of a morass". There is also a portrait of Brown at Burghley.

Capability Brown was involved in the design of grounds at the following properties included in Historic Houses Castles and Gardens:-

Audley End
Berrington Hall
Bowood
Burghley House
Burton Constable
Charlecote Park
Chilham Castle Gardens
  (reputed)
Clandon Park

Claremont
Chillington Hall
Corsham Court
Fawley Court
Highclere Castle
Longleat
Luton Hoo
Moccas Court
Petworth House

Sledmere House
Stowe (Stowe
  School)
Syon House
Warwick Castle
Weston Park
Wimpole Hall
Wrest Park and
  Gardens

UNIVERSITIES

CAMBRIDGE

NOTE: Admission to *Colleges* means to the Courts, not to the staircases and students' rooms. All opening times are subject to closing for College funtions etc., on occasional days. *Halls* normally close for lunch (12-2) and many are not open during the afternoon. *Chapels* are closed during services. *Libraries* are not usually open, special arrangements are noted. *Gardens* do not usually include the Fellows' garden. *Figures* denote the date of foundation, and existing buildings are often of later date. *Daylight hours* - some colleges may not open until 9.30 am or later and usually close before 6 pm - many as early as 4.30 pm. All parties exceeding 10 persons wishing to tour the college between Easter and October are required to be escorted by a Cambridge registered Guide. All enquiries should be made to the Tourist Information Centre, Wheeler Street. Cambridge CB2 3QB.

Terms: *Lent:* Mid-January to Mid-March. *Easter:* April to June. *Michaelmas:* 2nd week October to 1st week December. Examination Period closures which differ from one college to another now begin in early April and extend to late June. Notices are usually displayed. **Visitors and especially guided parties should always call at the Porter's Lodge before entering any College.**

CHRIST'S COLLEGE (1505)
Porter's Lodge, St. Andrew's Street   CB2 3BU
Telephone: (01223) 334900
Fax: (01223) 334967
Open: The College is closed to all visitors from May 1-mid June. At other times it is open as follows:- *College* daily 9.30-noon *Chapel* daily during Term *Hall* weekdays 9.30-noon *Library* by appointment with Librarian *Fellows' Garden* Mon-Fri 10.30-noon. (Closed Bank Hols, Easter week and weekends).

CLARE COLLEGE (1326)
Trinity Lane
Open: Hall Monday to Sat 9-12 (usually). Chapel Daily except Apr 17 to June 25. Library by prior arrangement with the Librarian. Gardens daily: 12-4.30. The College is closed for the Examination Term from Mid April to Mid June and an entry fee of £1.50 will be charged for each visitor between Mid June and 1st October.

CORPUS CHRISTI COLLEGE (1352)
Porter's Lodge, Trumpington Street   CB2 1RH
Telephone: 0223 338000
Fax: 0223 338061
Open: Opening times shown at Porter's Lodge.
Closed to large groups mid April-mid June during examinations

DOWNING COLLEGE (1800)
Downing College, Regent Street   CB2 1DQ
Telephone: (01223) 334800
Fax: (01223) 467934
Open: College Gardens daily daylight hours Chapel Term - daily vacation - by appointment. Hall closed to the public. Library by arrangement only.

EMMANUEL COLLEGE (1800)
Porter's Lodge, St. Andrew's Street   CB2 3AP
Telephone: (01223) 334200
Fax: (01223) 334426
Open: College Daily 9-6. Hall 2.30-5. Chapel 9-6 both daily except when in use. Library only by prior application to Librarian. Gardens & Paddock Daily 9-6 or dusk if earlier. Fellows' Garden Not open to visitors. (Closed for annual holidays, variable).

GONVILLE & CAIUS COLLEGE (1348)
Porter's Lodge, Trinity Street   CB2 1TA
Telephone: (01223) 332400
Open: College & Chapel Daily daylight hours. Library By appointment with Librarian. Closed during exams from early May to mid June and for short periods each day. Times shown at Porter's Lodge.

JESUS COLLEGE (1496)
Porter's Lodge, Jesus Lane   CB5 8BL
Telephone: (01223) 339339
Open: College daily 9-5.30. Chapel Hall closed to the public.
The college is closed to the public from 1 Apr-mid June. Groups of over 20 must make special visit arrangements in writing to the Domestic Bursar.

KING'S COLLEGE (1441)
Porter's Lodge, King's Parade   CB2 1ST
Telephone: (01223) 331212
Fax: (01223) 331315
Open: College weekdays 9.30-4.30 Suns 10-5. Adults £2 students/child (12-17) £1 (chidren under 12 free) cost includes Chapel during term time only. Chapel open weekdays 9.30-3.30 Suns 1.15-2.15 4.45-5.15 (Terms are from early Jan-mid Mar, late Apr-mid June, most of July and early Oct-Early Dec) from late Apr-mid June grounds are closed. Further informa-

tion may be obtained from the Cambridge Tourist Information Centre on (0223) 322640 or the Tourist Liason Officer at the College (0223) 331212.

MAGDALENE COLLEGE (1542)
Porter's Lodge, Magdalene Street
Open: College & Chapel Daily 9-6.30 (except during exams). Hall Daily 9.30-12.30 (except during exams). Gardens Daily 1-6.30 (except during exams). Pepys Jan 15-Mar 16 weekdays 2.30-3.30 Apr 23-Aug 31 weekdays (not Suns) 11.30-12.30 2.30-3.30.

NEWNHAM COLLEGE (1871)
Sidgwick Avenue
Open: College & Gardens Daily during daylight hours. College and gardens closed May 1-mid June and last 2 weeks of August.

PEMBROKE COLLEGE (1347)
Porter's Lodge, Trumpington Street   CB2 1RF
Open: Opening times shown at Porter's Lodge. Library by appointment with Librarian.

PETERHOUSE (1284)
Porter's Lodge, Trumpington Street   CB2 1RD
Telephone: 0223 338200
Fax: 0223 337578
Open: Guided parties of not more than 12. Chapel daily. Hall mornings only during term. Gardens Daily 10-5 (no dogs).

QUEENS' COLLEGE (1448)
Porter's Lodge, Silver Street   CB3 9ET
Telephone: (01223) 335511
Fax: (01223) 335566
Open: Open daily 1.45-4.30 & also 10.15-12.45 during July, Aug & Sept & for guided parties of not more than 20. Adm. charge.

ST. CATHARINE'S COLLEGE (1473)
Porter's Lodge, Trumpington Street
Open: College & Chapel Daily during daylight hours. (Closed May & June. Chapel Hall Closed to the public.

ST. JOHN'S COLLEGE (1511)
Tourist Liaison Office, St. John's Street   CB2 1TP
Open: *College* Daily 10.30 until 5.30. (Closed May & June). *Hall* Closed to the public. Admission charge July - October and March - April. £1 Adult, 50p Child/OAPs, £2 family ticket. Admission includes Guide leaflet.

SIDNEY SUSSEX COLLEGE (1596)
Porter's Lodge, Sidney Street   CB2 3HU
Telephone: (01223) 338800
Fax: (01223) 338884
Open: *College* Daily, during daylight hours. *Hall & Chapel*

TRINITY COLLEGE (1546)
Porter's Lodge, Trinity Street
Open: 10-6.
Admission: Adults £1.50 children/OAPs 75p families £3. UB40 form holders - free.

TRINITY HALL (1350)
Trinity Lane   CB2 1TJ
Telephone: (01223) 332531
Fax: (01223) 462116
Open: College, Chapel & Gardens Daily during daylight hours except during examination period (end April to mid June). Library - apply beforehand to College Librarian.

CONDUCTED TOURS IN CAMBRIDGE Qualified badged, local guides may be obtained from: Tourist Information Centre, Wheeler Street, Cambridge CB2 3QB. Tel: (01223) 322 640 or Cambridge Guide Service, 2 Montague Road, Cambridge CB4 1BX. Tel: (01223) 356 735 (Principals: John Mellanby MA., and Mrs E. Garner). We normally obtain the Passes and make all negotiations regarding these with the Tourist Office, so separate application is not needed. We have been providing guides for English, Foreign language and special interest groups since 1950. We supply couriers for coach tours of East Anglia, visiting stately homes etc. As an alternative to the 2 hour walking tour we can now offer half hour panoramic in clients' coach (provided there is an effective public address system) followed by 1 $^{1}/_{2}$ hours on foot or 1 hour panoramic only, special flat rate for up to 55 people.

UNIVERSITIES

OXFORD

NOTE: Admission to *Colleges* means to the Quadrangles, not to the staircases and students' rooms. All opening times are subject to closing for College functions etc., on occasional days. *Halls* normally close for lunch during term (12-2). *Chapel* usually closed during services. *Libraries* are not usually open, special arrangements are noted. *Gardens* do not usually include the Fellows' garden. *Figures* denote the date of foundation, and existing buildings are often of later date.

Terms: *Hilary:* Mid-January to Mid-March. *Trintiy: 3rd week* April to late June. *Michaelmas:* Mid- October to 1st week December. **Visitors and especially guided parties should always call at the Porter's Lodge before entering any College.**

ALL SOULS COLLEGE (1438)
Porter's Lodge, High Street   OX1 4AL
Open: College Weekdays: 2-4.30. (2-4pm Oct-Mar).

BALLIOL COLLEGE (1263)
Porter's Lodge, Broad Street
Open: Hall Chapel & Gardens Daily 2-5. Parties limited to 25.

BRASENOSE COLLEGE (1509)
Radcliffe Square
Open: Hall Chapel & Gardens Tour parties: Daily 10-11.30 2-5 (summer) 10-dusk (winter). Individuals 2-5. Hall 11.45-2.

CHRIST CHURCH (1546)
St. Aldate's, Enter via Meadow Gate   OX1 1DP
Telephone: (01865) 276499
Open: Cathedral daily 9-4.30 (winter) 9-5.30 (summer). Hall Oct-Mar daily 9.30-12 2-4.30 Apr-Sept daily 9.30-12 2-6 adm £2.50 chd £1 Picture Gallery weekdays 10.30-1 2-4.30 adm £1 Meadows daily 7-dusk hall published hours occasionally curtailed for College or Cathedral events.
Tourist Information: (24 hrs) (0865) 276499

CORPUS CHRISTI COLLEGE (1517)
Porter's Lodge, Merton Street
Open: *College, Chapel & Gardens* Term and vacations - daily 2-45.

EXETER COLLEGE (1314)
Porter's Lodge, Turl Street   OX1 3DP
Telephone: (01865) 279600
Fax: (01865) 279630
Open: College & Chapel, Fellows' Garden term and vacations daily 2-5. (except Christmas and Easter).

HERTFORD COLLEGE (1284, 1740 & 1874)
Porter's Lodge, Catte Street   OX1 3BW
Telephone: (01865) 279400
Fax: (01865) 279437
Open: College Hall & Chapel Daily 10-6. Closed for a week at Christmas and during exam periods.
Parties restricted to 10 people

JESUS COLLEGE (1571)
Turl Street
Open: *College, Hall & Chapel* Daily 2.30-4.30. *Library* special permission of librarian. (closed Christmas and Easter holidays).

KEBLE COLLEGE (1868)
Porter's Lodge, Parks Road
Open: *College & Chapel* Daily 10-7 (or dusk if earlier).

LADY MARGARET HALL (1878)
Porter's Lodge, Norham Gardens
Open: College & Gardens daily 2-6 (or dusk if earlier). Visitors must call at The Lodge before walking around the grounds.

LINCOLN COLLEGE (1427)
Porter's Lodge, Turl Street
Open: *College & Hall* weekdays 2-5. Suns 11-5. *Wesley Room   All Saints Library* Tues & Thurs 2-4.

MAGDALEN COLLEGE (1458)
High Street   OX1 4AU
Telephone: (01865) 276000
Fax: (01865) 276103
Open: College Chapel Deer Park & Water Walks daily 2-6.15. Parties limited to 25.

MANSFIELD COLLEGE (1886)
Porter's Lodge, Mansfield Road
Open: *College* Open May, June & July, Mon to Sat 9-5. Interior of Chapel and Library may be viewed by prior appointment.

MERTON (1264)
Merton Street   OX1 4JD
Telephone: (01865) 276310
Fax: (01865) 276361
Open: Chapel & Quadrangle Mon-Fri 2-4 Oct-Jun: Sat & Sun 10-4. Mon-Fri 2-5 Jul-Sept: Sat & Sun 10-5. Old Library Mon-Sat 2-4 admission £1. Apply Verger's office. Library not open on Saturdays Nov-Mar.

NEW COLLEGE (1379)
New College Lane
Open: College Hall Chapel & Gardens Daily 2-5. Vacation daily 11-5.

NUFFIELD COLLEGE (1937)
Porter's Lodge, New Road
Open: College only Daily 9-7

ORIEL COLLEGE (1326)
Oriel Square   OX1 4EW
Telephone: 01865 276555
Fax: 01865 276532
Open: College Daily 2-5. (closed Christmas and Easter holidays and mid Aug to mid Sept)

PEMBROKE COLLEGE (1624)
Porter's Lodge, St. Aldate's
Open: *College, Hall, Chapel & Gardens* Term - daily on application to the Porter's Lodge. Closed Christmas and Easter holidays and occasionally in Aug.

THE QUEEN'S COLLEGE (1340)
High Street   OX1 4AW
Telephone: (01865) 279120
Fax: (01865) 790819
Open: Hall Chapel Quadrangles & Garden Open to public by appointment or through Oxford Guild of Guides.

ST. EDMUND HALL (1270)
Queen's Lane   OX1 4AR
Telephone: (01865) 279000
Open: *College, Old Hall, Chapel & Garden* Daily, daylight hours. *Crypt or St. Peter in the East* On application to Porter.

ST. JOHN'S COLLEGE (1555)
St. Giles' Oxford   OX1 3JP
Telephone: (0865) 277300
Fax: (0865) 277435
Open: College & Garden Term & Vacation - daily 1-5 or dusk if earlier. Guided parties must obtain permission from Lodge. Hall & Chapel Summer 2.30-4.30. Apply Porter. Closed during conferences & college functions.

TRINITY COLLEGE (1554)
Main Gate, Broad Street   OX1 3BH
Telephone: (01865) 279900
Fax: (01865) 279898
Open: Hall Chapel & Garden daily 2-5 (summer) 2-dusk (winter).Opening hours may vary - visitors should check in advance.

UNIVERSITY COLLEGE (1249)
Porter's Lodge, High Street   OX1 4BH
Open: *College, Hall & Chapel* Term 2-4.

WORCESTER COLLEGE (1714)
Porter's Lodge, Worcester Street   OX1 2HB
Telephone: (01865) 278300
Fax: (01865) 278387
Open: College & Gardens Term daily 2-6. Vacation daily 9-12 and 2-6. Hall & Chapel Apply Lodge.

GUIDED WALKING TOURS OF THE COLLEGES & CITY OF OXFORD Tours conducted by the Oxford Guild of Guides Lecturers are offered by the Oxford Information Centre, morning for much of the year, afternoon, tours daily. For tour times please ring (01865) 726 871. Tours are offered for groups in English, French, German, Spanish, Russian, Japanese, Polish and Serbo-Croat. Chinese by appointment. The most popular tour for groups, Oxford Past and Present, can be arranged at any time. The following special interest tours are available in the afternoon only: Alice in Oxford; Literary Figures in Oxford; American Roots in Oxford; Oxford Gardens; Modern Architecture in Oxford; Architecture in Oxford (Medieval, 17th Century and Modern); Oxford in the Civil War and 17th Century. Further details are available from the Deputy Information Officer (018650) 726 871.

Supplementary List of Properties
Open by Appointment Only

The list of houses in England, Scotland and Wales printed here are those which are usually open 'by appointment only' with the owner, or open infrequently during the summer months. These are in addition to the Houses and Gardens which are open regularly and are fully classified. Where it is necessary to write for an appointment to view, see code (WA), * denoted owner/address if this is different from the property address.

The majority of these properties have received a grant for conservation from the government given on the advice of the Historic Buildings Councils. Public buildings, almshouses, tithe barn, business premises in receipt of grants are not usually included, neither are properties where the architectural features can be viewed from the street.

AVON

BIRDCOMBE COURT
(Mr.& Mrs. P.C. Sapsed (WA)
Wraxall, Bristol, Avon

EASTWOOD MANOR FARM
(Mr A.J. Gay)
East Harptree

PARTIS COLLEGE
(The Bursar (WA)
Newbridge Hill, Bath   BA1 3QD
Telephone: (01225) 421532

THE REFECTORY
(Rev. R Salmon)
The Vicarage
Telephone: (01934) 833126

WOODSPRING PRIORY
(WA)
Kewstoke, Weston-Super-Mare
*The Landmark Trust, Shottesbrooke, nr Maidenhead, Berks SL6 3SW.

BEDFORDSHIRE

THE TEMPLE
(The Estate Office (WA)
Biggleswade

WARDEN ABBEY
(WA)
nr Biggleswade
*The Landmark Trust, Shottesbrooke, nr Maidenhead, Berks SL6 3SW

BERKSHIRE

HIGH CHIMNEYS
(Mr & Mrs S. Cheetham (WA)
Hurst, Reading
Telephone: (01734) 34517

ST. GABRIEL'S SCHOOL
(The Headmaster)
Sandleford Priory, Newbury
Telephone: (01635) 40663

BUCKINGHAMSHIRE

BISHAM ABBEY
(The Director)
Marlow
Telephone: (016284) 76911

BRUDENELL HOUSE
(Dr H. Beric Wright (WA)
Quainton, Aylesbury   HP22 4AW

CHURCH OF THE ASSUMPTION
(Friends of Friendless Churches)
Hardmead, Newport Pagnell
Telephone: (01234) 39257
For key apply to H. Tranter, Manor Cottage, Hardmead, by letter or phone (0234) 39257.

IVER GROVE
(Mr & Mrs T. Stoppard (WA)
Shreding Green, Iver

REMNANTZ
(WA)
West Street, Marlow
*A. Wethered Esq., Brampton House 100 High Street, Marlow Bucks SL7 1A

REPTON'S SUBWAY FACADE
(WA)
Digby's Walk, Gayhurst
Telephone: (0190) 855564
*Mrs. J.H. Beverly, The Bath House, Gayhurst.

CAMBRIDGESHIRE

THE CHANTRY
(Mrs T.A.N. Bristol (WA)
Ely, Cambridge

THE CHURCH OF ST JOHN THE BAPTIST
(Friends of Friendless Churches)
Papworth St. Agnes
For key apply to Mrs. P. Honeybane, Passhouse Cottage, Papworth St. Agnes, Camb. by letter or phone (0480) 830631

THE KING'S SCHOOL, ELY
(WA)
Ely   CB7 4DB
Telephone: (01353) 662837
Fax: (01353) 662187
Bursars Office, The King's School, Ely.

LEVERINGTON HALL
(Professor A. Barton (WA)
Wisbech   PE13 5DE

THE LYNCH LODGE
(WA)
Alwalton, Peterborough
*The Landmark Trust, Shottesbrooke, nr Maidenhead, Berks SL6 3SW.

CHESHIRE

BEWSEY OLD HALL
(The Administrator (WA)
Warrington

CROWN HOTEL
(Prop. P.J. Martin)
High Street, Nantwich   CW5 5AS
Telephone: (01270) 625283
Fax: (01270) 628047

CHARLES ROE HOUSE
(McMillan Group Plc (WA)
Chestergate, Macclesfield   SK11 6DZ

SHOTWICK HALL
(Tenants: Mr & Mrs G.A.T. Holland)
Shotwick
Telephone: (01244) 881717
*Mr.R.B. Gardner, Wychen, 17 St. Marys Road, Leatherhead Surrey. By appointment only with the tenants Mr and Mrs G.A.T. Holland

TUDOR HOUSE
Lower Bridge Street, Chester
Telephone: (01244) 20095

WATERGATE HOUSE
(WA)
Chester
Telephone: (01352) 713353
*Ferry Homes Ltd. Barclays Bank Chambers, 48 High St. Holywell, Clwyd.

CLEVELAND

ST CUTHBERT'S CHURCH & TURNER MAUSOLEUM
(Kirkleatham Parochial Church Council)
Kirkleatham
Telephone: (01642) 475198 Mrs R.S. Ramsdale (01642) 485395 Mrs. D. Cook, Church Warden.

CORNWALL

THE COLLEGE
(WA)
Week St Mary
*The Landmark Trust, Shottesbrooke, nr Maidenhead, Berks SL6 3SW.

TOWN HALL
(Camelford Town Trust)
Camelford

TRECARREL MANOR
(Mr N.H. Burden)
Trebullett, Launceston
Telephone: (01566) 82286

CUMBRIA

PRESTON PATRICK HALL
(Mrs J.D. Armitage (WA)
Milnthorpe   LA7 7NY
Telephone: (0153) 956 7200

WHITEHALL
(WA)
Mealsgate, Carlisle   CA5 1JS
*Mrs. S. Parkin-Moore 40 Woodsome Road, London NW5 1RZ

DERBYSHIRE

ELVASTON CASTLE
(Derbyshire County Council)
nr Derby   DE72 3EP
Telephone: (01332) 571342

THE MANSION
(The Headmaster (WA)
Church Street, Ashbourne
Telephone: (01335) 43685

10 NORTH STREET
(WA)
Cromford
*The Landmark Trust, Shottesbrooke, nr Maidenhead, Berks SL6 3SW.

SWARKESTONE PAVILION
(WA)
Ticknall
*The Landmark Trust, Shottesbrooke, nr Maidenhead, Berks SL6 3SW.

DEVON

BINDON MANOR
(Sir John & Lady Loveridge (WA)
Axmouth

BOWRINGSLEIGH
(Mr & Mrs M.C. Manisty (WA)
Kingbridge

ENDSLEIGH HOUSE
(Endsleigh Fishing Club Ltd)
Milton Abbot, nr Tavistock
Telephone: (0182 287) 248
Fax: (0182 287) 502

HARESTON HOUSE
(Mrs K.M. Basset)
Brixton   PL8 2DL
Telephone: (01752) 880426

THE LIBRARY
(WA)
Stevenstone, Torrington
*The Landmark Trust, Shottesbrooke, nr Maidenhead, Berks SL6 3SW.

SANDERS
(WA)
Lettaford, North Bovey
*The Landmark Trust, Shottesbrooke, nr Maidenhead, Berks SL6 3SW.

THE SHELL HOUSE
(Endsleigh Fishing Club Ltd)
Endsleigh, Milton Abbott
Telephone: (0182) 287248
Fax: (0182) 287502

SHUTE GATEHOUSE
(WA)
Shute Barton, nr Axminster
*The Landmark Trust, Shottesbrooke, nr Maidenhead, Berks SL6 3SW.

TOWN HOUSE
(Tenant Mr & Mrs R.A.L. Hill)
Gittisham, Honiton
Telephone: (01404) 851041
*Mr. & Mrs. R.J.T. Marker.

WORTHAM MANOR
(WA)
Lifton
*The Landmark Trust, Shottesbrooke, nr Maidenhead, Berks SL6 3SW.

DORSET

BLOXWORTH HOUSE
(Mr T.A. Dulake (WA)
Bloxworth

CLENSTON MANOR
(Mr & Mrs J. Procter)
Winterborne, Clenston, Blandford Forum
Telephone: (01258) 880681

HIGHER MELCOMBE
(Mr M.C. Woodhouse (WA)
Dorchester   DT2 7PB

MOIGNES COURT
(Mr A.M. Cree (WA)
Owermoigne

WOODSFORD CASTLE
(WA)
Woodsford, Nr Dorchester
*The Landmark Trust, Shottesbrooke, nr Maidenhead, Berks SL6 3SW.

COUNTY DURHAM

THE BUILDINGS IN THE SQUARE
(Lady Gilbertson (WA)
1 The Square, Greta Bridge   DL12 9SD
Telephone: (01833) 27276

THE COLLEGE
(The Dean and Chapter of Durham)
The Chapter Office, The College   DH1 3EH
Telephone: 0191-386 4266
Fax: 0191-386 4267

*The Deanery No.6 The College no.9,10,11,15.All enquiries to the Chapter Steward. The Chapter Office Durham DH1 3EH

ESSEX

BLAKE HALL, BATTLE OF BRITAIN MUSEUM & GARDENS
(Mr R. Capel Cure, owner)
Chipping Ongar   CM5 0DG
Telephone: (01277) 362502

CHURCH OF ST ANDREWS AND MONKS TITHE BARN
(Harlow District Council)
Harlow Study & Visitors Centre, Netteswellbury Farm, Harlow   CM18 6BW
Telephone: (01279) 446745
Fax: (01279) 421945

COLVILLE HALL
(Mr C.A. Webster (WA)
White Roding

GRANGE FARM
(Mr J. Kirby)
Little Dunmow   CM6 3HY
Telephone: (01371) 820205

GREAT PRIORY FARM
(Miss L. Tabor)
Panfield, Braintree   CM7 5BQ
Telephone: (01376) 550944

THE GUILDHALL
(Dr & Mrs Paul Sauven)
Great Waltham
Telephone: (01245) 360527

OLD ALL SAINTS
(Mr R. Mill)
Old Church Hill, Langdon Hills   SS16 6HZ
Telephone: (01268) 414146

RAINHAM HALL
(The National Trust: tenant Mr I. Botes (WA)
Rainham

RAYNE HALL
(Mr & Mrs R.J. Pertwee (WA)
Rayne, Braintree

THE ROUND HOUSE
(Mr M.E.W. Heap)
Havering-atte-Bower, Romford   RM4 1QH
Telephone: (01708) 728136

GLOUCESTERSHIRE

ABBEY GATEHOUSE
(WA)
Tewksbury
*The Landmark Trust, Shottesbrooke, nr Maidenhead, Berks SL6 3SW.

ASHLEWORTH COURT
(Mr H.J. Chamberlayne)
Gloucester
Telephone: (01452) 700241

ASHLEWORTH MANOR
(Dr & Mrs Jeremy Barnes (WA)
Ashleworth, Gloucester   GL19 4LA
Telephone: (01452) 700350

BEARLAND HOUSE
(The Administrator (WA)
Longsmith Street, Gloucester   GL1 2HL
Fax: (01452) 419312

CASTLE GODWYN
(Mr & Mrs J. Milne (WA)
Painswick

CHACELEY HALL
(Mr W.H. Lane)
Tewkesbury
Telephone: (01452) 28205

CHELTENHAM COLLEGE
(The Bursar)
The College, Bath Road, Cheltenham   GL53 7LD
Telephone: (01242) 513540

THE COTTAGE
(Mrs S.M. Rolt (WA)

Stanley Pontlarge, Winchcombe   GL54 5HD

EAST BANQUETING HOUSE
(WA)
Chipping Camden
*The Landmark Trust, Shottesbrooke, nr Maidenhead, Berks SL6 3SW.

FRAMPTON COURT & GOTHIC ORANGERY (WA)
(Frampton Court Estate)
Frampton-on-Severn, Gloucester   GL2 7EU
Telephone: (01452) 740267 (home) or (01452) 740698 (office)
*Apply to Mrs. Clifford (0452) 740267 home (0452) 740698 office.

MINCHINHAMPTON MARKET HOUSE
(Mr B.E. Lucas)
Stroud
Telephone: (01453) 883241

THE OLD VICARAGE
('Lord Weymyss' Trust)
The Church, Stanway
Telephone: (0186) 735469
*Apply to Stanway House, Stanway, Cheltenham

ST MARGARET'S CHURCH
(The Gloucester Charities Trust)
London Road, Gloucester
Telephone: (01452) 23316
By appointment with the Warden. Tel: (01831) 470335

TYNDALE MONUMENT
(Tyndale Monument Charity)
North Nibley   GL11 4JA
Telephone: (01453) 542357
Fax: (01453) 548527
Keys available as per notice at foot of Wood Lane.

GREATER MANCHESTER

CHETHAM'S HOSPITAL AND LIBRARY
(The Feoffees of Chetham's Hospital & Library)
Manchester   MS 1SB
Telephone: 0161-834 9644
Fax: 0161-839 5797

SLADE HALL
(Manchester & District Housing Assn. (WA)
Slade Lane, Manchester   M13 0QP

HAMPSHIRE

CHESIL THEATRE (FORMERLY ST PETER CHESIL CHURCH)
(Winchester Dramatic Society)
Winchester
Telephone: (01962) 867086

THE DEANERY
(The Dean & Chapter)
The Close, Winchester   SO23 9LS
Telephone: (01962) 853137
Fax: (01962) 841519

MANOR FARM HOUSE
(Mr S.B. Mason)
Hambledon
Telephone: (01705) 632433

MOYLES COURT
(Headmaster, Moyles Court School (WA)
Moyles Court, Ringwood   BH24 3NF
Telephone: (01425) 472856

HEREFORD & WORCESTER

BRITANNIA HOUSE
(The Alice Ottley School (WA)
The Tything, Worcester
Apply to the Headmistress.

CHURCH HOUSE
(The Trustees)
Market Square, Evesham

GRAFTON MANOR
(Mr J.W. Morris)
Bromsgrove
Telephone: (01527) 31525

HUDDINGTON COURT
(Professor Hugh D. Edmondson (WA)
Droitwich

NEWHOUSE FARM
(The Administrator (WA))
Goodrich, Ross-on-Wye

THE OLD PALACE
(The Dean & Chapter of Worcester (WA)
Worcester
Apply to Diocesan Secretary.

SHELWICK COURT
(WA)
Hereford
*The Landmark Trust, Shottesbrooke, nr Maidenhead, Berks. SL6 3SW.

HERTFORDSHIRE

HEATH MOUNT SCHOOL
(The Abel Smith Trustees)
Woodhall Park, Watton-at-Stone, Hertford   SG14 3NG
Telephone: (01920) 830286
Fax: (01920) 830357

HOMEWOOD
(Mr & Mrs Pollock-Hill (WA)
Park Lane, Knebworth

NORTHAW PLACE
(The Administrator)
Northaw
Telephone: (01707) 44059

KENT

BARMING PLACE
(Mr J. Peter & Dr. Rosalind Bearcroft)
Maidstone
Telephone: (01622) 727844

FOORD ALMSHOUSES
(The Clerk to the Trustees (WA))
Rochester

MERSHAM-LE-HATCH
(Lord Brabourne)
nr Ashford   TN25 5NH
Telephone: (01233) 503954
Fax: (01233) 611650
Apply to tenant - The Directors, Caldecott Community.

NURSTEAD COURT
(Mrs S.M.H. Edmeades-Stearns)
Meopham
Telephone: (01474) 812121

OLD COLLEGE OF ALL SAINTS
Kent Music Centre, Maidstone
Telephone: (01622) 690404
Apply to Regional Director.

THE OLD PHARMACY
(Mrs Peggy Noreen Kerr)
6 Market Place, Faversham   ME13 7EH

PROSPECT TOWER
(WA)
Belmont Park, Faversham
*The Landmark Trust, Shottesbrooke, nr Maidenhead, Berks SL6 3SW.

YALDHAM MANOR
(Mr & Mrs J. Mourier Lade (WA)
Kemsing, Sevenoaks   TN15 6NN
Telephone: (01732) 761029

LANCASHIRE

THE MUSIC ROOM
(WA)
Lancaster
*The Landmark Trust, Shottesbrooke, nr Maidenhead, Berks SL6 3SW.

PARROX HALL
(Mr & Mrs H.D.H. Elletson (WA)
Parrox Hall, Preesall, nr Poulton-le-Fylde   FY6 ONW
Telephone: (01253) 810245
Fax: (01253) 811223

LEICESTERSHIRE

LAUNDE ABBEY
(The Rev. Graham Johnson)
East Norton

THE MOAT HOUSE
(Mr H.S. Hall)
Appleby Magna
Telephone: (01530) 270301

OLD GRAMMAR SCHOOL
Market Harborough
Telephone: (01858) 463201
*The Market Harborough Exhibition Foundation, 18 Springfield Street, Market Harborough, LE16 8BY

STAUNTON HAROLD HALL
(Ryder-Cheshire Foundation)
Ashby-de-la-Zouch
Telephone: (01332) 862798

LINCOLNSHIRE

BEDE HOUSES
Tattershall

THE CHATEAU
(WA)
Gate Burton, Gainsborough
*The Landmark Trust, Shottesbrooke, nr Maidenhead, Berks SL6 3SW.

EAST LIGHTHOUSE
(Cdr. M.D. Joel RN (WA)
Sutton Bridge, Spalding   PE12 9YT

FULBECK MANOR
(Mr J.F. Fane (WA)
Grantham   NG32 3JN
Telephone: (01400) 72231

HARLAXTON MANOR
(University of Evansville (WA)
Grantham

HOUSE OF CORRECTION
(WA)
Folkingham
*The Landmark Trust, Shottesbrooke, nr Maidenhead, Berks SL6 3SW.

THE NORMAN MANOR HOUSE
(Lady Netherthorpe (WA)
Boothby Pagnell

PELHAM MAUSOLEUM
(The Earl of Yarborough)
Limber, Grimsby

SCRIVELSBY COURT
(Lt. Col. J.L.M. Dymoke MBE.,DL (WA)
Scrivelsby Court, nr Horncastle   LN9 6JA
Telephone: (01507) 523325

LONDON

ALL HALLOWS VICARAGE
(Rev. R. Pearson)
Tottenham, London   N17

69 BRICK LANE
(The Administrator (WA)
London   E1

24 THE BUTTS, 192,194,196,198,202,204-224 CABLE STREET
(Mrs Sally Mills (WA)
London

11-13 CAVENDISH SQUARE
(Heythrop College (WA)
London

CELIA AND PHILLIP BLAIRMAN HOUSES
(The Administrator (WA)
Elder Street, London   E1

CHARLTON HOUSE
(London Borough of Greenwich (WA)
Charlton Road, Charlton, London   SE7 8RE
Telephone: 0181-856 3951

CHARTERHOUSE
(The Governors of Sutton Hospital (WA)
Charterhouse Square, London   EC1

17/27 FOLGATE STREET
(WA)
London   E1

36 HANBURY STREET
(WA)
London   E1

HEATHGATE HOUSE
(Rev Mother Prioress, Ursuline Convent)
66 Crooms Hill, Greenwich, London   SE10 8HG
Telephone: 0181-858 0779

140,142,166,168 HOMERTON HIGH STREET
(WA)
London   E5

HOUSE OF ST BARNABAS-IN-SOHO
(The Warden of the House (WA)
1 Greek Street, Soho, London   W1V 6NQ
Telephone: 0171-437 1894

KENSAL GREEN CEMETERY
(General Cemetery Company)
Harrow Road, London   W10 4RA
Telephone: 0181-969 0152
Fax: 0181-960 9744

69/83 PARAGON ROAD
(WA)
London   E5

RED HOUSE
(Mr & Mrs Hollamby (WA)
Red House Lane, Bexleyheath

SUNBURY COURT
(The Salvation Army)
Sudbury-on-Thames
Telephone: (01932) 782196

88/190 THE CRESCENT
(WA)
Hertford Road, London   N9

VALE MASCAL BATH HOUSE
(Mrs F. Chu)
112 North Cray Road, Bexley   DA5 3NA
Telephone: (01322) 554894

WESLEY'S HOUSE
(The Trustees of Methodist Church)
47 City Road, London   EC1Y 1AU
Telephone: 0171-253 2262
Fax: 0171-608 3825

MERSEYSIDE

THE TURNER HOME
(Mr R.A. Waring RGN.,CGN)
Dingle Head, Liverpool
Telephone: 0151-727 4177

NORFOLK

ALL SAINTS' CHURCH
(Norfolk Churches Trust)
Barmer

Keyholder - No 5 The Cottages.

ALL SAINTS' CHURCH
(Norfolk Churches Trust)
Dunton

Key of Tower at Hall Farm.

ALL SAINTS' CHURCH
Frenze

Keyholder - Mrs. Alston at farmhouse.

ALL SAINTS' CHURCH
(Norfolk Churches Trust)
Hargham

Keyholder - Mrs. Clifford, Amos, Station Road, Attleborough.

ALL SAINTS' CHURCH
(Rector, Churchwardens and PCC)
Weston Longville   NR9 5JU

Key holder - Rev. J P P Illingworth.

ALL SAINTS' CHURCH
(Norfolk Churches Trust)
Snetterton

Keyholder - at Hall Farm.

ALL SAINTS'CHURCH
(Norfolk Churches Trust)
Cockthorpe

Keyholder - Mrs. Case at farmhouse.

19-21 BEDFORD STREET
(Norwich City Council)
Norwich

BILLINGFORD MILL
(Norfolk County Council)
Scole

6 THE CLOSE
(The Dean & Chapter of Norwich Cathedral (WA))
Norwich

FISHERMEN'S HOSPITAL
(J.E.C. Lamb FIH Clerk to the Trustees)
Great Yarmouth
Telephone: (01493) 856609

GOWTHORPE MANOR
(Mrs Watkinson (WA)
Swardeston   NR14 8DS
Telephone: (01508) 570216

HALES HALL
(Mr & Mrs T. Read (WA))
Loddon   NR14 6QW
Telephone: (0150846) 395

HOVETON HOUSE
(Sir John Blofeld)
Wroxham

LATTICE HOUSE
(Mr & Mrs T. Duckett (WA))
King's Lynn
Telephone: (01553) 777292

LITTLE CRESSINGHAM MILL
(Norfolk mills and Pumps Trust)
Little Cressingham, Thetford, Norfolk
Telephone: (01953) 850567

LITTLE HAUTBOIS HALL
(Mrs Duffield (WA)
nr Norwich   NR12 7JR
Telephone: (01603) 279333
Fax: (01603) 279615

THE MUSIC HOUSE
(The Warden)
Wensum Lodge, King Street, Norwich
Telephone: (01603) 666021/2

NORWICH CATHEDRAL CLOSE
(WA)
Norwich

3,4,27,31,32,34,35,40,The Close. Contact Cathedral Steward's Office Messrs. Percy Howes & Co. 3 The Close, Norwich.

THE OLD PRINCES INN RESTAURANT
20 Prince Street, Norwich
Telephone: (01603) 621043

THE OLD VICARAGE
(Mr & Mrs H. Dance)
The Methwold, Thetford

ST. ANDREW'S CHURCH
(Norfolk Churches Trust)
Frenze

Keyholder - Mrs. Alston at farmhouse opposite.

ST. CELIA'S CHURCH
West Bilney

Keyholder - Mr Curl, Tanglewood, Main Road, West Bilney

ST. MARGARET'S CHURCH
(Norfolk Churches Trust)
Morton-on-the-Hill   NR9 5JS

Keyholder - Lady Prince-Smith at The Hall.

ST. MARY'S CHURCH
(Norfolk Churches Trust)
Dunton

ST. PETER'S CHURCH
(Norfolk Churches Trust)
The Lodge, Millgate, Aylsham   NR11 6HX

Keyholder - Lord & Lady Romney, Wesnum Farm or Mrs. Walker Pockthorpe Cottages.

STRACEY ARMS MILL
(Norfolk County Council)
nr Acle
Telephone: (01603) 611122 ext 5224

THE STRANGERS' CLUB
22,24 Elm Hill, Norwich
Telephone: (01603) 623813

THORESBY COLLEGE
(King's Lynn Preservation Trust (WA))
Queen Street, King's Lynn   PE30 1HX

WIVETON HALL
(D. MacCarthy (WA))
Holt

NORTHAMPTONSHIRE

COURTEENHALL
(Sir Hereward Wake Bt,M.C. (WA))
Northampton

DRAYTON HOUSE
(L.G. Stopford Sackville (WA)
Lowick, Kettering   NN14 3BG
Telephone: (01832) 732405

THE MONASTERY
(Mr & Mrs R.G. Wigley (WA))
Shutlanger   NN12 7RU
Telephone: (01604) 862529

PAINE'S COTTAGE
(Mr R.O. Barber (WA))
Oundle

WESTON HALL
(Mr & Mrs Francis Sitwell (WA)
Towcester

NORTHUMBERLAND

BRINKBURN MILL
(WA)
Rothbury

*The Landmark Trust, Shottesbrooke, nr Maidenhead, Berks SL6 3SW.

CAUSEWAY HOUSE
(WA)
Bardon Mill

*The Landmark Trust, Shottesbrooke, nr Maidenhead, Berks SL6 3SW.

CRASTER TOWER
Col J.M. Craster, Miss M.D. Craster, Mr F. Sharratt (WA)
Alnwick

HARNHAM HALL
(Mr J. Wake)
Belsay

MORPETH CASTLE
(WA)
Morpeth

*The Landmark Trust, Shottesbrooke, nr Maidenhead, Berks SL6 3SW.

NETHERWITTON HALL
(Mr J.C.R. Trevelyon (WA)
Morpeth   NE61 4NW
Telephone: (0167) 072 219

NOTTINGHAMSHIRE

FLINTHAM HALL
(Mr M.T. Hildyard (WA)
nr Newark

WINKBURN HALL
(Mr R. Craven-Smith-Milnes)
Newark   NG22 8PQ
Telephone: (01636) 636465
Fax: (01636) 636717

WORKSOP PRIORY CHURCH & GATEHOUSE
The Vicarage, Cheapside
Telephone: (01909) 472180

OXFORDSHIRE

26/7 CORNMARKET STREET AND 26 SHIP STREET
(Home Bursar)
Jesus College, Oxford

Shop basement by written appointment Laura Ashley Ltd. 150 Bath Rd. Maidenhead, Berks SL6 4YS.

HOPE HOUSE
(Mrs J. Hageman)
Woodstock

THE MANOR
(Mr & Mrs Paul L. Jaques (WA)
Chalgrove   OX44 7SL
Telephone: (01865) 890836
Fax: (01865) 891810

MONARCH'S COURT HOUSE
(Mr R.S. Hine (WA)
Benson

RIPON COLLEGE
(The Principal (WA)
Cuddesdon

30/43 THE CAUSEWAY
(Mr & Mrs R. Hornsby)
39/43 The Causeway, Steventon

SHROPSHIRE

BROMFIELD PRIORY GATEHOUSE
(WA)
Ludlow
Telephone: (01628) 825925

*The Landmark Trust, Shottesbrooke, nr Maidenhead, Berks SL6 3SW.

HALSTON
(Mrs J.L. Harvey (WA)
Oswestry

HATTON GRANGE
(Mrs P. Afia (WA)
Shifnal

LANGLEY GATEHOUSE
(WA)
Acton Burnell
Telephone: (01628) 825925

*The Landmark Trust, Shottesbrooke, nr Maidenhead, Berks SL6 3SW.

MORVILLE HALL
(The National Trust (tenant Mrs J.K. Norbury (WA)
Bridgenorth   WV16 5NB

OAKLEY MANOR
(Shrewsbury & Atcham Borough Council)
Belle Vue Road, Shrewsbury   SY3 7NW
Telephone: (01243) 231456
Fax: (01243) 271598

ST. WINIFRED'S WELL
(WA)
Woolston, Oswestry

*The Landmark Trust, Shottesbrooke, nr Maidenhead, Berks SL6 3SW.

STANWARDINE HALL
(P.J. Bridge)
Cockshutt, Ellesmere
Telephone: (01939) 270212

SOMERSET

COTHELSTONE MANOR AND GATEHOUSE
(Mrs J.E.B. Warmington (WA)
Cothelstone Manor, Cothelstone, nr Taunton   TA4 3DS
Telephone: (01823) 432200

FAIRFIELD
(Lady Gass)
Stogursey, Bridgwater   TA5 1PU
Telephone: (01278) 732251
Fax: (01278) 732277

GURNEY MANOR
(WA)
Cannington
Telephone: (01628) 825925

*The Landmark Trust, Shottesbrooke, nr Maidenhead, Berks SL6 3SW.

THE OLD DRUG STORE
(Mr & Mrs E.J.D. Schofield (WA)
Axbridge

THE OLD HALL
(WA)
Croscombe

*The Landmark Trust, Shottesbrooke, nr Maidenhead, Berks SL6 3SW.

THE PRIEST'S HOUSE
(WA)
Holcombe Rogus, nr Wellington

*The Landmark Trust, Shottesbrooke, nr Maidenhead, Berks SL6 3SW.

STOGURSEY CASTLE
(WA)
nr Bridgewater

*The Landmark Trust, Shottesbrooke, nr Maidenhead, Berks SL6 3SW.

WEST COKER MANOR
(Mr & Mrs Derek Maclaren)
West Coker, Somerset   BA22 9BJ
Telephone: (01935 86) 2646

WHITELACKINGTON MANOR
(Mr E.J.H. Cameron)
Dillington Estate Office, Illminster   TA19 9EQ
Telephone: (01460) 54614

STAFFORDSHIRE

BROUGHTONALL
(The Administrator (WA)
Eccleshall

DUNWOOD HALL
(Dr. R. Vincent-Kemp FRSA)
Longsdon, nr Leek   ST9 9AR
Telephone: (01538) 385071

THE GREAT HALL IN KEELE HALL
(Registrar, University of Keele (WA)
Keele

INGESTRE PAVILION
(WA)
nr Stafford

*The Landmark Trust, Shottesbrooke, nr Maidenhead, Berks SL6 3SW.

OLD HALL GATEHOUSE
(Mr R.M. Eades)
Mavesyn Ridware
Telephone: (01543) 490312

THE ORANGERY
(Mrs M. Philips)
Heath House, Tean, Stoke-on-Trent   ST10 4HA
Telephone: (01538) 722212

PARK HALL
(Mr E.J. Knobbs (WA)
Leigh

TIXALL GATEHOUSE
(WA)
Tixall, Nr Stafford

*The Landmark Trust, Shottesbrooke, nr Maidenhead, Berks SL6 3SW.

SUFFOLK

THE DEANERY
(The Dean of Bocking)
Hadleigh   IP7 5DT
Telephone: (01473) 822218

DITCHINGHAM HALL
(The Rt Hon Earl Ferrers)
Ditchingham, Bungay

THE HALL
(Mr & Mrs R.B. Cooper (WA)
Great Bricett, Ipswich

HENGRAVE HALL CENTRE
(The Warden)
Bury St Edmunds   IP28 6LZ
Telephone: (01284) 701561

MARTELLO TOWER
(WA)
Aldeburgh

*The Landmark Trust, Shottesbrooke, nr Maidenhead, Berks SL6 3SW.

MOAT HALL
(Mr J.W. Gray)
Woodbridge   IP13 9AE
Telephone: (01728) 746317

THE NEW INN
(WA)
Peasenhall

*The Landmark Trust, Shottesbrooke, nr Maidenhead, Berks SL6 3SW.

NEWBOURNE HALL
(John Somerville Esq. (WA)
Woodbridge

WORLINGHAM HALL
(Viscount Colville of Culross (WA)
Beccles

SURREY

CROSSWAYS FARM
(Mr C.T. Hughes (tenant) (WA)
Abinger Hammer

GREAT FOSTERS HOTEL
(Mr J. E. Baumann (Manager)
Egham   TW20 9UR
Telephone: (01784) 433822

ST. MARY'S HOMES CHAPEL
Church Lane, Godstone
Telephone: (01883) 742385

EAST SUSSEX

ASHDOWN HOUSE
(The Headmaster)
Ashdown House School, Forest Row   RH18 5JY
Telephone: (01342) 822574
Fax: (01342) 824380

LAUGHTON TOWER
(WA)
Lewes

*The Landmark Trust, Shottesbrooke, nr Maidenhead, Berks SL6 3SW.

WEST SUSSEX

CHANTRY GREEN HOUSE
(Mr & Mrs G.H. Recknell)
Steyning
Telephone: (01903) 812239

THE CHAPEL, BISHOP'S PALACE
(Church Commissioners)
The Palace, Chichester

CHRIST'S HOSPITAL
(WA)
Horsham
Telephone: (01403) 52547

TYNE & WEAR

CAPHEATON HALL
(Mr J. Browne-Swinburne (WA))
Newcastle upon Tyne   NE19 2AB

GIBSIDE BANQUETING HOUSE
(WA)
Newcastle

*The Landmark Trust, Shottesbrooke, nr Maidenhead, Berks SL6 3SW.

WARWICKSHIRE

BATH HOUSE
(WA)
Walton, Stratford-on-Avon
*The Landmark Trust, Shottesbrooke, nr Maidenhead, Berks SL6 3SW.

BINSWOOD HALL
(North Leamington School (WA))
Binswood Avenue, Leamington Spa　CV32 5SF
Telephone: (01926) 423686

FOXCOTE
(Mr C.B. Holman (WA))
Shipton-on-Stour

NICHOLAS CHAMBERLAIN'S ALMSHOUSES
(The Warden)
Bedworth
Telephone: (01203) 312225

NORTHGATE
(Mr R.E. Phillips (WA))
Warwick

ST. LEONARD'S CHURCH
(WA)
Wroxall
Mrs. J.M. Gowen, Headmistress, Wroxall Abbey School, Warwick CV35 7NB.

WAR MEMORIAL TOWN HALL
(The Secretary, Mr J.W. Roberts B.E.M.)
10 Haselor Close, Alcester　B49 6QD
Telephone: (01789) 762101
Open: View by appointment through secretary
Admission: Free

WILTSHIRE

CHINESE SUMMERHOUSE
Amesbury Abbey, Amesbury
Telephone: (01980) 622957

FARLEY HOSPITAL
(The Warden)
Church Road, Farley　SP5 1AH
Telephone: (01722) 712231

MILTON MANOR
(Mrs Rupert Gentle)
The Manor House, Milton Lilbourne, Pewsey
SN9 5LQ
Telephone: (01672) 63344
Fax: (01672) 64136

OLD BISHOP'S PALACE
(The Bursar, Salisbury Cathedral School)
1 The Close, Salisbury
Telephone: (01722) 322652

THE OLD MANOR HOUSE
(Mr J. Teed (WA))
2 Whitehead Lane, Bradford-on-Avon

ORPINS HOUSE
(Mr J. Vernon Burchell (WA))
Church Street, Bradford-on-Avon

THE PORCH HOUSE
(Mr Tim Vidal-Hall (WA))
6, High Street, Potterne, Devizes　SN10 5NA

NORTH YORKSHIRE

BEAMSLEY HOSPITAL
(WA)
Skipton
*The Landmark Trust, Shottesbrooke, nr Maidenhead, Berks SL6 3SW.

BROUGHTON HALL
(H.R. Tempest Esq.)
Skipton　BD23 3AE
Telephone: (01756) 792267
Fax: (01756) 792362

BUSBY HALL
(Mr G.A. Marwood (WA))
Carlton-in-Cleveland

CALVERLEY OLD HALL
(WA)
nr Leeds
*The Landmark Trust, Shottesbrooke, nr Maidenhead, Berks SL6 3SW.

CAWOOD CASTLE
(WA)
nr Selby
*The Landmark Trust, Shottesbrooke, nr Maidenhead, Berks SL6 3SW.

CHAPEL AND COACH HOUSE
Aske, Richmond

THE CHURCH OF OUR LADY AND SAINT EVERILDA
(WA)
Everingham
Telephone: (01430) 860531

THE CULLODEN TOWER
(WA)
Richmond
*The Landmark Trust, Shottesbrooke, nr Maidenhead, Berks SL6 3SW.

THE DOVECOTE
(Mrs P. E. Heathcote)
Forcett Hall, Forcett, Richmond
Telephone: (01325) 718226

HOME FARM HOUSE
(Mr G. T. Reece (WA))
Old Scriven, Knaresborough

MOULTON HALL
(The National Trust (tenant Hon. J.D. Eccles) WA)
Richmond

THE OLD RECTORY
(Mrs R.F. Wormald (WA))
Foston, York

THE PIGSTY
(WA)
Robin Hood's Bay
*The Landmark Trust, Shottesbrooke, nr Maidenhead, Berks SL6 3SW.

WEST YORKSHIRE

FULNECK BOYS' SCHOOL
(I.D. Cleland B.A. M.Phil Headmaster (WA))
Pudsey

GRAND THEATRE & OPERA HOUSE
(Warren Smith, General Manager)
46 New Briggate, Leeds　LS1 6NZ
Telephone: (0113) 245 6014
Fax: (0113) 246 5906

HORBURY HALL
(D.J.H. Michelmore Esq.)
Horbury, Wakefield
Telephone: (01924) 277552

TOWN HALL
(Leeds City Council)
Leeds
Telephone: (0113) 2477989

WESTON HALL
(Lt. Col. H.V. Dawson (WA))
nr Otley　LS21 2HP

WALES

CLWYD

FFERM
(Dr M.C. Jones-Mortimer)
Pontblyddyn, Mold　CH7 4HN
Telephone: (01352) 770876

GATEHOUSE AT GILAR FARM
(Mr P.J. Warbourton-Lee (WA))
Pentrfoclas

GOLDEN GROVE
(N. R. & M. M. J. Steele-Mortimer(WA))
Llanasa, Nr Holywell, Clywd　CH8 9NE
Telephone: (01745) 854452
Fax: (01745) 854547

HALGHTON HALL
(Mr J.D. Lewis (WA)
Bangor-on-Dee, Wrexham

LINDISFARNE COLLEGE
(The Headmaster (WA)
Wynnstay Hall, Ruabon
Telephone: (01978) 810407

NERQUIS HALL
(Mr A.W. Furse (WA)
Mold　CH7 4EB

PEN ISA'R GLASCOED
(Mr M.E. Harrop)
Bodelwyddan　LL22 9DD
Telephone: (01745) 583501

PLAS UCHAF
(WA)
Llangar, Nr Corwen
*The Landmark Trust, Shottesbrooke, nr Maidenhead, Berks SL6 3SW.

DYFED

MONKTON OLD HALL
(WA)
Pembroke
*The Landmark Trust, Shottesbrooke, nr Maidenhead, Berks SL6 3SW.

ST. DAVID'S UNIVERSITY COLLEGE
(Prof. Keith Robbins)
Lampeter
Telephone: (01570) 422351
Fax: (01570) 423423

TALIARIS PARK
(Mr J.H. Spencer-Williams (WA)
Llandeilo

WEST BLOCKHOUSE
(WA)
Haverfordwest, Dale
*The Landmark Trust, Shottesbrooke, nr Maidenhead, Berks SL6 3SW.

SOUTH GLAMORGAN

FONMON CASTLE
(Sir Brooke Boothby Bt)
Fonmon Castle, Barry　CF6 9ZN
Telephone: (01446) 710206
Fax: (01446) 711687

GWENT

BLACKBROOK MANOR
(Mr & Mrs A.C. de Morgan)
Skenfrith, nr Abergavenny　NP7 8UB
Telephone: (01600 84) 453
Fax: (01600 84) 453

CASTLE HILL HOUSE
(Mr T. Baxter-Wright (WA))
Monmouth

CLYTHA CASTLE
(WA)
Abergavenny

*The Landmark Trust, Shottesbrooke, nr Maidenhead, Berks SL6 3SW.

GREAT CIL-LWCH
(Mr J.F. Ingledew (WA)
Llantilio Crossenny, Abergavenny   NP7 8SR
Telephone: (0160) 825206

KEMYS HOUSE
(Mr I.S. Burge (WA)
Keyms Inferior, Caerleon

LLANVIHANGEL COURT
(Mrs D. Johnson (WA)
Abergavenny   NP7 8DH

OVERMONNOW HOUSE
(Mr J.R. Pangbourne (WA)
Monmouth

3/4 PRIORY STREET
(Mr H.R. Ludwig)
Monmouth

TREOWEN
(John Wheelock)
Wonastow, Monmouth   NP5 4DL
Telephone: (0160) 712031

GWYNEDD

THE BATH TOWER
(WA)
Caernarfon

*The Landmark Trust, Shottesbrooke, nr Maidenhead, Berks SL6 3SW.

CYMRYD
(Miss D.E. Glynne (WA)
Cymryd, Conwy   LL32 8UA

DOLAUGWYN
(Mrs S. Tudor (WA)
Towyn

NANNAU
(Mr P. Vernon (WA)
Dolgellau

PENMYNYDD
(The Rector of Llanfairpwll (WA)
Alms Houses, Llanfairpwll

PLAS COCH
(Mrs N. Donald)
Llanedwen, Llanfairpwll
Telephone: (01248) 714272

POWYS

ABERCAMLAIS
(Mrs J.C.R. Ballance (WA)
Brecon

ABERCYNRIG
(Mrs W.R. Lloyd (WA)
Brecon

1 BUCKINGHAM PLACE
(Mrs Meeres (WA)
1 Buckingham Place, Brecon   LD3 7DL   map **12** T22
Telephone: (01874) 623612

3 BUCKINGHAM PLACE
(Mr & Mrs A. Whiley (WA)
3 Buckingham Place, Brecon   LD3 7DL

MAESMAWR HALL HOTEL
(Mrs M. Pemberton, Mrs. I. Hunt)
Caersws
Telephone: (01686) 688255

NEWTON FARM
(Mrs Ballance (WA) to Mr. D.L. Evans, tenant)
Brecon

PEN Y LAN
(Mr S.R.J. Meade)
Meifod, Powys   SY22 6DA
Telephone: (01938) 500202

PLASAU DUON
(Mr E.S. Breese)
Clatter

POULTRY HOUSE
(WA)
Leighton, Welshpool

*The Landmark Trust, Shottesbrooke, nr Maidenhead, Berks SL6 3SW.

RHYDYCARW
(Mr M. Breese-Davies)
Trefeglwys, Newtown   SY17 5PU
Telephone: (01686) 430411
Fax: (01686) 430331

YDDERW
(Mr D.P. Eckley (WA)
Llyswen

SCOTLAND

BORDERS

OLD GALA HOUSE
(Ettrick & Lauderdale District Council)
Galashiels
Telephone: (01750) 20096

SIR WALTER SCOTT'S COURTROOM
(Ettrick & Lauderdale District Council)
Selkirk
Telephone: (01750) 20096

WEDDERLIE HOUSE
(Mrs J.R.L. Campbell (WA)
Gordon   TD3 6NW
Telephone: (0157) 874 0223

CENTRAL

CASTLECARY CASTLE
(Mr R.L.C. Hunter (WA)
by Bonnybridge
Telephone: (01324) 840031
By arrangement with current tenant.

DUMFRIES & GALLOWAY

BONSHAW TOWER
(Dr J.B. Irving (WA)
Kirtlebridge, nr Annan   DG11 3LY
Telephone: (01461) 500256

CARNSALLOCH HOUSE
(The Leonard Cheshire Foundation)
Carnsalloch, Kirkton   DG1 1SN
Telephone: (01387) 54924
Fax: (01387) 57971

KIRKCONNELL HOUSE
(Mr F. Maxwell Witham)
New Abbey, Dumfries
Telephone: (0138) 785-276

FIFE

BATH CASTLE
(Mr Angus Mitchell)
Bogside, Oakley   FK10 3RD
Telephone: 0131-556 7671

THE CASTLE
(Mr J. Bevan (WA)
Elie

CASTLE OF PARK
(WA)
Glenluce, Galloway

*The Landmark Trust, Shottesbrooke, nr Maidenhead, Berks SL6 3SW.

CHARLETON HOUSE
(Baron St. Clair Bonde)
Colinsburgh
Telephone: (0133 334) 249

GRAMPIAN

BALBITHAN HOUSE
(Mr J. McMurtie)
Kintore
Telephone: (01467) 32282

BALFLUIG CASTLE
Mr Mark Tennant (WA)
Grampian   NW8 9AT

Contact: 30 Abbey Gardens, London, Greater London, NW8 9AT.

BARRA CASTLE
(Dr & Mrs Andrew Bogdan (WA)
Old Meldrum

CASTLE OF FIDDES
(Dr M. Weir)
Stonehaven
Telephone: (01569) 740213

CHURCH OF THE HOLY RUDE
Broad Street, Stirling

CORSINDAE HOUSE
(Mr R. Fyffe (WA)
Sauchen by Inverurie, Inverurie   AB51 7PP
Telephone: (013303) 295
Fax: (013303) 629

DRUMMINOR CASTLE
(Mr A.D. Forbes (WA)
Rhynie

ERSKINE MARYKIRK - STIRLING YOUTH HOSTEL
St. John Street, Stirling

GARGUNNOCK HOUSE
(Gargunnock Estate Trust (WA)
Stirling

GORDONSTOUN SCHOOL
(The Headmaster (WA)
Elgin Moray

GRANDHOME HOUSE
(D.R. Paton Esq.)
Aberdeen
Telephone: (01224) 722202

GUILDHALL
(Stirling District Council)
Municipal Buildings, Stirling
Telephone: (01786) 79000

Also **John Cawane's House** contact above telephone number.

OLD TOLBOOTH BUILDING
(Stirling District Council)
Municipal Buildings, Stirling
Telephone: (01786) 79000

PHESDO HOUSE
(Mr J.M. Thomson (WA)
Laurencekirk

THE PINEAPPLE
(WA)
Dunmore, Airth, Stirling

*The Landmark Trust, Shottesbrooke, nr Maidenhead, Berks SL6 3SW.

TOLBOOTH
(Stirling District Council)
Broad Street, Stirling
Telephone: (01786) 79400

TOUCH HOUSE
(Mr P.B. Buchanan (WA)
Stirling   FK8 3AQ
Fax: 0786 464278

HIGHLANDS

EMBO HOUSE
(Mr John G. Mackintosh)
Dornoch
Telephone: Dornoch 810260

LOTHIAN

CAKEMUIR
(Mr M.M. Scott (WA)
Tynehead

CASTLE GOGAR
(Lady Steel-Maitland)
Edinburgh
Telephone: 0131-339 1234

FORD HOUSE
(F.P. Tindall OBE (WA)
Ford

FORTH ROAD BRIDGE
(The Bridgemaster)
South Queensferry
Telephone: 0131-319 1699

LINNHOUSE
(Mr H.J. Spurway (WA)
Linnhouse, Livingston   EH54 9AN
Telephone: (01506) 410742
Fax: (01506) 416591

NEWBATTLE ABBEY COLLEGE
(The Principal)
Dalkeith   EH22 3LL
Telephone: 0131-663 1921
Fax: 0131-654 0598

NORTHFIELD HOUSE
(Mr W. Schomberg Scott (WA)
Prestonpans

PENICUIK HOUSE
(Sir John Clerk Bt (WA)
Penicuik

ROSEBURN HOUSE
(Mr M.E. Sturgeon (WA)
Murrayfield

TOWN HOUSE
(East Lothian District Council)
Haddington
Telephone: Haddington 4161

SHETLAND ISLES

THE LODBERRIE
(Mr Thomas Moncrieff)
Lerwick

STRATHCLYDE

ASCOG HOUSE
(WA)
Rothsay

*The Landmark Trust, Shottesbrooke, nr Maidenhead, Berks SL6 3SW.

BARCALDINE CASTLE
(Roderick Campbell esq. (WA)
Benderloch

CRAUFURDLAND CASTLE
(J.P. Houison Craufurd Esq.)
Kilmarnock   KA3 6BS
Telephone: 0560 600 402

DUNTRUNE CASTLE
(Robin Malcolm of Poltalloch (WA)
Lochgilphead

KELBURN CASTLE
(The Earl of Glasgow (WA)
Fairlie, Ayrshire   KA29 0BE
Telephone: (01475) 568685 - Country Centre; (01475) 568204 - Kelburn Castle
Fax: (01475) 568121 - Country Centre; (01475) 568328 - Kelburn Castle

NEW LANARK
(New Lanark Conservation Trust)
New Lanark Mills, Lanark   ML11 9DB
Telephone: (01555) 661345
Fax: (01555) 665738

THE PLACE OF PAISLEY
(Paisley Abbey Kirk Session)
Paisley Abbey, Kirk Session, Paisley   PA1 1JG
Telephone: 0141-889 7654

SADDELL CASTLE
(WA)
Campbeltown, Argyll

*The Landmark Trust, Shottesbrooke, nr Maidenhead, Berks SL6 3SW.

TANGY MILL
(WA)
Campbeltown, Kintyre, Argyll

*The Landmark Trust, Shottesbrooke, nr Maidenhead, Berks SL6 3SW.

TANNAHILL COTTAGE
(Secretary, Paisley Burns Club)
Queen Street, Paisley
Telephone: 0141-887 7500

TAYSIDE

ARDBLAIR CASTLE
(Laurence P.K. Blair Oliphant)
Blairgowrie   PH10 6SA
Telephone: (01250) 873155

CRAIG HOUSE
(Charles F.R. Hoste)
Montrose
Telephone: (01674) 722239

KINROSS HOUSE
(Sir David Montgomery Bt (WA)
Kinross

MICHAEL BRUCE COTTAGE MUSEUM
(Michael Bruce Trust)
Kinnesswood

THE PAVILION, GLENEAGLES
(J. Martin Haldane Esq. (WA)
Gleneagles, Auchterarder   PH3 1PJ

TULLIEBOLE CASTLE
(The Lord Moncreiff)
Crook of Devon
Telephone: (0157) 74236

For further details on editorial listings or display advertising contact the
Editor: Deborah Valentine,
Windsor Court, East Grinstead House, East Grinstead,
West Sussex RH19 1XA
Tel: (01342) 335794 Fax: (01342) 335720

INDEX TO PROPERTIES
OPEN ALL YEAR

INDEX TO PROPERTIES
OFFERING ACCOMMODATION

INDEX
TO PROPERTIES

T

U

V

W

Y

NOTES

Orkney Is.

Scrabster
Wick

Isle of
Lewis

Ullapool

North
Uist

10 - 11

Inverness

Aberdeen

South
Uist

Isle of
Skye

Eigg
Mallaig
Fort William

Coll

Tiree
Mull
Oban
Perth
Dundee

Colonsay

Glasgow **15** Edinburgh
Berwick

Islay
Arran
Ayr
8 - 9
Newcastle

Londonderry
Larne
Stranraer
Carlisle

Dungannon
Belfast
Middlesbrough

Sligo
Isle of
Man
Scarborough

Douglas Heysham
Ripon
York

Fleetwood
Bradford Leeds
Hull

Galway
Blackpool
Manchester **15**
Doncaster

16
Liverpool
Sheffield
Lincoln

Dublin
Anglesey
6 - 7
Derby Nottingham

Dun Laoghaire
Holyhead
Stoke

Limerick
Shrewsbury
Leicester
Peterborough
Norwich

Wolverhampton
14
4 - 5

Killarney
Rosslare
Aberystwyth
Birmingham
Coventry
Cambridge

Warwick
Northampton
Ipswich

Cork
Banbury
Felixstowe
Harwich

Fishguard
Gloucester
Oxford

Pembroke
Swansea
Cardiff **14**
Swindon
LONDON

Bristol
Reading
Maidstone
Canterbury

Ilfracombe
Winchester
Crawley
12 - 13
Dover

Lundy
Bideford
Taunton
Southampton
Brighton
Folkestone

2 - 3
Poole
Portsmouth

Exeter
Weymouth
Isle of
Wight

Plymouth
Torquay

Penzance

Isles of Scilly

Channel
Islands

Key to Map Symbols

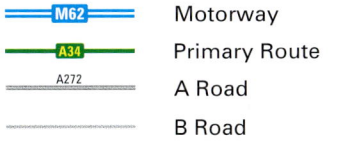

M62 Motorway	Property in the care of English Heritage
A34 Primary Route	Property in the care of The National Trust
A272 A Road	Property in the care of The National Trust for Scotland
B Road	

House with or without garden

Castle with or without garden

Garden

Scale : 16 miles to 1 inch (pages 2 -11)

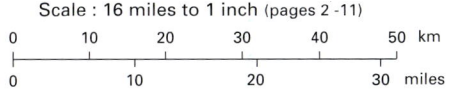

0	10	20	30	40	50	km

0	10	20	30	miles

Scale : 8 miles to 1 inch (pages 12 -15)

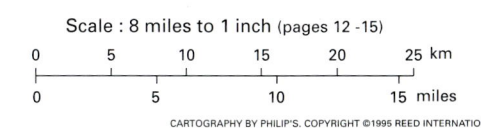

0	5	10	15	20	25	km

0	5	10	15	miles

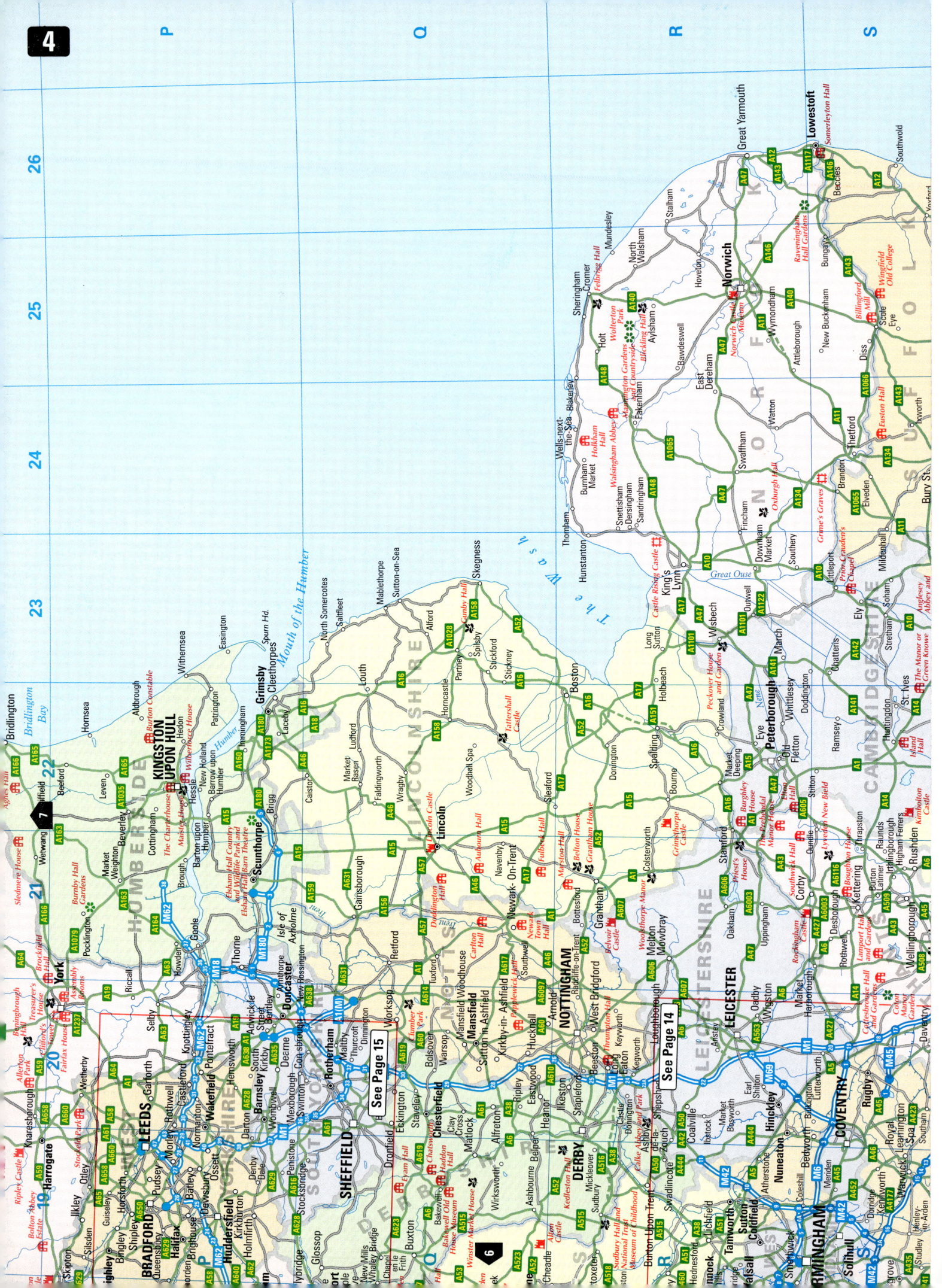

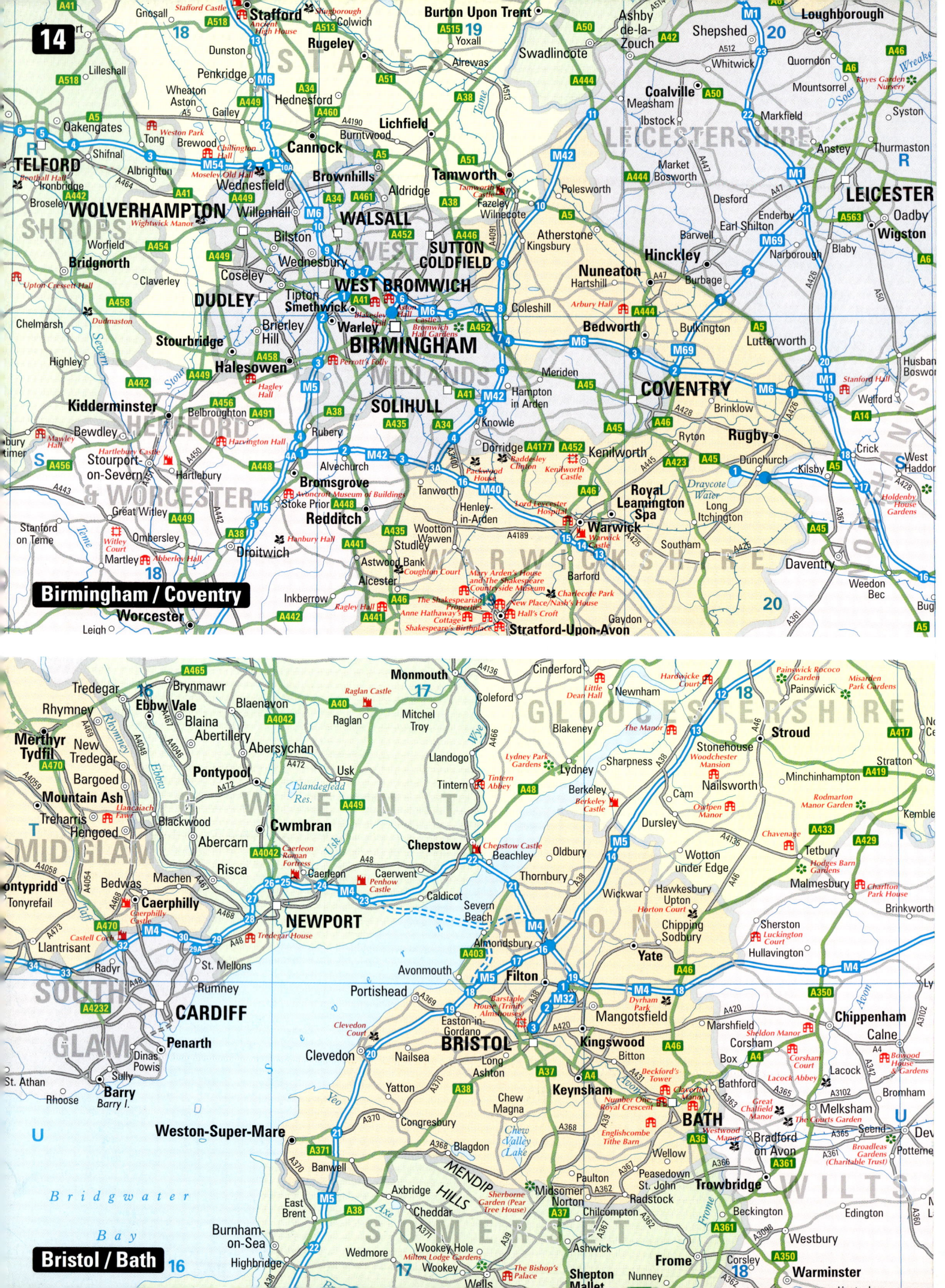

14

Edinburgh / Glasgow

Manchester / Leeds